Translating the Occupation

Translating the Occupation

The Japanese Invasion of China, 1931–45

Edited by Jonathan Henshaw,
Craig A. Smith, and Norman Smith

UBCPress · Vancouver · Toronto

30 29 28 27 26 25 24 23 22 21 5 4 3 2 1

Printed in Canada on FSC-certified ancient-forest-free paper (100% post-consumer recycled) that is processed chlorine- and acid-free.

Library and Archives Canada Cataloguing in Publication

Title: Translating the occupation: the Japanese invasion of China,1931–45 / edited by Jonathan Henshaw, Craig A. Smith, and Norman Smith.

Names: Henshaw, Jonathan, editor. | Smith, Craig A., editor. | Smith, Norman (Associate Professor), editor.

Description: Includes texts translated from Chinese, Japanese, and Korean.

Identifiers: Canadiana (print) 20200289659 | Canadiana (ebook) 20200289780 | ISBN 9780774864466 (hardcover) | ISBN 9780774864473 (softcover) | ISBN 9780774864480 (PDF) | ISBN 9780774864497 (EPUB)

Subjects: LCSH: Sino-Japanese Conflict, 1931–1933 – Sources – Translations into English. | LCSH: Sino-Japanese War, 1937–1945 – Sources – Translations into English. | LCSH: China – History – 1928–1937 – Sources – Translations into English. | LCSH: China – History – 1937–1945 – Sources – Translations into English. | LCSH: China – Social conditions – 1912–1949 – Sources – Translations into English.

Classification: LCC DS777.5 .T73 2020 | DDC 951.04/2 - dc23

UBC Press gratefully acknowledges the financial support for our publishing program of the Government of Canada (through the Canada Book Fund) and the British Columbia Arts Council.

This book has been published with the help of a grant from the Canadian Federation for the Humanities and Social Sciences, through the Awards to Scholarly Publications Program, using funds provided by the Social Sciences and Humanities Research Council of Canada.

Printed and bound in Canada by Friesens
Set in Museo, Warnock, Univers Black, and SimSun by Artegraphica Design Co.
Copy editor: Sarah Wight
Proofreader: Alison Strobel
Indexer: Noeline Bridge
Cover designer: David Drummond
Cartographer: Eric Leinberger

UBC Press
The University of British Columbia
2029 West Mall
Vancouver, BC V6T 1Z2
www.ubcpress.ca

In memory of our friend COLIN GREEN
and his scholarly devotion to Chinese military history.

Contents

Illustrations

Acknowledgments

This book was made possible through the hard work and important contributions of many people. The chapters for this volume were initially presented at two workshops hosted by the University of British Columbia's Institute of Asian Research in 2016 and 2017, and we as editors are grateful to the many scholars who presented and attended these workshops. We would like to express our appreciation to Timothy Brook, Timothy Cheek, and Diana Lary, whose scholarship has done much to inspire our own. We also thank the two anonymous readers at UBC Press who provided thoughtful insights and suggestions during the review process. We are grateful to the graduate students who contributed their time and effort to our project: Lisa Baer, who provided excellent organizational and administrative support; Jie Lu, who offered crucial help with the editing and formatting of the volume; and Shawn Sun, who did much to keep things running behind the scenes when we convened.

Funding for *Translating the Occupation* came from multiple sources: the 2016 workshop was generously supported by a Henry Luce Foundation/American Council of Learned Societies Program in China Studies: Collaborative Reading-Workshop Grant. The 2017 workshop was made possible through a Connection Grant from the Social Sciences and Humanities Research Council. We would also like to express our gratitude for additional funding and support from the University of British Columbia's History Department and Centre for Chinese Research, as well as the Department of History at the University of Guelph.

Finally, we would like to give our deepest appreciation to Randy Schmidt, Megan Brand, and Valerie Nair at UBC Press for supporting the project and shepherding us through the publication process and to Alison Strobel for her proofreading skills. Once again, David Drummond has created an evocative cover worthy of this work.

Translating the Occupation

Introduction

Discarding Binaries and Embracing Heteroglossia

JONATHAN HENSHAW, CRAIG A. SMITH, and NORMAN SMITH

Twenty years after Jiang Wen's 2000 film *Guizi laile!* (Devils on the doorstep!) captured the Grand Prix at the Cannes Film Festival, his tragic but sympathetic portrayal of those living in Japanese-occupied Hebei may no longer seem very surprising. At the time, however, Jiang's depiction of the assistance given to a Japanese soldier and this translator by Chinese villagers was not only controversial, it was banned by Chinese censors who were not able to look beyond the national narrative of a collaboration/resistance dichotomy.[1] Both historical memories and political directives have long held that narrative firmly in place. This national narrative delineates the rise of the Chinese nation through righteous battle and marginalizes alternative understandings of that era's history. In the 1930s, when the Japanese military began occupying large swathes of Chinese territory, China was in a state of disunity, with local elites presiding over a vast patchwork in which people lived different lives, spoke different languages, and encountered different experiences. While China today is by no means monolithic, the forces that shape historical memories have long emphasized the standard narrative that the occupation, and the greater war, galvanized the Chinese people as one in resistance to a common enemy – captured in the slogan *kangRi* (Resist Japan).[2] The enormity and simplicity of this narrative has shaped subsequent perceptions of the occupation, polarized understandings of the actions of the occupied, and homogenized an unequivocally heterogeneous cacophony of voices.

To excavate these voices, this volume introduces, contextualizes, and translates a broad range of primary sources written by a variety of men and women across China. The texts have been selected in order to deepen understandings of the myriad tensions, transformations, and continuities that persisted, seemingly heedless of monumental historical events during the Japanese occupation of China. Despite the enduring importance of that occupation to world history and contemporary East Asia, this is the first English-language volume to offer sources in such a way. Specialists on wartime history from institutions in six different countries were selected to provide expertise on a range of disciplines and subjects, and to translate sources from Chinese, Japanese, and Korean. Each scholar has provided a translation accompanied by a short, explanatory essay to contextualize the translation, speak to its importance, and place the occupation within a broader social, political, and cultural context.

This volume offers multifaceted views of the occupation that enrich knowledge of the period and encourage further much-needed comparative analysis. A dearth of English-language materials has resulted in the persistence of Eurocentric analyses of the Second World War in history and historical memories, just as nationalist realities have simplified and polarized discourses in East Asia. Despite its epochal importance and enduring influence in contemporary Asia, Japan's occupation of vast regions of China remains inadequately understood, both in the context of modern Asian history and the broader history of the Second World War. Indeed, it was only in 2013 that a history of the war that narrated events from Chongqing, Yan'an, and Nanjing was published in English, while such a work fully incorporating Manchukuo has yet to be written.[3]

In the decades immediately following the occupation, academic inquiries on the period were frequently shaped or stymied by shifting political agendas, with many scholars focusing on the rise of the Chinese Communist Party (CCP) and the revolutions it launched to transform the nation. In China, at popular levels and in overarching master narratives, portrayals of the war were seldom allowed to venture beyond nationalistic narratives of patriotic Chinese resistance or traitorous collaboration, amid horrific Japanese atrocities. Accordingly, by working to deepen understandings of how the war unfolded and to introduce previously marginalized voices, this volume is an effort to develop more complex comprehensions of China's twentieth-century history that go beyond the dominant national narratives.

In 1972, American historian Gerald Bunker gave voice to the lingering international contempt that obscured the occupation period in his assessment of texts produced by the 1940 to 1945 Reorganized National Government of the Republic of China under Wang Jingwei (1883–1944), dismissing them as "nothing more than the most mindless and trivial sort of propaganda with little historical value."[4] More recently, however, scholars have begun to engage more seriously with these texts in a way that places them within the complex moral landscape of wartime occupation.

In China, Japan, and across the English-speaking world, linguistic barriers, restrictions on access to source materials, and the fuelling of highly politicized nationalist narratives have left little room for developing a history of the war that is transnational, nuanced, and less bound by nationalist mythmaking or Eurocentrism. In China, historical memory of the wartime era has been reemphasized from the 1980s onward to form a cultural trauma of occupation that is continually relived and reinforced through popular media; according to cultural critic Zhu Dake: "War stories make up about 70 percent of drama on Chinese television."[5] The CCP continues to manipulate that history as a fount of bitter nationalism, enabled in part by the Japanese government's failure to fully accept responsibility for the very real atrocities perpetrated by its military on Chinese neighbours. Following the CCP lead, many Chinese-language studies have tended to focus on perspectives that promote nationalist narratives and avoid moral complexity, dismissing those who served in Japan's various occupation states as "traitors to the Chinese" (*Hanjian*) and viewing those who lived in occupied territory with suspicion.

However, in academic discourse, there have been efforts to complicate these narratives, and such work has accelerated in the twenty-first century. Yang Kuisong has related the surge of studies to the great release of source materials and published collections that has been ongoing since the reform and greater openness of the 1980s.[6] Even taking into account recent restrictions on access to primary sources in China, historians have more material to work with than ever before and have risen to the challenges on offer. Yang Kuisong is certainly not the only historian to investigate these issues. Take, for example, popular Hui scholar Zhang Chengzhi's moving discussion of Japanese Asianists who devoted their lives to the betterment of minorities in China's borderlands.[7] Han Chinese intellectuals in the 1930s inevitably interpreted these actions as acts of empire.[8] Indeed, whether well-intentioned or not, such actions contributed to the growing hegemony of the Japanese Empire (1879–1945), just as similar actions supported American hegemony in Afghanistan and, today, function for the Chinese state in Tibet, Hong Kong, Xinjiang, and elsewhere at its periphery. In terms of Japanese imperialism, literary scholar and historian Zhang Quan has recently argued that Chinese experiences of occupation differed by region, and that those differences must be critically examined – through Sinicizing Western methodologies and localizing Chinese research methods.[9]

In Japan, as in many post-imperial states, memories of the country's imperialist past have created fissures in today's society, fuelling controversies and continuing to influence the political realm and national identities.[10] Some Japanese textbooks tend toward nationalist narratives that shift blame away from even the most complicit individuals or organizations, but, as in China, the occupation is a popular (if fraught) subject for academic study and is profoundly political. Due to the sickening level of well-documented violence, the Nanjing Massacre of 1937–38 remains at the centre of divisive discourse on the war and the occupation. A litmus test of political perspective, particularly since the proliferation of historical studies in the 1980s, the Nanjing Massacre continues to divide what Takashi Yoshida labels as progressive and revisionist voices.[11] Revisionists such as Higashinakano Shudo continue to deny the massacre. A few historians, such as Kasahara Tokushi, fiercely oppose the revisionists with evidence of war crimes, while popular "centrists" such as Hata Ikuhito attempt to find a middle ground, by challenging the number of fatalities and questioning alleged atrocities, but still condemning the massacre in general.[12] This plurality is much preferred to the recent past, when historian Saburō Ienaga had to undertake a series of lawsuits against the Japanese government from 1965 to 1997 over state censorship of his work on Japanese war crimes.

With East Asia still riven by disputes over wartime history, leading Canadian scholars Diana Lary and Timothy Brook, both of whom participated in the workshops leading to this volume, have returned attention to the occupation and brought previously dominant narratives into question.[13] Scholarly studies, geopolitical change, and the desire to understand an era before those who experienced it are no longer with us have rekindled interest in the occupation, leading to collections such as this volume. Earlier source collections have concentrated on military incidents or diplomatic texts, for the most part ignoring other aspects of the occupation, and lack the contextualizing essays this volume offers, thereby making them less accessible to non-specialists. Timothy Brook's *Documents on the Rape of Nanking* sheds light on what many perceive to be the darkest period of the occupation through documents of the international community, the Nanking Safety Zone, and personal correspondence.[14] Suping Lu's *A Dark Page in History* is a collection of British diplomatic dispatches, Admiralty documents, and US Naval Intelligence reports.[15] Donald Detwiler and Charles Burdick's *War in Asia and the Pacific* contains mostly wartime secondary sources, especially military reports, troop movements, and statistical reports, more suited as a reference work than for reconsidering more varied aspects of the war and occupation.[16] Collections with a broader focus have touched on the occupation but again highlight political and military aspects. David Atwill and

Yurong Atwill's *Sources in Chinese History* includes three pages on the occupation, all of which are government pronouncements.[17] Sven Saaler and Christopher Szpilman's *Pan-Asianism: A Documentary History* has a number of excellent texts but is directed at intellectual and ideological essays and speeches, largely from Japan.[18]

In terms of sourcebooks on modern Chinese history, there are two main types: those that focus on primary sources, texts drafted by officials, ideologues, and literary people; and secondary sources produced from other forms of primary materials.[19] This volume falls firmly in the former category. The texts in this volume enable the reader to gain a firmer sense of how the occupation shaped official, intellectual, and popular cultures during a most tumultuous time.

As historians of twentieth-century China, we have an important goal in our work – to promote more fruitful comparative work and dialogue between East Asia specialists and our colleagues working on other areas. Beyond the barrier of language, a major challenge in this effort is the sheer complexity of working with texts produced under circumstances of invasion, occupation, or colonization. Accordingly, we have designed this project along very particular lines. A key feature of our approach is the use of scholarly translation, which lends itself well to the challenges of language, interpretation, and moral judgment that inevitably arise while researching a topic as charged as imperialist occupation. By drawing on the expertise of specialists working on wartime history, we place at the reader's disposal not only translations of primary source documents but the contextual information necessary to further interpret and make sense of them. This engagement with, and attention to, context invites the reader to begin evaluation of each text closer to the environment in which the author wrote, unburdened with the knowledge of how the war might end or what subsequent events might occur. More than that, the deep engagement involved in scholarly translation offers a useful bulwark against the rush to judgment that comes from nationalist narratives. The introduction to each translation enlarges on the meanings, contexts, and authorship of the text to draw us nearer to an understanding of the occupation as it unfolded, at particular points of time, as experienced by those who actually lived through it.

A long-standing problem in the study of wartime China has been the persistence of the collaboration/resistance binary as a means of positioning various individuals and factions during the conflict. Although that binary has long been called into question, it endures as an alluring form of analysis. A prime example of this is Pei-kai Cheng, Michael Lestz, and Jonathan

Spence's still-popular *The Search for Modern China: A Documentary Collection,* which condemns Wang Jingwei's "shameless collaboration," dismissing out of hand Wang's explanation of his beliefs in a 1941 radio address.[20] Such characterizations are not uncommon, even after the groundbreaking intervention of Poshek Fu, who proposed a tripartite mode of intellectual responses to the "grey zone" of Japanese occupation in his 1993 monograph *Passivity, Resistance, and Collaboration.*[21]

Rather than attempting further refinements or offering up additional schemas for the broad spectrum of wartime behaviour that historians have long grappled with, this volume is framed around "occupation." As suggested above, the terminology surrounding "collaboration" in China (as elsewhere) remains morally freighted, leading Dongyoun Hwang to aptly describe "traitor" and "*Hanjian*" as "term[s] in the rhetoric of power that legitimates other ideologies."[22] "Occupation," by contrast, is a less freighted term demarcating a period when the existing order of a state is swept away and a foreign power props up a new one, militarily, often in the face of local responses that ranged from armed resistance to passivity to self-serving acquiescence and shifted as the war unfolded. Within this framework, this volume represents an effort to spur further reflection on the thoughts and actions of individuals who remained active in public life under Japanese-occupied territory, with particular attention to the varieties of Pan-Asianism, Sun Yat-sen thought, Confucianism and Marxism that occupation officials, ideologues, politicians, and literary types advocated from within the various occupation states sponsored by Japan.

Scholarly translation and the application of a more analytical, less condemnatory approach to sources produced under and within Japan's occupation states reveal the intense ideological competition and blurring of boundaries that characterized the period. As the following chapters suggest, those who served in the occupation states were not a uniform group that emerged from nowhere. In many cases, their careers in prewar Chinese politics are crucial for understanding their occupation activities. At the same time, the work they did was more complex than simply regurgitating Japanese propaganda points. A more careful analysis reveals elements of subversion, either by advancing a covertly CCP world view, or by defending a China defined in terms of the prewar Republican state and its Three Principles of the People ideology, or by incorporating other indigenous streams of thought.[23] Accordingly, the individuals who staffed the occupation state and remained in public life, and who took the opportunity to advance an agenda (ideological or personal) that was stymied prior to invasion, should be recognized not only as more complex than the still-popular *Hanjian* caricatures allow but as representatives of the full complexity of prewar Chinese politics. If scholars accept the idea that the resistance/collaboration binary is (at least theoretically) insufficient to capture the complexities of occupation, then a contribution of this volume will be to provoke increasingly critical approaches to the full range of activity and personality that have hitherto been shoehorned into the categories of "collaboration," "*Hanjian*" and "puppet," to name a few.

Implicit in this approach, including the use of scholarly translation, is the issue of judgment. In 2005, Timothy Brook emphasized the ambiguity of decision-making processes, arguing that historians should refrain from making moral judgments on acts of so-called collaboration that cannot be fully understood today. Continuing this discussion, the February 2012 issue of the *Journal of Asian Studies* featured three articles revealing considerable disagreement on questions of moral judgment and the role of the scholar in studies of wartime collaboration, particularly as John Whittier Treat argued that moral adjudication is possible and understandable, taking Korean writer Yi Kwang-su (1895–1950) and his love for Japan as an example. Treat explains that this kind of judgment of those who work with the enemy "has to do with what we fundamentally are."[24] In the same issue, Timothy Brook emphasized that in due time regime changes further challenge questions of collaboration and resistance and repeated that historians should hesitate before making moral claims.[25] Whether historians should make moral judgments on their subject matter remains a question for many scholars. But how do our decisions to judge shape the histories that we construct?

Writing on the 1791 to 1804 Haitian Revolution, Michel-Rolph Trouillot asserted that the silencing of the revolution in Western historiography was "due to uneven power in the production of sources, archives, and narratives."[26] The same is true of the production of history in any time and place, yet regarding the Japanese occupation of China, the Chinese narrative – the victorious rise of the nation and people from tragedy – has taken on such power and is delivered with such apparent simplicity and "truth" that "Resist Japan" has dictated historical construction for decades. Putting aside moral questions, this dominance has inevitably obscured details that can inform, challenge, or even substantiate the master narrative. This volume addresses that paucity of details in the hope that it will inspire further work on the period.

Translating the Occupation: The Japanese Invasion of China, 1931–45 is divided into three parts: "Manchukuo," "East China," and "North China and

Beyond." In each region, Japanese imperialism in mainland China developed in a distinct manner. To accentuate these distinctions, we have selected readings from a wide variety of persons and topics, ranging from education to the "woman question," and much beyond and in between. Some of the authors were leading figures of their time, such as the well-known Chinese intellectual Zhou Zuoren. Others were less prominent, including Japanese agricultural colonists and Korean sex workers. By attending to the contexts in which these texts were produced and the varied perspectives they provide, we hope to shed valuable new light on life in China under Japanese occupation and demonstrate the utility of scholarly translation for advancing academic discussions on contentious historical topics.

Notes

1 Peter Hays Gries, "China's 'New Thinking' on Japan," *China Quarterly* 184 (2005): 835.

2 The term "Second Sino-Japanese War" is commonly used in English-language literature on the China-Japan conflict from 1937 to 1945. In mainland China, the conflict is called the "Chinese War of Resistance against Japan," and is sometimes dated from 1931. In Japan, the terms are "China Incident," "Japan-China Incident," or, from 1941, the "Greater East Asia War." We have encouraged contributors to this volume to decide what term is most appropriate in their work.

3 Rana Mitter, *Forgotten Ally: China's World War II, 1937–1945* (Boston: Houghton Mifflin Harcourt, 2013).

4 Gerald E. Bunker, *The Peace Conspiracy: Wang Ching-wei and the China War, 1937–1941* (Cambridge, MA: Harvard University Press, 1972), 272.

5 Cited in Aly Song, "China's World of Anti-Japan War Films," 23 August 2013, *Reuters: The Wider Image,* https://widerimage.reuters.com/story/chinas-world-of-anti-japan-war-films.

6 Yang Kuisong, *Guizi laile* [The devils have come] (Guilin: Guangxi Normal University Press, 2016), 173–75.

7 Zhang Chengzhi, *Zunzhong yu xibie: Zhi Riben* [Respect and reluctance at our parting: For Japan] (Beijing: Zhongguo youyi chuban gongsi, 2008).

8 Ge Zhaoguang, *What Is China? Territory, Ethnicity, Culture, and History,* trans. Michael Gibbs Hill (Cambridge, MA: Harvard University Press, 2018).

9 For example, see the 2018 essay by Zhang Quan, "Zhongguo lunxian qu wenyi yanjiu de fangfa wenti: Yi Du Zanqi de 'Manzhouguo' xiangxiang wei zhongxin" [Methodological problems in the study of literature and art in China's enemy-occupied territories: Taking Prasenjit Duara's imagination of "Manchuria" as the centre], *Wenyi piping* [Literary criticism], 30 July 2018, http://www.sohu.com/a/244095274_754344.

10 Akiko Hashimoto, *The Long Defeat: Cultural Trauma, Memory, and Identity in Japan* (Oxford: Oxford University Press, 2015), 3.

11 Takashi Yoshida, *The Making of the "Rape of Nanking": History and Memory in Japan, China, and the United States* (New York: Oxford University Press, 2006).

12 Hata Ikuhito, *Nankin jiken: "Gyakusatsu" no kōzō* [The Nanjing Incident: The structure of a "massacre"] (Tōkyō: Chūōkōronshinsha, 2007); Kasahara Tokushi, *Nankin jiken ronsōshi: Nihonjin wa shijitsu o dō ninshikishitekitaka* [A history of debates on the Nanjing Incident: On the Japanese people's understanding of the historical facts] (Tōkyō: Heibonsha), 2007.

13 For example, see Diana Lary and Stephen R. MacKinnon, eds., *The Scars of War: The Impact of Warfare on Modern China* (Vancouver: UBC Press, 2001); Timothy Brook, *Collaboration: Japanese Agents and Local Elites in Wartime China* (Cambridge, MA: Harvard University Press, 2005); and Diana Lary, *The Chinese People at War: Human Suffering and Social Transformation* (New York: Cambridge University Press, 2010).

14 Timothy Brook, ed., *Documents on the Rape of Nanking* (Ann Arbor: University of Michigan Press, 1999).

15 Suping Lu, ed., *A Dark Page in History: The Nanjing Massacre and Post-Massacre Social Conditions Recorded in British Diplomatic Dispatches, Admiralty Documents, and US Naval Intelligence Reports* (Lanham, MD: University Press of America, 2012).

16 Donald S. Detwiler and Charles Burdick, eds., *War in Asia and the Pacific, 1937–1949: A Fifteen Volume Collection* (New York: Garland, 1980).

17 David Atwill and Yurong Atwill, eds., *Sources in Chinese History* (Abingdon, UK: Routledge, 2009).

18 Sven Saaler and Christopher W.A. Szpilman, eds., *Pan-Asianism: A Documentary History, 1920–Present* (Lanham, MD: Rowman and Littlefield, 2011).

19 We thank an anonymous reader for drawing our attention to this significance. Two examples of the first type are Patricia Ebrey, ed., *Chinese Civilization: A Sourcebook* (New York: Free Press, 1981) and Wm. Theodore De Bary and Richard Lufrano, eds., *Sources of Chinese Tradition: From 1600 through the Twentieth Century* (New York: Columbia University Press, 1999). An example of the second type is Kenneth J. Hammond and Kristin Stapleton, eds., *The Human Tradition in Modern China* (Lanham, MD: Rowman and Littlefield, 2007).

20 Pei-kai Cheng, Michael Elliot Lestz, and Jonathan D. Spence, eds., *The Search for Modern China: A Documentary Collection* (New York: W.W. Norton, 2014).

21 Poshek Fu, *Passivity, Resistance, and Collaboration: Intellectual Choices in Occupied Shanghai, 1937–1945* (Stanford, CA: Stanford University Press, 1993), xiv.

22 Dongyoun Hwang, "Wang Jingwei, the Nanjing Government and the Problem of Collaboration" (PhD diss., Duke University, 1999), 20.

23 For a recent discussion of this, see Annika A. Culver, "Introduction" in *Manchukuo Perspectives: Transnational Approaches to Literary Production,* ed. Annika A. Culver and Norman Smith (Hong Kong: Hong Kong University Press, 2019), 1–10.

24 John Whittier Treat, "Choosing to Collaborate: Yi Kwang-su and the Moral Subject in Colonial Korea," *Journal of Asian Studies* 71, 1 (February 2012): 81–102.

25 Timothy Brook, "Hesitating before the Judgment of History," *Journal of Asian Studies* 71, 1 (February 2012): 112.

26 Michel-Rolph Trouillot, *Silencing the Past: Power and the Production of History,* 2nd rev. ed. (Boston: Beacon Press, 2015), 27.

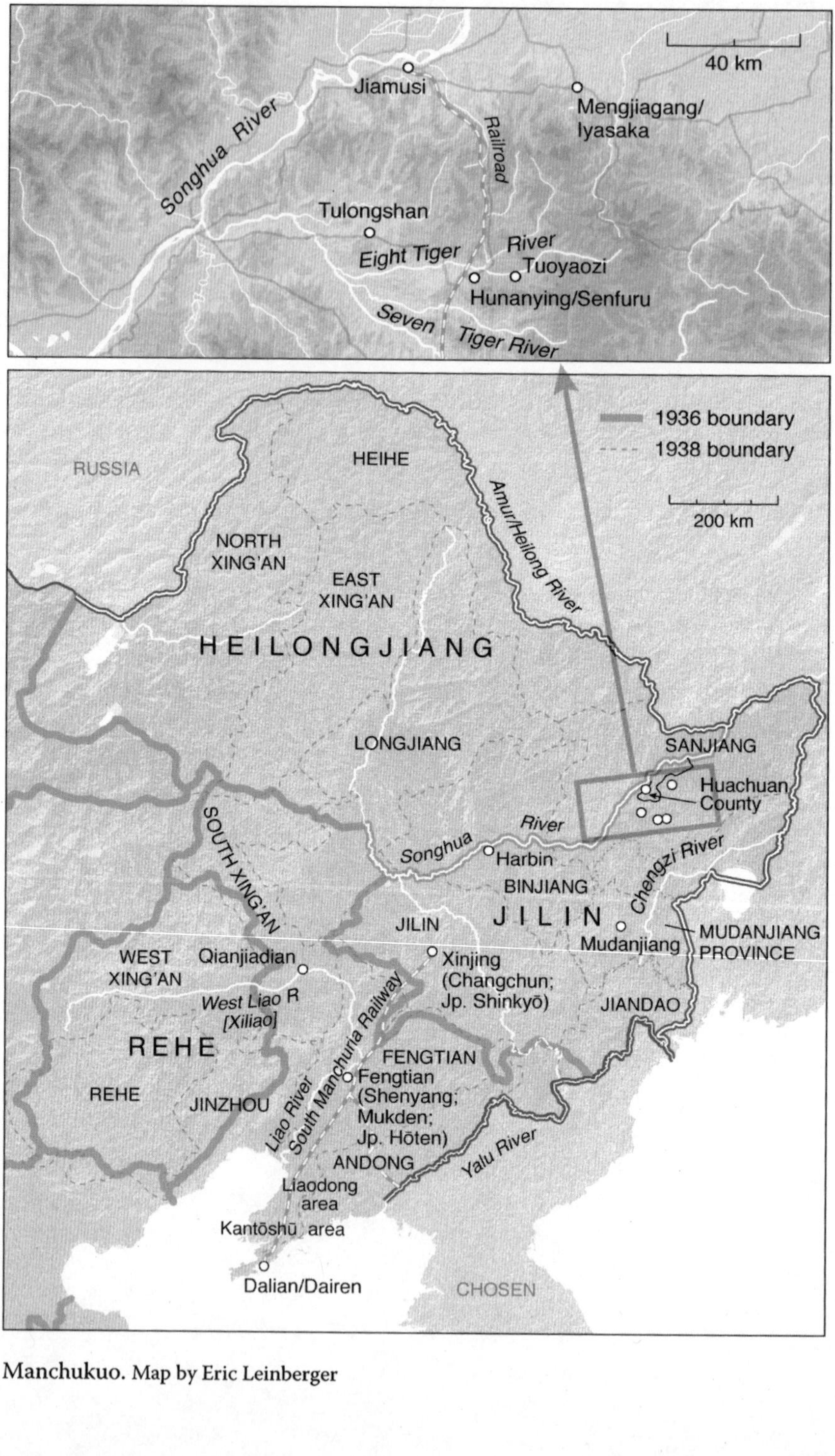

Manchukuo. Map by Eric Leinberger

Part 1
MANCHUKUO

—• MANCHURIA TIMELINE •—

1910	Korea annexed by Japan
1928	Japanese assassinate warlord Zhang Zuolin; his son, Zhang Xueliang succeeds him
1931	18 September, Mukden Incident. Japan begins invasion of Manchuria
1932	1 March, Manchukuo established, with Zheng Xiaoxu appointed prime minister
	August, north Manchuria, especially Harbin, floods for three weeks
1933	24 February, Japan withdraws from the League of Nations
1934	1 March, Puyi enthroned as emperor
1935	Prime Minister Zheng Xiaoxu resigns
1937	December, rationing and labour requirements increase from the start of the Chinese War of Resistance against Japan
1941	censorship deepens in Manchukuo's literary world
1945	August, Manchukuo dissolved

—• **MANCHURIA WAS THE FIRST** major region in mainland China to be occupied by Japan. The invasion that began on 18 September 1931 played a pivotal role in the mid-twentieth-century expansion of the Japanese Empire and in China exacerbated a sense of the nation's vulnerability. Japan's establishment of the puppet state of Manchukuo on 1 March 1932 contributed to a near-universal lack of faith in the League of Nations; Japan withdrew from the organization on 24 February 1933. Manchukuo fostered multitudes of "bandits," former warlord soldiers, and Communist insurgents who, in the aftermath of imperial Japan's collapse, would defeat the Nationalists in the region. Communist hatred of the puppet state was visited on the regime's capital during the horrific siege of Changchun (May to October 1948), in which Lin Biao (1907–71) caused as many as 200,000 civilians to die.[1] The highly decorated Communist general sought to turn Changchun into a "dead city."[2] The subsequent defeat of the Nationalists in Manchuria has been widely credited with Communist victory in the Civil War.[3] For decades after the collapse of Manchukuo, many in Japan mourned the loss of what they believed to be an idealistic state, one that featured prominently in popular culture and scholarship. In China, the state has been utterly condemned as "bogus" or "false," with the *de rigueur* addition of "*wei*" to the name of the state: *wei Manzhouguo* (bogus Manchukuo). In English-language scholarship, Manchukuo attracted little attention until the 1990s. Presently, there is considerable and growing interest in the multicultural state as an example of Asian imperialism.

The readings introduced and translated in this section highlight the ways that people lived in Manchukuo and the increasing levels of militarism that framed their lives. Ronald Suleski offers the first translation, of a roundtable discussion of Japanese migration to Manchukuo in the 1941 book *Manshū kaitaku monogatari* (Tales of opening Manchuria). The group of immigrant farmers is referred to as "armed colonists," because of their defensive positions against multitudes of armed "bandits" in the region. In 1933, these particular migrants had seized over fifty thousand acres of land from the original inhabitants. The subsequent, violent retaliatory attacks on the community lasted several months in the spring of 1934. The Japanese farmers were not soldiers or starry-eyed intellectuals set on improving Asia's status in the world but, rather, were impoverished labourers who often had no choice but to migrate to Japan's so-called lifeline of Manchukuo or be labelled unpatriotic. Their lives were hard and not to be envied, though the discussants put a positive spin on their experiences for propagandistic purposes back home in Japan.

One of the major institutions to promote the driving ideology of Manchukuo, the Kingly Way (Ch: *Wangdao;* Jp: *Ōdō*), was National Foundation University (established May 1938), which represented an alternate path for the puppet state. Bill Sewell and Norio Ota translate "The Light of Asia," written by Sakuta Shōichi (1878–1973), a professor of economics and law who, after retirement in Japan, moved to Manchukuo's capital to serve as vice-president of the university. Sakuta had a long-standing interest in China and was active in attempting to reform Japan, notably working in 1932 at a tuition-free National Institute of Spiritual Culture for left-leaning students who had been forced out of postsecondary education. With Manchukuo's second prime minister, Zhang Jinghui (1871–1959), as its nominal president, the university manifested an effort to create an elite Asian cohort to lead the multiethnic state. In "The Light of Asia," Sakuta describes how Japan could contribute to improving the lives of all Asians, a theme that motivated many educators and politicians in Manchukuo but failed to win the support of the dominant Japanese Kantō Army.

Hua Rui then introduces writings by the first prime minister of Manchukuo, Zheng Xiaoxu (1860–1938). Zheng, like Wang Jingwei (1883–1944), is one of the most contentious figures in modern Chinese history, known for his high-level collaboration with the Japanese, for which he has been condemned as a *Hanjian,* a traitor to the Han (Chinese). Zheng served from 1932 to 1935 as the figurehead of the State Council and a key defender of the ruling ideology, the Kingly Way. Zheng was a loyal defender of the Qing dynasty (1644–1912) and actively weaved late-Qing constitutionalism, pacifism, and Italian fascism into a quasi-Confucian utopian project to spur national development in the face of early twentieth-century nationalist modernity, which he, and his Japanese overseers, disdained. Realizing that he was politically impotent, despite his high-ranking political position, Zheng focused his energies on writing about the Kingly Way as a means of self-cultivation that he believed had universal application. Unfortunately, the Kantō Army preferred rule by racist, military force to the virtue that Zheng so eloquently wrote about.

In 1933, the Fengtian Education Bureau and the Fengtian Education Committee began publishing a Chinese-language journal, *Fengtian jiaoyu* (Mukden education review), featuring administrative announcements and education research; Wang Yu translates one of each, from the first issue. As Japan's domestic politics turned increasingly conservative and nationalistic in the early 1930s, some educators moved to Manchukuo, where they sought to implement what they believed to be the most appropriate and modern educational techniques. Their pedagogy reflected the Kingly Way espoused by Zheng Xiaoxu. As Wang makes clear, though, educators mixed Confucian-inspired ideals with philosophical, educational, and psychological theories from Germany and Switzerland. In an administrative announcement, Morita Ryōichi emphasizes labour education, with cooperative schools, short courses, and special classrooms – a form of education that contemporary critics disparaged as being anti-intellectual. Nakatani Sadaharu, education inspector of Fengtian province, introduced the theories of German philosopher, psychologist, and educator Eduard Spranger (1882–1963) in his speech on "Educational Love," which he reasoned was "scientific" and therefore not susceptible to social and political changes, effectively undermining Japanese notions that they could change Asia for the better.

Perhaps nothing epitomized the hypocrisy behind Japanese claims to the betterment of Asia more than the regulation and trade of opium. Janice Matsumura introduces a 1936 essay by Kaneko Junji (1890–1979), "The China Incident from the Perspective of Psychiatry," in which he decries Chinese "addicts" as "notoriously deceptive" in their rousing of anti-Japanese sentiments. He links widespread contemporary Chinese narcotics consumption with what he viewed as the Chinese "national character." Kaneko, a criminal psychiatrist, wrote on the dangers of narcotics and alcohol and was affiliated with the Tokyo Metropolitan Police Board. Yet, as Matsumura argues, it is difficult to gauge Kaneko's knowledge of Japan's opium trade as, for example, no evidence exists that he ever visited Manchukuo. Kaneko worked in Japan, where there was seemingly considerable support for censorship as well as state management of information, a system replicated in the puppet state.

From December 1941, the Manchukuo government tightened ideological control over literary and cultural production across the state. On 25 July 1942, the Department of Police Affairs in the Ministry of Public Security ordered an inspection of the activities and writings of ideologically suspect writers and cultural workers in Xinjing. Xie Miya Qiong translates "Documents Regarding the Investigation on Ideological Movements through Literature, Art, and Theatre" to provide a clear picture of official efforts to control cultural production. Three Chinese leftist writers from Harbin, who had been arrested and then half-heartedly obeyed Japanese officials' demands to identify suspicious writings and their authors, assisted in the investigation. Most notably, the officials sought intelligence on workers in the Manchuria Motion Picture Association and the publishing and broadcast industries. Contemporary tendencies in Chinese leftist cultural production reveal that critics of the state encouraged "Anti-Manchukuo, Resist Japan" (*fanMan kangRi*) sentiments in artful and circuitous ways.

Such leftist writers are rare in the *Collection of Literary Selections by Each Ethnicity in Manchukuo,* the introduction to which is translated here by Annika A. Culver.[4] In 1942, the Sōgansha press published the first of two planned Japanese-language collections of multiethnic literature that were to showcase thriving Manchurian cultural production under Japanese tutelage. Four Japanese editors comment on the significance of the collection and how it boded well for the future development of Manchukuo's literary world. Only one Chinese editor contributed: Gu Ding (1914/16–66), who was widely recognized as a favourite of the Japanese. Most of the essays in the introduction indicate aspirations for a particularly "Manchurian" literature that would put a positive spin on Sino-Japanese cooperation and cultural production.

In the early 1940s, Mei Niang (1916–2013), Wu Ying (1915–61), and Yang Xu (1918–2004) were writers whose lives and work epitomized the dream of a multiethnic state. Norman Smith translates three "open letters" published in popular journals in Japanese-occupied Manchukuo and Beijing, at a time when authorities stressed the ideal of a "good wife, wise mother" who was demure, obedient, and loyal to her father, husband, and son. Japan's colonial education system and media were enlisted to support the goal of cultivating such women – women were explicitly encouraged to "go back to the kitchen." But these young, educated women were not prepared to go back to the kitchen in their struggle against patriarchy and social injustice, as reflected in these translations. Mei Niang and Wu Ying penned letters to each other, while a writer using the name Jia Ren wrote an open letter to Yang Xu. Each of the letters remarks on the character of the writers, their professional lives, and the difficult circumstances in which they lived.

Jonghyun Lee has translated "Women Facing a Crossroads," a collection of Korean memoirs published in the *Mansŏnilbo* (Manchuria–Joseon daily news) in December 1932. As Lee points out, while there is no assurance that the memoirs were written by the authors named, they eloquently portray the lives and concerns of Korean women in Manchukuo. By 1945, Koreans in Manchukuo numbered almost two million, almost twice the number of Japanese, and the third-largest population following the Han and Manchus. As the memoirs make vividly clear, the Korean women endured colonializing influences from the Japanese as they became imperialists as well while still suffering from patriarchal norms.

Part 1 illustrates how varied individuals viewed their lives and ambitions in Manchukuo, striving to live in an order that was idealistic and militaristic, and that over time turned more and more to the latter, not to the Kingly Way or the "light of Asia" espoused by early propagandists and ideologues. The promises that the idea of Manchukuo may once have inspired were extinguished by activities of the military, an education system and ideology that many viewed with suspicion or contempt, and the opportunistic seizing of lands for Japanese "pioneers." Together, the readings demonstrate a complexity of life and cultural production that has often been overlooked, minimized, or condemned in accounts of the puppet state of Manchukuo.

Notes

1 Diana Lary, *China's Civil War: A Social History, 1945–1949* (Cambridge: Cambridge University Press, 2015), 126.

2 Quoted in Andrew Jacobs, "China Is Wordless on Traumas of Communists Rise," *New York Times,* 1 October 2009, https://www.nytimes.com/2009/10/02/world/asia/02anniversary.html.

3 For example, see Harold Tanner, *Where Chiang Kai-shek Lost China: The Liao-Shen Campaign, 1948* (Indianapolis: Indiana University Press, 2015).

4 Exceptions include Nogawa Takashi (1901-44) who contributed the short story "Tonsu he iku hitobito" [The people going to the hamlet]; he was later imprisoned for his sympathies toward Chinese villagers allegedly being stiffed by the cooperatives. Shimaki Kensaku (1903–45) is a converted leftist who helped edit the volume, too. For further information, see Stephen Poland, "The Literary Politics of Harmonization and Dissonance" in *Manchukuo Perspectives: Transnational Approaches to Literary Production,* ed. Annika A. Culver and Norman Smith (Hong Kong: Hong Kong University Press, 2019), 255–68.

1 Tales of Opening Manchuria

RONALD SULESKI

In September 1931, the Japanese Kantō Army (*Kantōgun*), with help from Japanese troops stationed in Korea, invaded Manchuria. Resistance quickly fell before the advancing Japanese, and by early 1932 Japan occupied all of Manchuria. In the summer of that year, civilian employees of the Japanese government arrived in the Manchurian city of Harbin. Their purpose was to identify areas where Japanese agricultural colonists (*nōmin kaitakusha*) could farm the land. More than just farms, the goal was to build Japanese village communities with schools, medical clinics, machinery repair shops, and regular communication with Japanese military units stationed nearby.

Nearly ten years later in 1941, a seminar was organized to celebrate the accomplishments of the early Japanese colonizers. Several of the men who had visited Jiamusi, a city about 350 kilometres east of Harbin where the first batch of colonists had been sent, were on hand to give their recollections of Japanese settlement in the region. The seminar transcript was published in the book *Manshū kaitaku monogatari* (Tales of opening Manchuria), a portion of which is translated here. Their comments are all in conversational Japanese. As I read them, devoid of political jargon or the honorific speech (*keigo*) often used at formal occasions, I felt as if I were attending the seminar, listening to this friendly and relaxed group of men (only men spoke at the seminar because the first groups of settlers consisted only of armed men) talk about the situation they faced from 1932. This text showed me how little conversational Japanese has changed since the 1930s.

I felt in a friendly mood toward these men as I read and translated their comments about hard work and scary times. Alas, a wider reading of materials about those early days of the Japanese colonists in Jiamusi revealed that, even beyond their assumptions that the Japanese occupiers had a perfect right to be in Manchuria, their recollections were very selective. The book turned out to be a well-edited piece of Japanese propaganda presenting convincing and human stories of sacrifice and hard work. When placed in the context of the wider story, the transcript is filled with clues about what was taking place. But when read in a relaxed way by a Japanese person at the time, the accounts were almost certainly accepted as sincere and admirable.[1]

In his first remarks, Katō Hisao refers to his group as "armed colonists" (*busō yimin*), the term used at that time. The government said arms were necessary due to the many armed "bandits" in the region, who were actually renegade former warlord military units. Unable to overcome the better-trained and more heavily armed invading Japanese troops, several Chinese units had moved into the swampy and hilly terrain south of Jiamusi, where they harassed incoming colonists. Historians in the People's Republic of China (PRC) today might classify them as anti-Japanese resistance forces. The Colonel Tōmiya that Katō mentions approvingly was Lt. Colonel Tōmiya Kaneo (1892–1937), who insisted the first settlers be armed with military rifles.

As the story unfolds, colonist Okada Takeba mentions the ruinous floods occurring along the banks of the Songhua River, flooding the streets of Harbin. Later during the occupation, the Japanese tried building dams to stop the periodic flooding, but it was not until 1958 that the Chinese government finally had enough water-control facilities to prevent the rampant flooding.[2]

According to the story below, the Japanese were encouraged by regional Chinese officials to take over large tracts of land and bring it into cultivation. When the group arrived south of Jiamusi, probably in trucks driven by soldiers of the Kantō Army, they took a horse cart up to an area of high ground in order to survey the lands available for the taking. They decided to claim twenty to thirty thousand *chōbu* of land, over twenty thousand hectares, for their use. This survey group was armed but, as Katō confirmed, they did not need survey instruments or maps in order to decide the lands to be designated for Japanese use.

Colonist Yoshizaki Senshū then talks about a bandit attack on the small settlement of Hunanying (renamed by the Japanese "Senfuru," or Thousand Waves of Prosperity), south of the Yongfengzhen area mentioned earlier in the text. The speakers conflate the towns of Mengjiagang and Yongfuzhen, but on current PRC maps these are

1.1 Cover of *Manshū kaitaku monogatari*.
Source: Author's collection

two distinct locations, although they are nearby each other, south of the city of Jiamusi. Both of these towns seem to have been walled market towns. The colonists took advantage of these walls, which defended their camp.

Why were the Chinese attackers so determined to overcome the Hunanying/Senfuru settlement? Most likely there were several reasons: in general, even the poorest Japanese settlers had better clothing, tools, medicines, and sewing machines compared to the neighbouring Chinese; the Japanese probably had food and grain in storage, which were always a pressing need for the Chinese renegade soldiers; and it seems that, in this case, the Japanese colonists had military-issue rifles and a lot of ammunition, while the scattered Chinese units were not receiving any resupply. These determined Chinese attacks lasted over a period of several months in the spring of 1934, a little over a year after the first Japanese colonists arrived.

On 18 April 1934, a small two-passenger DH.80A, a de Havilland Puss Moth aircraft manufactured in England between 1929 and 1933, landed in a field outside the besieged Japanese compound. Constructed of plywood, these planes had a deadly tendency for the struts supporting their overhead wings to break off – they would begin to flutter and buckle, and the plane would crash in a nosedive, which may have been how the plane later crashed that day. After forty days of siege and no contact with the outside world, the plane brought important treats such as letters from family in Japan and *yōkan* (a thick, jellied dessert made of red bean paste and sugar), to be eaten with tea. Among the items given to the colonists were some Ruby Queen (*rubii kuiin*), cigarettes that could be sold in the local commercial markets for a lot of cash. This supply may indicate that the local Chinese markets did not accept Japanese currency, which was also included in the shipment. On the other hand, trading in precious metals and stones was one of the main activities of the local Chinese markets in the Jiamusi area, so good negotiations would allow the Japanese colonists to raise a lot of cash.

Colonist Yoshizaki Senshū mentions a "Longshan Incident" (*Ryūsan jiken*). The correct name of this place is Tulongshan, an area west of the Japanese settlements discussed in this translation, today called Tulongshangzhen, in Huanan county. In January 1934, Japanese armed colonists were moving into the area, forcibly buying land from local Chinese farmers at low prices and taking away their firearms, over the strong objections of the local Chinese population, who used their firearms to hunt for food. A local gentry chief named Xie Wendong mobilized the local militia and, with other local people joining in, the Chinese forces soon numbered between three thousand and six thousand men.[3] Early in March, they drove out the Japanese, resulting in the deaths of at least nineteen Japanese soldiers sent to help the colonists. It was not until October 1934 that the Japanese forces regained control over the area, so the attacks against Hunanying being described here took place at the same time as the anti-Japanese revolt at Tulongshan. This was a (temporary) setback for the Japanese agricultural colonists and also for the plan of overrunning Heilongjiang with Japanese settlements. The event was strictly prohibited from being reported to the Japanese public, but of course people living in the area exchanged stories about it. In this case, Yoshizaki seems to be saying that the "bandit" attacks on Hunanying were part of Chinese anger against the Japanese who had tried to move into Tulongshan.[4]

Talk at the seminar then turned to the orchard the Japanese developed to help ensure that fresh fruits would be available to the colonists, named the Heaven Shining Garden (Ch: *Tianzhaoyuan;* Jp: *Tenshōen*).[5] A revealing point mentioned in the discussion is that the Japanese government in those days was not able to recruit enough farmers from Japan to move to Manchuria. So the government began to recruit unemployed labourers, especially younger men and boys in their teens, who were unable to find construction or factory jobs in Tokyo and who had to be trained in every aspect of preparing soil and planting trees. The discussion also reveals that because of the hard work and meagre meals, the weight of the average Japanese colonist working in the orchards dropped from fifty-nine to fifty-five kilograms. Most of these males were of slight stature and were skinny to begin with, so their bodies did not have any extra weight to lose, and they likely experienced medical problems as a result.

By the late 1930s, the Japanese government was sending recruiters directly to rural farming villages in Japan, and (as we now know) often intimidating portions of entire villages to move together to Manchukuo. One intimidation tactic was threatening to report these villagers as being "unpatriotic" and unwilling to aid the imperial war effort.[6]

In the translation below, I mix both Chinese and Japanese pronunciations for place names. This is because the Japanese speakers sometimes used the Chinese pronunciations for places (sometimes indicated by *kana* script next to the *kanji* in the text), and also because the Chinese pronunciation of most Manchukuo place names seem better known to English-speaking readers. But where Japanese place names were clearly used by the speakers, such as for the Iyasaka and Senfuru settlements, the Japanese pronunciations are given.

I am very aware of the narrative of the indignities and cruelties visited on Chinese, Koreans, Russians, and all the subject peoples of Manchukuo. That aspect of what the Japanese did cannot be explained away. Having said all this and having translated many pages from this book, I still find myself feeling a residue of sympathy for the men whose comments you will read below. They had no right to be in Manchuria, where they imposed themselves on the local population. Still, they gave up the prime years of their lives for the sake of the colonizing experiment. Even if they managed to survive the collapse of Manchukuo in 1945 and eventually got back to postwar Japan to continue their lives, they surely had lost more than they ever gained.[10]

TRANSLATION

Recalling the Early Days of Opening Manchuria: A Seminar[7]

MURAYAMA TŌSHIRŌ: We are talking about the early days of opening Manchuria, and as we all know this topic is one that continues to have historical importance. We are talking about the past ten difficult years in which each of you have been involved in this effort, so we have taken the opportunity to gather all of you together to discuss and relive the period.

As we know, this will be talk based on your concrete experiences, and recalling past times, and maybe some self-congratulation, but we want to give a clear and wide-ranging account to all our readers.

In the course of recalling these past times all of these events might not be clearly pulled together in our minds, but let's take the approach that we speak as clearly as we can.

The region of the initial opening that we are discussing is the first Japanese Iyasaka-*mura* (Prosperity Village) that was on the border of north Manchuria in the direction of Yongfengzhen. I heard that Katō-san was one of the first of the armed colonists involved in the initial survey of this area, so I'd like to begin by asking the person involved to speak.

Looking for Suitable Land near Yongfengzhen

KATŌ HISAO: I was a member of the survey team for immigration to Manchuria (*Manshū yijū tekichi chōsahan*) of the Ministry of Colonization (*Takumushō*). I came to Manchuria for that purpose, and as I recall that was in September 1932. As most of you know, at that time Jilin province (currently an area that includes the provinces of Sanjiang, Mudanjiang, and Binjiang) had a very bad public security problem since it was a time when thirty thousand followers led by Li Du and Ding Chao were on the rampage and no one could guarantee the safety of our survey team.

The first area considered for opening was the area of Yongfengzhen. There was a small village named Mengjiagang that had about one hundred Manchurian families who made their living by forestry work and extracting gold dust from surface deposits. But after the Manchurian Incident [1931] the village was attacked by bandits and the villagers scattered. Thus because of the very dangerous security situation, the plan of having settlers move into the area was by necessity made into having the settlers be armed.

When the first group of armed settlers moved into the area of Yongfengzhen (now renamed Iyasaka Village), it was through the foresight of Colonel Tōmiya, because the actual ability to move into the area had been thought about by Colonel Tōmiya at a time when no one else had made that consideration. There is an interesting story about how he made the decision to try this area.

The colonel (he was then a captain) was then in Jilin province as an adviser to the military. In the area east of Mudanjiang called Dongshi county there were about 30,000 bandits. Both the Japanese military and the Jilin military were engaged in trying to subdue them. The colonel was active by taking military action against the bandits in many areas. Because the bandits were hard to pin down, the colonel did a lot of reconnaissance in the region. Because he was a very discerning man, he was struck by the many areas of fertile land that was not under cultivation. He became convinced that these were areas where Japanese settlers ought to move into.

Just at the time that Colonel Tōmiya was commanding the Manchukuo Protection Army (*Manshūkoku gorogun*), the current minister of security (*chianbu daijin*), General Yu Chencheng, told the colonel that there were large fields of fertile uncultivated land within his jurisdiction to the southeast of Jiamusi in the area near to Mengjiagang. It was agreed that we could have up to a thousand families from Japan come to settle this area, which was a total of 20,000 *chōbu* [1 *chōbu* = 1 hectare], meaning that each family could be provided with 20 *chōbu* [20 hectares] of land without payment, and these conditions seemed appropriate to all sides so that was our proposal. At that time the county magistrate of Huachuan county, Tang Chunli, was also encouraging us. Under those conditions the colonel became excited about the idea.

Since the situation in the area was so dangerous, he returned to Changchun and – while saying it was imperative that the new settlers be armed, there also needed to be a plan for their protection – so he returned to Changchun and approached the Kantō Army.

MURAYAMA: So it appears that Colonel Tōmiya devised the plan to have Japanese settlers move into this area?

KATŌ: That's correct. And at the same time, we selected a possible area where the first group of settlers could move into. Both General Yu and Magistrate Tang recommended this area to Colonel Tōmiya, and also another place in the county, Beiliushu hezi.

So it was then the task of our survey team to decide which of the candidate areas would receive the first contingent of settlers. In order to survey the areas, our team left Harbin in the middle of September, and that year the waters of the Songhua River overflowed their banks, and there was a big flood.

OKADA TAKEBA: Yes, yes. Speaking of that year, in Harbin because of the flooding we had to ride in boats down Kitaiskaia Street.

KATŌ: I remember we had to ride in small boats down to the dock in order to board our larger boat to go down the Songhua River to Jiamusi.

MURAYAMA: How did you organize yourselves?

KATŌ: Our current director of Manchuria colonizing (*Mantaku*), Nakamura Kōjirō, was head of the survey team, Saitō was head of the Chengzi River group and others were also present; the guide was Colonel Tōmiya; and the Jilin bandit suppression chief of staff, along with Yang Yushu who had become a director of the Manchuria Colonizing Organization and Magistrate Tang of Huachuan county, all went together with us.

Our decision was to send the first group of armed settlers into the Yongfengzhen area. As I've just mentioned, in reaching this decision we listened to the opinions of Colonel Tōmiya, General Yu, and the magistrate. The final decision was up to us, based on what we had actually saw. Then we departed to inspect the area, each with our own concerns, which we repeatedly brought up and talked over among ourselves.

We arrived at Yongfengzhen for our inspection. We saw it was on a high plain with wild grasses of all sorts growing in profusion. Seeing that the soil was very fertile, we all agreed on that favourable point. We began to survey the surrounding area in terms of its suitability. We also saw the hill where the Iyasaka Shrine (*jinja*) now stands, and we climbed that hill, from where we could see the surrounding land out to quite a distance. We had not brought surveying instruments with us, and since we did not have maps of the area, we thought that we could only truly see the entire area from the nearby hilltop so we took a horse cart up there, and we could see the large area of land. That was how we surveyed the area. We saw the area consisted of twenty to thirty thousand *chōbu* of land, a great expanse.

On the second day we began to look at the other possible area, the nearby Beiliushu hezi. However, this area was very dangerous, and we noticed that it was narrower, so we ended up recommending the Yongfengzhen area.

1.2 Postcard of Harbin, flooded in 1932. *Source:* Author's collection

MURAYAMA: So the first area chosen for opening up was based on your conclusions after looking at the whole area. Katō-san has a story about tasting "mercury" that took place during your survey, didn't it?

KATŌ: Well, yes it did.

The Story of Drinking Mercury

OKADA: About this story of drinking mercury, what was that all about?

KATŌ: No, it wasn't really a big thing. It was a bit of a misadventure. In Director Nakamura's book *The Story of Manchuria Immigrants* (*Manshū imin monogatari*) he writes about the incident. But in leaving for our survey trip, we left Harbin and passed through an area where there was cholera. For those of us who were travelling through north Manchuria for the first time, that was all a scary business. As said earlier, we were on a boat travelling from Harbin to Jiamusi. That day following breakfast the boy (*bōi*) brought some water to gargle [to rinse out our mouths] and gave me some, and I rinsed my mouth. I thought: "This is not good," so I said to the boy: "What kind of water is this?" Later I thought it was a silly question to ask.

But the boy replied: "It was mercury (*shōkōsui*)." I panicked and wondered if I was about to die and thought: "I'm too young to die now." But one of the members of our group who could speak Manchurian [Chinese]

yelled over saying: "Katō, don't worry! That was just a mouthwash. In Manchurian a mouthwash is *soukoushui*. Take note of this, when we get back you'll still be alive and with us." (Laughter)

The Battlements of Hunanying and Group Leader Mune

MURAYAMA: Technician Yoshizaki, a member of the Colonization Agricultural Committee (*Takushoku inkai*) was a leader of the second group, and this is the first time we've invited him here. I'd like him to speak to us about life as a member of the agricultural group, about his outlook, and also about the bandit attack experienced by the second group, all in terms of his role as the group leader.

YOSHIZAKI SENSHŪ: As for speaking about leader Mune's attitude while on the battlements of Hunanying, we can sum it up in a phrase by saying he "had a bearing of sincerity and determination." Usually, when there is no wind blowing anyone can maintain a calm and steady demeanour. In the first year after joining the agricultural work, we worked hard to build something up, then returned [to our camp] with a sense of failure, and in this past year again we've not done well. It was because from the north and from the south, for days and nights at a time we were attacked by three thousand bandits. We had no food to eat, no way of communicating our situation, and never knew if we would live to see the next day. Almost all of us fell into deep depression and lost hope. At times like that, truly, human beings are reduced to people with no pretentions. In those times when it seemed we had no chance, the attitude of Group Leader Mune embraced all of us. We were in a situation when for two months straight the bandits attacked us every evening, and we had no way of communicating with the outside world. We could not conceive of any future for ourselves. The group leader refused to give in to hopelessness, and [therefore] we also could not fall into complete despair. The group leader would not countenance us giving up hope for the future, even when we approached him with our fears. I have to say that even I myself could not summon any vision of a future. I experienced the siege for two months with no contact with the outside world. It got to the point that I was criticizing our group leader.

We told our group leader that we could not see how we might build our camp (at that time we were called the Camp Building Unit [*Tonkondan*]). "Leader," I said, "we worked all last year to protect ourselves from the bandits, but this year things are just as awful for us." That was the way I had completed two months of work with our colonization group.

It was the exhaustion all of us group members had experienced because of the bandit attacks every day and every night for so long.

"Well, last year we could not finish our work because of the bandits, and this year the situation has gotten even worse. So far we've been here two years working hard. And it's true that all of us have become exhausted because of the bandit attacks and what you have been saying is all true. So I can see how you are thinking." The leader paused in his work of repairing our agricultural tools and was silent and thinking for a while. "Well, Yoshizaki-san, if things are so bad maybe all of us group leaders ought to slit our stomachs [kill ourselves] because of this."

That was the way he answered me. Then all of me, both my mind and my body, realized what he was saying. I regained my determination to preserve a spirit of hope for the future of our group.

It was 18 April. We were encircled by bandits for about the fortieth day. The ground was warming up because spring had come to north Manchuria, and there were green buds appearing on Tōmiya Mountain (*yama*). None of the people in our group had any idea what to expect of this spring. No one wanted to think about the coming year, and in those circumstances no one held out any hope. Although the black earth was loosening up and the green buds were appearing, beyond our protective walls there were three thousand bandits encamped.

All the members of our group were brave. Since joining the group in 1933, all our work of building by the five hundred members of our group [gave us] a sense of failure because of the Seven Tiger river bandits[8]. One winter we had walked thirteen *li* to the Xiaoshidao River (*hezi*) to cut trees for construction but at night, while returning, all our collected wood was set afire. So besides agricultural work, we could not accomplish any of the other tasks we had set for ourselves. The time for planting spring wheat was already past. In the face of our troubles and hard work, we all fell into depression.

At the same time, some of the members of our planting group had an idea to do the planting anyway, and they approached the group leader about it. The supervisor replied with the single phrase: "Let's try it." So the brave Japanese farmers began the spring planting of wheat even with the danger of the three thousand bandits waiting off in the distance.

KATŌ: It was really a case of planting in front of the enemy wasn't it? (Laughter.)

YOSHIZAKI: It was like the Imperial Army arrived in front of the enemy. When I think about it now, it seems like a very dramatic act, but at the time none of us felt that sense of glory. Our members ran out from behind the protective compound walls leading the horses and began the spring planting in the black earth.

On that day I didn't feel like going out into the fields, because I was feeling extremely exhausted. I stayed in my room by myself and was thinking about the agricultural work we would be doing when, I guess it was about two o'clock in the afternoon, for no reason I decided to go out to look at the fields. These days, we have a building used to repair our agricultural implements there, but at that time it was called the Fukuyoshi Brewery (*Fuji shaojiu gongsi*), and I walked among the pear trees growing in the ruins of the former brewery.

I happened to see our group leader standing in the shade of the pear trees, along with other group members all standing around without any wheat sprouts [i.e., they had all been planted]. I felt so much respect for them, it filled my breast. I didn't say a word but then quietly went away. All of the work that these Senfuru (Thousand Waves of Prosperity) settlers have done through their hard work and perseverance has resulted from the strong character and leadership of our group leader and from nothing else.

MURAYAMA: Indeed, thank you very much. The attitude of Group Leader Mune at the time has given me a deep impression. So, Yoshizaki, how did the other members of the group react to Group Leader Mune at the time?

YOSHIZAKI: The group members within the battlements had a strong spirit of wanting to take control of the land, and I would say that was the central conviction they all had.

In March, since we heard the bad news that the Seven Tiger river bandits were in the fields we planned to cultivate, one day we went to the ruins of Hunanying (today renamed Senfuru Town [*machi*]), where the earthen walls were battered and broken because of the constant day and night attacks from the three thousand bandits.

Beginning in May, the bandits started trying night attacks, when they sometimes penetrated the walls and started fires, and engaged in hand-to-hand combat. We later counted sixty bandit bodies and felt we had achieved a great victory. But the enemy was not ready to desist, and they continued to mount deadly attacks against us every day. With that reality, none of our group members could sleep at night or close their eyes in a restful way, so many stayed at the mud walls with a weapon by their side. Even now, it pains my heart when I think of those things.

But at least I'm still alive.

We all would get disheartened as the night would begin to turn into daylight. All our group members were extremely weary, having had no communication from the outside and none from Japan, and so we had no hope about tomorrow.

On about 10 May, our group members wondered what we should do because we all had wives or children or brothers back in Japan. Harbin was three hundred *li* distant, and even though Jiamusi was only twenty-three *li* away, we were out in the countryside. None of us had left this site in the two years we had been here. We wouldn't be able to do it this spring either. In this situation we had no idea what the coming year [the new growing season] would bring.

A senior group member said our government had forgotten us. That feeling about having no hope for the future was conveyed to the other members of the group, who began to say that there was nothing we could accomplish with this land. That opinion grew louder among our members, who began talking in earnest about returning to Japan. The conclusion we reached seemed to be that we had entered the road of sacrifices and the loss of blood, so we needed now to first get away from this area in order to decide what to do ultimately. We could do that by heading for Jiamusi, or we could go (farther south) to Lishuzhen, which was in Mudanjiang province.

Outside our walls were three thousand of the enemy, while within the walls was this disquiet. All sorts of danger awaited us, or not, but the work of opening up the land was surely the greatest danger facing us. This sort of extreme thinking was in the air at the time. Most people wanted to follow this course of action.

What was the way to solve our problem? Was there any other way out?

Weren't we the ones who had left our hometowns expecting our bones to be buried in north Manchuria? We couldn't know what would be coming the following year, let alone in two or three years' time. Will people say that the Japanese farmers put down their hoes and ran away because there were a lot of bandits? It seemed it would be good for us to get out of this area, but after we left wouldn't other Japanese farmers come to north Manchuria to farm? Were we like a rock embedded in the land that couldn't move away, or could we move away from this land? There was no one among us who could resolve these ideas. In the end, we all abandoned the idea of running away.

Even today, like a flame that will not be extinguished, I cannot forget the voices of those people. They were people who reached young adulthood and are now pillars in Senfuru, uncomplainingly doing the agricultural work they respect.

MURAYAMA: The bandit attacks were still continuing? Among the settlers was there anyone who was calm?

YOSHIZAKI: There was. In the very centre of our compound.

MURAYAMA: So, won't you tell us about the military hero, Nakamura-san?

The Calm Nakamura-san

YOSHIZAKI: As I remember, it was on 19 April [1934] just at the time of the Longshan Incident (*Ryūsan jiken*). The bandits who had organized the first attack on 10 April were doing so in reprisal for this incident, and we were surrounded by 3,000 bandits.

On 17 April, the bandits that were in the hills to the north of Hunanying three kilometres away had 2,000 men, four kilometres to the north of where the Senfuru train station (*eki*) is today they had 500 men; to the south in the Seven Tiger river area they had 100 to 150 men; and then to the southwest of us where the eighth colonizer group has now entered, they had 50 to more than 100 bandits all gathered for a second concerted attack on the Hunanying area. Everyone was aware of the coming attacks and, as I said before, the fierce attacks were unceasing both day and night against our bodies and our spirits. An especially bad point was that we could not communicate with anyone in Japan. We wondered if anyone in Japan knew of our plight, but then if they knew there was no way for them to contact us. If war with the Soviet Union were to suddenly break out, wouldn't we be quickly forgotten? All the people in our group were talking like that.

Fighting a defensive war is a very difficult thing.

Our group's funds were soon depleted. Food became more and more scarce. Tobacco had long before been used up, so we took to pulling grasses and rolling them up in newspaper in order to make a cigarette.

In that circumstance, on 18 April the bandits took over Tuoyaozi. There were three or four hundred bandits riding horses for about three thousand metres surrounding the area of Hunanying. On the following day there was no wind, and it was very sunny. The earth was so black [i.e., fertile and ready for planting]. Then many group members came running to our office where we were working. "An airplane!" they yelled. "It looks like it is searching for Hunanying." Our group leader (*tanchō*) dropped what he was doing, and his face lit up. Then all the people in the main office who were with us ran outside. It was a small Puss Moth plane that seemed to have been searching for us. People came running out of their homes and from every nook and cranny. How had that small plane found us? Probably it was confirming if we were the Hunanying settlement. The plane flew low overhead, and we saw someone dressed in khaki, so assumed it was a military plane. An arm tossed out a package. We ran to tear it open and found it was a memo from technician Nakamura (one of our colonization officials). "We express our thanks for your hard work." Inside were 30,000 yen in cash, sugar, cigarettes, and Japanese *yōkan*.[9]

But the plane did not land. It was honouring our strenuous efforts. That's all it was saying. But people seeing the plane from beyond the East Gate were jumping up to catch the heavy gunnysacks that were coming down from the plane. We opened them quickly to find Ruby Queen to sell on the open market to raise funds for our military supplies. The *yōkan* cakes were from the well-known Toraya store in Tokyo, and there were letters from our hometowns. The words in those letters were like gold falling from heaven, and it is hard to express how important they were to us or how good they made us feel.

"It's Nakamura-san, Nakamura-san!" everyone shouted, as with grateful eyes we watched the plane. That plane that had dropped the packages to us made another low pass over us, then flew off. The plane had confirmed our location, and in our joy we forgot about the bandits who were surrounding our position. What surprised us was that the plane then seemed to drop in altitude, and all of us uttered an exclamation of surprise when we saw that, with a spray of earth, the plane landed in a field to the north of us.

That was completely unexpected by us. It was already past mid-April, and the ice had all melted, but to see that plane land in our fields was something we had never even dreamed of. Probably the bandits had also seen it. Then, before I knew it, out of the airplane stepped Nakamura, broadly smiling. The group leader and others all ran over to shake his hand. We should have said something in greeting, but our emotions were strong, and we were at a loss for words, and we ended up not saying anything.

"You've been reckless," our group leader said to Nakamura, who replied simply: "I was worried about you so decided to land."

Nakamura was a cadre who had guided us and encouraged us many times as we planned for the Iyasaka and Senfuru settlements. He was someone we would never forget. Now he had once again engineered an adventure in order to save us. We simply could not express our gratitude to him.

After a while we began to talk about our situation and our plans going forward. Later the authorities in Tokyo announced that Administrator Ogawa and Nakamura, the two people who were in the airplane, were listed as missing. In taking off, the plane began to wobble in the field although there was no wind, and it was hard for the wheels to get traction. Somehow or other the plane was able to take off toward the north in spite of everyone's apprehensions. According to the reports made later, the wheels did not have good traction in the soft earth, and the plane was unable to achieve sufficient speed. About a thousand metres to the north, the wheels were spinning as the plane lifted off, but we could not see the metal struts [because of?] the tires. We were all intensely anxious. The plane with its heavy wing and tail sections seemed reluctant to leave us. It entered the air heading for Harbin and then seemingly without incident it disappeared. All of us group members tear up whenever we remember our last impression of that plane taking off.

He was a reckless guy! He is someone we are grateful to!

Heaven Shining Garden (Ch: *Tianzhaoyuan;* Jp: *Tenshōen*)

MURAYAMA: While listening to that interesting story I forgot all about the time moving on, but there are a few other topics I'd like us to cover, so let's move on to them. One of the things that very early on illustrated the attitude of the free immigrants (*jiyū imin*) in South Hsing'an province (*Xing'an nansheng*) were the fruit trees in Tianzhaoyuan. It is acknowledged that the development of this orchard was the result of the hard work of the Korean colonization (*sentaku*) Director (*riji*) Okada. I'd like us to hear something about those days.

KATŌ: Tianzhaoyuan? Eh? When did cultivation begin there?

OKADA: Well, it was around the end of May 1932, which means that nine years have already passed by since then, but it was in the following year that we planted trees in the orchard.

KATŌ: 1932 was the first year that we did any planting, wasn't it?

MURAYAMA: Those fruit trees are not old trees, are they? So Okada-san, about the Tenshōen, how was it that you brought in those unemployed people from Fukagawa? [Fukagawa was a working-class section of Tokyo at the time.] Wasn't that a difficult time for a lot of people?

OKADA: Yes it was. There are a lot of things I could talk about, but among the agricultural work that I manage in the Kantōshū area [in the southern part of the Manchurian peninsula], there are fields that have boys in training working them, which are always successful. The attitude of the

Japanese in Manchuria at the time was reflected by the young people who were ready to take on all problems. My friend Imai at that time was with the Mitsubishi Tenshōen and is now commissioned to work with the Korean colonizers. And Mr. Kōzaka from Tokyo's Fukagawa district is now the group leader of the Tenshōen. He told me that he had people from age eighteen to age forty-nine there living in the barracks, people he had not previously met. "Okay," he said. "If this is the situation, let's make it work." He asked them to do something that would help the agricultural colonization effort in Manchuria.

We have to say that their life was very hard, even to the point of dying, but they felt that if dying were necessary, they would do it. From what I heard them say, they came to Manchuria with that total determination. Seventy-three of them came on a cargo ship from Yokohama to Dalian in May, and my family also welcomed them with celebratory dishes of red rice (*sekihan*), thinking it might be the last rice they would be able to eat for two or three years.

They worked diligently for a year learning how to farm in Manchuria, and they built a camp in South Hsing'an province in the village of Qianjiadian. They were not receiving any financial assistance from the government at that time, but with assistance they got from the city of Tokyo they began to clear the land for cultivation. They could not develop wet paddy fields from the nearby West Liao River (*Xiliao he*) because the volume of water fluctuated much more than they anticipated. So they began to dig household wells, but the water was brackish. There were damages experienced from hail, and there were all these unexpected challenges as they tried cultivation. In 1937, they got some assistance from the Manchuria Colonization Company (*Mantaku kōsha*) that was newly established. They managed to bring about a great transformation and by good cooperation they set up the new orchard and the trees that are there today. Murayama-san, what is the latest news about the orchard trees?

MURAYAMA: The judgment is that the trees are very productive and are doing well. There are now fifty-four households there with 140 to 150 people, and they have built a wonderful community. We can really say that just as you reported, they have constructed a satisfactory community.

YOSHIZAKI: What kind of practical training did these Tenshōen immigrants have before they began to cultivate?

OKADA: Thinking about it from our current perspective, they certainly had a great will to succeed. It was a practical training facility that encountered a lot of obstacles, but in addition they received a monthly allowance of

6.50 yen. They had to invest 5 yen in the agricultural work, which means they could only save 1.50 yen to use for their own personal lives. That 1.50 yen was what they had to live on but, based on my research, most people used 1.29 yen [for expenses?], some could save only 0.30 yen [30 *sen*], meaning that the average was about 0.77 yen, which was not much money to live on. At that time, the typical cost for food for one month per person was 2.70 yen, or about 0.10 yen per day.

MURAYAMA: What kind of food can we eat with a budget of 0.10 yen per day? Especially if prices rise, then 0.10 yen is not very much for food.

OKADA: True, but remember that the amount had to cover three meals per day. For breakfast they ate corn (*baomi*) with beans, rice soup, maybe some pickles (*tsukemono*), and lunch was the same. For supper, they might add some miso soup or steamed vegetables. That was their typical menu. They might supplement that with a bit of pork or fish soup once a month. They would consider that a special treat.

KATŌ: Okada-san, what is the rice soup (*mitang*) you've just mentioned?

OKADA: It's just some rice boiled in water. You take one person's portion of dry rice, or twenty *momme,* and steam it and put it in water to make a thin soup.

YOSHIZAKI: So that is like saying they never eat white rice, isn't it?

OKADA: That's correct. They had to agree that in coming to Manchuria it was unlikely they would be able to eat white rice, and according to that condition they did not eat white rice. It was decided that the twenty-sixth of each month, the day they arrived in Manchuria, would be observed as Comfort Day (*Ian no hi*), and on that day they were able to ignore provisions and could eat white rice and a soup made from flour. Everyone began anticipating the twenty-sixth four or five days before it arrived, and the twenty-sixth was always noisy like a festival day. All the adults were running around like children. All the kids were running around with happy faces; you never saw them crying on that day. There never was a relief from the hard work, so it was a critical learning experience for us that we had to set up that day as our Comfort Day. It was an important lesson for us to learn.

KATŌ: Couldn't we say that carrying on for months at a time with such a hard life will have a negative effect on the health of the people?

OKADA: That was not a preferred situation, but it is one of the factors that I have investigated. I have paid special attention to this point in my investigations. The average weight of the settlers before they came to Manchuria was 15 *kan* 200 *momme* [roughly 59 kg], and after three months in

Manchuria their weight dropped to 14 *kan* 400 *momme* [55 kg], meaning that the average person lost 800 *momme* [4 kg]. The conclusion is that this drop in weight was because of the difficulty of life here in the first few months of their stay.

MURAYAMA: What about illness?

OKADA: Illness? Well, because of the changes they experienced in the geography, climate, and similar factors, initially there was a lot of sickness. But there were very few people who stopped work because of illness. I would say the most common ailments were problems of the digestive tract, but beyond that there were irritations like headaches, though we did have one person who suffered a cerebral hemorrhage while working and died. Fortunately we did not have other cases of severe illness. Based on our studies, the situation of farmers surviving on poor rations of 10 *sen* per day and yet not taking a rest from their work is a question that should be researched not only for the settlers but for the entire population of Japanese as well.

About being able to eat white rice, I do have a tearful story. It was in the autumn of the year I came to Manchuria, all of the settlers came to my house to help put on the roof, which was a very kind thing for them to do. When it came time for our meal, everyone had a good meal and ate their fill. We were all filled up, and I can't remember anything else about that meal. The next day people said: "If I die tomorrow, I'll have fulfilled my wishes," and saying so they returned to their homes. The strange thing is that the following day while we were in the fields working, we quietly passed away from this world. (Laughter)

YOSHIZAKI: It was in fact nothing to laugh about, we should say it was something to cry about.

Notes

1 For the wider context concerning Jiamusi, see Kuwajima Setsurō, *Manshū busō yimin* [Armed immigrants to Manchuria] (Tōkyō: Kyōikusha, 1979), 129–50.

2 An excellent article was provided to me by Xiaoran He, "The 'Baptism' of Manchukuo: The 1932 Deluge, State Building, and the Making of Local Memory in Harbin," presented at the Regional Meeting of the Association for Asian Studies in Boston, 2017. Cited here with the permission of the author.

3 The story is that Xie Wendong linked up with the Chinese Communist resistance. Due to his Communist connections, he was beheaded by the Kuomintang in 1946. See *Nimaru seiki Manshū rekishi jiten* [Dictionary of twentieth-century Manchuria history] (Tōkyō: Yoshikawa kōbunkan, 2012), 375.

4 For these events see Tsutsui Gorō, *Tetsudō jikeimura, shisetsu, Manshū yiminshi* [Railway self-defence villages, personal recollections, a history of Japanese immigrants to Manchuria] (Tōkyō: Nihon tosho kankōkai, 1997), 180–81. Also see Kuwajima, *Manshū busō*

yimin, 204–24. For brief accounts from both Chinese and Japanese sources of these events, see Liu Wenxin, ed., *Mengsui: Riben kaituotuan fumie qianhou* [Dreams of Manchuria: Before and after the Japanese colonizers] (Harbin: Heilongjiang renmin chubanshe, 1991), 266–83.

5 During the seminar exchange being translated here, Japanese colonist Murayama sometimes pronounced the garden's name in Chinese. For an account of the Japanese colonists living in the Jiamusi area during the 1930s, see Takarabe Toriko, *Heaven and Hell: A Novel of a Manchukuo Childhood,* trans. Phyllis Birnbaum (Honolulu: University of Hawai'i Press, 2018). This is a fictionalized account based on Takarabe's childhood memories and the stories she heard while growing up in Manchukuo near Jiamusi.

6 See Ronald Suleski, "Salvaging Memories: Former Japanese Colonists in Manchuria and the Shimoina Project, 2001–2012," in *Empire and the Environment in the Making of Manchuria,* ed. Norman Smith (Vancouver: UBC Press, 2017), 202.

7 *Hatsuki no Manshū kaitaku o kataru: Zadankai* [Recalling the early days of opening Manchuria: A seminar], in *Manshū kaitaku monogatari* [Tales of opening Manchuria], ed. The Manchuria Colonization Company (Manshū takushoku kōsha. Hsinking (Shinkyō) and Mukden (Hōten): Manshū jijō annaijo, 1941, 70. Pages 1 to 28 are translated here.

8 Yoshizaki referred to them as originating in the area of Qihuli, to the south of the new Japanese-controlled settlement areas.

9 A thick, jellied dessert made of red bean paste and sugar to be eaten with tea.

10 In the summer of 1998, a group of Japanese who had been born in the Senfuru colonizer's village at Hunanying were invited by the Chinese government to revisit the village. They were delighted to see the building where they had attended elementary school in the 1940s. The visit was officially to help them locate relatives who had been left behind in China in 1945. The movement of the Japanese groups was tightly controlled by PRC authorities, somewhat to their chagrin. See *Takuyū* [Colonizer's friend] 52 (October 1998).

2 Sakuta Shōichi, "The Light of Asia"

BILL SEWELL and NORIO OTA

Sakuta Shōichi (1878–1973) graduated from Tokyo Imperial University in 1905 – that heady year in which Japan ejected the Russian Empire from Korea and southern Manchuria. After graduate work in international law, he taught economics in China at Wuchang's new School of Law and Administration from 1908 to 1912. Returning to Japan, Sakuta taught in his home prefecture – in the former Chōshū domain, birthplace of many of Meiji Japan's elite – at the Yamaguchi Higher Commercial School. Accepting a position at Kyoto Imperial University in 1923, he made full professor in 1930 but retired in 1938 at age sixty to relocate to Manchukuo's new capital, Xinjing (Jp: *Shinkyō*) and serve as vice-president of Kenkoku Daigaku (Ch: *Jian'guo daxue;* National Foundation University).[1] "Kendai" opened in May that year, inspired by Ishiwara Kanji (1889–1949), one of the plotters behind the Manchurian Incident. Ishiwara had returned to Manchukuo the previous year as deputy chief of staff of the Guandong Army (Kwantung Army; Jp: *Kantōgun*). Concerned for the puppet state's management and fearing a looming confrontation with the USSR, Ishiwara preferred a less oppressive system so as to foster collaboration with Chinese in order to industrialize the region. His later disapproval of war in China and repeated clashes with then Guandong Army chief of staff Tōjō Hideki (1884–1948), among others, however, resulted in his return to Japan at the end of 1938 and assignment to the Japan Sea port of Maizuru. Continuing to denounce Tōjō, he was put on reserve in 1941.[2]

Kendai represented Manchukuo's potential for an alternate path. With the puppet state's premier its nominal president, it embodied a genuine, albeit limited, effort to create an elite cohort for Manchukuo's multiethnic society, idealized officially as the "harmony of five races"

(Ch: *wuzu xiehe;* Jp: *gozoku kyōwa*), and for the empire at large. Kendai recruited diverse students, including Russians, Mongolians, Koreans, and Taiwanese, for a university curriculum that included instruction in Pan-Asian ideology and martial arts. Tuition was free, and the university provided textbooks, room and board, and a small allowance. Sakuta, however, helped shift Kendai away from Ishiwara's initial hopes, resulting in a racial hierarchy ensuring Japanese pre-eminence. This problematized the effort, reproducing in microcosm the puppet state's conflicting realities. Tensions eventually led to mass arrests of students engaged in anti-Japanese activities in 1942, compelling Sakuta to resign.[3] Wang Zhixin has suggested that Kendai may have been a means of testing how to subordinate universities to the state, a trial run for universities in Japan.[4]

Sakuta's appointment to Kendai was due not only to his long-standing interest in China, but also to his work renovating Japan. At a tuition-free institute in 1932 he helped rehabilitate students forced to drop out of postsecondary education because of leftist affiliations.[5] That year he began working with the Ministry of Education developing a "national science" to challenge proliferating Marxist views, something he continued at Kendai.[6] Sakuta was also one of fourteen contributors to the ministry's *Kokutai no hongi* (*Cardinal Principles of the National Entity,* 1937), a widely distributed primer on Japanese identity centring on the imperial house. Written for educators, it provided the basis for the ministry's wartime propaganda, invoking the spirit of Japan's "national foundation" and describing Manchukuo's founding as an extension of prehistoric Japan's imperial unification.[7] In Manchukuo, Sakuta proposed a means of "mass rule" in which groups working within an umbrella organization might form a national organization that would supersede parliamentary politics. This concept helped enable Manchukuo's Concordia Association (Ch: *Xiehehui;* Jp: *Kyōwakai*), which served as a forerunner to Japan's own Imperial Rule Assistance Association of 1940.[8]

Written in a poetic style, the essay that follows was the lead article in the inaugural issue of Kendai's journal *Kenkoku* (National foundation).[9] It reflected not only contemporary propaganda but also themes long evident in the Japanese colonial imaginary, such as Japanese leadership, shared cultural traditions, and Asian liberation.[10] Sakuta, however, was not the first to identify Japan as the "light of Asia." Prewar Japanese Buddhists used the concept to reach out to other Buddhists through a common religious heritage and the promise of Japan's successful modernity. In so doing, some referenced *The Light of Asia* (1879), an epic poem by Sir Edwin Arnold (1832–1904) commemorating the historical Buddha.[11] The poem contributed to rekindling Japanese interest in the historical Buddha after its translation and provided the basis for a 1925 film shown internationally.[12] Arnold himself took an interest in Japan, marrying a Japanese woman and in 1892 receiving the Order of the Rising Sun.[13] Intriguingly, he defended Japan's first war with China by arguing that Japan was acting on behalf of the civilized world.[14] In his news magazine *Kokumin no tomo* (The people's friend), Tokutomi Sohō (1863–1957) showed a similar outlook, noting that Japanese

> have a duty to radiate the light of civilization beyond our shores and bring the benefits of civilization to our neighbors. We have the duty to guide backward countries to the point of being able to govern themselves. We have the duty to maintain peace in East Asia for this purpose. As a man has his calling, so too does a nation have its mission.[15]

This was part of a coherent world view – an unattributed leading article in the first issue of the new English-language edition of Tokutomi's journal in 1896 opined that Japan "was singularly prepared to receive the light from the West."[16]

Three months later, the liberal parliamentarian Ozaki Yukio (1858–1954) agreed with Tokutomi that "man can not live without ambition and the same is true of nations. Japan has her cherished ambition. It is to become the light of Asia and to spread the beneficent influence of civilization over the nations of the Far East."[17] A decade earlier he had even called for war with China to "cure the Chinese of the arrogance they maintained in spite of their lack of real power and their state of disorder, and to cure the Japanese of their excessive veneration of China." This was because "we have become the most advanced country of the Orient whereas China and Korea have fallen far behind ... It is now our turn to take the initiative to these two countries ... to repay all that we have benefitted from them in the past sixteen hundred years."[18] Significantly, Ozaki held favourable views of the United States and throughout his parliamentary career fought for representative democracy against lingering clan influences in Japan's military and government.[19]

Yet while Ozaki and Tokutomi are remembered as progressives, they clearly shared a sense of Japan's imperial mission. Tokutomi even applauded Japan's seizure of Manchuria and termed Japan's confrontation of Europeans and Americans in the 1930s a "heavenly calling," championing Japan's withdrawal from the League of Nations.[20] At the same time, Tokutomi and Ozaki also opposed "national purity thought" (*kokusui-shugi*) that maintained Japanese identity in opposition to "Westernization" – a view Sakuta dismisses below as well. While all three were internationalist in outlook, they all assumed Japan's leadership in Asia was natural and expected.

Identifying Japan as the "light of Asia" gained new life in the war era. Claiming that the light of spiritual culture came from the East, Sakuta justified an expanded war by echoing his theme below, but he was not alone.[21] Oka Ōji (also Daiji, unknown–1962), chair of the Manchurian Construction Society, reported that Manchukuo and its capital were "models" that shone with the "light of East Asia" (*tōA no hikari*).[22] A 1936 advertisement for the South Manchuria Railway indicated it was "carrying the light of civilization into Manchuria."[23] Similar views were expressed in a 1942 roundtable discussion (*zadankai*) of philosophers assessing Japan's new-found role and worldly significance published in the leading journal *Chūō kōron* (Central review).[24] In 1942 in the occupied Dutch East Indies, the short-lived Triple-A Movement (*Pergerakan Tiga A*) encouraged the liberated to see Japan as the "light of Asia," the "protector of Asia" ("mother" in the Japanese version), and the "leader of Asia."[25] In 1943, the *Asahi* newspaper published a photographic collection called *The Light of Asia* showcasing Japanese military successes and Asia's liberation, captioned in Japanese, Chinese, English, and Southeast Asian languages.[26]

Fostering Asian progress under Japanese tutelage was a longstanding goal, widely shared. Although Sakuta did not assert any racial superiority, he echoed a broad effort seeking to bring Asians together through Japanese leadership. His essay thus points to the arrogance with which non-Japanese had to contend. For Japanese, however, Sakuta suggested positive ways to perceive their actions, thereby providing a rationale for supporting the war effort. Popular acceptance of such views in turn helps explain why postwar Japanese views of wartime activities often remained positive, something men like Sakuta endeavoured to reinforce. In a postwar collective memoir on Manchuria, Sakuta reflected on the significance of Japanese civilians in Manchukuo, especially the "burning spirit" of student "trailblazers" who were "nation building in a new era," in effect "reconstructing a Manchurian nation."[27] Like many other elite participants in the puppet state, Sakuta looked back on his experience in Manchuria with pride.

Sakuta found postwar employment at Kyoto's private Ryūkoku University, writing chiefly about international affairs but also Shinto, which has gained him some posthumous recognition.[28] After profiling Sakuta in a series in *Gekkan Nippon* (Monthly Nippon) titled "Trailblazers of Japanese Civilization," journalist Tsubouchi Takahiko (b. 1965) called attention to the economic dimensions of Sakuta's thought.[29] A more earthy view of Sakuta can be found in a popular *manga* series set in 1938–39. Resurrecting also Ishiwara and Tōjō – as well as femme fatale Kawashima Yoshiko (1907–48) – it opens at Kendai, portraying Sakuta as a hesitant, perhaps anxious, university administrator. The series dramatized some of the tensions evident between the military on one side and Ishiwara and others on the other, but its popularity suggests that some of the era's passions continue to resonate in postwar Japan.[30]

TRANSLATION

The Light of Asia

SAKUTA SHŌICHI

The "light of Asia" – this shining slogan has been frequently praised and advocated by many people until now. Nevertheless, not only has it not been sufficiently explained, but it must also be discussed within the current context with current sentiments.

We can contrast the light of Asia with the light of Europe and the light of America. The light of America, however, is merely the projection and enlargement of European scenes brought by European immigrants. America has not yet undergone sufficient ordeals to emit its own light. While there were several places emitting their own light in ancient times, Europe accepted the light of west Asia from the beginning of antiquity and through the medieval era welcomed the religion of west Asia, with almost the whole of Europe praising and adoring it. Before long the outcry for a renaissance of the ancient culture, arising in resistance to it, managed to suppress the religion from the East in part, and displayed Europe's brilliance, but European culture, which had already been dualistic, was constantly torn between these two conflicting and interacting streams of brilliance and until now has not become a secure and stable state. Until the time comes when a feeble voice begging for God's mercy and a war cry roaring "I will defeat thee" should be resolved, the light of Europe will remain a succession of constantly oscillating waves.

The light of Asia is one that Asia emitted itself from prehistoric times. Initially, light started shining in several locations. The main sites were west Asia, India, China (*Shina*)[31] and Japan, excluding the Asia Plateau [central Asia], which we have no means to recall. Moreover, these lights gradually spread from west to east. The light of west Asia was transmitted widely to Europe, incorporating the light of Egypt as well, but it was partially transmitted to India and China; the light of India to China; the light of China to Japan. Furthermore, the weakening and waning of light also began from the West; first the light of west Asia, next the light of India, and in China the light of ancient civilization (*kodō,* literally "ancient way") has weakened greatly but not necessarily completely declined. Only the light of Japan has burned continuously, despite traces of occasional vacillation like adding oil to the eternal non-depleting light of ancient times and, moreover, has been gradually increasing in brilliance.

The reason why the light of west Asia went out so quickly was probably because it appeared early and external stimuli were scarce. The fate of the light of India was similar, and in comparison with the flash of west Asia, its light of truth and wisdom (*jakkō*) also failed to absorb energies from outside and ended up sinking below the horizon like a gigantic sun setting in the western mountains. While the light of China, which absorbed the lights of west Asia and India, later weakened remarkably, its jewelled light was transmitted for a long time and not only was it welcomed in Japan but also became known to Europeans in modern times. The light of Japan has a spirit like the rising sun rather than merely the light of the eternal lamp, which is probably the main reason why Japan has taken the path of daily improvements without submitting completely to the mature cultures of China and India, even while incorporating them. Moreover, although the light of Asia was transmitted from west to east and at the same time the light of west Asia was transmitted to western Europe, and Europeans said that the light came from the East, this does not mean that the transmission of light has any geographical direction, but, rather, was probably because light was transmitted from places where it shined earlier to places where it shined later. Alternatively, another reason may be that primitive light with potential for adding external light grows increasingly, [even when] exposed to light with no such potential.

As the lights of Asia were transmitted from west to east in this way, the farther east they went they became lights that grew increasingly and turned into ones with an inner glow, after adding external lights to each of their own unique lights. Japan, located in the Far East, inherited almost all the important aspects of the lights of Asia without losing much. Japan was exposed to the light of Europe after successfully putting the lights of Asia in order. Probably this is also the reason why Japan could persist in firmly maintaining an Asian soul without submitting completely to European culture, while assimilating it.

A match for Japan's accumulative culture (*ruiseki bunka*) might be ancient Greece, though Greece disappeared quickly from this world and did not do more than transmit its glorious inheritance to modern Europe. Japan absorbed that modern European culture as well. Japan's culture possesses uniquely complicated contents. Thus, in Japan there are not a few cases in which it is not possible to discern whether certain works of culture, life customs, and the like are of indigenous or foreign origin, or which elements of those are of indigenous or foreign origin. Thus, it is not uncommon that while national purists (*kokusui ronsha*) misjudge those of foreign origin as indigenous to Japan, worshippers of foreign cultures mistake the indigenous for having foreign origins.

Japan, which has long been on the receiving end in the Far East, has also begun to transmit its culture to the continent as part of the recent and rapid integration of the world: toward China after the Russo-Japanese War, and toward Manchuria and Mongolia after the Manchurian Incident. At that time, a group of Japanese said that the return of Japanese culture to the continent had begun. They meant that after the culture transmitted from the continent bore fruit in Japan, it has been brought back to the continent. However, this consideration is still insufficient. The culture that was transmitted to China after the Russo-Japanese War was not the indigenous Japanese one, but was the European culture Japanese learned, offered according to requests from China. The Japanese culture transmitted to Manchuria and Mongolia after the Manchurian Incident was also one learned from Europe as materialist culture, but as spiritual culture it was indigenous to Japan. Thus far, it has not been possible to consider that Japan returns what it absorbed from the continent to the continent. However, as Japanese culture has absorbed much of the culture of the Asian continent, there is no doubt that the Japanese culture that is transmitted to the continent includes continental elements.

Therefore, it is Japan's mission to convey Japanese culture itself to the people on the continent by taking these common elements as an opportunity as well as a medium. Even though China's Kingly Way (Ch: *Wangdao;* Jp: *Ōdō*)[32] entered Japan, where it was Japanized and put into practice, it would be troublesome for people on the continent for Japan to bring back to the continent Japanese culture with the Kingly Way omitted. What is more, it may not be an honourable task for Japanese either.

Europe at first received the light of west Asia, and after that emitted its own strong light and swept over the modern world. Asia emitted shining lights from ancient times, but they remained separate and disappeared one after another or atrophied without merging into one light of Asia. This is the main reason why Asian nations toppled over like dominoes under the pressure of modern Europe. However, fortunately only Japan was not only undefeated, but also rose up in rebellion. This was indeed because the good-quality light of Japan had for a long time scrupulously accumulated the lights of the Asian continent and, moreover, progressively added layers of the light of Europe on top. The lights of the Asian continent have been stored by Japan. The light of Japan is the grand sum of light from as much as possible of the entire Asian continent. As the light of Japan is taking charge of the lights of Asia, one should not be hung up on the name of Japan. It was for Japan itself that Japan consciously learned continental culture, but in reality it is the case that Japan learned more for the sake of Asia. Japan has been waiting for the opportunity to carry out its duty to open its treasury and share the lights of Asia accumulated over two thousand years with all Asians. And that opportunity has finally arrived.

In Europe the crisis of the decline of western European culture has been widely discussed and many feel that in order to restore Europe it must absorb the lights of Asia. At this time, Asian people feel that the lights of Asia are all the more precious. As these lights of Asia have accumulated in Japan, Japan has no choice but to take action. When Japan leads the lights of Asia to the continent, the most suitable region first of all is Manchuria and Mongolia (*ManMō*).[33] The light of Asia to be strengthened there will probably reach China next and before long will reach west Asia and India. Thus, the day of restoring (*fukkō*) Asia is nearing.

Asia's forefathers lit the shining lights of Asia separately. Several thousand years have passed, and the time has come for Asia's offspring to illuminate heaven and earth with the lights they inherited from their forefathers. For that, the Japanese people have risen first, and brought down the ancient heavenly fishing boat (*ama no tsuribune*)[34] to the earth to spread the lights of Asia to various places. It is also necessary to drop bombs and spread propaganda leaflets from planes, but it is more important to drop welcome rain and sweet dew from the air. When the time comes for the Japanese people to fly into the great sky, followed by the people of Manchuria, Mongolia, the Republic of China, and then west Asians and south Asians, all of Asia will leap forward.

I wonder if the time will come when the lights of all Asia are emitted again toward Europe, making Europeans cry out that the lights come from the East again. Since history does not repeat itself, there might not be the conflict between East and West as in ancient times. Nevertheless, it seems that the lights for which Europe is seeking will probably be transmitted from Asia.

When one considers change in world history, one finds that the mission of imperial Manchukuo, rising with its own Asian light, is critical. Manchukuo is not just for itself. The light that Manchukuo has been raising high to shine on its own way is not simply the light of the Kingly Way, but is also the light of the Heavenly Way (*tendō*) shining on the Kingly Way. Neither is the light of the Imperial Way (*kōdō*) simply that, but is also the Shinto light shining on the Imperial Way.[35] The light that shines on the earth is the light of the sun; the light in heaven that shines on the hearts and souls of the masses is the light of Amaterasu Ōmikami.[36]

Notes

1 Hayasaka Tadashi, "Sakuta Shōichi," in Heibonsha, ed., *Nihon jinmei daijiten* [Dictionary of Japanese biography] (Tōkyō: Heibonsha, 1979), vol. 3, 352. His surname is sometimes transliterated as Sakuda.

2 Mark R. Peattie, *Ishiwara Kanji and Japan's Confrontation with the West* (Princeton, NJ: Princeton University Press, 1975), 162–74, 311–16, 329–30.

3 Yuka Hiruma Kishida, *Kenkoku University and the Experience of Pan-Asianism: Education in the Japanese Empire* (London: Bloomsbury Academic, 2019); Shin'ichi Yamamuro, *Manchuria under Japanese Dominion,* trans. Joshua A. Fogel (Philadelphia: University of Pennsylvania Press, 2006), 198–202, 213–14. In Japanese, see Miyazawa Eriko, *Kenkoku Daigaku to minzoku kyōwa* [National Foundation University and ethnic harmony] (Tōkyō: Kazama shobō, 1997); Kawata Hiroshi, *Manshū* Kenkoku Daigaku monogatari: Jidai o hikiukeyō *toshita wakamonotachi* [Tales of Manchuria's National Foundation University: Young people taking responsibility for their times] (Tōkyō: Hara shobō, 2002); Yamane Yukio, *Kenkoku Daigaku no kenkyū: Nihon teikoku shugi no ichi danmen* [Studies on National Foundation University: A profile of Japanese imperialism] (Tōkyō: Kyūko shoin, 2003); and Shishida Fumiaki, *Budō no kyōikuryoku: Manshūkoku Kenkoku Daigaku ni okeru budō kyōiku* [The value of the martial arts training: Martial arts training at Manchukuo's National Foundation University] (Tōkyō: Nihon tosho sentā, 2005).

4 Cited in Emer O'Dwyer, "Heroes and Villains: Manchukuo in Yasuhiko Yoshikazu's *Rainbow Trotsky,*" in *Manga and the Representation of Japanese History,* ed. Roman

Rosenbaum (London: Routledge, 2013), 132. On growing oppression in Japan's universities after the outbreak of war in 1937, see Ben-Ami Shillony, "Universities and Students in Wartime Japan," *Journal of Asian Studies* 45, 4 (August 1986): 769–87.

5 "Akai seinen o sukū to" [A way to save red youth], *Kōbe yūshin nippō* [Kōbe daily news], 3 November 1932.

6 Hiromi Mizuno, *Science for the Empire: Scientific Nationalism in Modern Japan* (Stanford, CA: Stanford University Press, 2009), 98–101; Sakuta Shōichi, *Gendai kagaku to Manshūkokugaku* [Modern science and Manchukuo studies] (Shinkyō: Manshū teikoku kyōwakai kenkoku daigaku bunkai shuppanbu, 1942).

7 Robert King Hall, ed., and John Owen Gauntlet, trans., *Kokutai no hongi: Cardinal Principles of the National Entity of Japan* (Cambridge, MA: Harvard University Press, 1949), 5, 7, 8, 10–11, 30, 39, 59, 63, 75, 105.

8 Yamamuro, *Manchuria under Japanese Dominion,* 192–93.

9 Sakuta Shōichi, "Ajia no hikari" [The light of Asia], *Kenkoku* [National foundation] 1, 1 (August 1940): 2–5.

10 Barak Kushner, *The Thought War: Japanese Imperial Propaganda* (Honolulu: University of Hawai'i Press, 2006), 118–33.

11 Judith Snodgrass, "Performing Buddhist Modernity: The Lumbini Festival, Tokyo 1925," *Journal of Religious History* 33, 2 (June 2009): 133–48.

12 On Arnold's influence in Japan see Richard M. Jaffe, "Seeking Sakyamuni: Travel and the Reconstruction of Japanese Buddhism," *Journal of Japanese Studies* 30, 1 (Winter 2004): 69–70.

13 J.P. Phelan, "Arnold, Sir Edwin (1832–1904)," *Oxford Dictionary of National Biography* (Oxford: Oxford University Press, 2004; online edition, May 2008), https://doi.org/10.1093/ref:odnb/30455.

14 Sir Edwin Arnold, "China and Japan," *New Review* 64 (September 1894): 221–36.

15 John D. Pierson, *Tokutomi Sohō, 1863–1957: A Journalist for Modern Japan* (Princeton, NJ: Princeton University Press, 1980), 240–42.

16 "A Japanese View of Japan," *Far East* 1, 1 (20 February 1896): 9.

17 Yukiwo Ozaki, "Our Ambition," *Far East* 1, 4 (20 May 1896): 9.

18 Ozaki Yukio, *Shina shobun'an* [Proposal for dealing with China] (Tōkyō: Hakubunkan, 1895), 98, 219; and Yukio Ozaki, *The Autobiography of Ozaki Yukio: The Struggle for Constitutional Government in Japan,* trans. Fujiko Hara (Princeton: Princeton University Press, 2001), 76–81.

19 Ozaki, *Autobiography,* 111.

20 Pierson, *Tokutomi Sohō,* 371.

21 Sakuta Shōichi, *DaitōAsen no igi* [The significance of the Great East Asia War] (Tōkyō: Dōshi dōkōsha, 1942), 28.

22 Oka Ōji, "Manshū ni okeru shinkō kenchiku ni taibōsu" [Long-awaited rising architecture in Manchuria], *Manshū kenchiku zasshi* [Journal of Manchurian architecture] 13, 6 (June 1933): 1–3.

23 Annika A. Culver, *Glorify the Empire: Japanese Avant-Garde Propaganda in Manchukuo* (Vancouver: UBC Press, 2013), 17.

24 Harry D. Harootunian, *Overcome by Modernity: History, Culture, and Community in Interwar Japan* (Princeton: Princeton University Press, 2002), 34–94.

25 Shigeru Sato, *War, Nationalism and Peasants: Java under the Japanese Occupation 1942–1945* (Armonk, NY: M.E. Sharpe, 1994), 36–50.

26 Asashi Shinbunsha, ed., *Ajia no hikari* [The light of Asia] (Tōkyō: Asahi shinbunsha, 1943).

27 Sakuta Shōichi, "Manshū kenkoku no kaiko" [Reminiscing about Manchuria's National Foundation], in Manshū kaikoshū kankōkai, ed., *Aa Manshū: Kuni tsukuri sangyō*

kaihatsusha no shuki [Oh, Manchuria! Notes from country-building industrial development officials] (Manshū kaikoshū kankōkai, 1965), 65–66. This echoed Sakuta, *DaitōAsen no igi,* 69–71.
28 See, for example, Sakuta Shōichi, "Genshi no kami no michi" [The original way of the gods] *Shintōshi kenkyū* [Shinto historical studies] 1, 1 (1953): 25–44. His memoir is Sakuta Shōichi, *Michi no kotoba* [The language of the way], 6 vols. (Kyoto: Michi no kotoba kankōkai, 1963–67).
29 Tsubouchi Takahiko, "Sakuta Shōichi," *Gekkan Nippon* [Monthly Nippon] 13, 6 (June 2009): 76–83, and "Bōkyaku sareta keizaigaku: Kōdō keizairon wa shihonshugi o chōkoku dekiruka" [Forgotten economics: Can Imperial Way economics overcome capitalism?], *Shin Nihongaku* [New Japanology] 20 (Spring 2011): 118–32.
30 Yoshikazu Yasuhiko, *Niji-iro no Torotsukii* [Rainbow-coloured Trotsky] (Tōkyō: Ushio shuppansha, 1992–97); O'Dwyer, "Heroes and Villains," 121–45.
31 Replacing references to dynastic names, "Shina" became the common prewar Japanese term for China though it is now deemed pejorative. Lydia H. Liu, *The Clash of Empires: The Invention of China in Modern World Making* (Cambridge, MA: Harvard University Press, 2004), 79; and Stefan Tanaka, *Japan's Orient: Rendering Pasts into History* (Berkeley: University of California Press, 1995), 4–7.
32 The "Kingly Way" appears in the *Spring and Autumn Annals* and was a key term for Mencius to signify benevolent government. It was later appropriated by many, including Sun Yat-sen, and Japanese claimed it as a governing principle in Manchukuo.
33 Japanese in the prewar era often conflated the two regions under one label, though in reality much of western Manchuria was actually eastern Mongolia.
34 Reference uncertain, but likely to a poem or legend. Although the Chinese character for *ama* differs, possibly Sakuta refers to a poem by Ono no Takamura (802–52) in which he asks boats to inform a loved one that he has headed out toward the "innumerable isles." See Joshua S. Mostow, *Pictures of the Heart: The Hyakunin Isshu in Word and Image* (Honolulu: University of Hawai'i Press, 1996), 175–77. The poem also appears in the *Kokin Wakashū* [Collection of Japanese poems of ancient and modern times], no. 407.
35 "Heavenly Way" refers to the traditional Chinese perceptions, ethics, and practices as discussed by Confucius and other Chinese philosophers, and "Imperial Way" refers to Japanese perceptions of imperial rule as reimagined in the 1930s.
36 Japan's Sun Goddess. On 15 July 1940 – the month before Sakuta's article was published – Emperor Puyi promulgated a "Rescript on the Consolidation of the Basis of the Nation" attributing Manchukuo's establishment and success to the "divine blessing of the Sun Goddess." Puyi was likely seeking to secure his authority, but that year the capital's new National Foundation Shrine, modelled on Japan's Ise Shrine, began services. Amaterasu was enshrined there, as had been the case in other Japanese shrines overseas. Yamamuro, *Manchuria under Japanese Dominion,* 164–65; Michio Nakajima, "Shinto Deities that Crossed the Sea: Japan's 'Overseas Shrines,' 1868 to 1945," *Japanese Journal of Religious Studies* 37, 1 (2010): 21–46.

3 Writings of Manchukuo's Prime Minister Zheng Xiaoxu

HUA RUI

Zheng Xiaoxu (1860–1938) is a shadowy figure in modern Chinese intellectual history, best known for his collaboration with the Japanese in Manchukuo (1932–45). Zheng was the figurehead of its State Council and a key architect of its professed ruling ideology. His vision for an inclusive, developmental state in Manchuria marked the convergence of several prominent intellectual trends of early twentieth-century East Asia. Understanding his political thought is therefore critical for a fuller appreciation of the complex underpinnings of the Japanese colonial empire on the Asian continent.

Many remember Zheng as a devout follower of Confucian teachings. Historians have often attributed his choice to collaborate with the enemy to his desire to restore Qing dynastic rule.[1] The texts below, however, show that Zheng had developed a sophisticated, forward-looking theory about China's future before the outbreak of the war in 1931. I venture to call it Confucian developmentalism. This theory exhibits the intertextualization of three seemingly incompatible discourses: a radical offshoot of late Qing constitutionalism, post–First World War pacifism, and a misinterpreted version of Italian fascism. Zheng framed his utopia as a part of the global struggle to come to terms with the modern human condition.[2] These texts are a diary entry from July 1929 about a utopian frontier state in Inner Asia, a treatise outlining his developmental blueprint for China in 1930, and two essays about his vision for a pacifist Manchukuo in 1932.

Crucial to Zheng Xiaoxu's thinking was his early experience on the Qing frontiers. Born in Fujian province in 1860, Zheng received a neo-Confucian education, before joining Qing officialdom as the top-ranking candidate in the provincial exam of 1882. He earned a reputation in

Guangxi province, where he spearheaded efforts to modernize border defence.[3] His success notwithstanding, Zheng chose to leave officialdom and moved to Shanghai in 1906, where he advocated for the constitutionalist movement.[4] When the movement stalled in 1909, Zheng went to Manchuria to oversee construction of the Jinzhou-Aihun Railroad.[5] He almost succeeded in brokering an Anglo-American loan to counterbalance the ballooning influence of Japan in the region.[6] The constitutionalist moment and railway project sowed the seeds of open developmentalism in his mind.[7]

The 1911 Revolution dealt a blow to Zheng's political ambition. Throughout the 1920s, he remained in the inner orbit of the former emperor Puyi (1906–67). The Manchurian Incident in 1931 gave Zheng a fleeting sense of hope. Convinced that the Japanese takeover had created a power vacuum for his own ideals, he accepted the invitation to serve as prime minister of Manchukuo in 1932.[8] He soon found out, however, that he was just a puppet. The disenchanted Zheng redirected his energy to writing about the Kingly Way (*Wangdao*).[9] Zheng's contribution was twofold: he introduced an orthodox, conservative Song-learning thread and a profound modernist political critique into the Kingly Way.[10]

Zheng's idealistic advocacy for open borders and racial inclusiveness briefly earned him the sympathetic ear of the Japanese. His works were translated into Japanese and English and sold in metropolitan centres from Xinjing to Tokyo. However, as the Japanese Kantō Army tightened its grip on the colonial state, Zheng's pacifist ideas appeared increasingly out of sync. He was ousted from the government in 1935 and died a suspicious death in 1938.

Three key words define Zheng's utopian political thinking: race, development, and peacemaking.[11] In the late Qing, he viewed racial/ethnic tension as an imminent threat to the viability of multiethnic empires. He warned about the devastating effects of anti-Manchu sentiments for the fate of "China."[12] To him, race-based nationalism was the cause of total war. This sets Zheng apart from contemporaries who framed their thoughts about identity in racial-nationalist terms.[13] Zheng reached back to a mid-Qing discourse of racial relativism.[14] Paraphrasing the Yongzheng emperor (1678–1735), Zheng states: "The Shun emperor [r. 2233–2184 BCE] was an eastern barbarian. King Wen [1152–1056 BCE] was a western barbarian. They both fulfilled their aspirations in China."[15] For Zheng, China was a land open to experimentation, and the racial traits of its dominant population were background noise.

Anxiety over the politicizing of identity differences led Zheng to constitutionalism and, paradoxically, fascism. Zheng found in the constitutional polity the elimination of racial and class distinctions. As he said in a 1906 speech: "In the constitution is contained the universal truth of the philosophy of the collective; there is absolutely no trace of race and class: all those forms of repression [are gone]."[16] This unique view of constitutionalism continued in Zheng's writings in Manchukuo.[17]

Zheng's brief association with Italian fascism was similarly driven by a misguided desire to rid human society of differences.[18] Among his sources of knowledge about fascism was an Italian work, which promoted Mussolini's fascist theory as a cure for "weakness arising from social distinction and divisions."[19] Zheng was fascinated by the idea of moral restoration through the peaceful elimination of differences, but he grew disenchanted in 1932 after Mussolini made racist comments about the "yellow peril."[20]

The elimination of racial differences served Zheng's plan for China's open economic development. During his early stints on the frontiers, he was intrigued by the power of massive developmental projects: the Trans-Siberian Railway and the Panama Canal, for example, were to him "central nodes" that changed the whole world.[21] His developmental plan for Manchukuo had two parallel steps: the restoration of moral rituals and the construction of large-scale hydraulic projects.[22]

The final key word in Zheng's thought was peacemaking, as a direct response to treaties among European powers to curtail the use of force after the First World War.[23] Seeing the Kellogg-Briand Pact as a stillborn compromise among the great powers, Zheng offered an idealistic solution that substituted a neo-Confucian approach to interpersonal trust building for the Machiavellian balance of power. Manchukuo was to serve as a model of pacifism, a state focused single-mindedly on the welfare of its own people.

The haphazard conditions under which the texts were produced adds another twist to the story of Zheng Xiaoxu and Manchukuo. Between 1932 and 1934, Zheng hired two Chinese writers to interpret his opaque writings in classical Chinese for the popular audience. Their interpretations were featured in major publications on the Kingly Way. Unbeknownst to Zheng and his Japanese sponsors, however, these two men were Kuomintang spies operating under cover, with an express

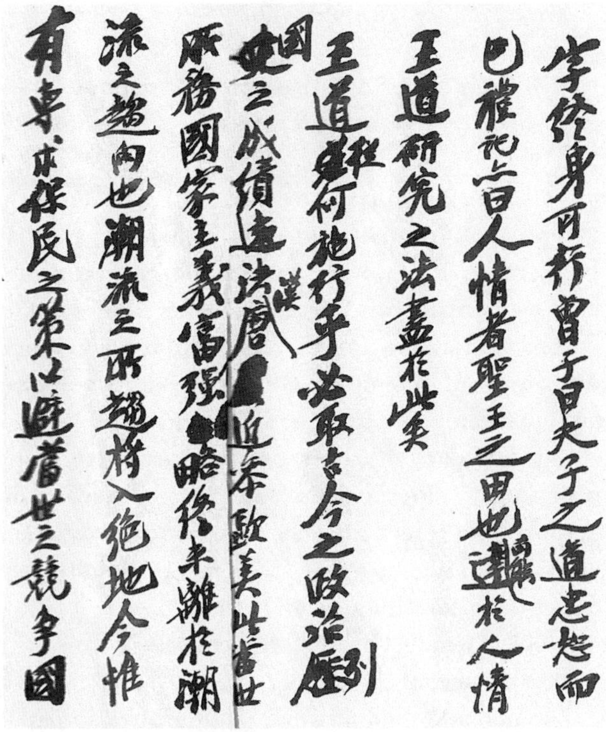

3.1 A page in Zheng Xiaoxu's last manuscript.
Source: Zheng Xiaoxu, Sukangong zuihou yigao, 8–9.

mission to sabotage Manchukuo.[24] Embedded in their interpretive texts were patriotic messages that encouraged resistance, hiding in plain sight waiting for the savvy reader to notice.[25]

This group of essays also demonstrates Zheng's mistrust of the interventionist modern nation state. Zheng grew wary of state power during the late Qing constitutionalist movement.[26] The brutalities of the First World War escalated his anxiety. He saw total war as a result of "state-centred, militaristic patriotic education." His last writing, composed only months before his death, reiterated the need to curtail state power.[27] Zheng presented his state critique as universally applicable.

These various lines of thinking converged into Zheng's unique theory of peaceful development. In Manchukuo, he was seen as a thorny critic of colonial policies. His poor political judgment sealed his tragic fate. His utopian theory, however, remains an important piece of the puzzle that is the intellectual underpinning of the occupation states in wartime China.

TRANSLATIONS

A Treatise on Rectifying the Wrongs[28]

ZHENG XIAOXU

The [degree of] disorder in China has reached 80 percent. From this moment onward, it will progress from 80 percent to 90 percent, and then from 90 percent to 100 percent. The rate of change will only accelerate. This is not something that we humans can foresee. However, things will turn to the opposite if pushed too far. The time for rectification may come sooner than we think. Now seven out of ten people under heaven resent chaos, but the rest still revel in mayhem. They stand as an insurmountable barrier – as tall as the mountains, as wide as the rivers – between us and the opportunity to rectify the wrongs. They have three mental illnesses. They feel shame in the illnesses, yet those who resent disorder have not gathered the courage to critique them. Now it is time to expose their mental illness. Then we might attempt to direct them back to the right track.

The first is reckless conduct against righteousness. After the 1911 Revolution, those who advocated civil rights saw the hierarchical relationship between the monarch and the minister as an embarrassment. They abandoned hierarchy for equality. [Now], sons are ashamed to serve their fathers; younger brothers are ashamed to serve their elder brothers; wives are ashamed to serve their husbands. They discard their traditional headwear, opting to dress and act outrageously. The disaster is unbearable. Those who resent disorder can no longer withstand the pain, but they do not have the courage to articulate it expressly. They cannot free themselves, yet they are reluctant to try out alternative approaches. This is the first obstacle to rectification.

The second is xenophobia. Since [we] sent students overseas, they have only learned about the superficial aspects of foreign [culture]. They resent the parochial outlook of our country, so much so that they dismiss our own advantages. They wish to wipe out everything and follow the European-American model, hoping to find a shortcut to overtake [Europe and America] overnight. When Russia descended into great disorder, [and its people were] preaching egalitarian values, the waves they made spread far and wide. They see their country as superior to the other great powers. This marks a new trend: republicanism will yield to communism. Now [our country] has lost its discipline and institutions. It cannot stand on its own. It would be impossible to restore order without bringing in external forces. The xenophobic thugs, however, are resisting [foreign influence] vehemently. This makes another obstacle for rectification.

The third is the erroneous theories of race. Yellow and White, Chinese and barbarian, Manchu and Han, south and north: these are all ways to exclude other groups from one's own. How is this different from warfare between great powers? How is this different from armed conflicts between villagers? Confucius said: "In education, there are no differences in kind."[29] This means that "those who keep to The Mean nurture those who do not; those with talent nurture those who lack it" and that "Heaven, in giving birth to the people, causes those who are first to know to awaken those who are later to know, and causes those who are first awakened to awaken those who are later to be awakened."[30] This is what differentiates humans, the highest order of living beings, from birds and beasts. This is not only true for teaching. Teaching is one element of politics. What Confucius preached was that there should be no discrimination in politics. To practise the politics of benevolence means to nurture all living beings. How can there be distinctions between groups? The Shun emperor was an eastern barbarian. King Wen was a western barbarian. They both fulfilled their aspirations in China. How can we expel them [from the Chinese world]? This is another obstacle to rectification.

The three mental illnesses have done much harm to the hearts and minds [of our people]. Therefore, the so-called National Congress movement is no more than begging for advice from strangers. If China fails to capture the opportunity to rectify the wrongs, it will be dismembered by the great powers. If such an opportunity presents itself, however, rectifying the wrongs in China would spare the world the perils of warfare. It would also effect a transformation of political morality across the world. The whole world will enter a new era of grand peace. These principles are crystal clear. The means to realize these goals are also easily within our reach. Now I shall present three proposals to show that rectification is feasible.

The first is about human talent. Talented people rise and fall with the ebb and flow of politics. When politics is in a good state, talented people abound. When politics is in disorder, talented people are nowhere to be found. Hunan and Hubei are known for producing talented people. This is because leaders [in the two provinces] promoted human talent during times of bandit pacification. So, talented people presented themselves spontaneously. The same holds true for all the other provinces of our country. Moreover, the Chinese people (*Hua ren*) are by nature wise and kind. They can thrive anywhere. The recent decades have seen a precipitous decline in the number of [available] talented people. However, if we look at Chinese emigrants in Southeast Asia and North America [things are different]. They were often taken overseas by slave traders and have enjoyed no state protection. They are easy prey for local bullies. Having endured all this hardship, they stand tall and proud nonetheless. There are hundreds of rich households in Southeast Asia, most of which attained their present status through honest hard work. The whole world marvels at their success. Since the opening up of trade ports [in China], foreign merchants have relied on Chinese compradors. The Cantonese served first; the Ningbo compradors followed. Foreigners have found the compradors to be worthy of their full trust. All the trade ports owe their prosperity to them. These people work faithfully even when not bounded by written contracts. Such is the nature of Chinese people. When politics is in disorder, these talented people eschew serving in the imperial court. Rather, they spread out to other fields, making their mark in industry and commerce. If the state brings them back to the right track, they will surely exert themselves for public good. [When that happens] China's human talent will surpass that in all other countries.

The second is about political teaching. The classics tell that those who rule must base their actions on benevolence and righteousness. Today's great powers, however, play by the rules of utilitarianism. Rulers have already started to find great power politics distasteful. Were China to rise and champion the ways of benevolence and righteousness, it would help rectify the excesses of utilitarianism. If practised for a few years, [this good form of politics] will shine over the world like the bright sun. Why is this? Those who strive for utilitarian ends always exert themselves for personal gains. This leads to inequality. At its very extreme, inequality causes annexation and deprivation. Those who strive for benevolence and righteousness, to the contrary, exert themselves to transform the world for the better. They strive to salvage the poor, leaving no one behind. Thus, the sages always say, Rule the state, pacify the world. Pacification means mitigating the excesses of power to follow what is best for the time and place. It means [using power wisely] to create peace and equality. When such goals are achieved, the imperial court's power should be curtailed, and self-governance [of the people] should be promoted. This is the right formula for world politics.

The third is about material wealth. Since the rise of scientific learning, heaven and earth have proffered their wealth for human consumption. However, the powers across the world have been exploiting their resources for so long that they may have to face the peril of resource depletion. China, however, is blessed with hidden resources that have remained untouched since the beginning of time. When the cause of rectification succeeds, we should work promptly to construct a major line of transportation between Asia and Europe. In the meantime, we should work on developing the northwest. If we made sure that national highways criss-cross our land within a few years' time, people from the southeast would all race to the northwest. China would then become a great power with a large territory and a sparse population. In a country with a large territory but a sparse population, the task of making a living would be urgent. If people invest all their energy in making their living, then disorder would diminish on its own. Order would spontaneously return. For [the talented people who have] academic ideas and capital that no other country would accept, we should allow them to experiment with the ideas and invest their funds in China. If they produce results, they should be allowed to naturalize as Chinese citizens. A decade from now, China will emerge as the strongest nation in the world, splendid and powerful. The whole world will look up to China as a paradise.

Those who are wise must regain their conscience and recognize the harm of disorder. They should take it upon themselves to restore order, address the urgent issues at hand, admit their prior mistakes, and give up their sense of embarrassment. They should ask themselves: How many more years do they have left in their lives to serve our country? They should conserve what is precious and apply it to practical matters. They should eschew anything that subtracts from their energy but does not yield practical benefits. If an opportunity presents itself, but nobody rises to the occasion, China will perish.

Editor's notes: The premier composed this treatise a few years ago, while witnessing unending disorder in China. It was a manifestation of his benevolent heart. We therefore publish it here. This is the true origin of Manchukuo politics, an ideal that is now becoming reality. It could even serve as a source of inspiration for grand world unity in the years to come.

Zheng Xiaoxu Diary, 5 July 1929[31]

I visited the provisional imperial residence[32] […] I proposed to send Akedi (who is a former Austrian naval officer. His full name is Xiao'e Akedi)[33] to Europe to establish a Zhendan Society.[34] The gist of the proposal reads: we cannot create a state of sustained peace and prosperity without the proper social hierarchy. The vast region in China's northwest holds wealth that has never been touched since the beginning of time. Now that we have four hundred million obedient people, a royal household that has governed [the realm] in peace for 270 years, and an emperor who has three years of experience ruling the Qing empire, we should unite to support them and create a new state [in the northwest]. There we shall abandon the shameful notions of discrimination in race/ethnicity, religion, and nationality. We shall share this moral way, this cause, and this glory with our comrades in arms. If we accomplish this [grand enterprise], we will surely change the whole world and put an end to the catastrophe of warfare. In the past, the British people launched a grand enterprise in the Americas on the basis of people's rule. Today we are starting another enterprise in Asia in the form of an imperial state: these two endeavours are the same in nature.

Questions about the Kingly Way[35]

ZHENG XIAOXU

States in today's world are all eagerly promoting patriotism, seeking to nurture citizens with qualities suitable for militarist nations. I nevertheless advocate the theory of the Kingly Way, which relies upon compassion as its foundation, rites and righteousness its weaponry. [States that practise the Kingly Way] do not produce arms. Nor do they maintain an army. Some may thus wonder, should world powers resent and oppress them, would they simply give up resistance? I would say that is not the case. Ours is a time of [territorial] annexations. [States] with no forces for self-defence will indeed find it difficult to preserve themselves. [Even powerful men like] Napoleon and Kaiser Wilhelm II [met their demise after] failures in wars of annexation. The reason why small states can still maintain independence today is that they are toothless and cannot cause harm. Thus, the great powers left them alone. This is probably because annexation would affect the balance of power. The security of small states is therefore tantamount to the security of the great powers themselves. The conference halls of Lausanne and Geneva are both set in Switzerland. Is this not because Switzerland never invites the animosity of other states and has consequently become the world's Goddess Huaxu?[36]

If a state of the Kingly Way arises in Asia, it will be of great benefit and no harm to the world powers. Even though it will not manufacture weapons or maintain an army, the weapons and armies of the entire world will come to its defence. Should [other states] conspire to bully it out of jealousy or act unreasonably against it, they would be violating the grand principles of All Under Heaven (*Tian xia*). It will be difficult to launch such baleful acts.

In recent years, the whole world has entered the era of pacifism. If the Kingly Way materializes, the thoughts of the world will change, which will significantly expedite the processes of arms control and peacemaking. The only thing to worry about is Communist policies. [The Communists] have developed plans to subvert the world and will surely take my thoughts as a forceful enemy. It is certain that [Communist policies and my theory] cannot coexist in peace.

The Theory on Preventing Wars[37]

ZHENG XIAOXU

Part I

The path of humanity is unclear. This is why state leaders are all striving for parochial interests. People are abused for profit; the strong bully the weak; the many are violent to the few. The disaster of war thus grows day by day, and the situation of humanity becomes worse and worse. People all over the world say that a country without arms cannot survive as a country. This theory only holds true for those who rely on armed forces to maintain the balance of power. For those who wrestle in such a way, if [their enemies] constrain one of their arms, they will surely fail: this is certainly true. However, should they continue fighting without end, they would both perish. Even those who rely only on physical force should understand this by themselves. Is it not therefore appropriate [for them] to come to the realization that [fighting] will lead to mutual destruction, and that they should relieve their animosity in order to survive? If they had stopped fighting but still could not ensure their survival, then we should reconsider our theory. However, the present situation is that [states] risk perishing because of their mutual rivalry. If [states] always resort to force in their attempts to eliminate others and preserve themselves, there will be no end to it.

Alas! Those states that rely on a military to defend themselves impose unbearable taxes on their people. They expose their people to the dim prospect of death. The king said, I heard that worthy men do not harm people with what is meant to preserve them (see *Mencius* for reference). Annihilating enemies by avoiding them, this is why the Zhou dynasty rose and the Di barbarians fell.[38] [Rulers of the Zhou] understood the path of humanity.

If there are indeed rulers today who are not obsessed with killing, it is certain that All Under Heaven will [eventually] belong to them. It is fine to give up arms.

Part II

Today's gentlemen are well aware of the danger inherent in attempts to prevent warfare. They are also concerned about the danger that the practice of the Kingly Way may bring about. This is why the disaster of war is difficult to avert. Those who clutch their swords with furious glares take retreat and compromise as signs of shame. They know nothing but deadly feuding. This is like chickens and insects fighting among themselves. If we propagate the idea of the Kingly Way on this day to prevent warfare, they will see such thoughts as deep humiliation. They will think of such ideas as nothing but an excuse for cowardly escape. If [we] can make them abandon arms and approach the Kingly Way, then those who are seeking to prevent warfare can do whatever they wish. They will be the beneficiaries. If such is not the case, and there are [militarists] who attempt to sabotage their endeavours with arms, then those seeking to prevent warfare would be committing suicide. This is not different from being killed by the Kingly Way. Wan Zhang told the following story: Song was just a small state but planned to practise politics of the Kingly Way. The kingdoms of Qi and Chu despised, and conspired to attack, Song. Mencius believed that there was nothing for Song to fear about Qi and Chu if the Kingly Way were indeed implemented. Mencius explained why the Kingly Way was not the way of harm and danger, but no one believed his theory. He [the ruler who did not believe in the Kingly Way] did not truly trust in the [Kingly] Way and therefore could not resolve this himself.[39]

Part III

Today's advocates of the idea of preventing warfare are all doing so in order to preserve themselves. Does this mean that they are not sincere in their effort? I must say no. However, if it is true that they are genuinely committed to this endeavour, why is it that they have failed to gain the trust [of the world]? I say this is because warfare involves deception. How do we know that those who advocate pacifism are not playing deceptive tricks? The language used in the oaths of alliance making always contain such lines as "I shall never deceive you; you shall never cheat me." However, how do we know whether such oaths are not just part of the art of war? Why is it that the world sees deception as the norm and sincerity as aberration? Those who discourage warfare in order to preserve themselves are not afraid of using such rhetoric as foil for deceptive strategy; it is this possibility that terrifies the whole world. Holding lethal weapons, entertaining baleful intentions – such people will end up engaging in violent fighting.

The agreement among Britain, Italy, Germany, and France aims at preventing all wars under heaven by firmly rejecting warfare.[40] Although this may in fact just be [their] strategizing, it does not contradict [my] idea of peacemaking. If the states that have abolished the military and those that have not can reach mutual trust without oaths of alliance making, and if [they can] discard the [said] thoughts about discouraging warfare merely for self-prevention, then [my] theory of warfare prevention will become reality even if I do not actively propagate it. This is the true foundation for a world of faith and sincerity.

Notes

1 Zheng's biographers have often framed his thoughts in negative terms: he resented republicanism and communism, wishing instead for a return to monarchical rule. See, for example, Xu Linjiang, *Zheng Xiaoxu qianbansheng pingzhuan* [A biography of the first half of Zheng Xiaoxu's life] (Shanghai: Xuelin chubanshe, 2003); Zheng Yingda, "Huiyi zufu Zheng Xiaoxu jiqi ersun" [Remembering my grandfather Zheng Xiaoxu and his sons and grandsons], *Ajia bunka kōryu kenkyu* [Studies of Asian cultural exchange] 3 (2008): 487–97; Aisin-Gioro Puyi, *Wo de qianbansheng* [The first half of my life] (Beijing: Qunzhong chubanshe, 2007); Lin Zhihong, *Minguo nai diguo ye: Zhengzhi wenhua zhuanxing xiade qingyimin* [The Republic is an enemy state: Qing loyalists and the transition of political culture] (Taipei: Lianjing chuban, 2010).

2 In his diary entry on 5 July 1929, for example, Zheng argued that his utopian cause was the parallel in Asia of the American cause of liberty in the West. In the preface to his 1934 anthology, his editor/interpreter suggested that Zheng's theory was the "newest" of all modern political thinking, because it merged the old and the new into an organic whole to address global problems. Zheng was not a believer in Chinese Confucian exceptionalism; he was a globalist in intellectual outlook. Zheng Xiaoxu, *Zheng Xiaoxu riji* [Zheng Xiaoxu's diaries] (Beijing: Zhonghua shuju, 1993), 2240; "Wangdao jiushi zhi yao" (Essentials of Worldly Salvation through the Kingly Way) in Zheng Xiaoxu, *Zheng zonglidachen Wangdao Jiangyanji* [An anthology of Prime Minister Zheng's speeches on the Kingly Way], ed. Cheng Kexiang (Xinjing: Fuwensheng yinshuju, 1934), 1–3.

3 Xu Linjiang, *Zheng Xiaoxu qianbansheng pingzhuan,* 142–57; Ye Can, Chen Bangzhi, and Dang Xiangzhou, *Zheng Xiaoxu zhuan ji nianpu* [The biography and annals of Zheng Xiaoxu] (Xinjing: Riman wenhua xiehui, 1939), 4.

4 Xu Linjiang, *Zheng Xiaoxu qianbansheng pingzhuan,* 169–80.

5 Ye Can, Chen Bangzhi, and Dang Xiangzhou, *Zheng Xiaoxu zhuan ji nianpu,* 26–27.

6 Wang Yunsheng, "Bubai: Zheng Xiaoxu yu Dongbei tielu jiaoshe" [Additional information: Zheng Xiaoxu and the railway diplomacy of the Northeast], *Guowen zhoubao* [National news weekly] 10, 29 (24 July 1933).

7 See, for example, Puyi, *Wo de qianbansheng,* 249. When introducing his political theory to Puyi in 1929, Zheng cited his Manchurian experience as evidence that his plan to bring in foreign capital for China's development would succeed. His early experience on the frontiers probably conditioned the way he understood the political situation of the 1920s.

8 On Zheng's political activities and frustration in the early years of Manchukuo, see Yamamuro Shinichi, *Kimera: Manshūkoku no Shōzō* [Manchuria under Japanese dominion] (Tōkyō: Chūō kōron shinsha, 2004), 209–21.

9 Rana Mitter, *The Manchurian Myth: Nationalism, Resistance, and Collaboration in Modern China* (Berkeley: University of California Press, 2000), 97–98.

10 On the conservative twist Zheng brought to the Kingly Way, see Komagome Takeshi, "Manshūkoku niokeru jukyo no iso" [The topology of Confucianism in Manchukuo], *Shisō* [Thoughts] 841 (1994): 57–82.

11 Zheng's thoughts have often been described in negative terms: he was resentful toward republicanism, nationalism, and communism, wishing instead for a return to the traditional dynastic era. Race, development, and peacemaking illustrate what drove his fear and desire. Understanding his perception of the specific historical moment he wanted to restore helps make better sense of his puzzlingly idealistic vision for the Japanese occupation state of the 1930s.

12 Zheng Xiaoxu, *Zheng Xiaoxu riji*, 25 December 1894, 455; 7 January 1910, 1222.

13 Frank Dikötter, *The Discourse of Race in Modern China* (New York: Oxford University Press, 2015), 107.

14 Wang Hui, *Xiandai Zhongguo sixiang de xingqi* [The rise of modern Chinese thought] (Beijing: Sanlian shudian, 2004), vol. 1, 86–87.

15 Zheng Xiaoxu, "Boluan fanzheng yi," in *Wangdao congkan* [Collected essays on the Kingly Way], ed. Wangdao xuehui (Fengtian: Fengtiansheng gongshu yinshuaju, 1934), 8.

16 Zheng Xiaoxu, "Zheng su'an jingqing yanshuogao" [Transcript of the speech by Zheng Xiaoxu], *Shenbao* [Shanghai news], 17 September 1906.

17 Zheng Xiaoxu, "Houteng Chunji wenba" [The afterword of Gotō Harukichi's article], in Zheng Xiaoxu, *Zheng zonglidachen,* 103–5.

18 On Zheng's fascination with fascism, see Lin, *Minguo nai diguo ye,* 335.

19 Caveliere Raffaele Muriello, *Mussolini: His Work and the New Syndical Law,* 3rd ed. (Edinburgh: MacNiven and Wallace, 1928), 1. Zheng's close friend Wu Aichen translated the book into Chinese. Zheng subsequently presented the work to Puyi for his perusal. Zheng Xiaoxu, *Zheng Xiaoxu riji,* 18 October 1929, 2254.

20 Zheng Xiaoxu, *Zheng Xiaoxu riji,* 6 May 1932, 2382.

21 Ibid., 8 March 1909, 1182.

22 Ye Can, Chen Bangzhi, and Dang Xiangzhou, *Zheng Xiaoxu zhuan ji nianpu,* 7.

23 These include the Locarno Treaties of 1925 and the Kellogg-Briand Pact of 1928. See, for example, Peng Shusu's interpretation of Zheng's peacemaking theory in the context of European great power diplomacy, Peng Shusu, "Kongyan heyue buruo shixing Wangdao" [The practice of the Kingly Way is better than empty talk about peace treaties], *Manzhou bao* [Manchuria newspaper], 9 December 1934.

24 On the pair's infiltration activities under the Wang Jingwei regime in Shanghai after 1938, see the memoirs of Kuomintang intelligence officials: Shen Zui and Kang Ze, *Qinlizhe jiangshu: Juntong neimu* [Witness accounts: Inside stories of the KMT Military Intelligence Bureau] (Beijing: Zhongguo wenshi chubanshe, 2009), 257.

25 See, for example, page 48 of Wangdao xuehui, ed. *Wangdao congkan.* The text described the misfortune of the citizens of weak states and implored its Chinese readers to take up arms. One would not notice that this was supposed to be ironic unless one turned to the next page and read to the last few sentences, which said "this old paradise will actually turn into hell."

26 See Zheng Xiaoxu, "Zheng su'an jingqing yanshuogao." An ardent supporter of Qing rule, Zheng nonetheless proposed that the constitutionalist movement should start from below.

27 Zheng Xiaoxu, "Sukangong zuihou yigao" [The last manuscript of Zheng Xiaoxu], 1937, Cornell University Library.

28 Wangdao xuehui, ed., *Wangdao congkan,* 8–10.

29 Confucius, *The Analects,* trans. Edward Slingerland (Indianapolis, IN: Hackett, 2002), 189.

30 Mencius, *Mencius,* trans. Irene Bloom (New York: Columbia University Press, 2009), 87, 106.

31 Zheng Xiaoxu, *Zheng Xiaoxu riji,* 5 July 1929, 2240.

32 Zheng Xiaoxu continued to think of Puyi as the emperor of China after the 1911 Revolution, as reflected by his choice to refer to Puyi's residence in Tianjin as the "provisional imperial residence" (*xingzai*).

33 According to Puyi's memoir, this former naval officer branded himself as a well-connected Austrian aristocrat, but never delivered on his promise to help with Puyi's plan for restoration. He also served in the municipal council of the Austrian leased territory in Tianjin. I have not been able to determine his German name. Puyi, *Wo de qianbansheng,* 229.

34 Zhendan is an ancient term for China.

35 Wangdao xuehui, ed., *Wangdao congkan,* 6–7.

36 Huaxu was the goddess who gave birth to China's mythical ancient ancestors. Zheng used this classical metaphor to emphasize the level of respect Switzerland commanded in the world.

37 Wangdao xuehui, ed. *Wangdao congkan,* 41, 49, 57.

38 This is a reference to Mencius's teaching to the duke of Teng. See *Mencius,* 25.

39 Wan Zhang was a disciple of Mencius. This story can be found in *Mencius,* 65.

40 This appears to be an allusion to the Four-Power Pact of 1933, which was a failed attempt to ensure international security in Europe through great power coordination.

4 Education Policies and Theories in Manchukuo

WANG YU

In recent years, scholars have pointed out that the ruling ideology of Japanese imperialism and colonialism was not monolithic; rather, it contained variety and conflicts.[1] In the case of Manchukuo, Rana Mitter argues that several coexisting strains of thought competed for local Han Chinese elites' attention as an effort at empire building in the late 1920s and early 1930s. These conflicting discourses, Mitter suggests, effectively produced two contrasting images of the Japanese Empire in the region, one being collaborative and the other nationalist and exclusive.[2]

The two translations presented here, produced by Japanese educators in Manchukuo, further complicate the picture of a multivalent empire depicted in existing scholarship. These two readings tell a fascinating story of Japanese colonialism from both structural and individual perspectives. In particular, the pedagogy promoted in the readings incorporates and modifies various scientific theories to legitimize colonialism but at the same time differentiates itself from the nationalistic and militaristic teaching styles then dominant in Japan proper.

These two texts were produced in the early 1930s, when political spheres in Japan became increasingly intolerant to ideas and influences that did not conform to the expansion of Japanese imperialism. Some educators, as a result, decided to move to Manchukuo, the newly developed frontier of the empire, to continue exploring the possibilities of innovative educational pedagogy.[3] Meanwhile, the Fengtian Education Bureau and the Fengtian Education Committee, established after the founding of Manchukuo in 1932, launched a journal titled *Fengtian jiaoyu* (Mukden education review).[4] The journal publicized guidelines and promoted colonial educational policies in Manchuria. It published fifty issues between 1933 and 1940, covering news events, political reports, speech drafts, research articles, and administrative announcements.[5] While the article "Fengtian jiaoyu jianshe si'an" ("Mukden Education Construction Project Proposal") was categorized as a research article, "Jiaoyu ai" ("Educational Love") was a reprint of the author's speech at a local educational institute.

The authors of both writings, Morita Ryōichi and Nakatani Sadaharu, advocated the New Education Movement that was popular in Europe and the United States in the 1920s. According to Andrew Reed Hall, the New Education Movement promoted "student-centered and hands-on teaching methods, an emphasis on practical and vocational learning over academicism, internationalism over nationalism, and the encouragement of individual talents over group conformity."[6] Morita particularly favoured physical participation education (*laozuo jiaoyu*), which, according to the author, marked "the pinnacle of education theory and action."[7]

To fully implement physical participation education in the colony, Morita suggested the establishment of cooperative schools, short courses, special classrooms, and celebratory days within the Fengtian education system. Such a diverse educational infrastructure not only took consideration of the spatial needs of certain learning and physical activities, but also created conditions for students to learn knowledge and practise it at the same time. Such a proposal entailed, in Tani's words, "colonial modernity."[8] That is, it showcased that the cultivation of colonial subjects was not merely a process of ideological indoctrination, but was also closely intertwined with the rise of modern citizenship and subjectivity.

Moreover, such a colonial modernity, according to Prasenjit Duara, contained East Asian characteristics. The best example of this would be the rhetoric and ideology of the Kingly Way (*Wangdao*). Initially raised by Sun Yat-sen but later appropriated by the Japanese military, the Kingly Way promoted the idea of a moral state that emphasized Confucian values such as loyalty, filial piety, and neighbourly harmony. Duara has aptly pointed out that such rhetoric and ideology functioned as a nexus connecting political leaders, Confucian monarchists, and religious and universalist societies.[9] The Kingly Way also served to criticize nationalism and communism and to legitimize the presence of the Japanese army in Manchuria.[10] Nakatani Sadaharu's article "Educational

Love" offers readers a fine specimen to examine how the moral state of the Kingly Way administered the hierarchy of love as the latter provided critical support to the full realization of one's self.

Nakatani, the education inspector of Fengtian province, introduced the theory of Eduard Spranger (1882–1963) to an audience in Manchuria in a talk on education and love. Spranger was a German philosopher, psychologist, and educator. In his famous book *Types of Men: The Psychology and Ethics of Personality* (1914), Spranger divides human personalities into six types in a hierarchy from what he believed to be the most elementary to the most complete: the theoretical self who focuses on the discovery of truth; the economic self who is interested in what is useful; the aesthetic self who values form and harmony; the social self who loves people; the political self who desires power; and the religious self who pursues unity.[11] Nakatani largely adopts Spranger's theory, but sets up a different hierarchy, reducing the six types to four and reordering them: the biological self, the aesthetic self, the theoretical self and the religious self. According to Nakatani, each type functions in its own territory and the only way for the self to cross the boundaries is to transcend its limits via love. Nakatani further designates five types of love to correspond to the four types of self: sexual love, parental love, educational love, neighbourly love, and Buddhist love.

Nakatani's articulation of these different types or, to be more accurate, levels of love, corresponded to not only modern psychological discoveries but also social norms and religious doctrines. Furthermore, according to Nakatani, the self was psychologically proven to be an unchanging subject; it contained no regional or historical traces and was immune to social and political changes. What is intriguing in Nakatani's theory is that science was significant only at the low-level ascendance of the self. In other words, science would hinder the self as the latter ascended. Only Confucianism (neighbourly love) and Buddhism (Buddhist love), which lay at the core of Manchukuo's Kingly Way, could further elevate the self once it reached the level of aesthetics and theory. This, then, repudiated contemporary idealizations of science.

Overall, these two readings demonstrate how the development of education in Manchukuo constituted an important part of colonial modernity with East Asian characteristics. The ideology and rhetoric of the Kingly Way not only administered the theory of love but was also consciously built into the modern educational infrastructure. As Morita claimed, the purpose of education in these varieties of new schools was to "let students have a real understanding of Manchukuo's Kingly Way." These texts illuminate the crucial position that education occupied in the building of modern Manchuria and the expansion of Japanese colonialism in early twentieth-century East Asia.

TRANSLATIONS

The Mukden Education Construction Project Proposal[12]

CHIEF EDUCATION INSPECTOR, MORITA RYŌICHI

Translator from Japanese to Chinese:
Provincial Education Inspector, Gao Wenyin

During the night of 18 September 1931, the righteous Japanese army quickly rose up following the sound of cannons that shook the Liutiaogou[13] in Mukden.[14]

Equipped with its internationally incomparable military rule and a historically exceptional Japanese spirit, the Japanese army drove the arrogant and stubborn warlord Zhang [Zuolin] out of the land of Manchus and Mongols with actions as swift as light emitted by electricity and fire emanating from the crashing of stones. Therefore, the thirty million people who have suffered from burdensome taxes and ferocious looting for twenty years are now rescued. Meanwhile, calls for "Independence for Manchus and Mongols" came to the Northeast. With devoted instructions from many of the early awakened, and enormous sympathy from the friendly neighbour Japan, the land of Manchus and Mongols turned itself in less than half a year into the only state in the world ruled in accordance with the Kingly Way.

The world viewed Manchuria with shock. The faces of the nearby Chinese turned pale; they gave up and ran away. Only Japan, the neighbour in the east, happily appreciated this and sent best wishes to the newly born Manchukuo.

On 1 March, the first year of the Great Unity [Datong] era, the thirty million masses stood under the five-colour flag. Their voices joyfully sang for the rule of right, filling up the space between Heaven and Earth. Glorious light and boundless happiness shall be bestowed upon Manchukuo forever.

Forget the bandits! Forget the League of Nations! Without them, Manchukuo developed its own path, going forward happily and joyfully.

Look at the military achievements of Manchukuo!

Listen to the voices of the thirty million people!

With a head of state that has inherited the Mandate of Heaven, and a government that supports the head of state, Manchukuo has the best type of politics. With its society at peace and all industries and businesses developing prosperously, should Manchurians not find themselves happy with their current life?

Tortured and humiliated by the bandit Zhang, the education system was destroyed after the roar at Liutiaogou. As a result, millions of tender students lost their schooling like lambs losing their way home. However, the elementary schools in Mukden province resumed on 1 March last year and rescued the homeless children. On 1 May, middle schools reopened. This comforted the hearts of the students, their brothers, and fathers.

Education in Mukden province has made comprehensive progress under the rule of glorious Manchukuo. It has now been operating for one year.

To celebrate the one-year anniversary of the establishment of Manchukuo and the one-year anniversary of schools reopening, the Bureau of Education and the Mukden Education Committee are honoured to release the journal *Mukden Education Review* on 1 March. This inaugural issue is a special one that carries profound meanings and important duties to celebrate the anniversary of the state's establishment. This is such a good and proper intention.

Since the inauguration of Manchukuo, we have taken over the responsibility of education in the country. We feel anxious whenever thinking about it. But when realizing that we have the support of thirty million people, the cooperation of tens of thousands of colleagues, the sympathy of the early awakened and our friendly neighbour [Japan], we immediately cheer up and become unprecedentedly courageous and ready to bravely march forward to carry out duties.

Concerning the problem of education construction in Mukden, I present here my view that contains proper and effective methods. I hope that the educated will not discard this and kindly offer corrections, so that we will together move this project forward. That is my hope.

Detailed Proposal of the Mukden Provincial Education Construction Project

1 Outline

1.1 The establishment of education policies. To students and children, etc., let them have a real understanding of Manchukuo's Kingly

Way. The guideline is to raise real talents for the development of Manchukuo culture. To realize this, it must be done under the principles of civic education and labour education. Below are the specific methods.

1.2 Revitalize vocational schools. Reform existing vocational schools.

1.3 Cultivate a career-oriented education system that produces capable talents.

1.4 Fundamental reform of teaching education.

1.5 Raise the quality of current faculties.

1.6 Change teaching school districts.

1.7 Engage in methodological studies to explore the theories of each discipline.

1.8 Study the local adoption of each discipline and textbook editing.

1.9 Fundamental reform of the previous education system to make it directly connected with the Manchukuo education project, to train future leaders for state reform and revival.

1.10 It is for the above purposes that the Mukden Education Committee organized societies for each discipline and uses the societies as centres of research, textbook editing, and other relevant teaching affairs.

2 Short courses

2.1 Since the establishment of Manchukuo, the Mukden Bureau of Education organized the following short courses to help current faculty build a deep understanding of Manchukuo and to help general audiences gain a broad sense of it.

2.1.1 Short course on the Mukden Provincial Education Project (the following were summoned: heads of the Education Bureau in the province's fifty-six counties, county education inspectors, and principals of provincial and municipal schools)

2.2 To revitalize the spirit of Manchukuo's construction and to reform the education reality, the following short courses were organized.

2.2.1 Short course on school management: Monday, Wednesday, Thursday

2.2.2 Short course on labour education: Monday, Wednesday, Thursday

2.2.3 Short course on physical education: Tuesday, Thursday, Saturday

2.2.4 Short course on school management: Monday, Wednesday, Thursday

3 Plan for the second year of Datong [1933].
   3.1 Types of short courses
      3.1.1 Short courses on common classroom facilities renovation (with on-site instruction at designated schools)
      3.1.2 Short courses on special classroom facilities renovation (with on-site instruction at designated schools)
      3.1.3 Short courses on activity room facilities renovation (with on-site instruction at designated schools)
      3.1.4 Short courses for school-employed instructors
      3.1.5 Short courses on civic education
      3.1.6 Short courses on national language education
      3.1.7 Each discipline organizes its lectures in order
   3.2 Types of meetings
      3.2.1 Meetings of the heads of the County Education Bureau and county education inspectors
   3.3 The province is divided into eight school districts centred around provincial normal schools to lead education development in each district. There will be at least three or four district short courses or meetings this year.
   3.4 In the future, the following proper periods will be prescribed at the convenience of each school to carry out physical education movements, intellectual education movements, morality education movements, and hygiene movements: Physical Education Day, Outdoor Day, Learning Crafts Day, Social Contribution Day, Cleaning Day.
4 In the second year of Datong, education committees in Mukden municipality and subordinate counties will be established to complete organization of the Mukden Education Committee. The following issues will be emphasized:
   4.1 Holding general meetings of the Mukden Education Committee
   4.2 Running activities of the teaching research societies under the guidance of each branch committee
   4.3 Having the teaching societies edit the most proper textbooks for each county

27 February, second year of Datong

Educational Love[15]

Mukden Provincial Education Inspector, Nakatani Sadaharu

Head of the Physical Education Team, Ba Kunduan

Today, I want to talk with you about educational love. Before I start, I want to introduce to you Eduard Spranger's "spheres of self and objects."

Our spirit contains different spheres, each of which stays at its own level. From these levels, one can assume different spheres of self. The objects corresponding to their respective spheres of self can be explained by the following diagram [Figure 4.1].

Although our selves may be different on the surface, they cannot separate themselves from objects in the course of real life. To be specific, located in the middle, the level of the biological self, which is also the level of the conscious self that concerns the body, corresponds to reality through direct sensorial contacts. It has limited territory. Second, there is the level of the aesthetic self that expands its territory through the function of imagination. It corresponds to the imaginative sphere, but it cannot go beyond the

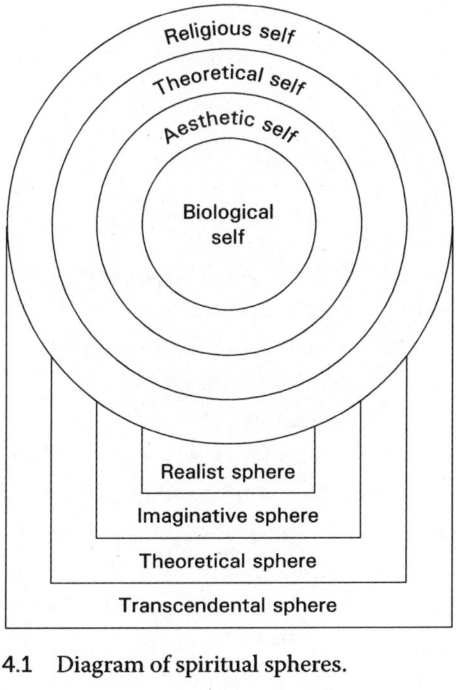

4.1 Diagram of spiritual spheres.

sphere of intuition. Third, with the help of logic to further expand its territory, the aesthetic self transcends the specific sphere of perception and reaches the level of the theoretical self. The layer of the theoretical self corresponds to the intellectual sphere. In the end, there is the layer of the religious self (the metaphysical self) that transcends the theoretical sphere via belief. Its territory is boundless. It corresponds to the transcendental sphere. In order to seek the focal point of all the above layers, one has to experience the spheres of reality, theory, imagination, and transcendence. Then, with the aid of experience, one can be sure that each of the above-mentioned layers of self has its own value. The value of the layer of the biological self is utility. The value of the layer of the aesthetic self is beauty. The value of the layer of the theoretical self is reality. The value of the layer of the religious self is sacredness.

These are the four basic values. In social life, there is hierarchy and equality. To communicate the ideas of people between different classes, one needs rightness. To connect the ideas of people within the same class, one needs love. Rightness, love, and the four basic values are the six focal points of the ideal life. See the following:

1 economic lifestyle
2 aesthetic lifestyle
3 theoretical lifestyle
4 societal lifestyle
5 rightful lifestyle
6 religious lifestyle.

These values cannot be divided into stages by type. They have to be divided by the strength of experience. Strength refers to the degree of experience that the self gets in relation to value. The closer that the fullness of life reaches ideal life, the higher and stronger the degree is.

Generally speaking, the religious value constitutes the skeleton (*guge*) of the ideal life. It is the strongest and highest among all the values. Then comes the economic value, which is secondary and also the value of utility. The economic value exists for the purpose of life preservation. The economic value is the weakest and the lowest because life only reaches the value of utility when it gains spiritual value. Between the two are aesthetic value, theoretical value, followed by the rightful value[16] and societal value (or the value of love). The two values are oppositional and purely formal. Their content has connections with other values, which, depending on the content, vary to some degree. When the self relates to the economic value, it is of the lowest degree. When the self relates to religion, it becomes higher in degree, the more connections it has with religion. Cultivation is the way to lead the lowest self up to the spheres of the highest self. When consciousness of the highest self awakens, one is able to use it to rule the subjective spheres of the self.

Assuming that there is a tunnel in the centre of each level that connects different levels of the self, hoping to pursue higher, deeper, and purer values, we climb up via the tunnel. That is the origin of love. With hope in our hearts, we are able to work together in a cooperative and integrative manner. In simple words, that is love. Under the layer of love is the biological self, the instinct to preserve life, which is simply greed. Above the layer of love is the religious self – the empathy of Buddha, the love of God. That is sacred love.

Between the two are sexual love, parental love, educational love, and neighbourly love. I will now talk about them.

Greed

Greed is the essence of the biological self. It is not only the essence of the human self, but also the essence of all animals' self. It is the desire of animals to preserve life. Desire only asks for the satisfaction of one's demand. It does not care how others might suffer or sacrifice for it. It excludes sympathy. It is egoistic and utilitarian. It can only be called desire. It does not qualify as love.

Sexual Love

Above greed is love. Love is a common phenomenon among humans. The first stage of love is sexual love. In order to distinguish sexual love and sexual desire, Spranger suggests that sexual love is man and woman doing something together in a cooperative and integrative manner, in the hope of reaching the sphere of aesthetics. But it is not only the male and female that can reach the sphere of aesthetics. The nature of sexual love is the sexual instinct between the two sexes. Before the sextual instinct turns into sexual consciousness, its aesthetic value is nothing more than a type of medium. For example, a beautiful appearance is only able to attract the other sex, and make it approachable. The sexual instinct is not only to satisfy oneself – it is willing to forget oneself, to sacrifice oneself to attract interest from others. This is a human instinct across races – that one is equal with others and that others are part of the self; this becomes an instinct. This is no longer greed. It is one level higher. It becomes spiritual once it transcends by the way of aesthetics. Once love is filled with moral consciousness, it becomes pure love that serves the entire human being. But sexual love essentially bases itself on sex, for the purpose of preserving posterity. Therefore, it cannot satisfy itself unless it monopolizes the other. This is the feature of sexual love. If that monopoly is interrupted and turns into triangular or quadrangular relationships, the members will feel upset. Love then turns into jealousy and hatred. This is where sexual love is impure. On this point, although sexual life can be very heartwarming, it only functions within a limited number of objects.

Parental Love

Although parental love and sexual love are instincts of the human race, the former bases itself on parents' instincts. It is a spiritualized and personalized human love. While sexual love preserves posterity, parental love develops the spirit and personality of that posterity. Parental love is not only pure, warm, and sacrificing; it is also liberating, equal, and sympathetic. These are the features of parental love.

What is liberation? It is not to monopolize, like sexual love. One does not feel upset or jealous if there are many people who love one's son. If the parents have many sons, they love the sons equally, with no discrimination – just as one cannot say any one of the ten fingers is useless. One loves the son who is excellent in virtue as much as one does one's son who is weak in body and mentality.

Sexual love develops through the medium of aesthetics. One loves the other because the other is lovable. Parental love is the opposite – it aims at something that has potential value in the future. The weaker and worse the son is, the stronger the love of the parents. That is sympathetic love.

Parental love is purer and higher than sexual love, but it is still limited by human instincts. Differences exist between one's own children and those of others. Therefore, although the territory of parental love is broader, it is still limited. Once parental love ascends through the sphere of theory and further extends itself, it becomes purer.

Educational Love

Educational love helps teenagers who are not yet developed and mature to complete the value of their personality. Therefore, the love of teachers is the same as parental love – both are liberating, equal, and sympathetic.

The love of teachers is altruistic and sacrificing. Although it is not as strong as parental love, it is a special emotion born out of the common values of teachers and students. Once theorized, this special emotion becomes purer and covers even broader areas. Parental love becomes educational love if it develops one step further. But differences still exist between students that teachers have and have not taught.

However, if one can make some spiritual effort to go beyond this sphere and treat the whole human race as one's sons, as one's own students, then educational love becomes religious love, neighbourly love. Neighbourly love in its extreme form becomes sacred love. It is the essence of the religious self. Sacred love in its extreme form becomes Buddha's love, God's love. It is equality between humans and animals, equality between grass, trees, fishes, and insects. It is the ultimate salvation of all human beings. It is the sphere of Buddha's empathy.

Conclusion

In this sense, the biological self (greed) purifies itself during ascendance until it reaches its completion in sacred love. This is the essential method to teach students how to be human beings. Whether it is possible to evolve from greed to sacred love and, if so, how to get there are difficult questions to answer. On the way to purification, there is an aesthetic value functioning on one side and a theoretical value functioning on the other. The aesthetic value concerns emotion, [while] the theoretical value concerns reason. They both can lead us and help us to reach the ultimate goal. In other to get there, we have to have the same ideals and cooperate with each other.

The purification process follows the order below:

1 greed
2 sexual love
3 parental love
4 educational love
5 neighbourly love
6 Buddhist love.

This is the general order of purification. However, low-level love cannot be simply changed into upper-level love. Yet the latter contains the former.

As educators, if we can pay attention to the purification of students' greed, we can claim that we are doing real education. If we teach students only technical knowledge, then that knowledge will become a tool to satisfy greed. If that is the case, then we better not teach them. Such instances are numerous.

I will stop here. Thank you for listening.

Notes

1 Andrew Hall, "The Word Is Mightier Than the Throne: Bucking Colonial Education Trends in Manchukuo," *Journal of Asian Studies* 68, 3 (2009): 895–926.

2 Rana Mitter, "Evil Empire?: Competing Constructions of Japanese Imperialism in Manchuria, 1928–1937," in *Imperial Japan and National Identities in Asia, 1895–1945,* ed. Li Narangoa and Robert Cribb (London: Routledge Curzon, 2003), 146–47. Similar contradictions existed in other parts of the empire as well. For instance, Jun Uchida describes a contradictory dynamic at work in colonial Korea between national autonomy and racial fusion in Japan's promotion of the "New Order in East Asia." See Jun Uchida, "Between Collaboration and Conflict: State and Society in Wartime Korea," in *Tumultuous Decade: Empire, Society, and Diplomacy in 1930s Japan,* ed. Masato Kimura and Tosh Minohara (Toronto: University of Toronto Press, 2013), 136.

3 On Manchukuo as a laboratory, see Louise Young, *Japan's Total Empire: Manchuria and the Culture of Wartime Imperialism* (Berkeley: University of California Press, 1998).

4 Andrew Reed Hall translates the title of the journal as "Fengtian education," while Wu Sihan translates it as "Education in Fengtian." On the back of the original journal, however, the title is translated as "Mukden education review." I therefore use this title to refer to *Fengtian jiaoyu*. See Andrew Reed Hall, "Constructing a 'Manchurian' Identity: Japanese Education in Manchukuo, 1931–1945," PhD diss., University of Pittsburgh, 2003, 38; Wu Sihan, "*Fengtian jiaoyu* yanjiu" [A study on *Education in Fengtian*] (master's thesis, Northeast Normal University, 2016), 2.

5 Guoqin Chu, "Preface," in *Wei Manzhouguo qikan huibian* [Collections of bogus Manchukuo periodicals], 2nd series, ed. Guoqin Chu (Beijing: Xianzhuang shuju, 2009), 21.

6 See Hall, "Constructing a 'Manchurian' Identity," 3.

7 Morita Ryōichi, "Fengtian jiaoyu jianshe si'an" [Mukden education construction project proposal], *Fengtian jiaoyu* [Mukden education review] 2, 1 (1933): 2.

8 Tani E. Barlow, "Introduction: On 'Colonial Modernity,'" in *Formations of Colonial Modernity in East Asia,* ed. Tani E. Barlow (Durham, NC: Duke University Press, 1997), 3–7.

9 Prasenjit Duara, *Sovereignty and Authenticity: Manchukuo and the East Asian Modern* (Lanham, MD: Rowman and Littlefield, 2003), 112.

10 Suk-Jung Han, "The Problem of Sovereignty: Manchukuo, 1932–1937," *positions: asia critique* 12, 2 (2004): 457–78.

11 Eduard Spranger, *Types of Men: The Psychology and Ethics of Personality* (New York: Hafner, 1928), 109–248.

12 Morita Ryōichi, "Fengtian jiaoyu jianshe si'an," 1–5.

13 The Japanese named the site Liutiao Ditch or Liutiao Bridge.

14 Mukden, Fengtian, and Shenyang refer to the same city in Northeast China. The name Shenyang dates to the Ming dynasty. When the Manchu leader Nurhaci captured Shenyang in 1625, he assigned the city the Manchu name Mukden. The name Fengtian initially referred to the prefecture where the city is located but gradually became applied to the city. During the Manchukuo period, the puppet state officially named the city Fengtian. All three names were used in the republican period, but Shenyang became the official, singular name of the city in the 1950s.

15 Nakatani Sadaharu, "Jiaoyu ai" [Educational love], *Fengtian jiaoyu* [Mukden education review] 2, 1 (1933): 5–11.

16 In Chinese, this was printed as *quanli jiazhí* (power value). But it should be *quanli jiazhí* (rightful value), as rightful value is discussed in the text while power value is not.

5 The Second Sino-Japanese War, Propaganda, and Medical Publications

Kaneko Junji's "The China Incident from the Perspective of Psychiatry"

JANICE MATSUMURA

In February 1933, the editors of the *Chinese Medical Journal* issued the following statement: "Not content with misleading the world in their relentless campaign of subjugating China through Manchuria, Shanghai and Jehol, the Japanese Government and their propaganda machine have enlisted the help of even the medical profession in running down the praiseworthy efforts of Chinese and missionary organizations in that region."[1] The editors referred to a communication entitled "News from Manchuria" by a Japanese correspondent that had appeared a month earlier in the *Journal of the American Medical Association*. Ignoring the contributions of Chinese and Western personnel, the correspondent credited Japan with any medical progress in the region and asserted that the "natives at large, most of whom are said to have received medical treatment for the first time, are grateful."[2]

As Barak Kushner observes, the postwar Tokyo war crimes trials, in promoting the vision of an all-powerful military establishment that duped and oppressed the Japanese people, effectively negated the role of non-official groups in advancing wartime policies.[3] Individuals in Japan, as elsewhere, denied their own mastery of propaganda, suggesting that other peoples were more duplicitous and thus adept at the task.[4] The scope of propaganda activities proves otherwise. "Proposals and suggestions for improved propaganda products," Kushner explains, "came from around the Japanese nation and from a variety of organizations."[5] Annika A. Culver, for example, has uncovered the participation of avant-garde artists and writers, whose leftist ideological history would seem to make them unlikely spokespersons for the goals of the authorities.[6]

This translation draws attention to another group who may not be immediately associated with state ideologues. While there are works in English on how medical professionals lent their skills to wartime research projects, the most notorious being for the manufacture of bacteriological and chemical weapons, less attention has been given to their involvement in the production of propaganda.[7] One reason this topic may have stayed under the radar is the stereotype of medicine and medical knowledge, which, to quote Julie V. Brown, "is presumed to be derived from supranational scientific principles and hence to be impervious to such influences as culture, politics, or individual idiosyncrasy."[8]

Historians such as Miriam Kingsberg have refuted this presumption, demonstrating the intricate ties between medical personnel and Japan's informal colony of Manchukuo, which was one of the world's first "narco-states," being financially dependent on the opium trade.[9] These experts included Tokyo Imperial University professor of physiology, Dr. Sakai Yoshio, who was a notable presence in the Japanese anti-opium crusade of the 1930s that, Kingsberg points out, functioned as pretext for contesting China's sovereignty.[10] Sakai went on speaking tours throughout Manchukuo and north China and published works in Japan enjoining the Japanese people to refrain from opium consumption and asserting that, without the intervention of Japan, the Chinese were doomed to extinction due to widespread addiction. He also worked with the municipal Police Sanitation Bureau in Tokyo, supervising addiction cases as well as setting up in occupied China a factory to produce an analgesic known as IM, which was used to treat addiction. Investigating the charge that Japanese policy makers had adopted a policy to drug China into submission, prosecutors at the Tokyo war crimes trials determined that IM was no different from opium.[11]

Medical experts such as physiologists figured more prominently in the research and discourse on addiction before 1945, and it was only after the war that psychiatrists in Japan claimed addiction as their area of specialty.[12] Throughout much of the twentieth century, a constant complaint of its practitioners was that officials and the public dismissed psychiatry as a minor branch of medicine that simply provided custodial care for an unfortunate minority of individuals. In response, activists within the profession sought to demonstrate psychiatry's greater relevance, often melding medical and national interests in making their case. In opposing in the late 1930s the government's growing support for a eugenic sterilization law, Kaneko Junji (1890–1979), the author of the article translated below, argued that such legislation was premised on goals of racial purification that could only encourage ethnic hatreds and thus undermine the mission to promote the Japanese spirit among the Chinese people.[13]

Kaneko's foray into the discussion of Chinese opium addiction illustrates the range of medical experts who became involved in a propaganda war between China and Japan, as well as demonstrating the ripple effect of propaganda generating propaganda.[14] Although there is no evidence of a direct connection between Kaneko and other propagandists such as Sakai Yoshio, it is highly likely that the former was familiar with the work and views of the latter. A specialist in criminal psychiatry who had written on the dangers of narcotics and alcohol and who was affiliated with the Tokyo Metropolitan Police Board, Kaneko enjoyed the same civil police connections as Sakai, who in 1936 similarly scorned Chinese addicts as "notoriously deceptive" and skilful in using "tricks and charms" to foment anti-Japanese sentiments.[15] However, it is difficult to assess Kaneko's knowledge of Japan's opium traffic in China as, unlike Sakai, he appears to have operated strictly in the metropole, where members of the public approved of state control of information, especially that coming from foreign critics.[16]

Chinese and Westerners charged Japan with encouraging addiction, and in September 1938, the wife of Jiang Jieshi (Chiang Kai-shek), Song Meiling, accused Japanese policy makers of a plot "to drench the land with opium and narcotics with the primary object of so demoralizing the people that they would be physically unfit to defend their country, and mentally and morally so depraved that they could easily be bought and bribed with drugs to act as spies when the time came in order that their craving might be satisfied."[17]

In January 1938, the Chinese authorities appeared to have won a propaganda war to influence foreign opinion by succeeding in having Jiang and Song featured on the cover of *Time* magazine as husband and wife of the year.[18] In the very same month, Kaneko published in *Tōkyō iji shinshi* (Tokyo medical journal), a major Japanese medical publication,[19] the following article attributing the enemy's skill at propaganda to a national character perverted by an endemic opium addiction that had long predated the Japanese invasion of Manchuria.

TRANSLATION

The China Incident from the Perspective of Psychiatry[20]

KANEKO JUNJI

Since the start of the war, it is often said that "China is skilled at propaganda." When hearing this, one is immediately reminded of Lenin's observation: "Religion is the opium of the masses."

The Roman Catholic Church's Congregation for the Propagation of the Faith of 1622 is said to be propaganda. But it is not just propaganda's etymology or the fact that successful religions were those skilled at propaganda that makes one see a relationship between China's talent for propaganda and Lenin's statement: "Religion is the opium of the masses."

The premier intellectuals of their time, missionaries had extensive knowledge of opium and so used opium smoke when proselytizing. The psychological state that overcame visitors exposed to opium smoke in resplendent temples and monasteries was captured by [Thomas] De Quincey, the author of *Confessions of an English Opium-Eater,* who wrote that "opium truly is like carrying bliss in one's waistcoat pocket."[21] To peoples ignorant of opium, missionaries promoted as a reward for the faithful the narcotic effect of opium, which allowed one to forget all spiritual anguish and physical pain. In this respect, there is much truth in Lenin's observation that "Religion is the opium of the masses." But, aside from this, one may note another connection between opium and propaganda.

From the perspective of psychiatry, the Chinese skill at propaganda, even though not a case of religious propaganda, is profoundly related to opium. Ancient peoples had discovered opium's pleasurable qualities, and, while it is not known when exactly, it was originally used as a recreational drug. In Homer's epic poem, there is mention of "'a drug for forgetfulness' called Nepenthes, which was cast into wine and caused those who consumed it to lose all memory of worry, anguish, sadness, to forget the deaths of their fathers and mothers, and, until the end of their day, to never shed tears." This was not a product of Homer's imagination and reveals that opium was already present in ancient Greece. In particular, [the German pharmacologist Louis] Lewin proposed that opium had been transplanted in Greece, being originally produced in Egypt, by the age of Homer and that there existed a place called Mekone, which means Town of Poppies (Mohnstadt), during the eighth century BCE.

It is not known if opium was first used as a recreational drug and then as a medical treatment, or vice-versa, but, regarding its use in treating enteropathy and convulsions, Greece's Diagoras [of Melos] and Episistaratus [Peisistratus?] warned of its abuse. Consequently, there is no doubt that opium has not only been used as medicine, but has aroused medical concerns about its harm since ancient times.

Opium as a medical drug has appeared in Chinese documents since 973, but Arabs first imported it into China as a recreational drug between 1280 and 1295. Thereafter, opium smoking quickly spread, and already by 1368 a ban was imposed against opium. The injunction was ineffective and, since 1739, similar bans were repeatedly issued. However, the import of opium increased annually, with over 4,054 boxes entering the country in 1796. England was the main supplier for these imports.

The Chinese government at the time issued a ban against opium that imposed the death penalty on opium smokers, but this failed to eradicate the problem. It threatened the excessive profits that England enjoyed from the opium trade, and, as a result, it marked the first step toward the Opium Wars. With its disastrous defeat in the Opium Wars, China was forced to conclude the Treaty of Nanking with England. England acquired Hong Kong, a huge indemnity, as well as the freedom to export opium. China thus demonstrated that "a country where opium as a recreational drug flourishes will collapse."

The prevalence of opium smoking in China, of course, differed depending on the period and, as it was a practice that had to be conducted in secret due to bans that imposed severe penalties, exact figures are unavailable. However, specialists have roughly estimated that between 25 and 33 percent of adults were opium smokers. Moreover, there are sources that propose that 50 to 75 percent of Chinese adults were opium smokers. There is no agreement for these high and low figures. In any case, written down somewhere, there is a saying in China that illustrates how opium has permeated life in the country: "Life is fortunately bearable because of opium and love and, so, opium is love and love is opium."

There are not only many smokers of the narcotic known as opium in China, but, as can be expected, a proportionate number of addicts. Of course, ever mindful of the enormous profits that it enjoyed through the export of opium to China, England established in 1893 the Royal Commission on Opium, which declared that "opium posed no danger to health." Concerned about the effect that a duty on opium would have on the revenue of its Asian colonies, England's conclusion was self-serving denial of opium smoking's irrefutable psychological and physical harm. As Britain's Royal Commission on Opium at that time did not include medical doctors among its committee members, the findings of this commission were bogus and without authority, and in no way can counter recent psychiatric research.

The degree to which opium smoking is hazardous may be illustrated by what occurred during the establishment of Manchukuo, when Japanese bought and moved into homes previously occupied by long-time opium smokers. The mice in the homes would disappear. That is, mice that had been long addicted to opium could not live in a home without opium smoke and would leave and follow the opium smokers. This anecdote is useful as evidence of the prevalence of chronic addiction among opium smokers.

However, an assessment of the calamity of opium in China from the perspective of psychiatry cannot be limited simply to calculations of "such-and-such a percentage of present-day Chinese are opium smokers." In calculating the percentage of addicts among opium smokers but not taking into consideration the widespread impact of addiction, one overlooks the harm that opium smoking has on national character.

Moreover, when investigating in terms of psychiatry the relationship between opium smoking and the Chinese national character, one must not forget how long ago it was that opium smoking was introduced into China. The great impact of opium smoking on the national character becomes apparent as one counts the number of generations that have smoked opium, and just because one set of parents were not addicted to opium smoking, this does not safeguard the next generation from the scourge of opium.

In psychiatry, it is imperative to trace a patient's medical history, and opium, which was imported into China from 1280, has been used as a recreational drug for about 660 years. If one calculates one generation as amounting to thirty years, then the symptoms of opium addiction could be traced back for twenty-two generations, which is long enough for it to have become fixed in the national character. There is thus a relationship between this national character influenced by opium addiction and the skill of the Chinese at propaganda. Accordingly, from the perspective of psychiatry, the Chinese skill at propaganda is simply symptomatic of the influence of opium addiction. This will be made more evident by comparing the symptoms of opium addiction and the Chinese national character.

No. 1, the Chinese national character is feminine. A unique trait of the Chinese national character is the absence of anything that can be deemed masculine. Chinese foreign policy has traditionally pitted barbarians against barbarians and, even during the China Incident, China has relied on England, the United States, or the Soviet Union. This lack of courage to act independently is a symptom of opium addiction that has been implanted in the national character.

No. 2, in China, the national character lacks a sense of responsibility, and this is a pre-eminent feature of chronic opium addiction. China has unilaterally broken agreements with Japan and does not respect international agreements. What is notable about this lack of responsibility is that it reveals how chronic opium addiction has seeped into the national character.

No. 3, a strong sense of victim consciousness may be considered fundamental to the Chinese national character, and this is also a tendency notable in chronic opium addiction. This strong victim consciousness in the Chinese character, which ensures the unquestioning acceptance of the absurd notion that Japan is an invading force, is a product of chronic opium addiction.

No. 4, the Chinese number more than four hundred million, but it is said that they do not have a state. In truth, the utter egoism of the Chinese is rare among races. Because of this strong egoism, social morality has no way of developing. There are military cliques that function as private armies, but there is no national army in China. Causing misery for the masses, huge war expenditures and hundreds of millions in private funds are expropriated. Given this selfishness, this glaring flaw in the Chinese national character, bribery has become the driving force behind politics. Opium addiction invariably dulls a sense of social morality and makes selfishness extremely obvious. The inculcation of selfishness in the national character of the Chinese is directly related to the prevalence of opium addiction in China.

No. 5, those who are untrustworthy and mendacious have been considered "wretches like the Chinese," and the Chinese are an unreliable people who are skilled at lying. The Chinese do not believe that there is anything wrong with lying, and a propensity for falsehoods is also symptomatic of chronic opium addiction, which has spread among the masses so much that it has affected the national character.

No. 6, although scholars throughout the world have grappled with the question, Is China truly a nation state?, an important feature of the Chinese national character is the insistence on Middle Kingdom as the name for China. On the one hand, this is a manifestation of great conceit; on the other hand, it indicates that China lacks the judgment required for self-evaluation. This is also evidence of a national character that has evolved from opium addiction. Even during the present war, the Chinese have vainly overestimated their country's strength and underestimated the actual power of Japan, and, in such a narcissistic mental state, they have commenced hostilities that they are bound to lose. Extremely conceited and lacking judgment, chronic opium addicts are doomed to self-destruction.

No. 7, the vanity of the Chinese is famous and usually figures in their national character. It is apparent when examining the history of Chinese foreign relations that China is content to revere form over substance.

Although Sinkiang and Outer Mongolia have been invaded by the Soviet Union and Tibet is being offered up to England, China remains content to say that it has not lost its suzerainty. But, when it comes to its honest neighbour, Japan, hostility erupts over trivial matters and, despite losing its capital city of Nanjing, China continues to indulge its vanity through anti-Japanese resistance. Excessive vanity is a special characteristic of chronic opium addicts, and China's vanity may be attributed to the proliferation of this special characteristic.

No. 8, the Chinese national character also lacks a spirit of independence. Successive generations of Chinese diplomats have used barbarians against barbarians and, while this tactic usually ended in failure, China customarily depends on another's power rather than its own. China has contrived to simply borrow the power of England, Russia, the United States, and France. China's lack of independence and excessive reliance on others is, once again, representative of a national character emanating from chronic opium addicts. In truth, chronic opium addicts, having lost their spirit of independence, must rely on others for their salvation.

No. 9, in Chinese diplomatic history, even though the use of barbarians against barbarians has been painfully unsuccessful, it continues to be applied, and this policy of using barbarians against barbarians is used because there is a lack of willpower in the Chinese national character. The Chinese national character is such that individuals, once enticed by the momentary benefits offered by other countries, become utterly incapable of resisting the sweet words of foreigners. Taking advantage of this weakness in the Chinese national character, the strong susceptibility to suggestion, the Soviet Union has seduced China, and England has instigated it into undertaking anti-Japanese activities. The psychological peculiarity of chronic opium addicts, their lack of willpower and their great susceptibility to suggestion, is so widespread among the Chinese people that it has become their national character.

No. 10, notable in the Chinese national character is the absence of a sense of duty. China is representative of nations that insist on their rights but disregard their duties. Chronic opium addicts insist on their rights but never live up to their obligations, and chronic opium addiction has made the Chinese devoid of a sense of duty.

By comparing from the vantage point of psychiatry the Chinese national character and the symptoms of chronic opium addiction, the preceding ten points of similarity are discernible. Given this national character, China's vanity has reached a high point as result of the instigation, flattery, and deception of the Soviet Union, England, France, and the United States. Entertaining an unjustifiable sense of being victimized by Japan, China remains suspicious of its honest neighbour. It is inevitable that China's overestimation of its strength and reckless reliance on others to achieve its objectives has given rise to a vehement anti-Japanese spirit. Feminine in its vanity and penchant for falsehoods, utterly selfish and devoid of a sense of accountability, irresponsible and dependent on foreigners, China has started an ill-advised war. Consequently, rather than saying that the Chinese have a talent for propaganda, it is more apt to say that they are skilful at broadcasting misinformation. There will be no victory for chronic opium addicts, unless a country can triumph when its people have become addicted to opium, and, using the language of psychiatry, China's condition is such that it must be immediately placed under complete protective care. Unless the Chinese national character, which is permeated with the psychology of chronic opium addicts, is thoroughly reformed, China will share the same fate as chronic opium addicts and be destined to self-destruct. It is more than just troublesome for Japan to have as its neighbour a country of opium addicts, and no matter what, Japan cannot simply abandon China. Japan's great act of benevolence, which it must undertake, is to thoroughly administer treatment.

Notes

1 "Medical Works in Manchuria," *Chinese Medical Journal* 47, 2 (1933): 187, cited in Miriam Kingsberg, "Legitimating Empire, Legitimating Nation: The Scientific Study of Opium Addiction in Japanese Manchuria," *Journal of Japanese Studies* 38, 2 (2012): 344.

2 "News from Manchuria," *Journal of the American Medical Association* 100, 1 (1933): 56.

3 Barak Kushner, *The Thought War: Japanese Imperial Propaganda* (Honolulu: University of Hawai'i Press, 2006), 19, 24.

4 Ibid., 23.

5 Ibid., 21.

6 During a workshop, Annika Culver kindly provided information on a restricted-access government publication, *Senbu geppō* [The Monthly Report on Pacification]. Among its

contributors was the head of the Home Ministry's Bureau of Education, Tamura Toshio, whose September 1938 article included a section entitled "Senden-sen ni okeru: Bunkajin no batteki" (The selection of cultural figures for the propaganda war). See Annika A. Culver, *Glorify the Empire: Japanese Avant-Garde Propaganda in Manchukuo* (Vancouver: UBC Press, 2013), 147, 149.

7 The English-language literature on medical weapons research has become considerable. One more recent title is *Japan's Wartime Medical Atrocities: Comparative Inquiries in Science, History, and Ethics,* ed. Jing-Bao Nie (New York: Routledge, 2010). Of the various definitions of propaganda, I use the definition provided by Jacques Ellul, who focused on the aim of propaganda "to provoke action." Jacques Ellul, *Propaganda: The Formation of Men's Attitudes* (New York: Knopf, 1965), 25.

8 Julie V. Brown, "Revolution and Psychosis: The Mixing of Science and Politics in Russian Psychiatric Medicine, 1905–13," *Russian Review* 46 (1987): 284.

9 Miriam Kingsberg, *Moral Nation: Modern Japan and Narcotics in Global History* (Berkeley: University of California Press, 2013), 7.

10 Ibid., 2–3.

11 Ibid., 53, 167–68, 175–76. Because the prosecution eventually attributed responsibility for war crimes to policy makers, little effort was made to go after individuals who did not hold office, and Sakai's postwar fate is unknown. Regarding the alleged plot to drug the Chinese into submission, Kingsberg illustrates the shift in attributed responsibility to the army, referring to the statements of prominent American officials stationed in Japan. For example, in the early 1950s, Richard Deverall stated that "the opium-pushing activities of the Japanese Army in Korea, Manchuria, and, later, in China proper was part of the planning of a military group that at times behaved as if it were beyond the control of the civilian government in Tokyo." Ibid., 185.

12 Ibid., 196.

13 Kaneko Junji, "Shakai mondai toshite no seishinbyōsha no yūseigakuteki danshuhō" [The law for the eugenic sterilization of the mentally ill as a social problem], *Nihon iji shinpō* [Japan medical practice news] 893 (1939): 23.

14 Kingsberg, *Moral Nation,* 189. Kingsberg discusses Kaneko Junji's work on addiction after but not during the war with China and the other Allied powers.

15 Ibid., 78–79.

16 Kushner, *Thought War,* 19. Kushner describes the results of a January 1940 survey conducted by the conservative magazine *Bungei shunjū* (Age of art and literature) in which two-thirds of the respondents recommended tighter social controls – which would have further limited the public's ability to assess the political and military situation – in order to ensure the achievement of Japan's aims in China.

17 Quoted in Timothy Brook, "Opium and Collaboration in Central China, 1938–1940," in *Opium Regimes: China, Britain and Japan, 1839–1952,* ed. Timothy Brook and Bob Tadashi Wakabayashi (Berkeley: University of California Press, 2000), 323, 339. Regarding Song's accusation, Brook states that he has found "no evidence on the Japanese side that there was a plot to narcotize the Chinese people, although many Japanese regarded the extent of addiction in China as grounds for treating Chinese with contempt."

18 Kushner, *Thought War,* 27.

19 Kishio Kondō, "*Tōkyō iji shinshi* – Meiji shoki no igaku zasshi ni tsuite kōsatsu" [*Tokyo Medical Journal:* An investigation of early Meiji medical journals], *Igaku toshokan* [Tokyo library] 20, 2 (1973): 141. A pioneering journal established in 1877, *Tōkyō iji shinshi* remained a leading medical publication throughout its eighty-three-year history.

20 Kaneko Junji, "Seishinbyōgaku kara mita Nisshi jihen" [The China Incident from the perspective of psychiatry] *Tōkyō iji shinshi* [Tokyo medical journal] 3065 (1 January 1938): 50–52.

21 "[H]ere was the secret of happiness, about which philosophers had disputed for so many ages, at once discovered: happiness might now be bought for a penny, and carried in the waistcoat pocket; portable ecstacies might be had corked up in a pint bottle, and peace of mind could be sent down in gallons by the mail-coach." The Project Gutenberg ebook, *Confessions of an English Opium-Eater,* by Thomas De Quincey http://www.gutenberg.org/files/2040/2040-h/2040-h.htm.

6 An Inspection Report on Ideological Movements in Literature and Arts Activities

XIE MIYA QIONG

After the Greater East Asia War broke out in December 1941, the Manchukuo government tightened its ideological control over literary and cultural production across the country. On 25 July 1942, the Department of Police Affairs in the Manchukuo Ministry of Public Security ordered the Capital Police Bureau to launch a long-term inspection of the movements and works of ideologically suspicious Chinese writers and cultural workers in the capital of Xinjing. A series of reports were drafted and submitted to the central police in response to this order under the title of "Documents Regarding the Investigation on Ideological Movements through Literature, Art, and Theatre" (hereafter, the Investigation). In the late 1980s, Howard Goldblatt, a renowned scholar of Chinese literature from the Northeast, found one of these reports in an archive in Taiwan. Dated 29 November 1943, this report was marked as the fourth report of the series. Drafted in Japanese, it is an invaluable and unique source attesting to Japanese ideological control over Chinese intellectuals in Manchukuo.

This document has attained considerable fame: Okada Hideki, the leading Japanese scholar of Manchukuo literature, has studied the document extensively over the past thirty years. He owns a copy of the original document, and this English translation is based on his transcription of the document.[1] The document has to date been quoted numerous times by East Asia–based and North American scholars in the field, including the Chinese scholar Liu Xiaoli's monograph *Yitai shikong de jingshen shijie: Wei Manzhouguo wenxue yanjiu* (Spiritual world in a time of alienation: Research on bogus Manchukuo literature) and the Canadian scholar Norman Smith's monograph *Resisting Manchukuo: Chinese Women Writers and the Japanese Occupation.*[2] It has also been translated into Chinese three times. Translated by Yu Lei, it first appeared in 1987 in the journal *Dongbei wenxue yanjiu shiliao* (Historical materials for the study of Northeast literature).[3] In 1993, a new translation was included in *Wei Man xianjing tongzhi* (Police rule in bogus Manchukuo), a volume from the series *Riben diguozhuyi qinhua dang'an ziliao xuanbian* (Selected archival materials on Japan's imperialist invasion of China).[4] The latest translation, by Deng Lixia, is included in the Chinese translation of Okada Hideki's monograph *Zoku bungaku ni miru "Manshūkoku" no isō* (The topology of Manchukuo: A literary perspective, continued) and was published in 2017, as one of the thirty-three volumes in *Wei Man shiqi wenxue ziliao zhengli yu yanjiu congshu* (Bogus Manchukuo literary materials compilation and research collection).[5]

The Investigation is divided into three parts. Part 1 provides intelligence information about major movements of Chinese writers and cultural workers in the Manchuria Motion Picture Association (Ch: *Manying;* Jp: *Man'ei*), the publication and broadcast industry, and the "Chinese embassy" in Manchukuo. Part 2 summarizes contemporary tendencies in Chinese leftist literature in Manchukuo based on the inspection of a number of Chinese literary journals. Part 3 consists of a close reading of nine selections from this set of journals. The censors believed that these selections encouraged anti-Manchukuo and anti-Japanese sentiments in artful and circuitous ways. There is also a cover sheet, an original introduction, and a conclusion attached to the report.

As is shown in the document, parts 2 and 3 were drafted by three leading Chinese leftist writers from Harbin, namely Li Jifeng (1917–45), Guan Monan (1919–2003), and Wang Guangti (1918–81). The three writers had been arrested in two consecutive 1941 crackdowns targeting Manchukuo's Chinese leftist intellectual organizations. The first, commonly referred to as the December Thirtieth Incident, was a national (in the sense of Manchukuo) motion to undermine a self-organized underground anti-Japanese reading group across Manchukuo in which Li was involved.[6] The second took place on 31 December, the following day. Commonly referred to as the Harbin Leftist Literature

6.1 Group photograph from a symposium organized for Manchurian writers and members of the Manchuria Motion Picture Association. *Front row:* Shan Ding (*centre*). *Back row:* Manchuria Film Production director and writer Wang Ze (*farthest left*), writer Wang Qiuying (*third from left*), actor Meng Hong (*fifth from left*), writer Ren Qing (*middle, behind Shan Ding*), actor He Qiren (*second right*). This photograph was taken at the film studio, without notable participants in the symposium: Gu Ding, Mei Niang, Wu Ying, and Xiao Song. *Source: Manshū eiga* (Manchuria film) 2, 7 (August 1938): 33. Norman Smith collection

Incident, it targeted a Marxist reading group in Harbin that had a secret connection to Communists in China proper. Guan was its organizer and Wang was an ardent supporter.[7] Shortly after the two incidents, the three writers, together with many other arrestees, were transferred to a prison in Xinjing. Beginning in the summer of 1943, the three were required to read Chinese literary journals provided by the police and to report any suspicious contents they came across. Their reading reports were later compiled as parts 2 and 3 of the document here.

There are many possible readings of the two parts. The imprisoned authors were otherwise the colleagues of the writers they reported on in the document. The document therefore shows how colonized intellectuals made sense of the principles of ideological control that their colonizers used against them, and how they reacted to the difficult assignment of censoring work that they would personally support out of the prison. Okada Hideki believes that in writing this report, the three writers tried their best to protect young and new Chinese writers in Manchukuo. They reported only on experienced, well-established Chinese writers in Manchukuo, while minimizing the impact of other writers in the following statement: "There are two to three other new writers who have written sporadically on antifeudalism. The negative impact of such works on our citizens should be limited. As for the rest of the authors, they merely depict the pain and grief of life and can hardly qualify as targets of police censorship."[8]

As Okada notes, the report likely also contains the three authors' nuanced satire of the Japanese censors:

> There will be cases in which someone pretends to collaborate with the government but in effect promotes anti-state thoughts. However, because the form and content of such literature will become all the more complex and ambiguous, it will be very difficult to grasp its themes without a good understanding of the local circumstances and customs in Manchuria and the sentiments of the intellectuals.[9]

Here, the writers seem to imply that, because the Japanese were essentially outsiders who imposed their domination on the local Chinese in Manchuria, the linguistic, cultural, and social divisions between the two groups made complete ideological control nearly impossible. When the writers remind the Japanese censors that covert anti-Manchukuo and anti-Japanese tendencies in Manchukuo's Chinese literature "cannot be elucidated through theory; rather, the job left for the censors is to study and scrutinize the literature" – they know better than anyone that this would only frustrate Japanese censors who, had they been able to "study and scrutinize the literature" in meaningful ways themselves, would not have needed to conscript imprisoned Chinese writers to compile the report.

Certainly, it is also possible to read the report in ways that are more critical of the three Chinese writers who drafted it. For this reason, Okada disclosed their names only after they had all passed away, for fear that such disclosure would bring a new round of criticism to them in their later years.

Below is a selective translation of the introduction, the headings in part 1, the complete part 2, and the conclusion of the original report.

TRANSLATIONS

Capital Police Bureau Special Duties Section
Secret Document No. 3650

AN INSPECTION REPORT ON IDEOLOGICAL MOVEMENTS IN LITERATURE AND ARTS ACTIVITIES (FOURTH REPORT)

29 November, Kangde 10 [1943]

Vice Inspector General of the Police to the Director
of the General Bureau of Police Affairs

Please see attached for reports under the above-mentioned title regarding the inspection required by the Special Duties Section of the Department of Police Affairs in the Ministry of Public Security, Secret Document No. 545 issued on 25 June, Kangde 9 [1942].

Contents

1 Updates on cultural work (information acquired through staff members)
2 Latest literary trends among Manchukuo's left-wing writers
3 Findings regarding the works of left-wing literature.

Note: Items 2 and 3 are based on other inspections.

Part 1. Report on the Current Status of Investigation Regarding Literature and Arts

As has been reported, former Manchuria Motion Picture Association writer Wang Ze has escaped to north China after our August First Initiative.[10] As the situation has recently seen objective improvements, he has become active again. Since last year, he has travelled between Manchukuo and north China twice. His purpose is to establish a Manchukuo-oriented work base inside the Department of Literature and Arts of the Manchuria Motion Picture Association and to collaborate with An Xi and Shan Ding, his ideological comrades.[11] He intends to take advantage of the special nature of the Chinese embassy to maintain contact with his comrades through messengers. He came to Xinjing from Tianjin on 14 October with the excuse that he had difficulty sustaining a living there. He attempted to resume his position in

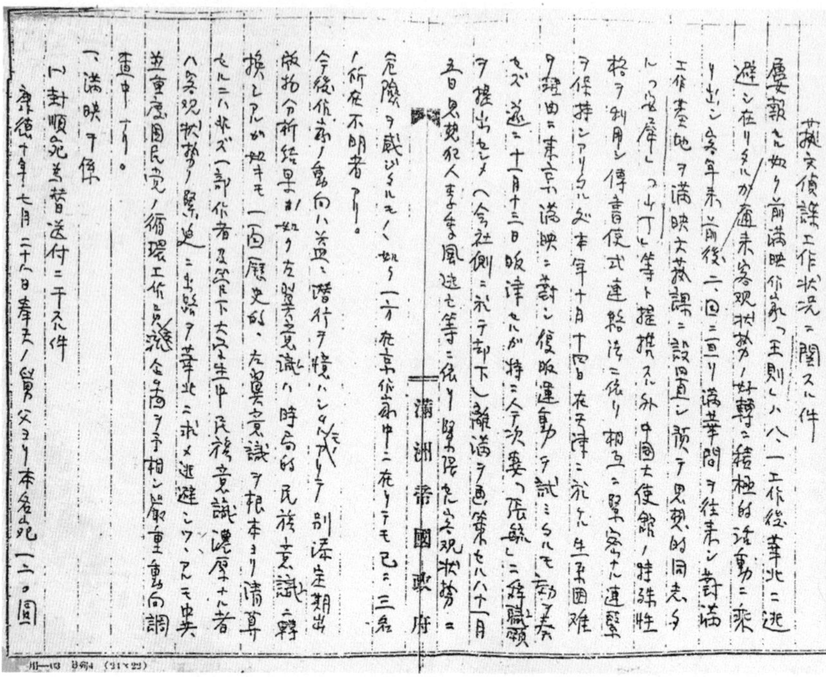
葉文偵諜工作状況ニ関スル件
憂鬱ナル如ク前満映作家ハ王則ト八八一工作從華北ニ逃
避シ在リタルガ通未客観状勢ノ好転ニ積極的活動ニ乗
リ出シ客年末前後二回ニ亘リ満華間ヲ往来シ對満
工作基地ヲ満映大欽課ニ設置シ殆テ思想的同志ヲ
シテ「盗窃」「山丁」等ト提携スル外中国大使館ノ特殊性
格ヲ利用シ傳言使式連絡法ニ依リ相互ニ緊密ナル連繋
ヲ保持シアリタルモ本年十月十四日在天津ニ於ケル生活困難
ヲ理由ニ東京満映ニ對シ復職運動ヲ試ミタルモ効ヲ奏
セズ遂ニ十一月十三日帰津セルガ特ニ今次妻ノ張敏ヲシテ辞職願
ヲ提出セシメ（会社側ニ於テ却下）離満ヲ画策セルハ十一月
五日思想犯人李季風逃亡等ニ依リ緊張化セル客観状勢ニ
満洲帝國政府
危険ヲ感ジタルモノゝ如ク一方在京作家中ニ在リテモ已ニ三名
ノ所在不明者アリ。
今後作家ノ動向ハ益々潜行ヲ續ハルヽモノト別添定期出
版物分析結果ノ如ク左翼意識ハ時局的民族意識ニ轉
換シアルガ如キモ一面歴史的左翼意識ヲ根本ヨリ清算
セルニハ非ズ一部作家及學下大学生中民族意識濃厚ナル者
ハ客観状勢ノ緊迫ニ其ノ路ヲ華北ニ求メ逃避シツヽアルモ其
並重慶国民党ノ循環工作員ト気脈ヲ通ジ相ニ厳重動向調
査中ナリ。
一、満映ヲ係
一、封順充為替送付ニ干スル件
康徳十年七月二十八日奉天ノ賀父ヨリ本名充一二〇圓
用一13 B64 (21×23)

6.2 First page of the Inspection Report. *Source:* Okada collection

the Manchuria Motion Picture Association, but the plan did not work out. He then went back to Tianjin on 13 November. He also has had his wife Zhang Min submit her resignation (which was then rejected by the association) and has planned for her departure from Manchukuo. This is likely because he sensed danger in the current tension that emerged after the escape of thought criminal Li Jifeng on 5 November.[12] In addition, among all the writers in Xinjing, there have already been three who have gone missing.

Writers' manoeuvres will become more obscure in the future. As the attached analysis of periodicals indicates, left-wing consciousness seems to have been shifting to nationalist consciousness, which corresponds more closely with the current political situation. However, this does not mean that historical left-wing consciousness has been thoroughly uprooted. Circumstances have compelled a number of writers and college students under our jurisdiction, who have demonstrated strong nationalist consciousness, to flee to north China to seek a way out. It is likely that they will try to communicate with the mobile agents of the CCP and KMT. Such serious developments are under (our) investigation.

[The following translation includes only the headings of the detailed report in part 1.]

1 Manchuria Motion Picture Association related
  1 The remittance to Feng Shun[13]
  2 The founding of the Manchuria Motion Picture Association Stage Play Society
  3 Wang Ze's departure to Beiping
  4 The Manchuria Motion Picture Association Stage Play Study Group and its external relations
  5 Wang Du's visit to Xinjing[14]
  6 The meeting for critiquing Manchuria Motion Picture Association films
  7 The current status of the Manchuria Motion Picture Association Stage Play Society
  8 The latest state of staff members in the Department of Literature and Arts in the Manchuria Motion Picture Association
  9 Wang Ze's conditions and activities in Xinjing
  10 Manchuria Motion Picture Association actors'/actresses' attendance at a dinner event at the Chinese embassy
  11 Prosecution of the actor Zhang Yi[15]
  12 Shan Ding's recent movements

2 General matters
  1 Personnel constitution of Changcheng Bookstore
  2 Communications between bookstores in Xinjing and censors at the Bureau of Publicity and News
  3 Movements of Song Yi from Manchurian Books[16]
  4 Activities of the Literature and Arts Broadcast Association
  5 Conditions of the constitution of the intelligence network at the Chinese embassy
  6 Shan Ding's movements after the Greater East Asia Writers' Congress
  7 Shanghai's Yinxing Troupe's visit to Xinjing
  8 *Qingnian wenhua* (Youth culture), a magazine newly created by the Concordia Association
  9 Movements of writers in Xinjing after Li Jifeng's escape.

Part 2. Latest Literary Trends among Left-Wing Writers in Manchukuo

The above-mentioned inspection is limited to an extremely narrow scope, conducted only by the left-wing activists and former writers Jifeng, Monan, and Guangti; nevertheless, some conclusions can still be made based on the inspection of periodical and non-periodical publications each month. It is of course dangerous to conduct general censorship in this way, but we believe under the current circumstances (in the next year or two), this could be used as a point of reference for publication censorship.

Due to the political circumstances it confronted in its early stage, the left-wing literature of Manchuria started with an abstract and seemingly ambiguous formal style. Consequently, for alien nationalities that entertain no appreciation of such literature, it is even more difficult to grasp its central themes.

In particular, after the outbreak of the Greater East Asia War, the government's persecution and oppression of those involved in Anti-Manchukuo/Resist Japan activities has made the left-wing writers more cautious. As a result, they tend to write in even more abstract and ambiguous ways.

At the same time, one needs to be mindful of the fact that, for those who subscribe to theories of left-wing literature, sudden changes in their environment will not suffice as reasons for them to completely abandon the essence of such theories. Accordingly, Manchukuo literature will probably evolve along the lines of New Romanticism in the future.

Digressive as it may be, here we would like to discuss New Romanticism a little. New Romanticism is a literary form typically associated with the initial stage of the proletarian movement. Its contents aim to promote liberal thoughts, raise antifeudalist consciousness, envision an ideal society, and analyze the old society as a way to suggest directions for the future. Compared to the individualistic way of thinking that is often associated with Old Romanticism, a style that negates all customary forms of legal, moral, and social relations and is only enthusiastic about the world of the ego, New Romanticism is more active and embraces a socialist consciousness. Mindful of this difference, Maxim Gorky (1868–1936) calls the former Bourgeois Romanticism and the latter Proletarian Romanticism.[17]

Now we have investigated the possible future directions of Manchukuo left-wing literature on the basis of the inspection of several available books and periodicals. It seems that renowned left-wing writers like Gu Ding and Shan Ding have been rather silent; when they do occasionally publish, they have, like Xiao Song, shifted completely to national literature.[18] There are two to three other new writers who have written sporadically on antifeudalism. The negative impact of such works on our citizens should be limited. As for the rest of the authors, they merely depict the pain and grief of life and can hardly qualify as targets of police censorship.

However, it remains an undisputable fact that, although they have all tried their best to avoid radical depictions for fear of censorship, they are still working hard to inculcate their readers with political consciousness. Based on a comprehensive consideration of the above-mentioned factors, we are predicting that they may employ the following literary techniques in the future:

Works That Oppose the Government

They depict the involvement of corrupt officials at the Living Necessities Cooperatives, Agriculture Development Cooperatives, and other local offices in cheating, bribe taking, and extorting, and expose defects in the operations of the current government, so as to foster anti-state thoughts against the government among the people. However, with regard to the techniques, they try their best to avoid explicit expressions of mass enlightenment. Rather, they pretend to criticize the immoral officials and sympathize with their victims from the government's standpoint; doing so would evade the eyes and ears of officials yet at the same time garner sympathy from people.

Works That Oppose the Bourgeoisie

They depict the involvement of house owners, capitalists, and merchants in illegal trading, hoarding, or speculating, and implicitly criticize the individualism and egoism of the bourgeoisie, imbuing readers with class-struggle consciousness and deepening the gap between capitalists and proletariats, all in the name of such beautiful words as "the War" and "the present political situation."

Moreover, they criticize landlords, village heads, and country gentry for practices that are at odds with the implementation of state policies. They may at the same time imply that the current government often makes compromises to accommodate them. This way of representation further deepens class-struggle consciousness among the people.

They are willing to use all kinds of stories about defects in the familial system to reflect inequality in the present society while expressing hope for the future and desire for the construction of a new country and even a new society.

Although the above-mentioned literary techniques are all similar to those in New Realism, in stories, essays, and critiques by these writers, the central themes are generally not presented in a transparent manner but are rather depicted in ambiguous and obscure ways. However, with regard to this point, it cannot be elucidated through theory; rather, the job left for the censors is to study and scrutinize the literature. In order to deceive the censors, in addition to the ambiguousness in literary representation, the above-mentioned left-wing writers probably also drop theoretical jargon and use emotional expressions unique to educated Manchurian nationals.

Moreover, besides the aforementioned issues, we also project that there will be cases in which someone pretends to collaborate with the government but in effect promotes anti-state thoughts. However, because the form and content of such literature will become all the more complex and ambiguous, it will be very difficult to grasp its themes without a good understanding of the local circumstances and customs in Manchuria and the sentiments of the intellectuals.

1 They aim to raise antigovernment sentiments among the people through ostensibly advocating disciplinary supervision of the government and criticizing the misconduct of corrupt officials.
2 They aim to foster antigovernment sentiments by ostensibly collaborating with the government's command-economy initiatives but in effect crystalize its contradictions through literary representation.
3 They pretend to embrace totalitarianism and emphasize the need to denounce egoism in modern society. At the same time, they would criticize the decline of the bourgeoisie on the basis of a historical materialist world view, prophesize the eventual advent of a world of grand harmony, and therefore inspire popular passion for socialism.
4 They state that Anglo-American imperialism has conquered Asia and oppressed the Chinese people, and then skilfully depict the pain of the Chinese people under oppression. This would cause (readers) to also see Japan as an imperialist aggressor and thus nurture Anti-Manchukuo/Resist Japan thoughts.
5 They draw on examples from the national independent movements in Burma, India, the Philippines, and other countries that emerged after the outbreak of the Greater East Asia War to denounce the violence of the British and the Americans. At the same time, they implicitly connect these movements to the current situation [in Manchuria] and

thereby further nationalist consciousness and Anti-Manchukuo/Resist Japan thoughts.

In addition, there is also a form of anti-state literature that refuses to compromise with reality. It is antigovernment, antibourgeoisie, and nihilist. These kinds of people assign the resolution of problems to fate or divine power, stage active opposition against the government, and disagree with its policies. Literature as such will encourage passive resistance among readers and pave the way for future socialist enlightenment.

Part 3. Findings Regarding the Works of Left-Wing Literature
[Detailed analysis of literary works is omitted here.]

Conclusion
To comprehensively review this inspection, we can see that left-wing colouring has almost become latent, yet nationalist consciousness is on the rise. This is possibly because the Greater East Asia War has reached a stalemate, and because the Allies have made partial progress in their anti-Axis offensives in the Mediterranean. To approach the issue from a more theoretical perspective, however, [the cause of the transition may be that] left-wing intellectuals have lost their ideological home ground after the dissolution of the Comintern; as a result, they have been compelled to switch to the nationalist resistance front. Therefore, if we may conclude based on a comprehensive consideration of the above two points, we believe that future development will probably take the following forms:

1 Promotion of nationalist and anti-Japanese consciousness through the slogan of "Beat the British and the Americans"
2 We may predict that they would integrate the presses and promote collaboration among writers of the various factions so as to move forward in the form of a united front. In other words, from their activities in the press and their publication plans we may outline their sphere of influence as follows (see table, Spheres of Influence).

In particular, with regard to literary publication, they all exhibit a "pan-Manchukuo" colour. We may observe the integrated character of each press from it.

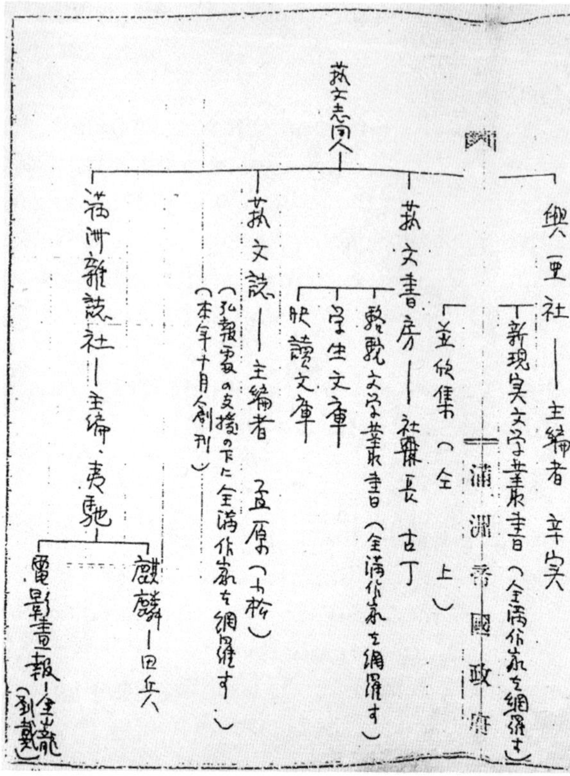

6.3 Final page of the Inspection Report. *Source:* Okada collection

Notes

1 Okada Hideki, *Zoku bungaku ni miru "Manshūkoku" no isō* [The topology of "Manchukuo": A literary perspective, continued] (Tōkyō: Kenbun shuppan, 2013), 412–38.

2 Liu Xiaoli, *Yitai shikong de jingshen shijie: Wei Manzhouguo wenxue yanjiu* [Spiritual world in a time of alienation: Research on bogus Manchukuo literature] (Shanghai: Huadong shifan daxue chubanshe, 2008), 257; Norman Smith, *Resisting Manchukuo: Chinese Women Writers and the Japanese Occupation* (Vancouver: UBC Press, 2007), 49–57.

3 Yu Lei, trans., "Di wei mijian" [A secret document from the enemy], *Dongbei wenxue yanjiu shiliao* [Historical materials for the study of Northeast literature] 6 (1987): 153–59.

4 Zhongyang danganguan, "Shoudu jingcha fu zongjian zhi jingwu zongjuzhang de baogao" [A report by the vice inspector general of the police to the director of the General Bureau of Police Affairs], in *Wei Man xianjing tongzhi* [Police rule in bogus Manchukuo], ed. Zhongyang danganguan (Beijing: Zhonghua shuju, 1993), 588–610.

5 Okada Hideki, *Wei Manzhouguo wenxue: Xu* [The literature of bogus Manchukuo: Continued], trans. Deng Lixia (Harbin: Beifang wenyi chubanshe, 2017). This is the Chinese translation of Okada's monograph *Zoku bungaku,* issued as a volume of *Wei*

Man shiqi wenxue ziliao zhengli yu yanjiu congshu [Bogus Manchukuo literary materials compilation and research collection] (Harbin: Beifang wenyi chubanshe, 2017).

6 Li Jifeng's original name was Li Fuyu. Other pen names include Jifeng, Fangjin, and Lei Leisheng. Li was an influential leftist essayist in Manchukuo and was known for his repeated successful jailbreaks after being arrested and imprisoned by the Japanese in the December Thirtieth Incident in 1941. For more details about the incident, see Zheng Xinheng, *Yi'er sanling yundong shimo* [The beginning and end of the December Thirtieth Incident] (Shenyang: Shenyang daxue chubanshe, 2010).

7 Guan Monan's original name was Guan Dongyan. Other pen names include Pogai and Menglai. An influential Chinese leftist intellectual in Manchukuo, he had secret connections with Communist organizations in China proper. He organized the Harbin Marxist Study Group of Literature and Art and was consequently arrested by the Japanese during the Harbin Leftist Literature Incident on 31 December 1941. Wang Guangti used the pen name Jinming before 1945. In Manchukuo, he worked as a journalist for *Da Bei Xinbao* (New newspaper of the greater north), Guan Monan's company. He is most well-known as Sima Sangdun, a pen name he used after he became a Kuomintang member and moved to Taiwan in 1948. See Okada, *Zoku bungaku,* 289–91.

8 Ibid., 292.

9 Ibid., 293.

10 Wang Ze (1916–44) was a Chinese screenwriter and director at the Manchuria Motion Picture Association. He also edited several literary journals in Manchukuo, including *Manzhou yinghua* (Cinema in Manchuria) and *Yiwenzhi* (Record of arts and literature), and was an active writer. In 1944, he was persecuted to death by the Japanese police. For more about Wang Ze, see Yamaguchi Takeshi, *Aishū no Manshū eiga* [Melancholic Manchurian cinema] (Tōkyō: Santen shobō, 2000), 77–118.

11 An Xi (1916–72) was a leading Chinese playwright, director, actor, and critic in Manchukuo. He launched several influential performance groups, including Fengtian Xiehe Jutuan (Fengtian Concordia Troupe) and Fengtian Fangsong Huajutuan (Fengtian Broadcasting Play Troupe). He also held positions at the Manchuria Motion Picture Association and *Shengjing shibao* (Shengjing times). For more about An Xi, see He Shuang, "Wei Manzhouguo juzuojia An Xi lun" [A study of the bogus Manchukuo playwright An Xi], *Shenyang shifan daxue xuebao shehui kexue ban* [Journal of Shenyang Normal University, social science edition] 4 (2016): 11–15. Shan Ding (1914–95) is the pen name of Liang Shanding, an influential and prolific Chinese writer in Manchukuo. He was known for his promotion and practice of native soil literature (*xiangtu wenxue*) and also worked at the Manchuria Motion Picture Association as a screenwriter. He was awarded the Literary Award of the *Shengjing shibao* in 1942 but had to flee to Beijing the following year due to tightened ideological surveillance in Manchukuo. For more about Shan Ding and his work, see Niu Gengyun, ed., *Shan Ding zuopinji* [Collected works of Shan Ding] (Harbin: Beifang wenyi chubanshe, 2017).

12 As mentioned in n6, Li, an influential leftist essayist in Manchukuo, was arrested by the Japanese on 30 December 1941 and transferred to a prison in Xinjing. He was able to escape on 13 January 1942, but was soon arrested again. On 5 November 1943, he broke out from prison for the second time but was rearrested in April 1945. He was assassinated on 23 August 1945 after the Japanese surrendered; the Kuomintang was said to be responsible. Okada, *Zoku bungaku,* 290.

13 Little is currently known of Feng Shun, apart from Manchukuo police apprehension of his mail.

14 Wang Du (1918–2014) was an active Chinese writer in Manchukuo and also a screenwriter at the Manchuria Motion Picture Association. He used the name Jiang Yan at the

Manchuria Motion Picture Association and changed his name to Li Min after 1948. For more about Wang Du, see Okada, *Zoku bungaku,* 198–218. For his own memoir of his experience in Manchukuo, see Wang Du, *Ryūnichi gakusei Ō Do no shishū to Kaisōroku: Manshūkoku Seinen no ryūgaku kiroku* [Poem collection and memoir by Wang Du, a Chinese student in Japan: Records of studying abroad by a Manchukuo youth], ed. Okada Hideki and Xie Qiong (Tōkyō: Manshūkoku bungaku kenkyūkai, 2015).

15 Zhang Yi's (1921–2006) original name was Zhang Zhixin. He was a leading actor at the Manchuria Motion Picture Association and was arrested in 1943 by the Martial Police Unit of the Japanese Kwantung Army for suspected anti-Japanese political involvement, but was soon released. This section of the report provides a summary of the incident. For Zhang Yi's memoir of his experience at the Manchuria Motion Picture Association, including the arrest, see Zhang Yi, *Manying shimo* [The beginning and end of the Manchuria Motion Picture Association] (Changchun: Changchunshi zhengxie wenshi ziliao weiyuanhui, 2005).

16 Song Yi was the owner of Yizhi Bookstore (*Yizhi shudian*), a major Chinese publisher in Manchukuo.

17 Maxim Gorky, the founding literary theorist of Soviet literature, distinguishes two types of Romanticism. The first type, which he calls "the Old Romanticism," "the Passive Romanticism," or "the Bourgeois Romanticism," is "based on individualism" and is "sundered, detached from reality." He refers to the second type as "the New Romanticism," "the Active Romanticism," "the Revolutionary Romanticism," or "the Proletarian Romanticism." He considers it "the teaching of an active attitude towards life, of the dignity of labor and the will to live, as the source of inspiration in the building-up of new forms of life and as hate of the old world." See Maxim Gorky, "Soviet Literature" (1934) and "How I Learn to Write" (1928), in Maxim Gorky et al., *On the Art and Craft of Writing* (Hawaii: University Press of the Pacific, 2000), 44–45, 10–17, and 17 in particular. For the dissemination of Gorky's theory of Romanticism in China in the 1930s and the 1940s, see Yu Zhaoping, "Meixue de langmanzhuyi he zhengzhixue de langmanzhuyi" [Aesthetical romanticism and political romanticism], *Xueshu yuekan* [Academe monthly] 4 (2004): 68–77.

18 Gu Ding's (1914/16–66) original name was Xu Changji. Arguably the Chinese writer from Manchukuo most well-known among the Japanese, Gu Ding was known, and often denounced by, the Chinese for his close collaboration with the Japanese in Manchukuo. For a collection of Gu Ding's work, see Li Chunyan, ed., *Gu Ding zuopinxuan* [Selected works of Gu Ding] (Shenyang: Chunfeng wenyi chubanshe, 1995). Xiao Song's (1921–unknown) original name was Zhao Mengyuan. A close companion of Gu Ding, he was an active Chinese writer and editor in Manchukuo. For more information about Xiao Song and his work, see Chen Shi and Xie Chaokun, eds., *Xiao Song zuopinji* [Collected works of Xiao Song] (Harbin: Beifang wenyi chubanshe, 2017).

7 *Collection of Literary Selections by Each Ethnicity in Manchukuo-1,* "Statements by Selectors"

ANNIKA A. CULVER

In wartime Manchukuo, leading Japanese literary authorities of the allegedly independent state planned two collections of multiethnic literature to serve as a means to showcase a thriving cultural production by writers under Japanese tutelage. Published in Japanese and edited by six intellectuals, of whom only one was Chinese, this endeavour privileged imperial Japan's language as well as literature, while seemingly uniting all the different ethnic groups to create a framework for propagating literature in the new state.[1] In 1942 and 1944, the Japanese press Sōgansha published both collections in Tokyo, the empire's cultural, economic, and political capital, whose central locus cast an imperialist shadow on the project. During this time, the Second Sino-Japanese War (1937–45) had been waged on the Chinese for over half a decade, with Manchukuo increasingly serving as a base of military operations and ramped-up agricultural production. In late 1941, after Japanese military forces simultaneously attacked the American Pearl Harbor naval base in Hawaii and others in the US-controlled Philippines, imperial Japan declared war on the United States and further enlarged its battlefronts into the Pacific to fight American allies. Against this backdrop of Japanese invasion and occupation, and amid planning for the Greater East Asia Co-Prosperity Sphere, the propaganda-like nature of the literary project in Manchukuo becomes starkly apparent when examining the essays that introduce the first collection, translated here.

This introduction frames a volume compiled in 1941 under the head editorship of Japanese literary establishment (*bundan*) writer Kawabata Yasunari (1899–1972), and published a year later by Sōgansha.[2]

Kawabata's high literary stature in domestic Japan lent credibility to this initiative, in which he as an imperialist agent showcased the talents of writers from a colonized area under Japanese occupation since 1931. Along with Kawabata's remarks, which follow a short essay by the domestic Japanese writer Kishida Kunio (1890–1954), the introduction includes statements by the Manchukuo-based Japanese writers Yamada Seizaburō (1896–1987) and Kitamura Kenjirō (1904–82). In addition, the shortest passage represents the sole Chinese writer, Gu Ding (1914/16–66). Due to his strong connections with Japanese writers and participation in collections such as these, scholars have often characterized him as pro-Japanese, a claim arising out of debates among Chinese intellectuals as early as 1939.[3]

Most of these essays, including Kawabata's, still indicate the aspirational nature of a particularly "Manchurian" literature, even a decade after Manchukuo's 1932 establishment, and evidence a tension between an independently formed literature and one guided by Japan.[4] Kishida believes that, in Manchukuo, he had discovered the voicing of "a mutual history of myriad peoples" with national consciousness "to surpass ethnic particularities" (1). He, however, defers authority to Kawabata and the converted leftist writer Shimaki Kensaku (1903–45), who had travelled to Manchukuo in 1939 and subsequently wrote a well-received travelogue, for actually choosing the works in the collection. Kawabata views Manchukuo as a potential model for the "ideals of greater East Asia" (5–6) when imperial Japan "advanced the war southwards"; he also envisions literature created in Manchukuo not as "a distant foreign country's literature" but considers the collection as "oriented toward Japan" (5) and by implication, as revealing the paternalism intrinsic to its imperial project. Yamada, as a converted leftist and contemporary proponent of the Japanese-led regime's cultural projects, is more cautious about his praise and intentions toward a literary scene still in the process of maturation. However, he hopes the first collection will become an annual publication to showcase the efforts of Manchukuo-based writers that he implies could become more inclusive.

Interestingly, Kitamura dates the "birth" of a uniquely Manchurian literature to sometime in 1938, a year notable for the intensification of the Second Sino-Japanese War and growing anti-Japanese sentiments among Chinese intellectuals and others. He also refers to the thriving literary debates in Manchukuo, and points to 1940 as a key date when the Manchukuo-themed works he proposes first emerged. On the other hand, Gu Ding somewhat deflects responsibility for the literary selections included in the volume by noting that Liu Jueqing (1917–62)[5] actually chose the stories by four of Manchukuo's most well-known Chinese writers as representing a kind of microcosm of "Manchurian literature" (13). Liu had been an active participant in debates on the role of literature through the Yiwenzhi (Record of Arts and Literature) faction formed with his friend. Gu Ding also asserts in an oblique critique that 80 percent of the Manchurian population is illiterate, despite a growing number of youth who "love literature," and posits that "truly significant literature" in Manchuria will depend on Japanese "enterprises like Sōgansha." The latter seems like superficial flattery of the literary collection's press, possibly meant to curry favour for future projects. Unfortunately, only one subsequent volume was published, in 1944, at a date when Tokyo became the target of Allied bombing campaigns, and deep restrictions on non-essential paper usage became the norm for most media.

However, the editors of the first collection frame their endeavour by communicating grand intentions that also intersected with the Japanese-led regime's propaganda goals. Transmitted to Manchukuo's populace by organizations like the Kyōwakai (Concordia Association), for which Yamada had worked as a journalist beginning in 1938, these included *minzoku kyōwa* (racial/ethnic harmony) to be expressed within a utopian space described as *Ōdō rakudo* (Kingly Way paradise land). Literature could aid in unifying the new nation's peoples, while literary production advanced forward a harmonious new multiethnic culture unique in East Asia to serve as a model wherever imperial Japan extended its reach. Kawabata saw this as arising first in Manchukuo, while envisioning collaboration with Chinese and peace with China (proper), but cautiously emphasizes that "those who could be our greatest friend, or our greatest enemy, are none other than the Han ethnicity" (6).

Intended to signify Manchukuo's multiethnic literary production, fourteen of the twenty selections in the collection, or the majority, are written by Japanese writers, of whom the most well-known is Akutagawa Prize finalist Nogawa Takashi (1901–44). Four are by Chinese: Shan Ding (1914–95), Shi Jun (1912–unknown), Yi Chi (1913–unknown), and Wu Ying (1915–61).[6] Two are by Russians, Boris Yu'ilski

(1911–unknown) and Arseny Nesmelov (1880–1945), and none by Koreans – who were sometimes subsumed under the "Japanese" category in Manchukuo or had assumed Japanized names by choice or coercion. Interestingly, by the time Nogawa's story "Tonsu e iku hitobito" (People going to the hamlet) appeared in this volume, the author was imprisoned and under investigation for allegedly Communist activities, while Yamada had firmly switched his loyalties from early 1930s proletarian activism in domestic Japan to active support of a fascist state within the Manchukuo context by the late 1930s. Around the time of the June 1942 publication of this first volume, Shan Ding serialized his novelistic magnum opus *Lüse de gu* (Green valley) from May to December on the front page of *Datong bao* (Great unity herald), the Manchukuo state's government mouthpiece. Economic considerations seemingly motivated Shan Ding's decision to publish his novel in a state-sponsored media organ, while Nesmelov firmly belonged to the Russian Fascist Party, which supported Japanese rule as a bulwark against Soviet communism, and viewed his poetry as a craft to combat this.[7]

Published a decade after the "founding" of the new state, this multi-authored introduction reveals certain Japanese propaganda aims for Manchukuo's new literature: a means to unite disparate ethnicities in a harmonious way through mutual cultural endeavours, and to apparently create an independent literature representative of the "country" as it creates a "myth of national construction" (6). Most of all, as Kawabata proposes, the project exemplified by this initial volume attempted to help build a thriving literary culture under Japanese tutelage that would serve as a model for other regions taken over by the imperial Japanese army, which he describes as having "advanced" into southern regions in Asia, such as Singapore.

The fact that this lofty endeavour ended with the publication of volume two in 1944 shows the impact of imperial Japan's burgeoning, multifront war on even cultural production in occupied areas. However, the Allied firebombings of Tokyo – the literal centre of the Japanese Empire – most likely represented the largest negative factor, causing publishing to become a spotty enterprise. Efforts toward literary promotion in occupied territories increasingly became subsumed under survival measures enacted during total war as the domestic Japanese home front also became a battlefield.

TRANSLATIONS

Collection of Literary Selections by Each Ethnicity in Manchukuo, Volume 1, Edition from the Eighth Year of Kangde, Shōwa 16 [1941], Statements by Selectors

KISHIDA KUNIO[8]

We are making it so that in Manchuria, literature shall be born. Much of it is in the hands of the people who are giving birth to literature in Manchuria.

Last year, I walked all over in Manchuria, where a new country is arising from among the completely different traditions and lifestyles of so many ethnicities; I sensed that everywhere a mutual history of myriad peoples is already beginning to be voiced, and if before long this could not help but form into national consciousness to surpass ethnic particularities, then it could lead to indicating a type of extremely diverse and unprecedented spirit, which I suppose is the kind of expectation that I brought back.

In whatever many languages they are written, their works are perhaps already understood respectively as Japanese literature, Chinese literature, and Russian literature. However, regardless of whether or not the writer is conscious of the environment that births literature or [of] the era's influence, above all I cannot help but clearly reflect upon that reasoning and sensibility. I say that even though Manchurian literature might be young, as young as it is, great hopes can be tied to it. This is because such things as true traditions always have no old age, I believe.

As for the literary expression "torn up by the roots," one cannot say that this is not in their works at all. However, in the future, if viewed from a personal standpoint, and even viewing this from Manchuria itself, we should soon try to dispel such an expression; and the writers with this achievement will probably also, through the cooperation of multiple ethnicities, yearn to reach that which can arise from the development of the national land. Thanks to this becoming thus,[9] the history of Manchurian literature has first begun to occupy its own page, and each of these works can literally arrive at holding classic value.

The problem is only that, in the manipulation of ideas, one cannot grasp associated tendencies, particularly in literary works.[10] Through perceiving directly the complicated visage of reality, we truly must arrive at feeling what should be called the era's fetal movements. Here is one path for separating doubts from hopes. And now, because of my love of how writers should correctly stand upon this path, I am bearing this role of indicating a way for them.

And thus, as I have not had the time to read all the works assembled in this collection in their entirety, I relied on the other two honourable gentlemen, Kawabata and Shimaki, for their selections; regarding this result, I who have depended on these two gentlemen definitely intend to bear this collective responsibility.

As Manchurian writers, the talent of the individuals named here in this anthology is unmistakably such a beautiful talent. We all consider the significance of the yearly repeatability of this same enterprise as a serious thing. That is, at the same time that it becomes a clear sign that each separate talent grows, is it not because we pay absolute attention to the healthy ascension of an allied culture that hereby should be properly recorded?

One can say more than ever before that Sōgansha's plan is to introduce Manchurian writers to Japanese readers; if one considers the multiple effects encompassing this enterprise, I as one of the people carrying responsibility as selectors, here in addition to craftspeople of literary establishments from the two countries of Japan and Manchukuo, expect that one should pay much attention regarding this anthology.

(At an inn in Fukushima, 21 March 1942)

KAWABATA YASUNARI[11]

In the spring of a decade since the nation's construction, having regarded the first publication of this yearbook of collected literary works, our congratulatory mood is fortunately the most appropriate expression and, moreover, I believe it is something that has certainly attained fruition. The editors without a doubt privileged all of the writers on the Manchurian side, and though we on the Japanese side are subordinate, we are not at all holding on to it as a faraway foreign country's literature; in a new broad sense we are making it our literature, and this book can also be said to be oriented toward Japan. And thus, this belongs to [is of] today's glory. Isn't this book a symbol of beautiful ideals where multiple ethnicities are weaving into history the milestone of a harmonious culture? Isn't it also a voice calling upon a great future?

Japan has now even advanced the war southwards, but constructing a nation together with other ethnicities and reviving [their] culture does not yet exist outside of Manchukuo. Because the ideals of greater East Asia were first enacted in Manchukuo, if these are not attained here, then we should not just consider that they cannot be attained anywhere, but we must accomplish these together with the Han ethnicity; this is Manchuria's important raison d'être. It goes without saying that this is because there is no other kind of superior ethnicity like the Chinese ethnicity. In regarding the cultural domain, it is clearly so. Now, as Manchukuo is participating to aid in Japan's Greater East Asia War and is constructing itself, we are led to splendid southern victories and, moreover, must reflect upon this honourable northern valour, but especially writers and so on require this sense of meaning. Many of Japan's writers are moving to live in the southern countries, but when will be the day when they might create those countries' literature together with those countries' ethnicities? Now, from the point of crystallization of this book, we should tread firmly. Moreover, we should hope for peace with China. I, who went to Beijing, also found that there were Chinese who extended their hands to Japanese writers who must cooperatively construct the path of literature. Those who could be our greatest friend, or our greatest enemy, are none other than the Han ethnicity.

As a traveller, I briefly had two viewpoints about Manchurian literature. One of them is the problem of Manchurian literature's lofty high ideals. Along with the country, a new literature, as said by this nation's writers, might be creating a myth of national construction, or guiding history from a point of genesis. Besides, five ethnicities are coming together to raise up this type of literature. In this virgin land, the significance and message of literature was extremely easy to see. The other point was the problem of Manchurian literature's everyday reality. The country's exhortations and general hopes are still shallow, organizations to publish literature haven't been maintained, and the market is constricted. Consequently, a strong and widespread critique has not expanded, writers have received little proper criticism and praise, [and] readers demand domestic Japanese literature; [thus] there was an inclination to disdain this country's literature. The new continental literature that should be great in scale is on the contrary not even under a bureaucratizing gaze in a provincial world. Domestic Japan's market and critique are still today inspiring and developing the motivations for Manchurian literature. The domestic publication of Manchurian works is desirable. Even in this sense, this book's role is precious. One could say that Manchurian literature and even the works of ethnic Japanese writers should not only be an extension of Japanese literature. One could carelessly propose that it must not be enslaved to Japanese literature. In such a way I am not opposing Japanese literature, but am myself expecting the planting of an independent Manchurian literature. Manchurian writers' connection to Chinese literature is also similar. Is it not so that White Russian authors even moreso take a different path from Soviet literature, and that they pride themselves that they are the ones continuing the correct orthodoxy of Russian culture? We really wish of course for the birth of an independent Manchurian literature on the one hand; beyond the intimacy of the phrase "Japan-Manchukuo cultural exchange" and so on, regarding a mutual independence, I wonder if rather we should not strengthen it? By now, should we not know a bit about Manchurian culture and literature? Should [we] not suppose that our thoughts are superficial? It would be fortunate if this book can become a recompense.

For the works in the first volume of this annual publication, it is hard to say that we have completely expended all of our aspirations for Manchurian literature. If that becomes so, one can consider it a level of necessity that Manchurian literature will also receive harsh critique in domestic Japan. Additionally, we have to correctly view the true form of Manchurian literature. However, it will not do to view it like a distant foreign country's literature, with cold eyes. If one whips, that whip will hit one's own body. Are we not also the ones who should take part in the construction of Manchurian literature? On the occasion of such a book's completion, we should extend renewed respect toward the bitter labour of creation attained by writers in Manchuria. I suppose that the path of Manchurian and White Russian authors moreover must overstep this suffering. Now, where in the world is the beauty of multiethnic writers bringing their arms together for a new nation's literature in the annual publication of selected works? Possibly in the bright victory of successive volumes over the years, [and] without a doubt I believe it is this book's fine future.

(February 1942)

YAMADA SEIZABURŌ[12]

This collection is a compilation from among Manchurian literature's achievements to date, and for each author who gains acclaim for this selection, I have chosen representative works and those deserving our gaze. I think that, in the decade since the nation's construction, one cannot exhaustively say this [represents] the whole picture of Manchurian literature, but we can glimpse enough of such an outline through only the works gathered here.

This collection is, in the way that I just mentioned, like a collective memorial tower of Manchurian literature until today; yet at the same time, if this is also seen as one historic step in the ten years of the nation's construction, from here onward, moreover, the newest in the utmost development of Manchurian literature progressing by leaps and bounds must signify this foothold. In considering it like this, the import of this collection truly has depth.

Frankly speaking, in this collection, Manchurian literature's true characteristics still have not yet achieved the pioneering point of the Greater East Asian new order as the literature of a newly arisen multiethnic nation – what one should say is that works have not yet sufficiently appeared. Many of them, those that grasp the new Manchuria following the nation's construction and, moreover, the writers who give birth to this founding spirit of the country, regardless of their desires to move forward, many of them still had no choice but to suffer the negative aspects of ad hoc cultivation and literary influences from the past, but is this no small achievement, I am wondering?

However, this aspect somehow has until now not hindered the robust development and flying leaps of Manchurian literature, and even within each work assembled here, in terms of the futurity of Manchurian literature, is a tendency to move forward and [with] plural developmental factors, and the fact that it is pregnant with multiple forms, on one hand comes from within Manchuria's new reality and new literary players, but I already know the truth that it has already enough matured.

For these reasons, this *Collection of Selected Works by Each Ethnicity in Manchukuo* is made into an annual publication, a task until now accumulated in layers over the years, and together with a plurality of readers, I leave here my boundless hopes and expectations.

Above all, in the editing of this collection, we have arrived at making most important the editors on the Manchurian side, and formed it with the assent of the three gentlemen Kawabata, Kishida, and Shimaki; but, from the next collection onwards, beyond broadly holding up works for candidacy, via the collective responsibility of all the editors, I await an editing that is as prudent as possible, and am considering making this annual publication into one with substantial authority.

KITAMURA KENJIRŌ[13]

The coming into usage of the name Manchurian literature is not at all old, because it arose extremely recently. I suppose it is good to see it as something that arose four years ago in 1938.

Within this time, one could think that were not the debates concerning Manchurian literature for the most part exhaustively discussed? These were primarily debates concerning the qualities of Manchurian writers, as well as the uniqueness of Manchurian literature, and its relationship to Japanese domestic literature and so on, but presently as a natural tendency, I have been steadily extending the opinion that the most important thing is that writers write works, and in order not to cut off or end debates as debates, above all to make work production activities thrive is the only remaining way. In order to make work production activities thrive, it is not that I do not have an opinion that debating activities should accompany them, and it is not even that debating activities are completely in decline, rather that each writer, in lieu of superficial research into debates, must come to tread upon and advance along a path of realizing works that is internal, objective, and concrete; this is the actual condition of the Manchurian literary and art world. I believe [that] it would be good to say this.

From about the beginning of a year ago (Shōwa 15 [1940]) until the end of last year, I brought up that we should see multiple results of efforts toward a process of realizing works.[14] While mentioning Manchurian literature's uniqueness, when it comes to the actual works, if one were to emit a reply of how one can amply show the characteristics of what one is so proud of, this is expressed in extremely subtle grounds, because it only gradually shows itself sprouting. It is probably through penetrating observation and deeply rooted investigation that we believe we will first arrive at seeing a big result.

The path toward the process of realizing works is thus also a path toward investigating the place of the writers' souls.

Now, while my country, Japan, is engaged in a glorious incomparable battle and advancing a huge step in construction, the lifestyle of Manchurian writers and problem of spiritual development, as something at once unshakable, can become anew a resource for internal reflection, I suppose.

The issue of coming into contact with other ethnicities truthfully casts great power over Manchurian writers. Also, the power that the northern nature and climate wields is also great. How do they deal with this, and as Japanese, how should we go about loving Manchuria?

Such a large problem as this, lying static over the path of a process of realizing works, only they [Manchurian writers] must clearly understand.

GU DING[15]

The one who arrived at the choice of the Manchurian works among this collection was Mr. Liu Jueqing. I want to multiply his labour. I want to believe

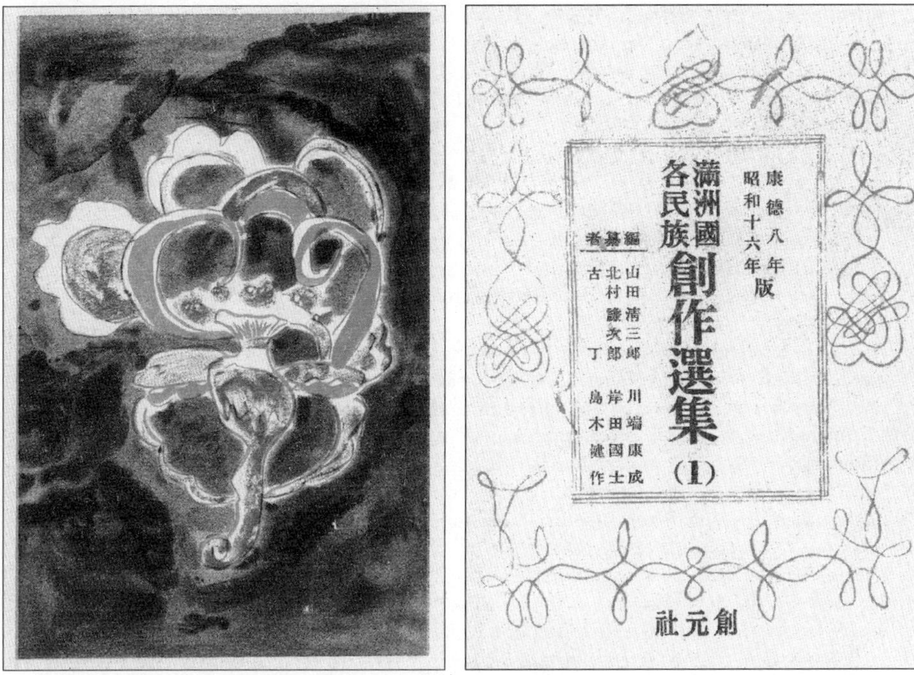

7.1 Box cover (*right*) and book cover (*left*) of *Manshūkoku kaku minzoku sōsaku senshū* (Collection of literary selections by each ethnicity in Manchukuo), vol. 1. *Source:* Author's collection

that, through the four stories collected and recorded within this volume, the whole picture of Manchurian literature can be promoted and made known.

Up to 80 percent of Manchuria's people are illiterate, so generally they do not have a close connection to this literature. However, it is also true that there are so many youth who love literature; I believe that there is no doubt that a future blossoming and coming to fruition is something that should be promised.[16]

In terms of truly significant literature, though I don't know about previous years, I believe that certainly in Manchuria it will come to be produced, and not only in this sense, but also I think that the most important thing is that it depends on enterprises like Sōgansha.

Notes

1 For a detailed discussion of this state-led project, see Annika A. Culver, "The Legitimization of a Multi-Ethnic Literary Culture in Manchukuo," in *Glorify the Empire: Japanese Avant-Garde Propaganda in Manchukuo* (Vancouver: UBC Press, 2013), 169–92.

2 Yamada Seizaburō, Kitamura Kenjirō, Gu Ding, Kawabata Yasunari, Kishida Kunio, and Shimaki Kensaku, eds., "Sensha no kotoba" (Statements by selectors), in *Manshūkoku kaku minzoku sōsaku senshū (1)* (Collection of literary selections by each ethnicity in Manchukuo, vol. 1) (Tōkyō: Sōgansha, 1942). Parenthetical page numbers in the text refer to this volume.

3 For more about these issues, see Chao Liu, *The Matrix of Modernity and National Identity in Manchukuo Literature from 1937 to 1941* (New York: Peter Lang, 2019).

4 For a comprehensive treatment of the complex, politically layered history of literary endeavours in Manchukuo, from the perspective of scholars from East Asia and North America, see Annika A. Culver and Norman Smith, eds., *Manchukuo Perspectives: Transnational Approaches to Literary Production* (Hong Kong: Hong Kong University Press, 2019).

5 Also known as Jue Qing. In March 1939, Liu Jueqing joined with Gu Ding and his associates to launch the journal *Yiwenzhi* (Record of arts and literature); this intellectual literary group also became known by the same name. The focus of their writing was criticized as too formalistic, lacking in social import, and "pro-Japanese" by their rivals, the Wenxuan (Literary Selections) group, formed by Qiu Ying (1914–95) and others in December 1939.

6 Wu Ying is a subject of Chapter 8 in this volume.

7 Olga Bakich, "In the Sunken Submarine: Russian Émigré Poetry in Manchukuo," in Culver and Smith, *Manchukuo Perspectives,* 227.

8 Kishida Kunio, *Manshūkoku kaku minzoku sōsaku senshū (1),* 2–4.

9 In other words, dispelling the expression "torn up by the roots" and reaching a point where works arise from the development of the land.

10 In this passage, Kishida uses *hiragana* for *torashimeru,* which can be alternatively read as "to get rid of" or "to grasp, to capture," so this phrase appears to have a double meaning. *Kotosara* can mean "particularly," but written in kanji, *kotosara* means "deliberately, intentionally, especially." *Kakaru shisei* (associated tendencies) can be read as "residual political attitudes," or literally, "attitudes hanging on." One could translate this sentence as: "The problem is, however, in the manipulation of ideas; associated tendencies are deliberately not elided in literary works."

11 Kawabata Yasunari, *Manshūkoku kaku minzoku sōsaku senshū (1),* 5–8.

12 Yamada Seizaburō, *Manshūkoku kaku minzoku sōsaku senshū (1),* 9–10.

13 Kitamura Kenjirō, *Manshūkoku kaku minzoku sōsaku senshū (1),* 11–12.

14 The phrase *sakuhin jissen-ka* (the process of realizing works) is repeated three times within the section, revealing Kitamura's preoccupation with the matter.

15 Gu Ding, *Manshūkoku kaku minzoku sōsaku senshū (1),* 13.

16 When writing in Japanese, Gu Ding uses many Chinese-sounding expressions, with classical Chinese influence, which give a heterodox feel to his language. For example, he uses *chengyu: kaika keshitsu,* a four-character phrase common among educated Chinese but also used by Japanese familiar with *kanbun* (classical Chinese read with Japanese grammar). At this point, a long vernacular tradition in Chinese prose did not yet exist; it had developed slowly in the late teens and twenties around the time of the May Fourth Movement.

8 Open Letters from Women Writers of Manchukuo

Mei Niang and Wu Ying, Jia Ren to Yang Xu

NORMAN SMITH

In the early 1940s, during the height of the Chinese War of Resistance against Japan, three women published "open letters" in Japanese-occupied Beiping (now Beijing) and Manchukuo, at a time when authorities stressed an ideal of "good wife, wise mother" (*xianqi liangmu*), who was to be demure, obedient, and committed to her father, husband, and sons.[1] Men were raised to be "the national backbone" (*guomin gugan*) while women were encouraged to "go back to the kitchen" (*zouhui chufang*).[2] In Beiping, colonial authorities encouraged similar agendas. But many educated young women were not prepared to go back to the kitchen in their struggle against patriarchy and social injustice. Progressive women writers in Beiping and Manchukuo (as elsewhere in East Asia) questioned or outright violated what they believed to be outdated Confucian ideals.

During the late 1930s and early 1940s, regulations governing literature were aimed at structuring literary worlds and local culture. In areas under Japanese occupation, draconian measures increased vigilance over writers who engaged in social criticism. In Manchukuo, on 21 February 1941, the "Eight Abstentions" (*Ba bu*) were issued. Severe sanctions were prescribed for those who wrote in the following ways:

1. Rebellious tendencies toward the current political situation
2. Criticism of the shortcomings of national policies or non-constructive suggestions
3. Stimulation of a mood of opposition to the nation
4. Singular focus on describing the dark side before and after establishment of the country
5. Decadent thoughts as the theme

6 About love and desire, descriptions of killing, love triangles, love games that denigrate chastity, lust, love's sexual desire, or dying for love, incest, and adultery
7 Description of the cruelty of crimes or being too explicitly upsetting [in doing so]
8 Use of matchmakers or maids as themes, exaggerated descriptions of the peculiar state of affairs in red-light (*huajie liuxiang*) districts.[3]

Nonetheless, each of the "Eight Abstentions" was present in popular literature, manipulated by writers to express criticism of the colonial state. Xie Miya Qiong introduces and translates additional examples in Chapter 6.

Persecution increasingly grew after 1934, when noted writers Xiao Hong (1911–42) and Bai Lang (1912–94) left Manchukuo. While some male writers were forced into exile (Liang Shanding, 1914–95), jailed (Yuan Xi, 1920–79), or executed (Jin Jianxiao, 1910–36), before 1944, censors usually paid little heed to writing by women. Zhu Ti (1923–2012) and Ke Ju (Li Zhengzhong) (1921–2020), prominent writers of the Manchukuo era, later attributed officials' lax attitudes to a misogyny that blinded them to the significance of women's writings.[4] But in the final year of the occupation, the critical tone and controversial content of women's literature was targeted for persecution, especially Yang Xu's (1918–2004) second volume of collected works, *Wo de riji* (My diary, 1944), most copies of which were destroyed.

The first prominent woman writer to emerge in Manchukuo in the mid-1930s was Wu Ying (1915–61), who was hailed by contemporaries as "Manchuria's miraculous writer" (*Manzhou baimiao shengshou*).[5] Born into a declining Manchu household, she began to publish fiction in 1934 while she worked at the journal *Simin* (This people). In 1939, the literary group Wenxuan (Literary Selections) awarded her story "Liang ji" (Two extremes) its annual literary prize. From 1939 to 1940, she worked as an editor at *Simin* and published in the most important government newspaper, *Datong bao* (Great unity herald). In 1941, she was a contributor to the officially sponsored journal *Xin Manzhou* (New Manchuria), and she was a special editor of the June edition, featuring works of fiction by Manchukuo's women writers. Also in 1941, she coedited with Zuo Di (1920–76) the critically acclaimed *Shijie ming xiaoshuo xuan* (Selection of world famous novels), which conflicted with the official promotion of Japanese literature as the sole legitimate base for literary development. In 1942, she was an editor at *Manzhou wenyi* (Manchuria literature and arts) and began work at *Xin Manzhou* in the same capacity, a position that she maintained until 1944. Also in 1942, at the age of twenty-seven, she was named a delegate to the first Greater East Asia Writers' Congress (Ch: *DadongYa wenxuezhe dahui;* Jp: *DaitōA bungakusha taikai*) in Tokyo. In 1943, her short story "Xuyuan" (Dilapidation) was awarded the Yiwen (Arts and Literature) prize, and her short story "Ming" (Howl) was published in *Xin qingnian* (New youth); "Ming" made her a target of censors, who questioned the story's anti-Japanese stance.[6] She subsequently stopped writing fiction.

In 1944, in a review of Manchuria's women writers, Wu noted that Mei Niang (1916–2013) established "liberalism" (*ziyouzhuyi*) in the local literary world while Yang Xu was praised for her "bold and unrestrained" manner of writing.[7] Contemporaries called Wu Ying and Mei Niang "a pair of bright jewels of Manchuria's literary world" (*Manzhou wentan shuang bi*).[8]

Mei Niang was born into a wealthy Han Chinese family in Vladivostok and was raised in Xinjing (now Changchun).[9] She published her first volume of collected writings, *Xiaojie ji* (Young lady's collected works) in 1936, and was an occasional contributor to *Datong bao*. After graduating middle school, Mei Niang attended Kobe's Women's College for two years, where she met her husband, fellow Manchurian Liu Longguang (1916–49). In 1938, she worked as a proofreader at *Datong bao*. Liu followed her to Xinjing and, in 1939, their home became a salon for literati, as they became key members of the literary faction Wencong (Collection of Literature).

In 1940, Mei Niang published her critically acclaimed second volume of collected writings, *Di'er dai* (The second generation). At the end of 1940, she and her husband moved to Japan, for his work as an editor at the journal *Daban Huawen meiri* (Chinese Osaka daily). In Japan, Mei continued to write short fiction and translated Japanese fiction into Chinese. In 1942, the couple moved to Beiping, where Liu helped found the Huabei zuojia xiehui (North China Writers Association). Mei Niang continued to write, publishing two more volumes of collected writings during the occupation, *Xie* (Crabs) and *Yu* (Fish); she also worked as an editor and reporter at *Funü zazhi* (Lady's journal).[10] In November 1944, *Xie* was awarded the prize for novella of the year at the final Greater East Asia Writers' Congress, in Nanjing.

8.1 Mei Niang and Wu Ying, late 1930s. Mei Niang stands behind Wu Ying. *Source:* Author's collection

Yang Xu was born into a Hui household, and became one of Manchukuo's foremost celebrities, famed for her *yema xing* (wild horse character).[11] In 1936, in middle school, Yang began to publish poems and essays in *Xin qingnian* and *Shengjing shibao* (Shengjing daily).[12] By 1940, she was a staple of the music scene. Gracing the covers of magazines such as *Qilin* (Unicorn; in June 1942), Yang made frequent radio broadcasts, personal appearances, and recorded songs on the Shanghai-based *Victory* label. Her writing appeared in the most prominent journals in Manchukuo, including *Manying* (Manchuria film), *Xin Manzhou*, and *Qilin*. In 1942, she worked as a reporter and editor at *Guomin huabao* (Citizens' paper). In 1943, Yang Xu's first volume of collected works, dominated by negativity, *Luoyingji* (Collection of fallen blossoms), was published. In direct defiance of regulations such as the "Eight Abstentions," Yang described herself as "plodding onto the rugged road of pessimism" (*maizai beiguanlu shang tazhe qiqu*).[13] For such writings, she encountered significant problems with Manchukuo censors, and in 1944 *Wo de riji* (My Diary) was banned for its intense introspection, discussion of sexuality, and rejection of "traditional Confucian" constructs of womanhood.[14] Among Yang's most provocative works in *Wo de riji* is

8.2 Yang Xu on the cover of *Qilin* (Unicorn), June 1942. *Source:* Author's collection

"Gongkai de zuizhuang" (Open indictment), in which she wrote: "I am not a person who can accept society's demands. I never think that I am a woman and I cannot bear for other people to see me as a woman."[15] In her letter below, Jia Ren describes Yang's public behaviour and responds to some of Yang's assertions regarding womanhood and modernity.

To various degrees, the open letters that they crafted (Mei Niang, Wu Ying, and Jia Ren) or received (Yang Xu) remark on the character of these writers, their professional lives, and the difficult circumstances in which they lived. These women gave a face to the multicultural environment that officials sought to promote with Han, Hui, and Manchu writers. Yet the letters clearly criticize the status quo and the morality that officials sought to implement; the letters also suggest the degree to which officials attributed a lack of agency to the women, a disempowered position that also characterizes the Korean women who are introduced by Jonghyun Lee in Chapter 9.

— TRANSLATIONS —

A Letter for Wu Ying[16]

MEI NIANG

Wu Ying:

Since you left last year, I moved from my home where you visited me to this new residence. Other than that, my life is the same. Within the last three months, I gave birth to a daughter and she took my freedom away. My current situation is the same as when we lived in Xinjing, just managing the house and parenting.

When you came, I felt as though the words we spoke did not come from the bottom of our hearts, but I understood your unspoken feelings and emotions; I think that you and I are the same. I often think: Only women can understand women, can sympathize with women. A considerable distance always lies between men and women. When in love they have one heart; this is an affectation of puberty. I now realize "love" is so pure and beautiful, a rare moment together between life and death. Life is not leisurely enough to allow love, but it is just at this time that those feelings are real, eternal, and resplendent. If you now still feel wifely loneliness, then let me comfort you this way – [can you] take the [merciful heart] of Sakyamuni as your own? If you have the resolution to enter into hell, you can conquer everything, you can transform everything. I often encourage myself this way. Perhaps you think that what I am saying is good to hear, yet empty. But this is exactly what I think. Often when I am bored and cannot inspire myself, [when] reading a story about Sakyamuni, subconsciously tears fall. I think that women are the saviours of this world. Only women can change this world into heaven. [If] a girl has the compassion of Sakyamuni, her siblings will certainly receive benefits; a mother like that will certainly make her household peaceful, happy, really beautiful, and really kind. Her daughter will naturally become a most complete person among the people. This is the fundamental significance of women being born into this world. This is the glory of females.

Naturally, this is difficult work – indeed it is tough. The women in our society suffer more hardship and pain than men can imagine. This hardship and pain that men need not suffer tempers women, awakens women, makes women determined, and urges women to forge ahead. It completes this greatest task of those born as women.

I often cry by myself, but I am unwilling to let others know. This weeping is saved-up depression after being wronged for a few days. Just like this, I think

I could cry to make myself feel better. So, when completely alone, my tears, tame and docile as an obedient child, flow out. After crying, I feel even emptier and enter a state of melancholy. Then I think of Jesus. I think of Sakyamuni. I think I am really being tempered and my disturbed emotions subside.

But we are basically ordinary people – ordinary women in a patriarchal society. Life is always lonely and boring, it can never be ideal. But this idea is enough to save us, do you not think so?

Beijing's autumn has just deepened, and the chrysanthemum flowers are flourishing. Although the mornings and evenings are a bit cold, the noon sun still makes people sweat. Three *yuan* can buy four pots of big yellow chrysanthemums, with ten flowers in each pot. On the street, there are many people pulling carts selling flowers. I fear that in our native land [Manchukuo], this time [you are] already wearing cotton jackets? The freezing native land makes me even more attached to beautiful Beijing, with its many flowers. I cannot forget that desert wind with its bold and unconstrained, open and upright atmosphere. I am always afraid that Beijing is too affected, perhaps because I am a child of the mountains. For this precise reason, my course and crude temperament cannot come to terms with this capital city on a [flat] plain! On the surface, Beijing's women, compared with the women of our native land, are more enchanting, beautiful, refined, and courteous. In fact, I think that living in the same city as them, more affectation is less honest. Perhaps this is my preference. Naturally not all here are like that. I just feel like that. Perhaps, in a sense, perhaps this is really a kind of merit. The people who love writing are not a few: Lei Yan,[17] Dong Fangjuan,[18] and Ouyang Feiya,[19] and others' writings, I think you have already read them.

Everybody has gotten together to buy coal to pass the winter. Perhaps in our native land the fires have already been lit; if you do not grasp this leisurely mood, I really admire your freedom and willpower. I have several times thought about completely giving my child to someone else, to take [up] my personal freedom to live. Several times – I could not do it, so most of my time is taken up. So many things that I would like to do cannot be done.

The day before yesterday, Longguang[20] and Professor Shen Qiwu[21] – you know this gentleman – returned from Nanjing. They are busy preparing a "National Chinese Literature Report Meeting" (*Zhongguo wenxue bao guo hui*). This meeting will strengthen the North China Writers Association organization, gathering together China's literati, strengthening Chinese literati's refined loyalty to protect the country, to work for the whole Chinese literary world and the nation. We are excitedly looking forward to its early realization.

When you come again, at that time I will certainly invite several eloquent writing sisters for a discussion, to let Beijing ladies come to look with reverence at Manchuria's first-class woman writer, Madame Wu Ying.

How do you feel about your new career? Give my greetings to Wu Lang,[22] and your children.

Mei Niang, End of October

A Reply to Mei Niang's Letter[23]

WU YING

Mei Niang:

Many days ago, I read your letter from the faraway ancient capital [Beijing]. I remember it as if I read it several times. Mei Niang, only women can understand women, sympathize with women. Sometimes a person can receive real understanding, sympathy, and flowing tears from a friend – this has value, is noble. Just this bit of nobility is the most real, most beautiful emotion in the world.

Several times, after I heard that you had given birth to a little girl, I wanted to write you a letter; perhaps this idea has been since coming back from yours the year before last in the fall. I am ashamed to tell you what few things I have done all day.

You know, my professional life has been long. This kind of tossing aside the family, tossing aside a child is a selfish desire I have harboured for a long time. Yet my inadequate preparation is not enough to dispel the grief of abandoning my child. And the meagre rewards are not enough to fill up the void left by that abandonment.[24]

You say that you manage the household and teach your child. I cannot help thinking that women, can [they] only find comfort through caring for their own children as they grow up? Last year, I wrote in a letter to my child [that] I would really expose my loneliness and the void that I felt after leaving her. If you have some spare time, you should read this piece of writing. You have said that you several times thought about completely giving your child to someone else, to free yourself to live. Mei Niang, do not have these selfish thoughts again. You give me no comfort. Should we not take Sakyamuni's heart as our own? Through this, a mother's household certainly will have peace, happiness, real beauty, real kindness, [and] her daughter will naturally become a complete person [that stands out from] the crowd. Do you not want your child to become complete?

Recently, I have often thought about how to guide one's daughter toward honesty and goodness, how to make one's daughter engage with society, how to make her resist all the temptations that society offers. These many questions vex me, depressing me without any peace. No matter what, we have arrived at the time of liberating children – do you not think so?

You often shed tears, but are not willing to let others know. I think about so many things, so many women. Did Jesus not say that women come into this world to suffer? I could not help but think that when I became a mother, I would thus reduce my senseless thoughts. Mei Niang, why can't we use a mother's heart as our hearts? Precisely because we are after all normal people, we ought to use a mother's heart as our hearts.

Three months ago, I quit my job and returned home. Shopping for rice, for oil. This life is not at all as peaceful as you imagine: cooking food, cleaning clothes; that so-called housewife life. Engaging with these trivial household matters restricts people from exposing honest emotions, that this is not an easy life. Perhaps this type of lifestyle exposes emotions that are real – yes, life does not permit us to have leisure.

Two months ago, our house was very cold. To think of doing something, it just can't be done. Just at that time, my troubled (*fanluan*) thoughts strongly occupied (*zhanju*) me.[25] Then, I found myself bored.

Wu Ying

To Ms. Yang Xu[26]

JIA REN

Time, just like artillery shells, flies by. Life is like unpredictably wandering around (*zhao Qin mu Chu*).[27] *Shaobing*[28] with a wine pot is heaven and earth, the vast sea has changed into farmland, how unpredictable is the world! Remember when we parted two years ago, and now? Brave you, [you] can run with great courage back to your nostalgic national capital [Xinjing] – what about me? Still the same as in the past – sitting around waiting to die (*hunchi dengsi*)[29] – I do not know to move up or wait here. Although you and I are now breathing the same air in this national capital, we have not spoken together once. Twice, when I saw you, I was in no position to talk to you; till now my heart is still not calm!

Two years ago, you abandoned a group of friends who were counting on you and left Xinjing.[30] At that time I did not know why you had to go. No, I did know, but I thought you were not at all the same as women in general.

Other women around you have no courage, [yet] you have determination to not fear social rejection and not tolerate Confucian ethics. I thought that you would definitely have fought that evil environment (*e huanjing*) suppressing you. Even more, I believed that you would win. But what was the result? It was contrary to all that I had hoped for, [and] you really did just pick up and go. Then I saw news of your return in the papers. At that time, I placed my previous expectations on you. Although there were many people on different sides criticizing you, stepping on you, I believed that you were a modern new female who would dare to dare and that this time you would. Working in literature, this gave me even greater hope and, at the same time, brought our women compatriots even greater expectations because, I think, your answer to us this time – it will never dare to disappoint us?

Yesterday I read the July *New Manchuria* and saw your masterpiece ["My indictment"]. From start to finish, I carefully read it three times. The reason was to soothe my choking breath. I realized that the more I read, the more I choked. The result was that I felt wronged and did not read more, but I still could not breathe, there was nothing to do but fart! I spent two nights thinking about this fart – [should I] let it go? Because holding it in was too dangerous, I decided to let it out, but who can put it in your name, and I was afraid that you would not understand my intention? So, finally, with great courage I publicly send this little to you. I hope you can read it and forgive [me].

Recorded in the masterpiece is this paragraph:

> Myself, I am sowed into this group of female colleagues who the whole day only know sitting around waiting to die – all in a heap. [They] let others see them as dubious and, in fact, it actually is that – more or less. What exactly do my female colleagues know – they are fantasizing about a foreign-style house and banknotes, fantasizing about cars and rings. Besides that, they know nothing about the regularization or the meaning of life.

When I read this grandiose theory above, it really made me sorrowful. For thousands of years, men have used us as playthings – is this not entirely like a feudal opinion? It is a pity that you published this talk after you got the worst of it, but really it is a bit too late and so, when I read it, I could see that you are also part of it, pitiless. Actually, you – this knowing the regularization of life and knowing the meaning of life – to be mixed up with us, this group of people sitting around waiting to die – really, God is blind! In the end, I am tired of you, this knowing the regularization of life and the meaning of life, yet you are also fantasizing about a foreign-style house and currency, cars, finger rings and, besides, even more when compared to us, this group of people sitting around waiting to die, you are fantasizing about lovely foreign students. The result is that you had to leave Xinjing but us, this group of people sitting around waiting to die, who do not know the regularization of life and also do not know the meaning of life, we make no trouble and did not have a predicament to leave Xinjing! If you were willing to go, very well, go. This makes me really afraid – life can be so hypocritical!

Sometimes my faith in you is shaken, but I still consider you a brave female. If all women in society were like you, why worry about men and women not being equal? Us, this group of people sitting around waiting to die, our group of people are really ashamed of you. However, my country until now has not become a male country. This must be said to be a credit to us, this group sitting around waiting to die, because this group of things sitting around waiting to die cannot like you open a convenient door, using the world for one's own amusement, although I really do admire your brave spirit.

After you read the above words, do not think that I am accusing you or attacking you, because you and I have not criticized each other and, I, this sitting around waiting to die stubborn [one], also how dare [I] ask Sakyamuni Buddha to say it? But before your masterpiece, "My Indictment," had been completely revealed, I admired your bravery to its core. This penetrating confession finally reveals your taciturn behaviour over the past two years.

Jia Ren, relating to Yang Xu's "My Indictment"
(the original writing was in this magazine, volume 4,
July–August two-month issue).

Notes

1 "Shidai xiaojiemen" [Contemporary girls], *Datong bao* [Great unity herald], 5 November 1936, 7.

2 Wang Yeping, *Dongbei lunxian shisinian jiaoyushi* [The history of education in the Northeast's fourteen years of enemy occupation] (Changchun: Jilin jiaoyu chubanshe, 1989), 114.

3 Yu Lei, "Ziliao" [Data], in *Dongbei lunxian shiqi wenxue guoji xueshu yantaohui lunwenji* [Collection of papers from the International Research Conference on Literature of the Enemy-Occupied Northeast], ed. Feng Weiqun, Wang Jianzhong, Li Chunyan, and Li Shuquan (Shenyang: Shenyang chubanshe, 1992), 181.

4 Zhu Ti and Li Keju, "1942 yu 1945 nian Dongbei wenyijie yi wan" [A glimpse of the world of arts in the Northeast from 1942 to 1945], in *Dongbei lunxian shiqi wenxue.*

5 Li Ran, "Wu Ying yu di'yi ci 'DongYa caoguzhe dahui' – yi 'Dong you hou ji' wei zhongxin" [Wu Ying and the "First East Asian Manipulators' Conference" – Focus on "Remembrance of the Eastern Tour"], 28 August 2017 on website "Wei Manzhouguo yanjiu zhongxin" [Bogus Manchukuo Research Centre], http://www.sohu.com/a/167938517_713945. Wu's work is collected in Norman Smith and Li Ran, eds., *Wu Ying zuopin ji* [Collection of Wu Ying's writings] (Harbin: Beifang wenyi chubanshe, 2017).

6 For details, see Norman Smith, *Resisting Manchukuo: Chinese Women Writers and the Japanese Occupation* (Vancouver: UBC Press, 2007), 126–27.

7 Wu Ying, "Manzhou nüxing wenxue de ren yu zuopin" [Female writers and writings of Manchuria], *Qingnian wenhua* [Youth culture], May 1944, 24–28.

8 Literally, the double wall of Manchuria's literary world. Li Ran, "Wu Ying yu di'yi ci 'DongYa caoguzhe dahui' – yi 'Dong you hou ji' wei zhongxin."

9 Zhang Quan is the foremost scholar on Mei Niang's life and career. See Zhang Quan, "Searching for Memories of Colonial Literature in Republican History: Centring Mei Niang's Border Crossing and Intergenerational Situation" in Annika A. Culver and Norman Smith, eds., *Manchukuo Perspectives: Transnational Approaches to Literary Production* (Hong Kong: Hong Kong University Press, 2019), 189–201; and Smith, *Resisting Manchukuo,* especially 190–91.

10 For further discussion of Mei Niang's literary activities in Beiping, see Chen Yan, "Acculturation and Border-Crossing in Manchukuo Literature: Mei Niang, Liu Longguang, and Yuan Xi," in Culver and Smith, *Manchukuo Perspectives,* 175–88.

11 Yang Xu, *Wo de riji* [My diary] (Xinjing: Kaiming tushu gongsi, 1944), 151.

12 Her work is collected in Norman Smith, Xu Jianwen, Hu Di, and Li Ran, eds., *Yang Xu zuopin ji* [Collection of Yang Xu's writings] (Harbin: Beifang wenyi chubanshe, 2017).

13 Yang Xu, *Wo de riji,* 144.

14 In 1946, Yang argued that if she had been nicer to the Japanese authorities (going to dinners and entertaining them more often), her book would likely not have been banned, recalled, and destroyed.

15 Originally published as "Wo de zuizhuang" [My indictment], *Xin Manzhou* [New Manchuria], July 1942; republished as "Gongkai de zuizhuang" [Open indictment] in Yang Xu, *Wo de riji,* 89–90.

16 Mei Niang, "Ji Wu Ying shu" [A letter for Wu Ying], *Qingnian wenhua* [Youth culture] 1, 5 (December 1943): 84.

17 Lei Yan (1911–52) was a Beijing-based writer in the 1940s. In 1935, she graduated from Beijing University Women's College of Arts and Sciences, Department of English Literature. Among the group of women mentioned by Mei Niang, she is considered to have been the most successful. For more information, see Zhang Quan, "Cong lunxian qu wenxue jieshou xian kuang kan jiaqiang shiliao gongzuo de zhongyao xing – Yi Beijing nü zuojia lei yan wei zhongxin" [The importance of strengthening work on historical materials to the current reception of literature of the occupied areas: Focus on Beijing woman writer Lei Yan] in *Kangzhan wenhua yanjiu, san* [Anti-war culture research, 3] ed. Li Jianping and Zhang Zhongliang (Guilin: Guangxi shifan daxue chubanshe, 2010), 231–42.

18 Fangjuan (1917–unknown), was a Beijing-based writer, noted for writings in *Funü zazhi* (The Ladies' Journal), during the occupation.

19 The birth and death dates for Ouyang Feiya are currently unknown. Ouyang published four major novellas in the early 1940s, including Nü Shen (Goddess) in *Funü zazhi* (The Ladies' Journal) 3.2 (February 1942): 80–89.

20 Mei Niang's husband, a pre-eminent journalist and editor in north China, died in 1949, when his ship sank in the waters between Taiwan and China. For further details, see Chen, "Acculturation," esp. 180–85.

21 Shen Qiwu was a student of Zhou Zuoren, and a professor at Beijing University during the Japanese occupation; he was considered one of the four most promising of Zhou's students. See *Qingnian wenhua* [Youth culture] 2, 6 (1944): 56.

22 Wu Ying's husband, Wu Lang, was a famous writer and editor in Manchukuo. He is said to have committed suicide due to political persecution during the Cultural Revolution in 1968.

23 Wu Ying, "Fu Mei Niang shu" [A reply to Mei Niang's letter], *Funü zazhi* [Ladies journal] 5, 4 (1944): 20–21.

24 Wu Ying had a child at the age of seventeen; the child was raised by her parents.

25 Words such as *fanluan* and *zhanju* would most likely have been censored in a Manchukuo magazine, but were not in this journal published in Beiping.

26 Jia Ren, "Zhi Yang Xu nüshi" [To Ms. Yang Xu], *Xin Manzhou* [New Manchuria] 5, 2 (February 1943): 96–97. The identity of Jia Ren is unknown, but she had apparently worked with Yang Xu at a bank in Xinjing. She was not a frequent contributor to the magazine. Li Zhengzhong, personal interview, Shenyang, 9 May 2017.

27 This set phrase literally means "to serve the state of Qin in the morning and the state of Chu in the evening," meaning quick to switch sides, or unpredictable.

28 *Shaobing* is a baked, unleavened, layered flatbread popular in north China.

29 A more literal translation of *hunchi dengsi* is "drift around, eat, and wait to die."

30 Yang Xu left Xinjing in the aftermath of a failed romantic relationship, in which she was betrayed by a man.

9 The Lives of Korean Women in Manchukuo

JONGHYUN LEE

What was it like to live in Manchukuo as a Korean woman? Many Koreans migrated to the region, fleeing from poverty and encouraged by the Japanese authorities that had occupied Korea since 1910. When arriving in Manchukuo, Koreans had to deal with not only Japanese, the invading forces in the region, but also with the local Chinese people.[1] Because of their gender, Korean women in particular had to endure additional challenges including the patriarchal oppression that limited their opportunities to better their lives. However, less is known about the life experiences of Korean women in Manchukuo than those of their male counterparts, and they must be differentiated.

"Shipcharoe panghwanghanŭn yŏindŭl" (Women Facing a Crossroads) is a collection of eight memoirs written by anonymous Korean women that appeared in the December 1939 *Mansŏnilbo* (Manchuria–Joseon daily news). There is no way to verify that these memoirs were written by the women themselves. They might have been created or modified by the editors of the newspaper.[2] However, their accounts reflect the widespread patriarchal social norms in Manchukuo, where Korean women were mostly invisible in the public sphere.[3] At the same time, these Korean women suffered from political marginalization as the colonial subjects of Japanese imperialism. Korean women in Manchukuo faced a crossroads where patriarchal oppression and colonial exploitation intersected.

The migration of Koreans to what is now Northeast China started well before modern times. Beginning in the 1620s, some Koreans moved to Chinese territory fleeing from starvation, debts, and government oppression. Often, they settled in the Liaodong area just north of the Korean border, where they collected ginseng or engaged in farming.[4]

In the late nineteenth century, the Qing government implemented a policy that promoted migration to the borders (*Yimin shibian*) to attract Koreans to Manchuria in an attempt to protect the region from Russia.[5] By 1904, there were at least fifty thousand Koreans living in the area of Beijiandao, just north of the border with Korea.[6]

After the Japanese annexation of Korea in 1910, the number of Koreans who lived in Northeast China increased, ranging approximately from 200,000 in 1910 to almost two million by 1945.[7] Between 1910 and 1931, Koreans migrated internationally to this region from colonized Korea. In Manchuria, Koreans were a marginalized group, exploited by the Japanese who were trying to colonize the region and viewed as exploiters by the Chinese who were resisting Japanese encroachments. During the Manchukuo era from 1932 until 1945, the migration of Koreans was considered intercolonial within the Japanese Empire as they moved from Korea, an official colony of Japan, to its unofficial colony of Manchukuo.[8]

Advocating Korean migration to Manchukuo was an economic strategy of the Japanese colonial authorities. They recognized that the cost involved in migrating to Manchukuo was lower for Koreans than for Japanese. At the same time, Japanese authorities wanted to prevent the influx of Koreans into Japan since they could pose a threat to its labour market.[9]

For many Koreans, Manchukuo might have seemed an idealized land where they could find opportunities for better lives.[10] Following the slogan of Naesŏnilch'e (Japan and Korea Together), some Koreans decided to assimilate themselves to Japanese colonial power in the hope of achieving better economic opportunities and social status.[11]

Despite their hope for a better life, most Koreans in Manchukuo were unable to access the same opportunities as Japanese migrants. Unlike the Japanese, the Koreans in Manchukuo tended to reside predominantly in rural areas while engaging in farming. For instance, by the end of 1938, 87.9 percent of Japanese residents in Manchukuo were concentrated in urban areas such as Dairen (currently Dalian), Fengtian (currently Shenyang), and Xinjing (currently Changchun), which were protected by Japanese military and police forces. In contrast, the majority of Koreans resided in rural villages across the Jiandao area of Jilin, in Fengtian province, and even in the lightly populated lands of Mongolia.[12] Moreover, the daily average wage of Koreans in Manchukuo was 1.05 *yuan* in 1939, almost two and half times lower than that of

Japanese, which was 2.56 *yuan*.[13] Thus, "Japan and Korea Together" was nothing more than a political slogan of the Japanese colonial authorities who wanted to utilize Korean labour in the region.[14]

Korean women in Manchukuo had to endure multiple marginality due to their ethnicity and gender. Just like Korean men, they suffered from the colonial oppression imposed by the Japanese authorities while being confronted by discriminatory practices exercised by the Chinese people. In addition, these women had to endure patriarchy that offered only fringe opportunities for survival. The wages of Korean women demonstrate their economic deprivation. Their average daily wage was 0.65 *yuan*, almost three times lower than that of Japanese women in Manchukuo, which was 1.65 *yuan*.[15]

Combined with poverty, limited education and scarce resources pushed many Korean women into involuntary prostitution. The work of prostitutes was often called *inyukchangsa* (the human flesh trade).[16] Many slang terms were used to refer to the women engaging in prostitution. For instance, the term *yŏgŭp* refers to waitresses at cafés who provided erotic services to their male patrons.[17] *Kisaeng* is a Korean word that is equivalent to the Chinese term *jinü*, a term that often refers to professional women who entertain male patrons through song and dance; *yegi* is another term especially used for female entertainers. In contrast, the term *ch'anggi* was designated for those who engaged exclusively in prostitution. *Chakpu* is another term used to refer to those engaged in prostitution at *yorijŏm* (restaurants), whereas *taensŏ* were women who served male patrons at a dance hall.[18]

In Manchukuo, the term *ch'anggi* was not in use.[19] As they did in Korea, the Japanese authorities in Manchukuo tried to hide their involvement in the licensing and management of prostitution. They were afraid that state-regulated prostitution could tarnish their international reputation in their colonies. Instead of *ch'anggi*, new terms such as *yŏgŭp*, *chakpu*, and *taensŏ* were adopted to refer to women engaging in prostitution, along with more traditional terms such as *yegi* or *jinü*.[20] These new terms represented the proliferation of prostitution catering to the increasing numbers of Japanese soldiers in the region. In order to prevent the spread of sexually transmitted diseases among its soldiers, the Kantō Army, together with Japanese consulate offices, tried to regulate the people and places involved in prostitution.[21] At the same time, the Japanese police oversaw the operation of prostitution since it was categorized as a security-related business.[22]

9.1 Advertisement for White Gold: Korean Café in the International City of Harbin. *Source: Mansŏnilbo* (Manchuria–Joseon daily news), 10 December 1939, morning edition, 3.

The Fourth Annual Statistical Report prepared by the Police Affairs Office in 1942 provides useful information relevant to prostitution in the region.[23] According to the report, the number of Korean women engaged in prostitution across Manchukuo was 5,075 in 1940. This means that Koreans represented 11.2 percent of the 45,323 women engaged in prostitution. The actual number of Korean women engaged in prostitution was lower than the number of Chinese or Japanese women. According to the report, while Chinese women represented approximately 54.3 percent of those who engaged in prostitution, Japanese women represented about 33.5 percent. Also noted in the report were the types of prostitution that Korean women were involved in. The largest proportion of Korean women (14.2 percent) worked as *chakpu* (in restaurants) followed by *yŏgŭp* (9.9 percent; at cafés), and *taensŏ* (0.3 percent, at dance halls). In addition, Koreans made up 12.9 percent of women engaging in prostitution at cafés and 8.5 percent of those who engaged in prostitution at restaurants.[24]

9.2 Advertisement for Oasis Café: Your Place for Pleasure. Your Place for Rest. *Source: Mansŏnilbo* (Manchuria–Joseon daily news), 12 January 1940, evening edition, 2.

Due to the higher income in comparison to other professions, many Korean women decided to remain in prostitution.[25] The monthly income of Korean women engaged in prostitution was much higher than those of other professional women. According to a report made by the *Mansŏnilbo* on 21 September 1940, the average monthly income of Korean *chakpu* in Jiamusi was 261 *yuan,* which was more than thirteen times higher than the monthly salary (20 *yuan*) of kindergarten teachers in the capital, Xinjing. Even compared to the monthly income of nurses (50 to 60 *yuan*), typists (65 *yuan*), or office workers (55 *yuan*), the monthly income of Korean *chakpu* was four to five times higher. Since they had limited education and professional skills, these women had few options. Prostitution might have often been the only available means for their survival.

Korean women had to face a patriarchy that disallowed them to be agents of their own will. Chastity was their virtue; happiness could be secured only through marriage. Korean women in Manchukuo faced a crossroads not because of some supposed moral inferiority but because of the oppressive Japanese colonial power, discrimination against migrants, and patriarchy that perpetuated the economic and occupational barriers against them. Their limited access to opportunities, resources, and privileges deprived Korean women of the ability to reach their potential, while reinforcing their subjugation to Japanese colonists, xenophobia, and the pervasive patriarchal system.

"Women Facing a Crossroads" was written by anonymous authors who represented all walks of life. They were students, nurses, housewives, and entertainers. In each account, these women are portrayed as victims of their own shortcomings. Since they had limited ability to become independent, these women were at a loss when abandoned by their husbands, and had to live as concubines, or turn to prostitution. These eight stories of "Women Facing a Crossroads" provide a view of the life circumstances of Korean women in Manchukuo.

—• TRANSLATIONS •—

Women Facing a Crossroads

A Poor Caged Bird Yearning for Freedom: In the Midst of Devastating Sorrow, Remembering the Sweet Home I Used to Have[26]

I am a so-called caged bird. Day and night, I have to pretend that I am happy by giving a smile and acting charming for strangers. My life is devastatingly pitiful as I have to sell my chastity, the most important virtue for women, to a man I do not know.

Chastity

Pretending to be happy and acting charming is distressful. But what agonized me most was to give my chastity to a man that I had no emotion for. Unfortunately, I had no other choice. I am caged like a bird.

Miracle

I am a woman chained up with misery. Without finding a miracle, day and night, I have to put oil on my hair and wear makeup to please a man that I do not know. As I think back, I have been living this caged life for three years of shedding tears. I was seventeen and lived in Taegu, in Kyŏngsang-Do, when I met a driver, K, who came from another place. I fell in love with him and we courted secretly to avoid gossip.

Conjugal Tie
In the fall of that year, we exchanged vows of marriage and committed to live together till death would us part. It was a marriage built by a loving man and woman. We kept our marriage happy through loving and by understanding each other's flaws. However, a demon must have been jealous of our happiness. Less than half a year after our marriage, I lost my husband in a car accident. I felt devastated by this tragedy, which caused my current despair that I cannot escape. My suffering might not have been as painful if I had not gotten a taste of a happy marriage.

Happiness
My current suffering is devastating because of the happiness that I enjoyed in the past. If I had not enjoyed such happiness, I might not perceive my current circumstance as such a misfortune. The happiness in my past rankles in my heart and causes my current sorrow. I see all kinds of people. Some of them are losers while others are successful. At times, I encounter people with a gruff manner and at other times I serve people who are considerate. Despite their diversity, I cannot find anyone whom I can trust or share my feelings with. They are just frequent visitors to the red-light district.

Someone Else
Even when I find a man whom I want to be intimate with, he is most likely to be a married man with a wife and a child. I should not be intimate with any stranger, no matter if he is successful or a failure. The only man that I can trust would be my husband. Although missing a man who is no longer alive will not help, I find comfort when I cry over his spirit.

Sympathy
People often say that one should not listen to prostitutes. Who will listen to my unfortunate tale or even believe my adverse life circumstances? No one will have sympathy for me. I am the only one who can listen to and understand my own circumstances. As time goes by, the amount of debt that I am responsible for continually grows. I will not be able to make a family like other ordinary people. I feel suffocated and agonized by the thought that I have to continually suffer from my current circumstances.

Fate

I blame fate that forced me into my current life circumstances. However, I seek solace in the hope that I have. Although there is only a slight chance, our lives spin over and over again. I hope to find a miracle that will lead to a brighter future.

– CCHA IN THE MIKASA-CHŌ, UNKNOWN CITY (*SHINAE, MIKASA-CHŌ, CCHA*)

A Virgin Who Lost Her Virginity to the Man She Was Engaged To: Did He Only Want the Girl's Virginity? All Men Are Untrustworthy[27]

Engagement

I am a nineteen-year-old, inexperienced girl. About a year ago, I met C through a matchmaker and eventually my parents approved of our engagement. He had been working as a driver. After we got engaged he frequently visited my home. He always wanted to be alone with me and did not want to have my parents around. He probably was worried my parents would keep an eye on him. My parents knew that C did not like their supervision when we were meeting. Whenever he, their future son-in-law, would visit us they let us be alone.

Parents

My parents have told me that although we were engaged, I needed to be cautious until after the marriage and guard myself from him. However, they left us alone in order not to interfere and this made me feel that the soldiers who could protect my body had backed off. I did not know how to answer his questions nor did I know how to respond when he made impolite requests.

Courtship

Due to his frequent visits to our home and our extended courtship, my concerns about being left alone with him gradually disappeared. I began to appreciate my parents' consideration for creating opportunities for us to be alone without supervision. This might have been the first step of my love affair. Whenever we found opportunities just as he planned for, we took a walk to the park or went to movies together. My parents let us do these things. They even appeared to be satisfied with what we were doing.

Love
Without having any parental supervision, nothing could interrupt our love affair. This was only a passionate love shared by a young man and woman. Because of the strong love that we shared, I lost my virginity. Although I decided to give my virginity to him, I found a sense of regret lingering in my mind. After our affair, his visits to our home became less frequent. Initially I thought it might be because he was shy. I also thought that he might be tied up with his work.

After That
The truth that I found was devastating. Less than half a month after seducing me, he was madly in love with a bar girl. I was not able to believe it until I witnessed it. I asked about this and learned that his affair with the bar girl was not new but was an ongoing one. If only I had known this earlier, I would not have made the mistake of giving up my virginity.

Truth
A few days after I found out about his affair, C sincerely apologized to me for his wrongdoing. He said that there was no way his temporary love affair with a bar girl would interfere with our marriage. He knew that I would understand about his affair with the girl. How devious and shameless the man was! I would not be feeling satisfied even if I could spit in his face. No matter how much I cried, I felt suffocated due to the pain caused by a sense of betrayal.

Crying
I just cried for several days without even eating at all. Initially, my parents harshly admonished me. However, they felt pity for my many days of suffering and began to offer words of comfort. My parents soothed my mind with their benevolence. The power of parental care was mighty and, with their support, I decided to start my life anew. Finally, I was able to recover from many days of nightmarish suffering.

Awakening
Here is the reason I could recover. Not long ago, I heard news about C. He married the bar girl. On the one hand, I became resentful of her as she was a rival in love and I thought of her as my enemy. On the other hand, I worried about her and her future because I see her as a woman just like me.

— A WOMAN LIVING IN THE CITY
(*SHINAE IL YŎSŎNG*)

A Woman's Hysteria Made Her Husband Leave Home: Couples' Spats Never Last, Come Back to the Arms of Your Wives[28]

Husband and Wife

Couples' spats never last. However, my husband left home about half a year ago after we had a quarrel, which was nothing serious. I am concerned about his well-being and no one knows his whereabouts. At the same time, I feel bitter about his heartlessness. A sense of lonesomeness has built up in my mind. This might be the real end of our togetherness. I think about what happened to us day and night and realized that I am the one who is wrong.

Husband

My husband and I got into fights almost every two or three days. Each time, my tight-lipped husband could not manage his anger. He broke household goods and left home. Every time my husband left home, I wandered around searching for him. After a day or two, my husband came back home after calming himself down.

Affection

"How foolish I am living with a hysterical woman like you! It is right for us to be separated and lead our own lives." Although he used to talk to me like this, he continually showed his affection for me. My husband was twenty-nine years old and I am thirty-one years old. I expressed my gratitude for his affection and apologized for my wrongdoing to my two-years-younger husband. However, regretting my own wrongdoing was a momentary thing. I started another quarrel with him. I am upset with myself since I cannot control my own behaviour. When I married my husband, I confessed to him that I was not a virgin.

Wife

My husband generously accepted me as his wife. I determined that I would remain his wife by believing that he is the only person who could save my life. But we were often on edge and regularly got into fights over trifles. Initially, he was able to suppress his anger. But he left home after kicking, hitting, and breaking household goods because of the anger caused by my offensive evil tongue. It would have been nicer if I were a little more patient. Why should I pick a fight with my husband?

I Don't Know the Reason
Although there should have been some reason for our fights, I still do not know what they were. I was not dissatisfied with my husband's affection nor was I unhappy about our limited financial means. Instead, I am appreciative of what we have now and consider us lucky. I cried a number of times because I did not like myself. Once a woman gets into a wrong circumstance, she may easily get into a state of hopelessness.

Personality
When I was twenty-one years old, I worked as a nurse at S Hospital in Kyungseong. I lost my virginity to a twenty-seven-year old male patient whose name was K. Ever since that time, my personality completely changed. I became irritable and short tempered with my colleagues and got into fights over trifles. Therefore, my colleagues tried to avoid me and I did not try to approach them. That fall, I left the S Hospital and moved to A City where I worked as a sales clerk. I got married to my current husband when I was twenty-three years old and it was in the late spring. It was entirely my fault, as I think carefully about what had happened to us on that cold winter stormy night under the lonely lamplights.

Overcome
I was not able to overcome my hysteria no matter how hard I tried. Because of the hysteria, I lost my husband. I do not know where to find my husband, and he doesn't respond although I call out for him. Whenever I think of him, my mind is aching and I am heartbroken.

— O-YŎNG KIM FROM A CITY
(*A-SHI KIM O-YŎNG*)

A Glowing Passionate Love Frozen by Jack Frost: A Woman Who Sympathized with the Heroines in Tragic Novels, Leading a Sorrowful Life When Abandoned by a Lover[29]

School Uniform
A virgin girl's innocence is wrapped in a blue school uniform. However, it turns into ash grey as soon as she graduates from a school and takes off her uniform.

Suffering
Escaping from my parents' gaze, I used to read romance novels that my schoolteachers warned us students not to read. I sympathized with those

unfortunate heroines in the stories. Although they were fictional, there are countless women in our society suffering from much harsher lives than those appearing in the stories, women who were abandoned by men who toyed with them. Each time I read such unfortunate stories, I assured myself that "I would not be such an unfortunate heroine in this society." Such a determined girl like me would never have thought that I, too, could be abandoned as worthless by a man. A couple of years ago, when I was eighteen years old, late in the spring, I was a student at X women's school. I became particularly close to a student in my class whose name was Kim Sukcha (pseudonym).

Intimate
We became close friends, and if she did not come to visit my home, I went to hers. By the way, Sukcha had an older brother who was five years senior to her and worked for a company. He was the very man who brought misfortune to me. I just took a first step into social life with a beautiful dream after graduating from school and no longer in a school uniform. Whenever I visited Sukcha's home, her brother greeted me more warmly than Sukcha would. He always treated me in a soft, friendly, and kind manner. At the beginning, I was annoyed by him and guarded myself against him. As I got to know him more, he appeared not to be a mean-spirited man.

Wariness
As time went by, I began to let my guard down. I concluded that he treated me in a friendly and kind manner because I was a special friend of his sister Sukcha, and for no other reason. I interacted with him just like I would with my own brother. Therefore, along with Sukcha, we sometimes took a walk to the Taedong River and Moran Peak. Also, at other times, we went to the movies.

Him
After many frequent encounters and outings, I began to dislike our brother-and-sister type of relationship. Honestly speaking, I began to develop affection toward him. Also, he treated me in a kind and tender manner not because I was a friend of his sister, but because he took an interest in me as someone he wanted to be intimate with. That year in the fall, when the trees' leaves began turning red, our love was also aglow like the ruddy red leaves.

Proud
I cannot forget the very date, the fourteenth of October. It was the date I surrendered my virginity, which I had proudly preserved, to him. After this,

I was thrown out of our home by my parents and stayed at my uncle's house for a few days. After much consideration about my future, I decided to ask Sukcha's brother for an engagement. My parents finally realized that harsh scolding or other punishments would be useless and approved my decision.

Engagement
I went to see him to explain my circumstances. I was able to receive his verbal consent by desperately asking him to be engaged to me. However, around the early winter of that year, I heard a rumour circulating that he was engaged to a woman whose name is P and they had even set their wedding date. I hesitate to share with others what happened after that. I do not even want to talk about my problems anymore.

– A FOOLISH WOMAN IN PYONGYANG
(*P'YŎNGYANG ARISŎKŬN YŎJA*)

An Anguished Girl Trapped in a Triangular Relationship: No Matter How Hard I Tried to Get Away, the Power of Love Was Irresistible[30]

Love
I am an anguished teenage girl in the midst of a triangular relationship. I feel foolish and even pity myself for competing with another woman in order to win the love of a man named H. However, what else can I do? The power of love is absolute and I became its prisoner. "Let me break away from him and give him up!" "Let me be courageous and allow my friend to be with him! Let me sacrifice myself!" I agonized with myself in order not to stay in a conflicted triangular relationship. Instead, I tried to break away from him as soon as possible. However, no matter how hard I tried to distance myself, I found myself getting closer to him. It may be love. Indeed, it is a shame that I am not able to give him up.

I Began
Starting this spring I began to love H. I do not know when my friend YŏngX started to love him. One day in the summer, I found him and YŏngX walking side by side. Not only was he embarrassed when he found me watching them but also YŏngX blushed when she saw me there. YŏngX blushed because she

was ashamed of herself taking a walk with a man. She might not have known that H loves me and I still love him.

My Friend
I believed that H would not have anyone he loves other than me. From the day when I found that H loves my friend YŏngX, I began to develop not only a fierce jealousy toward my friend but also a rebellious spirit against H. Such an extreme defiant attitude was a helpless thing in the face of love. Numerous times I tried to stop my friendship with YŏngX, but such attempts were useless.

I Back Down
After many days of agony, I decided to ask YŏngX how much progress she had made in regard to her relationship with H, or when they began dating. After that, I planned to sincerely request that she back down from H and give a chance to me. Finally, I visited YŏngX and asked about her relationship with H, after talking about all sorts of other matters. Initially, YŏngX denied the relationship by saying: "What do you mean by love?" However, as soon as she heard that H and I were lovers, YŏngX's face turned blue with shock. Based on her confession, I realized that the relationship between YŏngX and H had begun before I entered the picture.

Not Less
Also, I realized that the affection of YŏngX toward H was not less than mine. Moreover, I learned that, unlike me, she did not have the courage to sacrifice herself for me, her friend. I thought that it was not appropriate for me to be jealous that YŏngX loves H. I tried to overcome my moral scruples by backing away myself from H. However, those attempts were only momentary.

Absolute
No one will ever surrender love because of morals or sympathy. I blame H who unexpectedly loved two different women at the same time. But, it is extremely sad to know that I do not possess the courage to reject him. It is a great pity for me that I cannot control myself the way I want to.

– AN AGONIZED WOMAN IN KYŎNGSŎNG
(*KYŎNGSŎNG KOMINHANŬN YŎJA*)

To Avoid Marriage a Woman Runs Away from Home and Cries Out Her Misfortune: Does Men's Sympathy Always Hide a Conspiracy? Lost Virginity in an Instant[31]

Misfortune

I am a twenty-one-year-old ill-fated woman. I protested against my parents who forced me to become engaged to a man that I had no affection for by not eating for a few days. My mother expressed her sympathy by saying that "affection keeps a relationship stable and we were wrong to force you to get engaged with a man you have no affection for. If you are really against this engagement there is not a thing we can do. However, there is no better mate than him."

Engagement

My father insisted that I should get engaged to the man. He scolded me by saying: "He has money, social status, and is good looking. What more can you ask for? Why do you resist your parents' arrangements?" I am not ignoring my parents' intention to secure their daughter's happiness by forcing her to marry a wealthy man. However, this society tells us that a person cannot enjoy happiness only with money. After careful consideration, I decided to run away from home because my parents could not understand my stance on marriage and happiness. Last year, one summer night I left Seoul with tears in my eyes by taking a train to Xinjing station from Kyŏngsŏng Station.

Tragedy

The journey without a purpose threw me into a trap. The following evening I got off the train at Xinjing Station and checked into XX hotel near the station. As a young woman, when I walked into a hotel alone, male customers looked at me like something they should not see. Among those, there must have been poisonous attention aimed at my body. By spending a couple of nights there, I wondered about my future.

The First Time

That was the first time that I ever agonized over the ways I could overcome the challenges posed by society. The hotel demanded that I make a deposit for my meals. After paying the deposit of 5 won by using all the money I had at that time, I felt desperate without knowing what to do with my future.

I was aware of what others say: "Money is all you can trust when you are away from home." As time went by, people began to discover that I had run away from home. Through watching every behaviour of mine, those men who gave attention to me probably learned about my circumstances. Those men began to seduce me as they found I was in need.

Money

Some asked me how I could stay in a hotel without money and others told me that they could help me find a job. At other times, people were curious about the amount of money that I owed for the accommodation and why I stayed in a hotel by myself. There were people who tried to seduce me by asking to go out to see a movie. I was able to learn about the hideous psychological state of men even at this small hotel. But I did not have the determination to overcome all these temptations. Moreover, my circumstances did not allow me to do that.

Employment

One day, I was hired by the XXX department store as a sales agent in the city through the help of K, a man who stayed in the same hotel. I was sincerely thankful to K whose help enabled me to pave my future. However, the fact that he helped me with finding a job became another stain on my life. One night, it was an extremely brief moment, and I still tremble even thinking about it.

K came into my room and talked about various things until late at night. He later went back to his room since he saw me yawning. I made the bed and fell into a deep exhausted sleep. I began to vaguely sense discomfort and opened my eyes.

Too Late

But it was too late. K came back into my room while I was sleeping to satisfy his sexual desire. Despite such a traumatic accident, all I could do was cry under the covers. Because I was scared of other people's blame, I was not even able to yell or scream. I spent that unfortunate night in tears. I went out to the store to work in order to survive. K, the man who ruined my life, disappeared from the hotel a few days later.

– A WOMAN LIVING IN THE CITY
(*SHINAE IL YŎSŎNG*)

A Beloved and Trustworthy Husband Has Another Wife and Children: Can Warm-Heartedness Be a Problem? He Gets into Another Affair – A Troubled Woman Fooled by Love[32]

Marriage
I am a thirty-five-year-old housewife. I married my husband two years ago. He is four years older than I am and currently works at a company located in the city. After our marriage, my husband showed his passionate affection toward me so much it could even melt my body. He loved me so much that he stopped drinking only because I did not like it. I was grateful in my mind to have such a rare husband like him. My mind was filled with pride and happiness whenever I thought that my husband was exactly who I had idealized to marry.

Wife and Children
When happiness reaches its peak, one may have to suffer from some misfortune. Less than half a year after our marriage, I learned that my beloved husband had a wife and children in his hometown. After I learned about his other family, tornado-like worries began to rise in my mind. "Do I have to continue this life? Or is it better for me to run away from home in order to cut off this ill-fated relationship?" I repeatedly asked myself these questions several hundred times. However, I was not able to gather the courage to run away from home. This might be because my husband's love discouraged me from making such a decision. I felt that I would not be able to live without him.

Surrender
Therefore, my effort to surrender to him was useless no matter how hard I tried. My husband acknowledged that he had lied about his marital status when he married me and accepted my rage at him. Also, he tried to calm me down and comfort me. As time went by, our troubles settled down. Our lives filled with love started again. I should not say that I did not worry about his former wife who might unexpectedly come to us and cause trouble for us. However, this concern was nothing in comparison to the love shared between us.

Husband
But such an affectionate husband of mine had a problem. Every night he came home late from his work. Since I was suspicious about his behaviour,

I learned that he was dating another woman. At that time, I worried a lot about this issue. I felt helpless. I not only loved him but also kept a marital relationship with him even after I learned that he had a wife from his previous marriage. I could not complain at all even if he fell in love three or four times with different women. I was able to understand the suffering of his former wife whenever I remembered what others say: "Understand the pains of others through your own hardships."

Separation

After that, a number of times I asked my husband to separate from me. But each time he responded to me by saying: "My infidelity is a sort of illness. Please do not worry and wait until I can recover from it." Because he talked to me this way, leaving him was difficult even though I wanted to. However, his infidelity did not seem to get better. I had to wait for him until eleven or twelve o'clock every night. But I could endure such suffering each day because of the brief sweet encounter that I could have with him.

Someone Else

No matter how much I love him or he loves me in his entire life, he is the husband of someone else. Whenever I think of this, I become sad with tears. However not many people would offer sympathy with my circumstances. Except for those who are in a similar situation to mine, everyone would blame me by saying I was paying for what I had done. Because of that I do not dare to speak about my pain. Instead, I tried to console myself with a deep sigh. But now I have told this story of mine to the world.

– A TROUBLED WOMAN IN FENGTIAN
(*PONGCH'ŎN IL KOMINNYŎ*)

A Woman Betrayed Again after Her First Heartbreak: The Man She Is Engaged to Has a Wife and Children – A Woman Crying in North Manchuria[33]

After reading the articles "Women Facing a Crossroads" published in your newspaper, I decided to write my story – that was never to be told – in the hope that it might help other women.

I Am

Although my hometown is Pyongyang, I went to a women's high school located in Kyŏngsŏng because of a personal reason. One day in my sophomore year, I went with classmates to a picnic in Ch'anggyŏngwŏn.[34] While walking around the palace, we enjoyed our time by singing songs originating from the sentimentality of teenaged girls. I saw a male student walking by who did not know he had dropped a book. I immediately picked up the book and handed it to him. He repeatedly expressed his gratitude several times and walked away. During that time, I commuted to the school from my uncle's home. The male student attended a middle school while staying at a boarding house located next to my uncle's home. His name was A.

An Encounter

Due to our encounter at the palace, I went out with him a number of times. While dating, we became passionately affectionate with each other. When we first fell in love it was autumn, and our affection became pigmented in red just like all the leaves one could see in the mountains. One year passed by and another autumn came to us. 24 September is the date that I cannot forget. It is the date that I gave my virginity and everything to him. At that time, I was seventeen years old. I wish I could have been more temperate. I would not have allowed him to take my virginity even though we were passionately in love. Because I became blind with love, I was not able to make an appropriate judgment. When our love reached its peak, we were separated.

In Pyongyang

The following year in March, he graduated from the middle school and went back to his hometown Pyongyang. There was nothing we could do, but we had to face our separation while making a pledge to keep our love. After that, we exchanged letters three or four times. From the letters, I saw that his affection toward me gradually changed. Our communication stopped as he no longer responded to my letters. This was the time when I stepped into a wrong path. But I was able to graduate from the school under the supervision of my uncle. He might have told my elder brother about my behaviour. My elder brother came to my graduation to pick me up and took me back to Pyongyang with him. However, I was not able to start a new life but fell into a vicious life more and more. I eventually became a *kisaeng.*[35]

As a Kisaeng

After I became a *kisaeng,* I saw A in a city. Not only was I calm that time but also he did not recognize me. He just passed me by. I had migrated to north Manchuria in order not to encounter A. In addition, my elder brother forced me to move. However, life in north Manchuria was not as I expected. There were other Koreans who were in more desperate circumstances than mine. I finally started to regret my wrongdoing but knew that resentment would be useless. While agonizing over my resentment, I fell in love a second time. He was from south Korea and in this area he was an influential man, called T. After three or four months of dating, we decided to get married and began to start a new family. But I must be an ill-fated woman. I thought that T was single but later I learned that he had a wife in his hometown.

Pregnant

But when I heard this news, I was already five months pregnant. Even though I had followed a wanton life, I was determined that I would never become a concubine under any circumstances. But my determination is no longer effective. I cannot separate from my husband because of my pregnancy. My only hope is that T will continue to love me. However, I feel extremely sad whenever I think of his wife, who leads a lonely life in his hometown, and his children, who miss their father. In fact, my pain is bigger than the time I found out that I was fooled by A. How can I ask for forgiveness for the pain that I caused? I am tormented by a guilty conscience. I live my life with tears because of a child growing in my womb.

A Memoir

If A reads this memoir, I wonder what his emotion will be? With what sentiment would he read the story of a woman he abandoned three years ago? Please understand my poor and incomprehensible writing.

— A FOOLISH WOMAN IN NORTH MANCHURIA (*PUKMANŬI ŎNŬ PABOYŎJA*)

Notes

Acknowledgment | This study was supported in part by the Faculty and Librarian Research Grant award by Bridgewater State University in Massachusetts, United States.

1 Sŏkchŏng Han, "Manjuguk shigi chosŏninŭi sahoejŏkchiwi" [The social status of Koreans in the Manchukuo period], *Tongbugayŏksanonch'ong* [Journal of northeast Asian history] 31 (March 2011): 21.

2 Yŏngju Kim, "Mansŏnilboŭi chendŏjŏk t'ŭksŏnggwa ŭimi" [The meaning of gendered characteristics in the Mansŏn daily news], *Ŏmunhak* [Korean language and literature] 120 (June 2013): 365.

3 Keongil Kim, Hwytak Yoon, Dongjin Lee, and Sungmo Yim, *Tongasiaŭi minchokisankwa tosi* [Korean diaspora in Manchurian cities in the early twentieth century] (Seoul: Yŏksabip'yŏngsa, 2004), 263–67.

4 Chŏngpong Cho, "Ilche kangjŏmgi chosŏninŭi kando ijuwa yahagundong" [The migration to Jiandao among Koreans and the night school movement during the Japanese occupation], *Han'gukkyoyuk* [Journal of Korean education] 34, 1 (April 2007): 160.
5 Kyŏngsuk Pak, "Shingminji shigi (1910nyŏn-1945nyŏn) chosŏnŭi in'gu tongt'aewa kujo" [Population and structure during the colonization between 1910 and 1945], *Hankukinkuhak* [Korea journal of population studies] 32, 2 (August 2009): 33.
6 Sangch'ŏl Ch'oe, "Kwangbokchŏn chunggugŭi han'gŭl shinmun" [Pro-Japanese Korean-language newspapers in China before independence], *Sinmun'gwa pangsong* [Newspaper and broadcasting] 263 (November 1992): 100.
7 Han, "Manjuguk shigi chosŏninŭi sahoejŏkchiwi," 1,8.
8 Kihun Kim, "Manjuguk shigi chosŏnin imindamnonŭi shironjŏk koch'al – Chosŏnilbo sasŏrŭl chungshimŭro [Study on the discourses about Korean migration during the Manchukuo period – Focusing on the editorials of the Chosŏn daily news], *Tongbugayŏksanonch'ong* 31 (March 2011): 103.
9 An'gi Chŏng, "Manjugukki chosŏninŭi manju imin'gwa dŭtgyumlpbyaet (chu)" [Joseon people's immigration into Manchuria and Sŏnman Colonization Co. Ltd. during the Manchukuo period], *Tongbugayŏksanonch'ong* 31 (March 2011): 48–49.
10 Han, "Manjuguk shigi chosŏninŭi sahoejŏkchiwi," 28–33.
11 Yŏngbok Chin, "Chaemanjosŏninŭi naesŏnilch'e tamnon'gwa kyunyŏl – I Sŏkhun ŭi ilbonŏ sosŏrŭl chungshimŭro" [A study on imperialistic desire and colonial subject in Manchuria: Centring on Lee Seok-Hoon's novels in Japanese], *Hanminjogŏmunhak* [Language and literature of the Korean people] 58 (June 2011): 138–48.
12 Kim et al., *Tongasiaŭi minchokisankwa tosi*, 72–90.
13 Han, "Manjuguk shigi chosŏninŭi sahoejŏkchiwi," 21–22.
14 Ibid., 21–28.
15 Ibid., 21–22.
16 Hyŏnchin Ch'a, *Chungangŭnhaengbyŏlgok: Hondonŭi shidae* [Unofficial story of the Korea Central Bank] (Seoul: Inmulgwa sasangsa, 2016), 193–95.
17 Hyosun Kim and Wŏnju Kang, eds. and trans., *Chaejo ilboninyŏgŭp sosŏl* [Waitress novels among the Japanese in Joseon] (Seoul: Yŏngnak, 2015), 5–10.
18 Dongjin Lee, "Minjok, chiyŏk, seksyuŏllit'i – Manjugugŭi Chosŏnin Sŏngmaemaejong-sajarŭl Chungshimŭro" [Nation, region, and sexuality: Focusing on Korean prostitute in Manchukuo], *Chŏngshinmunhwayŏn'gu* [Korean Studies Quarterly] 28, 3 (2005): 28–30.
19 Jungae Park, "Manchu chiyŏkŭi ilbonkun wianso sŏlch'iwa chosŏnin 'wianpu'" [Establishment of a Japanese military comfort centre in Manchuria and Korean "comfort women"], *Ashiayŏsŏngyŏn'gu* [Journal of Asian women] 55, 1 (May 2016): 11–13.
20 Lee, "Minjok, chiyŏk, seksyuŏllit'i," 27–34.
21 Park, "Manchu chiyŏkŭi ilbonkun wianso sŏlch'iwa chosŏnin 'wianpu,'" 11–13.
22 Lee, "Minjok, chiyŏk, seksyuŏllit'i," 30.
23 Ibid., 37–41.
24 Ibid., 37–41.
25 Ibid., 48–54.
26 "Chayuŭi segye tonggyŏnghanŭn kayŏpsŭn nongjungjijo: Kwagŏe talk'omhan kajŏng-saenghwari itkittaemune hyŏnjaeŭi koeromi tŏukk'ŏyo" [A poor caged bird yearning for freedom: In the midst of devastating sorrow, remembering the sweet home I used to have], "Shipcharoe panghwanghanŭn yŏindŭl" [Women facing a crossroads], *Mansŏnilbo* [Manchuria–Joseon daily news]. (1 December 1939), morning edition.
27 "Yak'onnamjae chŏngjobach'in ch'ŏnyŏgaanin ch'ŏnyŏ – Kŭŭi yogunŭn ch'ŏnyŏŭi sunjŏng kŭgŏt ppuniyŏnnŭn'ga – Mitchi mot'algŏsŭn sanaeŭi maŭm" [A virgin who lost her virginity to the man she was engaged to: Did he only want the girl's virginity? All men

are untrustworthy], "Shipcharoe panghwanghanŭn yŏindŭl," *Mansŏnilbo,* 2 December 1939, morning edition.

28 "Namp'yŏnŭl chibesŏ naetchoch'ŭn yŏjaŭi hisŭt'eri – Pubussahom k'allo Mulgallŏ Nonjari Kattanŭnde – Anhaeŭi p'umŭro Toraora" [A woman's hysteria made her husband leave home: Couples' spats never last, come back to the arms of your wives], "Shipcharoe panghwanghanŭn yŏindŭl," *Mansŏnilbo,* 3 December 1939, morning edition.

29 "Tanp'ungdŭlttae pulget'an sarang sŏrimajŏ naenggak'aenna – Sosŏlsok nunmurŭi yŏjuin'gongege tongjŏnghadŭn yŏja – Yŏninege pŏrimbatko nunmullo sewŏl" [A glowing passionate love frozen by Jack Frost: A woman who sympathized with the heroines in tragic novels, leading a sorrowful life when abandoned by a lover], "Shipcharoe panghwanghanŭn yŏindŭl," *Mansŏnilbo,* 4 December 1939, morning edition.

30 "Samgagaee p'orogadoeyŏ kominŭrhanŭn yŏsŏng – Amuri ijŏbŏrigo tannyŏmharyŏgo aessŏdo mullich'ilsuŏmnŭn sarangŭi himiyŏ [An anguished girl trapped in a triangular relationship: No matter how hard I tried to get away, the power of love was irresistible], "Shipcharoe panghwanghanŭn yŏindŭl," *Mansŏnilbo,* 5 December 1939, morning edition.

31 "Kyŏrhonhoep'ik'i wihae ch'ulga yŏch'angeunŭn pangmyŏngnyŏ – Namsŏngŭi tongjŏngŭi kŭnŭrenŭn ŭmmoman sumŏ innŭn'ga – Ilsun'gane ch'ŏnyŏsŏngŭl ppaeatkyŏ" [To avoid marriage a woman runs away from home and cries out her misfortune: Does men's sympathy always hide a conspiracy? Lost virginity in an instant], "Shipcharoe panghwanghanŭn yŏindŭl," *Mansŏnilbo,* 7 December 1939, morning edition.

32 "Mitko saranghanŭn namp'yŏnen ch'ŏjakkaji itsŏyo – Tajŏngi haniralkka taŭmyŏnaerŭl ttohago itsŏ – Sarange sogasanŭn kominnyŏ" [A beloved and trustworthy husband has another wife and children: Can warm-heartedness be a problem? He gets into another affair – A troubled woman fooled by love], "Shipcharoe panghwanghanŭn yŏindŭl," *Mansŏnilbo,* 8 December 1939, morning edition.

33 "Ch'ŏtsarange ssŭnmasŭl pogo tolchae sarange ttosoga – "Paengnyŏn'gayakŭl maejŭn namp'yŏnen ch'ŏjakkaji itsŏ – Pukmanesŏ unŭn nunmurŭi yŏin" [A woman betrayed again after her first heartbreak: The man she is engaged to has a wife and children – A woman crying in north Manchuria], "Shipcharoe panghwanghanŭn yŏindŭl," *Mansŏnilbo,* 10 December 1939, morning edition.

34 Ch'anggyŏngwŏn was a former royal palace that was converted into a public venue by the Japanese. It contained a zoo, a botanical garden, and a museum and opened to the public starting 11 November 1909.

35 The Korean word *kisaeng* refers to professional women who entertained male patrons by performing songs and dances at an event.

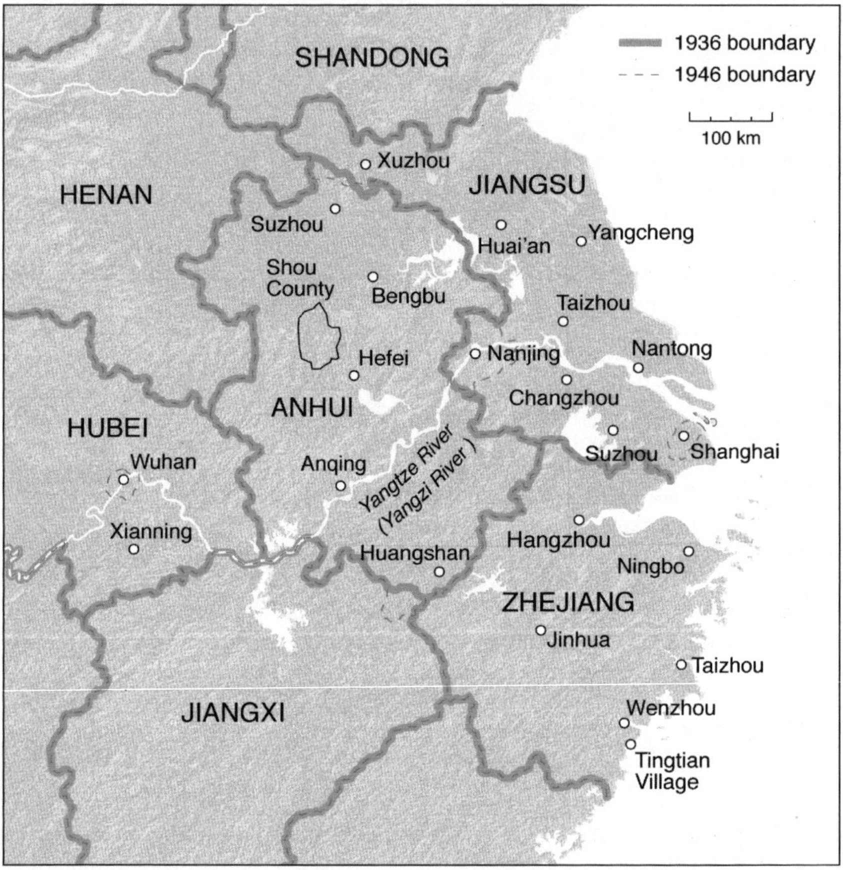

East China. Map by Eric Leinberger

Part 2
EAST CHINA

—• EAST CHINA TIMELINE •—

1932 28 January, Shanghai Incident. Japanese forces clash with the Chinese Nineteenth Route Army in the Shanghai International Settlement

1936 19 October, Lu Xun dies of illness in Shanghai

1937 13 August, Battle of Shanghai

12 November, Japanese army occupies Shanghai

13 December, Japanese army occupies Nanjing, and Nanjing Massacre begins

1938 3 November, Prince Konoe announces a "New Order in East Asia"

1939 8 May, Wang Jingwei arrives in Shanghai

1940 30 April, Reorganized National Government of the Republic of China (RNG) established in Nanjing under Wang Jingwei. Zhou Fohai appointed minister of finance, Kiang Kang-hu as minister of personnel, Lin Baisheng as minister of propaganda, and Fu Shiyue as minister of rail

1941 1 March, Japanese forces occupy Wenzhou for the first time

8 December, Japanese forces occupy the International Settlement in Shanghai

1942 24 March, Zhang Gang dies from illness

15 May, inaugural issue of ***Nü sheng*** (Women's voice) published in Shanghai

1943 30 October, Nanjing gains further autonomy after signing Treaty of Alliance with Japan

1944 10 November, Wang Jingwei dies in Nagoya, and Chen Gongbo takes over as acting president in Nanjing

1945 16 August, responding to the Japanese surrender the day before, RNG acting president Chen Gongbo announces the dissolution of the RNG and its replacement by a provisional political affairs committee in Nanjing

1946 April, trials of major collaborationist officials in East China commence in Shanghai, Suzhou, and other major cities

1947 10 November, Xu Zhuodai publishes "Remarkable Soy Sauce!"

1948 28 February, Zhou Fohai dies in prison while serving a life sentence

THE JAPANESE OCCUPATION of east China, commencing with the attack on Shanghai on 13 August 1937, was marked by massacre, gave way to an occupation of considerable complexity, and bequeathed a legacy that continues to haunt survivors and Sino-Japanese relations – as well as challenge historians. Contributors in this section analyze this period with an emphasis on the multiple layers of ambiguity and range of experiences involved in the occupation.

For the Republic of China, the fall of the lower Yangtze delta entailed the loss of a major economic centre, Shanghai, as well as a larger cultural heartland, home to writers, artists, and intellectuals, not to mention the universities, publishing houses, and studios that employed them. This was capped by the brutal Nanjing Massacre and the deeply symbolic loss of the national capital; in short order, the Nationalists lost most of the territory that they had controlled in the so-called Nanjing Decade (1927–37). The emergence of a series of Japanese-sponsored administrations in the region was not simply a response to both the Japanese need for local partners in administering the territories of east China, and the need for Chinese living in this area to re-establish some form of order. Rather, it was also the outcome of efforts by Chinese intellectuals and politicians who remained in or returned to the region with a vision for establishing a new order in the wake of Japanese invasion.

Such multiplicity makes the lower Yangtze delta and the surrounding region a fascinating case study for scholars examining the challenges and difficult choices that occupation posed, not only for ordinary Chinese people and elites, but the Nationalist state as well. In contrast to the northeast, where Manchukuo masqueraded as an independent nation in and of itself, and north China, which was only a region, albeit an important one, under the Republic of China, east China was home to the national capital of Nanjing. It was there that the Reorganized National Government (RNG), with its pretentions of representing the whole of China and its claims to Nationalist orthodoxy, eventually emerged.

Over the course of 1937 and 1938, in line with the Japanese advance, international safety zones for civilians sprang up in Shanghai, Nanjing, Hangzhou, Hankou, and other cities, all operating with varying degrees of success and varying degrees of responsibility in providing food, water, and shelter for the local population. After Japanese military forces swept up the Yangtze River, invasion gave way to occupation and a series of occupation states and statelets took shape, sponsored by the Japanese and staffed by local elites. These ranged from the strictly local and provisional, in the form of "Self-Governance" or "Order Maintenance" committees that were established in the immediate aftermath of the takeover, up to the grandly named Great Way Government of Shanghai (1937–38) and from there the Reformed Government of the Republic of China (1938–40). This in turn gave way to the Reorganized National Government (1940–45) of Wang Jingwei (1883–1944).

This rapid turnover at an administrative level was accompanied by a complex situation on the ground, where the rural-urban divide, uncertain political loyalties, and the continued tumult of the war complicate any straightforward narrative of the period. As Diana Lary has observed, and as the following pieces suggest, there was no "standard experience" of occupation that could be defined by geography alone.[1]

This section opens with an abridged translation from the work of the celebrated Republican-era humourist, Xu Zhuodai (1880–1958), by Christopher Rea. Xu's account of his wartime career selling soy sauce offers an important reminder that, quite apart from questions of ideology, collaboration, or propaganda, for many the wartime era was dominated by the struggle for survival and the search for life's more basic necessities. Lighthearted and told through humour, Xu's account of how he managed to "get by" through the war years redirects attention to questions of everyday life, and offers a reminder that it is possible to recount the history of occupation in multiple ways.

In the countryside, the full extent of Japanese occupation could ebb and flow, creating contested spaces and reoccupations that left ample opportunity to "settle the score" with those who served in deposed regimes. Such is the situation described by Weiting Guo in his analysis of the diary of Zhang Gang (1860–1942), a local educator in the hinterland of Zhejiang, who witnessed the turmoil brought on by multiple occupations and retreats among contending forces. In the course of capturing the confusion and disorder brought on by invasion, Zhang's diary also demonstrates how complex narratives run the risk of being simplified in the victor's recounting of occupation.

Adhering to a narrative of national resistance is a journalistic account by Fan Shiqin (n.d.), introduced by Jennifer Lau. Like Zhang, Fan's focus is on events in the countryside, in this case rural Anhui, at a time when the distance from front line to home front was perilously short. As Lau describes, Fan's reportage, intended for readers in the interior, was an effort to conjure the strength of China's soldiers and the spirit of civilians, one meant to inspire hope in the future and a sense of national unity amid national crisis.

Shifting to urban China, Naoko Kato turns our attention to Shanghai and the Uchiyama Bookstore, which played an important role in knowledge transmission and cultural life in the city, particularly during the lead-up to war. For Kato, the bookstore as salon, serving as a site of transnational cultural and intellectual exchange, is a reminder that the Japanese in China during the war, and the relationships that they forged as individuals with individual Chinese, was variegated and complex. Over the course of the war, however, public spaces for such exchanges shrank and were eventually snuffed out.

Above the shifting situation on the ground, Chinese intellectuals working further up in the occupation state hierarchy were tasked with the need to adopt new propaganda and articulate new ideological positions. As Timothy Brook has observed: "Managing needs and interests within the new order might well mean parroting the hyperboles of Japanese propaganda in order to get what one needed."[2] Applying this observation to the RNG and media more broadly, it is worth considering how Nanjing's propaganda represented the adoption of appropriate formulations beneath which other agendas might be more subtly deployed. The following pieces offer a starting point for considering these and related issues.

Torsten Weber introduces two early examples of such subterfuge by Fu Shiyue (1891–1947) and Lin Baisheng (1902–46), both of whom played important roles in the RNG. Fu puts forth an effort to position the Greater Asianism of Sun Yat-sen (1866–1925), and with it China itself, at the heart of the proposed "New Order in East Asia," while Lin emphasizes Sun as a means of explaining Chinese involvement in Japan's East Asian League. Common to both texts, as Weber points out, is the sense of ambiguity and the challenge of interpretation, particularly around whether to view their writings as propaganda for domestic audiences or as an attempt, directed at Japan, to find space for Chinese autonomy within a Japanese order by adopting the rhetoric of the occupier.

Other elements of RNG propaganda drew much more heavily on existing Nationalist Party doctrine and political campaigns. Craig Smith reflects on the RNG's signature political campaigns and efforts to promote a "Wang Jingwei-ism" ideology, which turned out to be very much in line with the Nationalists' New Life Movement of the 1930s, incorporating elements from Confucianism, Sun Yat-sen's Three Principles of the People and, somewhat less directly, the Japanese-led East Asian League. In other instances, as Smith shows, the ideological work of collaboration involved less the importation of Japanese influences in the form of the League, and more a judicious re-emphasis of neglected aspects of the prewar Nationalist creed. For this, Smith considers the case of Yang Honglie, an intellectual who, unlike Lin Baisheng and Fu Shiyue, had no direct connection with Wang prior to joining his peace movement. Yang did, however, have a Japanese education and a long-standing intellectual interest in Asianism. Having joined the peace movement, he then began penning a series of speeches outlining his interpretation of Great Asianism and his vision for China in the East Asian new order.

Alongside the ambiguity of interpretation in these texts is the complex network of personal relationships in which they were produced. As in many other contexts, the political agendas and loyalties of those who staffed the occupation states cannot be assumed. Personalized factional groupings were one feature of the RNG, as was the presence of individuals of varying ideological stripes along the Chinese political spectrum, some of whom held important public positions but were in fact working as operatives for the Communist Party or the Nationalist Party.[3] While the writings above point toward the ideological refashioning that took place under occupation, the following are particularly striking, not only for their content, but the careers and positions of those who wrote them.

First among them is Zhou Fohai (1897–1948), whose career began in the Communist Party and continued in the orbit of Chiang Kai-shek (1887–1975) and the Nationalists, before finally reaching its highest point as a paramount figure among those who followed Wang Jingwei in advocating peace.[4] Brian Martin's translation of an extract from Zhou's diaries not only highlights the breadth of Zhou's social network within the many factions of the Nationalist Party, but also offers an insider's look at the personal relationships between various figures, the formation of the RNG in its early stages, and the personality of Wang Jingwei.

By comparison, the subject of the next submission, Kiang Kang-hu (1883–1954), founder of the Chinese Socialist Party (established in 1911) and an early advocate for women's education, stood at a remove from the leading figures of the RNG, and offered a voice of dissent from within the occupied territory. His essay, published in 1941 and translated by Jonathan

Henshaw, critiques the RNG's failure to deal with the problem of starvation, and reflects Kiang's disillusionment with the RNG and its collaboration with Japan.

These writings are followed by works from two authors whose private affiliations lend ambiguity to their public writings. The first is an exploration of youth, capitalism, and the "woman question" written by underground Communist agent Guan Lu (1907–82) and translated by Norman Smith. Guan's work is of interest not only for her complicated pre- and postwar biography, but also as a platform for considering cultural production under occupation, the role of personal relationships between "occupier" and "occupied," and the space available for critique and discussions of gender under the RNG.

Yuan Shu (1911–87) was another Communist Party spy operating within the RNG. Yuan's essay on constitutionalism, translated by Matthew Galway, offers a critique of Euro-American imperialism, with reference to the Three Principles of the People and Marxist class categories, which reviews the causes of China's semicolonial predicament and outlines a way forward – through constitutional development. Despite his public position and invocation of RNG talking points on imperialism and the need for constitutionalism, Yuan's arguments and use of Marxist class categories would have likely caused some consternation to a careful Japanese reader.

Taken together, the documents translated in this section point to the complex geographic, intellectual, and personal dynamics at work over the course of the occupation of east China. Geographically, the continued resistance from Nationalist-held Chongqing and Communist-held Yan'an meant that Japanese control was contested, which contributed to the continued shuffling of occupation states, one replacing another, as the war unfolded. Intellectually, Japanese failure to put forward an ideology with local appeal left Chinese writers, thinkers, and politicians to raid the storehouse of recent Chinese political thought, resulting in a propaganda landscape of reworked messaging subject to multiple interpretations. Finally, the occupation states themselves were staffed by individuals whose allegiance was not always assured, including reluctant, wavering converts to the Japanese cause and underground agents whose political loyalties lay elsewhere. This is not to say that the translations included here are representative of all places, all propaganda, or all individuals. Instead, they draw out the full range of activity that took place under occupation and offer a platform for considering what occupation in east China meant for those who sought to live through it.

Notes

1 Diana Lary, "Introduction: The Context of War," in *China at War: Regions of China, 1937–1945,* ed. Stephen R. MacKinnon, Diana Lary, and Ezra F. Vogel (Stanford, CA: Stanford University Press, 2007), 7.

2 Timothy Brook, *Collaboration: Japanese Agents and Local Elites in Wartime China* (Cambridge, MA: Harvard University Press, 2005), 8–9.

3 Other high-profile Communist Party agents within the RNG include Li Shiyu in the Shanghai mayor's office and Zhang Ke in the Propaganda Ministry. Nationalist Party agents included Tang Shengming and Li Wenzhai in Nanjing.

4 For Zhou Fohai's ties with Chongqing, see Brian G. Marin, "Collaboration within Collaboration: Zhou Fohai's Relations with the Chongqing Government, 1942–1945," *Twentieth-Century China* 34, 2 (2009): 55–88.

10 Xu Zhuodai, "Remarkable Soy Sauce!"

CHRISTOPHER REA

Xu Zhuodai (born Xu Fulin, 1880–1958) was one of Republican Shanghai's most famous comic writers.[1] His stories, essays, plays, jokes, translations, and advice columns appeared in over three dozen periodicals. In a literary career spanning five decades he also authored two dozen books and edited a variety of fiction and general-interest magazines. Xu was a cultural entrepreneur who, in addition to his literary activities, founded and ran gymnastics academies, theatre troupes, and film companies, acted in plays and movies, recorded phonograph records, hosted radio shows, and wrote everything from advertising copy for amusement halls to memoirs of the modern drama scene to textbooks on sports physiology, martial arts, and film-making technique. Xu was one of those self-made men who embraced all that modern city life had to offer. He relied on this considerable resourcefulness to make a living in Shanghai during the Japanese occupation.

In 1946, the Shanghai tabloid *Jipu* (Jeep) put Xu Zhuodai second on their list of the "108 Leaders of Shanghai Literature." Next to a caricature of Xu, a caption dubbed him "Dr. Do-It-All, a Man of Innumerable Clever Tricks," and also hailed him as a "tycoon of the tofu industry and modern Dongfang Shuo," alluding to a celebrated wit of the Han dynasty.[2] The profile is proof that Xu's celebrity as a comedian extended across the eight-year Anti-Japanese War, which he was perhaps uniquely positioned to survive.

For one thing, he spoke fluent Japanese. In the 1900s, Xu had studied in Japan, but whereas many contemporaries studied medicine or engineering, he chose physical education. By the 1940s, he had decades of experience translating works from Japanese as varied as *Zhongxue yuedian jiaokeshu* (Middle schools foreign musical course, 1914),

Xuexiao jubenji (Stage plays for the classroom, preface dated 1924), and a popular textbook on Japanese martial arts (1917; 8th ed., 1935) based on the curriculum of the Kodokan Judo Institute. During the war, Xu remained in Shanghai and continued to write and translate for magazines such as *Wan hsiang* (Wanxiang) and *Dazhong* (The masses). Between 1943 and 1945, he translated at least nine stories from Japanese for *Dazhong,* including works by Tsutsumi Chiyo (1917–55), Kimura Ki (1894–1979), Yokomizo Seishi (1902–81), and four works by Kikuchi Hiroshi (1888–1948), who was an ardent supporter of the Japanese war effort.

Xu's versatility and productiveness as a writer was another asset during the war. He kept people informed and entertained. In its early years, he published a how-to book, *Cinematography* (*Dianying sheyingfa,* 1938) and two editions of *Xiaohua xiao hua* (Jokes with cartoons, 1937; 2nd ed., 1938). (He'd earlier published thousands of jokes and another book on film-making, and in the 1920s ran two film companies.) In the 1930s, Xu wrote an advice column under the pen name Dr. Li Ah Mao (Li Amao boshi), and he later developed Li Ah Mao into a trickster-detective figure who provides advice to his downtrodden friends and the general public. Xu wrote screenplays for several film comedies based on the character (no longer extant), including *Li Amao yu Tang xiaojie* (Li Ah Mao and Miss Tang, 1939) and *Li Amao yu jiangshi* (Li Ah Mao and the zombie, 1940).

When the Pacific War broke out, Xu was in the middle of serializing the twelve-part series *Li Amao waizhuan* (The unofficial story of Li Ah Mao, July 1941–June 1942) in *Wan hsiang.* In several stories, Ah Mao helps his unemployed friends make money by duping gullible urbanites with scams advertised in the newspaper. In one, he solves the case of a stolen pearl necklace just by having a friend read him a news report. In another, he stimulates demand for the book *Socializing Techniques for Men and Women* by penning fake reviews labelling it pornographic. Military conflict is never mentioned, but several stories allude to a general climate of economic hardship and food scarcity that encourages scheming for survival.

The most topical story in the series is the eleventh, "Riyu xuexiao" (Japanese school). Ah Mao's friend Ah Yang spends his entire salary on rice and has no money left over for rent, clothes, or transportation expenses. Ah Mao's solution is to open a Japanese-language school (having just read *Japanese in One Day*) and recruit students by advertising free tuition. Instead, he charges each student one bag of rice, and then spends an entire month teaching them one word, *kome* (rice). Month two he charges them four catties of cooking oil and, in exchange, teaches them the word *abura* (oil). When students complain about the slow pace of the lessons, he points out that they're getting what they paid for, and furthermore that he's been forced to eat raw (and then oily raw) rice. The third month's tuition and lesson is to involve charcoal briquettes, but "yesterday I took one to ask a Japanese person what they were called but he didn't know either." Ah Mao closes down his home school and replaces the sign on his door with the notice *Seeking charcoal briquettes. Will trade rice or cooking oil.*

This concern with the basic necessities reappears in Xu's other writings of the Japanese occupation period. The same magazines that carried his fiction and plays also published his home economics advice pieces, such as "Shengmi chifan fa" (How to make your rice last) and "Baojian shiliao" (Healthful foods), which contained tips on home economics and nutrition. The latter included a table listing foods high in protein, vitamins, and carbohydrates.[3]

Yet even with such language skills, literary talent, industry connections, and common sense, Xu Zhuodai, by his own account, still had to branch out into other enterprises in order to make ends meet in occupied Shanghai. "Remarkable Soy Sauce!" (1947), about half of which is represented in this abridged translation, is something of an infomercial for a home business that Xu Zhuodai and his second wife, Hua Duancen, started in Shanghai during the Japanese occupation manufacturing "scientific" (*kexue*), or artificial, soy sauce. (Xu's first wife, Tang Jianwo, died in 1932 in the Japanese bombing of Shanghai's Zhabei district.) Xu jokes that "the second wives that men took in the interior during the War of Resistance were called 'wartime wives'; for the same reason, you could call me a 'wartime businessman.'" The phenomenon of wartime polygamy that Xu refers to was dramatized that same year in the two-part epic film *Yi jiang chunshui xiang dong liu* (Spring river flows east, 1947).

Since at least the 1910s, magazine writers routinely wrote autobiographical pieces and biographical sketches of their colleagues both to make copy and to boost their celebrity. In the 1920s, for example, Xu wrote an essay about why his two film companies failed.[4] Xu's wartime soy sauce business was apparently still a going concern in 1947, as he devotes much of his energy to building his "Good Wife Brand" and touting the quality of his product. His complaints about the machinations of cooks and servants demanding kickbacks for buying his product suggest that everyone in 1940s Shanghai was trying to make a little extra on the side. Also symptomatic of wartime pressures in Shanghai – in Xu's words, "an age when everyone is a businessman" – is the impulse to make one's own home economically productive, whether by renting out rooms (and subletting parts of rooms), or by operating a home business, scenarios depicted in films like *Huanxiang riji* (Diary of a homecoming, 1947) and *Wuya yu maque* (Crows and sparrows, 1949).

More particular to Xu Zhuodai's personality is the extroverted advice giving. Xu mentions a text within the text: a "Guide to Preventing Soy Sauce from Going Mouldy" that was popular with customers and competitors alike. Xu's essay illustrates what makes the writer-businessman different from the regular businessman: you don't just do business; you also sell the story of your business.

A sense of literary flair is evident too in the title (and refrain) of Xu's essay, which puns on the phrase "Too remarkable for words!" (*miao buke yan*): "words" (*yan*) sounds like "salt" (*yan*) and soy sauce is salty. Xu refers to himself several times as "Maiyou lang," one of his many jocular pen names. Oil and soy sauce are both *you* in Chinese, so "Maiyou lang" alludes both to Xu's occupation as a soy sauce seller and to the Oil-Peddler, a figure appearing in literature and drama of the imperial period, who saved up his meagre earnings so that he could spend one night with a famous prostitute.[5] While struggling to fill our bellies, why not have a little fun too?

TRANSLATION

Remarkable Soy Sauce![6]

XU ZHUODAI

How, you ask, did I become the Soy Sauce Seller? I used to make soy sauce purely for my own consumption. I made it myself and ate it myself. It was so delicious – so much better than anything on the market – that I let a few friends and family members have a taste. They were all full of praise (were they just being polite?) and I was delighted. The more people praised it, the happier I felt and the more I gave away. But prices kept creeping up, and my costs were increasing by the day. I just couldn't give it away anymore, so I copied the technique of calligraphers who curtail sponging from friends and family by setting a fee to "moisten the brush," and started out-and-out selling my soy sauce to recoup my costs.

During the War of Resistance I originally made my living with my pen, but I really couldn't continue to support myself by writing alone. In an age when everyone is a businessman, the only thing for me to do was to take a stab at business myself. Having nothing else to sell, I sold the soy sauce I made, and began this irretrievably vulgar life as the Soy Sauce Seller. The second wives that men took in the interior during the War of Resistance were called "wartime wives"; for the same reason, you could call me a "wartime businessman."

A greenhorn who takes up a certain line of business is bound to make a regular fool of himself. That's even more the case in this business (if you could call it that) of mine. I wasn't speculating in securities or stocks, where all you have to do is chomp down on your cigar and make a few phone calls. Nor was I underwriting a major business someone else would be running for me, where I could just kick back as the big boss. In my trade, I was both worker and owner, producer and seller. Boss, assistant, technician, worker, salesman, everything – it was all me. My operation really couldn't have been any smaller; it was such a tiny organization that if it were any smaller no one would probably even notice it. But the product that came out of this teeny-tiny outfit of mine tasted so delicious to me that I couldn't help dancing a jig. As far as I was concerned, it beat every product on the market. Size didn't matter to me; so long as the product was good, I was happy.

[...]

The fourth of the four methods for producing soy sauce is called the "scientific method" and involves a completely different approach from the three fermentation-based methods. With this method you don't create a fermented paste and then extract soy sauce; instead, you produce a seasoning powder, and turn the powder into soy sauce by adding water. It's the most time-efficient process, requiring only four or five days.

[...]

Ninety-nine percent of soy sauce consumers, however, are not experts, and your average person has a hard time telling good soy sauce from bad. Pour a cup of water into a litre of soy sauce and it's still soy sauce – few people can tell that it's been diluted. Soy sauce is an unregulated product, so on the market you'll find people making a buck with bogus soy sauce made with the dregs of seasonings, or with salt water. Some shops will even pass off coloured salt water as soy sauce, and no one detects the fraud. Remarkable soy sauce indeed!

Your average person judges the quality of soy sauce solely by price. If the price is high, they think the product must be good. Instead of judging the flavour with their mouth, they hear the price with their ears and determine the quality based on that. This puts me at a disadvantage. I come to this business as an outsider, and my goal is to sell superior goods at an affordable price, so my constant priority is product quality. No matter how expensive the ingredients are, I never cut corners, while always keeping my price slightly below the competition. In this period of fluctuating commodity prices, my prices track the ups and downs of the market, and yet there are some people who hear my price and remark: "With a price as low as that, it must be inferior goods." What an injustice! When customers hear the price but don't taste the flavour, I lose out.

Be that as it may, though I've had many long-time customers mysteriously stop buying my soy sauce all of a sudden, after two or three months they inevitably come back. This is because they've tasted the competition's soy sauce, compared it to mine, and discovered that mine tastes better and is cheaper to boot. So these old customers end up returning as new customers.

At the start, I sold my soy sauce to others cheaply out of the goodness of my heart. But later I experienced two types of invisible losses: First, when I set my price low, people would buy a lot with the intention of hoarding it. But people stockpiling eight or ten crocks of soy sauce obviously won't be able to finish it all, and as soon as the weather warms up, the soy sauce starts going mouldy. The customer invariably blames the quality of my soy sauce, never allowing the possibility that the mould grew because the soy sauce was stored for too long, or that it might have had something to do with the muggy weather. Second, customers buying a lot of soy sauce in one go rarely have their own containers to store it in, so they insist on borrowing my crocks. To them, the loan is a trifle, but for me it's a huge pain in the neck. Over the course of one month, I might use a single crock to sell thirty jars of soy sauce. If I lend it out for a month I'm losing thirty orders, so I have to go and buy another crock. If one hundred customers each borrow a crock, that's one hundred crocks, and I have to shell out a fortune. No small matter.

Furthermore, when I, out of the goodness of my heart, lend a customer a crock, that crock is always like the proverbial yellow crane – "once gone, never to return." Soy Sauce Seller suffers a humongous loss if he isn't careful. A couple weeks or a month later when I send someone to retrieve the crock, he might have to make as many as five or six trips. Other crocks end up broken or missing. The maidservant might sell it to the second-hand goods man, and the customer then claims that he never borrowed one in the first place. My losses mount, since the profit I made from selling one crock's worth of soy sauce is less than the price of the crock itself. So lending out crocks is a real pain in the neck for Soy Sauce Seller.

But that isn't Soy Sauce Seller's only sorrow! Should a cook or a housekeeper take enemy action against him, his business in that household is kaput. Imagine, say, that the head of a household is a friend of mine, or the friend of a friend. He decides to buy soy sauce from me, but his cook or housekeeper is one of those people who tries to make a little on the side. The latter will object to buying from me, because if they buy from one of the nearby shops instead, they can get a kickback. But if the vendor is a friend of the Master or was introduced by the Master's friend, there's no kickback to be had. And it goes without saying that if I'm the one standing between them and their kickback. I'm the enemy, and they take enemy action. Their simplest method of revenge is to pour out a certain portion of the soy sauce and then to weigh it out in front of the Master, claiming that they're being shortchanged and should switch to a different vendor. Just like that, their revenge is complete.

I remember a certain household on Anfu Road that someone or other had recommended as a customer. Three days after they bought my soy sauce, I suddenly received a letter from the household saying that the soy sauce was bad and that I should send someone to exchange it. I immediately sent someone over with a new crock and brought the original one back, but as soon as I opened the container my nose was hit by a foul stench that smelled like some sort of mineral oil. How on earth could I be responsible for something like this? So I took that crock of soy sauce myself and sought out the head of household. No sooner had I stepped through the door and explained my purpose, however, then the cook came out and said: "This concerns me. It has nothing to do with the Master. If you have something to say, say it to me." His attitude was high-handed and intimidating, and he refused to let me see his Master, even physically blocking me from going upstairs. I'd pretty much figured out the score, so I told him:

> Bad soy sauce warrants an exchange, but this crock smells like kerosene. It would be impossible for me – or any soy sauce maker – to produce something

> like this. I'm positive this isn't my original product, so I'm unwilling to exchange it. I'll be taking back the crock of soy sauce that was delivered just now, and if you really believe that this soy sauce is bad because of me, you can take me and the product to the police station.

My goal at the time was to cancel the exchange, and I thought he'd be unwilling to agree, but it turned out he had nothing to say, and so I held on to the kerosene soy sauce and returned home with that and the replacement crock. I was well aware that the cook had sabotaged me in retaliation for losing his kickback, but since there was no chance of doing business there again anyway, why should I suffer the loss of yet another crock of soy sauce? The unfortunate thing is that the master of the house continued to be hoodwinked by his cook and never discovered the mischief. I expect that the cook wasn't doing this just with soy sauce either, and that the head of household was losing vast sums on his account. Sticking to the principle of selling authentic goods at a reasonable price, I would rather not do business than make an exception and pay kickbacks. Soy sauce shops that give kickbacks to cooks and serving girls are fleecing their customers; they may not be providing an inferior product, but they're shorting on quantity, even if the shop itself suffers no loss. Such an arrangement between cooks or housekeepers and small businesses may be common, but I'm completely opposed to it. A cook buying on a budget, however, is always delighted to buy my soy sauce because it's such a good deal.

[...]

Does adding preservatives guarantee that soy sauce won't grow mould? Preservatives do discourage mould but don't prevent it. How the consumer stores it is also a factor. One household I know would keep their soy sauce in the kitchen where it was extremely hot and humid, and it developed mould due to improper storage. Another family kept theirs in a storeroom and hung a ham above the open container. The ham had gone mouldy, and the mould travelled through the air into the soy sauce, making it go mouldy too. Then there's the maidservant who ladled soy sauce out from the container every day and who accidentally introduced unboiled water into the container, which of course made the soy sauce go mouldy. Yet another household hoarded an immense quantity of soy sauce, which, if kept too long in hot weather, naturally goes mouldy. In each case, it's the environment and not the soy sauce itself that's creating the mould. That's why I say that use of preservatives can only discourage mould, since storage conditions are also important. When soy sauce has preservatives in it and storage conditions are good, it'll never go mouldy.

[…]

The foolproof way to prevent soy sauce from going mouldy is to transfer the soy sauce from the crock it came in into a bottle and seal it tightly with the cork for the months between early summer and early fall. This will prevent mould. An even more advanced method is to drip one drop of sesame oil into the soy sauce, which will prevent mould from growing.

The rich flavour of soy sauce comes entirely from protein. The more protein it has, the greater its richness. My soy sauce's flavour is superior to other people's because it contains more protein. On that score, let me share a couple of secrets: the Japanese tonic Polytamin will make you fat if you eat too much of it because it's made completely of protein. Its ingredients and production method are identical to that of artificial soy sauce; you could say it's just essence of soy sauce without the salty taste. The product they sold ten years ago had a good, rich flavour, but you can't taste it in what they're making nowadays. Put another way, they're basically selling essence of soy sauce as medicine, but at a tremendous premium. I call my soy sauce "nourishing" because its protein is so abundant that it could be used as a substitute for tonic. Here's another secret: some of the beef broth on the market these days has essence of soy sauce secretly added to it. It's got a great rich flavour and is extremely nourishing. Beef broth and essence of soy sauce are similar in that both contain protein – the sole difference is that one comes from animals and the other from plants.

[…]

The most important person in the household when it comes to soy sauce is the lady of the house. If she's not attentive or takes only a cursory interest in domestic affairs, then her cook and housekeeper will have the run of the kitchen. In such circumstances, all the ingredients that go into what the family eats and drinks, including soy sauce and the like, can be manipulated by the housekeeper and cook as they see fit. They'll report inflated prices and take kickbacks, such that the family ends up shortchanged and the quality of their food declines. They'll pay big bucks to eat poorly. If, however, the lady of the house is well educated or has a good mind for running a household, no cook or housekeeper will ever undermine her authority when it comes to the running of the kitchen. So long as she inspects all the food purchases personally, quality is assured, and the whole family will be able to eat three delicious meals every day for a reasonable expenditure. My soy sauce customers are probably this type of housewife. Those who don't have much of a personal hand in domestic affairs are unlikely to buy my soy sauce, and I don't welcome their business. They're blind to quality and are not my true target customers. That's why I call my brand of soy sauce "Good Wife Brand" – it's for the superior housewife.

The Chinese attitude toward prepared foodstuffs could be called: "It's all good, so long as you don't see what goes into it." What you put in your mouth might taste delicious, but if you were to see how it's really made it would turn your stomach. Nine times out of ten, it's unbearably filthy. That's why I don't delegate any soy sauce making to other people. I do the whole thing myself, so as to keep everything clean. The reason is that my family eats what we make. My constant worry nowadays is: "If one day I were to quit the soy sauce business, where would I buy reliably delicious soy sauce?" Nobody else's could be as clean as ours.

Moreover, soy sauce is typically made with unboiled water. When cooked with food, there's no problem of course, but it's unhygienic to eat raw as a condiment. My soy sauce, in contrast, is precooked. I pasteurize it by bringing it to a boil, so it can be eaten raw with no problems. What with fuel being so expensive these days, who but me is willing to do this work that the consumer never sees?

"Remarkable soy sauce!" Soy sauce is a remarkable thing indeed. Businessmen tend to be experts in their products. Soy sauce is the sole exception – a trade in which all the people involved are laymen. Should you run into someone who makes or sells soy sauce, just query him about a few basic principles or facts related to soy sauce and he'll always be unable to respond. Remarkable, wouldn't you say? As for the big players that have not a single technician and rely entirely on the recipe of some venerable chef, just ask them how an age-old soy sauce recipe might be improved. Last summer, I printed a small booklet called "A Guide to Preventing Soy Sauce from Going Mouldy," and advertised it in the newspaper as a freebie for housewives, intending to teach them a few basic facts. I received quite a few letters, but to my surprise over half of them were actually from not housewives but fermenters at soy sauce factories as far away as Henan province. The people in need of this advice turned out to be my colleagues in the business. So, you see, most people involved in the soy sauce trade are not experts at all. Remarkable as soy sauce, wouldn't you say?

Notes

1 Not to be confused with the Republican politician Xu Fulin (1879–1958). On Xu Zhuodai's life and works, see Christopher Rea, *The Age of Irreverence: A New History of Laughter in China* (Oakland, CA: University of California Press, 2015), ch. 5. Translations of several of Xu Zhuodai's stories and plays, including *The Unofficial Story of Li Ah Mao,* mentioned below, appear in Christopher Rea, ed., *China's Chaplin: Comic Stories and Farces by Xu Zhuodai* (Ithaca, NY: Cornell East Asia Program, 2019).

2 Shi Nan'an (text), Dong Tianye (illustration), "Doufuye juzi, jindai Dongfang Shuo Xu Zhuodai" [A tycoon of the tofu industry and modern Dongfang Shuo: Xu Zhuodai], #2 in series "Haipai wentan yibailingba jiang" [108 leaders of Shanghai literature], *Jipu* [Jeep] 15 (1946): 5.

3 Xu Fulin, "Shengmi chifan fa" [How to make your rice last], *Dazhong* [The masses], 1 December 1944, 115–16; Xu Fulin, "Baojian shiliao" [Healthful foods], *Dazhong,* 1 January 1945, 113.

4 Xu Zhuodai, "Wo ban yingxi gongsi shibai tan" [On my failed film companies], *Mingxing yuebao* [Star monthly] 2 (1928): n.p.

5 For one Ming dynasty version of the Oil-Peddler's story, see: "The Oil-Peddler Wins the Queen of Flowers" [Maiyou lang duzhan huakui], in *Stories to Awaken the World: A Ming Dynasty Collection,* vol. 3., ed. Feng Menglong, trans. Shuhui Yang and Yunqin Yang (Seattle: University of Washington Press, 2014), 38–77.

6 Xu Zhuodai, "Miao buke jiangyou" [Remarkable soy sauce], *Chahua* (Tea talk) 18 (10 November 1947): 40–48.

11 The Diary of Zhang Gang

An Excerpt

WEITING GUO

During the Second Sino-Japanese War (1937–45), Japanese troops occupied Wenzhou, Zhejiang, three times.[1] Although brief, these occupations devastated Wenzhou's infrastructure and disrupted the local order and economy. In 1941, the Japanese army occupied Wenzhou and destroyed the goods transportation network of this port city over fourteen days. Prior to this, Wenzhou had never experienced Japanese occupation, as many other coastal cities already had. The quick takeover not only disturbed local order, but also sent a warning signal to the Nationalist government. A year later, after the United States bombarded several Japanese cities, Japan fought back by occupying Wenzhou and destroying the main airbases in southern Zhejiang. This time, the Japanese army occupied Wenzhou for over a month. Yet it encountered fierce resistance as the Nationalist army fought to retake this strategic port. The third occupation took place from September 1944 to June 1945. Fearing that the Allies would take the southeast coast as a strategic base, the Japanese army took Wenzhou and constructed military fortifications.[2] Frequent occupations reflected how the Japanese military approached the battles and handled the changing circumstances. To survive Japan's attacks and atrocities, Wenzhou people and government officials also created strategies for managing their daily lives and navigating the competing military groups and political factions that operated in their region.

Facing east to the sea, Wenzhou had long served as a hub for goods transportation and as an important fishing port.[3] Despite the rugged terrain that separated this area from the prosperous Jiangnan region, Wenzhou had frequent contact with neighbouring Fujian province, and had a rich history of maritime trade and smuggling with the surrounding regions.[4] After 1876, when Wenzhou became a new treaty port open to foreign countries, it became a major trade centre on China's southeast coast. During the early twentieth century, Wenzhou continued to develop its foreign trade and had increased sea routes for both import and export.[5] Primarily due to its geographical location and its distinctive role in coastal trade, Wenzhou became a target of Japanese occupation, particularly when the Japanese army adjusted its plans against the Nationalists and the Allies.

Zhang Gang, who spent his entire life in Wenzhou's Tingtian village,[6] witnessed the first occupation in 1941 and observed the rivalries between the Nationalist authorities, Japanese armies, and local elites. Born to a lower gentry family in 1860, Zhang Gang obtained the *shengyuan* (licentiate) degree and was noted for his prose and poetry.[7] He played a positive role in literati circles and opened his own school in 1887.[8] He was also active in the introduction of new ideas and made great efforts in introducing new books from Shanghai to local academies (*shuyuan*). Throughout his life, he actively engaged in literature, education, communal activities, and the practice of village mediation.[9] More importantly, Zhang Gang's rich experiences with local affairs became an asset in his remarkable account of local history. For over fifty years, from 1888 to his death in 1942, Zhang Gang recorded almost every development of his life and local community in his diary.[10]

Due to its remarkable record of daily life in a Chinese village, Zhang Gang's diary reveals how local people acted, perceived, and responded to the Japanese occupation. It reflects the complex layers of occupation experiences, including how local officials fled, causing havoc, and then shamelessly returned to present themselves as heroes. Through his daily observations, Zhang depicts how government officials persecuted those who negotiated and collaborated with the Japanese after the occupation, and how opponents of these collaborators joined the persecution and exacerbated political struggles. He also describes how local elites offered food and supplies to Japanese troops in exchange for security, and how bandits and government officials disturbed local communities during and after the occupation. For example, Zhang records the entire existence – from its formation to its termination – of the Committee for Maintaining Order (*Weichihui*), a Japanese-sponsored organization that invited locals to participate in various public affairs, and the consequent political struggles within local society. He also describes the interesting case of Ye Fuquan, a Wenzhou native who worked as a woodworker in Taiwan, then a Japanese colony.[11] After the Japanese occupied Wenzhou, Ye returned to his hometown and served as an interpreter in the Japanese army. Just before Japanese troops departed from Wenzhou, he leaked some key clues to the locals that enabled Zhang Gang and other elites to predict the departure of the Japanese soldiers before they left. Moreover, throughout his diary, Zhang Gang chronicles how he maintained his life, gathered information, encountered the Japanese army for the first time, contacted friends and relatives, helped relatives escape from war-ravaged areas, and heard how his relatives bribed Japanese soldiers to avoid being executed. This diary provides a first-hand window into life and local politics under Japanese occupation in a key centre for trade along China's southeast coast.[12]

Zhang Gang entitled his diary *Duyinyuan riji* (Duyinyuan diary), following his literary name, the Old Man at Duyinyuan. The original manuscript of this diary is stored in the Rare Book Department of the Wenzhou Municipal Library.[13] An excerpted version was published by Shanghai Social Sciences Press in 2003, including about one-fourth of the original manuscript.[14] Below is a translation of selections from this excerpted version.

TRANSLATION

Diary of Zhang Gang

1 March (4 February on the lunar calendar) 1941

At six o'clock, just as I woke up, I heard the roar of aircraft overhead. Again, seven airplanes appeared in the sky. They flew from east to north, and then intensively bombarded Yongjia area [Yongjun, a.k.a. Yongjia]. Now it's still unknown which place was damaged. In the afternoon, Tongqing[15] came and told me that [the Japanese army] dropped bombs in Changqiao salt field and raked Tangxia with machine-gun fire. One was reported killed by gunfire in Tangxia. Places around Yongjia area, such as Nantang, Baixiang, and the county's East Gate, South Gate, and Xiguo (close to the West Gate), were each hit by around fifty or sixty bombs. There were over a hundred casualties from the bombing. Rumour has it that four out of six people in a family were killed in the bombing. One may well say that it's extremely tragic.

4 March (7 February on the lunar calendar)
I have read the *Wenzhou News* (*Wenzhou bao*) from the past two days. It said that the crazed bombing by the Japanese dwarves' planes (*woji*) led to damages to gates and buildings and high casualties in Yongjia. Since the members of the Patrol and Protection Corps (*Xunhudui*), Xue Yinkui and Lin Liansheng, lost their entire families during the bombing, people in the county raised around 300 [national] dollars in compensation (*fuxujin*) to help these two soldiers get by. Fortunately, there has been no [air-raid] alarm today.

5 March (8 February on the lunar calendar)
Today, the noise of airplanes in the sky came once again. Some observers said the first batch had five airplanes, the second seven, and the third ten. In total, there were twenty-two airplanes. They all flew from north to south. Fortunately, they didn't drop any bombs.

15 March (18 February on the lunar calendar)
Today, I sold out my stored shredded potato (*shusi*). For 100 *jin*, the sale price is 14 *yuan*. I sold about 825 *jin*, so I got 140 *yuan* and 1 *jiao* in national dollars. Recently, 100 *jin* of good, clean, and white shredded potato cost 26 to 27 *yuan* in *xiaoyang* (*yang* or *xiaoyang;* "small foreign-style money"). One hundred *jin* of shelled rice would cost 40 *yuan* in *dayang* ("large foreign-style money"). For table salt, the price is 1 *yuan* for 4 *liang.* A handful of good firewood would cost 6 *yang* or 7 *jiao.* When daily necessities become so extraordinarily expensive, what could anyone with a household do?

27 March (30 February on the lunar calendar)
Tongqing came and told me that two of the enemy's small motorboats entered the Feiyun River in Rui'an yesterday.[16] They realized that there is military defence in the area, so they left right away. The county government then warned people to evacuate. Many people in the county capital were so panicked that they were eager to run away. My third daughter-in-law also fled to the village from the county capital.

4 April 4 (8 March on the lunar calendar)
Today, the fifth *fang* branch of the family (*fang*) was dividing its sacrificial meat offerings (*fenzuo*). Tongqing is on duty for doing this for this year. It cost around 300 *yuan* in national dollars. Now the price of meat is a dollar for only 14 *liang.* The price of rice is a dollar for only 11 *liang.* For shredded

potato, a dollar only gets you 1 *jin* of the good-quality stuff, or only 2 *jin* of the average stuff. Prices are skyrocketing. For thousands of years, this has never happened.

15 April (19 March on the lunar calendar)
I went to [my cousin] Haoqing's[17] house, and talked to his wife's uncle, Chen Apu, for a bit. Now, the price for shelled rice is 1 *yuan* for only 4 *jin* in market scale. For firewood, 1 *yuan* can only buy three armfuls. For taxpaying with new grain, 1 *mu* of land is now exchangeable for 25 *jin* of grain, which is equivalent to around 6 *yuan* in *dayang*. Compared to the previous price of grain, the current rate has increased seventy to eighty times. Ordinary people like us who have some business and properties all complained about this in great pain. Poor people who have nowhere to turn find it impossible to survive in times like this. The world has gone mad such as it has never gone before!

17 April (21 March on the lunar calendar)
It is said that over ten airplanes came to Yongjia one after another yesterday, hovering over the area and bombarding it. The Ouhai hospital, which is close to the end of Fuxue Lane, was also bombarded. The Xiguowai area also reported causalities, and six people were reported dead.

In the afternoon, I heard that Xia A'dong's son, Zhesheng, was fatally shot by the dwarf pirates (*haikou*) while working on the sea for his fishing business.

19 April (23 March on the lunar calendar)
This morning, before I got up, I heard the sound of the enemy bandits' planes up in the air. I can't imagine what they were spying on.

At eight o'clock, I saw several Japanese airplanes flying from north to south. They continuously bombed the area. All the people in Rui'an county fled. At this moment, Tang Leshui[18] and his third brother, along with his third brother's wife, sons, and daughters, fled to the house of my third son through the trails on Wansong Mountain. They were really agitated and could hardly sleep [in this situation]. Last night at ten o'clock, there were already hundreds of Japanese soldiers landing outside the South Gate of Rui'an county. People in the city all fled. As they fled, a mob formed, and some of the very young and old were trampled to death. Some fell into the riverways. All this misery – it is too much even to put into writing. The officers, clerks, and guardians of the county government office scattered like birds and beasts, and the government offices are now deserted. Some clerks fled with their female family members into the township office (*xiang gongsuo*) in our village. They only stayed temporarily and left after breakfast. In the afternoon, airplanes were almost constantly circling around in the skies. It didn't quiet down until nightfall. Now, Rui'an county has become an area under enemy occupation!

20 April (24 March on the lunar calendar)

Today, the enemy occupied the [Rui'an] county. Under the command of Japanese soldiers, various sorts of thugs entered the county to rob wealthy families who hoarded goods. Many rich families, such as those of Xiang Yinxuan,[19] Xiang Gengyu, Wang Kai, and Wang Chaoliu,[20] and many family-owned shops, such as those of Chen Zhipu, Cao Xuqing, Wang Yuda,[21] and Li Datong,[22] were robbed of everything. Also, countless families were separated, not knowing if their missing relatives are alive or dead. To date, [my cousin] Leisheng's[23] younger brother's eldest son Yucong and third daughter A'he, and, outside the East Gate, his fourth son's mother-in-law Woman Cai, wife's younger sister, and younger female cousin all went missing – their whereabouts still remain unknown. One may well say that it's extremely tragic.

Tonight, someone said that the Yongjia area had also been occupied by the enemy. It is still not certain if this news is true.

21 April (25 March on the lunar calendar)

This morning, I heard that Yongjia was occupied by the enemy and all the people there had fled. However, the ferry [to Yongjia] could not sail, the phone could not connect, the newspaper office could not open, and the transportation between north and south has been completely disconnected. [Under such circumstances,] the rumours spread here are really unreliable. Before dawn, Tang Yunting's[24] wife, along with her female servants, went to Rui'an to check on their belongings in their residence. At ten o'clock, over ten thousand *jin* of shredded potato, which was stored by the township office, was unexpectedly taken by the local people and distributed among themselves. The country is in turmoil, and the people are in panic. The government has no solutions [for this]. What is there that can be done about it? In the afternoon, I went by my nephew Zhang Zucheng's place, Wancha.[25] It is said that most wealthy families in Rui'an have been robbed of everything.

It is also said that Rui'an's Cai Pingzhou has been selected by the Japanese to serve as the county magistrate. It is not certain if this plan has been realized.

22 April (26 March on the lunar calendar)

My nephew, Gongying,[26] came to my place and talked about his life on the run in the past few days. On 23 March [on the lunar calendar], at ten o'clock in the evening, he heard the alarm at Zhongxin Elementary School[27] and fled through the North Gate with his fellow instructor, Shen Gongpu. [As they fled], they were menaced by aircraft overhead more than ten times. When this happened, they threw themselves down on the ground in the grass and the fields. Fortunately, they were not under direct fire. But the day was dawning. Later they asked the peasants in the mountains for directions and took the long route to flee to Dong Zhenliu's home in Xianju [a.k.a. Xianyan].[28] At that time, the county magistrate Lü Lü also brought a few soldiers as guards all the way there. [These officers] sat and asked for wine and meals. In the beginning, Gongying wanted to return home immediately. Yet because there were Japanese soldiers stationed at Tangxia, he did not dare to go down the hill, so he stayed at Gong's house for a night. Today, he was finally able to return home. He is quite fortunate.

23 April (27 March on the lunar calendar)

In the morning, it was said that the Committee for Maintaining Order's meeting on military rations (*Bingshi weichihui*) was going to be held in Rui'an. I then called my nephew, Xingtong [a.k.a. Zucheng], to come to Rui'an for drinks and snacks. He [came to my place and] stayed until late at night. When I went out this morning and asked around, I learned that the committee meeting was held, but the people who chaired the meeting were so hesitant that they did not dare to make any decisions. The committee then nominated Cai Pingzhou, Shen Gongzhe,[29] and He Luofu as the representatives to request the locals to prepare a food supply in order to prevent the Japanese soldiers from disturbing the community. Since Rui'an is full of Japanese soldiers, all its shops have been shut down and no goods are for sale. It has suddenly become a ghost town, and it is extremely gloomy and miserable. At midday, my nephew Xingtong asked someone to collect eggs from various families. He had Cai Yuanchu send the eggs to Jin'ao village[30] in order to supply them to the Japanese soldiers.

At one o'clock in the afternoon, I suddenly heard consecutive rounds of artillery from the lower part of Daishi Mountain. A few small motorboats crossed the river and the border. I also saw over ten Japanese soldiers who arrived in this area and went on an inspection tour. As I was sitting in the main room, I saw a Japanese soldier in uniform carrying a rifle enter our front entrance, have a glance around and then leave. At that time, an ignorant villager, Luansheng, fled in a panic.[31] Japanese troops immediately opened fire and gunned him down. The son of Pock-face Chang (*Chang Malian*) was among those who were shot and killed. This is indeed an unexpected tragedy.

Due to the occupation of Rui'an and the early escape of the local officials that led to the tragedy [of the city], I cannot stop my anger and could only compose a poem to express my painful memories:

Over a night, our military dropped their weapons
The entire city sang in chorus the Flight of Town Father Dong
(Dongtao ge) song.[32]

24 April (28 March on the lunar calendar)
It was said yesterday that Cai Yuanchu went to Jin'ao to pay respects to the Japanese army and ask for instructions. The Japanese, in their reply, asked every district to offer five hundred cows, five hundred pigs, and five hundred beauties. I really don't know if the local communities could afford such cruel extortion. But what is there to do about it?

At two o'clock in the afternoon, I was sitting in the west study room practising chess with the chess manual. My widowed daughter was cooking in the kitchen again. The house was empty, with no one else inside. All of a sudden, a Japanese soldier, carrying a sword, entered my room and searched every table, drawer, chest and wardrobe. Fortunately, he took only a scarf and left.

26 April (1 April on the lunar calendar)
In the morning, the newly arrived Japanese soldiers landed in Dongshan.[33] Several hundred soldiers came across the border. From there, they advanced to Meigang and Yongjia Chang. Some locals in the mountains had just woken up by this time, and were caught [by the Japanese soldiers] and forced to guide them along the road. This is because some guerrilla forces reportedly came to fight the enemy near Taiping Hill (*Taipingling*) in Yongjia.

Before noon, my clan brother in Huabiao, Zhang Mingdong,[34] accompanied ten Japanese soldiers to visit my nephew Xingtong's home. They intended to invite Xingtong to join their discussions. [But] at that time, Xingtong, the township chief Cai Yuanchu, and my son Feng [Yufeng] had gone to Zhiluo to visit his friends. [Zhang Mingdong and the Japanese soldiers] did not get a chance to meet Xingtong, so they left. In the afternoon, they gathered the village gentry and elders to discuss the matter [for the local community]. Then, they visited the Japanese troops that were stationed at the Baotan Temple (*Baotansi*) of Jin'ao.[35] They begged the soldiers not to expropriate the farm cattle so that the villagers could transplant dry seedlings and increase grain production. On the other hand, they also promised that they would supply vegetables [to the Japanese soldiers] and hoped that the soldiers would not disturb the community or frighten the women. Fortunately, this request was approved by the Japanese military. The Japanese army also granted the interpreter, the woodworker Ye Fuquan, a certificate for passage with six words on the side, "Cenqi Mountain Guard Reserve Unit" (*Cenqishan jingbei-dui*), sealed with a stamp reading [the Japanese surname] "Iguchi." After completing these discussions, all of them returned to the village.

28 April (3 April on the lunar calendar)

In the morning, Cai Yuanchu came to visit my son-in-law, Dai [Dai Tengqiu]. Then, these men from the Baotian village [Baotian] also admitted that they and the people from the surrounding five villages had supplied [food to] the Japanese military in order to prevent disturbances.

29 April (4 April on the lunar calendar)

Yesterday, I heard that Rui'an's wealthy families, such as Xiang Yinxuan's, Xiang Weichen's,[36] [Xiang] Weifu's,[37] and Lin Zizhen's families, and wealthy merchants, such as Li Datong, Wang Yuda, and Ren Jishan stores, were robbed of everything by ne'er-do-wells who followed in the steps of the Japanese soldiers. Also, numerous women were raped by the Japanese, and no one can tell how many such cases happened. In this chaotic world, all order is lost. [As ordinary people were so panicked to leave], our corrupt officials escaped first. Such unscrupulous officials deserve to die a thousand deaths. Even this harsh punishment could not compensate for the injustice that has been done to our people.

30 April (5 April on the lunar calendar)

I heard that yesterday, Ye Fuquan [Cai Fuquan] accompanied the Japanese soldiers to walk around Qianci.[38] [The Japanese soldiers] saw many peasants crowding around in order to see them, and then one soldier randomly shot [at the crowd] and killed someone. [Human] life in a chaotic time is really worse than that of chicken or a dog. How sad! Today, before noon, the Japanese came to inspect the area around Qianci. They saw a woman and robbed her. The woman's sixty-year-old father knelt down to beg to the Japanese, but to no avail, and he was then bayoneted to death.

2 May (7 April on the lunar calendar)

This morning, Tang Wenbo came to talk to me. He said that he had walked from the East Gate of the county to here. Since there were Japanese soldiers stationed at the Baihe bridge (*Baiheqiao*), he then turned to Longquan lane and the small lane of Zhouhu village around the hillside of Wansong Mountain, and that is how he eventually arrived here. Tang also said that the Japanese have broken and disconnected the Beimenwai bridge (*Beimenwaiqiao*) and the Yangjia bridge (*Yangjiaqiao*) in Rui'an. Barbed wire has been installed everywhere, outside every city, in order to corral people travelling on foot. Goods and silver found [by the Japanese] were all loaded onto Japanese ships and sent across the sea. I think [the Japanese] must have had the idea of abandoning the city and fleeing.[39]

Today, thousands of Japanese soldiers came from Yongjia to Rui'an. All of them went through the mountain roads on the west bank [of the Feiyun River]. In the sky, airplanes circled around in order to prevent any attack. Since the Japanese army encountered massive forces and strong resistance around the Kuozhou and Chuzhou areas, it cannot advance and attack [through this way]. Now that they have robbed over ten million dollars of property in Dong'ou [Wenzhou], they can return with fruitful results. So are they still fascinated with our tiny city that is as small as a ball? These Japanese planned their schemes so cleverly, while our Wenzhou merchants, who intended to hoard and profit, met with karma so quickly. Speaking of this, our two corrupt officials – Yongjia magistrate Zhang and Rui'an magistrate Lü – [have committed so many offences] that even cutting their bodies to pieces could not compensate for the injustice that they have done to our people.

It is also said that all of the Japanese soldiers are going to cross the sea tonight. They are going to burn down Baotan Temple.

4 May (9 April on the lunar calendar)

Today, since the [Japanese] bandits have retreated, my relatives and friends who took refuge at my home are returning to where they came from. At ten o'clock, Pan Zhimin came from Jiuli to visit me. During our chat, Zhimin vividly described what happened during the occupation. He was in deep sorrow regarding the suffering of his hometown. [This occupation] occurred mainly due to the ignorance of the former maritime defence commander, Huang Quan. Huang neglected the repair of cannons and batteries at the strategically important areas of Dongshan.[40] He did not make enough of an effort to strengthen our garrison, but rather blocked the bridges of the inner rivers by installing bamboo embankments. He also dug trenches at the major traffic ways. Such actions were a waste of money and made zero contribution to maritime defence. His guilt was so manifest that everyone reviled him. [On the other hand], Rui'an magistrate Lü Lü who, as an official, had the responsibility to live or die with the city together like a father over his people. But when the Japanese bandits entered Rui'an on 19 April, Lü Lü had already led his troops far away the day before. The entire city was left with no government, and the estuaries of the rivers had no soldiers standing guard. This facilitated the quick entry of the Japanese bandits into the city, and caused thousands of people to flee from the town in panic. Countless people drowned or got trampled to death on their way; powerful families and wealthy merchants were all stripped of their possessions; jails released their prisoners. Lü Lü fled from the wild mountains all the way to a township chief's home in Xianju [Xianyan]. This demonstrates that [he only cares about his own safety] and never sympathized with the lives of the people. Moreover, when he hid in the harbours and the countryside, he compelled people to make monetary contributions and pretended that these were all being collected for counterattacking the enemy. Now, after the enemy bandits have retreated, Lü still enjoys his leisure time without returning to the county. He has failed to discharge his duties and has caused nothing but hardships for the people. Even cutting his body into pieces could not expiate his guilt. After Rui'an was occupied, the Japanese army attacked Yongjia one day later. It quickly occupied Yongjia without the loss of even a soldier or an arrow. [At that time], the subregional prefect, Zhang Baochen [d. 1951], was still unaware of the presence of Japanese soldiers. It was not until he heard the sound of artillery that he hastened to the road and rushed away. Seeing the officials fleeing, the people also ran away in a rush. The enemy bandits took all the county valuables away. Even regulating these officials with the state's law and beheading them with the sharp sword of Huanshou (*Huanshou jian*)[41] would still leave a margin of their inexpiable guilt. As to the staff at the custom and salt offices, they followed the lead of superior officers and were unworthy of blame. Being here in his hometown, Pan Zhimin witnessed the tragedy and felt deeply sorrowful. If these three corrupt officials were not punished by law so that the government could choose another virtuous person to govern Wenzhou, how could people feel calm and rest assured in such an abyss of suffering? As a result, Pan Zhimin asked me to draft a telegram report on his behalf and file this report via telegram with the higher authorities. This man is really a good-hearted person. In the afternoon, upon the completion of the telegram report, Pan Zhimin departed.

5 May (10 April on the lunar calendar)

This afternoon, I heard that Yongjia and Rui'an's magistrates have returned to their posts. They have arrested many rioters who robbed the people [during the occupation]. At four o'clock, several soldiers dressed in plain clothes and carrying pistols suddenly came to my nephew Xingtong's house, Wancha. They took Xingtong to the county office, and stated that they acted under the secret warrant of the county. The entire village was frightened. The masses were all discussing this incident. I then went to talk to them, stating that when Japanese soldiers occupied the county, several Rui'an people who had studied in Japan – such as Shen Gongzhe – convened an emergency meeting to maintain local order. Xingtong was also called to attend the meeting, and every attendee signed their names [on the document]. No one expected that this fleeing official, after returning to Rui'an, instead of repenting for his sin, would unrestrictedly use authority and harsh policies to frame various gentry members as *Hanjian* and detaining them. As a result, my nephew Xingtong was also drawn into this persecution. Alas! What an injustice! I really wonder how Xingtong could settle down tonight after being arrested.

6 May (11 April on the lunar calendar)

At four o'clock this afternoon, after I took a boat from town to home, I heard that Pan [Zhimin] had begged the militia commander, Chen Hongliu, to ask the government for leniency, and that Xingtong had been brought from the detention centre to Chen Hongliu's home. It is said that after the county's interrogation, Xingtong could be released in two to three days.

18 May (23 April on the lunar calendar)

Yesterday, [Lin] Jian'an told me that the Rui'an magistrate, Lü, concealed his failure [during the occupation] and sought rewards for his merits. Using an extravagant approach to magnify his own achievements, Lü urged over seventy *bao* villages[42] in Rui'an to organize a lantern festival to celebrate the victory (*tideng shenghui*) recovery of Rui'an from the Japanese military and compelled each *bao* to contribute 10 *yang* dollars. How could the shamelessness of a person reach such a level?! The ancient poet's "Looking at a Rat" (*Xiangshu*)[43] is just the right poem to be sung for this man. Yesterday I read the *Wenzhou Daily* (*Wenzhou ribao*), learning that the Yongjia magistrate also held a victory meeting for the great triumph (*dajie shenghui*). The attendees of that meeting were scathing in their criticism, claiming that Rui'an brought about disaster that led in turn to Yongjia falling into the enemy's hands. The chief culprit [as they claimed] was Lü Lü, and Lü must be punished immediately. However, [to me], evils usually collaborate with one another. To be servile is very nearly the same as to be obsequious.

19 May (24 April on the lunar calendar)

I woke up this morning and read in the *Zhejiang-Wenzhou Daily News* (*Zhe'ou ribao*) that in Yongjia hundreds of shops, companies, and banks had registered their losses from the Japanese occupation. Critics of this newspaper only stated that civilians must stay alert and that *Hanjian* must be spat on and cursed, but they did not dare to call the [government officials] who [were supposed to] safeguard our territory to account for their dereliction of duty. They feared that critiques may call down calamity upon themselves, and thus neglected the universal principles (*gongli*); they fawned upon their superiors, and thus abandoned public commentary (*gongping*). Thinking of all this, one can't help but to stop reading news and sigh.

Yesterday, Lin Jian'an told me that a few days before Rui'an fell into enemy hands, he suddenly received a letter from a distant nephew, and was inspired to compose a poem in a happy mood [as his nephew was found alive]. The poem read:

An evil atmosphere spread amid the Risen Sun[44]
The land was in turmoil and singing a sorrowful song
Our army, navy, and air force shed their blood in hundreds of battles
Nine out of ten houses were empty [as people fled and died]
Families separated from their flesh and blood
Our old country's mountains and rivers [a metaphor for national territory] are now fragmented
Walking under the moon and standing in a quiet night
[I see] a lonely goose flying south in the sky[45]

Jian'an pasted this poem on the wall. After Rui'an was occupied, his entire family fled and left the house empty. A Japanese soldier entered the house to search around. He spotted the poem on the wall and slowly appreciated the lines. He then used a pencil to cast out the first line, make a mark on the second, put an *x* on the third, circle the fourth, and keep the fifth. He changed the sixth line to "Rearranging the old mountains and rivers" (*Chongzheng jiu shanhe*). While keeping the seventh line, he changed the eighth to "This morning, it was fortunate that I passed through here" (*Jin zhao xi wu guo*) and signed his name at the bottom as "Mishima Shibaka." Alas! Our enemy has such an elegant and cultured soldier. This really makes the people of our country deeply ashamed.

24 May (29 April on the lunar calendar)
A day before yesterday, I heard that lawyer Yu Zhixia [d. 1941], who was living in Neihe,[46] next to Baotian, drowned in the night for unknown reasons. Yesterday, I further heard that Yongjia and Rui'an's district courts performed an autopsy on the body. Judging by its shape and condition, [the viewers] said that Yu appeared to have been murdered and then dumped in the river. Some claimed that after the Japanese bandits occupied Yongjia, local people invited Wang Yongshan, Yu Zhixia, and about thirty people in total to organize the Committee for Maintaining Order. After the enemy bandits left, the magistrate returned to the county, concealing his failure and seeking reward for his accomplishments. He framed these committee participants as *Hanjian*. As a result, Yongshan fled, and Zhixia's property was seized. When Zhixia fled to his hometown alone, detectives suddenly came in order to catch him. In great panic, Zhixia committed suicide. Others argued that Zhixia had once taken another's wife as his own concubine. The husband of that woman feared Zhixia's wealth and power, so nursed his hatred and lived outside the city for years. Recently, this man suddenly returned. He found Zhixia hiding in a village. During the night, he had someone lure him to a desolate place for a chat, and then took him by the throat and killed him. They worried that a body on the road would cause people to investigate, so they peeled off his clothes and threw the naked body into the water, thus making it appear as a suicide to the public. These people made their deliberate plan and committed such a cruel crime. Alas! Zhixia was the son of [Yu] Demu in Dadianxia. Demu worked as a trade broker (*ya lang*). He once visited the county capital and the Xu Taihe Hotel (*Xu Taihe jiudian*). Since he got along well with my mentor, Xu Zhuyou, his son Zhixia, at the age of thirteen, was adopted by Master Xu as a foster son. Master Xu thus taught him to prepare for the civil service exams, and I was fortunate to have him as my playmate [during my childhood]. Later on, since Master Xu's fourth brother [Xu] Yangyi was a barrister in Hangzhou and had a great reputation, Zhixia studied law with Yangyi, and then registered as a litigation master (*zhuangshi*)

to deal with registration and legal affairs. With his bright and clever character, Zhixia frequently handled big cases and earned a plentiful fortune. [With this fortune], he was able to purchase a house in Yongjia. And so a poor scholar became a wealthy man! Yet in recent years, he aged and became fond of women. He paid to get a mistress, and kept this woman in a love nest. He failed to stay on good terms with his wife, and this cost him a great deal of money. Unexpectedly, ghosts and spirits haunted his house and brought misfortune to him. He died [of such misfortune], and his wealth was totally dispersed. Isn't this retribution for being a lawyer?

27 May (2 May on the lunar calendar)

According to the precedent that all that is heard needs to be recorded, we never expected to accuse newspapers of making untrustworthy historical records. If a thing has been viewed and heard by nearby people, and has been known to everyone already, why should one suppress the facts and recklessly publish unreliable reports? In this regard, the recent news reports in the *Wenzhou News* are particularly shocking. For example, Yongjia and Rui'an fell into enemy hands for half a month. Then, the Japanese retreated from the town by themselves. But the Rui'an government made an announcement saying: "After chasing the enemy back and forth for fourteen days, we finally repelled our ferocious enemy and recovered our county." Alas! How could anyone possibly ever trick us this way? Are they going to fool Heaven? Are they going to fool the people? Now our country has no political deliberation, and someone has done such a self-deceptive thing, just like the act of stealing a bell [and making loud noise] while covering his ears [to deceive himself]. Who can be as shameful as this?

Notes

1 Although Wenzhou has abundant sources for local history, few studies have explored its history during the Second Sino-Japanese War. Most studies repeat either the grand narratives of nationwide development or the stories of military tactics and atrocities. The most important exception is Lo Shih-Chieh's research, which combines historical and ethnographical approaches to explore Wenzhou's wartime history and local politics. See Lo Shih-Chieh, "Chenghuang shen yu jindai Wenzhou difang zhengzhi: Yi 1949 nian Huang Shisu dang chenghuang wei taolun zhongxin" [Communal religious tradition and "de-centralized" local politics: Reconsidering the Wenzhou Jinqianhui Incident (1850–1862)], in *1898–1949: Gaibian Zhongguo zongjiao de wushi nian* [1898–1948: Fifty years that changed Chinese religions], ed. Paul Katz and Vincent Goossaert (Nangang: Zhongyang yanjiuyuan jindaishi yanjiusuo zhuankan, 2015), 101–39. In addition, Keith Schoppa's study of refugees in wartime Zhejiang provides a thorough and comprehensive view of the socioeconomic circumstances of wartime Wenzhou and other regions of

Zhejiang. See R. Keith Schoppa, *In a Sea of Bitterness: Refugees during the Sino-Japanese War* (Cambridge, MA: Harvard University Press, 2011). As to the process of the Japanese occupation of Wenzhou, Zhang Jie's articles outline its major developments and general context. See Zhang Jie, "Kangzhan shiqi Wenzhou di'yi ci lunxian de beijing, jingguo ji tedian" [Wenzhou's first occupation during the Resistance War: Background, process, and characteristics], *Wenzhou shifan xueyuan xuebao* [Wenzhou Normal College journal] 19, 2 (1998): 38–41; Zhang Jie, "Kangzhan shiqi Wenzhou di'er ci lunxian de beijing, jingguo, ji tedian" [Wenzhou's second occupation during the Resistance War: Background, process, and characteristics], *Wenzhou shifan xueyuan xuebao* 22, 4 (2001): 43–48; Zhang Jie, "Kangzhan shiqi Wenzhou di'san ci lunxian de beijing, jingguo, ji tedian" [Wenzhou's third occupation during the Resistance War: Background, process, and characteristics], *Wenzhou shifan xueyuan xuebao* 16, 4 (1995): 15–18, 40. Other studies include Xu Dingshui, "Kangzhang shiqi de Wenzhou gongshangye" [Industry and commerce of Wenzhou during the Resistance War], *Hangzhou shifan xueyuan xuebao* [Hangzhou Normal College journal] 10, 5 (1988): 25–31; and Feng Jian and Liu Zhangjin, "Kangzhan shiqi Wenzhou sanci lunxian jiyao" [Essential chronicle of Wenzhou's three occupations], *Wenzhou luntang* [Wenzhou forum] 4 (1987): 53–56.

2 See Zhang Jie, "Kangzhan shiqi Wenzhou di'yi"; Zhang Jie, "Kangzhan shiqi Wenzhou di'er"; and Zhang Jie, "Kangzhan shiqi Wenzhou di'san."

3 During the Qing dynasty, Wenzhou prefecture was mainly composed of Yongjia, Yueqing, Rui'an, Pingyang, Taishun, and Yuhuan. In 1913, the Republican government abolished the prefecture-level unit. This administrative division continued throughout the Republican era, including the period of the Second Sino-Japanese War. In 1949, the Chinese Communist Party re-established the prefecture-level unit and renamed the unit a "city." Thus Wenzhou became a prefecture-level city, and is now called Wenzhou city.

4 See Weiting Guo, "Living with Disputes: Zhang Gang Diary (1888–1942) and the Life of a Community Mediator in Late Qing and Republican China," *Journal of the Canadian Historical Association* 24, 2 (2013): 224.

5 Hu Zhusheng, *Wenzhou jindai shi* [The modern history of Wenzhou] (Shenyang: Liaoning renmin chubanshe, 2000), 344.

6 Tingtian village is in Rui'an county.

7 Zhang Junsun, Zhang Tiesun, and Dai Ruolan, eds., *Duyinyuan shiwen jicun* [Collected essays and poems from the Duyinyuan] (Hong Kong: Xianggang chubanshe, 2005), 433–35, 531–22.

8 With the help of prominent scholar-official Sun Yirang, Zhang Gang also extended his teaching career to other private schools, and taught at a new public school, Rui'an Middle School. See Zhang Zucheng, "Congfu Zhenxuan Zhang fujun xingzhuang" [The biography of my uncle Zhang Zhenxuan], ibid., 521–22.

9 For Zhang Gang's activities in local academies and mediation, see Guo, "Living with Disputes," 218–62.

10 For the potential limitations of this diary, see ibid.

11 Ye Fuquan, also known as Ye Qianshui, is sometimes called Cai Fuquan. According to Zhang, Ye could speak Japanese after his long stay in Taiwan. See Zhang Gang, Zhang Junsun, and Dai Ruolan, *Zhang Gang riji* [Zhang Gang's diary], unpublished, 27 April 1941 (MG30/4/2). "MG" here refers to the Chinese era name "Minguo" (Republican). The unpublished verison of this diary was originally written by Zhang Gang, and was re-arranged, typed, and annotated by Zhang Junsun and Dai Ruolan.

12 Few studies have utilized this diary. See, for example, Shih-Chieh Lo, "The Order of Local Things: Popular Politics and Religion in Modern Wenzhou, 1840–1940" (PhD diss., Brown University, 2010); You Yuhao, "Zai jiuxue yu xinzhi zhijian: Yi ge xiangcun shishen de yuedu shijie" [Between old learning and new knowledge: The reading world of a village

gentryman], *Lishi jiaoxue wenti* [History research and teaching] 4 (2011): 93–100; Guo, "Living with Disputes"; Feng Xiaocai, "'Zhongshan chong': Guomindang dangzhi chuqi Rui'an xiangshen Zhang Gang de zhengzhi guangan" [The "Sun Yat-sen bug": Political views of Rui'an's village gentryman Zhang Gang during the early period of Nationalist rule], *Shehui kexue yanjiu* [Social science research] 4 (2015): 156–69; Lo Shih-Chieh, "Chenghuang shen yu jindai Wenzhou"; Qu Jun, "Xiao chengzhen li de 'da dushi': Qingmo Shanghai dui Jiangzhe difang dushuren de wenhua fushe" [A "big city" in a small town: The cultural influence of Shanghai toward local literati in Jiangsu-Zhejiang regions], *Shehui kexue yanjiu* 5 (2016): 160–72.

13 Wenzhou Municipal Library, Rare Book Department, MS 4506, Zhang Gang, *Duyinyuan riji*, 1888–1942.

14 Yu Xiong, ed., *Zhang Gang riji* [Zhang Gang diary] (Shanghai: Shanghai shehui kexue chubanshe, 2003). In addition to this excerpted version, part of the diary was published in a volume compiled by Zhang Gang's grandsons Zhang Junsun and Zhang Tiesun, and granddaughter-in-law Dai Ruolan, titled *Duyinyuan shiwen jicun*. A reprint version of this diary has also been published in a sixty-volume collection, *Wenzhou shi tushuguan cang riji gao chaoben congkan* [Wenzhou Municipal Library's collection of diary drafts and manuscript copies], ed. Wenzhou shi tushuguan [Wenzhou Municipal Library] (Beijing: Zhonghua shuju, 2017).

15 Tongqing is the courtesy name of Zhang Yutong, a nephew of Zhang Gang. For the relationship between Zhang Gang and Zhang Yutong, see the genealogy of Tingchuan's Zhang family in Zhang Junsun, Zhang Tiesun, and Dai Ruolan, *Duyinyuan shiwen jicun*, 557.

16 Flowing from inner Wenzhou to the East China Sea, the Feiyun River has long served as a major water route in the area. Various towns relied on the river to connect with one another and transport goods to other regions and provinces. During the first occupation of Wenzhou, the Japanese army entered the region via the Feiyun River due to its significant role in water transportation.

17 Haoqing is the courtesy name of Zhang Zailü (1867–1944), a cousin of Zhang Gang. See ibid.

18 Tang Leshui (1861–1959), also known as Tang Zengzhi, lived in Xiaoxia, Rui'an. He was the brother-in-law of Zhang Gang's third son, Zhang Yufeng. After Yufeng's marriage in 1924, Tang frequently contacted Zhang Gang and became Zhang's close friend.

19 Xiang Yinxuan and his cousin, Xiang Xiangzao, were the founders of Tongji Ferry Company on the Feiyun River. See Yu Zhentang, ed., *Rui'an lishi renwu zhuanlue* [Brief biographies of Rui'an's historical figures] (Hangzhou: Zhejiang guji chubanshe, 2006), 169–71. In his diary, Zhang described how Xiang Yinxuan eagerly engaged in local competition over fishery, transportation, and various types of business.

20 Wang Chaoliu (1909–91) was the wartime principal of the Wenzhou Middle School. Zhang Gang also described in his diary how he discussed his friend's son's school housing issue with Wang. For a description of Wang's life, see Yu Zhentang, *Rui'an lishi renwu zhuanlue*, 531–33.

21 Wang Yuda was a company mainly operated by a Rui'an merchant, Wang Zhijian, during the war. The company's business included insurance, medicine, dairy products, and food production. See Rui'an shi difangzhi bianzuan weiyuanhui, *Rui'an shi zhi* [Gazetteer of Rui'an City] (Beijing: Zhonghua shuju, 2003), vol. 2, 1352; Wenzhou shi baoxian hangye xiehui, ed., *Wenzhou baoxianye bainian shiliao, 1894–1996* [Sources of Wenzhou's insurance industry in the past hundred years, 1894–1996] (Wenzhou: Wenzhou shi baoxian hangye xiehui, 2012), 67.

22 Founded in Rui'an in 1889, Li Datong is one of the most famous traditional pastry shops in Wenzhou. See Rui'an shi difangzhi bianzuan weiyuanhui, *Rui'an shi zhi*, vol. 2, 953, 1556.

23 Leisheng is the courtesy name of Zhang Zaitong. See Zhang Junsun, Zhang Tiesun, and Dai Ruolan, *Duyinyuan shiwen jicun,* 556.

24 Tang Yunting is also known as Tang Yunchui in Zhang Gang's diary.

25 Zucheng is the official name of Zhang Yuliu (1886–1951), a nephew of Zhang Gang. Zhang Zucheng had his own diary, titled *Wancha riji* [Wancha diary]. He has two courtesy names: Shengtong and Xingtong. In both Wenzhou and Rui'an dialects, the pronunciations of Shengtong and Xingtong sound very similar. Both courtesy names – particularly the latter one – were frequently used by Zhang Gang in his diary. For Zucheng's place in Zhang's family tree, see Zhang Junsun, Zhang Tiesun, and Dai Ruolan, *Duyinyuan shiwen jicun,* 557.

26 Gongying is the courtesy name of Zhang Yucong, the eldest son of Zhang Gang's cousin Zhang Zaitong (a.k.a. Leisheng). See ibid., 556.

27 Zhongxin Elementary School, in Xincheng, was previously Juxing Academy, where Zhang Gang coordinated local educational affairs and founded the Civil Service Examination Aid Association. For Zhang's involvement in a dispute pertaining to this academy, see Guo, "Living with Disputes," 238–41. The school is located right beside a *tang* river (a small canal-style river across the Wenzhou region) that links Feiyun River in the south and the Wen-Rui-Tang river network in the north. On 31 December 2015, I visited this school and its surrounding area. The canal's route was well preserved, and the river's flow was still rapid. Most of the historical relics had vanished except for a stone inscription dated in the founding years of the Juxing Academy. The security staff told me that the stone was soon to be discarded.

28 Xianyan is a mountainous area located at the north of Tangxia, close to the boundary between Rui'an and Ouhai. According to the diary, Rui'an magistrate Lü Lü escaped from the county capital in the south (close to the Dongshan area) to the northern district of the county.

29 In August 1937, when the Second Sino-Japanese War erupted, Shen Gongzhe was elected as one of the directors of the Committee for War Relief in Wenzhou. Wenzhou shi zhengxie wenshi ziliao weiyuanhui, "Linshi jinji huiyi (1937 nian 8 yue 5 ri)" [Provisional emergency session, 5 August 1937], in *Wenzhou wenshi ziliao* [The historical materials of Wenzhou], Vol. 22: *Wenzhou lǚ Hu tongxianghui shiliao* [Documents of the Wenzhou Sojourners Association in Shanghai], ed. Wenzhou shi zhengxie wenshi ziliao weiyuanhui (Wenzhou: Wenzhou shi zhengxie wenshi ziliao weiyuanhui, 2007), 63.

30 According to my interview with Zhang Gang's granddaughter-in-law, Dai Ruolan, on 21 July 2017, Jin'ao here refers to a place beside a mountain in Cenqi, Rui'an, rather than any of the other Jin'ao in Wenzhou, such as the ones in Yongjia and Longwan. On 22 July 2017, I visited Jin'ao in Rui'an, which is located between Jinqian and Jinhou. This area is close to Tangxia, Tingtian, Xincheng, and Baotian, where Zhang Gang had activities and connections. The Cenqi Mountain (Cenqishan) is right on the side of the street market. The Jin'ao Road is now in Jinhou right beside the main canal of the area. On the other side of the village, which had a small lane leading to a factory-like facility, is the place where Japanese army stationed the Baotan Temple (Baotansi). As Zhang Gang mentions below, the Japanese troops set up a unit called the Cenqi Mountain Guard Reserve Unit (Cenqishan jingbeidui). This unit was probably located around this area because it's close to Jin'ao and the Baotan Temple.

31 Many relatives of Zhang Gang had a "Sheng" in their names, such as "Leisheng."

32 "The Flight of Town Father Dong" is a folk song that describes how Dong Zhuo, a military general in the late Eastern Han dynasty, oppressed ordinary people, deposed the emperor, and then fled and retreated to Chang'an due to his defeat by opposing forces.

33 Located beside the Rui'an County Government and the estuary of the Feiyun River, Dongshan was one of the first strategic points taken by the Japanese army. On 31 December

2015, I visited the Xincheng watergate (*Xincheng shuizha*), and then drove southward along Binhai boulevard (*Binhai dadao,* literally the "seaside boulevard"), passing by the Shangwang seawall (*Shangwang haitang*) and Shangwang watergate (*Shangwang doumen*), and then reaching the Feiyun River and crossing the Rui'an bridge (*Rui'an daqiao*). The entire trip went along Rui'an's previous shoreline, which is now filled with sand and reclaimed land, as well as packing factories. The shoreline, seawalls, watergates and the nearby *tang* canals indicate the significant role of this area in strategy and local transportation.

34 Zhang Mingdong (1899–1963) was born in Huabiao (now part of Xincheng), and then moved to Wenzhou prefecture (now city). He was a renowned lawyer who served as president of the Law Society in Wenzhou. In 1940, when Wenzhou had a rice riot, Zhang Mingdong negotiated with the Yongjia government on behalf of the citizens. He continued to engage in various public affairs during the war. See Rui'an shi difangzhi bianzuan weiyuanhui, *Rui'an shi zhi,* vol. 2, 1674.

35 As Zhang Gang mentions in his diary entry of 7 November 1941 (MG29/10/8), a regiment of the Nationalist army once stayed in this temple. In the following battles, all the soldiers of this regiment were killed.

36 Xiang Weichen (1880–1944), also known as Xiang Xiang, was a renowned politician during the Republican era. In his hometown, Rui'an, Xiang was very active in education and various public affairs. In 1926, when Chiang Kai-shek's army set out on the Northern Expedition, Xiang was also involved in local fundraising for the Nationalist troops. See Zhang Gang, Zhang Junsun, and Dai Ruolan, *Zhang Gang riji,* unpublished, 29 December 1926 (MG15/11/225).

37 Xiang Weifu, also known as Xiang Zhui, studied at the Tōkyō Shinbu Gakkō with Chiang Kai-shek. See Zhongguo shehui kexueyuan jindaishi yanjiusuo zhonghua minguo shi zu, ed., *Zhonghua minguo shi ziliao conggao* [Collections of historical resources of Republican China] (Beijing: Zhonghua shuju, 1978), vol. 2, 339.

38 According to my interview with Dai Ruolan on 21 July 2017, Qianci here refers to the one beside Tingtian rather than the one in Baotian.

39 In the complete version of this diary, Zhang Gang notes Ye Fuquan's remark that "the Japanese gave him several rewards today [2 May] and told him not to come [to visit the Japanese army] again; they also asked him to forward their appreciation to our township chief for his supplies and hospitality." See Zhang Gang, Zhang Junsun, and Dai Ruolan, *Zhang Gang riji,* unpublished, 2 May 1941 (MG30/4/7).

40 Again, Dongshan refers to the district where the Japanese army landed and established its military base, rather than its literal meaning, "the eastern mountains."

41 The sword of Huanshou was primarily developed in the Western Han dynasty, replacing the previous long swords. Its literal meaning – "the decapitation sword" – was borrowed by Zhang Gang in this critique of local officials.

42 *Bao* was a unit in the *baojia* system, which had been used in China mainly since the Song dynasty and was inherited or modified in different periods. In 1934, the Nationalist government re-established the *baojia* system, maintaining the existing household system and the lowest quasi-officials in local society. In Rui'an as well as in other regions, ten family *hu* made a *jia,* and ten *jia* made a *bao.* The head of a *bao, baozhang,* was held responsible for checking residency, collecting taxes, organizing local defence, and promulgating policies and propaganda. See Rui'an shi difangzhi bianzuan weiyuanhui, *Rui'an shi zhi,* vol. 3, 2117, 2199.

43 *Xiangshu* is an ancient poem compiled in the *Book of Songs* (*Shijing*). Describing officials as rats, this poem criticizes the government for violating moral principles and deceiving ordinary people.

44 Here, the Risen Sun (*bairi,* or "broad daylight") also refers to Japan, whose national flag is the rising sun flag.

45 In Chinese literature, the goose usually represents those who are displaced, banished, or separated from their family or friends.

46 While the term *neihe* literally means "inner river," Neihe here may refer to the Fengwan inner river (*Fengwan neihe,* located in north Baotian) or Qianfeng inner river (*Qianfeng neihe,* located in south Baotian). Yu Zhixia is a native of Dadianxia, which is near the southern region of Baotian. Zhang Gang's village, Tingtian, is also close to south Baotian.

12 Two Indestructible Pillars of the Great Wall

JENNIFER JUNWA LAU

In the face of Japan's attacks against China during the 1930s, Chinese wartime reportage increased dramatically, and the progression of the conflict became a major topic of public discussion in the news following the Manchurian Incident in September 1931.[1] Thereafter, the patriotic narrative surfaced time and time again in wartime writings. However, as scholar Parks M. Coble notes: "The vast legacy of their wartime writings had long disappeared from public view for it celebrated China's wartime resistance (led by Chiang [Kai-shek])."[2] Only within the past three decades are these writings being newly "remembered." The Deng Xiaoping era saw the repurposing of the memory and history of war for a new narrative of patriotic nationalism.[3] To be sure, wartime writings were also incorporated into this new narrative.

During the war, Chinese reporters realized that with Japan's continued advances into Chinese territory, the situation was bleak. Nonetheless, newspapers and journals emphasized "the heroic resistance concept" in order to support morale.[4] In other words, because of its expected patriotic character, wartime reportage did not entirely give "objective" facts about the circumstances. As a result, wartime reportage is now perceived as a rich archive to study the "aesthetics of historical experience," as put forth by Charles Laughlin. He goes on to explain: "Reportage authors attempt to make actual historical experience meaningful, to rescue the truth of actual events from the hollowing, reifying effects of journalistic objectivity."[5] Perhaps unsurprisingly then, strong emotions were infused into wartime reportage and much creativity was involved.

Although the literary merit of this genre of writing cannot be overlooked, English audiences do not have access to these articles and reports in full. Translations of these wartime writings are scarce or piecemeal in secondary research. But this large body of writing carries deep implications for China's cultural history as readers consider the tropes and themes of Chinese reportage as a genre.

A reportage piece written about districts in Anhui, an eastern Chinese province, is translated below. This geographical location is noteworthy because contemporary research on the Sino-Japanese War commonly focuses on sites such as Nanjing, Shanghai, and Manchuria. Yet Anhui was deeply affected by the war as advances continued. With much of northern China in the hands of the Japanese by 1938, the Nationalist leader, Chiang Kai-shek, opened the dykes of the Yellow River as a "strategic interdiction" to halt Japanese advancement.[6] The flood caused a reported 300,000 deaths, and most of these casualties were in Anhui.[7] The value of this decision has been contested; the Japanese were able to find other routes toward their goal of Wuhan later that year. Nevertheless, destroying land was perceived as preferable to risking its loss to the enemy. Ultimately this decision proved that these eastern Chinese districts held great significance in the minds of both nations' leaders. As such, the following piece of reportage describing Anhui brings to light this area affected by the war in material reality as well as in literary representation. This article is presented in its entirety for interested readers to perform close critical readings via translation.

The writer of this article is Fan Shiqin (n.d.). In 1934, Fan published and established a school for reporters to learn shorthand methods and note-taking. He had self-studied English, German, French, and Japanese and was known to be a great storyteller. At the time of writing, he served as a special news correspondent for the official organ of the Kuomintang, the *Zhongyang Ribao* (Central daily news), which would later relocate its headquarters from Guangzhou to Taipei. This piece, which covers stories from Shou county (*Shou xian*) and Fengyang district, depicts the atmosphere in the 1930s through incorporating various incidents showing the national morale of the soldiers and civilians in Anhui province.

Entitled "Two Indestructible Pillars of the Great Wall" (*Liangzuo buneng cuihui de Changcheng*), the five-page essay has many of the common characteristics of wartime reportage. First, the fundamental task of a reporter to "foster unity and strength of the Chinese people"[8] is lucidly seen in Fan's title. The metaphor of the indestructible Great

Wall symbolizes the strength of a united Chinese front. Second, the confident presentation of heroic facts, which are often exaggerated with larger-than-life reactions and testimonies, makes evident the patriotic nature of this reportage genre. Third, the idea that China's children are significant in the war is echoed in Fan's discussion of the nameless children on the streets who are portraying themselves as soldiers fighting against the Japanese. Lastly, the hopeful future (yet to be obtained) is constantly renewed in his writing, which follows the common narrative that China's resistance to Japan was to be celebrated and that China's victory was imminent.

Yet this incontestable victory is challenged by the parallels between reportage writing and travel literature. There is an "allegorical dimension" of late Qing travel literature, Laughlin explains, which aligns the travel writer's actual journey abroad "as a surrogate for China's journey into the modern world."[9] The writer through his writing observes, accepts, and rejects other cultures. In the same way, the writer of wartime reportage acts as a surrogate for the psychological collective consciousness. I argue that the temporal shifts and collapsing of time and travel by the reporter betrays the celebratory rhetoric of Chinese victory and reveals the psychological struggle to represent the chaotic reality of war. The narrative timeline fluctuates from "a few days ago," to "currently," to "the eighteenth of last month," "a couple weeks ago," and "last month," and then returns to "a few days ago" when the reporter is visiting the wounded soldiers. And there is no clear mention of how the reporter could verify these stories or how reliable his sources are. While one could argue that the overlapping timelines suggest the imaginative construction of reportage with "its own historical agency" to change the reader's mind about historical events in their own historical moment,[10] the fact that Fan does not recount the events in a linear form suggests the difficulties of penning the war and what I term the "fog of wartime writing."

This fog of wartime writing is loosely based on the phrase "fog of war," which references confusion of location and perspective on the front lines by soldiers. Here, the writers of war are the ones disoriented by the news they are called to write. The shifting chronological pendulum in the narrative suggests the struggle Chinese reportage writers faced when composing an organized representation of the everyday experience of the Sino-Japanese War. Instead of a linear narrative about Anhui, the author produces a disorganized timeline – which can be understood as representative of the chaos felt by the author on inscribing this new genre. As with late Qing travel literature, the writings represent more than a personal and individual account and reflect a collective, cultural consciousness,[11] which here, I argue, reveals ruptures in the celebrated patriotic content of wartime reportage.

Although Fan Shiqin is not as well-known as wartime reporters as Zou Taofen (1895–1944) or Fan Changjiang (1909–70), Fan Shiqin covers the wartime experience of southern Chinese districts and counties that more prominent writers did not have the opportunity to visit, and leaves a small corpus for further analysis and comparison. Fan Shiqin also exemplifies the influence of wartime writing on Chinese reporters-on-scene. This translation of his short article will hopefully draw more attention to the literary merits and readings of texts written during the Second Sino-Japanese War and give them new meaning.

—• TRANSLATION •—

Two Indestructible Pillars of the Great Wall[12]

FAN SHIQIN

I received a letter from a friend a few days ago asking this reporter about what he saw and heard about morale on the front lines. These questions, the reporter believes, are those that the people of the whole nation are concerned about. Taking on the task of finding news about the war and reporting about the morale of the civilians, the reporter feels the need to report the answers to all these questions for the whole nation's peoples.

Currently, Shou county is where the front lines come closest to the rear area, which is to say it is the rear area that is closest to the front line. The bombing of enemy aircraft and the shelling of enemy artillery on the front lines cannot be seen from here, but there is not a single day when the sounds of battle are not heard here.[13] Fifty to sixty *li*[14] to the east of here, our courageous soldiers are defending the front lines. Thus, the atmosphere and morale on the front lines can be seen and heard from here.

Whether the spirit here is lively, or whether civilian morale is strong, the reporter does not need to first explain to the whole nation's peoples. As long as the people of the whole nation consider the stories this reporter tells below, they will understand the liveliness of the atmosphere and the strength of civilian morale here!

On the eighteenth of last month was exactly when our enemy was fiercely fighting in Shangyao,[15] and that day we found out that four of our soldiers were missing. In those four days, there was no news about the four missing soldiers – without a doubt they had been killed by the enemy's hands. On the fifth morning, there was a soldier who happened to enter the bamboo forest of the beach by the Luo River and suddenly found four soldiers lying on the ground, which was covered in bamboo leaves. Getting closer for a better look, they were the four soldiers who had gone missing for the past few days! But those four comrades strangely did not speak, did not move, and were already like wooden figures without sense and feeling. Their hands were still tightly holding two grenades; they looked like they were ready to throw and attack at any moment. These four soldiers, after having some water given to them by people, slowly began to awake and gain consciousness. After fighting an intense battle, these four soldiers lost contact with the camp and ran to the bamboo forest to wait for the enemies. Even though they consumed all the dried food they brought with them that day, they still did not wish to leave the forest. And so, on the fourth day, they fainted and lost consciousness. This story about waiting in the forest for the enemy might seem much like the proverb "waiting in the forest for a rabbit."[16] But this story tells of, and underscores, the determined hearts to defeat the enemy.

A few weeks ago, we had over a dozen soldiers fighting the enemy in an intense battle in a small village of Dingyuan. The result was that the gunpowder was used up and the enemies were quickly approaching. At the time under pressing conditions, several soldiers quickly improvised and took off their battle garments, threw away their guns, pretended to be a group of refugee men and women, and secretly ran to the rear of the enemy camp. Coincidentally the enemy had hand grenades, and they went up toward them and grabbed the hand grenades of the enemy and threw them one after another toward the enemy camp. *Pi-pi-pa-pa!*[17] "Using the enemy's hand grenades to kill over fifty enemies," is the phrase they bring back to their comrades upon their return from the battle.

Everyone still remembers the four hundred enemies in Shangyao that were surrounded by us, right? To resolve this dangerous situation, the enemy sent soldiers to assist them along the Fifth Route. But our soldiers successfully surrounded them and killed off one-half. On the day war trophies from the battle were distributed among the soldiers, this reporter was coincidentally there to celebrate at the banquet. Those soldiers, who received high praise from officials and were rewarded with war trophies and monetary rewards, all suggested using the money to buy shoes and socks for all the comrades on the front lines. At the time, this reporter felt such shame and such joy – it was really indescribable, a story that can never be forgotten!

Last month in Hefei, a turncoat organization was found and a traitor, a well-known person, was captured. When he was sent to Lu'an, he had a "filial daughter" (a graduate of Peking University) who insisted on following her traitor father to Lu'an. After fifty to sixty *li*, the two feet of the "filial daughter" could no longer move. An official felt compassion in his heart and gave a horse for her to use. At the time when this "filial daughter" mounted the horse, there were three thousand troops and soldiers in charge of accompanying the traitor, and the three thousand troops all stopped their feet and did not advance. It was not until that "filial daughter" dismounted that they then continued forward. The mind of a soldier might be simple and unsophisticated, but it really is worthy of respect and lovable.

There was a succession of soldiers who in the middle of last month took orders to create confusion among the enemy's rear in Quanjiao.[18] In order to gain access to the targeted area, they had to cross three lines into the enemy camp. Crossing the first lines of the enemy camp, more than fifty soldiers were sacrificed. The main strength of their army was in the second and third lines of their front. Those soldiers separated into eight on the front lines. At that moment, they confused the sight and sound of the enemy soldiers and so under this disorder and chaos, they crossed into the targeted area. However, by that time there were only forty or so soldiers left. But there they played a farce with the enemy. They were firing in a circle around a mountaintop. One day the enemy went to Mountain X, and they would go to Mountain Y. The next day the enemy would go to Mountain Y, and they would be at Mountain X. They played this game of hide-and-seek for half a month and again passed through the three lines of the enemy camp to return to their own original station. Even though at the end there remained only several dozen soldiers, it was enough to express our unyielding and unrelenting spirit!

A few days ago, this reporter visited a hospital for wounded soldiers. One incident scared the reporter. In a patient's room, there were two soldiers who were badly wounded and who had placed two heads dripping blood by their sides. After the reporter's investigation, they said they had just returned from Shangyao and had used a huge knife to cut off the enemy's head and brought it back. Even though they had several bullet wounds, they were unwilling to throw away the prize they obtained. They had to place this thing beside them to be content.

The morale is so strong, but how is the civilian spirit? The following describes the general populace. In the few days in which Fengyang was lost last month, the military advised the people living there to expedite their migration elsewhere. But when the troops moved back, there was an old woman, more than seventy years of age, who would not leave the village. Someone asked her if it was because she could not move, and she shook her head. When asked whether she did not have any money to use, she also shook her head. When asked if she was unwilling to leave her home, she still shook her head. In the end she loudly exclaimed: "My eldest son died in the hands of the enemy. My second son also died in enemy hands. Now our chance for revenge has come. I have to entice the enemy to my home, and then close the door, and set the house on fire – burning even me within it!" Someone wanted to take this old lady from this place, but still was rejected. So this tragedy of warmth and courage must have been performed before the enemy's eyes!

Whenever a village or a town fell into enemy hands, moving events written with tears and blood always appear. The few days before Dingyuan fell, the people of the village, for the sake of avoiding the contamination of the enemies, erected the flag of army volunteers. Because many young married couples from various families had to participate in this great work, they were willing to abandon their very own children at home. In this tragedy beyond comparison on earth, a great spirit is held and embodied that plants the seeds of immeasurable strength!

In Shou county, what makes one the proudest is what is seen of the children on the streets. These poor children pester you and make you uncomfortable, but what is surprising is how they are not afraid of the enemy and how they do not hate the sound of cannons. Even more surprising is how a child from a typical family commonly uses bamboo shoots as guns. Placing the bamboo shoots on their backs, they march along the streets like they are patrol officers. This is already enough to rejoice in the future of China! The most reflective of the times in Shou county is the people's self-protection army. Every few houses, there is bound to be one civilian standing who is clothed in a short-sleeved shirt. The local kids who play this game are everywhere. At a glance, it seems like the civilians in this attire standing outside the houses have suddenly shrunk to half their height. Moreover, the way they hide in the corners of the air-raid shelters and pretending to intensely perform field operations? This shocks you! Although these expressions are just play-pretend for children, but they are also a miniature reflection of the civilian spirit.

Yesterday in one place I met with a youth who escaped from Fengyang. When speaking, this youth was very excited and impassioned. One look and it was easy to discern that he was someone who had gone through something traumatic. This reporter asked why he was so worked up. He suddenly burst into tears and said: "The day Fengyang fell, my seventy-six-year-old father told me several times to leave Fengyang. And he sternly told me, 'Until the last victory is won and Fengyang is reclaimed, don't you dare come back home! No matter what changes happen in the family, you must defend until death.'" His words touched a nerve of the reporter; it was really like heaping burning coal on the reporter's head.

Shou county is only eighty *li* away from the battle lines, but generally the people are calm and it does not appear that they have any worry. The reporter found their town's composure strange and constantly asked them foolish questions. They would always respond with the same answer, claiming: "Our Shou county is not easily challenged: from the battle lines to the city, there is the power of ten thousand civilian guns!" Their confident hearts are really harder than iron and firmer than rocks.

Ultimately, the morale and civilian spirit here have already formed two indestructible pillars of the Great Wall. No matter how violent and fierce the enemy's gunfire, it will never destroy these two pillars of the Great Wall!

Notes

1 Parks M. Coble, *China's War Reporters: The Legacy of Resistance against Japan* (Cambridge, MA: Harvard University Press, 2015), 11.
2 Ibid., 7.
3 Ibid., 2.
4 Ibid., 28.
5 Charles A. Laughlin, *Chinese Reportage: The Aesthetics of Historical Experience* (Durham, NC: Duke University Press, 2002), 10.
6 Diana Lary, "Drowned Earth: The Strategic Breaching of the Yellow River Dyke, 1938," *War in History* 8, 2 (April 2001): 191.
7 Ibid., 205.
8 Coble, *China's War Reporters,* 57.
9 Laughlin, *Chinese Reportage,* 43.
10 Ibid., 271.
11 Ibid., 44.
12 Fan Shiqin, "Liangzuo buneng cuihui de Changcheng" [Two indestructible pillars of the Great Wall], *Zhongyang Ribao* [Central daily news], in Wang Xunzhi, ed., *Huoxian shang de wu lu jun* [The Fifth Route Army on the front lines] (Guangzhou: Zhujiang ribao, 1938), 68–72. Also in *Mengzang Yuebao* [Mongolia and Tibet monthly] 8, 2 (1938): 29–32, and *Guoji wenzhai* [International digest] 1, 4 (1938): 20–22, and *Da Mei wanbao* [Shanghai evening post and mercury], 28 March 1938.
13 The text literally says "do not arrive here."
14 A *li,* or Chinese mile, is commonly thought of as being one-third of an English mile or five hundred metres.
15 Shangyao is a town in Anhui province, not be to confused with Sheung Yiu in Hong Kong.
16 This is a Chinese classical idiom found in the classical text of *Han Feizi:* a man waits for a rabbit in the forest because he once captured a rabbit there in hopes of the same outcome

(*shou zhu dai tu*). It points to the inaction of man and the lack of practicality in leaving things to chance.

17 The onomatopoeia may stand for the sound of repeated throwing of the grenades or the explosion of the grenades themselves.

18 Quanjiao is in Chuzhou, Anhui.

13 Uchiyama Bookstore

Sino-Japanese Cultural Exchanges in the Midst of War

NAOKO KATO

Shanghai's Uchiyama Bookstore[1] operated between 1917 and 1945 in the midst of heightened nationalism and antagonism between Japan and China. The store became known as a Sino-Japanese cultural salon because its owner, Uchiyama Kanzō (1885–1959), focused on new Japanese publications that Chinese intellectuals sought. Returned Chinese students from Japan, such as Lu Xun (1881–1936), and visiting Japanese writers frequented the bookstore, particularly to obtain the latest Marxist literature. As Shanghai became a war zone, Uchiyama Bookstore's role shifted to become a safe haven for many Chinese and Japanese left-wing activists. Even during the war, the bookstore continued to act as a hub for Sino-Japanese intellectual exchanges. Chinese intellectuals absorbed knowledge through Japanese books, and Japanese customers actively sought information about China and Chinese.

I have chosen three primary sources that illustrate the daily face-to-face Sino-Japanese intellectual exchanges that occurred through the bookstore.[2] The first is "Yimian" by A Lei (1909–87), which is a short story written in memory of Lu Xun soon after his death. It describes A Lei's experience of going to Uchiyama Bookstore and interacting with Lu Xun and the bookstore owner. The second is a sample of Lu Xun's diary with numerous references to the bookstore. The third is a report written by a Japanese in 1937, on the books and customers at Uchiyama Bookstore and other Japanese bookstores in Shanghai.

"Yimian" ("An Encounter") is one of many stories that have been used in Chinese high school textbooks to educate students about the founder of modern Chinese literature, Lu Xun. I include it as an example of how Chinese students generally come to know of Uchiyama Bookstore. The fact that this story is set at a bookstore is appropriate, given the importance Lu Xun placed on the role of literature in changing China. Yet the little-remarked-on setting was none other than the Japanese-owned Uchiyama Bookstore. Probing deeper, a logical question is: Why did A Lei, Lu Xun, and many other Chinese writers at this time frequent Uchiyama Bookstore?

In "Yimian," the protagonist of the story, A Lei, recounts his encounter with Lu Xun at Uchiyama Bookstore. A Lei has thirty minutes to spare before work, and decides to go to Uchiyama Bookstore. The casual mention of the bookstore here implies that going to Uchiyama Bookstore was something that A Lei often considered. In A Lei's words, Uchiyama, a "Japanese gentleman" whom he refers to as "Sir," is portrayed as somebody who is sympathetic to China, and is an acceptable person despite being Japanese. A Lei also notes that the two people in the store, one of whom is Chinese (Lu Xun) and the other Japanese (Uchiyama Kanzō), talk to each other in Japanese. Just as A Lei's frequent visits to Uchiyama Bookstore were nothing out of the ordinary, so too is the use of Japanese in communicating with the bookstore owner, and in reading books.

On entering the bookstore, A Lei observes that it is dark, and he can only make out that there were two people behind the counter. Uchiyama had around seven houses that he rented in order to hide Lu Xun from the Kuomintang; at least three of them were rented under his name, including one where Lu Xun kept his books. As soon as Lu Xun entered the bookstore, he sat at the back of the store as a precaution, and Uchiyama sat toward the entrance. Those who came to the bookstore to correspond with Lu Xun would pretend to search for some books, signal, and Lu Xun would come out. This was how they exchanged letters or talked behind the bookshelves.[3]

"Yimian" was written in 1936, but A Lei's encounter with Lu Xun is stated as four years prior, which would be 1932. In the story, Lu Xun recommends two books by Russian proletariat writers: *The Iron Flood* by Alexander Serafimovich (translated by Cao Jinghua) and *The Rout* by Alexander Fadeyev. *The Rout,* which Lu Xun himself translated, was published in 1932.[4]

The second translation below is a diary entry, written in 1932, which demonstrates the frequency with which Lu Xun went to Uchiyama Bookstore. In May 1932 alone, there are twelve entries on it. Lu Xun visited the bookstore over five hundred times, and the number of books he purchased is said to number over a thousand.[5] The diary also shows Lu Xun's close relationship with Uchiyama, beyond that of a bookstore owner and patron. Examples include gifts received as well as gifts bought for people associated with the bookstore; purchases of books including the price; postcards or correspondence with Uchiyama and his friends; and routine afternoon visits to the bookstore.

The diary entries also show how closely intertwined Lu Xun's personal networks were with the operations of the bookstore and Uchiyama Kanzō's network of friends. Uchiyama Bookstore acted as Lu Xun's post office: Lu Xun directed all his mail there and paid his manuscript fees there.[6] Lu Xun was forced to use pseudonyms from about 1933, because he was writing pieces critiquing the Kuomintang's crackdown on the Communists. In order to find ways to publish underground, Lu Xun resorted to translating, commissioning, and publishing through Uchiyama Bookstore. Masuda Wataru (1903–77), mentioned in this diary, was one of Lu Xun's translators; Uchiyama introduced them in 1931. Masuda published the first biography of Lu Xun in Japanese in 1932, and translated many of Lu Xun's works thereafter.

Among the correspondence Lu Xun received at Uchiyama Bookstore were woodcut prints, as Uchiyama provided assistance in organizing woodcut print exhibits. In the early 1930s, woodcut artists faced intense persecution from the Kuomintang with many societies disbanded, exhibits banned, artists jailed, and prints confiscated. Kakichi, who appears in this diary, was Uchiyama Kanzō's brother and an art teacher in Japan. During his visit to Shanghai in 1931, he was asked by Lu Xun to lead a woodcut workshop to teach young Chinese artists. Kakichi led a woodcut workshop at the Japanese-language school run by Uchiyama, with Lu Xun acting as the interpreter.

Uchiyama rented rooms on behalf of Lu Xun, paid for utilities such as water and electricity,[7] and assisted in evacuating Lu Xun on three separate occasions. Kamata, who is featured in this diary, was the bookstore's shop assistant and played an important role in securing Lu Xun's safety. Lu Xun hung the nameplate "Kamata Seiichi" in front of his house for safety reasons, around the time that members of the League of Left-Wing Writers were executed in 1931. Following the January 28 Incident in 1931, Uchiyama was forced to temporarily flee to Japan, leaving Lu Xun in the care of Kamata.

Uchiyama Bookstore appeared in a March 1937 governmental report, excerpted and translated as the third item below, which was compiled by Uezaki Kōnosuke, who was assigned to lead the Shanghai Japanese Modern Science Library that same year. The 1936 establishment of the Modern Science Library was part of Japan's cultural policy in China (*tōhō bunka jigyō*) headed by the China Cultural Affairs Division under the Ministry of Foreign Affairs.[8] The objective of the report was to assess Japanese-language books and Japanese-language learning in China.[9] The report assessed the distribution of Japanese books and magazines in Shanghai through a comparison of major distributors, noting the percentage of Japanese versus Chinese customers.

Uezaki's report highlights the significance and uniqueness of Uchiyama Bookstore, not only noting the mere numbers of books and magazines distributed, but also by examining its intellectual impact, especially on the Chinese populace. Uchiyama Bookstore had the largest percentage of Chinese customers (70 percent) in terms of book purchases, surpassing the number of Japanese customers (30 percent), and it distributed the largest number of books among its competitors. In terms of the number of magazines sold, Uchiyama Bookstore sold the least. However, Uezaki lays out the types of magazines Chinese customers purchased from Uchiyama Bookstore. He emphasizes that they are not entertainment magazines but are widely popular journals focusing on intellectual content, ranging from social and labour problems to literature and diplomacy.[10]

Writer Kaneko Mitsuharu (1895–1975) describes the bookstore as the "nipple" from which Chinese literati acquired nourishment – namely, knowledge.[11] For example, Uchiyama Bookstore ordered 1,000 copies of the *Complete Works of Japanese Literature,* 400 of the *Complete Works of World Literature,* 350 of the *Complete Works of Marx and Engels,* 200 of the *Complete Works of New Economics,* and 200 of the *Complete Works of Law.*[12] Out of the left-wing published materials in China, those that were originally in Japanese (330 of the publications) were almost exclusively available through Uchiyama's store.[13] Kaneko asserts that Japanese translations of *Das Kapital* and numerous other works on socialist thought poured into Chinese society from the bookshelves of Uchiyama Bookstore, and became "the blood and body of revolutionaries."[14]

Despite its significance, Uchiyama Bookstore has been mentioned either only in passing as a place where May Fourth writers purchased books, or in the context of Lu Xun's friendship with the bookstore owner, Uchiyama Kanzō. This is due to the fact that nationalist or postcolonial paradigms that essentialize the relationship between individuals and the imperial project have dominated past historical interpretations. Uchiyama Bookstore's Sino-Japanese networks transcend national divisions and borders, and its continual cultural exchanges do not fit into these dominant narratives. Further investigation into the activities of the bookstore reveals how intricately Chinese and Japanese intellectual histories were intertwined.

—• TRANSLATIONS •—

Yimian (An Encounter)[15]

A LEI

In the fall of 1932, I was working as a bus conductor for the Shanghai British Transportation Company.

One afternoon, it was drizzling as I went to take over my shift. There was still half an hour left. I thought to myself: "Why not go to Uchiyama Bookstore? That way, I can find shelter from the rain and take a break as well."

There was not a single customer inside the store, only two people chatting with each other behind the counter. I took a look inside – it was very dark and blurry. I could only identify a thin Chinese man, who looked about fifty years old, sitting at the south end of the shop.

I stood in front of the bookshelves and began to look through the books.

Outside, light rain twirled around like smoke as the autumn wind blew it in all directions.

The store was as chilly as a cellar and cold air came up through my pants.

Suddenly I noticed the title *The Rout* in a row of Chinese books.

The Rout? I remembered this book being positively discussed in a magazine.

The spine of the book had three words, *Translator: Lu Xun,* which provided a sense of guarantee. I immediately took a copy down from the bookshelf.

I took a look at the postscript first, but after reading the first page, I was unable to open the book further because the pages were not trimmed open at the side. A stocky middle-aged Japanese gentleman entered – Mr. Uchiyama, the owner.

"Sir, how much is this book?" I always addressed the owner Mr. Uchiyama respectfully as "Sir," as he was sympathetic toward China.

He nodded politely, took the book, flipped to the bottom page, and said: "One *kuai* [*yuan*] forty."

I smiled with embarrassment and felt around in my shirt pocket; I had only one *yuan* and a few coins left, enough for a few days of food for my unemployed roommate and myself. I regretted my hastiness and said with a reddened face: "It's too expensive."

He did not notice my embarrassment, and twiddled the green thick cloth-pattern book cover with his stubby fingers: "How is that expensive? Take a look at this paper."

It was a fairly solid book with thick paper and clear letters. It was an oddly comfortable feeling to hold it in my hands.

"Go ahead and buy one. This is a very good book."

I really hesitated. On the one hand I had to eat, but the book was really good as well. If I were to buy a copy and place it at the head of the bed, I could curl up with it and read a few pages after coming home feeling exhausted from work – how wonderful it would be! I kept stroking the book, unwilling to let go. I did not say I would buy it but nor did I say that I would not.

The owner Mr. Uchiyama could figure out what was going on. Smiling, he turned and said a few words in Japanese to the person inside.

The old man who had been chatting with him earlier came out with a cigarette filter chomped between his teeth. His face was yellowish, pale, and worrisomely thin as if he had just recovered from a serious illness. He was in good spirits and did not seem the least disheartened. His hair was about an inch long. It was obvious that he had not cut it for a long time and it stood straight up. His moustache was eye-catching like the Chinese character "—" ("one") in black ink.

"Do you want to buy this book?" He took a look at me. His honest and kindly gaze landed on me like a father's touch, stern and affectionate. "Yes," I said quietly.

He took a book from the shelf which had the identical paper format as *The Rout,* except it was thicker. The cover had two words printed: *Iron Flood.*

He handed the book to me with his bamboo-like fingers, sleeves wrapped tightly around his wrists. "You should buy this book," he said. "This one is better than that one."

Who could he be? Why is he giving such sincere advice to me – a routinely disdained blue-collar worker? I was somewhat puzzled when I first walked in, and was even more so now. Although I could not figure out who he was, I was sure he was someone extraordinary.

I turned to the page with the marked price: one *yuan* eighty.

"Sir, I cannot afford it. I do not have enough money."

My voice was so low even I could not hear it myself, and I did not know what to do.

"Do you have one *yuan* – just one?"

"Yes!" I raised my head and instantly regained my courage.

"I'll sell them to you – two copies for one *yuan*."

What? With surprise I observed his yellowish-pale complexion, worrisome thinness, inch-high spiky hair, long yellowish long robe, "—" moustache, and yellow cigarette filter which blackened at the end held in his left hand. It was at this moment that I suddenly recalled an interview in a magazine.

"Oh, you are ..." I stammered in exhilaration. It had to be him, no mistake, it had to be! That name bounced around madly around in my heart as I looked all about, but failed to bounce right out.

He smiled and nodded in acknowledgment as if he fully understood what I had meant to say. This indicated to me that I could not be wrong. It was him – the warrior who detested darkness as if it were the devil, who devoted his lifetime to the betterment of our nation, and grew increasingly determined as he advanced in age. I looked at his face carefully and it was thin. Our warrior's health had almost been ruined by restless toil. He smiled encouragingly, pointed to the book *Iron Flood*. I will only charge you one *yuan* for Mr. Cao's book. My book is a gift to you."

With much effort, I took the one *yuan* silver coin, still warm from my shirt pocket, and placed it in his hand. His hand felt so very thin. I felt a sudden surge of emotion as if I were going to break out in tears. I bowed respectfully and stuffed the books inside my canvas bag, placed the bag on my back and walked out of the bookstore.

This incident happened four years ago, today. In these four years I experienced many hardships and suffered through the most inhumane abuses. But I clenched my teeth and did not utter a single complaint. I always held my head up high and said to myself: "Lu Xun is with us!"
10 June 1936.

An Extract from Lu Xun's Diary, May 1932[16]

2nd Went to Uchiyama Bookstore[17] in the afternoon, bought a copy of *Friendship*, 2 *yuan* 5 *jiao*.

4th Went to Uchiyama Bookstore, bought one copy of *World Art Collection* and 2 copies of *Supplemental volume 11 & 14*, in total paid 6 *yuan* 4 *jiao*.

6th Went to Uchiyama Bookstore in the afternoon, bought *Gudong-duowan,*[18] in total five copies, 7 *yuan* 4 *jiao.* Also, a copy of Guan Tianpeng's *Modern Chinese Studies,* 6 *yuan* 8 *jiao.*

7th Gift given to Uchiyama Kakichi[19] – Masereel's *Selection of Woodblock Prints.*

12th Heard from Uchiyama.

19th Went to Uchiyama Bookstore, received a copy of *Calligraphy Collection* (25), 2 *yuan* 4 *jiao.*

20th In the morning, Uchiyama gave me one box of seaweed. Received from Uchiyama, cigarette tools and a lion-dance toy that belonged to Masuda.[20]

21st Bought clothes for Uchiyama, Yamamoto,[21] Kamata,[22] Hasegawa, and Uchiyama Kakichi's wife.

22nd Went to Uchiyama Bookstore, received one copy of Qiaoben Guanxue's *Shitao* (Waves of stone), 3 *yuan* 2 *jiao.*

25th Postcard from Uchiyama Kakichi.

26th In the afternoon, went to Uchiyama Bookstore and bought two books, 3 *yuan* 5 *jiao.*

31st Went to Uchiyama Bookstore in the afternoon and bought *The Consistency of Literature,* 5 *jiao.*

March 1937 Report by Librarian Uezaki on Japanese Books and Japanese Language in Shanghai, Uezaki Kōnosuke

Report Index

1 Investigation of Japanese Books and Japanese Language
2 Investigation of Exchange Students in Japan
3 Investigation of Chinese Libraries.

Item 1. Investigation of Japanese Books and Japanese Language

1. Investigation of Japanese Book Sales in Shanghai

There are four bookstores that sell Japanese books in Shanghai: Uchiyama Bookstore and Uchiyama Bookstore Magazine Section[23] on North Sichuan Road, Shiseidō on Wusong Road, and Nihondō. The most prominent and successful is Uchiyama Bookstore.

I have listed the amount sold, the numbers sold, and the types of patrons (Japanese and Chinese) for the past year.

Monographs

Bookstore	Number of books/year	Amount per year ($)	Patrons – Percentage Japanese	Patrons – Percentage Chinese
Uchiyama Bookstore	100,000	200,000	30	70
Nihondō	4,000	6,000	100	0
Shiseidō	13,500	25,000	85	15

Note: The subject fields sold at Uchiyama Bookstore range from mental science, history, social sciences, natural science, engineering, industry, art, language, and literature. Social sciences was the most popular field among Chinese customers.

Journals/Magazines

Bookstore	Numbers per year	Amount per year ($)	Patrons – Percentage Japanese	Patrons – Percentage Chinese
Uchiyama Bookstore	18,000	9,000	65	35
Shiseidō	120,000	60,000	80	20
Nihondō	54,000	27,000	100	0

Note: Chinese customers at Uchiyama Bookstore's magazine section do not purchase entertainment magazines but are interested in *Kaizō* (Restructure), *Bungeishunju* (Literary magazine), *Chūōkōron* (Central review), *Nihonhyōron* (Japan review), and *Gaikōjihō* (International affairs). Chinese customers subscribe to approximately eighty journals per month.

Notes

1 Neishan Shudian in Chinese and Uchiyama Shoten in Japanese.

2 This work is based on my PhD dissertation, Naoko Kato, "Through the Kaleidoscope: Uchiyama Bookstore and Sino-Japanese Visionaries in War and Peace" (University of Texas at Austin, 2013).

3 Fujii Sōsen, "Rojin no shin no deshi" [Rojin's true disciple], in *Michi* [Path] (Tōkyō: Ko Uchiyama Kanzō nitchū yūkō sōgi iinkai, 1959), 6.

4 Mark Gamsa, *The Chinese Translation of Russian Literature: Three Studies* (Leiden; Boston: Brill, 2008), 23.

5 Shin Gō, "Senzen shuppan media no shanhai rūto: Uchiyama Shoten to Kaizōsha no umi o koeta nettowāku," Qin Gang, [Transmission of Japanese publications through Shanghai in the prewar period: The tie between two publishers, Uchiyama Shoten and Kaizōsha] *Nihon kindai bungaku* [Japanese modern literature] 89 (2013): 200–7.

6 Hanchao Lu, *Beyond the Neon Lights: Everyday Shanghai in the Early Twentieth Century* (Berkeley: University of California Press, 1999), 369.

7 Koizumi Yuzuru, *Rojin to Uchiyama Kanzō* [Lu Xun and Uchiyama Kanzō] (Tōkyō: Kōdansha, 1976), 217.

8 See Heng Teow, *Japan's Cultural Policy Toward China, 1918–1931: A Comparative Perspective* (Cambridge, MA: Harvard University Asia Center, 1999), 199.

9 Uezaki Kōnosuke, *Shanhai chihō no Nihon tosho oyobi Nihongo ni kansuru Uezaki shisho no shisatsu hōkoku* [Inspection report on Japanese books and Japanese language in Shanghai region by Uezaki Librarian, March 1937], Diplomatic Archives of the Ministry of Foreign Affairs, H-7–1–0–6_002.

10 Ibid.
11 Kaneko Mitsuharu, *Dokurohai* [Skull-cup] (Tōkyō: Chūō kōronsha, 2004), 160–61.
12 Uchiyama Kanzō, *Kakōroku* [Recollections from the past] Tōkyō: Iwanami shoten, 1960), 145.
13 Shin Gō, "Senzen shuppan," 200–7.
14 Ibid.
15 Cao Juren, ed., *Lu Xun nianpu* [A chronology of Lu Xun] (Beijing: San lian shu dian, 2011), 202–4.
16 Lu Xun, *Lu Xun Ru Ji* [Lu Xun diary] (Beijing: Ren min wen xue chu ban she: Xin hua shu dian Beijing fa xing suo fa xing, 1976), 781–84.
17 Lu Xun said about Uchiyama Bookstore, "I have been frequenting the place for the past three years. It is safer than dealing with some of the Shanghai literati, as he is in the business of making money. He is not in secret investigations and sells books for money, and I am convinced he will not be selling blood." Maruyama Noboru, *Shanhai monogatari: Kokusai toshi Shanhai to nitchū bunkajin* [Shanghai stories: International city Shanghai and Sino-Japanese literati] Tōkyō Kōdansha Gakujutsubunko, 2004), 189.
18 A Chinese journal edited by the Japanese writer Satō Haruo, who was also a translator of Lu Xun's works.
19 Uchiyama Kanzō's brother.
20 Masuda Wataru, translator of Lu Xun's works. From March to December of 1931, Masuda went to Uchiyama Bookstore on a daily basis, followed by three-hour Chinese literature sessions with Lu Xun.
21 Yamamoto Sanehiko, editor of Kaizōsha, which published socialist and communist articles such as the *Complete Works of Marx and Engels* (sold at Uchiyama), as well as fiction. Yamamoto also introduced many of the Chinese returned students from Japan and like-minded Japanese revolutionaries to Marxism.
22 Kamata Seiichi, bookstore shop assistant, 1930–33. In 1933, Lu Xun rented the second floor of Kamata's house on Dixwell Street (renamed Liyang Road) as his "secret reading room" for Marxist-Leninist books and leftist journals that he could not keep at home.
23 The Magazine Section is located on the same road as the main bookstore, close to Foo Ming Hospital. Uchiyama Masao, Uchiyama Yoshie, Kojima Noboru, and Kojima Shizuko, *Robin to Shanhai Uchiyama Shoten no omoide* [Memories of Lu Xun and Shanghai Uchiyama Bookstore], 1996, 17.

14 Finding China's "Asia" in Japanese Asianism

TORSTEN WEBER

Many of the publications of the collaborationist government of Wang Jingwei (1883–1944) focused on reconciling China's status in Asia and its domestic situation with 1) Japan's imperialist policies toward China and 2) Japan's anti-Western and Pan-Asianist propaganda. As the title of this chapter suggests, these efforts could be described as the search for China's "Asia" in Japanese Asianism.[1] In other words, publications and other activities sought to portray Japanese Asianism in general as well as concrete Japanese declarations and activities regarding Japan's Asia policy as based on China's – not Japan's – central role in Asia. In this effort, Sun Yat-sen's (1866–1925) visions of Asianism and of Sino-Japanese cooperation played a particularly prominent role.

The two sources translated below, originally published in 1940 and 1941, are examples of such attempts at rhetorical harmonization and appropriation. They focus on the 1938 declaration of a "New Order in East Asia" by the Japanese prime minister Konoe Fumimaro (1891–1945) and on the East Asian League, founded in 1939 to promote a union of Japan, China, and Manchukuo.[2] In both cases, the main medium of reading "Chineseness" into these Japanocentric approaches is Sun Yat-sen's conception of Sino-Japanese cooperation, in particular his famous speech on Greater Asianism delivered in Kobe in November 1924.[3]

Both texts selected – and the majority of writings published in journals such as *Da Yazhouzhuyi yu dongYa lianmeng* (Greater Asianism and East Asian League, published in Nanjing) or *DongYa lianmeng huabao* (East Asian League pictorial, published in Guangzhou) – aim at portraying

Japanese approaches to East Asia as either complying with China's own domestic and foreign policy agenda or even as originating in China itself. While such logic could simply be dismissed as pro-Japanese propaganda, different interpretations are also possible. Directed at Japan, they could be seen as skilful acts of diplomacy by a weak government in an occupied country toward a strong, occupying country. By adopting official Japanese rhetoric of "Japanese-Chinese friendship" and "East Asian Co-Prosperity," Chinese writers attempted to navigate between complying with a Japanese-dictated regional order and proactively seeking autonomy for China within this order. Directed at a Chinese audience, these texts may be seen as attempts to appeal to as many Japanophile Chinese as possible in order to recruit support for Wang's Nanjing government and its conciliatory political stance toward Japan. Probably more importantly, references to Sun Yat-sen's conception of Asianism and Sino-Japanese cooperation were means of seeking legitimacy for Wang's regime within the domestic and internal party power struggle; after all, following the logic of collaborationists, as a true follower of Sun and in the spirit of a Chinese patriot, Wang only continued the work that the founder of the Chinese republic had begun decades earlier and had left uncompleted when he died in 1925. Collaboration with the Japanese, therefore, was the only way to implement Sun's legacy and complete the unfinished revolutionary task. In addition, as Wai Chor So explains, Wang "revived" Sun's Asianism "to instigate anti-British and anti-American sentiment among his countrymen for the purpose of expelling the Anglo-American powers from China."[4] In both texts this anti-Westernism is expressed in the typical contemporary manner of criticizing "Euro-America" (*Ou-Mei*) for its aggressive policies.

The originality of the texts published in Nanjing journals should not be underestimated. They included criticism of Japan (e.g., Fu Shiyue's attack on the Nine-Power Treaty of which Japan was a signatory, as in the essay below), and in many cases where texts from these journals later appeared in translation in Japan, they were altered to de-emphasize Chinese nationalism or to decentre China's role in the joint Asianist project.[5] The fact that the Japanese considered it necessary to edit these texts before publication in Japan contradicts the assumption that they were exclusively written as reproductions of Japanese propaganda or lip service to the Japanese.

Fu Shiyue (1891–1947), a native of Yueqing in the southeast of Zhejiang province, was a scientist, professor, and Kuomintang (KMT) politician, and served as the minister of railways in Wang's government from 1940 to 1941. He first went to Japan in 1905, and he later graduated from the engineering department of Tokyo Imperial University. In 1922 he became professor at Xiamen University and helped establish Daxia daxue (Great China University), a private institution in Shanghai of which he also temporarily served as president. He was also an executive board member and president of the *Zhonghua xueyishe* (officially known in English as the China Learning Society) in Shanghai, an organization composed mostly of Chinese exchange students returned from Japan. In addition to several posts in Wang's government, from 1940 onwards Fu also served as a board member of the Zhong-Ri wenhua xiehui (Sino-Japanese Cultural Association), an organization set up by the Japanese government to promote Japanese culture and policies in China. In 1943, he was made provincial governor of Zhejiang province and in 1944 became head of the Construction Ministry in Wang's government. After Japan's defeat, Fu was captured in Shanghai by Chiang Kai-shek's government in September 1945 and sentenced to death as a *Hanjian* in the following year. Fu was executed in Shanghai on 19 June 1947.

In the first text below, Fu tries to explain the Japanese concept of a "New Order in East Asia" that Prime Minister Konoe Fumimaro had declared the new guideline of Japan's foreign policy in East Asia in November 1938. While in reality the New Order was a propaganda term to conceal Japanese expansionist and hegemonic ambitions in the region, Fu argues that it was based on Sun Yat-sen's conception of Asianism and would help China's independence by overcoming the "old order" of Euro-American white dominance in East Asia. Since China was the largest country in Asia, Fu argues, it would naturally be at the core of this new order.

Lin Baisheng (1902–46), from Xinyi in Guangdong province, was a journalist and KMT politician who served as propaganda minister in Wang's government. As his former secretary and one of Wang's closest followers, Lin's writings are seen as particularly representative of the regime's political and ideological stance. In 1920, Lin became a student at the private Lingnan University in Guangzhou but was expelled after participating in a strike in 1923. In 1925, he became Wang's secretary but left China to study abroad in Moscow. After a dispute with Chiang Kai-shek, Lin together with Wang went to France in 1927. On his return, he founded several newspapers in Hong Kong and Shanghai. In 1937, Lin became a member of the KMT's Central Propaganda Division. With the establishment of Wang's government in 1940, Lin was appointed propaganda minister, a post he held until he became governor of Anhui province in December 1944. In August 1945, together with Chen Gongbo (1892–1946), Lin fled to Japan but was deported back to China two months later. He was sentenced to death in May 1946 and executed in Nanjing in October. Lin was a prolific writer whose essays were also widely distributed in newspapers and journals Japan. A collection of his writings was published in 1942 in Japanese as *Meihō no tomo e* (To our allied friends).[6]

In this 1941 interview-styled text, Lin tries to explain the rationale of China's participation in Japan's East Asian League. The league had been founded in 1939 by the Japanese lieutenant general Ishiwara Kanji (1889–1949) and quickly grew in membership and branches but proved short-lived. Prime Minister Tōjō Hideki (1884–1948) viewed Ishiwara's activities and prominence with suspicion and started to suppress the organization as early as 1940. It took two more years before it was dissolved, after which it managed to partly reorganize under a similar name (East Asian League Comrades Association). It continued to publish its monthly journal *TōA renmei* (East Asian League) until 1945. The China General Assembly of the East Asian League was founded in Nanjing in February 1941 as a merger of different East Asian League associations that had been founded in China during the previous year, including two China East Asian League Associations in Beijing and Guangzhou, with Nanjing's East Asian League China Comrades Association. Wang Jingwei became president of the assembly. Its main publication, the monthly *DongYa lianmeng* (East Asian League) was published from 1941 to 1944.

In order to mask the strong Japanese influence and Japan's leadership in the East Asian League movement, Lin argues that the East Asian League was in fact based on Sun Yat-sen's revolutionary and Asianist ideals. Therefore, according to Lin, committing to the East Asian League movement not only meant realizing Sun Yat-sen's legacy of Sino-Japanese friendship and Asianist cooperation but also completing the revolutionary task of securing China's independence.

TRANSLATIONS

Greater Asianism and the New Order in East Asia[7]

FU SHIYUE

The term "Greater Asianism" was proposed by Sun Yat-sen in a speech in Kobe in 1924. But the idea of Greater Asianism had already existed around the time of the founding of the Chinese Revolutionary Alliance (*Tongmenghui*). Sun Yat-sen clearly explained its content and significance in his speech on Greater Asianism. The term "New Order in East Asia" appeared during the course of this war from the public debate in Japan. In December last year,[8] the Konoe Declaration also officially declared the plan to establish a New Order in East Asia. The Japanese side has been using this slogan, but the definition and contents of the so-called New Order in East Asia is neither very clear nor very fixed. From my point of view, the so-called New Order in East Asia aims at initiating actions, namely to build a nonconfrontational order in Asia by us Asians ourselves and for the benefit of us Asians. In most cases, any action must depart from a clearly defined thought, which guides and instructs that action so it can accomplish its expected results, whereas blind action is unlikely to bear any fruit. But what is the intellectual base for this action to establish the New Order in East Asia? We think that Greater Asianism should be the intellectual base for the New Order in East Asia. Precisely understanding the thought of Greater Asianism will allow us to complete the important task of establishing a New Order in East Asia. This means that realizing the thought of Greater Asianism and completing actions for the establishment of the New Order in East Asia are two sides of the same coin. Merely possessing a belief in Greater Asianism but not displaying actions to establish the New Order in East Asia renders belief an empty thought. Simultaneously, not having Greater Asianism as the basis of the New Order in East Asia, but forcibly establishing it just the same, would also not conform to our ideal order. Therefore, the realization of Greater Asianism will be achieved by conforming actions to construct a New Order in East Asia, and this New Order in East Asia we want to construct must be an Asianist New Order in East Asia.

There are three preconditions to constructing an Asianist New Order in East Asia:

First, we must destroy the old order in East Asia. What is this old order? More than one hundred years ago, the whites from Euro-America, relying on military, economic, and cultural invasion, turned East Asia – with the exception of Japan, which had already emerged as an independent country – into a more or less complete colony or semi-colony of Euro-America. Therefore, one can say that East Asia's old order is a colonial order in which China – mainly because of its location in East Asia and, importantly, because unfortunately over the past decades it has not been able to complete the revolution[9]– has not yet managed to strip off its semicolonial status until today. Therefore the old order in East Asia remains deep-rooted until today. In recent years the Nine-Power Treaty[10] between the capitalist powers has preserved this colonial order. [...]

As the second precondition to establishing an Asianist New Order in East Asia, we must build a thriving China. In order to understand the importance of China in Asia, we only need to have a look at the map. Its location is central, its territory vast, and its population is big. Also, its history is long and its culture is superior. Summed up, China is the only great country in Asia. If this only great country cannot break away from its semicolonial status, in other words, if it continuously suffers under Euro-American colonialism and the demagogy of Soviet communism, it cannot achieve political independence and economic autarky. Then, without doubt, China itself and at the same time the liberation of all East Asia comes under threat; all encounter great difficulty or even become impossible.

Japan is the only strong country in East Asia. But it is merely one single link in the chain of peoples in East Asia. Even if as a part it is incomparably strong, if China as its neighbouring, large link is weak and powerless, it [Japan] will naturally be affected too. Therefore in order to establish a healthy New Order in East Asia from now on we must first strengthen and raise the big link of China day by day. Then we can join together with the Japanese and other segments to start making efforts for the creation of a new paradise in East Asia. As was clearly laid out in the Konoe Declaration: "Japan desires of China to share the task of establishing a New Order in East Asia"; "Japan's real desire is not China's ruin but its revival, not the conquest of China but cooperation with China"; "Japan recognizes the passion of the Chinese nation and accepts China as an independent country." All of these statements deeply express the essence of Greater Asianism. [...]

The third precondition is a thorough cooperation between China and Japan. Sun Yat-sen pointed this out to us in his Greater Asianism speech when he said: "The greatest people in the East of Asia are the Chinese and Japanese. The motor behind this movement is China and Japan." By "this movement" he meant the movement for the independence and liberation of the different peoples in Asia. Unless both countries that form this motor cooperate, Greater Asianism cannot be realized and the New Order in East Asia cannot be established. As I have already said before, China is the largest country in Asia and Japan is the strongest country in Asia. Between these two countries of size and strength, for the past forty years not only could we not help and cooperate with each other but, on the contrary, we have frequently clashed and at times engaged in political infighting. And recently this has even turned into a bloody war that we are unable to stop. Sun Yat-sen's thought of Greater Asianism, which he had proposed for so long, was practically shelved and no one realized its significance. Although the Japanese side has issued the slogan to establish a New Order in East Asia, the Chinese people on the contrary harbour doubts and curse bitterly. This non-cooperation between China and Japan is the most painful phenomenon in East Asia. The reason why the whole of East Asia has not yet been able to achieve its liberation lies in the inability of China and Japan to cooperate. As a consequence, Euro-American capitalism and Soviet communism have come to inflict invasions and to instigate disorder with the result that until today East Asia has remained in the status of a colony and has been unable to free itself. [...]

To conclude, in order to establish the New Order in East Asia we must first destroy the old order in East Asia. In order to destroy this old order, it is indispensable for China to achieve liberation and independence and to improve the country's condition. Improving China's condition naturally requires efforts by China itself. But one important condition is to acquire sincere support from Japan for profound cooperation between the two countries of Japan and China. In the final analysis this means that in order to realize Greater Asianism and in order to build the New Order in East Asia, we must have Sino-Japanese cooperation as its basis. As Sun Yat-sen said in his speech on Greater Asianism after he had explained that China and Japan are the motors of the movement for the liberation and the independence of the Asian peoples: "Neither we Chinese nor you Japanese know the consequences once this motor has started. After all, China and Japan have not yet formed a great alliance. But the tides of the time indicate that we peoples in the East of Asia by all means must also form an alliance." When Sun spoke these sentences his heart must have been in great grief since, at that time, in 1924, the [Kuomintang] Party had decided to adopt a policy to ally with Russia and to acknowledge the Communists. Although, considering the historical context, he had adopted a policy of acknowledging the Communists, Sun had always considered Chinese-Japanese relations as the cornerstone of safety and decided not to abandon the fundamental ideal he had held for many years, namely, that of cooperation between China and Japan. Therefore, on his way from Shanghai to Beijing he made a stop in Kobe and propagated Greater Asianism to the Japanese people as the final teaching of his life. He said that at the time many people in China and Japan did not know the principle of Greater Asianism but he believed that against the tides of time an alliance between China and Japan had to be created in the future. Unforeseeably, it has now come as far as this bad war, but from this sea of blood the two countries can take a first step onto the road of cooperation. I wish that from now onwards we may realize peace, unbroken cooperation, and shared respect for Sun Yat-sen's great legacy in order to realize Greater Asianism, and revive China and East Asia in accordance with our ideal of establishing a New Order in East Asia.

On the East Asian League Movement[11]

LIN BAISHENG

Today, in our capital, promoted by pacifist patriots and East Asianists, the China General Assembly of the East Asian League was established. It builds on the legacy of Sun Yat-sen's Greater Asianism and is guided by Wang Jingwei. From Chinese and foreign journalists we have recently received several questions about the character and the intentions of this assembly.

(QUESTION) *What is the central thought of the East Asian League movement and where does it start from?*
(ANSWER) Although the East Asian League movement has only recently evolved in a concrete process, the central thought of the East Asian League movement actually takes its origins from the theoretical system of Sun Yat-sen's revolutionary stance. The aim of the Republican Revolution was to realize China's freedom and equality. To achieve this aim it was necessary to raise the masses and to work hard for the revolution. And we also aimed at uniting with all the peoples in the world who treat us as equals in order to fight together. As two countries located in East Asia, China and Japan have both experienced the force of suppression by the Euro-American powers. Therefore, we feel the responsibility to plan together the revival of East Asia. Already in the early days of the revolution, led by Sun, this view was expressed clearly and can be found everywhere in early revolutionary writings. For example, three years before the founding of the republic, Mr. Wang [Jingwei] already said in his "On Why the Revolution Will Not Lead to the

Disaster of Splitting the Melon"[12] that "Any country must have beneficial relations with other countries. If countries have contradictory interests this will lead to hostility, but if they have common interests they possess the sentiments of allies ... No country can exist in isolation in this world. All countries must form alliances with countries of common interests to be able to check others and in order to not be suppressed by others." And he continued: "Countries seek alliances to gain mutual support." In the same text he also mentions the situation in East Asia and states that because of shared interests an alliance between China and Japan was necessary. But in Japan there were conservatives and people advocating aggression with different opinions. They claimed that because China had no ability to become independent it would inevitably meet the fate of invasion. The blame was put on China and we had to abandon our hopes in Japan. In 1917, in the piece *The Question of China's Survival* (*Zhongguo cunwang wenti*),[13] which Sun Yat-sen asked Zhu Zhixin[14] to write, it says:

> Because China and Japan have mutual relations that really concern their survival, there can be no China without Japan and no Japan without China ... China and Japan must under the banner of Asianism develop the resources west of the Pacific as the United States unites the east of the Pacific under its Monroe Doctrine. In this way we make sure that we achieve growth and will not have a conflict within the next hundred years. In the future, we must cooperate as three countries [that is, China, Japan, and the United States], restrain our armies, and set aside enmity to secure eternal world peace. This will bring happiness not only to China.

In 1924, after he had completed his lectures on the Three Principles of the People, Sun travelled north via Japan and in detail set out his Greater Asianism. He called for the awakening of the two great peoples of the East and to take the Three Principles of the People as the guiding principle for the establishment of a new China, with Greater Asianism as the guiding principle for the establishment of a new East Asia. He said:

> China and Japan are the two greatest nations in the East of Asia. China and Japan should be the motors of this movement (movement for the independence of nations). Neither we Chinese nor you Japanese know the consequences once this motor has started. After all, China and Japan have not yet formed a great alliance. But the tides of time indicate that we peoples in the East of Asia by all means must also form an alliance.

And he continued: "What will be the result of Greater Asianism and what problem does it aim to solve? The problem is how the grieving Asian peoples can resist the powerful European peoples. To put it simply, it is the problem of how to help the oppressed peoples to destroy injustice." From this we can see again that Sun's revolutionary claims are not only concerned with China but take into consideration all of East Asia. In fact, this is the historical origin of the core thought of the East Asian League (*DongYa lianmeng*).

In Japan, similar claims have been made by people since the First Sino-Japanese War [1894–95]. Their motivations and points of discussion have not necessarily been the same. But an alliance between China and Japan and the view that both countries must cooperate for the defence of East Asia have been considered natural in theoretical terms and inevitable in practical terms. In the course of events, this has eventually resulted in the contrary of the anticipated aims. But from the grief and bloodshed since the past incident,[15] the peoples of both countries have awakened to their mission in East Asia. From there, the peace movement was born, a Sino-Japanese treaty was concluded and a Joint Declaration was issued.[16] We are now proceeding on to the movement of the East Asian League, on the basis of the thus-far-held revolutionary ideals toward China and East Asia. In the preamble of the assembly's statutes we explain the purpose of the founding of the organization. The first point is that Greater Asianism is the guiding principle of the East Asian League movement. The second point is that the East Asian League movement is the concrete implementation of the Joint Declaration. The third point is that "common existence and common prosperity" and the revival of East Asia are the common objectives of the East Asian League. These may be plain words, but the central thought of the East Asian League is probably covered by these points.

What are the characteristics of the East Asian League movement that are developed from the above-mentioned core thought?
The founding of the East Asian League China General Assembly corresponds to the developments of our times. Adapting to the needs of our people it has started the great East Asian League movement, which displays the following three characteristics:

1 It unfolds as a people's movement with the KMT at its core.
2 The East Asian League is an intellectual movement that takes Greater Asianism as its guiding principle and the Joint Declaration as its basic spirit to promote precise policy proposals.

3 It is an international movement to establish a new system of coexistence and cooperation by awakening the great peoples of East Asia (taking China as its standard and Japan as its axis).[17]

In light of the characteristics you have explained above, can the assembly be seen as a kind of political party?
No. The East Asian League China General Assembly is not a political party. As a movement it is a national organization, which takes the party as its core and unites with other parties and factions and non-political organizations. The establishment of a central force is what China needs most at this moment, both internally and externally. Without doubt, one result of this movement will be the increase and strengthening of the base of the central force. However, this will be an extension of the party, not a replacement of it.
[...]

The first paragraph of the East Asian League China General Assembly statutes defines political independence, economic cooperation, military alliance, and cultural exchange as its four guiding principles. These four points are in line with the Konoe Declaration, the yandian (December 29 Telegram),[18] *and the Joint Declaration. There can be no doubt they are necessary conditions for the revival of East Asia. But regarding its concrete implementation, what kind of practical formation will the East Asian League take?*
We are not concerned with form but with spirit. As for political independence, the East Asian League can be seen as a league of nations if the different national states in East Asia unite, cooperate, and uphold the existence of independence. As for economic cooperation, the East Asian League can be viewed as an economic league if the different national states in East Asia form a fair and mutually beneficial economic union based on principles of mutual support and exchange. As for a military alliance, the East Asian League can be seen as a military alliance if the different national states in East Asia share tasks and cooperate to work together for a common defence. In cultural terms, the East Asian League can be seen as a cultural league if the national states in East Asia, based on the original culture of East Asia, plan to blend their respective cultures within East Asia and promote the culture of East Asia to the world.

Sun Yat-sen said: "We Chinese people want to unite with the Japanese people to use the joint power of both people to support the situation in East Asia" (Conversation with journalists from the Kobe Newspaper on board the

Shanghai Maru, 24 October 1924), and he also said: "If Japan helps China the Chinese people will be deeply moved by the Japanese and the two countries can even further help each other and cooperate. This includes additional treaties for mutual help, such as treaties for economic or military alliances. If both countries would conclude a military alliance, the benefits that Japan gained would natural multiply a hundredfold" (24 October 1924). And he said: "Our Greater Asianism aims at destroying inequality by taking *Wangdao*[19] as its base ... The culture we are now advancing is an antidespotic culture, a culture that represents the demand for equality and liberation of the ordinary masses" (Greater Asianism speech in Kobe, 28 November 1924). The league that we are proposing today has exactly this meaning. If in this spirit the great nations of East Asia jointly fight for a common purpose, "there are many ways to ally the two peoples," as Sun Yat-sen said. There may be people who think the East Asian League is like the League of Nations or a different kind of supranational authority but those people are wrong. The former is a weak and incapable fabrication, while the latter is impairing the sovereignty of independent countries and therefore nothing we are pursuing. As I said before, what we are focusing on now is spirit not form.

Notes

1 On the interactions between Japanese and Chinese Asianism, see Craig A. Smith, "Constructing Chinese Asianism: Intellectual Writings on East Asian Regionalism (1896–1924)" (PhD diss., University of British Columbia, 2014); and Torsten Weber, *Embracing "Asia" in China and Japan: Asianism Discourse and the Contest for Hegemony, 1912–1933* (Cham, Switzerland: Palgrave Macmillan, 2018).

2 On Konoe's declaration, see Roger Brown, "The Konoe Cabinet's 'Declaration of a New Order in East Asia,' 1938," in *Pan-Asianism: A Documentary History, 1920–Present,* ed. Sven Saaler and Christopher W.A. Szpilman (Lanham, MD: Rowman and Littlefield, 2011), 167–73. On the East Asian League, see Michael A. Schneider, "Miyazaki Masayoshi: 'On the East Asian League,' 1938," in Saaler and Szpilman, *Pan-Asianism,* 179–83; and Roger Brown, "Ishiwara Kanji's 'Argument for an East Asian League,' 1940," in Saaler and Szpilman, *Pan-Asianism,* 201–7. Although the East Asian League was only founded in 1939, it was first proposed as a tripartite union in the context of the founding of Manchukuo in 1932. For a detailed history of the East Asian League, its origins, and its development in Japan and China, see the excellent essay by Katsuragawa Mitsumasa, "TōA Renmei Undōshi shoron" [Short essay on the history of the East Asian League movement], in *Nitchū Sensō shi kenkyū* [Research on the Japanese-Chinese War], ed. Furuya Tetsuo (Tōkyō: Yoshikawa kōbunkan, 1984), 363–439. For contextualization of the movement in the activities and ideology of Wang's Nanjing government, see Shibata Tetsuo, *Kyōryoku, teikō, chinmoku. Ō Seiei Nankin seifu no ideorogī ni taisuru hikakushi-teki apurōchi* [Cooperation, resistance, silence: A comparative history approach to the ideology of Wang Jingwei's Nanjing government] (Tōkyō: Seibundō, 2009), especially chs. 1 and 2.

3 On the speech and its legacy, see Smith, "Constructing Chinese Asianism," ch. 6; and Weber, *Embracing "Asia,"* ch. 5.

4 See Wai Chor So, "Race, Culture, and the Anglo-American Powers: The Views of Chinese Collaborators," *Modern China* 37, 1 (January 2011): 69–103, esp. 78.

5 On this aspect see also Torsten Weber, "Nanjing's Greater Asianism: Wang Jingwei and Zhou Huaren, 1940," in Saaler and Szpilman, *Pan-Asianism*, 209–20.

6 Lin Baisheng, *Meihō no tomo e* [To our allied friends], trans. Fujita Hideo (Tōkyō: Ikubundō, 1942).

7 Fu Shiyue, "Da Yazhouzhuyi yu dongYa xin zhixu" [Greater Asianism and the new order in East Asia], *Da Yazhouzhuyi* [Greater Asianism] 1, 3 (1940): 3–9.

8 Actually in November 1938.

9 "The revolution has not yet been completed" (*geming shangwei chenggong*) is a reference to Sun Yat-sen's last will, in which he encouraged his comrades to continue his work for "China's freedom and equality," including the abolition of the unequal treaties.

10 This 1922 treaty, signed at the Washington Naval Conference by the United States, United Kingdom, Belgium, China, France, Italy, Japan, the Netherlands, and Portugal, confirmed the Open Door Policy that was meant to preserve China's territorial integrity from Western or Japanese colonial ambitions. However, it facilitated the continuation of great power rivalry for special rights in China and failed to prevent the Manchurian crisis and the founding of Manchukuo.

11 Lin Baisheng, "Guanyu dongYa lianmeng yundong" [On the East Asian League movement], *Da Yazhouzhuyi* 2, 2 (1941): 4–9.

12 Wang Jingwei's "Shenlun geming jue buzhizhao guafen zhi huo" (On why the revolution will not lead to the disaster of splitting the melon), published in 1908, is based on Wang's earlier "Geming jue bu zhizhao guafen shuo" (On why the revolution will not lead to splitting the melon), published in the *Minbao* (People's newspaper) in 1906. The metaphor "splitting the melon" (also "carving up the melon") refers to the division of China into spheres of interests or quasi-colonial entities by the powers. On its origins and legacy, see Rudolf G. Wagner, "'Dividing Up the [Chinese] Melon (*guafen*)': The Fate of a Transcultural Metaphor in the Formation of National Myth," *Transcultural Studies* 1 (2017): 9–122; and Marc A. Matten, *Imagining a Postnational World: Hegemony and Space in Modern China* (Leiden: Brill, 2016).

13 Reprinted in *Sun Zhongshan quanji* [Complete writings of Sun Yat-sen], ed. Zhongguo shehui kexueyuan jindaishi yanjiusuo Zhonghua minguoshi yanjiushi, et al. (Beijing: Zhonghua shuju chuban, 1985), vol. 4, 39–99.

14 Zhu Zhixin (1885–1920) was a scholar and revolutionary from Panyu in Guangdong province, considered to be Sun's ghostwriter. Zhu first met Sun when he, together with Wang Jingwei, went to Tokyo to study at Hosei University in 1904. In the following year he became a founding member of Sun's Revolutionary Alliance.

15 The so-called July Seventh Incident (also Marco Polo Bridge or Luguoqiao Incident) of 1937, which is seen as the starting point of the full-scale war between China and Japan.

16 In the so-called Japan-China Basic Relations Treaty (Ch: *RiHua jiben tiaoyue;* Jp: *Nikka kihon jōyaku*), concluded in November 1940, Japan acknowledged the Wang government as China's central government. Further clauses included friendly relations, joint defence, and economic cooperation between both countries. The Japan-Manchukuo-China Joint Declaration (Ch: *RiManHua gongtong xuanyan;* Jp: *Nichi-Man-Ka kyōdō sengen*) was issued together with this treaty. The three parties jointly declared the erection of a new order in East Asia, resting on moral principles, as their common ideal and mutually acknowledged their sovereignty and territorial integrity.

17 In a Japanese translation of this text in the official journal of the East Asian League, published one month after the Chinese original, the part in brackets, which appears to subordinate Japan to China, was omitted. See Lin Baisheng, "TōA Renmei undō no honshitsu" [The essence of the East Asian League movement], *TōA renmei* [East Asian League] 3, 3 (March 1941): 84–88.

18 *Yandian* refers to Wang Jingwei's telegram of 29 December 1938 to Chiang Kai-shek, which Lin published on Wang's behalf the following day. It explains Wang's motivation for adopting a peaceful stance toward Japan.

19 In his Kobe speech, Sun Yat-sen made several references to the Confucian ideal of *Wangdao,* often translated as the Kingly Way or Rule of Right, in opposition to *Badao,* the Despotic Way of the Hegemon. In Sun's speech, the former represented the traditional Asian way of rule, whereas the latter signified the Western, imperialist way. Sun appealed to the Japanese to remain true to their Asian origins by adopting *Wangdao,* not *Badao,* as their guiding principle. On Sun's use of this pair and its origins, see Seki Tomohide, "'Tōyō=Ōdō' 'Seiyō=Hadō' no kigen. Ō Seitei, In Jokō, Son Bun" [The Origins of "East= Kingly Way" and "West=Despotic Way": Wang Zhengting, Yin Rugeng, Sun Yat-sen], *Son bun kenkyū* [Research on Sun Yat-sen] 59 (2016): 1–13. In the 1930s, Japanese propaganda utilized the term *Wangdao* to justify Japan's de facto rule in Manchuria. See Weber, *Embracing "Asia,"* ch. 7.

15 Collaboration and Propaganda

Yang Honglie and His Eight Speeches on Greater Asianism

CRAIG A. SMITH

In the early days of the Reorganized National Government of the Republic of China (1940–45), Wang Jingwei's (1883–1944) Propaganda Ministry was employed to justify collaboration with the Empire of Japan. Led by Lin Baisheng (1902–46),[1] the propagandists published dozens of journals and newspapers that were focused on explaining the theoretical side of collaboration, usually turning to Sun Yat-sen's theories of Nationalism and Greater Asianism (1866–1925) to find legitimacy for their actions. Unlike news articles produced for the daily newspapers under the occupation, particularly the *Zhonghua Ribao* (Central China daily news) and the *Nanhua Ribao* (South China daily news), theoretical articles were produced for elite reading in monthly or biweekly journals. Many intellectuals contributed articles to journals such as *Xin Dongfang* (New Orient, 1940–44), *DaYazhouzhuyi* (Greater Asianism, 1940–42) and *DaYazhouzhuyi yu DongYa lianmeng* (Greater Asianism and the East Asian League, 1942–43). Leading theorists of this movement included Zhou Huaren (1902–76), a minor political figure in the Kuomintang (KMT) and the author of *An Outline of Asianism*;[2] Li Shiqun (1905–43), a Russian-trained intelligence officer and one of the leaders of the infamous security service at 76 Jessfield Road;[3] and Yang Honglie (1903–77), a Japanese-trained academic researching legal history.

Yang's contributions to this propaganda are particularly interesting because he was a celebrated academic and had no evident relationship with the core collaborators before the establishment of Wang Jingwei's Peace Movement. His earlier writings were both nationalist and Asianist. And although he had moved from Japan to Hong Kong in the late 1930s when the Peace Movement began, he hurried to join Wang Jingwei and support the movement. In a 1940 article, he recalled:

> I remember the early spring of 1939, not long after Mr. Wang sent out the December 29 Telegram (*yandian*),[4] I left Hong Kong's Kowloon with my entire family in tow, and set off for the Route Tenant de la Tour[5] area of Shanghai's Foreign Concessions, what has been called the area with the most assassinations. Two or three friends suffered the entire day under a drizzling winter rain ... as they prepared a secret publication called "Discourse for the Masses," the front cover of which outlined the main points of Mr. Wang's suggestions to the central government. It was followed by my article, "The Sino-Japanese War and Sun Yat-sen's Greater Asianism," written under my pen name Zhang Gang.[6]

Like most Chinese intellectuals in the interwar period, Yang was a fierce supporter of Sun Yat-sen. In his eulogy of Sun, he expressed his excitement that an East Asian thinker had made Euro-American intellectuals take a step back.[7] This faith in the words of Sun Yat-sen was widespread in Chinese intellectual society, and Sun had been the focus of Kuomintang propaganda since his death in 1925.

After the split with the Chongqing KMT in 1939, it was important for Wang Jingwei to show himself as following in the footsteps of Sun Yat-sen and the true heir to Sun's legacy. To do this, a team of propagandists turned to Sun's Greater Asianism speech of 1924 and related it to the Three Principles of the People, an ideology that had not lost popularity across China. Wang explained: "For China, the Three Principles of the People is an ideology to save the country. For East Asia, the Three Principles of the People is Greater Asianism."[8] These words were echoed by his minister of propaganda, who unabashedly connected Sun's philosophy to Japan's New Order in East Asia and encouraged Chinese citizens to accept the Japanese rule as a phase in the Asian revolution: "The basic theory of the Chinese revolution is the Three Principles of the People, and the canon that leads the Asian revolution is Greater Asianism." As Japan's "New Order" is a phase in the revolution, "the Chinese people should not fear Japan's establishment of the New Order in East Asia as masked imperialism."[9]

The application of Sun's theories to a united Asia was not a stretched reinterpretation. For the most part, it was not a reinterpretation at all, at least not a new one. It had always been interpreted in this way by his closest intellectual associates and protégés: Dai Jitao (1891–1949), Hu Hanmin (1879–1936), and Wang Jingwei himself. Therefore, the majority of the propaganda from this period is not very different from 1930s writings that posited China as the leader of Asia. Kuomintang-sponsored journals such as *Xin Yaxiya* (New Asia, 1930–37) and *Yazhou Wenhua* (Asian culture, 1932–37) had remarkably similar content. However, after 1937 the political context was different and this propaganda was used to justify Japanese domination. Although Yang had lived in Japan for four years, this does not explain his actions. However, his earlier publications do offer clues to his support of a united East Asia.

Yang Honglie had first made a name for himself when his 1,248-page *Zhongguo falü fada shi* (History of the development of Chinese law, 1930) became a seminal work in legal history. Before this he had taught at Beijing Normal University and Nankai University, to which he was recommended by Liang Qichao and Hu Shi, both of whom were influential in his writings and life.[10] He received his PhD after studying at Tokyo Imperial University from 1934 to 1937, when he published *Zhongguo falü sixiang shi* (Intellectual history of Chinese law) and went on to teach at numerous universities.[11]

On the eve of the war in 1937, Yang published his third book on Chinese law, further cementing his position as a top scholar of legal history. *Zhongguo falü zai dongYa zhuguo zhi yingxiang* (The influence of Chinese law in all the countries of East Asia) presented a detailed study of the legal history of countries within the traditional Sinosphere, showing how regional legal practices were based on the civilizational centre of China. In his introduction, Yang explicitly discussed the unity of East Asia, as he exclaimed: "The author resolutely believes that, because East Asia was originally all one family, we should all help one other (*huxiang tixie*) and work together to plan for development and to maintain the lasting glory of East Asia."[12] After Wang's Peace Movement was established, National Central University employed Yang as a professor of history. At the same time, he also served as department chief for the Propaganda Ministry's Censorship Department.[13]

Like Zhou Huaren, Yang was not tried as a war criminal after the fall of the empire. It is unclear why Yang was not arrested, as his wartime work and his postwar location in Shanghai were common knowledge in 1946. His wife, Wan Mengwan (n.d.) was not so fortunate. Labelled a "female *Hanjian*" (traitor to China) for her role as principal of the National Model Girls' School, she was tried in Suzhou and sentenced to thirty months in prison, which was later commuted to six months.[14] After her release, Wan joined Yang in Hong Kong, where they remained throughout the Civil War.[15] Yang returned to China in 1955 or 1956 and continued to teach at universities. He was labelled a rightist in the Anti-Rightist Movement and sent to a labour reform camp, but survived until 1977.[16]

In 1942, Yang delivered eight speeches on Greater Asianism, ostensibly in his role as an academic at the National Central University. The eight speeches were serialized across the first four editions of *DaYazhouzhuyi yu DongYa lianmeng*, and the first three speeches are translated here. The first two discuss the theory of Sun Yat-sen's Asianism and Nationalism. The third speech relates the war and the New Order in East Asia to the intellectual thought of Sun Yat-sen, as well as of Japanese military and political elites. The fourth speech criticizes the Far Eastern Monroe Doctrine for not being proper Asianism. The sixth, seventh, and eighth speeches offer historical narratives of Asianist thought from the Opium War to the 1940s. And the eighth speech also discusses the need for economic and cultural unity with Japan from the perspectives of Sun Yat-sen and Kodera Kenkichi (1877–1949).

TRANSLATIONS

Eight Speeches on Greater Asianism

YANG HONGLIE

The First Speech: Defining Greater Asianism[17]

What is Greater Asianism? For now I offer the following working definition: Greater Asianism is a form of self-defence policy that resists the aggression of Euro-American imperialists through the power of all the nations of Asia. Therefore, all the independent nations of Asia, including China, Japan, Manchukuo, and Thailand, must first engage in mutual cooperation[18] and unite in an alliance (*tongmeng*). All of us must unanimously draw out the spirit of the Kingly Way (*Wangdao*)[19] to revive the glorious history of Asia and forge lasting peace for Asia and the entire world.

We should all be well aware that there now exist innumerable "isms" that harbour an emotional bias toward a particular race. Foremost among these is the overbearing arrogance of the Euro-American imperialists' belief in their own superiority. We find Greater Americanism (*Da Meizhouzhuyi*), Great Britishism, Russian pan-Slavism, and French pan-Latinism to be repulsive. They are entirely adopting an offensive that is ruthless, violent, and utterly abominable. Perhaps none will deny that Americans are most wont to profess their wonderful-sounding doctrines, including "God-given rights," and "emancipation of the black slaves." However, in the twenty years from the fifth year of Xianfeng [1855] to the second year of Guangxu [1876], the Americans took advantage of China's troubles, which included the Taiping Heavenly Kingdom, the Franco-British united army [Second Opium War], and the Nian Rebellion. While China's homelands were in disarray, the Americans persecuted and humiliated those tens of thousands of overseas Chinese who have drifted across the ocean. Those forced into exile by hardships at home found themselves thrust into a hopeless twilight. Therefore, although Dr. Wu Tingfang has often been called pro-American, he criticized the Americans thus:

> It will be seen that by the treaty of 1868, known as the "Burlingame Treaty,"[20] the United States government formally agreed that Chinese subjects, visiting or residing in the United States, should enjoy the same privileges and immunities as were enjoyed by the citizens or subjects of the most favoured nation; that being so ...[21] the continuation of the exclusion of Chinese labourers and the restrictions placed upon Chinese merchants and others seeking admission to the United States are not only without international authority but in violation of treaty stipulations.
>
> The enforcement of the exclusion laws against the Chinese in the Hawaiian and Philippine Islands is still more inexcusable. The complaint in America against the immigration of Chinese labourers was that such immigration was detrimental to white labour,[22] but in those islands there has been no such complaint; on the contrary the enforcement of the law against the Chinese in Hawaii has been, and is, contrary to the unanimous wish of the local government and the people. Free intercourse and immigration between those islands and China have been maintained for centuries.[23]

Actually, American anti-Chinese legislation is not limited to the country and its colonies, but has even influenced the countries of Central and South America, stirring up some of the most violent actions against Chinese in Cuba, Peru, and Mexico. This continues today with no good means for resolution. Its influence is far-reaching and extends across the entire planet, including South, North, and Central American countries, including Canada, Argentina, El Salvador, Chile, and the Dominicans; the Pacific islands of French Tahiti and British Samoa; Vietnam and the British, Dutch, and French colonies of Southeast Asia; Australasian countries of New Zealand and New Guinea; and countries of South Africa, such as Sheshengya.[24] One after the other, all these countries followed the American model and issued ruthless orders to ban Chinese. From this we can see that the spirit of Euro-American imperialism is still the violent Way of the Hegemon (*Badao*) from head to toe, while the Greater Asianism that we call for is the Kingly Way. The two are polar opposites of each other, as Greater Asianism advocates benevolent virtue and morality (*renyi daode*), while imperialism advocates self-interest and dominance (*gongli qiangquan*). Greater Asianism leads by virtue, while imperialism leads by force. Those who lead by virtue must inevitably and invariably promote peace, while those who lead by force will inevitably bring about widespread aggression. Therefore, delving deeply into the matter, we can say that Greater Asianism is a product of Eastern culture, while imperialism is a representative of Western culture. In his speech on this matter, Mr. Sun Yat-sen explicated most clearly and succinctly on these most important of differences.

[Here, Yang quotes twelve hundred words of Sun Yat-sen's 1924 speech, "Greater Asianism." Sun connected Western imperialism in Asia to the Way of the Hegemon, and he connected Asian political culture to a China-centred Kingly Way as the foundations of Greater Asianism.][25]

It could not be more appropriate that Mr. Sun Yat-sen employed the spirit of Eastern culture to explain Greater Asianism and clarify the extent of its scope.

The Second Speech: Greater Asianism and Nationalism[26]

Now that we have illustrated the definition of Greater Asianism, are there any contradictions between Greater Asianism and the Nationalism found in the Three Principles of the People? And if there are no contradictions, then what are the interconnections and indivisible relations? We are all aware of the position of Nationalism in China, and of the hope that with the realization of Nationalism, China can achieve the independence, equality, and freedom of the Chinese people. Therefore, it is imperative that we must oppose the aggression of Euro-American imperialism. From research into Mr. Sun Yat-sen's speeches on Nationalism, we can induce the following two points:

The first point concerns the domestic perspective. Nationalism opposes feudal forces and promotes complete equality among all the nationalities of China. This is because the remaining feudal forces are continually compelling us along the path to mutual destruction and depriving us of the ability to construct a modern state. So the domestic implications of Nationalism are the opposition to feudalism and the promotion of complete equality among the nations for the advancement of peaceful unification.

The second point concerns the international perspective. Since we demand an equal and independent position for the people of China in the international arena, it is in Nationalism's nature to oppose imperialistic aggression. Therefore, casting off the shackles of international aggression has become a crucial strategy for our people. If these shackles are not one day eradicated, then all our efforts for the revolution are not even worth mentioning. Therefore, the international significance of Nationalism is the opposition to imperialist aggression. However, here we should point out that Nationalism is entirely different from those narrow-minded doctrines of racism, statism, and other xenophobic doctrines. It most certainly does not include any concept of aggression. This is because the basis of Nationalism can be found in the intrinsic peace and morality of China. In his sixth speech on Nationalism, Mr. Sun Yat-sen explained:

> The Chinese people are great peace-lovers. Indeed our people are the only people in the world who are real peace-lovers. All other big nations are imperialistic and warlike ... Our people are by nature peace-lovers! ... sincerity and righteousness, and especially peace-loving are good characteristics of our people; and they have become a part of our spirit of Nationalism. We should not only carefully preserve this spirit, but develop it to its highest excellence, whereby the glorious position of our people among the nations can be restored.[27]

The true spirit of Nationalism resides in this peaceful morality (*heping de daode*).[28]

The true content of Nationalism is just and honourable, yet we have unfortunately been as yet unable to realize it. Remember the strong indignation with which Chairman Wang opened his "Outline of the New Citizens' Movement":

> Why are we unable to realize Nationalism? It is because we have forgotten Asianism. "If China cannot achieve freedom and equality, then we will be unable to do our part in the construction of East Asia. And to fully achieve freedom and equality for China, East Asia must be liberated." The truth of these words was only realized at the onset of the peace movement, yet they were earnestly expressed in Greater Asianism much earlier. Why did we

forget this and allow China to fall into this plight? From this day forth, we shall meld the love of China and the love of East Asia into one heart. With mutual love between all the nations of East Asia, we shall unite for the protection of East Asia. This is the main point of Nationalism.[29]

The original goal of the Chinese revolution was the realization of freedom and equality for China, but in our efforts to achieve this goal we cannot consider merely arousing the masses and striving for the revolution to be a success. In addition to this, we must unite all the nations of the world that treat us as equals and struggle onwards together. Remember what Chairman Wang wrote in his article, "Revolution Must Never Lead to the Calamity of Dividing China," in the first year of the Xuantong reign [1909]:[30]

The interests of all countries around the world are connected. If one profits at the other's expense then they feel themselves to be enemies. If their interests are the same, then they feel themselves to be allies ... A country cannot isolate itself from the world, but must unite with those of matching interests. Then that country can govern, rather than be governed ...

Countries seek alliances for mutual benefit. Those that fawn [on the foreign powers] cannot be autonomous, how can they be of help? And who would want their help?[31]

Finally, Chairman Wang expounded on the state of affairs in East Asia, explaining that the interests of China and Japan lie together, and that there is actually a need to ally. In the sixth year of the republic [1917], Mr. Sun Yat-sen encouraged Zhu Zhixin to write the pamphlet *The Vital Problem of China,* which clearly and specifically stated:

The relationship between China and Japan is one of common existence or extinction. Without Japan, there would be no China; without China, there would be no Japan ... Under the principle of Pan-Asianism, Japan and China can together develop the natural resources in the West of the Pacific, while under the Monroe Doctrine the United States can unify authority in the East of that ocean ... By a concerted effort of these three Powers disarmament might some day be affected, and, going one step further, permanent peace of the world secured.[32]

Later, after Mr. Sun delivered his speeches on the Three Principles of the People in the thirteenth year of the republic [1924], he made a special detour to Japan on his journey north and specifically advocated Greater Asianism in order to advance the awakening of the two great nations of East Asia. He hoped to use the Three Principles to construct the guiding principles of new China, and use Greater Asianism to construct the guiding principles of new East Asia. Therefore, Mr. Sun explained:

> In East Asia, China and Japan are the two greatest peoples. China and Japan are the driving force of this Nationalist movement. What will be the consequences of this driving force still remains to be seen. [We Chinese do not yet know. You Japanese also do not yet know. Therefore, China and Japan have not yet united together.] The present tide of events seems to indicate that not only China and Japan but all the peoples in East Asia will unite together to restore the former status of Asia.[33]

He continued: "What problem does Pan-Asianism attempt to solve? The problem is how to terminate the sufferings of the Asiatic peoples and how to resist the aggression of the powerful European countries. In a word, Pan-Asianism represents the cause of the oppressed Asiatic peoples."[34] From this we can see that Mr. Sun's revolution is not only for the country of China, but is also for all of East Asia.

To summarize, Nationalism is not at all so-called narrow-minded statism, but is truly the collectivization of states. This is what we mean by Greater Asianism. Therefore, these two principles are in no way in conflict or contradiction. In fact, they are so closely related that one could even say they are two sides to the same coin. This is because from China's perspective, we resolutely oppose the incursion of imperialism and fight for the independence and freedom of the Chinese people. Therefore, we urgently require the realization of Nationalism. On the other hand, if we are to examine this from the perspective of all Asia, then we must be completely united to fight against the invasiveness of Euro-American imperialism in the hope that all the nations of Asia can achieve a united and mutual liberation. Therefore, we urgently require the realization of Greater Asianism. What I have just said is merely for the convenience of explanation. In truth these two principles are one and the same and have no discernible differences in terms of their advantageousness.

The Third Speech: Greater Asianism and the New Order in East Asia[35]

We all know that since the advent of the Marco Polo Bridge Incident of five years ago, the people of both China and Japan have had to engage in introspection as they have become deeply aware of a readjustment in relations between the two countries. There is also a renewed need for the establishment of an East Asian order, which led to calls for an East Asian community in Japan's public discourse. However, due to the ambivalent nature of this term, the people of China have rarely made mention of it. More recently the slogan "Establish the New Order in East Asia" has appeared, the meaning of which has been much clearer. In a special broadcast on 3 November in the twenty-seventh year of the republic [1938], Prince Konoe[36] explained Japan's true intention is not the destruction of China, but rather the prosperity of China. Japan hopes to share the responsibility for the construction of the New Order in East Asia with China. In a further broadcast on 12 December of the same year, he announced the three principles of "friendly relations with our neighbour," "joint efforts against communism," and "economic mutual assistance,"[37] This brought about the Chinese people's interest in the future prospects of all East Asia. They have been continuously examining this slogan of establishing an New Order in East Asia. Yet still there remain those who either hold senseless doubts or treat the plan with cold indifference.

And why do they hold these senseless doubts? Because they "view the ambitions of the noble through the eyes of the lowly,"[38] imagining that Japan only promotes this slogan to disguise its mainland policy or to cover up its plot for the merging of China and Japan. However, we need only to hear the words of Itagaki Seishirō[39] to gain a clear impression of the establishment of the New Order in East Asia: "To return China to China, Japan to Japan, and East Asia to East Asia." If we are then to listen to the words of General Nishio Toshizō,[40] we then see that the construction of the New Order in East Asia is not by some happenstance method but is a concept that has been actively and specifically pursued: "China must take China into consideration, but also take Japan into consideration. Japan must take Japan into consideration, but must also take China into consideration. Both countries must take East Asia into consideration." And then on 13 March in the twenty-ninth year of the republic [1940] we read the following lines in the declaration of Prime Minister Yonai Mitsumasa:[41] "We will make the Chinese people find contentment. Close neighbours must help each other." Through "mutual respect for the nature of the other country's nation" and "mutual defence against the infiltration of materialist communization," "we will establish peace in East Asia, a mutually beneficial economy, and reciprocal financial assistance in large and small forms." This gives us a much more firm and precise understanding of the substance of the establishment of the New

Order in East Asia. After this the Japanese expeditionary commander-in-chief expressed in a "Report to Officers and Soldiers":

> When the national sovereignty and independence of China has been threatened, this has led to turmoil in East Asia and also led to the intimidation of Japan as well. In Japan there are those intellectuals who hope to divide and weaken China, and to manipulate China's doom. We are not lacking in such people, but this kind of thinking is no different from that of the various Euro-American countries that invade China. This is not the objective of our military operations ... The amiable integration of China and Japan must await the firm resolution of the Japanese to devote themselves to the assistance of China in the realization of unification and to satisfy the enthusiastic demands of the nation. Only then can we be successful. If some among the Japanese hope to trick the Chinese people and gain inappropriate profits, or treat China as Japan's colony as the foreigners do, this would go against the respect for morality that is intrinsic to Japan and would result in Japan being unable to uphold its once unassailable beliefs.

This offers us unlimited hopes for the spirit surrounding the establishment of the New Order in East Asia. Every day the meaning of this establishment becomes more and more concrete and ever clearer. Therefore, although there are still those who doubt our slogan of "establish the New Order in East Asia," these people become fewer by the day.

However, perhaps there still remains a segment of the population that sees no good in the establishment of New East Asia, which feels today's China is struggling to survive [so] how could there be the time and energy to talk about establishing the New Order in East Asia? Therefore, Japanese people view the Chinese people's indifference and believe that the Chinese are only aware of their own nation's independent existence, and think nothing of the shared responsibility for East Asia. This leads to the Japanese castigating the Chinese for being too myopic, to which the Chinese retort that the ideals of the Japanese people are too unrealistic. Investigating this impasse between the Chinese and Japanese peoples, we find that it is due to these reasons that there is not yet any mutual understanding between the two peoples, neither is there mutual trust. Therefore, Lin Baisheng, minister of propaganda, explained:

> The establishment of a strong new world order must be based upon strong parts. Conversely, a country's independent existence much be protected

> through a powerful international order. Both parties should achieve this mutual understanding, to establish the New Order in East Asia and pursue the independent existence of the nation; if we consider them individually, these are plans for the independent existence of each one; if we consider them together, these are plans for mutual and safe development – this means success through unity, with not the least division. For Japan, in order to achieve the goal of establishing the New Order in East Asia, the country must assist with the governance of China so that China may achieve independent existence, followed by development and prosperity. In order to share the responsibility of establishing the New Order in East Asia, China must strive toward the nation's independent existence, and particularly must unite and struggle together based upon the equal treatment of our nation. The starting point for each nation may be different, but our path is the same, and, therefore, so is our objective. So today in China, we must understand and acknowledge that the establishment of the New Order in East Asia and China's independence are one and the same. China's independence must be pursued through the New Order in East Asia. And in Japan, they must understand and acknowledge this same fact [...] that the establishment of the New Order in East Asia can only be successful with the independent existence of China as a cornerstone. In China, we must make Japan aware that the independent existence of China not only poses no obstacle to the establishment of the New Order in East Asia, it is actually beneficial to the order. And then both sides can come to understand each other and advance together.

These words are both appropriate and valuable! From this we see that the goals of Greater Asianism and the New Order in East Asia are one and the same, and so too are the guiding principles. Then what are the differences between the New Order in East Asia and Greater Asianism? To put it simply and precisely, we can say that the New Order in East Asia is the realization of Greater Asianism, and Greater Asianism is the ideal of the New Order in East Asia before its realization.

Notes

1 Lin Baisheng's name is also romanized as Lin Bosheng.

2 See Torsten Weber, "Nanjing's Greater Asianism: Wang Jingwei and Zhou Huaren, 1940," in *Pan-Asianism: A Documentary History, 1920–Present*, ed. Sven Saaler and Christopher W.A. Szpilman (Lanham, MD: Rowman and Littlefield, 2011), 209–19.

3 Frederic Wakeman Jr., "The Puppet Police and 76 Jessfield Road," in *The Shanghai Badlands* (Cambridge: Cambridge University Press, 1996), 85.

4 The "Telegram of the 29th" (*yandian*) was issued by Wang Jingwei on 29 December 1938, indicating his permanent separation from the Chiang Kai-shek government. *Yan* indicated the twenty-ninth day of the month in classical numerology.
5 Ladu Road, now known as Xiangyang South Road.
6 Yang Honglie, "DaYazhouzhuyi yu Yingguo" [Greater Asianism and Britain], *DaYazhouzhuyi* [Greater Asianism] 1, 1 (1940): 39–46.
7 Yang Honglie, "Shelun: Zhongshan xiansheng shishi yaochuan zhengming hou de suogan" [Editorial: My feelings after the rumour of Sun Yat-sen's death were proven to be true], *Jiaoyu zhoubao* [Education weekly (Shanghai)] 11 (1925): 2.
8 Wang Jingwei, "Sanminzhuyi zhi lilun yu shiji" [The Three Principles of the People in theory and practice (23 November 1939)], in *Wang Jingwei guomin zhengfu chengli* [The establishment of the Wang Jingwei Nationalist government], ed. Huang Meizhen (Shanghai: Shanghai renmin chubanshe, 1984), 210.
9 Lin Baisheng, "Qianyan" [Preface] to Zhou Huaren, *DaYazhouzhuyi gangyao* [An outline of Asianism] (Nanjing: DaYazhouzhuyi yuekanshe, 1940), 1, 3.
10 The Hu Shi archive at Academia Sinica retains family pictures that Yang sent to Hu Shi (1891–1962). Yang also frequently quoted Hu in his writings, and turned to Hu for financial support for his studies in Tokyo. He was a student of Liang Qichao (1873–1929) and turned to him for mentoring and advice. See Ye Shuxun, ed., *Yang Honglie wencun* [The writings of Yang Honglie] (Nanjing Shi: Jiangsu renmin chubanshe, 2016), 3.
11 He Qinhua, "Yang Honglie qiren qishu" [Yang Honglie, the man and his writings], *Faxue Luntan* [Legal forum] 18, 3 (2003): 89.
12 Yang Honglie, *Zhongguo falü zai dongYa zhuguo zhi yingxiang* [The influence of Chinese law in all the countries of East Asia] (Shanghai: Commercial Press, 1937), 9.
13 He Qinhua, "Yang Honglie qiren qishu," 89. Also see Ye Shuxun, *Yang Honglie,* 8.
14 The Shanghai media were merciless in condemning Wan, describing her as "skinny like a gristly pork chop, and ugly to match." Wu Fu, "Wan Mengwan congqingfaluo" [Wan Mengwan let off easily], *Xin Shanghai* [New Shanghai] 41 (1946): 9. Also see "Wan Mengwan zhuan jiang kaiyi" [Wan Mengwan to be released], *Hai Jing* [Shanghai crystal] 10 (1946): 11.
15 See Hung Lieh Yang, "A Lonely Evening," *Guoguang yingyu* [English fortnightly] 3, 1 (1946): 31.
16 He Qinhua, "Yang Honglie qiren qishu," 90; Ye Shuxun, *Yang Honglie,* 42.
17 Yang Honglie, "DaYazhouzhuyi zhi jieshuo" [Defining Greater Asianism], *DaYazhouzhuyi yu dongYa lianmeng* 1 (1942): 7–9.
18 Yang was using this term, *huxiang tixie,* and calling for East Asian nations' mutual cooperation before the outbreak of the Sino-Japanese War. See the above quotation from his 1937 book, *Zhongguo falü zai dongYa zhuguo zhi yingxiang.*
19 *Wangdao,* or *Ōdō* in Japanese, is the "Kingly Way" by which Confucian sages governed the people through *ren* (benevolence). In 1924 Sun Yat-sen posited *Wangdao* as the root of Asian civilization in opposition to *Badao* (Way of the Hegemon), which utilizes violent coercion and represents Western civilization. *Wangdao* was also a concept for Japanese propaganda in Manchukuo and China.
20 This treaty amended the Treaty of Tientsin and gave China Most Favoured Nation status.
21 Yang did not include the clause "and as the convention of 1894 has expired, according to the legal opinion of Mr. John W. Foster, and other eminent lawyers." Many Chinese immigrants were able to legally challenge American restrictions on their entry until 1894, when Congress passed a bill greatly restricted the right to challenge immigration decisions.
22 Yang added: "This protest was raised by the Republican Party."
23 Wu Tingfang originally published this work in English with Frederick Stokes Press in 1914. It has recently been republished with an introduction by Jonathan Spence: Wu

Tingfang, *America through the Spectacles of an Oriental Diplomat* (London: Anthem Press, 2007), 30–31.

24 I have not been able to find any African country by this name.

25 I will not reproduce the entire text here. Sun Yat-sen's "Greater Asianism" speech can be found in a 1941 English translation at https://en.wikisource.org/wiki/Sun_Yat-sen%27s_speech_on_Pan-Asianism.

26 Yang Honglie, "'DaYazhouzhuyi' yu 'Minzuzhuyi'" [Greater Asianism and Nationalism], *DaYazhouzhuyi yu DongYa lianmeng* 1 (1942): 9–11.

27 I have used an existing English translation: Sun Yat-sen, *San Min Chu I: The Three Principles of the People,* trans. Frank W. Price (Taipei: China Publishing, n.d.), 3.

28 Yang had actually been arguing this long before the war. In 1933 he argued for the special nature of Chinese culture as peace-loving and moral, based on *Wangdao* and in opposition to Western *Badao.* See Yang Honglie, "Zhongguo wenhua yu shijie wenhua" [Chinese culture and world culture], *Suijing Xukan* [Appeasement weekly] 5 (1933): 22.

29 This paragraph is a quotation from Wang Jingwei's "Xinguomin yundong gangyao" (A summary of the New Citizens' Movement), originally published 1 January 1942, reprinted in *Wang Jingwei guomin zhengfu 'qingxiang' yundong* [The rural pacification movement of the Wang Jingwei National government], ed. Zhu Jinyuan (Shanghai: Shanghai renmin chubanshe, 1985), 371.

30 Yang may have an incorrect date for this article as it is listed as 1908 elsewhere.

31 By "those that fawn on foreign powers," Wang is referring to the Qing government, but Yang uses this quote to indicate the Chongqing Kuomintang and the Communist Party. He did not view Japan as foreign, but as part of a united East Asia. Wang Jingwei, "Shenlun geming juebu zhizhao guafen zhi huo" [Revolution must never lead to the calamity of dividing China], in *Wang Jingwei quanji,* vol. 2, 72–118 (Shanghai: Sanmin gongsi, 1929), 116.

32 Sun Yat-sen, *China and Japan: Natural Friends – Unnatural Enemies: A Guide for China's Foreign Policy by Sun Yat-sen,* with a foreword by Wang Jingwei and edited by T'ang Leangli (Shanghai: China United Press, 1941), 116. Originally published in the 1917 pamphlet *The Vital Problem of China,* and republished in Taiwan in 1953. In the Chinese original, the term for "Pan-Asianism" was "Asianism" (*Yazhouzhuyi*). Sun Yat-sen, *Sun Zhongshan quanji* [Complete writings of Sun Yat-sen], ed. Zhongguo shehui kexueyuan jindaishi yanjiusuo Zhonghua minguoshi yanjiushi, et al. (Beijing: Zhonghua shuju chuban, 1985), vol. 4, 95.

33 Translation taken from the 1941 *China and Japan.* I have added the sentences that were not translated in 1941 in [brackets].

34 Ibid., 151–52.

35 Yang Honglie, "DaYazhouzhuyi yu 'DongYa xin zhixu'" [Greater Asianism and the New Order in East Asia], *DaYazhouzhuyi yu DongYa lianmeng* 1 (1942): 11–12.

36 Prime Minister Konoe Fumimaro was officially known as Prince Konoe in English. However, the title was not equivalent to the English term "prince" and was also regularly translated as "duke." This speech in November, known as the Second Konoe Address (*dai niji seimei*) was the first official call for the New Order in East Asia. See Marius Jansen, *The Making of Modern Japan* (Cambridge: Harvard University Press, 2009), 623.

37 Known as the Third Konoe Address (*dai sanji seimei*), this was an important declaration for establishing the Wang Jingwei government.

38 This is a popular expression from the *Zuozhuan.*

39 Although minister of war in 1939, General Itagaki Seishirō (1885–1948) was the commander of Korea's Chōsen Army at the time of this article. He was hanged for war crimes in 1948.

40 General Nishio Toshizō (1881–1960) was commander of the Second Army (*dainigun*), an army mobilized to secure north China after the Marco Polo Bridge Incident. He served in north China and Manchukuo before retiring in 1943.

41 Yonai Mitsumasa (1880–1948) was a commander of the Japanese navy before being appointed to the position of prime minister for six months in 1940. He was the third of the military-appointed prime ministers after Konoe Fumimaro stepped down in January 1939, but he was unpopular and replaced by Konoe, who returned for his second term in July 1940 and stayed in power until Tōjō Hideki became prime minister in October 1941.

16 The New Citizens' Movement and Wang Jingwei-ism

CRAIG A. SMITH

On 1 January 1942, the Reorganized National Government (RNG) officially began a nationwide movement to revitalize the spirit (*jingshen*) of the Chinese people. Wang Jingwei (1883–1944) and his government designed the New Citizens' Movement (NCM) as a means to penetrate all levels of society to enforce correct thought and morality in individuals. Published in journals and newspapers across the nation, Wang's "Xinguomin yundong gangyao" (Outline of the New Citizens' Movement) listed eight points to develop the strengths and amend the shortcomings of the Chinese people. By following these eight points, the Chinese people would create a "new spirit," which would be able to "realize the Three Principles of the People" and "protect East Asia." At the same time, the Wang government attempted to develop a cult of personality around Wang, called Wang Jingwei-ism.

Having an acute understanding of the importance of such a construction, propaganda ministry chief Lin Baisheng (1902–46) called his office the "Publicity Bureau" in English and assembled a team of able propagandists and academics to create an image of both Wang and the RNG that was in contrast to the governments of Chiang Kai-shek (1887–1975) and Mao Zedong (1893–1976). An examination of this official propaganda from the RNG at its strongest moment shows that, although Wang's government constructed the NCM on the existing models of three related movements, this movement largely employed the moral and political authority of both Confucianism and the nationalist image of Sun Yat-sen to motivate the people and encourage loyalty to the collaborationist regime.

RELATED MOVEMENTS

The New Citizens' Movement was built on the previously established frameworks of Chiang Kai-shek's New Life Movement, Ishiwara Kanji's (1886–1949) movement for an East Asian League, and the Wang regime's existing Rural Pacification Movement.

The connection with Chiang's New Life Movement, which began eight years earlier in 1934, has been well-documented by scholars.[1] David Barrett explains: "Both movements stressed spiritual, or ideological, training as essential to the creation of a disciplined, unified people. Both movements fostered the idea that a properly motivated populace would spur material development of the nation ... Both movements testify to the strong tradition of Confucian inner rectification and social harmonization present in the Kuomintang."[2]

As in the New Life Movement, NCM efforts to control the people were focused through a combination of nationalism and Confucianism and attempted to turn the populace into agents of the state with fascist populism centralized on an absolute leader. However, the NCM took this a step further, making Wang's rule into the first example of an East Asian cult of personality, which I will return to below. Hans van de Ven describes the New Life Movement as an "attempt to propagate a new Chinese identity around which to make the armed forces and society cohere," matching modernity and Confucianism for a new China.[3] The same definition could be applied to the New Citizens' Movement.

The second movement connected to the NCM was the Rural Pacification Movement. This effort to root out communism and "cleanse" rural areas of east China had begun six months earlier. The NCM was, in part, an urban extension of the effort, which Wang had been very supportive of. "Model peace zones" would be cleared of Communist guerrillas, through the *baojia* collective responsibility system, and then economically developed.[4] The Rural Pacification Movement was more effective than the NCM, but failed to extend the territory of the government or deepen its reach as Wang had hoped.[5]

The NCM was also connected to the movement to construct an East Asian League, which had first been propagated by Ishiwara Kanji and Miyazaki Masayoshi (1893–1954) as an Asianist plan to integrate the five nationalities of Manchukuo in an egalitarian union based on the

Confucian concept of the Kingly Way.[6] Sun Yat-sen's "Greater Asianism" was also based on the understanding that East Asia was fundamentally opposed to the West due to its political and moral basis in the Kingly Way.[7] Therefore, the East Asian League and Greater Asianism overlapped conveniently. Shibata Tetsuo has shown that the NCM arose out of the movement for an East Asian League, but that Wang concentrated on the political independence that Ishiwara had maintained was crucial for the development and integration of Asian states.[8] The Wang government did gain greater autonomy throughout 1942 and 1943, yet never managed to convince citizens of its authority, despite consistent attempts to do so through invocations of Confucianism and the symbolism of Sun Yat-sen.

CONFUCIANISM AND SUN YAT-SEN'S THREE PRINCIPLES

The position of Confucianism in Wang's "Outline of the New Citizens' Movement" is evident in the emphasis on loyalty and ethics in general, and in references to the *Great Learning* in the introduction in particular. Although these references were strategically placed to draw on both traditional and modern authorities to validate the party state, some historians have accentuated other Confucian elements evident in the NCM and the Wang regime. As Poshek Fu argues, movements such as the NCM "promoted a collectivist, forward-looking outlook defined by an amalgam of the Confucian virtues of 'loyalty' and 'propriety' with Western scientism."[9] Still, the most important discourse evident in the New Citizens' Movement was Sun Yat-sen's Three Principles of the People.

Although once a leader of the left-wing cadres in the Kuomintang, Wang became a fervent anticommunist in the 1930s. He also held no sympathy for liberalism. This can be seen in points three and four of the translation below, as he rails against "Communist bandits" as a reason for China's lack of material development while also arguing that "in the face of danger, we must sacrifice the individual in order to save the state." He made a number of other speeches denouncing liberalism and individualism in 1942, arguing that the survival of the state must be paramount.[10] This stemmed from Wang's understanding of Sun's Three Principles as offering a third way, an alternative to liberalism and communism in the form of nationalism. He was not the only disciple of Sun

Yat-sen to see the ideology in this way, although he may have pushed the limits of interpretation, crossing the line to statism and fascism. Hu Hanmin (1879–1936), Dai Jitao (1891–1949), and others had also criticized the "red imperialism" of communism and the "white imperialism" of Europe, arguing for Sun's nationalism as an alternative to both.[11] The wartime Propaganda Bureau employed almost identical criticisms of red and white imperialism.[12] However, Wang was not attempting to reinterpret Sun's ideology in this text; rather, he was limning the methods that could encourage China to achieve the ideology.

The first three points of Wang's outline are brief explanations of the means by which to achieve Sun Yat-sen's Three Principles of Nationalism, Rule by the People, and the People's Livelihood (*minshengzhuyi*). However, Wang went beyond Sun's original texts, asserting that Greater Asianism was the path to the realization of Nationalism; democratic centralism was the path to Rule by the People; and anti-communism was the path of the Principle of People's Livelihood. Deriving a sense of legitimacy from his long apprenticeship under Sun Yat-sen, Wang propagated his understanding of the Three Principles, and his team in turn propagated him as a new Sun.

Alongside the NCM, the propaganda bureau developed a cult of personality around Wang, seeking to both bolster his authority and to contradistinguish him from Chiang Kai-shek and Mao Zedong.[13] Wang Jingwei-ism was first detailed in an article by, oddly enough, a Communist spy in Wang's employ. Yuan Shu published "Wang Jingwei-zhuyi" (Wang Jingwei-ism) in *Xin Zhongguo bao* (New China) on 21 December 1941, highlighting four main points: the correct understanding of the Three Principles of the People, Greater Asianism, peace, and Action over Words.[14] The propaganda of Wang Jingwei-ism was almost inseparable from that of the NCM. However, the particular effort to develop these ideas under the leader's name merits further consideration and has left behind sufficient sources for analysis. In 1942, Yuan Shu made efforts to define the central texts through a two volume *Wang Jingwei-zhuyi duben* (Wang Jingwei-ism reader) that compiled many of Wang's published political texts.[15] This campaign, which included Nanjing residents wearing buttons with Wang's image on their lapels, was short-lived and ineffective, but resulted in a plethora of images of Wang Jingwei being made available across the areas under the control of the Reorganized National Government.

The NCM and Wang Jingwei-ism ultimately failed. Education campaigns were carried out, but due to the lack of loyalty and organization in the RNG, they were slowly implemented and ineffective.[16] As Wang himself notes in the introduction and conclusion to the essay translated here, this movement was never intended to be an ideology, but instead brought together a number of rules and guidelines intended to boost spiritual (non-material) and material development in China. However, the government did not have the authority or support to mobilize the people with such a campaign, and the war was gradually but definitively slipping away from the Nanjing government during these years. Still, the movement defined in these texts reveals the efforts of the collaboration regime to establish itself as an independent and legitimate state. It shows the importance of Sun Yat-sen as a symbol for the RNG and the importance of Confucianism in the field of ethics, both of which point to continuity in propaganda and discourse with the government before it. These texts also show change, particularly the efforts to employ Greater Asianism as a justification for participation with, and inevitably domination by, the Empire of Japan. And, finally, they show the haphazard attempts to make sense of the regime's position and situation in the world, attempts that would soon be meaningless.

TRANSLATIONS

Outline of the New Citizens' Movement[17]

WANG JINGWEI

War is like a military review of citizens, or, to put it more precisely, it is a military review of the spirit (*jingshen*)[18] of a country's people. These four years of turmoil have brought both the strengths and the shortcomings of our compatriots to light. The strengths should be developed and glorified, while the shortcomings should be amended. With more than four years passing since the Sino-Japanese Incident,[19] we have now entered the Great War to Protect East Asia.[20] If we fail to have a new spirit at this junction, how can we live up to our new responsibility and accomplish our new mission? Calling this a new spirit does not simply imply that it should be manufactured. We must dispel our old debasements and engage in self-renewal.[21] This can be understood to mean that we must bravely acknowledge our deficiencies, and then rectify these deficiencies. In particular, we must bravely root out and sweep away our worst attributes. This is the emphasis of the New Citizens' Movement.

The New Citizens' Movement is not another ideology, as we already have the Three Principles of the People for the foundations of the Republic of China. The question we must now consider is why we cannot realize the Three Principles of the People. It is not due to a lack in our ability to implement, but in our ability to research this ideology. In short, the strength of our spirit (*jingshenli*) is lacking. The New Culture Movement's resolve and measures to deal with these failings must be a treatment that matches the ailment. I therefore propose the following outline:

1 Why are we unable to realize Nationalism? Because we have forgotten Asianism. "If China cannot achieve freedom and equality, then we will be unable to do our part in the construction of East Asia. And to fully achieve freedom and equality for China, East Asia must be liberated." The truth of these words was only realized at the onset of the peace movement, yet they were earnestly expressed in Greater Asianism much earlier. Why did we forget this and allow China to fall into this plight? From this day forth, we shall meld the love of China and the love of East Asia into one heart. With mutual love between all the nations of East Asia, we shall unite for the protection of East Asia. This is the main point of Nationalism.
2 Why are we unable to realize Rule by the People (*minquanzhuyi*)? Because we ignored the system of democratic centralism.[22] Therefore, although we praised the people's rule (*minzhi*) on the surface, in practice we created a dictatorship by an individual. From this day forth, our group must be organized, our action must be disciplined. Matters of great importance shall be thoroughly researched before any decision is made. And once a decision is made, implementation shall be uncontested. At all times, we must remember that something may be "difficult to understand, but easy to implement," and we should dare to implement. This is what is meant by truly and loyally seeking knowledge, and is the main point of Rule by the People.[23]
3 Why are we unable to realize the Principle of the People's Livelihood (*minshengzhuyi*)? Because we ignored the development of the state capital. If we are able to emphasize this and develop the country's capital, then private capital will fall in line. The Communist bandits will then have no excuse to promote class struggle; and the British and American economic invasion will have nowhere left to play its tricks. Operating in concert, the Communist bandits and the British-American invasion have

formed a pincer movement uniting the left and the right. From this day forth, through the aggregation of spirit, we must develop the country's capital. This is the main point of the Principle of People's Livelihood.

4 If we are to pursue the three main points described above, then it is imperative that we enhance our spiritual power by bolstering all that we can and researching all that we can. Therefore, we must first promote the public spirit and forget the individual spirit. The individual must give to the state rather than receive from the state; must be sparing to oneself to be prodigal to the state. In the face of danger, one must sacrifice oneself in order to save the state.[24]

5 The key to uniting the strength of the nation is amicable relations between people. We must remember the following points concerning amicable relations: speak honestly; do not conceal your thoughts; employ virtuousness and dispel malevolence. It is important that we hear of people's goodness, then happiness will prosper. If we hear of people's ills, then a negative spirit will prosper. Let people take pleasure in the good and shame in the bad. Particularly those working together must collectively weather hardship, labouring together and resting together, to foster amicable relations. One should acknowledge others' achievements and not take undue credit. One should admit fault and not blame others. Failing in this, we cannot say that we have united in an ardent spirit.

6 Our nation has been ruined by impetuous and superficial actions. We are aware of our many shortcomings, and that the greatest of these are that our actions cannot be disciplined and our knowledge cannot be made scientific. From this day forth, discipline will extend from the individual to the multitude; science will not only be made universal, it will be deep-rooted.

7 The majority of Chinese people remain mired in poverty. And now, it is needless to say, they must be ever frugal. Therefore, increasing production is of the upmost importance for us. Yet prudence in consumption and the policies of People's Livelihood are both still advantageous. For example, we can increase the production of grains as a substitute for rice. Only a small minority of people are currently trying to live a spartan life, but there are both economic and ethical reasons for them to do so. The economic reasons are the passive restriction of unnecessary consumption and the active apportioning of resources to effective means. From a moral perspective, to observe this many people mired in poverty with our eyes yet still not economize would be absolutely unconscionable.

8 In the political realm, we must drive out corruption in the shortest possible time. All public servants and all soldiers must have guarantees on their livelihood, yet it is entirely inexcusable for them to use dissatisfaction with their living conditions as an excuse for corruption and negligence. We must aspire to the spirit of "the cries of one family do not compare to the cries of the entire district."[25] We must exterminate the corrupt and negligent as mercilessly as we do locusts.

The points raised above, including total mobilization for spiritual purposes and economic construction for material purposes, are simple words with no lofty theory; however, we seek to save China, to protect East Asia, to depart from this impossible path, and so we launch the New Citizens' Movement as a means of encouraging ourselves and also encouraging each other. All of the items listed above should be persistently discussed and persistently implemented.

(New Year's Day of the thirty-first year of the republic)

Wang Jingwei-ism[26]

YUAN SHU

Before today, no one used the term "Wang Jingwei-ism," yet the concept was actually formed much earlier. We take up this term now to raise this standard of a common belief and united efforts that we aspire to.

An "ism" is a mixture of thought (*sixiang*), belief (*xinyang*), and power (*liliang*). The formation of an ism stems in part from the great character of an individual, and in part from the ability of this great character to fit the needs of a society and become the representative figure in a particular history and environment. Therefore, to truly be called an "ism," this ism must be an objective of a common belief and united efforts. This goes without saying.

The formation of Wang Jingwei-ism began three years ago with the December 29 Telegram.[27] Through these three years of development, the content of Wang Jingwei-ism has been clearly stipulated. And what is this content?

1. Wang Jingwei-ism is based in the Three Principles of the People. Since the time of the president's death,[28] people have been distorting the Three Principles. In Chongqing, people of the likes of Dai Jitao have interpreted the Three Principles entirely from the perspective of philosophy, making it

a vacuous and abstruse ideology, while others cite it to collaborate with British and American imperialists and to discriminate against others. As for those in the Chinese Communist Party, they too cheer for the Three Principles in order to support the reunion of their United Front and their pipe dreams of wresting political power. However, distinguishing their words from those in Chongqing, they invariably add "the revolutionary" before "Three Principles of the People." These kinds of interpretations and applications are entirely a matter of strategic employment and sink under the quintessence of the Three Principles of the People. And what is the quintessence of the Three Principles? In "The Theory and Practice of the Three Principles of the People," Mr. Wang explains very clearly. Simply put:

> Nationalism is not the same as the statism of Europe and the United States. Statism is narrow-minded and xenophobic, while Nationalism is produced upon the intrinsic peaceful thinking of China and has no xenophobia.
>
> Rule by the People is not the same as the "natural rights" of Europe and the United States, neither is it the same as the social democracy of these countries. Natural rights promote individual liberty, while Rule by the People promotes collective liberty (*quanti ziyou*). Social democracy is an economic concept, while Rule by the People is political. In terms of quality, the goal of Rule by the People is a politics of all the people (*quanmin zhengzhi*).
>
> Likewise, the Principle of People's Livelihood is not the same as socialism or communism. Marxist communism promotes class struggle, but Mr. Sun's Principle of People's Livelihood promotes class coöperation. One method is violent, while the other is peaceful, and on this point they remain completely different. Marxist communism aims to entirely abolish private property, while Mr. Sun's Principle of People's Livelihood aims to develop the state's capital while protecting personal capital under a planned economy. On this point too they remain completely different.[29]

This is the special nature of the Three Principles of the People. The Three Principles "has the goal of saving the country and sets off from this standpoint of saving the country." This can be understood from the lines: "The Three Principles are principles for saving the country"; "The goal of the Three Principles of the People is to save the country, and liberating China from the economic invasion and economic oppression of Europe and America is the first requirement for saving the country"; "How can we liberate China from the position of semicolonialism and achieve freedom and equality for

China? Mr. Sun prepared two methods for this: The first was through the efforts of China; the second was through mutual cooperation with the advanced country of Japan." Wang Jingwei-ism is based on this quintessence of the Three Principles of the People.

2. Wang Jingwei-ism is based on the president's Greater Asianism. For three years now, Mr. Wang has repeatedly expounded on the essential meaning of Greater Asianism, the speech that our president made in the thirteenth year of the republic [1924]. Mr. Wang believes that the significance of Greater Asianism "is to rouse our love for China, as well as our love for Japan and East Asia." He also explained:

> Done in accordance with the Three Principles of the People, China will inevitably gain freedom and equality, as well as the power to shoulder the burden for bringing stability to East Asia alongside Japan, establishing our sense of responsibility for East Asia. Therefore, for China, the Three Principles of the People are principles to save the country. For East Asia, the Three Principles of the People are Greater Asianism."

In Chongqing, where they rely on British-American imperialism, Greater Asianism has long been forgotten. Yet Mr. Wang explained through theory and contemporary conditions: "From beginning to end, Mr. Sun maintained the belief, the perpetual belief, that Sino-Japanese cooperation lies at the heart of solving the problems of East Asia." Wang Jingwei-ism is based on this belief.

3. Wang Jingwei-ism is based on peace. In the December 29 Telegram, Mr. Wang explained: "With such a sincere declaration from the Japanese government, if we follow the peaceful approach, not only will the northern provinces be safeguarded, the territory lost since the War of Resistance [began] can be regained, allowing Chinese sovereignty, administrative independence and integrity to be maintained."[30] Mr. Wang's adoption of peaceful means toward Japan is the consistent spirit that he continues to maintain. This consistent spirit is formed by loyalty to the president's dying command for "Peace, struggle, and save China"[31] as well as adherence to the proverb "It is better to dissolve enmity than to let it bear fruit."[32] After 1931, Mr. Wang advocated "Resistance and diplomacy"[33] to rectify the climate of "Oppose direct diplomacy," successively concluding the [1932] Cease Fire Agreement in Shanghai and the [1933] Tanggu Truce. Mr. Wang explained his intentions thus: "At the time, my intentions were rooted in the concept of 'it is better

to dissolve enmity than to let it bear fruit.' From the localized and temporary cessation of hostilities, I hoped to expand to peace across the entire country." The December 29 Telegram also advocated resolution through peaceful means. However, it was upon seeing the three principles of the Konoe Declaration, which, he stated, "are the ideal of Greater Asianism and the underlying spirit of the Three Principles of the People,"[34] that he believed the time had truly come in which we must rely on resolution through peaceful means. Wang Jingwei-ism is based on this consistent spirit of peaceful means.

4. Wang Jingwei-ism is based in action. Mr. Wang is not a dreamer but a doer. We need not discuss his spirit shown here: "Among the crowds of [Beijing] I chaunt elate, Tranquilly, I enter the prison-house."[35] Nor do we need speak of the numerous times he was forced into exile or shot at. We just need to consider the courage of his escape from Chongqing. This is enough to make us sigh in admiration, because we know that, were Mr. Wang to remain in Chongqing and falsely shout out "Fight the War of Resistance," he would easily have received blind praise. However, he had to brave countless dangers and endure spite and abuse while promoting the peace movement. This is the true spirit of action. This is why Mr. Wang is not a scholar, but a man of action,[36] and this is why he has become the leader. Wang Jingwei-ism is based on the spirit of action.

Of course, the content of Wang Jingwei-ism does not stop with the four points discussed above. From the sincerity of "honest words and responsible actions"[37] and progressing to a "polite dignity" externally and a "harmonious sense of responsibility" internally, these are all concrete expressions of the great personality of Mr. Wang. However, it is the four points listed above that encompass the most basic elements in Wang Jingwei-ism. Wang Jingwei-ism continues the final will of the president, but through Mr. Wang's subjective efforts and objective historical environment, Wang Jingwei-ism has the value and inevitable development of an independent existence.

Mr. Wang has said: "When I left Chongqing, all I had was the shirt on my back. I relied on thought and belief. And today, my power has manifested and it grows day by day. These are not subjective but objective words." This describes the formation of Wang Jingwei-ism. Mr. Wang continued: "For example, if all those in this hall today are united in thought, united in belief, then we can naturally surge forth with united strength. This hall could be like this, and the entire country could be like this." This describes how Wang Jingwei-ism must become the standard for our common belief and united efforts. We have created this term "Wang Jingwei-ism" today in order to raise this standard of a common belief and united efforts for our aspirations.

Notes

1 Rana Mitter, *China's War with Japan, 1937–1945: The Struggle for Survival* (New York: Allen Lane, 2013), 229; David P. Barrett, "The Wang Jingwei Regime, 1940–1945: Continuities and Disjunctures with Nationalist China," in *Chinese Collaboration with Japan, 1932–1945,* ed. David P. Barrett and Larry N. Shyu (Stanford, CA: Stanford University Press, 2001), 105–6.

2 Barrett, "Wang Jingwei Regime," 105.

3 Hans J. van de Ven, *War and Nationalism in China: 1925–1945* (London: Routledge, 2003), 163–68.

4 John Hunter Boyle, *China and Japan at War, 1937–1945: The Politics of Collaboration* (Stanford, CA: Stanford University Press, 1972), 314–16.

5 Barrett, "Wang Jingwei Regime," 108.

6 Shibata Tetsuo, *Kyōryoku teikō chinmoku: Ō seiei nankin seifu no ideorogī ni taisuru hikakushiteki apurōchi* [Cooperation–opposition–silence: A comparative history approach to the ideology of Wang Jingwei's Nanjing government] (Tōkyō: Seibundō, 2009), 18. Also see Michael A. Schneider, "Miyazaki Masayoshi: 'On the East Asian League,' 1938," in *Pan-Asianism: A Documentary History, 1920–Present,* ed. Sven Saaler and Christopher W.A. Szpilman (Lanham, MD: Rowman and Littlefield, 2011), 179–83.

7 See Chapters 14 and 15 in this volume.

8 Shibata, *Kyōryoku teikō chinmoku,* 22.

9 Poshek Fu, *Passivity, Resistance, and Collaboration: Intellectual Choices in Occupied Shanghai, 1937–1945* (Stanford, CA: Stanford University Press, 1993), 148.

10 Lo Jiu-jung, "Survival as Justification for Collaboration, 1937–1945," in Barrett and Shyu, *Chinese Collaboration with Japan,* 120.

11 Hu Hanmin, "Minzu guoji yu disan guoji" [The International of Nations and the Third International], transcribed by Zhang Zhenzhi, *Xin Yaxiya* [New Asia] 1, 1 (1 October 1930): 18.

12 Shibata, *Kyōryoku teikō chinmoku,* 23.

13 Jeremy E. Taylor, "Republican Personality Cults in Wartime China: Contradistinction and Collaboration," *Comparative Studies in Society and History* 57, 3 (2015): 665–93.

14 Yuan Shu, "Wang Jingwei-zhuyi" [Wang Jingwei-ism], reprinted in: *Zhengzhi yuekan* [Monthly report of political affairs (Shanghai)] 3, 1 (1942).

15 Dongyoun Hwang, "Wang Jingwei, The Nanjing Government and the Problem of Collaboration" (PhD diss., Duke University, 1999), 298–99.

16 Barrett, "Wang Jingwei Regime," 106.

17 Wang Jingwei, "Xinguomin yundong gangyao" [A summary of the New Citizens' Movement], originally published 1 January 1942, reprinted in *Wang Jingwei guomin zhengfu 'qingxiang' yundong* [The Rural Pacification Movement by Wang Jingwei's National government] (Shanghai: Shanghai renmin chubanshe, 1985), 371.

18 *Jingshen* is an important keyword in modern China, but also a defining concept in the New Citizens' Movement. *Jingshen* referred to the spirit, zeitgeist, energy, or intellect of a group or individual.

19 The Sino-Japanese Incident refers to the Marco Polo Bridge Incident, usually called the 7–7 Incident in Chinese.

20 Although Wang was already attempting to prepare his citizens to enter the war with the Allies, the Reorganized National Government did not declare war until January 1943.

21 This is a slight edit of a popular line from Zhu Xi's commentary on the *Great Learning.* Explaining why he changed *qin min* to *xin min,* Zhu Xi explained that *xin* or "'Renewing' means stripping away what is old. This part means that, having already enlightened one's own enlightened Virtue, one should then extend it to reach others, making it so that they too have the wherewithal to *get rid of impurities from their old contaminations*" (my emphasis of the relevant phrase in Bryan Van Norden's translation). Liang Qichao used

this phrase to explain his own understanding of *xinmin* (new citizens), and Sun Yat-sen employed the phrase to explain revolution in "On the Significance of Revolution." Zhu Xi, "Collected Commentaries on the *Great Learning*," trans. Bryan W. Van Norden, in *Readings in Later Chinese Philosophy: Han to the Twentieth Century*, ed. Justin Tiwald and Bryan W. Van Norden (Indianapolis, IN: Hackett, 2014), 188.

22 Democratic centralism (*minzhu jiquan*) was a Leninist concept that encouraged democratic discussion within the party, but demanded united action. It was formally taken up by the Kuomintang in the First National Congress, 1924.

23 "Difficult to understand, easy to implement" (*zhinan xingyi*) was a phrase that Sun Yat-sen constantly employed to explain the importance of "seeking knowledge" (*qiuzhi*). For example: "The fundamental aim of Marxism is to overthrow capitalism, but whether the capitalists should be overthrown or not is a question which still needs serious study. Indeed, it is easy to act but difficult to know." See his 3 August 1924 speech, "The Social Question: Definitions and Solution," in Sun Yat-sen, *San Min Chu I: The Three Principles of the People* (Taipei: China Publishing, undated), 124, 125.

24 Wang was fond of reminding readers of his own sacrifice and his attempt to assassinate the emperor's regent in 1910. The act was certainly suicidal, but Wang was released from prison after the 1911 Revolution.

25 The Northern Song anticorruption official Fan Zhongyan (Fan Wenzheng) wrote this famous line to indicate the necessity of punishing corrupt officials without mercy. Fan Zhongyan, "Fan Wenzheng nianpu" [A chronicle of Fan Wenzheng], in *Fan Wenzheng gongji* [Collected writings by Fan Wenzheng (Fan Zhongyan)] (originally published in 1043) (Taipei: Taiwan shang wu yin shu guan, 1968), 29.

26 Yuan Shu, "Wang Jingwei-zhuyi."

27 The December 29 Telegram, known in Chinese as the *yandian,* was the proclamation issued by Wang on 29 December 1938, to indicate his "Peace Movement" in opposition to Chiang Kai-shek's War of Resistance.

28 Sun Yat-sen died in 1925, followed by an explosion of books and articles explaining the Three Principles of the People. Like numerous other Kuomintang writers, Yuan Shu included a space before every mention of Sun Yat-sen or "the president," a custom reserved for references to the emperor in texts from imperial China.

29 *Sanminzhuyizhi lilun yu shiji* (The theory and practice of the Three Principles of the People) was a speech Wang made to a conference for Japanese Imperial Army Propaganda Officers on 23 November 1939. The speech is available in *Shidai wenxuan* [Times selection] 2, 1 (1940): 25–28. Unattributed quotations in this essay are taken from *Sanminzhuyizhi lilun yu shiji.*

30 The entire December 29 Telegram has been translated into English and is available in David G. Atwill and Yurong Y. Atwill, eds., *Sources in Chinese History: Diverse Perspectives from 1644 to the Present* (Upper Saddle River, NJ: Prentice Hall, 2010), 226–27.

31 These are commonly believed to be Sun Yat-sen's dying words.

32 Wang used this Ming dynasty idiom to refer to Sun Yat-sen's willingness to work with Japan after the Twenty-One Demands in "Theory and Practice," 28.

33 This policy is outlined in English in T'ang Leang-Li's uncredited translation: Wang Ching-wei, "National Defence and Dictatorship," *China's Problems and Their Solution* (Shanghai: China United Press, 1934), 59–60.

34 Noted in *Sanminzhuyizhi lilun yu shiji.*

35 This is an excerpt from Wang's famous poem composed after his arrest in 1910, while he awaited his death sentence. This translation is based on Seyuan Shu's 1938 translation. Seyuan Shu, "On Being Arrested, I Improvise," *Poems of Wang Ching-Wei* (London: George Allen and Unwin, 1938), 16.

36 The term *zhishi,* more commonly known by the Japanese term *shishi* in English, refers to men of action that fought against the Qing.

37 This was one of Wang Jingwei's favourite sayings. Just before his death, he wrote the booklet *My Final Feelings,* in which he returned to the concept. Boyle, *China and Japan at War,* 395–97.

17 The Diaries of Zhou Fohai

Selected Translations from 1938

BRIAN G. MARTIN

The career of Zhou Fohai (1897–1948) demonstrates in microcosm the extreme volatility and uncertainty of politics in China in the first half of the twentieth century, and especially the complexity and contingency of collaboration in the Sino-Japanese War. He began his career as a founding member of the Chinese Communist Party (CCP), and was a member of the CCP-Kuomintang First United Front in the 1920s. Later he became a stalwart of the Chiang Kai-shek (1887–1975) regime, becoming a senior member of the so-called CC Clique, named for the two brothers Chen Guofu (1892–1951) and Chen Lifu (1900–2001), which controlled the party on Chiang's behalf and that was a factional rival to Wang Jingwei's (1883–1944) group, the so-called Reorganizationists (*gaizu pai*). Finally, he joined Wang Jingwei in collaboration with the Japanese, becoming minister of finance, head of the regime's central bank, minister for police (in 1940) and deputy head of its Executive Yuan.

Zhou Fohai placed great importance on his political and social networks. During the 1930s he forged close links with the political factions around Chiang Kai-shek, such as the CC Clique, and enjoyed good relations with the Renaissance Society (*Fuxingshe*), founded by right-wing nationalist Huangpu graduates, many of whom Zhou taught when he was an instructor at the Huangpu Military Academy in the mid-1920s. He also maintained good working relations with two of Chiang's closest confidants, Shao Lizi (1882–1967) and Chen Bulei (1890–1948). And he developed close relations with a constellation of military commanders around Chiang, including Gu Zhutong (1893–1987), He Yingqin (1890–1987), and Xiong Shihui (1893–1974). As the CC Clique's point man on relations with the Communists in 1937–38, he maintained correct relations with the Communist representatives on the United Front, Zhou Enlai (1898–1976) and Guo Moruo (1892–1978). In his efforts to seek a diplomatic exit from the war, Zhou developed relations with like-minded individuals such as Mei Siping (1896–1946), Gao Zongwu (1905–94), and Tao Xisheng (1899–1988). At the same time, he also began to develop closer relations with Wang Jingwei on this same issue, as well as with those in Wang's entourage. These included Chen Gongbo (1892–1946), Zeng Zhongming (1896–1939, Wang's secretary), Lin Baisheng (1902–46), and Chen Chunpu (1900–66, Madame Wang's nephew), although his relations with Chen Bijun (1891–1959, Madame Wang) remained correct but distant.

Zhou Fohai's diaries are one of the most valuable sources for the Wang Jingwei government in that they provide a first-hand account of the personalities and policies of that regime. They also provide a unique insight into the motivations of one of the key collaborators in the Wang regime.

Zhou's decision to keep a diary was influenced by his deep respect for his fellow Hunanese, the Qing statesman Zeng Guofan (1811–72), who played a leading role in the suppression of the Taiping Rebellion, and who also kept a diary. The late Cai Dejin (1935–99), the leading authority on Zhou's diaries, believed that Zhou only began to keep a diary at the beginning of 1937, and not earlier. Cai also noted that Zhou stopped his diary on 9 June 1945 when he had to attend to his mother's obsequies.[1] In the intervening years Zhou, who was a facile writer, proved to be a meticulous and assiduous diarist. He used two of the more popular annual diaries produced by the Commercial Press to write up his entries, devoting a page to each daily entry, no matter how short, and a book to a year. Normally he would write up the diary on a daily basis, but when pressure of work intervened he would occasionally write up his entries after an interval of several days. The writing up of his diary was almost an obsession with Zhou, as his son, Zhou Zhiyou (1922–85), noted: "If he had not written up his diary he could not sleep."[2]

Zhou attached great importance to his diaries, and in some way, saw them as his political testament. When a fire broke out in the family home in Nanjing in January 1943, Zhou's first thought was to save his diaries. Immediately after the Japanese surrender, Zhou sought to ensure the safety of his diaries by entrusting them to the father-in-law of General Gu Zhutong, commander of the Third War Zone, with whom he had a long-standing personal relationship. However, with his formal arrest in September 1945, Zhou's diaries were handed over to the Juntong (National Bureau of Investigation and Statistics), along with his other household goods, to be used in his prosecution; once he had been sentenced, they were stored in the Office for the Management of Enemy, Puppet, and Traitors' Property. When a Juntong officer was prepared to sell Zhou back the diaries for ten ten-ounce gold bars, Zhou was keen to purchase them, but his wife resolutely opposed this as being too expensive.[3]

The fate of the diaries became somewhat obscure after the collapse of the Kuomintang state in the Civil War (1946–49). According to Professor Cai, the former head of the office managing traitors' property fled to Hong Kong in 1950, taking with him two volumes of Zhou's diaries – those for 1939 and 1940. He lent the 1940 volume to an acquaintance, who later sold it to a local publishing house. What happened to the 1939 volume remains a mystery.[4] The loss of the diary for 1939 is a major blow to scholarship on the Wang Jingwei regime. This volume would have covered a crucial period in the formation of that regime – the discussions both with Japanese intelligence officials in Shanghai and with the Japanese government in Tokyo on the formation of a "National Government" (*guomin zhengfu*) under Wang Jingwei – and Zhou Fohai played a key role in these discussions.

After his trial and sentencing, Zhou resumed keeping a diary, and he kept writing up entries for almost nine months in 1947 until ill health forced him to stop. After the Communist takeover in 1949, Zhou's diaries enjoyed a rather sinister afterlife. With the fall of Liu Shaoqi (1898–1969) during the Cultural Revolution they were used by the Central Investigation Group as criminal evidence against Communist underground members active in the "White Areas" during the Sino-Japanese war.[5]

To provide an analytical context for the translations that follow, an overview of the events of 1938 is helpful.[6] This was the year of decision for Zhou Fohai. In the course of 1938 his earlier efforts to seek a negotiated peace with Japan within both the structures of the Kuomintang government and the parameters of the War of Resistance[7] were progressively replaced by a search for peace in spite of Chiang Kai-shek's government and in lieu of the War of Resistance. By year's end, Zhou Fohai, like other members of Wang Jingwei's group, had taken the fateful decision to leave Chongqing and to seek separate negotiations with the Japanese.

Zhou Fohai grew to believe that the only way to secure China's sovereignty was to seek a negotiated settlement to the Sino-Japanese War, which was necessary both for the survival of China and for the survival of the Kuomintang as a party and as a government. The mounting military defeats and the continued retreat of China's armies in the face of superior Japanese military power only strengthened his conviction that China could not win militarily. At the same time, he believed that, as conditions worsened, the only political beneficiary of the United Front would be the CCP. So, despite the setback of Konoe Fumimaro's (1891–1945) statement refusing to deal with Chiang, Zhou's pessimistic assessment of the prospects for the Kuomintang and China persuaded him of the urgent necessity for reopening communication channels with the Japanese.

Zhou's senior governmental positions in 1938 – deputy head of Chiang's Personal Office and acting director of the Kuomintang's Propaganda Department – gave him a broad overview of the situation that only reinforced his views. It was during the second quarter of 1938 that Zhou began to have regular official dealings with Wang Jingwei, and gradually came to share his views. The attempts to open up back channels were conducted initially within the structures of the Kuomintang state and with Chiang's backing. Zhou played an important role in facilitating the activities of Gao Zongwu (1905–94), China's unofficial go-between with the Japanese, and in encouraging him to deepen his contacts. Even when Chiang withdrew his support in mid-year, after Gao made an unauthorized visit to Tokyo, Zhou and the others believed that continuing the contacts clandestinely was in the best interests of the party state, and there was no consideration yet of developing a peace party separate from the Chongqing government.

The change in the nature of prosecution of contacts with the Japanese by Zhou and the Wang group was the result of the general crisis of morale within the Kuomintang government that followed the double blow of the fall of Guangzhou and Wuhan. In an atmosphere where many right-wing members of the government thought that China had to make terms with Japan, the Wang group reassessed its approach. They decided to actively pursue peace discussions with Japan on 30 October, deputed Gao Zongwu and Mei Siping (1896–1946) to hold discussions with Japanese representatives in Shanghai in November, and made an in-principle decision to leave Chongqing on 21 November. The key period, therefore, for the emergence of the Wang Jingwei "peace movement" was thus October–November 1938.

Zhou Fohai was one of the strongest advocates of the decision to leave and was disturbed by Wang Jingwei's last-minute procrastination. In the first half of December, while Zhou prepared the ground in Kunming, Wang frequently postponed his departure from Chongqing. This demoralized Zhou, who decided to return to Chongqing the day before Wang finally arrived in Kunming. With Wang's failure to persuade Long Yun (1884–1962), governor of Yunnan, to actively support his "peace movement," Zhou and the Wang group quickly left for Hanoi, where Zhou was actively involved in drafting Wang's telegram to Chiang explaining his motives; Zhou oversaw its publication in Hong Kong. Despite the formal expulsion of Wang from the Kuomintang on 1 January 1939, Zhou continued to believe that contacts could be maintained with Chongqing, and he was concerned that the Japanese not treat the "peace movement" as on a par with the existing pro-Japanese governments in north and central China. The die, nevertheless, had been cast.

TRANSLATION

Zhou Fohai's Diaries for 1938

Sunday, 3 April 1938

[In Wuhan] I heard Gao Zongwu report on the circumstances of his consultations in Shanghai and Hong Kong. In the afternoon I went over to Mr. Wang [Jingwei]'s residence and we discussed the issue of the director of the Propaganda Department, where I expressed my unwillingness [to take it up], and issues concerning the party and politics for about half an hour. In the evening I was summoned by Mr. Chiang [Kai-shek] and I went across the River, where I met Chen Guofu, Chen Lifu, Chen Bulei, Chen Cheng [1897–1965], He Zhonghan [1900–72], and Zhang Daofan [1897–1968], and we were strictly ordered [by Chiang] to dissolve the two organizations [i.e., the CC Clique and the Renaissance Society (*Fuxingshe*), also known as the Blue Shirts (*Lanyishe*)] and henceforth all are to work openly [...]

Friday, 8 April 1938

Chen Bulei telephoned to tell me that the plenum had passed a resolution this evening appointing Gu Mengyu [1888–1972] as director of propaganda,

[…] and Dong Xianguang [Hollington Tong, 1887–1971] and myself as deputy directors. Since Gu could not come to Hankou, I am to act as director. On hearing this I was extremely anxious, and as a result I spent a sleepless night.

Saturday, 9 April 1938

Shao Lizi [the outgoing director of propaganda] came over and we discussed the handover and I laughingly thanked him; I briefly enquired about the situation in the Department of Propaganda. I went directly to the residence of Zhang Qun [1889–1990] to request that he act on my behalf with Chiang and Wang and to do all he could to persuade them that Chen Gongbo or Wang Shijie [1891–1981] should be acting director and that I could be appointed deputy director; we talked for an hour and a half, as there were a great many party and political issues that were involved. In the afternoon, I called on Mr. Wang. I emphatically declined [the acting post], and he continued to express his agreement but told me that it was not convenient to recommend Chen Gongbo to Mr. Chiang. I then crossed the river and had a detailed discussion with Chen Bulei, and then I telephoned Zhang Qun and informed him of Wang's desire, and requested him to talk forcefully with the chairman [Chiang].

Wednesday, 13 April 1938

[I] went to the residence of Gao Zongwu, with whom I discussed our methods toward Japan in the immediate future, as Gao Zongwu was flying to Hong Kong tomorrow charged with a secret mission.

Saturday, 14 May 1938

[…] Cheng Cangbo [1903–90] and Xiao Tongzi [1895–1973] came over and we all had lunch together, and then we discussed the reorganization of the Kuomintang's *Central Daily* (*Zhongyang ribao*). Because there are a lot of hidden dangers to do with its finances and personnel, we do not dare to hope that it can go smoothly […] I had arranged to meet [Wuhan] Defence Commissioner Guo Huiwu, and we discussed matters concerning press censorship in Wuhan. Guo went back on his word; he made me angry, but for the time being we have just to put up with it.

Friday, 20 May 1938

I went to the Central Party Headquarters to attend the Three People's Principles Youth Corps Preparatory Committee […] I received a letter from Gao Zongwu, but the contents were vague [regarding Gao's negotiations with the Japanese]. This was only what I anticipated, but I had only heard about it [previously]; without doubt I am very anxious and losing hope.

Saturday, 28 May 1938

In the evening I was summoned to an appointment by the chairman, it was a meeting and a banquet. The chairman himself had just returned from the front, and he was in excellent spirits, and selfishly I was relieved to see him.

Monday, 6 June 1938

I remember the time we were in Nanjing, and we would talk frequently about the fifteen [actually thirteen] years when Nanjing was the capital of the Taiping Heavenly Kingdom; however, did we not know how many years we would stay there? Now we have evacuated the capital unexpectedly only ten years after its establishment, and so, suddenly it fulfills a prophecy! I do not know when we will be able to recover [the capital].

Saturday, 18 June 1938

Tao Xisheng and Chen Bosheng [1891–1957] came back to my home, and we discussed the future of the current political situation; I am extremely pessimistic. My generation do not want to be the running dogs of Russia or to join the Communist Party, and we certainly are not willing to be the puppets of the Japanese, so, apart from suicide, what is to be done?

Saturday, 25 June 1938

I discussed with Tao Xisheng and Mei Siping the ways of handling the unblocking of the impasse in Sino-Japanese relations [...] Mei Siping returned from a call on Mr. Wang, and we speculated on Gao Zongwu's trip to Japan [Gao secretly went to Tokyo on 23 June, on the orders of Wang and Zhou]. Tao Xisheng came over at 6 p.m., and we crossed the river together to go for dinner at the residence of Mr. Chiang, and afterwards we had a roundtable discussion.

Thursday, 7 July 1938

I read Konoe's statement, and not only does it not seek to win over the Chiang regime, but it does not even seek to woo the National Government; even if Mr. Chiang stepped down, the Japanese politicians who are in power will not negotiate with the National Government. So any gleam of hope for peace has been eradicated.

Friday, 22 July 1938

Gao Zongwu had sent Zhou Longxiang [1905–69, who had accompanied Gao to Tokyo] to present his report to the chairman; I summoned him [i.e., Zhou Longxiang] to come over and discuss it, and then I invited Tao Xisheng to come over for a discussion. I delegated someone to hand the report over to Chen Bulei. The other side [i.e., Japan] insists that the chairman must step down, which caused us disappointment. I called on Mr. Wang, and we talked for half an hour.

Tuesday, 26 July 1938

I had a brief conversation with Zhou Longxiang. I telephoned Zhang Qun and we discussed the Gao Zongwu affair [...] At 5 p.m. I called on Mr. Wang, and we discussed China's future for about an hour. I heard that Mr. Chiang had ordered Wang Liangchou [1881–1958] to request the British and American ambassadors to try to get Britain and the United States to propose a ceasefire to China and Japan, or to propose the hope of an early cessation of hostilities to China and Japan. If the Japanese would not accept this, then Britain and the United States should demonstrate their absolute [intention] to protect their rights and interests in China, and not to recognize any organization imposed by force. I heard that Britain could agree to the first measure but that the United States would not, and that both agreed to the second measure; but I fear that it is too late to implement this, and that it will not be easy to succeed [...] I talked with Zhou Longxiang for half an hour, and I urged him to go to Hong Kong tomorrow, and to transmit everything.

Friday, 12 August 1938

Chen Bulei telephoned to say that the chairman had indicated that there have been no propaganda successes over the past three months. I am scared out of my wits, and from now on I must make a real effort. I summoned Xu Xiaoyan [1900–80], and we discussed the means of unifying propaganda. In the evening I accepted an invitation from Hollington Tong [...] and I had a brief talk with Hollington Tong and Xiao Tongzi on various propaganda questions. I returned home at 9 p.m., where I answered He Zhonghan's telephone call regarding the chairman's profound dissatisfaction with the Communist Party propaganda outline published in today's *New China Daily,* and I immediately telephoned Commander Guo to stop the publication of the newspaper for three days. There were several telephone calls back and forth on this matter.

Sunday, 14 August 1938
Xu Xiaoyan came over, and we discussed the report that Mr. Chiang is extremely dissatisfied with propaganda in the [enemy-]occupied areas in Hebei and Chahe'er. Naturally I need to pay attention to this fact, because in the past I did not pay attention to it, for which I am now suitably reprimanded.

Thursday, 1 September 1938
In surveying the current political situation, I became uncontrollably angry; through this long, long night, when will dawn break? In the future, difficulties and misery will increase greatly. If, for argument's sake, Wuhan does not hold out, then news from Hong Kong will become relatively sluggish, and news from Hankou will be basically cut off; reading this aloud makes me twitchy.

Monday, 12 September 1938
In the evening I was invited to a banquet by Mr. Wang, where I drank a great deal of French white wine, and it was really precious. Mr. Wang talked about a great many things, and I deeply admired his very good memory. Mr. Chiang has an exceptionally good memory, which I have come to know and admire, and Mr. Wang is also like that, and it goes to show that great figures have special gifts. I have a very weak memory: I always forget past events, and I cannot completely remember what I have read; this is a reason why my life is commonplace. I returned [to my residence] at 9 p.m., and I drafted a telegram to the National Office for Examining Newspapers banning newspapers from defaming the German leader Hitler, and I telegraphed a warning to the *New China Daily.*

Saturday, 24 September 1938
I returned to my residence at 11:30 a.m. Just then I received a telephone call from Yang Tianyun telling me that Zhu Jiahua [1893–1963] had sent a telegram in which he stated that the chairman stressed the importance of propaganda, and still urged me to go to Wuhan immediately [...] This action forces me to take risks, and clearly he will not tolerate my refusal, but I fear that the chairman fails to understand my situation, and has been too critical of my administrative responsibilities, which has put me into a sulk. But sulking is not the way to escape from this dilemma, and one can only submit and accept it [...]

Tuesday, 27 September 1938
Tomorrow I have an audience with the chairman, and there will be a lot of criticism of propaganda [policy]. I have heard recently that he is very bad tempered, and that he cannot avoid hurling insults; if he injures my dignity I certainly will not accept it.

Thursday, 6 October 1938
I need to consider carefully the very uncertain discussions that Mei Siping had [in Tokyo; after Gao Zongwu became incapacitated with tuberculosis, Mei was given responsibility for the secret talks with Japan] [...] In the evening I accepted a summons from Mr. Chiang for dinner, and we had an informal discussion on the international situation.

Friday, 7 October 1938
I sent a letter to Mei Siping, requesting him to be my department's special representative in Hong Kong.

Monday, 17 October 1938
I went to the home of Chen Bulei, and we discussed [the fact] that the situation from now on looks increasingly grim, and we can only heave a great sigh as there are no means to remedy [it]. China is completely lost at the hands of the Kuomintang [as the result of] one past mistake after another; for generations to come we will certainly not be forgiven; we are the guilty men of history! With the outbreak of conflict at Shanghai last year, I, together with Tao Xisheng, Mei Siping, and Gao Zongwu, early on foresaw [this outcome], but, alas, we were the only ones and our words were too subtle, and no one was won over to see the gravity of the situation! From the present circumstances there is only collapse, we cannot find any other way out.

Tuesday, 18 October 1938
[...] The republic has been established for twenty-seven years, but now, quite unexpectedly, the trend is toward the conquest of the nation, and I cannot help being desolated and wishing for the end. At the moment we are preserving our actual strength in order to prepare for a protracted war of resistance, so there is no intention to defend Wuhan to the death. Before we say goodbye to Wuhan, we should all feel crestfallen.

Saturday, 22 October 1938

The airline office telephoned saying that there were no flights to Chongqing tomorrow, and that it could give no guarantees for the next two to three days; there was, however, a flight to Chengdu this evening, but I must get there [to the airline office] by 6 p.m. It was already 5 p.m. when I received this telephone call! I hurriedly made preparations, and by 6:15 p.m. I got to the [airline] office, with a friend accompanying me. I got to the airport by 7:30 p.m. and by 8:30 p.m. I was in the air. Farewell Wuhan! ... This morning at 10 a.m. Guangzhou fell. The enemy forces took only ten days to land, and so Guangzhou fell before Wuhan. Who would have expected such an outcome? From now on the situation will grow worse. Recalling with feeling my sad lot and my concern about the nation, I could not get to sleep, and I only began gradually to fall asleep after 4 a.m.

Tuesday, 25 October 1938

Mei Siping and Tao Xisheng came over to discuss a number of things, and we had a detailed discussion concerning our propaganda in Hong Kong.

Thursday, 27 October 1938

I was startled awake by the telephone at 7 a.m.; it was Mr. Wang who summoned me to a meeting, as he had some instructions to give me. When I returned to my residence, Chen Gongbo came over for a chat.

Friday, 28 October 1938

[...] In the evening I went to Mr. Wang's place for an informal dinner, where we had a detailed discussion of China's situation and a fairly detailed discussion of [possible] ways out. But it is in fact difficult to predict exactly what changes will occur in the future.

Saturday, 29 October 1938

Wang Shaolun [1902–82] came over and in addition to the Communist Party we discussed the general public mood, which almost entirely hopes for peace, and I regard this as right. But Japan cannot rescind its declaration of 16 January [Konoe's "no dealing with Chiang Kai-shek" policy]; moreover, Mr. Chiang is unable to, indeed, cannot step down from office, so how can talks about peace begin? The British ambassador has gone to Hunan, but although there is a lot of speculation, it is really no more than an exploratory visit, and it is unlikely that he will recommend mediation. *In that case the path to peace lies on a different road* [emphasis added]

Tuesday, 1 November 1938
I discussed with Mei Siping and Tao Xisheng various propaganda questions, and tomorrow Mei Siping goes to Hong Kong via Yunnan. I went to bed at 11 p.m. My whole body is itching, and there are red spots; according to what I am told it is nettle rash. I am terribly upset and I cannot sleep.

Wednesday, 2 November 1938
Whatever the changes in the overall situation, there is a clear trend that they could occur in the course of this month [emphasis added].

Thursday, 3 November 1938
I heard that today Japan had issued a declaration the gist of which is: Japan's aim is to create a new order and permanent peace in East Asia, and if the National Government renounces its policy of opposing Japan and close relations with the Communists, and fundamentally reorganizes its governing authorities, then Japan would not reject the National Government's participation in this creative work. But the implication is that the National Government and the two puppet organizations in Beiping and Nanjing would be considered on an equal basis – this is really bitter.

Tuesday, 8 November 1938
Luo Longji [1896–1965] came over for a talk, and he said that if this procrastination dragged on, it must surely result in the destruction of the nation. I said that to break out of it is very difficult, and it will require extraordinary action. It [such action] does not seek understanding from the state, but it surely will obtain the understanding of future generations. If the nation can be saved, then it is inappropriate that I should be bothered about temporary damage to my reputation; the Communist Party opposes peace, and its theory is to persevere in resistance until the nation is destroyed, which is not worth thinking about. Luo considered this to be correct.

Monday, 21 November 1938
As regards the matter [the secret discussions in Shanghai between Mei Siping and Gao Zongwu and Kagesa Sadaaki (1893–1948) and Imai Takeo (1900–82)], there is a slight prospect of success, but I cannot predict whether or not there will be [further] changes.

Saturday, 26 November 1938
I rose at 8 a.m. Mei Siping has come from Hong Kong and we had a brief chat, and I then went with him to Wang's mansion, where he reported on

the progress of his trip with Gao Zongwu to Shanghai, and he then brought out the agreement signed by both sides and the draft of Konoe's declaration, and we discussed these matters until noon, when we dispersed [...] I returned to Wang's mansion at 4 p.m., where Wang suddenly wanted to totally reverse our past decisions, and said that we needed to have a discussion. I waited coolly for him to begin, and I listened to his self-justification, but I did not offer any suggestions [...] I talked to Mei Siping about Wang's temperament; everyone knows very well that he is indecisive, and that it is easy for him to change [his mind], and as a result for over ten years he has been repeatedly defeated by us [i.e., Chiang's group]. But concerning this matter, then, despite his vacillation, we decided that the outcome must be that we stick with the original plan. [Entry made in the diary on 31 December in Hong Kong.]

Sunday, 27 November 1938

At 5 p.m., I went with Mei Siping to the Wang mansion, and we had a discussion with Mr. Wang and his wife [Chen Bijun]. Mr. Wang had suddenly changed his attitude and raised very many difficult questions. I immediately suggested that we give up the previous views, so that all discussions would indicate one conclusion. To retrieve the situation Wang, however, said that he could agree to sign part; the rest [of the "Record of the Secret Agreement between Japan and China"] would wait until further discussions in the future, so he decided in accordance with this [decision] to send a telegram in reply. In the course of numerous meetings Mr. Wang's reluctance to take responsibility, his irresolution, his vacillation in doing things are increasingly revealed, as are his easy and modest actions. But this affair is momentous, so it is understandable that he turns it over in his mind and looks at it from different perspectives. I myself have considered this matter repeatedly from all directions, and I am mentally and physically exhausted.

Tuesday, 29 November 1938

At 9 a.m., I again went with Mei Siping to the Wang mansion, and he had just summoned Chen Gongbo, who will arrive by airplane from Chengdu. After we had again studied all of the documents we decided that we could agree [to them], and then we sent a telegram to Hong Kong to let them know ... At four in the afternoon I went again to the Wang mansion, where I had a discussion with Chen Gongbo and the others, and we decided that Wang will go to Chengdu on the eighth [of December], and then go to Kunming on the eleventh; I will go first to Kunming and wait [...] [Entry made on 31 December in Hong Kong].

Thursday, 1 December 1938

[...] Lately I have felt that Wang's shortcomings are at times vacillation and at other times [engaging in] restless activity, and his strong point, by contrast, is his considerable ability with words.

Friday, 2 December 1938

Today I consulted the news report in the Tongmeng News Agency, that the Japanese Cabinet on 28 [November] had agreed on the key points in Sino-Japanese relations, and this had then passed at an imperial conference; and then Konoe issued his formal statement, but I do not yet know what it contains.

Monday, 5 December 1938

At 10:15 a.m., I boarded the airplane and we took off. Farewell Chongqing! The existence or the destruction of the nation and the making or breaking of myself hinge on this trip! But, since I have been early resolved to sacrifice myself, therefore I cannot shirk the dangers of the trip. At the very moment the aircraft left the ground I thought, Have I now destroyed my political career? I slept for an hour on the aircraft, and an hour before we landed at Kunming we experienced some bad turbulence [...] I contemplated the vastness of the future, in which the nation's destiny and my own are equally uncertain.

Thursday, 8 December 1938

After lunch, Chen Chunpu [1900–66] came himself from Chongqing, and said that Chen Bulei had arrived yesterday [in Chongqing], Mr. Chiang could arrive today, and Mr. Wang urges caution in everything, as he will cancel his trip [scheduled for] tomorrow. I wrote to Chairman Long Yun reporting on the postponement of the date of [Wang's] trip, and I then sent a telegram to Hong Kong, urging them to delay the issuing [of a statement]. There have been many setbacks in national affairs, but this is usually the case, as success and failure are truly determined by fate, and are beyond the power of man's capacity to plan for. I took my afternoon nap, but I could not sleep as I painfully racked my brains in a way that I have not usually done. Should I break immediately with the present situation? Should I return to Chongqing for the time being to observe the situation? I thought hard and deep, but I decided not to return. The reasons were very many, but two were most important: first, sooner or later he must make a break, if sooner then he will suffer a great deal of abuse for a number of days, if later it only will be a few days of abuse, but I fear that he will not be able to leave when the time comes; second, the clues to Mei Siping's two visits to Chongqing are being sought everywhere and they will be discovered shortly, so the nation would then not be saved and it would be led to its funeral! *On the 21st of last month the decision was taken to go to Hong Kong* [emphasis added], and if fate will not destroy China, then perhaps Mr. Wang will be able to leave Chongqing within ten days.

Sunday, 11 December 1938

Tao Xisheng and Chen Chunpu came over, and we speculated about whether or not Mr. Wang has the freedom to move. In the present circumstances, even if the secret perhaps does not leak out, nevertheless there are suspicious aspects, and even if its details are not known, yet I fear that a long delay is fraught with trouble. If Mister Wang cannot leave Chongqing before the twentieth, then the affair is finished. A telegram came from Hong Kong urging me to wait for Wang and stating that [information on] the situation had been passed on to other parties.

Saturday, 17 December 1938

Chen Chunpu came over for a talk, and he said that Wang had sent a telegram cancelling the railway tickets to Hanoi for the nineteenth. This then [demonstrates] that he will be unable to leave Chongqing before the twentieth. After all what should I do? It is in fact difficult to decide, as I am not in control [of events ...] I thought it over again at four, and I am still determined to return to Chongqing [...] Today my mood is 80 percent in favour of returning to Chongqing, and 20 percent for going to Hong Kong.

Sunday, 18 December 1938

I thought hard about it, and I felt that it would be appropriate if I did not care at all about going to Hong Kong. A variety of difficulties were now resolved, and I would put off for the time being [replying] to the Hong Kong telegram. At 9 a.m. I went to the Air Force Academy to give a lecture. I took my leave at 10 a.m. and, as I was passing the airport, I saw troops and a military band, and all along the way there were neatly turned out gendarmerie. Very strange! Does this mean that Mr. Chiang or Mr. Wang is coming to Kunming? If Chiang is coming it must be on a special aircraft, so why did the Air Force Academy not know? And If Wang is coming then why did Chen Chunpu not let me know? Later I walked out with Long Tiyao [1904–89] for lunch, and we ran into the police chief so we asked him whether he knew [what was going on] and he told us that Wang has come. I was very happy

[...] For over ten days I have had a piece of stone in my heart and now it has gone [...] I just received a written summons from Mr. Wang to call on him immediately. We met and shook hands happily greeting one another, and I then learned that Mr. Chiang was still in Chongqing, and that this trip was extremely dangerous [for Wang]. We talked for thirty minutes and then I took my leave, and I sent a telegram to Hong Kong to inform them [of Wang's arrival]. From now on whether or not we are able to leave Kunming certainly depends on Long Yun's attitude, but we probably cannot make things difficult for him. This evening Mr. Wang and Long Yun had a discussion, and the outcome was very good.

Monday, 19 December 1938
At 9 a.m., I returned to my residence, where Tao Xisheng was waiting for me, and I went with him to call on Mr. Wang, and I heard that at 2 p.m. this afternoon we were guaranteed an airplane to fly to Hanoi [...] At noon I went to Wang's place, and Long Yun was there, and we talked together for an hour [...] At 2:30 p.m. we went to the airport, and Long Yun personally saw us off [...] On the airplane I thought about my mother not being settled, and I fear that from now on it will not be easy for us to meet, and I shed tears. In one hour we crossed the frontier into Annam, and I now felt safe; at 5:30 p.m. we arrived. I was now overseas, and it is very difficult to predict when my exile will end. I am housed in the Hotel Metropole along with Tao Xisheng and Zeng Zhongming, and the language is different and I am extremely embarrassed!

Sunday, 25 December 1938
Mister Wang requested the others and I to visit him in the hills for two or three days, and change our flight to Hong Kong to the twenty-ninth [...] From the outset we stayed at Mr. Wang's residence there. Wang is unable to walk for two weeks because a few days earlier he had fallen and hurt his leg, and it is an unexpected calamity; at this time the full text of Konoe's statement arrived, and we read the translation and then studied it.[8] Mr. Wang will issue a statement on the contents [of Konoe's statement], and tomorrow after Wang has done a draft, we will again discuss it.

Monday, 26 December 1938
I drafted a written submission to Mr. Chiang and I sent a letter to Chen Bulei, explaining the meaning of this trip. Of course I know that it will certainly be unlikely to gain their understanding, but I put everything into it

[...] We returned to [Wang's] residence at 11 a.m. Mr. Wang had just drafted a statement and suggested that after we studied it we should meet for a discussion this afternoon. I first had a discussion with Chen Gongbo and Tao Xisheng, and we added and revised two points: Japan must renounce both its invasion of China and its humiliation of China's traditions and thought; the War of Resistance seeks the nation's independence and well-being, and now the peace measures will be able to fully protect the nation's independence and well-being, so the aims of the War of Resistance will have been attained. In the evening we resumed our discussion of the future implementation of policy and future measures, but we did not make concrete decisions.

Thursday, 29 December 1938

[...] At noon, we reached Hong Kong; when we had just got out of the aircraft, Chen Gongbo was immediately discovered by a British journalist who enquired as to the purpose of this trip. Tao Xisheng and I left immediately. Mei Siping came to greet us and took us to the Peninsula Hotel, where we went in by the front door and immediately went out by the back door. Tang Shoumin's [1892–1974] motorcar was waiting there to receive us, and we went directly to his home [...] Just as I was going to bed, Chen Gongbo and Lin Baisheng came over, and said that Gu Mengyu insisted that it was inadvisable to publish Mr. Wang's statement, and then urged Lin Baisheng to stop publication, and prevented him [i.e., Lin] from sending a telegram to Wang. I disagreed deeply with this, as I believed it had to be published immediately. Chen Gongbo maintained that no matter whether Wang replied to the telegram or not, it would be published tomorrow, and I agreed with this.

Friday, 30 December 1938

I had a discussion with Chen Gongbo and we decided that we would inform the Japanese that we would not consent to be a puppet organization in response to Konoe's statement, otherwise Mr. Wang would have the same position as a puppet organization! [...] Mei Siping telephoned at 7 p.m. and I heard that there were still problems with [Wang's] statement, as it could not be published today and I still did not know why, so I then asked him to go to the offices of the *Nan Hua* [a newspaper controlled by Wang] to supervise and urge Lin Baisheng to publish it immediately. I waited until 8:30 p.m. but still no telephone call [from Mei Siping], and I was very anxious! If it is not published today, then all our plans will be destroyed and we will have nothing left! So I telephoned Lin Baisheng to ask about it, and it was then that I learned that it had been published, and I could relax.[9]

Notes

1 Cai Dejin, foreword to *Zhou Fohai riji quanbian* [The complete edition of Zhou Fohai's diaries], ed. Cai Dejin, 2 vols. (Beijing: Zhongguo wenlian chubanshe, 2003), 2; hereafter cited as ZFHCD.

2 Zhou Zhiyou, "Guanyu Zhou Fohai riji" [On Zhou Fohai's diaries], preface to ZFHCD, 1.

3 Ibid., 2–3.

4 Cai Dejin, foreword, ZFHCD, 3; Zhou Zhiyou, "Guanyu Zhou Fohai riji," 4.

5 Cai Dejin, foreword, ZFHCD, 4.

6 This overview is based on my conference paper: Brian G. Martin, "Leaving Chongqing: Zhou Fohai and the Origins of the 'Peace Movement' 1938," presented to the International Conference on Modern China in Global Contexts, Institute of Modern History, Academia Sinica and the Historical Society for Twentieth-Century China, 11–13 August 2014, Taipei. The events of 1937 as they affected Zhou Fohai can be followed in Brian G. Martin, "The Dilemmas of a Civilian Politician in Time of War: Zhou Fohai and the First Stage of the Sino-Japanese War, July–December 1937," *Twentieth-Century China* 39, 2 (May 2014): 144–65.

7 Martin, "Dilemmas of a Civilian Politician," passim.

8 Konoe's third declaration on China policy, issued on 22 December, outlined the principles for future Sino-Japanese cooperation: both China and Japan would regard the creation of the New Order in East Asia as a common goal, and would cooperate to achieve mutual friendship and good neighbourliness, joint defence against communism, and economic cooperation.

9 This was Wang's so-called amorous telegram, or *yandian* [December 29 Telegram].

18 Kiang Kang-hu, "Starvation Is a Serious Matter"

JONATHAN HENSHAW

The following essay, written in 1941 by Kiang Kang-hu (1883–1954), was first published in *Minyi yuekan* (The people's will), a monthly journal that Kiang founded in 1940 and for which he served as editor. As the minister of personnel (Quanxu buzhang) in the Reorganized National Government (RNG) of Wang Jingwei (1884–1944), Kiang was a prominent figure in occupied Nanjing, but remained something of an outsider, in office but out of power among the capital's movers and shakers. In this essay, Kiang laments widespread starvation in China, offers a critique of cooperation with Japan, and levels a warning of what the occupation authorities and the Japanese can expect if the problem of hunger is not resolved. While more recent scholarship has dealt with the problem of hunger through Japan's grain extraction processes or the Chongqing Nationalist policy on grain control at a regional level, Kiang wrote as an insider to the occupation state, concerned with all of China and outlining the consequences of failing to feed the people.[1] The Chinese press under Japanese occupation is not typically remembered for pointed dissent, but by broaching the subject of hunger and committing his dissent so explicitly to print, Kiang offered a clear example of the discontent that lurked beneath the surface in occupied China.[2]

As a historical figure, Kiang Kang-hu remains somewhat obscure. He enjoyed a flash of early celebrity after establishing the Chinese Socialist Party in 1911 (the first organization to call itself a *dang,* or "party") before fleeing the country as a fugitive following the party's dissolution by decree of Yuan Shikai (1859–1916) in 1913. Kiang thereafter led a peripatetic existence, advocating his political views while travelling mostly between China and North America and never quite managing to secure employment for more than a few years at a time.[3] During these wanderings, Kiang collaborated with the American poet Witter Bynner (1881–1968) in translating a famed collection of Tang dynasty poems, published in English in 1929 as *The Jade Mountain*. In 1939, Kiang travelled from Hong Kong to Shanghai, by then under Japanese occupation, where he joined Wang Jingwei's peace movement. Following the inauguration of the new government in Nanjing, Kiang held a series of government posts and served as president of Southern University. In March 1940, he was appointed as minister of personnel, a peripheral post that he held until succeeding Wang Yitang (1877–1948) as president of the Examination Yuan two years later. After Wang Jingwei's death in Japan in 1944, Kiang retired and wrapped up his affairs in Nanjing. Thereafter, he lived in Beijing with his family until he was arrested by Nationalist agents after the war, put on trial, and sentenced to life imprisonment. In 1954, he passed away while incarcerated in Shanghai's Tilanqiao Prison (formerly the Ward Road Gaol).

Food supplies and starvation were contentious issues during the occupation. They bedevilled the RNG from its establishment and also challenged the returning Nationalist administration after the war.[4] In 1940, Nanjing was struck by a rice shortage, with prices doubling in a matter of days, while the nearby agricultural hub of Wuxi was struck by a wave of "rice robberies" as Japanese demand induced popular panic.[5] In response, the RNG established a Foodstuffs Administration Commission in an effort to stabilize prices.[6] Scarcity, forced extraction, and hunger also gave rise to profiteering. In 1943, the president of Nanjing's National Central University, Fan Zhongyun (1901–89), was dismissed after student protestors marched on Wang Jingwei's official residence to petition for his removal amid accusations of corruption in the campus dining halls. That same year, a major corruption scandal engulfed the minister for foodstuffs, Gu Baoheng (1903–85), and his deputy, who were both removed from office and later sentenced to life imprisonment.[7]

By his own account, Kiang's criticism of Japanese policy toward China and the measures taken by the RNG circulated widely and brought him into conflict with Wang Jingwei. As Kiang recalled at his postwar trial in 1946, the RNG's Ministry of Propaganda prohibited the circulation of "Starvation Is a Serious Matter," and ordered the police to seize and destroy copies from newsstands. Ultimately, however, the Capital

High Court paid no heed to these or Kiang's other writings, dismissing them as "momentary outbursts" that were insufficient to absolve Kiang of his criminal culpability as a *Hanjian* (traitor to China). Despite multiple appeals, including one from the procurator, who sought the death penalty, the verdict handed down from the bench remained unchanged – life imprisonment.[8] Verdict aside, it is useful to consider Kiang's essay from the lens of conditions within occupied territory, with regard to starvation itself; as part of the full range of opinion or dissent within the RNG; and as an indicator of the focus of the postwar collaboration trials.

Fittingly for one who began his career advocating education for women, Kiang opens his essay by reversing a well-known quotation from the neo-Confucian scholar Cheng Yi (1033–1107). Asked about the propriety of a widow who remarries after the death of her husband in order to avoid starvation, Cheng proclaimed: "To starve to death is a minor matter, but to lose one's integrity is a major matter indeed" (*e'si shi ji xiao, shijie shi ji da*).[9] Educated readers of Kiang's claim that "to starve to death is a major matter" would likely recall the second half of Cheng's declaration and wonder at the implied loss of integrity Kiang is suggesting, be it large or small. Certainly this was the reaction of one author, based outside occupied territory, who acknowledged reading only the title of Kiang's essay and immediately completed the thought, assuming that the unspoken "loss of integrity is a minor matter" was Kiang's attempt at a rationale for collaboration.[10]

In fact, Kiang makes an entirely different critique. By highlighting the problem of starvation under a regime founded ostensibly to protect the people during wartime occupation, Kiang calls into question its very raison d'être. As for the implied loss of integrity, Kiang remains circumspect, although his readers might well have been inspired to question just what exactly Wang and his associates achieved by compromising themselves before the Japanese.

Citing famous figures from Chinese history, Kiang argues for tolerance for the vast majority of people who, unable to match the high moral standards of exemplars from antiquity like Boyi and Shuqi, or Kiang's own townsman, Xie Fangde (1226–89), instead choose the path of compromise.[11] Rather than offering a self-serving defence of the compromises made with Japan by the RNG leadership, however, Kiang pivots to issue a direct warning to the Nanjing leadership and its Japanese backers over the consequences of starvation in occupied territory.

Failure to address the issue of starvation, Kiang warns, will undermine the government's efforts in other areas, be it the anti-communism trumpeted by the RNG, the Co-Prosperity Sphere proposed by the Japanese, or the great task of national rejuvenation. In closing his argument, Kiang invokes Li Zicheng (1606–45) and Zhang Xianzhong (1606–47), two well-known leaders of peasant revolts against the Ming dynasty, in order to illustrate the danger of neglecting the basic needs of the people. This was not an uncommon rhetorical move. As Geremie Barmé has noted, the Nationalists repeatedly likened Mao Zedong (1893–1976) and the Chinese Communist Party to Li Zicheng and his forces. It is likely that Kiang, an anti-communist literatus writing only three years shy of the three hundredth anniversary of Li Zicheng's entry into Beijing and the fall of the Ming, was making a similar rhetorical move. Soon after Kiang, the left-wing writer Guo Moruo (1892–1978) marked the anniversary with an influential essay of his own, "Jiashen san bai nian ji" (In commemoration of the three hundredth anniversary of 1644). Guo drew a much different historical lesson than Kiang or the Nationalists did, however, using the failure of Li's undisciplined forces to hold the capital as a cautionary tale for the Communist leadership as they sought to seize power through a rebellion of their own.[12]

Despite the brutality of Japan's invasion of China, the Japanese met with little success in eliminating voices of dissent or enforcing ideological compliance within occupied territory; indeed, factionalism, based on both personality and politics, ran rampant even within the RNG, let alone across the full spectrum of Japan's client states. More broadly, Chinese intellectuals remained alive to the plight of their countrymen and, as Kiang's essay suggests, occasionally committed their critiques to print. At the same time, such outspokenness was not without consequence. Gadflies find few friends in high places, and Kiang's refusal to join the Nationalist Party, the independent streak that characterized his prewar career, and his criticisms of the RNG, such as the ones contained in this essay, undermined his influence in a government that was already circumscribed in what it could do.

TRANSLATION

Starvation Is a Serious Matter[13]

KIANG KANG-HU

The neo-Confucianists tell us: "Starvation is a minor matter." Alas! How easy for them to say, and how different from what I know of Mencius. As Mencius says:

> It is only scholars who, without a certain livelihood, are able to maintain a fixed heart. As to the people, if they have not a certain livelihood, it follows that they will not have a fixed heart. And if they have not a fixed heart, there is nothing which they will not do in the way of self-abandonment, of moral deflection, of depravity, and of wild license.[14]

The neo-Confucianists demand, then, that everyone be a gentleman, that everyone be a saint, a sage, a Boyi or a Shuqi, yet they do not know that in all of Chinese history, there have only been these two sons of Guzhu who rose to fame by starving to death. Thereafter, from the Spring and Autumn period down to the end of the southern Song, there was only one perfect person who starved rather than accept a scornfully offered handout – my fellow villager, Xie Fangde, who likewise earned renown throughout the ages by starving himself to death. From ancient times down to the present, those who have endured starvation have been so few, and have done so with such hardship; how can [starvation] be called a minor matter? Yet in these years of hardship, of civil war and foreign conflict, of natural and human calamity, and of political and economic oppression, not a day goes by and not a place is spared from the death of those who cannot help but starve unwillingly. It is the same for our people and for all humanity; with so many starving, and so easily, how can this be called a minor matter?

In today's China, we are truly in an age without hope of saving the dying. In the past three years, the price of grain that northerners live off of and the rice that southerners rely on for their subsistence has risen tenfold and continues to rise today. The same is true of other grains and produce. The occupied territories will starve, and so will the guerrilla districts; those in the resistance will starve, and so will those in the peace movement. Those without kith and kin to call upon will starve, as will those with work, with hearth and home. The common people will starve and the civil servants will starve. Of course, there is no hope of making a man on the brink of starvation resist foreign aggression or safeguard the country. Should he establish the New Order through mutual assistance, it would still be impossible. Even with pencil-pushing bureaucrats and flag-waving minions, only those who are not ravenous with hunger could gladly do such tasks. Unless the problem of sustenance is resolved first, it is foolishness, if not self-delusion, to pass each day in anticipation of victory and to babble about rejuvenation.

Today I am speaking out to warn the authorities, and to warn our friendly ally: "Starvation is a serious matter!" As the Western proverb goes: "Hunger knows no law." Hunger knows no culture, no education, no foreign or domestic affairs, nor does it know anything of friendly neighbours, economic cooperation, joint anti-communism, or other principles. Therefore, for those who wish to bring about a Sino-Japanese cooperation treaty, or to achieve the ideal of an East Asian alliance, or to realize the slogan of clean governance or the great enterprise of national rejuvenation, the first step is to attend to food for the people. Luxury goods can be banned and jewellery done away with, entertainment expenses can be halted and banquets refused. Daily expenses can be economized, with only two meals per day to fill one's stomach. Redundant offices can be merged, idle personnel dismissed, and official salaries reduced. The defence forces can rely on powerful neighbours, but to the best of their ability, these officials must always follow the path of caring for the people from cradle to grave. Moreover, the lives of the ordinary people, compared with the select few in officialdom and the military, are especially gruelling, and especially important. It is necessary to enable the planters to tend their fields, the merchants to ply their markets, and the artisans to practise their crafts, and only then will the majority be able to fend for themselves without relying on government granaries and donations from charity for support. Never mind that neither government nor charity has the power to provide such support. Even if they did, and all the strength of the nation was bent toward providing disaster relief, with our great cities made over into congee factories, what form of government would we have then? And what kind of nation?

Our country's people – docile, law-abiding and capable of arduous labour – have for thousands of years had the habit of relying on their own efforts, with no need for the government's aid or for philanthropists to open their purses. For the people to live and work in peace and contentment, their only requirement is to "benefit by that which is beneficial to them," nothing more. The path to their prosperity lies in agriculture, industry, commerce, and trade. The simple, ordinary people dare not concern themselves and are unwilling to become involved in the schemes of great powers, in foreign policy, in culture, and in thought. When the farmers are left to their farms, the workers to their work, the merchants to their usual business, and the hawkers to moving their goods as always, only then will the problem of food naturally be resolved, and the nation's destiny will be prosperous. And what of today? The farmers' crops, the workers' goods, the merchants' capital, and the hawkers' wares are monopolized, seemingly frozen. Leaving aside for a moment the larger issues, even the gifts exchanged between rural scholars in the distant countryside and the everyday goods of the street peddlers are viewed as hoarding or smuggling.[15] Carts and boats cannot carry their cargo, the post cannot make deliveries, and the banks cannot send remittances. Under these conditions, how can the cost of goods not soar? How can resources not grow scarce? How can life be anything but hard? How can the people not go hungry and perish? Alas! Freedom and independence are all well and good, yet many vassal states have also been well-protected. At minimum, however, the people must not be driven to starvation. If one is not a Boyi or a Shuqi, one will be a Li Zicheng or a Zhang Xianzhong. But in a world where the likes of Boyi and Shuqi are seldom seen, the Li Zichengs and Zhang Xianzhongs will run amok. And so I say: "Starvation is a serious matter." What, then, are those who call for anti-communism, who speak of close and friendly ties, still thinking about?

Notes

1 For exacerbating factors surrounding the problem of food, see Odoric Wu, "Food Shortage and Japanese Grain Extraction in Henan," in *China at War: Regions of War, 1937–45*, ed. Stephen R. MacKinnon, Diana Lary, and Ezra F. Vogel (Stanford, CA: Stanford University Press, 2007), 181; and Jin Pusen, "To Feed a Country at War: China's Supply and Consumption of Grain During the War of Resistance," in *China in the Anti-Japanese War, 1937–1945: Politics, Culture and Society*, ed. David P. Barrett and Lawrence N. Shyu (New York: Peter Lang, 2001): 157–69.

2 Edward M. Gunn describes quips at Nanjing's expense, and also credits Zhou Zuoren as the source of "serious, direct dissent with Japanese policies." See Edward M. Gunn, *Unwelcome Muse: Chinese Literature in Shanghai and Peking, 1937–1945* (New York: Columbia University Press, 1980), especially 46–48.

3 Apart from public lecturing and organizing art exhibitions, Kiang worked primarily in education, teaching at the University of California, Berkeley and at McGill University. He also had an intermittent affiliation with the Library of Congress during the 1910s and 1920s. For a discussion of Kiang and socialism, see Edward S. Krebs, *Shifu: The Soul of Chinese Anarchism* (Lanham, MD: Rowman and Littlefield, 1998), 79–85. A partial discussion of Kiang's career in Canada is available in Macy Zheng, "Principal Sir Arthur Currie and the Department of Chinese Studies at McGill," *Fontanus* 13 (2013): 75–77.

4 The RNG-appointed mayor of Shanghai, Chen Gongbo (1893–1946), for example, surprised his British and American counterparts on the Shanghai Municipal Council by engaging them on the topic of rice supplies for the city. See "Visit of Shanghai Mayor to H.M. Consul-General," 1941, FO 371/27713, "Foreign Office Files for China, 1919–1980,"

http://www.archivesdirect.amdigital.co.uk.ezproxy.library.ubc.ca/FO_China; and Norwood F. Allman, *Shanghai Lawyer: The Memoirs of America's China Spymaster,* ed. Douglas Clark (Hong Kong: Earnshaw Books, 2017), 328. For the situation faced by the postwar returning government in terms of depleted granaries, disrupted distribution networks, and poor harvests, see Hsu Kan, *Report on Food Problem* (Nanjing: International Department, Ministry of Information, 1946), 1–4.

5 For the case of Wuxi and the complex dynamic that developed between Japanese occupiers, Chinese officials, and local elites over the course of occupation, see Toby Lincoln, "From Riots to Relief: Rice, Local Government and Charities in Occupied Central China," in *Food and War in Mid-Twentieth-Century East Asia,* ed. Katarzyna J. Cwiertka (Surrey, UK: Ashgate, 2013), 12.

6 See Huang Meizhen, ed., *Wei ting youying lu–dui Wang wei zhengquang de huiyi* [Hidden records of the bogus court: Remembering the bogus Wang regime] (Beijing: Dongfang chubanshe, 2010), 140.

7 For an account of the scandal by two former officials, see Xu Xilin and Zhao Tianyi, "1943 nian 'liangshi tanwu an' zhenxiang" [The truth about the 1943 foodstuffs corruption case], *Jiangsu wenshi ziliao* [Jiangsu literary and historical materials] 29 (December 1989): 289–95.

8 Nanjing dang'anguan, ed., *Shenxun Wang wei Hanjian bilu* [Interrogation records of the traitors from the bogus Wang regime] (Nanjing: Fenghuang chubanshe, 2004), 374, 376.

9 For further discussion, see Lydia He Liu, Rebecca E. Karl, and Dorothy Ko, eds., *The Birth of Chinese Feminism: Essential Texts in Transnational Theory* (New York: Columbia University Press, 2013), 133.

10 See Yun Qing, "E'si shi da" [Starvation is a serious matter], *Da feng ban yuekan* [Great wind bimonthly] 101 (1941): 1.

11 The brothers Boyi and Shuqi were natives of the state of Guzhu who lived during the Shang dynasty and became renowned for their willingness to starve rather than compromise their principles. Xie Fangde was a southern Song loyalist at the time of the Mongol conquest who was unwilling to take office under the new regime. After being forcibly brought to Beijing and incarcerated, he refused all food and succumbed to starvation.

12 See Geremie R. Barmé, *The Forbidden City* (Cambridge, MA: Harvard University Press, 2008), 143–44. For a more in-depth overview of Guo's historical analogies, see Hans van de Ven, *China at War: Triumph and Tragedy in the Emergence of the New China, 1937–1952* (London: Profile Books, 2017), 200–2.

13 Kiang Kang-hu, "E'si shi da" [Starvation is a serious matter], *Minyi yuekan* [The people's will] 1, 9 (15 February 1941): 1–3. Reprinted in Kiang Kang-hu, *Huixiang dongfang* [Return to the Orient] (Nanjing: Minyi she, 1941), 97–101.

14 James Legge, ed. and trans., *The Works of Mencius* (New York: Dover Publications, 2011), 49.

15 On this point, Kiang might well have been writing from personal experience. Long after the war, Wang Manyun, an attaché who worked in the RNG's counterinsurgency campaigns, recalled an incident in which Kiang was caught by Japanese gendarmes illegally transporting hog bristles (considered at that time to be a military resource). As president of the Examination Yuan, Kiang was normally exempt from being searched when boarding a train as part of the privileges accorded at that time to anyone of ministerial rank or higher. By Wang Manyun's account, Kiang had the misfortune of boarding a train from Nanjing to Shanghai that was being used to transport Wang Jingwei himself as part of an inspection tour to one of the cleared districts. As an added security measure, the Japanese imposed additional checks and consequently discovered the bristles in two of Kiang's suitcases. See Huang Meizhen, *Wei ting youying lu,* 276.

19 Guan Lu, "How to Be a New Woman"
Shanghai, March 1942

NORMAN SMITH

Guan Lu (1907–82) was an "editor, a journalist, a writer, a social critic, and first and foremost, a 'new modern urban woman.'"[1] Her writings include novels, essays, poems, and even the lyrics for a popular song.[2] From 1942 to 1945, during the Japanese occupation of Shanghai, Guan worked undercover, at the behest of the Chinese Communist Party (CCP), for the Japanese-owned and -operated journal *Nü sheng* [Women's voice]. In the preface to its first issue, the editors describe it as a journal "by women, about women, and for women." However, the journal was also widely viewed as a "Japanese propaganda tool for Chinese women."[3] After the war, Guan Lu was denounced by the Kuomintang (KMT) as a *Hanjian* traitor to the (Han) Chinese and later by the CCP in the 1950s and 1960s as an "educated traitor" and "cultural traitor."[4] Guan Lu spent ten years in prison for her social activities in Shanghai and her work at *Nü sheng*. The translation provided below, "How to Be a New Woman," is considered by scholar Nicole Huang to be "probably the centerpiece of the entire journal collection."[5] In it, Guan critiques new youth and especially new women for adopting the worst aspects of capitalist culture in a much more explicit, and Marxian, manner than did women writers in Manchukuo.

Guan Lu was born Hu Shoumei in Youyu (currently in Shanxi province). Both of Guan's parents died while she was young, and she moved from relative to relative, acquiring whatever education she could. In 1928, she enrolled in Nanjing's Zhongyang University to study philosophy. After a year, she transferred to the foreign languages department. While at university, she began to write and befriend left-wing writers, such as Ouyang Shan (1908–2004) and Zhang Tianyi (1906–85), while also establishing her own reputation as a left-wing writer. After three years at university, she was expelled on the grounds that she had submitted a fake high school diploma, though her growing reputation as a leftist was more likely the deciding factor.[6] In the summer of 1931, she moved to Shanghai. In the spring of 1932, recruited by Zhou Enlai (1898–1976), the future premier of the People's Republic, Guan joined the CCP.[7] That same year, Guan joined the League of Left-Wing Writers and on 14 May 1933, when Ding Ling (1904–86) was arrested, she assumed Ding's committee duties. Guan also joined the Shanghai Association of the Cultural Circle and Women's Circle to Resist Japan and Save the Nation, and served on its board of directors.

In the early thirties, Guan Lu met and wed Shen Zhiyuan, a CCP member since 1925. They were married for three years before divorcing, as Shen apparently sought a domesticated "good wife, wise mother" (*xianqi liangmu*), a role that Guan could not commit to.[8] She did not remarry. After 1949, she requested permission to marry a diplomat, and Zhou Enlai would not allow it.[9]

In the 1930s, Guan Lu worked at various magazines, including *Funü shenghuo* (Women's life) and *Shanghai funü* (Shanghai women). The latter was first published in April 1938, and was edited by Guan Lu, Xu Guangping,[10] and underground CCP members; it was published by the Eighth Route Army Office.[11] At the same time, she began writing her most famous novel, the autobiographical *Xin jiu shidai* (New and old eras). In 1939, Guan was instructed to go to Shanghai, a city under the control of the Reformed Government of the Republic of China, to gather intelligence on the occupation government and, eventually, from her Japanese coeditor at *Nü sheng*.[12] Subsequently, she began to drop out of her leftist social circles.[13] She became a regular at the infamous secret service "No. 76" social gatherings and became close friends with the wife of the head of the unit, Li Shiqun (1905–43).[14]

The first issue of *Nü sheng* was published on 15 May 1942; its final issue was volume four, number two in July 1945. Co-sponsored by the Japanese embassy and the Navy publication department, *Nü sheng* printed approximately thirty-four hundred copies per month.[15] The journal has been named "the most important and long-running women's periodical in the central regions of China."[16] According to Nicole Huang,

19.1 Guan Lu in the 1940s. *Source:* Author's collection

the journal was to "create, restructure, and propagate a discourse on domesticity that transcended national and ethnic boundaries."[17] The journal's motto was *Women de di'yi sheng* (Our first voice).

Guan Lu worked at *Nü sheng* as an editor as well as a writer.[18] Her co-editor was leftist woman writer Satō (Tamura) Toshiko (1884–1945), who had been influenced by the women's movement when she lived in Vancouver, Canada, from 1918 to 1936. The CCP sought information from her, believing that she could be sympathetic to their anti-imperialist, leftist agenda.[19] Tamura and Guan lived as housemates for one year and seven months; their relationship, to date, has not been a focus of scholarly analysis.[20] Nicole Huang has argued that Guan "played a more crucial role in producing every page of the journal."[21] Guan also hired many undercover CCP members as editors and advocated for socialism; in her view, "the nation" and "society" were of the utmost importance – "individual issues" were secondary.[22] Kishi Yōko argues that Guan was covertly telling Chinese female readers to call for the freedom of women and the Chinese, in opposition to Japan.[23] Thus, while the journal could be seen as a form of Japanese propaganda, its call for women to be "progressive" and "new" implicitly challenged contemporary political, social, and economic circumstances that prevented such behaviour – and Japanese imperialism was likely foremost in readers' minds. Over time, Guan Lu assumed most editorial duties, and she published two final issues after Tamura died on 16 April 1945.[24]

After the collapse of the Reorganized National Government in 1945, Guan was denounced as a *Hanjian* by the KMT, and the CCP removed her from Shanghai. After 1949, Guan fared no better as she was jailed for over ten years. Her supervisor, Chinese intelligence leader Pan Hannian (1906–77) was tried after the war as a double agent and traitor. Guan's reputation was tarnished by association with him as well as by her own high-profile activities during the occupation – despite having undertaken her duties at the order of the CCP. Guan was imprisoned in Beijing's infamous Gongdelin (Virtuous Forest) prison from 15 June 1955 to 26 March 1957. During the Cultural Revolution, she was arrested again, on 1 July 1967, and remained incarcerated until 20 May 1975.[25] It was not until 23 March 1982 that Ding Ling personally took the news to her that the unjust prosecutions had been overturned. Emotionally scarred by her decade of imprisonment, Guan Lu killed herself with an overdose of sleeping pills.[26]

The post-1949 treatment received by Guan Lu was very similar to that visited on the writers who created successful careers in other parts of Japanese-occupied China. Although many wrote highly critical accounts of the societies within which they lived, all were severely persecuted by the Maoist regime. Guan Lu's case stands out because she was punished for working as a CCP member as directed by one of the party's most powerful leaders, Zhou Enlai.

As evident in the translation below, Guan Lu's writing focuses on gender self-awareness, individualism, and social responsibilities, within a Marxist narrative. In the translation, Guan criticizes "modernized youth" "for their superficial understanding of capitalism and ignorance of its essence."[27] She especially urges young women to "use the correct kind of perspective," cautioning that many have only adopted "decadent and degrading" activities from a capitalist civilization on the decline. Guan Lu advocated for "new women of substance" to be in step with the "historical development of the times." For this, she was mercilessly persecuted by the CCP during the Maoist era, as were the women writers of Manchukuo.

TRANSLATION

How to Be a New Woman[28]

GUAN LU

With the arrival of a new atmosphere of equality and the arrival of freedom in China, there are now many "modernized" youth among the Chinese people. We can divide these modernized youth into two groups. The first group entertains new thinking and resists feudalizing, decayed institutions. For example, they resist the old Confucian ethics in their homes, resisting arranged marriages. Not only do they resist, but they can even help their sisters to resist and fight against old-style family marriages. They respect women and love their own wives. In terms of the nation, they labour [for it with] their bodies. They are not pale-faced scholars and do not quote the sages from morning to night, like some kind of bookworm that can do nothing but read. Sometimes they suddenly show their spine with mighty acts that shock and awe. And the other style of modern youth? They wear exquisite Western clothes, they comb their hair so bright it glistens like a mirror, and they throw on cologne. They joke, tease women, and talk trash in front of them. They pry their long legs open and dance till dawn. They not only throw on cologne, they use perfume and candy to cheat women; they take a young woman to a hotel to pass the night and, the next day, change her for another. And sometimes, even cleverer, they talk new economics; they may discuss dialectical materialism. They say that one of the three great principles of dialectical materialism is that everything changes with the times, and that nothing in the world is cast in stone. And so, equipped with their ideal, their theory of dialectical materialism, it is natural that they long to put it into practice, and change love for a long-faced woman today for a round-faced woman tomorrow.

Above are some "modernized" young men. As for whether their "modernization" is correct or not, we will not discuss that now, because it is beyond the scope of this essay. What we need to talk about now is the "modernized" woman, the so-called modern woman (*modeng funü*), or new woman (*xin funü*) for short.

Since the raw material for "modern" youth first arrived from abroad, China has had new youth, and naturally also the new woman. The new woman, similar to the previously discussed new youth, can be divided into two types. The first one? They also can resist the old kind of family, its ethical teachings and system, and arranged marriages. They use many methods to respect themselves, and also make men respect them. They have a good ideal, that is, one day they want equality with men in all respects. They want to enjoy equal rights with men, and fulfill the same types of obligations. The other kind? That is the now-trendy so-called modern girl (*modeng nülang*). Their good points? The first is their fashionable dress. They can go from a short *qipao* to a long *qipao,* a long *qipao* to a three-quarter-length *qipao,* from a three-quarter-length *qipao* to wearing a foreign-style long skirt and a blouse.[29] From round-toed leather shoes to wearing pointed leather shoes, from pointed leather shoes to square-toed leather shoes. They have to wear different kinds and colours of jackets – long and short, red and green. And they need to have matching colours for their outer clothes, *qipao,* leather shoes, and leather purses. Second, they use cosmetics. They use foreign, imported brands. The foreign brands are not only good quality, but famous. Using famous cosmetics for oneself, one can also become famous. Besides using cosmetics, they would state the original name of the makeup (although, in their mouths, the foreign word pronunciation is a combination of Chinese and Western [languages] – or seemingly right but actually wrong, or simply outright wrong. Take "cold cream," for example. Instead of saying "cold cream" [*lengshuang*], they would think about the English and say "icy cream" [*leng qi lin*]). Not only that, they would periodically announce the cost of a long list of makeup. And then, they could see a movie and go to a coffee house. Drinking coffee, they would naturally have to go to a foreign shop. To see a film, if one is to say it is really modern, it has to be a foreign film. Although they cannot fully understand the foreign film, when discussing it with other people, they would inevitably spit out a long list of film stars' names.

Also, this kind of modern female (*modeng nüxing*) must enjoy life: they have inherited the freedom of western European capitalist society. They have broken the shackles of the old family ways, they enjoy equality between husband and wife, and they consider themselves new women in society. Besides the above few material enjoyments, there are even more non-material benefits for them to enjoy. Through their qualifications as modern women, they throw off the old traditions of a woman's lifestyle and duty. They do not go into the kitchen. The kitchen has oil and smoke, and that oil and smoke can ruin their beautiful clothes and looks. In the kitchen, any little thing can damage their hands, so kitchen work would destroy their elegant appearance.

Besides these, they have other things to do at certain times, and it changes with the weather. When the weather is good, they will find themselves friends to go out with, and apart from going to places for pleasure, they go to all sorts of shops: candy and fruit shops, leather shoe stores, and clothing boutiques. Sometimes they will go to hair salons, where they not only have their hair done, but also paint their nails, from fingers to toes, which is to say, not only their hair and face have to look good, their four limbs and nails all have to look good as well. When it is bad weather, they naturally do not fancy going outside for a walk, and just do indoor work, the most trendy and common type of which is mah-jong. Naturally, when they play mah-jong it simply cannot be dull, and at all times they must have candy, snacks, and fruit to eat.

The lives of this large group of women described above can be seen as lives of extreme freedom and enjoyment. In their lives, there is not the slightest trace of the pain and bother brought on by the old family ethics. In the eyes of the average person, they are a kind of fortunate new woman.

However, in order to critique something, we should use the correct kind of perspective, and work to create a deeper episteme. To do this, we have to focus on reality; we cannot just look at its surface. We must look at it now and think about the future. We cannot just look at it and limit it to present aspects. We must use this kind of method to see it all, and also use this way to look at the woman question.

Since capitalist culture came to China, owing to changes in the Chinese mode of production and relations of production, the lifestyles of the Chinese people have undergone tremendous changes, becoming more capitalist day by day. The elderly are usually conservative, but because young people are restless and they harbour no assumptions, they are easily swayed by new influences. Above, we discussed new tendencies among modern youth in general that are due to the new desire to absorb capitalist culture. Under this kind of cultural environment, they became the morbid new woman discussed above.

Originally, capitalist culture was progressive compared to China's old feudal culture, and young men and women could toss aside old lifestyles and ideas, could go and receive a kind of new baptism – this was a good thing. However, to accept this new kind of culture is a choice and, regardless of what kind of thing we are accepting, we should never accept it in its entirety, but should accept it in a critical manner. This is to say, no matter what kind of culture, it must have its advantages and shortcomings. We have to take in its advantages and discard its shortcomings. If we talk about feudalism, "loyalty" and "piety" are feudal society's advantages, but "autocracy" is its shortcoming. Also, no matter what kind of system a culture has, when the kind of system arises, it must have good points; when it falls, it must have many shortcomings. Capitalist culture is also the same – when capitalism began to emerge in Europe, it brought much positive culture. For example, those working on literature and art opposed classicism, praised freedom, and praised the progressive spirit of youth. In terms of science, the Europeans brought about many inventions. They used scientific methods to advance social production. They developed both material and spiritual culture. In their ways of living, they were very frugal. They were not only careful with money, but [also] careful with time. In their lives, there was no wasted time and money. They had scientific, rational thinking, and science became a part of their lives in all respects. With scientific and disciplined lives, they found happiness and joy. In recent years, capitalism has already developed to its highest level and, in many respects, it is already at the stage of breaking down and collapsing. So in this recent century, European capitalist culture, besides those few good things left behind from its first rising, is defined by tragic and decadent hedonism, such as crazy nights in bars, the sexualization of the movie business – Hollywood movies – enticing and perverted pleasures, like the fleshpots of Paris – all is decadent and degrading, such as dance halls, gambling dens, and all kinds of improper, unnatural entertainment.

We must understand that to receive and absorb advanced nations' culture is a good thing. If we are to see this from the position of a young woman, to think first of the self, we naturally have to wash away and resist the spread of toxic Chinese feudal holdovers and absorb advanced capitalist nations' science and material culture, because society and history must progress every day, and people's lives also must move forward every day. Because of this, accepting advanced capitalist nations' culture is a principle of our individual lives. But we have to pay attention – we must accept the good parts from the emerging period, and we have to avoid the bad parts from the declining era. All those modern women that we see today are the opposite of what we hope for. They misunderstand capitalist civilization. They have not used grander or deeper points of view to look at the good things in the early era of capitalist society. They only, on the basis of their laziness and lowly habits, accept those decrepit, decadent enjoyments and morbid beauty, the decrepit culture of capitalism. These women are then the Chinese new women that average people imagine. They have the external appearance of capitalism, wearing trendy European clothes and using foreign cosmetics. They dance, bet on jai alai and other games, truly lacking the essence of capitalism.[30] They have neither scientific minds nor scientific epistemes. They lack a disciplined lifestyle as well as the defining features and independent skills of women in capitalist societies. The Chinese new woman.

We are all young women, and naturally we want to be new women. We need to follow the example of advanced countries, to absorb progressive culture. However, we have to pay attention to our own choices, to make our episteme firm. We have to think deeply to analyze our own lives and reality, so we do not become superficial, but are new women of substance. We have to focus on the significance of the new woman and think about the individual's relationship with society and the future. In viewing your own life, do not stop and be satisfied with the current appearance of life. Think about and consider life now and in the future. Do not be excited or sad about your current material life and enjoyment, but plan on how to exist and structure life in this changing society and with historical developments of the times. Otherwise, if we appear as the perfect embodiment of the indulgent new women, yet are in fact empty, then nothing but tragedy lies in our future.

Notes

1 Nicole Huang, *Women, War, Domesticity: Shanghai Literature and Popular Culture of the 1940s* (Leiden: Brill, 2005), 98.

2 Guan wrote the lyrics for the theme song of the popular 1937 film, *Shizi jietou* [Crossroads]. Amy Dooling, *Women's Literary Feminism in Twentieth-Century China* (New York: Palgrave Macmillan, 2005), 227n41.

3 Anne Sokolsky, *From New Woman Writer to Socialist: The Life and Selected Writings of Tamura Toshiko from 1936–1938* (Leiden: Brill, 2015), 46.

4 Louise Edwards, *Women Warriors and Wartime Spies of China* (Cambridge: Cambridge University Press, 2016), 140.

5 Huang, *Women, War, Domesticity,* 115.

6 Ibid, 98.

7 Edwards, *Women Warriors,* 140.

8 Luo Jiurong, *Ta de shenpan* [Her trial] (Taipei: Zhongyanyuan jin shi suo, 2013), 87.

9 Ibid., 174.

10 Xu Guangping (1898–1968) was the widow of Lu Xun (1881–1936). In 1941, she was arrested by the Japanese, tortured, and jailed for two years.

11 Dooling, *Women's Literary Feminism,* 305.

12 See Peichen Wu, "Satō (Tamura) Toshiko's Shanghai Period (1942–1945) and the Chinese Women's Periodical Nü-Sheng," *U.S.–Japan Women's Journal* 28 (2005): 122.

13 Nicole Huang, "Fashioning Public Intellectuals: Women's Print Culture in Occupied Shanghai (1941–1945)," in *In the Shadow of the Rising Sun: Shanghai under Japanese Occupation,* ed. Christian Henriot and Wen-hsin Yeh (Cambridge: Cambridge University Press, 2004), 305n4.

14 Number 76 was the regime's intelligence and secret police centre, established in April 1939 at 76 Jessfield Road in Shanghai. Edwards, *Women Warriors,* 141.

15 Dooling, *Women's Literary Feminism,* 306.

16 See Wu, "Satō," 109n4.

17 Huang, *Women, War, Domesticity,* 103.

18 Guan Lu published over seventy essays in the journal; her pen names included Fang Jun, Fang, Lan, Mengyin and Lin Yin, Huang. *Women, War, Domesticity,* 101.

19 Wu, "Satō," 111.

20 Rumours of a same-sex relationship between Guan Lu and Bai Yang (1920–96), one of China's "Four Great Actresses," were dismissed in a short article in *Nü sheng* in 1942. Both women were jailed during the Cultural Revolution.
21 Huang, *Women, War, Domesticity,* 97.
22 See Wu, "Satō," 110.
23 Cited in Sokolsky, *New Woman Writer to Socialist,* 47.
24 Huang, *Women, War, Domesticity,* 97.
25 Luo Jiurong, *Ta de shenpan,* 123.
26 Huang, *Women, War, Domesticity,* 101.
27 See Wu, "Satō," 114.
28 Guan Lu, "Zenmeyang zuo yi ge xin funü" [How to be a new woman], *Nü sheng* [Women's voice] 3 (1942): 12–13.
29 A *qipao,* or *cheongsam,* is a Chinese body-hugging dress, inspired by Manchu clothing of the Qing dynasty, which was popularized in the 1920s and 1930s. In the 1934 silent film *Shennü* (The goddess), a *qipao* is hung on the wall to indicate that the lead female character is a "lady of the evening."
30 Jai alai is a sport in which a handheld wicker basket is used to throw a ball against a walled space, and thereby accelerate it. For more on jai alai in Shanghai, see Tina Kanagaratnam, "Dangerous Game: Shanghai's Hai Alai Auditorium," 20 February 2015, *Shanghai Art Deco,* http://www.shanghaiartdeco.net/lost-treasure-shanghais-jai-alai-auditorium.

20 Yuan Shu, "The Current Stage of the Chinese Revolution and the Problem of Constitutional Government"

MATTHEW GALWAY

The true allegiance of Yuan Shu (1911–87), the famous five-faced spy (*wumian jiandie*), is difficult to pinpoint.[1] He infiltrated as many as five major organizations during his career as a spy. Yuan wrote the essay below in 1941, while he was a card-carrying Chinese Communist Party (CCP) member and intelligence officer infiltrating the Kuomintang (KMT) and Reorganized National Government of the Republic of China (RNG) of Wang Jingwei (1883–1944) during the tenuous Second United Front (1937–46).[2] In the two years that preceded the release of his article, "The Current Stage of the Chinese Revolution and the Problem of Constitutional Government" (*Zhongguo geming xian jieduan yu xianzheng wenti*), Yuan (under the alias Yan Junguang) "established the headquarters of the 'Movement for Asiatic Regeneration and National Reconstruction' (*Xingye jianguo yundong*)," which called for Chinese coexistence and co-prosperity with Imperial Japan.[3]

In his article, Yuan proposes his vision of a rejuvenated China in which a peaceful movement for constitutionalism and against reactionaries, Communist or otherwise, precludes revolutionary victory. The article reflects the ideological machinations of a networked individual responding to the crises of a China in uncertainty. Although Yuan, in his guise, argues for cooperation with Japan in uniting all oppressed peoples against Euro-American imperialism, he criticizes KMT stagnation and the United Front's failures. He decries the CCP (presumably his main party of affiliation at the time) for propagating falsities and stresses the vision of Sun Yat-sen (1866–1925) for Asian unity. Yuan concludes that China must cooperate with Japan to create a new East Asian order and expel Euro-American imperialists who impede the constitutional movement.

Importantly, his writing captures his viewpoint as an intellectual-spy who pairs Sun's rhetoric with leftist class categories to contextualize China's historical situation while invoking Pan-Asianism as the solution to China's "state of backwardness, semi-development, and semicolonial subjugation." Yuan draws from Marxist class categories and Lenin's criticism of imperialism to frame China as "semicolonial, semifeudal," identifying Euro-American imperialism as the cause of China's "economic backwardness, political corruption, low standard of living, inability to defend itself, and inertial policies." Solutions, he urges, lie in the Three Principles of the People (*Sanminzhuyi*) and Sun's ideal of "equal political, economic, and international status" that forms the basis for Yuan's advocacy of constitutionalism. He concludes that only a peaceful constitutionalist movement that collaborates with Japan in an East Asian order uniting all oppressed persons will uplift China from its state of weakness. The article also broadens our understanding of critiques of Chinese society before the foundation of the People's Republic, and throws light on the complicated internal dialogue of a committed spy who wrote *for* collaboration with the Japanese occupiers while simultaneously working to undermine them.

Yuan Shu (born Yuan Xueyi, a.k.a. Yuan Junguang, Zeng Dazhai, Zeng Huaming) was a writer and intelligence officer. He was born in Qizhou town, Hubei, where his father, Yuan Xiaolan, served as a Chinese United League (*Tongmenghui*) member before joining the KMT.[4] At sixteen, Yuan participated in the 1926 Northern Expedition, and in 1929 he studied journalism at the University of Tokyo, where he first encountered Marxist works. After returning to China in 1931, he founded *Art news* (*Wenyi xinwen*) magazine and met leading CCP Central Special Service Section (*Zhonggong zhongyang teke*) cadre Pan Hannian (1906–77), who hired him as a special party member (*tebie dangyuan*).[5] Yuan went underground as a Communist whose fluency in Japanese led him to serve as a Japan specialist for the KMT and CCP, sometimes simultaneously.[6] His spy career began shortly after joining the CCP in 1931 and lasted to 1955.[7] Pan facilitated Yuan's infiltration of the Japanese Foreign Ministry through contact with Japanese vice-consul general Iwai Eiichi's (1899–unknown) "Intelligence Agency."[8] Yuan's connections at news agencies also brought him into the orbit of the Japanese consulate, where he collected intelligence. From the consulate, Pan "worked out all the information about the CCP to be transferred to his different employers."[9]

To strengthen his intelligence sources, Yuan joined the Qinghongbang (Green and Red Gangs) secret societies in 1933. After the Battle of Shanghai broke out, Du Yuesheng (1888–1951), a leading Green Gang figure and Yuan's "co-brother" within the society, used his KMT connections to introduce him to Dai Li (1897–1946), the acting head of Chiang Kai-shek's intelligence services.[10] Dai oversaw a bureau collecting intelligence on Japan that included nearly twenty thousand spies, and his reputation as a fierce anticommunist later earned him the nickname "Himmler of Nationalist China."[11] Including espionage work on Soviet Red Army Intelligence officer Yakov Bronin (1900–84), Yuan held affiliation with and spied on five organizations, earning him the nickname "five-sided special service agent" (*wufang tewu*): the KMT Juntong (Bureau of Investigation and Statistics), which he infiltrated in 1932 through his cousin Jia Botao (1902–78) and politician Wu Xingya (1892–1936); the Japanese consulate in Shanghai; the CCP; the Soviet Union, on which he spied in 1935 and, in 1940, aided through his reports on the Japanese "southern march"; and the secret service of Wang's RNG.[12]

Yuan also authored reportage literature during this time; his July 1931 "On reportage literature" (*Baogao wenxue lun*) represented "possibly the first published article after the League of Left-Wing Writers' August 1930 resolution promoting reportage along with other genres to define reportage and link it with recent worldwide literary trends."[13] His writings betray a proletarian-internationalist leaning, credentials as a Marxist cognoscente, preoccupation with factory labourers, and commitment to broadening leftist readership. Such works are reminiscent of those by Kawaguchi Hiroshi (pseudonym for Yamaguchi Tadayuki, 1905–84), a Japanese Marxist literary theorist whose "more extensive treatment of the genre (translated by Xia Yan) ... was published the following year."[14] Kawaguchi's stylistic imprint on Yuan highlights Yuan's views at the time. Yuan also wrote on larger political issues – the article below among them – while working simultaneously as a CCP member and spy.

Yuan published the article translated below in the Shanghai-based *Constitutional Monthly* (*Xianzheng Yuekan*). He also operated undercover, serving Wang Jingwei as a KMT Central Committee member, deputy minister in the Propaganda Department, and education minister of Jiangsu province.[15] Yuan's discussion of constitutionalism was not in isolation; intellectuals outside of the Japanese-occupied zone concerned themselves with similar issues. The choice to publish in *Constitutional*

20.1 *Left:* Yuan Shu in Shanghai, Autumn 1939. *Right:* Sixteen-year-old Yuan prepares for the Northern Expedition. *Source:* http://www.xinhuanet.com/politics/2015–12/29/c_1117606731.htm.

Monthly was fitting because its coverage was mainly of the development of, and obstacles to, constitutionalism in China. In response to the mounting constitutional movement, which developed into a push for more general political research, *Constitutional Monthly* reorganized in 1941 at 308 Henan Rd., Shanghai, as *Political Monthly* (*Zhengzhi yuekan*). Yuan was editor-in-chief and publisher, and the Jiangsu Education Department operated, in name only, as producer; *New China Newspaper* (*Xin Zhongguo baoshe*) a pro-Japanese outlet, handled production. Wang Jingwei viewed *Political Monthly* as especially important for the RNG. The first issue included essays by Wang himself, and by Xingzheng Yuan (Executive Yuan) second-man Zhou Fohai (1897–1948) and politician Lin Baisheng (1902–46). Virtually every *Political Monthly* issue contained a Wang-written essay, and it became one of his most important media outlets in Shanghai.[16]

By October 1945, Yuan had relocated covertly to the northern Jiangsu liberated areas. In 1949, he was repositioned to the Central Intelligence Department responsible for Japan-US research. The "Pan Hannian case" on 3 April 1955, in which the People's Republic of China Ministry of Public Security charged Pan with collusion with Wang Jingwei and Japanese intelligence, led to Yuan's incarceration for twelve years (until 1967). Because the end of his prison sentence coincided with the early Cultural Revolution,[17] however, Yuan served another eight years that the CCP tacked onto his sentence, whereas Pan died in prison in 1977. On

15 May 1975, the CCP granted Yuan clemency, after which he moved to a farm in the mountains of Wuchang to reform through labour (*laodong gaizao*). He returned to Beijing in 1980, and the CCP declared him rehabilitated. On 26 November 1987, he died in People's Liberation Army Hospital 309, after which his ashes were placed in Beijing Babaoshan Revolutionary Cemetery.[18]

TRANSLATION

The Current Stage of the Chinese Revolution and the Problem of Constitutional Government[19]

YUAN SHU

Presently, China is a republic that safeguards the people's freedom to speak their minds. I supported peaceful reunification, "an open solution," at the National Assembly that was attended by groups of representatives of organizations to discuss and solve national affairs.

I. Euro-American Imperialist Aggression and Developments in China

China is an important country, with great territory, a large population, and rich history, and today stands as the geographical centre of Asia and an Eastern political culture with important contributions for future generations. Yet China is not a very progressive or developed country. China can and should progress, and it is making progress. But today's China is among the world's backward countries, a semicolonial and semifeudal society. This does not prove that the Chinese people do not want to make progress; rather, China's backwardness is merely due to imperialist aggression and the oppression of the Chinese people, who have remained "static" instead of progressing toward a new era.

Over the past century, China has become a semifeudal, semicolonial society, with European countries building capitalism that has been intrusive to China. In this process, 450 million Chinese have fought against Euro-American imperialism. Their effort reflects an inevitable desire to progress, and has laid the foundation for progress now and in the future. In the development of Euro-American capitalism during the nineteenth century, commodity output gave way to seizing fertile Chinese lands for the market. Capitalism in Europe was still in a fledgling state, so capitalists assaulted

China through trade. Sporadic local trade developed thereafter, which required producing for larger trade requirements. The development of commerce led to the consolidation of power necessary to protect Euro-American interests and to maintain their advantage over competing world powers. Thus economic aggression on the political stage, and again through mediums such as missionary schools, led these capitalist hegemons to develop the Chinese comprador class, whose innate reliance on Euro-American capitalism for survival meant that they stand only for Euro-American imperialism.

Naturally, China's economic backwardness, political corruption, low standard of living, an inability to defend itself, and inertial policies have all benefited capitalist countries. The Manchu government, for instance, sealed China's fate with many unequal treaties. But the Chinese people have not been willing to be conquered, so the national revolutionary movement in the private sector emerged in various forms, and everywhere around the country it has spread. This process began under Manchu government rule and to succeed required a powerful new political system to represent the people's interests, to resist imperialist aggression, and to revive the Chinese nation. The Manchu government had brought the country to near total collapse, with its fragile structure, complex bureaucratic problems, widespread corruption, and imperialists demanding repayment of huge debt. To suppress rural rebellion, which had emerged in response to government weakness, and to prolong its rule, the Manchu government made a transition from exclusion to capitulation, a so-called policy of "allies with gifts, not with slaves." The imperialist conflicts of interest in China made it so that no single foreign or domestic party could monopolize the country. China was thus divided into spheres of influence and, ultimately, imperialist-related conflicts arose with no clear end in sight. Why, then, does China still exist?

Sun Yat-sen once said that "China today still has reason to exist, because its own strong resistance against the powers that want China refuses to give in to other states' forces in China. It has become a state of equilibrium, so China still exists."[20] Indeed, the Chinese people's national revolutionary movement opposed the Qing government and indirect European imperialism, which led both to collapse in the face of the Chinese national revolution. Ever since, our movement has been in the interest of self-reliance. The arrival of a new imperialism – which is supported by the very foreign powers that eroded the Manchu government, weakened its policies, and established indirect rule in China – is responsible for China's semicolonial status and for cementing the unequal treaties that have allowed such nations to achieve their interests. As Sun Yat-sen states: "These treaties are nothing short of bonds signed by the former Chinese government selling the Chinese people into slavery to the foreigners."[21] Thus began China's semicolonial status.

II. China's Semicolonial Economy and Political Affairs

Imperialist aggression, surprisingly, had the effect of stimulating China's economic development. The Qing government's defeat led it to change its military requirements, and with the arrival of foreign powers on Chinese soil and the subsequent establishment of factories and other undertakings, China was forcibly inserted into a capitalist mode of production. One may evaluate how modernizing industry, financial industry, and business undertakings developed gradually. But imperialism did not, and does not presently, help China's progress, since imperialists will always be in a position to repress China. If China is to modernize, imperialists cannot dominate the country. Due to societal developments, China's progress is not a part of the reactionary rulers' subjective will; there are objective laws. To prevent imperialism, China must develop its capitalist economy, even though capitalism established a comprador class. We cannot ignore the powerful forces of imperialism. China is developing its national capitalism, but outside of the resistance there has not been a positive move forward. China has therefore stagnated, with semifeudalism dictating socioeconomic relations in the rural sector even today.

China's economy is indeed underdeveloped although, objectively, imperialist aggression brought it into the capitalist mode of production. Accordingly, many Chinese cities became commercial centres and the development of relatively large-scale modern enterprises and financial institutions followed suit. Across the country, however, the places in which such technological innovations benefit the people compose only a very small part of China. The majority of mainland China's population is still dominated by agricultural production, and productivity has stagnated, with large numbers of people not benefiting from outdated and insufficiently mechanized production methods. In terms of the development of modern enterprises, most are subjected to Euro-American control, especially with Chinese currency relying heavily on capitalist countries. So strong is international capitalism that it has dominated, and will continue to dominate, the world financial industry.

China will not be politically independent under this system of exploitation either. Although nominally a "government," and not taking orders from Europe or the United States, Chinese economic imbalances as reflected by political disunity have led to feudal separatism and government corruption.

Before the 1926–28 Northern Expedition, warlords divided China in opposition to the ruling Nationalist Government. The Northern Expedition crushed warlordism and brought about administrative factional differences with the Central Army, in which many military wings were manipulated by Red Moscow [the Soviet government].

Although the Three Principles of the People were nominally its foundational principles, the Nationalist Government remained simply a one-party military dictatorship, which is a powerful political force. The Nationalist Government, of course, does not have active public support. We certainly cannot achieve real unity in China to complete the revolution (*Xinhai geming*) that began in 1911. Despite Chiang Kai-shek's courage, China cannot achieve independence, freedom, and equality, for he and his party represent different political forces of imperialism in China that account for the major imperialist powers. They fear that democracy will improve the knowledge and power of the Chinese people and guide them onto the anti-imperialist road toward a true national government. Chiang also fears that democracy will present strong competition in the country's political sphere and bring an end to one-party dictatorship and political disunity. Citizens always strive to educate themselves, organize, and support a political party. Modern Chinese society definitely does not welcome private political appointments, crony politics, exploitation, the absence of civil rights, and limited freedom of speech, among others. Poverty has also worsened peoples' lives and limited their political liberty and civil rights. Our international status, too, is behind other nations. No wonder the Communist Party of the Soviet Union has taken advantage of China's weakness to incite anxious civilians, frustrated intellectuals, and weakened public services to carry out their plot to influence our politics. No wonder Chinese politics are even more of a spectacle than ever! But the Chinese people move forward, engaged with and coming to understand Chinese demands and consciousness through the lens of Sun Yat-sen's Three Principles.

III. China's Path to Rejuvenation

China has excellent qualities, but today, it suffers from the illness of imperialism. The only way to treat this illness is to break the Euro-American imperialist chains and obtain true independence! This is the basic principle of China's revival. This basic principle includes two major components: 1) A democratic, multiparty state and representative government; and 2) equitable international relations and exchange.

First, Chinese politics must get on the right track, and the Chinese government will turn into a genuine representative of the interests of the Chinese people. For it is only in this way that the government can obtain genuine public support, reunify China, end one-party rule, develop China's economy, defeat Euro-American imperialism, and achieve Sun Yat-sen's ideals of "equal political, economic, and international status."[22] Past Chinese governments were one-party and military dictatorships that marshalled foreign imperialism to deceive people and control public opinion. In a system wherein only a dictator and imperialism are welcome, whereas the very Chinese people it claims to govern are not, we ask what one-party politics since Sun Yat-Sen's death has achieved? Have we failed to resolve the myriad problems of the Chinese people's livelihood? Have we failed to obtain national independence? What about our civil liberties? Has our economy failed to develop? The true liberation of the Chinese nation and the elimination of imperialist oppression requires an end to one-party rule. The Chinese people do not need to draw from nineteenth-century democratic politics. Indeed, the Declaration of the First Congress of the Kuomintang [KMT] declared that "modern/contemporary provisional states of the so-called civil rights system often benefit the bourgeoisie, and this becomes suitable as a tool of repression of civilians." Hence why Sun Yat-sen stated: "We stand for civil rights, but these rights are not necessarily the same as those in Europe or the United States; we draw from Euro-American history for inspiration without studying solely Euro-American progress and following in their footsteps."[23] But people of import have the right to vote, the right of initiative [one of the four civil rights in Sun Yat-sen's doctrine], and to call for a referendum; the government has executive/administrative power, legislative power, judicial power, and supervisory power over the politics of the Three Principles of the People system. But it is the people who ought to have the power to continue Sun's legacy of carving a Chinese course from diverse sources so that one day China will no longer be governed by a one-party dictatorship.

But what do national politics mean? Before addressing this issue, four hundred million people must come to influence the man in charge. How can we do this? We need the four civil rights of the people to manage our national affairs. The people have four powers with which to supervise the government, whereas the government must concentrate its efforts on handling its affairs. What methods can we use inside the government? The government must be a full working body, work efficiently, and use its five branches effectively. Sun

Yat-sen recognized the inherent contradictions and the future decline of democracy in Europe and America, and present history confirms that Sun Yat-sen predicted correctly. Our task is to learn from Euro-American democratic decline to establish a democratic system that works in China for the Chinese people.

Second, since China is a semicolonial and semifeudal country, it will need foreign assistance to obtain true independence from imperialism. Sun Yat-sen spoke repeatedly about "my nation among equals in a united world."[24] Because China's major industrial and financial lifeblood is in the hands of imperialism and its agents (the comprador class), the Chinese national economy is underdeveloped, and the dictatorial Chinese Communist Party has seized control of all cultural enterprises for its sole benefit. The knowledge of the masses is still not enough. To be a truly independent nation, apart from intensifying the organization and education of the masses, foreign support and assistance are essential. But external assistance goes against the CCP's propaganda of a "Proletarian China" like the Soviet Union, and does not factor into the European and American *imaginaire* of "China's Anti-Japanese War of Resistance making for an advantageous international situation" for Euro-American imperialism. All oppressed nations of East Asia must therefore unite and strive for new political systems. As Sun Yat-sen once said:

> In the future, the general trend indicates that our East Asian people will achieve cooperation, with only the issue of time as a constraint. People have to realize this trend before the possibility of ameliorating the status of Asia and Africa is no longer available. This current shines brightly and warmly in the eyes of European and American people. An American scholar [Dr. Lothrop Stoddard, author of *The Rising Tide of Colour against White World Supremacy* (1920) and *The Revolt against Civilization* (1922)] even predicted the rise of the coloured races. Japan defeated the Russians, as Asians defeated the Europeans. The future trend is to expand, with people of colour uniting hand in hand to attack Europeans and Americans. This is their greatest calamity, and they may strive to prevent this from occurring. The scholar later attacked the cause of all national liberation movements as an inversion of the cultural movement ... This notion is that almost all the Euro-American privileged classes share a common ideology, and that they, as a minority, may suppress a majority from their continent. But now they come to Asia to oppress nine hundred million people. The minority demands that the

> great majority becomes their slaves. It is truly a cruel and hateful ideal. As the scholar said: "In a short time the Asian nations will awaken and rebel against Euro-American culture and, so it seems, consider themselves equals. People outside the Euro-American cultural sphere are at the point of rebelling against it."[25]

We must ultimately gain a deep understanding of Pan-Asianism.

IV. The Position/Status of Constitutionalism in the History of the Chinese Revolution

To accomplish this undertaking, Sun Yat-sen advocated for constitutional government. The implementation of constitutionalism guarantees democracy and allows for further discussions on helping small nations. The implementation of constitutionalism also guarantees freedoms of speech, assembly, and association to the Chinese people, and as we have said in the past, although the Chinese government is a one-party dictatorship with little to no support, it has not actually unified China. Rights of the people to assembly and political participation will make it possible for the Chinese government to end one-party dictatorship and all past drawbacks, and ultimately unite and mobilize 450 million people. Indeed, the implementation of constitutionalism shall mark an era of great action in Chinese history, a summary process of the Chinese revolution. We believe that the drafting of a constitution, though not the Chinese revolution's end goal, will at least initiate the implementation of constitutionalism and progress the Chinese nation to a higher stage than when the Chinese revolution began. In a previous stage, the people's rights, political achievements, our regulated economic system, and improvement to the people's standard of living formed pillars to a foundation that held for many years with clearly defined regulations in a constitution. Further implementation of constitutionalism will yet again bring us forward and consolidate people's livelihood, and only on that day, though likely not the day of finalizing the constitution, can the Chinese people achieve real independence, freedom, and happiness. The total liberation of the Chinese people thus does not rely solely on drafting a constitution; rather, liberation can be obtained through a constant struggle, by fighting continuously against domestic and international evils.

The delicate relationship between domestic and international evils in China, which are inextricable, has made it so the Chinese people are indeed capable of defeating the evil scourge of Euro-American domination. In a declaration to foreign business groups in China, Sun Yat-sen stated that

> the veil of imperialism seeks to destroy the KMT government, so China must strive to uphold and maintain the unequalled revolutionary spirit of the government, and only then can we combat counterrevolutionaries. [...] First was the overthrow of the Qing dynasty, and today, a period of wiping out the greatest hindrance to China's revolutionary history – imperialism – has begun.[26]

This task does not mean that China relies solely on its own strength to achieve it; rather, it means relying on the genuine solidarity of all Asian nations in a new representative body for the interests of Asians, united under a common ideal, working together and committed to the long-term achievement of such goals. Thus Sun Yat-sen held forth time and time again the vision of "a thorough awakening of our own people" and the need to "ally ourselves in a common struggle with those peoples of the world who treat us on the basis of equality."[27] His words teach us especially to emphasize among Asian peoples the principle of working together to achieve his ideal of Pan-Asianism. The implementation of constitutionalism will elevate the Chinese revolution to a new and higher stage. And at this stage, the task of national liberation in China will unite with the task of liberating Asia and its nations! Only in this way will international and domestic imperialists be unable to defeat it.

To implement constitutionalism and realize the provisions of Sun Yat-sen's ideals, we must not break into military, political, and constitutional branches, for this is a great struggle for the Chinese nation. We must strive to achieve constitutionalism soon, so that the Chinese people may someday live peaceful lives. Thus as Sun said in the early Republican era:

> Now the whole country is for the members of the legislature, which is completely disappointing for citizens; to resolve the state's affairs, we cannot rely on those members. We ought to rely on our own citizens. So I initiated this meeting so that people may understand the current status of the state, and so the people can know the relationship between politics and people's interests, with the decency to maintain the Republic of China. Since its name is the Republic of China, it must always be people-oriented and let the people speak.[28]

Unfortunately, soon after Sun Yat-sen died, those who held power surrendered to Euro-American imperialism; thus the Chinese revolution has faced an enormous obstacle! Constitutionalism, which would have given Chinese people independence, freedom, and improved their livelihood for many years, was never realized.

V. A Peaceful Movement for Constitutionalism/Constitutional Government

At present, the implementation of constitutionalism is required more urgently than ever before. Yet some people are rather skeptical and say: "China is in a period of war and total peace has not been achieved, so how can we implement constitutionalism?" Such a view indeed represents the perspective of a considerable number of people. But the problem that surfaces is, in fact, not a problem at all, because in the current domestic and international environment, to achieve a comprehensive peace is just a possibility, and to be only close to success is not genuine or true success. And just as now in this moment of near, yet incomplete, success, all reactionary and war-prone forces are in the process of using their greatest powers of influence to struggle on to their final destiny. They understand that if they can struggle against current difficulties, they can have a chance to recuperate their health temporarily and swell their ranks. They can pose a greater threat to peaceful factions and dupe the people as they establish a new type of control over the whole country. Especially clear is the CCP's intensified propaganda campaigns, and the comprador class's pro-American policy, which plans to obstruct peaceful movements, including expansion; meanwhile, the Soviet Union and Chongqing authorities hesitated, so as to use a number of petty favours such as bribes to perpetuate the War of Resistance. Since the CCP understands that the beginning of a comprehensive peace will initiate a wave of anti-communism, the Soviet Union understands that after a comprehensive peace the Communists will no longer occupy a prominent position in China. Hence Moscow's orchestration of the CCP plot to seize political power in China, though they have thus far been unable to realize their goals. The Soviet Union's eastern border will also be at risk under a comprehensive peace since it will rebuff Moscow's attempt to establish a greater "Red Asia." Both motivations have prompted Moscow's use of propaganda that incites the Chinese people to prolong the war, raving wantonly and singing the "persist in the war, insist on the war" fallacy.

But empty words cannot hide the pain of war. The CCP's all-domineering attitude shall put the pressure squarely on the people for further warfare, and ultimately make them give up all hope for the war and for communism. Thus as the days go on, if the peace movement is inspired and stimulated theoretically, in political practice it can resolve the real problems of the people, who will themselves now experience in China that only a peaceful movement is necessary for the country! War is good only for the CCP. Therefore, the implementation of constitutionalism, the democratic rights of the people, our security and stability, the development of the national economy and solving the unemployment problem, among other livelihood issues, is not an empty slogan; rather it is the goal of the peace movement. These problems can be resolved by implementing constitutionalism.

Each year, we support fully the establishment of a new constitutional central government, for we support constitutionalism today as China prepares mentally and materially for its implementation. We believe that only through constitutionalism will we meet the people's political demands and link the central government to its people closely. Only through constitutionalism will the central government be a strong, well-rounded government, and only then will the people, in fact, discover that the central government is the representative of the people's interests. Only then will it be possible to expose the CCP's malicious class hatred and the central government may move to repair its prestige among the people.

VI. The Possibility of a Peaceful Movement of Constitutionalism

Is it possible under the current domestic and international situation to implement constitutionalism? Our answer is yes. Some characteristics of the current international situation are: the ruling imperialist forces are already weakening, and in the current large-scale war in Europe, they will continue to weaken. A British and German encounter is still quite far away today, because of terrain restrictions, so Germany is not able to mobilize its lightning tactics in the United Kingdom, whereas the British navy cannot yet play a decisive role in the European theatre. Both are looking to strike at each other's weaknesses, making peace between the two less likely, while air force bombings during the war have yet to play a decisive role. The first offensive for the Germans may appear to be relatively large, thus England cannot but attempt to bring about peace in France alone and, later, make great efforts to break itself out of an isolated situation. And for England, the most likely and reliable new ally is the United States, which is aiding England's fight, but is unable to take military responsibility at present. Modern warfare is total warfare, with the military as only one aspect alongside economic and political power, and to succeed a military must show great acumen. The United States, although by no means making any progress in granting direct military aid, has enhanced the English war effort economically and through propaganda, in part because in the American ruling class's opinion,

Anglo-American competition is better than a future German-American competition. Thus in their view, it is better if the British prevent the German rise, which serves US interests in maintaining Britain at least, and maintaining the balance of power in Europe more generally. To do the inverse will lead to Germany achieving Europe-wide and, soon, worldwide hegemony. Yet the cost of American aid to England, by political means, can win a lot of interest from English abroad. The US desire to replace the British for domination of the world today is not merely beginning, and in fact has a great chance to come to fruition.

In this international situation, the circumstances for us in East Asia are clear. The old imperialist forces will increasingly weaken in Asia, which will give Asian people a great opportunity for resurgence. Although American resistance is likely, as long as we Asian people have determination we will achieve close unity and mutual assistance for each other with a common interest, and then under this common vision it will be completely possible for China to achieve its independence. Hence China's position is, first, to oust Euro-American imperialism. Historically, the power of white people has yet to weaken. In Asia today, the innate power of white people is weakening and has been unable to maintain a dominant position amid new and emerging forces. This is China's opportunity to break from the shackles of Euro-American imperialism, repeal all unequal treaties, and eliminate all unfair means to obtain so-called legitimate interest in the best of times! Sun Yat-sen laboured for great causes in his lifetime, yet never had such a great chance as today. This responsibility is on our shoulders, and the problem is whether we have the determination today to capitalize on it. In practice, will Sun Yat-sen's thought struggle steadfastly and assiduously? Or be used by those in power to deceive and cheat people to maintain their dominant status over the people's livelihood? Do we or do we not want to be responsible for Sun Yat-sen and his legacy? What about our history? Or the needs of all the world's people? Or the Chinese Communist Party's needs?

Second, one of Japan's positions during its occupation of Asia is to reach out to us, expecting us to cooperate with them. Japan's new cabinet has expressed full commitment to building a new order in East Asia: the Greater East Asia Co-Prosperity Sphere. However, a true statesman cannot incite others merely because of a slogan; this is an evil attack. We do need to establish a new order. But what does the Greater East Asia Co-Prosperity Sphere mean for us? The establishment of a new East Asian order is precisely what Sun Yat-sen envisioned with his doctrine of Pan-Asianism. In today's environment, "Pan-Asianism" has to be modified so that the Japanese understand Sun's intention. As Japanese diplomat Toshio Shiratori [1887–1949] once said: "In Japan's new political system, the people will profit from Asianism, and will strive toward realizing the ideal of building a new order in East Asia. [Asianism] conforms to the ideals for which Sun Yat-sen advocated; shall we not cooperate with them?"

VII. The War of Resistance against Japanese Aggression, Constitutionalism, and the Chinese Revolution's Reactionaries

In China, several members of the comprador class now regard Britain and France as powerless. But they were once victim to a pro-British habit of stereotyping about inferiority, so they do not see themselves as Asians in a united sense, and would nonetheless like to switch from relying on British imperialism to relying on American imperialism. This type of pro-American thinking is truly unclear, as the United States is still trading flirtatious glances with China's comprador bourgeoisie, maintaining the status quo, and enabling China's War of Resistance against Japan with the compradors hoping that it [the United States] will strike a blow in the future. In addition, those who hold a deep prejudice toward pacifists are singing loudly for a War of Resistance without end. Since foreign aid in support of China's War of Resistance is necessary, they blindly use force. However, the result of using force leads to exploitation by external forces, as those who condone the Communists do not recognize that the CCP's followers dance to the Soviet Union's tune. These people ignore completely the true peace-loving nature of the Chinese people, and ignore our all-around need for a peaceful and stable life. Regardless of how hypocritical white people in China are today, when their purpose is nothing more than to maintain a presence in China's economic and political spheres, they will ultimately eat their own words and their own hand will seal their fate. They advocate for constitutionalism today, but only insofar as it benefits their purpose.

The intermediary that is clamouring to cause the most destruction is the CCP, whose members advocate for "democracy" and urge recognition of its equal status with the KMT. The Communists demand the legal acknowledgment of the Shaanxi-Gansu Communist regime, and call for greater expansion of the Eighth Route and New Fourth Armies and the permanent maintenance of its regime's independence and institutional system. In essence, the CCP wants China to become a "Democratic Republic of the Three

People's Principles" in correspondence with a Marxist critique of democracy with a "socialist future." It also wants the Chinese revolution to comprise two stages: the stages of "bourgeois democratic" and "socialist" revolution. For the CCP, the War of Resistance against Japan belongs to the first stage, and must be completed during China's first revolutionary stage, after which China will enter a political stage with the proletarian and petty bourgeoisie classes participating in a joint dictatorship. Specifically, the CCP wants to seize state power and government. Then, the joint dictatorship will make the transition to the second revolutionary stage: the Chinese socialist revolution. But specific measures precede the joint dictatorship of the proletariat and petty bourgeoisie turning into a dictatorship of the proletariat. One such measure is the transformation of the coalition of the CCP, KMT, and other "anti-Japanese resistance" parties into a one-party dictatorship of the CCP. This is the current and most harmful Communist Party propaganda of "New Democracy"! The CCP at once opposes the current one-party dictatorship and democracy. To pander to popular feeling, they speak more favourably about democracy than do certain others. But as we can see, their current Communist regime in the Shaanxi-Gansu border region is merely a so-called "resistance," as official KMT newspapers, the *China Daily, Saodang Daily,* and *Dagong Daily,* all characterize it.

While this is their approach, our conclusion is the following: to complete the Chinese revolution, we must accomplish the first stage of the bourgeois class and the second stage of the socialist class. So it must be the CCP succeeding and developing a hundredfold, and the Eighth Route and New Fourth Armies succeeding and developing a hundredfold. Various Communist regimes, of regions of every shade and stripe, will establish themselves everywhere, for the sake of their so-called "fight for final victory"! (Of course, any discerning person can see that the CCP's final victory does not belong to all of the Chinese people, who are led by Mr. Chiang Kai-shek, and does not belong to the KMT in Chongqing, but belongs instead to the CCP, which belongs to the Comintern of Moscow and Stalin!) China does not belong to the proletariat because today, it has suffered through unemployment, displacement, countless sufferings, and high costs of living! Today's Chinese proletariat needs peace, not the War of Resistance!

We have discussed the true substance of the CCP's advocacy for constitutionalism, and now we examine the contents of the KMT's case for the same. The CCP has already sacrificed constitutionalism, which succeeded in obtaining the support of many progressive activists, and over the course of this movement's development the Communists will become increasingly powerful. The KMT, accordingly, will be weakened slightly, but again, one cannot allege arbitrarily that constitutionalism is bad, and cannot speak frankly saying that a one-party dictatorship is good. Hence, the use of a method of fighting fire with fire, as the Chongqing-based KMT advocated for a constitutional movement. But the constitutional movement requires several local self-governing bodies to be accomplished fully. It needs support for future movements such as KMT leader Chiang Kai-shek's Association for the Promotion of Constitutionalism.[29] Although we do not see any indication that it will conflict directly with New Democracy, it will give orders to various local parties and associations, thereby preventing different party activities, namely the CCP's ideologically tempered propaganda, and if necessary, it will catch a few CCP members, the Eighth Route Army, and the New Fourth Army. The KMT's faithful comrades cannot stand idly by and watch Communist Party aggression, and there is no small number of them proceeding from a standpoint of justice. Yet despite the KMT's handling of, general approach to, and proclamations on constitutional issues, they are still unable to assert emphatically a concrete position, wanting to maintain their one-party leadership. In other words, they want to implement constitutionalism as a smokescreen under a new name, and then continue the one-party dictatorship, which for the KMT is a military dictatorship.

Today, the Chongqing KMT and the CCP are both talking about constitutionalism and democracy, and each have their own intentions for their own benefits and plans. Evidently, they are most afraid of the Chinese popular will, not as a tool of the constitutional political struggle, but as a powerful driver to resolve the Chinese people's problems and carry out anti-communism clearly and the movement for constitutionalism peacefully. Thus both parties attack a peaceful constitutional movement not only in words, but also in action, attacking our constitutional peace movement's cadres. But we persist in working for peace and implementing constitutionalism peacefully. As representatives of the Chinese public opinion, we know how to solve the problems of our people and complete the Chinese revolution. For these reasons, we will inevitably obtain widespread popular support.

VIII. Conclusion

Although the peace movement is progressing, we are still far away from the requirements that we need, because old forces have not been eliminated, and part of the strength of our faction has not awoken. Our movement is the future of peace and national reconstruction, whereas these evil forces cause a shortfall of confidence and no group consciousness among the masses, as public opinion cannot be developed. Yet in the middle of this very short three-year period, the development of the peace movement has taken a great leap. Its work and message has changed tremendously, as the movement demands peace, but lacks confidence in its own movement for peace; it lacks foresight/vision, as it only sees its immediate difficult environment/surroundings. It therefore needs to reform this environment even though it does not yet understand how to go about realizing reform. Henceforth, we must redouble our great efforts and our important constitutionalist movement must smash to pieces all heresies and fallacies, so that we may destroy once and for all Euro-American imperialist manipulations from behind the scenes.

We have to understand the actual situation and the reality of Chinese societal needs, to learn, to study how to apply skilfully Sun Yat-sen's theory in all the revolutionary processes. We have to study the relationships between China, Asia, and the world, and should bear the responsibility of understanding how China, through such methods, can cooperate with Asian nations to achieve universal unity. We believe that China can progress since it possesses abundant objective conditions, and we have to grasp these objective conditions and put them on the right track toward completing the Chinese revolution, regardless of forces that may bring our movement down, which will collapse in the course of the peaceful constitutional movement. China's revolutionary success will liberate Asia's one billion Asians, whose task will be to rise up in unity. Today, we are committed to the constitutional movement for peace, not only because of the needs of Chinese society, the objective needs of the Chinese people, and the need for the peace movement itself, but also because of the need to combat all disinformation and slander against the peace movement. The present peaceful constitutional movement is a specific task of the Chinese revolution and today's domestic as well as international situation. The constitutional peace movement will inevitably move the Chinese revolution to a stage of great rejuvenation, and shorten the distance to the completion of the Chinese revolution and liberation of the Asian peoples. Then, all peoples of the world shall take a great breath of relief.

We revisit the Chinese revolutionary leader Sun Yat-sen's ingenious teachings, in which we can see that:

> We advocate pan-Asianism in order to restore the status of Asia. Only by the unification of all the peoples in Asia on the foundation of benevolence and virtue can they become strong and powerful. But to rely on benevolence

> alone to influence the Europeans in Asia to relinquish the privileges they have acquired in China would be an impossible dream. If we want to regain our rights, we must resort to force. In the matter of armaments, Japan has already accomplished her aims, while Turkey has recently also completely armed herself.[30]

In short, Sun Yat-sen's many teachings were entirely correct. The problem is: Do we have the determination to put theory into practice? And how do we organize and determine the concrete means of practice? On the former, we have illustrated time and again that the ultimate aim of the constitutional peace movement, its "determination," will without a doubt answer this question. On the latter, the Nationalist Government has contributed positively since returning to the capital after its exile. It has stood genuinely among the people, who are united under its leadership and its efforts to carry out progress. Especially in China and Japan, the premise of our inseparable relationship means constructing a new order in East Asia to achieve the Greater East Asia Co-Prosperity Sphere, to realize Pan-Asianism, and to receive the friendly nation of Japan's active support in carrying out our national movement. Now we should put these forces together to fight for a new China and the birth of a new Asia.

Notes

1 Shen He, "Zhongguo juewu jinyoude hongse 'Wumian Jianjie'" [The uniquely red "five-faced" spy in China], *Chuangji* [Legend] 6 (2015): 11–12; Zeng Long, *Wode fuqin Yuan Shu* [My father Yuan Shu] (Nanning, Guangxi: Jieli chubanshe, 1994); and Tan Yuanheng, "Zhonggong qingbao shi shangjuewu jinyoude 'wufang jiandie'" [The only 'five-layered spy' in the CCP intelligence history], *Dangshi bolan* [Party history overview] Part 2 (March 1999): 36–38.

2 Zeng Long, *Wode fuqin Yuan Shu,* 280–81; and Yuan Chengliang, "Yuan Shu: Nande di qingbao rencai" [Yuan Shu: The valuable intelligence talent], *Jingdie chunqiu* [Stories of the police and spies] 6 (2004): 44.

3 Joseph Yick, "Yuan Shu: Chinese Special Service Agent and Spy, 1931–1945," *Southeast Review of Asian Studies* 39 (2017): 92.

4 Zeng Long, *Wode fuqin Yuan Shu: Huanyuan wumian jiandiede zhenshi yangmao* [My father Yuan Shu: Restoring the five-faced spy's true identity] (Taipei: Duli zuojia, 2016), 10, 82; and Po Meisheng, "Juewu jinyoude 'wufang jiandie'" [The unique "five-faced" spy], *Dangan jiyi* [Archives and memories] 5 (2016): 45.

5 Yick, "Yuan Shu," 88; and San Mu, "Dageming qinhoude Zhonggong 'tebie dangyuan' he 'mimu dangyuan'" [CCP "special party members" and "secret party members" before and after the great revolution], *Dangshi bolan* [Overview of party history] 6 (2007): 49.

6 Chen Yung-fa, *Making Revolution: The Communist Movement in Eastern and Central China, 1937–1945* (Berkeley: University of California Press, 1986), 83, citing Chin Hsiung-pai, *Wang zhengquande kaichang yu shouchang* [The beginning and end of the Wang regime] (Hong Kong: Ch'un-ch'iu tse-chihshe, 1959), vol. 3, 27–31.

7 Yick, "Yuan Shu," 84–113.
8 Xiaohong Xiao-Planes, "The Pan Hannian Affair and Power Struggles at the Top of the CCP, 1953–1955," *China Perspectives* 4 (2010): 116–27.
9 Barbara Barnouin and Yu Changgen, *Zhou Enlai: A Political Life* (Hong Kong: Chinese University of Hong Kong Press, 2006), 81.
10 Zeng Long, *Wode fuqin Yuan Shu: Huanyuan wumian jiandiede zhenshi yangmao,* 175–81; and Yick, "Yuan Shu," 89.
11 Frederic Wakeman Jr., *Spymaster: Dai Li and the Chinese Secret Service* (Berkeley: University of California Press, 2003), 1.
12 Gu Xueyong, "Zhenshide 'weizhuangzhe': 'Wufang tewu' Yuan Shu" [The real 'pretender': 'Five-sided special service agent' Yuan Shu], *Wangshi* [Past events], December 2016, 73–74. See also Zeng Long, *Wode fuqin Yuan Shu: Huanyuan wumian jiandiede zhenshi yangmao;* and Yick, "Yuan Shu," 85–86 (on names), 89–92 (on Yuan's espionage on the Soviets and later intelligence aid to Moscow).
13 Charles A. Laughlin, *Chinese Reportage: The Aesthetics of Historical Experience* (Durham, NC: Duke University Press, 2002), 22, 285n33, 286n43.
14 Ibid., 22.
15 "'Sanmian Jiandie' Yuan Shude hongse rensheng: Duochong shenfen ru diying gongxian zhuoyue" [Triple agent Yuan Shu's revolutionary life: Multiple identities in the enemy camp and outstanding contributions], *Xinhua xinmen* [New China news agency], 23 March 2010, https://news.qq.com/a/20100323/002064.htm.
16 Ma Guangren, *Shanghai xinwenshi (1850–1949)* [The history of Shanghai journalism] (1850–1949) (Shanghai: Fudan daxue chubanshe, 2014), 926.
17 Quan Yanchi, *Zhongguo miwen neimu* [Secrets and insider stories of China] (Lanzhou: Gansu wenhua chubanshe, n.d.), 44; and Warren Kuo, *Analytical History of the Chinese Communist Party,* vol. 2 (Taipei: Institute of International Relations, 1969), 285–87.
18 "Sanmian Jiandie"; and "55 Nian Pan Hannian: Fangao qingbao gongzuode daduo dou meihao xiachang" (55 Years of Pan Hannian: Most of those who did intelligence work met a bad end), *Liaochen wanbao* [Liao Shen evening news], 2 March 2012, https://news.qq.com/a/20120302/000614.htm.
19 Yuan Shu, "Zhongguo geming xian jieduan yu xianzheng wenti" [The current stage of the Chinese Revolution and the problem of constitutional government], *Xianzheng yuekan* [Constitutional monthly] 1, 2 (18 September 1941): 9–24.
20 Sun Yat-sen, "Sanminzhuyi: Minzuzhuyi diwujiang" [Three People's Principles: Fifth lecture on nationalism], 24 February 1924, in *Zhongshan xiansheng jian'guo honggui yu shijian* [Sun Yat-sen's foundational plans and practices], ed. Sun Yat-sen Academic and Cultural Foundation of the Republic of China (Taipei: Caituan faren zhonghua minguo zhongshan xueshu wenhua jijinhui, 2012), 278.
21 Sun Yat-sen, "Riben yingzhu Zhongguo feichu bupingdeng tiaoyue: Dui shenhuge tuanti huanying yanhui yanshuoci (shiyiyue nianbari zai Shenhu Dongfang fandian)" [Japan should help China abolish the unequal treaties: Address delivered by Dr. Sun Yat-sen at a welcome banquet on 28 November 1924 at the Oriental Hotel in Kobe, Japan], in *Sun Zhongshan xiansheng you Shanghai guo Riben zhi yanlun* [Mr. Sun Yat-sen's Speeches from Shanghai to Japan] (Guangzhou: Minzhi shudian, 1925), 25–36.
22 Sun Yat-sen, "Sanminzhuyi: Minzuzhuyi diyijiang" [Three Principles of the People: First lecture on nationalism], 27 January 1924, in *Zhongshan xiansheng jian'guo honggui yu shijian,* 227. Mao referenced Sun's Three Principles of the People and their pursuit of "equal international status, equal political status, and equal economic status for China" several times, most notably: Mao Zedong, "Interview with a Correspondent of New China News in Yan'an (on One-Party Dictatorship)," 2 February 1938, in *Mao's Road to Power: Revolutionary Writings, 1912–1949,* vol. 6: *The New Stage, August 1937–1938,* ed. Stuart

R. Schram (Armonk, NY: M.E. Sharpe, 2004), 202; and Mao Zedong, "Mobilize Our Forces on Every Hand to Defeat the Enemy's Encirclement of the Shanxi-Chahar-Hebei Border Region," 2 October 1938, in *Mao's Road to Power,* vol. 6, 513.

23 Sun Yat-sen, quoted in Li Yunhan, "Sun Zhongshan Xiansheng sixiang tixi zhongde Meiguo yinsu" [American elements in Dr. Sun Yat-sen's ideological system], in *Zhongshan xiansheng jianguo honggui yu shijian,* 272.

24 Sun Yat-sen, "Zai Beijing-Meng-Cang tongyi zhengzhi gailiang huanyinghuide yanshuo" [Speech at the Beijing-Mongolia-Tibet political reform and unification welcome party], in *Sun Zhongshan quanji* [Complete works of Sun Yat-sen] (Beijing: Zhonghua shudian, 2011–15), vol. 2, 340.

25 This speech was also translated under the RNG slightly differently. See Sun Yat-sen, "Speech on Pan-Asianism: Translation of a speech delivered in Kobe, Japan on 28 November 1924," in *China and Japan: Natural Friends, Unnatural Enemies* (Shanghai: China United Press, 1941), 144.

26 Sun Yat-sen, "Wei Guangzhou shangtuan shijian duiwai xuanyan" [Manifesto regarding the Guangzhou Merchant Corps Incident], 1 September 1924, "Collected Works of Sun Yat-sen Online Full Text Retrieval System," http://sunology.culture.tw/cgi-bin/gs32/s1gsweb.cgi/ccd=cLGSg9/record?r1=240&h1=0, http://www.sunyat-sen.org/index.php?m=content&c=index&a=show&catid=46&id=6703. See also Sun Yat-sen, "Dayuanshuai fandui diguozhuyi ganshe wu guonei zhengzhi xuanyan" [Declaration of Grand Marshal Sun Yat-sen's opposition to the internal affairs of our country against imperialism], *Minguo ribao* [Republic of China daily], 1 September 1924, 2.

27 Dr. Sun Yat-sen's Will, quoted from Sun Yat-sen and Tang Leang-li, ed., *China and Japan: Natural Friends—Unnatural Enemies; A Guide for China's Foreign Policy* (Shanghai: China United Press, 1941), viii.

28 Sun Yat-sen, "Zai Shanghai xinwen hizhe zhaodaihuide yanshuo" [Speech at a Shanghai news press conference], 19 November 1924, in *Sun Zhongshan xiansheng you Shanghai guo Riben zhi yanlun,* 67–68.

29 Not to be confused with the *Association for the Promotion* of Constitutional Government, which Mao discussed on 20 February 1940. Mao Zedong, "New Democratic Constitutional Government," in *Selected Works of Mao Zedong* (Beijing: Foreign Languages Press, 1965), vol. 2, 407.

30 Sun Yat-sen, "Speech on Pan-Asianism," 149.

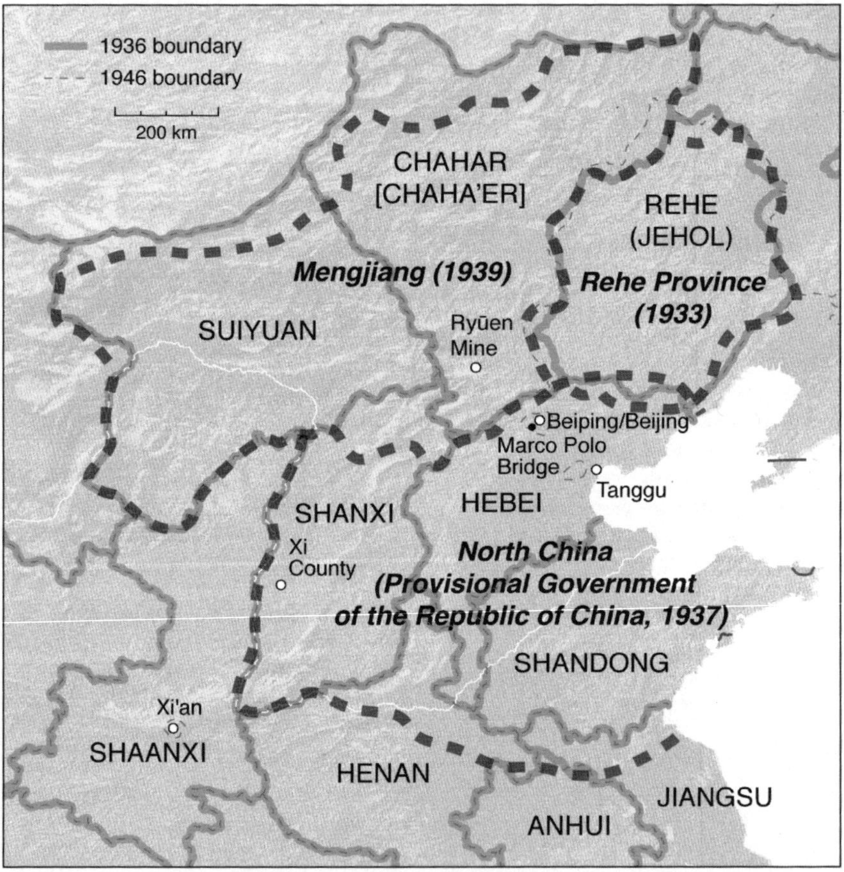

North China and Beyond. Map by Eric Leinberger

Part 3
NORTH CHINA AND BEYOND

NORTH CHINA TIMELINE

1933 21 January, Japanese invade Rehe, which is then annexed by Manchukuo

1935 25 November, Hebei Autonomous Government established as the first collaborationist government in north China

9 December, Beiping students stage the December Ninth Movement to protest increasing Japanese influence

1937 7 July, Marco Polo Bridge Incident. The Japanese military begin occupying much of north China

12 December, Provisional Government of the Republic of China established and Beiping renamed as Beijing

1939 Chiang Kai-shek's Chongqing government issues "Resolutions on Presenting Hanjian Activities and Espionage"

1 September, Mengjiang United Autonomous Government established

December, Western Shanxi Incident. The United Front enters difficult times when Yan Xishan turns against Communist Party forces

1940 30 March, the Provisional Government of the Republic of China dissolves and its members join the Reorganized National Government led by Wang Jingwei in Nanjing

1942 18 November, Zhou Zuoren publishes "The Problem of Chinese Thought"

1945 15 August, Japan surrenders and occupying forces begin withdrawal

1949 4 July, Zhou Zuoren appeals to Zhou Enlai in an open letter

1 October, Mao Zedong announces the foundation of the People's Republic of China in Beijing

THE DATE 7 JULY 1937 is a traumatic day in the Chinese historical memory. After years of tension and gradual encroachment on Chinese soil and sovereignty, Japanese troops surged across the Yongding River in what is known in English as the Marco Polo Bridge Incident but referred to in Chinese as the 7 July or Double Seven Incident (*Qiqi shibian*). Although the Japanese army had occupied Manchuria since 1931, this incident marked the beginning of the occupation of China proper, land long established as Chinese territory despite having been occupied by the Manchus for over two hundred years.

In the years leading up to 1937, Japan had gained valuable experience with the benefits of collaborationist governments from its efforts in Manchukuo, beginning in 1932, and the Hebei Autonomous Government, beginning in 1935. The autonomy of these governments fluctuated wildly, and ambiguity surrounded decision-making procedures. However, whether control was directly or indirectly actualized, the might of the Japanese military presence was undeniable.

After 7 July, the invasion proceeded quickly. The troops overwhelmed Chinese defenders and, throughout the remainder of 1937, quickly streamed across the north and then the east of China. Unlike the south and east of China, north China had spent most of the years since the fall of the Qing dynasty in 1912 relatively disconnected from the Nationalist government. Some rural areas remained largely under the control of warlords and, when the Japanese invasion began in full force, Nationalist armies and politicians in the region immediately retreated south to be closer to their power bases.

The hastily thrown together Provisional Government of the Republic of China (Zhonghua minguo linshi zhengfu), led by President Wang Kemin (1879–1945) and his close ally Tang Erhe (1878–1940), nominally controlled North China from 14 December 1937 until 30 March 1940, temporarily restoring Beiping to its former name of Beijing, the northern capital. For the final five years of the war, Beijing was subordinate to the much larger Nanjing government of Wang Jingwei (1883–1944), but just as in many places across China then, and for millennia before, the people adapted to the situation and continued to live their lives.

Conditions varied dramatically across this region. Some areas were repeatedly decimated throughout the eight years of conflict, while others were quickly and peacefully occupied by the Japanese. The chapters to follow capture this variety by presenting voices from inside and outside of relevant political institutions, as well as inside and outside of the geographic zone of north China. They represent the ambiguous and mercurial nature of these experiences in a textual voyage from the centre to the periphery, consistently returning to the concept of colonized life under duress.

This section begins in Beijing, a city that remained one of China's cultural and political capitals during the war and occupation. The first four chapters introduce and translate works by Tang Erhe, Zhou Zuoren (1885–1967), and Lin Yutang (1895–1976), three of China's most renowned intellectuals of the time. These are followed by two chapters concerning the rural areas of north China before turning to external perspectives on the occupation and the obligations of those living under it.

To begin this section, David Luesink examines the work of Tang Erhe, who played an important role in the development of medical and educational modernity in addition to his role in establishing a collaborationist government. Revealing Tang's intellectual importance, as well as the complexity of his roles in government, Luesink translates archival records of Tang's directives during his time as minister of education and in other important positions in the Provisional Government. This chapter ends with the notes of a Japanese political cartoonist, whose candid descriptions of Tang indicate the difficulty that the Japanese had in working with this collaborator. The cartoonish image of a collaborator sits in stark contrast to his complicated intellectual agenda, as found in Tang's Chinese texts.

After the Japanese government removed Tang Erhe as the minister of education, an even more famous and troublesome collaborator took his place. Zhou Zuoren's years of working with the Provisional Government, as well as his later trial and release, perhaps embody the ambiguities of colonial life better than any other wartime example. One of the most influential intellectuals of his generation, and the brother of iconic writer Lu Xun (1881–1936), Zhou's apparent support for the regime posed an arduous dilemma for patriotic Chinese elites to deal with after the war. The two texts introduced and translated here were at the heart of debates over Zhou's culpability. They put to rest any simplistic or binary understandings of his activities, and they reveal the difficulty of attributing fault to those who worked with the Japanese.

First, Xue Bingjie introduces and translates "Zhongguo de sixiang wenti" (The Problem of Chinese Thought), Zhou's 1942 defence of Chinese thought, which he essentialized as "Confucian." As Xue explains, this pivotal article was an important element of Zhou's defence at his postwar trial. During the war it prompted Japanese intellectuals to angrily denounce Zhou for perceived opposition to Japan's War for Greater East Asia. Second, Timothy Cronin discusses Zhou's spirited and fecund assertion of his own innocence in a letter addressed to Communist Party leader Zhou Enlai (1898–1976) just months before the establishment of the People's Republic of China in 1949. In a thoughtful consideration of Zhou Zuoren's intention and strategy, Cronin outlines his calculating and timely gambit. Perhaps this letter played a role in the respite from retribution afforded to Zhou until, like many accused of collaboration with the Japanese, he lost his life in the Cultural Revolution.

The fourth chapter of this section examines Lin Yutang, an intellectual who lived in the north for many years. Lin expresses his dismay at the Japanese occupation in his usual style of sarcasm and criticism. Son Yoo Di examines two works, "Wuzi de piping" (Criticism without Words), an analysis of the occupation of Shenyang, and the 1936 article "Guanyu Beiping xuesheng 'yier-jiu' yundong" (On the "December 9" Students' Movement in Beiping), a vocal support of the students' resistance to Japanese control. Reflecting Lin's sensitivity to the human element, these articles highlight the danger of accepting legal and rational argumentation over moral realities.

These four chapters examine texts by those living at the urban heart of the occupation of north China. But what of those on the margins of the occupation? To what extent do they add to diverse understandings of the occupation?

Timothy Cheek translates a report from the *Jiefang Ribao* (Liberation daily) on Yan Xishan (1883–1960), a warlord in control of territory strategically situated between the Communist Party stronghold of Yan'an and the Japanese puppet regimes of north China and Mengjiang. The ambiguities of life and loyalty in such an imbricated space can be seen through Cheek's translation of this report, which was personally revised by Mao Zedong (1893–1976) in 1944, highlighting the text as an unquestionable statement of the Maoist perspective on the issue of cooperation with the Japanese.

Also moving away from Beijing's centripetal magnetism, Zhang Yuanfang turns to the rural areas of north China with an analysis of the *batou* system, the local work-recruitment system adopted by wartime Japanese enterprises. Zhang offers a portrait of Japanese thought and research on work conditions in the empire through a study of *batou* by Japanese researcher Nakamura Takatoshi (n.d.). Resurrection of the *batou* system was a rejection of modern or Western labour practices, yet it was in no way a reaffirmation of feudal practices. Rather, it was an indication of the accommodating fluidity of the empire as it brought labourers into its ever-burgeoning means of production.

Following Zhang's study of Japanese intellectual discourses on occupied China, Morgan Rocks and Yun Xia offer two chapters on Chinese intellectual perspectives beyond the occupation. In a study of the Chengdu-based anarchist journal *Jingzhe* (The awakening), Rocks shows that, despite the unwillingness of anarchists to work with either the Nationalist or the Communist Parties, they were adamant in their call for resistance to the Japanese occupation. Surprisingly, these international-minded revolutionaries turned to the Spanish Civil War (1936–39) for their inspiration, even establishing a branch of the Solidaridad Internacional Antifascista in 1938, explicitly connecting events in Spain with those in East Asia. The anarchists were clear in calling for resistance and condemning collaboration. Like Rocks's study of anarchist thought, Yun Xia's examination of Nationalist laws regarding those who worked under or with the Japanese is relevant to all of China and is a crucial text for understanding wartime and postwar China. Xia explains the creation of *Hanjian* (traitors to China) laws and regulations, arguing that they exemplified and amplified existing prejudices in Chinese society by succumbing to populist paranoia that typified wartime society.

From the centre to the periphery, and then beyond the occupation, these eight articles do not offer a comprehensive picture of the Japanese occupation of China, but rather limn the frustration, fear, violence, and abuse that traversed wartime China in response to Japanese occupation. Unlike most perspectives on this time and place, these chapters are not limited to any political party, but offer myriad voices from inside and outside of the political institutions, as well as inside and outside of the region. Collectively, these chapters confirm that the occupation was a many-faceted fact of life that needed to be accepted, often in the face of harsh physical and intellectual violence.

21 Tang Erhe's Educational Collaboration with Japan in North China, 1937–40

DAVID LUESINK

On 12 December 1937, the Provisional Government of the Republic of China was established by a group of Chinese elites with close ties to Japan. One of these Chinese collaborators was Tang Erhe (1878–1940), physician, anatomical researcher, educator, and politician, who served on the Peace Preservation Committee, then as chairman of the Legislative Council of the Provisional Government, minister of education, chairman of the East Asian Cultural Association, and chancellor of National Peking University before his death in 1940. Although a key figure in many events of Chinese politics, education, and medicine between 1905 and 1940, Tang, like the north China wartime regime itself, has remained largely ignored by scholars.

Beginning during his student days in Japan, and throughout his life, Tang Erhe's relationship with Japan was complicated, but as a fluent Japanese speaker with a Japanese wife, he inevitably moved within its powerful orbit. He became a fierce antimonarchist revolutionary before the Republican Revolution and devoted himself to establishing the National Medical School in Beijing. After returning from an educational mission to Germany in 1921, Tang resigned as head of the National Medical School and took up a cabinet-level role as minister of education among a group of reformers known as the "cabinet of able men." He was made minister of the interior in 1926, and served as minister of finance under Zhang Zuolin (1875–1928) before the latter's assassination by the Japanese.

In 1929 Tang travelled to Japan and studied to receive a doctorate of medicine from Tokyo Imperial University. When Zhang Zuolin's son Zhang Xueliang (1901–2001) took over Manchuria, Tang Erhe became his adviser and liaison with Japan. After the Manchurian Incident of

1931, Chiang Kai-shek (1887–1975) ordered Zhang and his army to retreat and allow the Japanese occupation of Manchuria. When the Japanese army invaded Rehe, in 1933, they sought to establish a demilitarized zone all the way to Beijing and Tianjin, south of the Great Wall. Tang served in the Northeast Political Affairs Council, from which position he helped negotiate the Tanggu Truce in 1933. In 1935, Tang became a member of the Hebei-Chahar Political Council, which worked with the Japanese while nonetheless not making any vital concessions toward their goal of setting up a puppet state in all five northern provinces of Shandong, Hebei, Shanxi, Chahar, and Suiyuan.[1] Tang Erhe became a leading collaborator after the Marco Polo Bridge Incident on 7 July 1937 led to open war with Japan,[2] when he decided that the retreating Nationalist government had abandoned its responsibility to care for the common people and was cooperating with the Communist "troublemakers."

There were major debates in Japanese military and government circles in the opening months of the war about whether they should come to terms with Chiang Kai-shek and the Nationalists or rely on new local regimes and control China region by region. These divisions, between the Kantō Army in Inner Mongolia, the North China Army centred in Beijing and Tianjin, and Tokyo government offices such as the Foreign Ministry, allowed collaborators like Wang Kemin (1879–1945) and Tang Erhe to play various groups of Japanese against each other in the defence of Chinese interests.[3] Yet the proclamation of the inauguration of the Provisional Government read by Tang Erhe distinguished it from the collaborationist government that would develop in Nanjing under Wang Jingwei (1883–1944) in that it was completely contemptuous of the Nationalist Party. The Nationalist government, according to Tang, had brought the war on itself with a hostile attitude to Japan, and then demonstrated its incompetence, disorganization, and corruption in its inability to defend China. Crucially, the inauguration speech emphasized the unity of the Chinese and the Japanese races and focused squarely on an anticommunist stance.[4] Tang then supported a revival of Confucianism and its ideal of the "Kingly Way" as an ideology to do battle with Western materialism, liberalism, and communism.

Japanese and collaborationist attempts at ideological control in education were stymied by the anti-Japanese nature of student life in the years preceding the Marco Polo Bridge Incident.[5] The Nationalist Party under Chiang Kai-shek and especially under Dai Jitao (1891–1949) had long attempted to "partify" schools (*danghua*) by emphasizing the Three Principles of the People of Sun Yat-sen (1866–1925): nationalism, democracy, and people's livelihood. By the mid-1930s, the focus was on an antiforeign and especially anti-Japanese nationalism, given that democracy had been diluted by Sun's later emphasis on "tutelage" or party dictatorship. Dai Jitao saw the first function of primary and secondary schools as political inculcation.[6] Tang Erhe sought to use education for the same purposes, but against the Nationalist "partification."

A brief surviving order appears to demonstrate that in early 1938 Tang ordered the removal and dispersal of all archival equipment from the Academia Sinica Institute of History and Philology and the International Library, but whether he was trying to protect it from soldiers or follow orders from the Japanese command is not clear.[7] Students of elite north China universities were driven out of their campuses, and many left with faculty to a branch campus of Tsinghua in Changsha, and later marched on foot to Yunnan as Japan occupied the central Yangtze region as well.[8] While the Japanese Foreign Ministry hoped to use financial support of institutions of higher learning to influence the remaining educated classes, the overall lack of funding meant that the North China Army's policy of suppression and occupation of these institutions would continue.[9] The initial Committee for Public Safety was tasked with taking control of, and financing, the government educational institutions in Beijing.[10] The Japanese Foreign Ministry eventually convinced the North China Army to cooperate on educational and cultural affairs, although in reality, the army was able to ignore the Foreign Ministry. When the committee was replaced by the Provisional Government in December 1937, Tang Erhe became head of the Ministry of Education of the Executive Committee and early in January of 1938 announced that some funds were available and that classes would resume in April. A large slate of education officials was announced, in Beijing and as far away as Shandong,[11] while all former universities were combined into one teaching university and one research institute.[12] Textbooks were rewritten and censored for any evidence of anti-Japanese sentiment, although the rest of the content was barely touched.[13]

At the newly unified Peking University, the first two faculties to resume were medicine and agriculture, and by 1942 only engineering and science had been added.[14] In this choice of faculties, a clear pattern can be seen of focusing on professional education and avoiding the ideologically more suspect subjects of the humanities and liberal arts, such as history, philosophy, or the social sciences. And yet eventually Tang appointed his old friend Zhou Zuoren as dean of literature and another friend as head of philosophy.[15] In his New Year's speech of 1938, soon after becoming minister of education, Tang railed against the Nationalist Party's toleration of Communists and its "hoodwinking of the gullible" students and their "extinguishing of the personal standards of the youth."[16] This tirade was aimed directly at the by then long tradition of Chinese Communist Party organization among students. Although Tang had supported his students in the 1919 protests by securing their release from prison, at that time and even more so in 1938 he felt that protesting was a waste of time and claimed that students were merely manipulated by "those people" – meaning the Communists.[17] Demonstrations of Chinese nationalism aimed against Japan were counterproductive to academic goals.

Although available records are not clear, several sources indicate that Tang eventually found Japanese military dominance of the Provisional Government unbearable.[18] In 1938, a Japanese manga artist, Tsutsumi Kanzō (1895–1972), met with the three top Chinese collaborators and wrote brief impressions to match his cartoons. When it was time to meet the sixty-year-old Tang Erhe, Tsutsumi found him on the upper floor of a German restaurant eating a relatively cheap set menu meal with two friends. In the final translation below, Tsutsumi writes that Tang eventually became difficult to handle, and that he was sent to Japan as part of a political "castration." This anecdote points to the possibility that Tang pushed as far as he could against the Japanese military authorities who came to dominate Sino-Japanese relations in Beijing. Tang died not long after returning to Beijing, and his long-time colleague, Zhou Zuoren, took over his position.

TRANSLATIONS

Government Gazette

[The first six documents were selected from among hundreds signed by Tang Erhe and found in a search of the *Government Gazette*, published in Beijing. Decrees 48 and 49 seem to indicate concern to limit the circulation of archives and library sources to employees of the Ministry of Education.]

29 January 1938, Ministry of Education Decree #48
Regarding the decree to Academia Sinica Institute of History and Philology/ formerly Beijing Research Institute
Immediately cancel all requests for archival files from this ministry dispatched to employees and carefully hold in the warehouse. We hope you will act accordingly.

MINISTER OF EDUCATION, TANG ERHE

29 January 1938, Ministry of Education Decree #49
Regarding the decree to the International Library
Immediately cancel all requests for library materials from this ministry dispatched to employees appropriately and carefully hold in the warehouse. We hope you will act accordingly.

MINISTER OF EDUCATION, TANG ERHE

18 February 1938, Ministry of Education Decree #49
[Decree 49 is an example of many decrees making new appointments to various educational institutions.]
Dispatch Xu Zuzheng to fill the position of president of National Beijing Teacher's College.

MINISTER OF EDUCATION, TANG ERHE

27 February 1938, City Government Order / Provisional Government Order
[As minister of education, Tang led a group of fellow collaborators to offer the sacrifices to Confucius at the spring festival in 1938 as an attempt to establish ideological cohesion. This follows the patterns developed in Japanese-dominated Manchukuo.]
For this period's Spring Confucian Sacrifices, dispatch the following people to Government Affairs Committee member and education minister, Tang Erhe, who should respectfully go to the sacred temple to prostrate himself. Dispatch Beijing Special Government mayor, Yu Puhe, to conduct the ceremony in the side hall and to the two porticos of twelve wisdoms, and also send the following to attend: Jiang Chaozong, Ji Yuanzhu, Zhu Tutu, Wang Yitang, Zhang Xiaoyi, Wang Yongquan, Li Shiheng, Zhu Shuyuan, Fang Zongbie, Tao Zhuxia, Qing Yi, Liu Qian, Wu Chengshi, Li Xuanwei, Yang Yanpu, Xiong Zhengyuan, Zhang Xinpei, Liu Shiyuan, Zhang Shuiqi, Shen Yunchang, Hou Yuwen.

HEAD OF ADMINISTRATIVE COUNCIL, WANG KEMIN
MINISTER OF EDUCATION, TANG ERHE

1 March 1938, Ministry of Education Order #104

[Order 104 indicates the concern Tang Erhe had to control editorial processes for school textbooks.]

Now formulating the promulgation of the organizational rules of the Editorial Commission under the jurisdiction of this ministry.

MINISTER OF EDUCATION, TANG ERHE

12 November 1938, Provisional Government Order #293

[Order 293 indicates that Tang Erhe's ministry had jurisdiction as far as Shandong province. Order 985 of 9 September 1939 lists all regions under control of Beijing at this time, specifically the provinces of Shanxi, Hebei, Shandong, and Henan, and the cities with independent educational bureaus: Tianjin, Beijing, and Qingdao.]

Decree ordering Deputy Hao Shuxuan to become education minister for the Shandong government.

HEAD OF ADMINISTRATIVE COUNCIL, WANG KEMIN
MINISTER OF EDUCATION, TANG ERHE

[The next two documents aimed to implement the reversal of a policy established under the Nationalists to instill allegiance to the Nationalist Party, a policy known as "partification." The main goal was to reverse the schools' role as centres for anti-Japanese sentiment.]

15 April 1938, Ministry of Education Order #245

To all schools in Beijing; all provincial schools; each city's education department:

A decree ordering compliance with the educational plans of the new government has already circulated as notification about this issue, which should now be implemented by conducting or paying attention to each item below:

1 This incident gradually arose from the means of the implementation of the former Nationalist Government's Partification Education Plan. Henceforth, the program of "Daily Partification Education" will be severely suppressed.
2 Regarding the resumption of classes from primary school to middle school and also including university, in order to get to work, schools should first apply to the government to receive from this ministry guidance with the new regulations for each level of school, which will then be promulgated.

3 The length of primary and middle school will remain of short duration, with three years for middle school and three years for primary school, compared to four and two in the old system.
4 Education can have the positive function of transforming lifestyles for the better; therefore, the implementation of education must ensure the implementation of policies to ensure lifestyle preservation. Hereafter, beginning in the primary school stage, educators must conscientiously emphasize lifestyle functionality so that education and lifestyle can merge into an organic whole. At the same time, educators must especially emphasize hygiene education.
5 Secondary schools should be based on the principle of separate schools for boys and girls. Universities and colleges had to admit women before since there were no women's universities and women's technical schools.
6 Girls have their vocation in the family and in society, so it is suitable that the education they receive is not quite the same as the education boys receive. In addition, the insecurities of girls mean that it is necessary that they receive a suitable education, one that especially emphasizes the cultivation of moral character.[19]
7 For those schools established by foreigners, it is appropriate to earnestly supervise and lead them to make sure they adhere to the educational plan of the new government.[20]
8 The physical education classes in primary and middle schools, now called physical education in all the textbooks, should now consider being divided up into gymnastics exercises and martial arts.
9 Boy Scouts should change its name to Youth League, with the practical goals of group drilling, disciplined training, and service spirit. Military-style joint organization and personnel will be abolished and each school will establish its own general "Youth League of Such-and-such School."
10 Previously, school textbooks of various levels were improper in many places. The publisher has revised editions that are already being sold, but they should all be the same, and so revising the not-yet-perfect books from here on should be according to the new government's educational plan, and the ministry's senior editor should compile these independently of the publisher.
11 Corrupt practices in the examination system have multiplied and should be abolished. The principal of each school should study the academic records repeatedly and conscientiously investigate, increasing the number of school inspectors who conduct meticulous inspections of each field of study.

12 After the [Marco Polo Bridge] incident [7–9 July 1937], if students of each province and city want to transfer schools because their school had ceased to operate, but cannot obtain their transfer document or other transcripts, they can transfer by undergoing a rigorous inspection and examination.

13 Elementary and middle school teachers should add new drills to enable the correction of ideological errors. The educational administration organization of each place should organize lectures by the senior official of that locality. All of the short lecture courses sponsored by this ministry for Beijing elementary and middle school teachers have already been promulgated and can be consulted as reference.

The most pressing matter among the above points is to conscientiously pursue this policy and handle and implement them according to conditions while making timely reports back to the ministry.

MINISTER OF EDUCATION, TANG ERHE

15 April 1938, Education Ministry Order #246
To: Beijing academies; all provincial schools; all urban departments of education; General Order

Since the [Marco Polo Bridge] incident [7–9 July 1937], education in the entire nation and each province and city has ceased and even school buildings have been reduced to ruins, and so young people have discontinued their studies. The cause is nothing more than the result of the former Nationalist government's policy of the "partification" of society, permitting the Communist errors of using the absolutely sincere patriotism of the youth to instigate national feeling, and at the same time promoting class struggle and advocating a war of the people's front in order to harm the people, including the Nationalist use of floodwater.[21] To think about the influence of these policies is to be grieved.[22]

This ministry has learned from past errors to avoid future mistakes and knows well the East Asian people have a heartfelt close connection in history, geography, culture, and thought that is long cherished. For states that were brothers and mutually dependent, how could there be no mutual guidance and support? Is it not important to recognize that antiforeign thought should not be guiding our policies? Yet one can see it grow vigorously and still not be able to root it out. From now on, the aim of Eastern cultural tradition, and its relations of benevolence and good neighbourliness regarding the people's impressions, are suitable to make a radical reform with regard to international friendship. We should sincerely bring it into line with true, general education.

In this way, we will be able to establish a national base of administrative politics, to select a level road and stride forward, the masses mutually assisting each other, and to work in unison and help one another if possible, all advancing in proper sequence step by step. In this way it will not even be difficult to plan a world commonwealth. Each province and city and place would be responsible for its own educational administration organization. We should take the essence of these ideas and wash away all that is exerting a pernicious influence: the old attempts of the Nationalists at "partification" of society, Communist appeasement, and antiforeign sentiment. In a variety of ways we can bring order out of chaos and lead youths to accept discipline and standards – a matter of fundamental importance for generations to come. But it will also be advantageous if we declare that the educational laws and decrees from the past are not in conflict with the purposes of the provisional government, thus we can allow the use of the old method.

Tojiwa[23] (Mr. Tang Erhe)

TSUTSUMI KANZŌ

Please remember, he is the equivalent of vice-premier, because he is leader of the deliberative council. Close to the Hatamen neighbourhood in Beijing, in a foreign restaurant run by Germans called Kalatsuas with sweets on the first floor and a restaurant on the second.[24] It is a place where criminals gather, white palace dancers perform, and "modern boys" are to be found.[25] The restaurant lets one eat a fixed menu of three items for 1 *yuan*. I happened to see Mr. Tang eating together with a friend. It is said that he graduated from Kanazawa Medical Vocational School, has a Japanese wife, and he speaks Japanese very well. Anyway, Mr. Tang is friendly with Japan, which puts him in a dangerous position, but he had not even one security guard. In this kind of situation, anything can happen in Beijing.

At the time of the Great Kantō Earthquake [1923], he was a representative of the Red Cross and came to Japan and, before the Manchurian Incident,[26] he was a member of the Chinese cabinet. For the sake of building a friendly relationship between Japan and China, he has accomplished good results for many years. His characteristics as chancellor of Peking University are warm and good. However, at times in the past we could not handle him when he did not follow the official agenda. If he returned to being a doctor, then there would be no problems, so he was sent to Kanazawa and was politically castrated.

Notes

1 Xu Youqun, *Minguo renwu dacidian* [Republican dictionary of biography] (Shijiazhuang: Hebei renmin chubanshe, 1991), 1188.
2 The Marco Polo Bridge Incident is described merely as an "incident" (*shibian*) in some of the documents below.
3 John Hunter Boyle, *China and Japan at War, 1937–1945: The Politics of Collaboration* (Stanford, CA: Stanford University Press, 1972), 10.
4 Ibid., 91.
5 Rana Mitter, *The Manchurian Myth: Nationalism, Resistance, and Collaboration in North China* (Berkeley: University of California Press, 2000), 130–56.
6 Peter Zarrow, *Educating China: Knowledge, Society and Textbooks in a Modernizing World* (Cambridge: Cambridge University Press, 2015), 35–36; Wen-hsin Yeh, *The Alienated Academy: Culture and Politics in Republican China* (Berkeley: University of California Press, 2000), 172–79.
7 Jiaoyubu ling [Ministry of Education order] no. 48–49, *Zhengfu gongbao* [Government gazette], 29 January 1938.
8 John Israel, *Lianda: A Chinese University in War and Revolution* (Stanford, CA: Stanford University Press, 1998), 7–60.
9 Lincoln Li, *The Japanese Army in North China, 1937–41: Problems of Political and Economic Control* (Oxford: Oxford University Press, 1976), 99.
10 Ibid.
11 Lingshi zhengfu ling [Provisional government order], *Zhengfu gongbao,* 1 January 1938; Lingshi zhengfu ling no. 293, *Zhengfu gongbao,* 12 January 1938; Jiaoyubu ling no. 82, *Zhengfu gongbao,* 18 February 1938.
12 Jiaoyubu ling no. 82, *Zhengfu gongbao,* 18 February 1938.
13 Jiaoyubu ling no. 104, *Zhengfu gongbao,* 1 March 1938.
14 Li, *Japanese Army,* 100.
15 Zhou Zuoren (1885–1967) was the estranged brother of Lu Xun (Zhou Jianren), and a major literary talent in his own right. Zhou read a eulogy for Tang at a memorial in Tokyo one year after his death. Tang Yousong [Tang Qi], *Tang Erhe xiansheng* [Mister Tang Erhe] (Beijing: Jinhua shuju, 1942), 175, 184–90. See chapters 22 and 23 in this volume for more information on Zhou.
16 Ibid., 103.
17 Ibid., 171.
18 Sophia Lee, "Education in Wartime Beijing: 1937–1945" (PhD diss., University of Michigan, 1996), 100.
19 This appears to indicate a need to educate young women to avoid sexual encounters. Chinese schools throughout the twentieth century have attempted to inculcate abstinence-only sexual education. The administration was also antifeminist.
20 For more on missionary education during this period, see Lee, "Education in Wartime Beijing," 146–219.
21 This refers to the blowing up of the Yellow River dikes in 1937 that killed half a million people and created at least three million refugees.
22 No mention is made of Japanese bombings and other violence.
23 Tsutsumi Kanzō, "Tojiwa" [Mr. Tang Erhe], *Chūō kōron* [The central review] 53: 6 (1938): 257–58.
24 Hatamen was a neighbourhood of Beijing from the Yuan dynasty to the Republic, now part of the Chongwenmen area. "Kalatsuas" is a Japanese spelling of a German word of uncertain provenance.
25 This seems to indicate that unsavoury types might gather at this restaurant.
26 The Manchurian Incident, known in English as the Mukden Incident, initiated the Japanese creation of the puppet state of Manchukuo in 1931.

22 The Transformation of Zhou Zuoren's Thought and Rhetorical Strategies Found in His Writing

"The Problem of Chinese Thought"

XUE BINGJIE

The renowned essayist and translator Zhou Zuoren (1885–1967) was one of the most influential intellectuals in modern China. During the Second Sino-Japanese War (1937–45), Zhou collaborated with Japan and held office in the North China Political Affairs Council as director of the Department of Education, following in the footsteps of Tang Erhe (1878–1940), discussed by David Luesink in the previous chapter. Zhou also served as chief librarian and chair of the Department of Literature at National Peking University, and president of the East Asia Cultural Council. This period of Zhou's life led to divergent assessments of the man and his work.[1] After the war, Zhou was arrested by the Nationalist government of Chiang Kai-shek (1887–1975) and stood trial in Nanjing for treason, for which he was sentenced to ten years in prison. Zhou was released in 1949 and returned to Beijing, where he made a living by writing and translating. He died in 1967 at the age of eighty-two.

Zhou wrote "Zhongguo de sixiang wenti" (The Problem of Chinese Thought) on 18 November 1942, and originally published it in 1943, in *Zhonghe yuekan* (Zhonghe monthly).[2]At that time, Japan was waging the Greater East Asia War, and its propaganda organs were agitating for the revival of traditional Chinese thought and advocating "coexistence and co-prosperity." In his later years, Zhou explained his reasons for writing this piece:

> That article advocated original Confucianism, as I often was wont to do, but I had a special intention for this text, which was to prevent the New People's Association (*Xinmin hui*) [a Japanese-backed political group organized in 1937] clamouring to set up a core school of thought to cooperate with the principles of Greater East Asia. Like the braying

> of donkeys and the barking of dogs, their activities would disappear with the passing of time, so they were not worth paying attention to, but their braying was annoying to have to listen to at that time, so I determined to strike a blow against it.[3]

In this article, Zhou made it clear that there was no problem with Chinese thought, which was Confucianism as represented by Confucius (551–479 BCE), Mencius (c. 372–289), and the legendary sages Yu and Ji.[4] Zhou writes:

> Some think that China is always lacking a "central thought" and they labour to find China a new one. This is a difficult task to accomplish and naturally leads to failure. In my opinion, there is no need for such efforts because China's central thought has existed and has not changed for thousands of years. In brief, it is Confucian thought (*Ruxue sixiang*).

As a representative of Chinese intellectuals, Zhou's actions and words exerted great influence on other intellectuals' decisions to advance or withdraw. He retained his moral integrity at the early stage of Japan's occupation but, as time went on, he finally cooperated with Japan, for which he was accused of being a traitor by successive generations of Chinese. Zhou tried to relieve his moral pressure by advocating Confucianism.

Chinese scholar Zhao Jinghua has explained:

> Since the 1930s, Zhou Zuoren was deeply disappointed in the political government of China, and therefore his national identity and national consciousness began to convert to a cultural and historical understanding of China; one could also say that his thoughts gradually changed from viewing China as a "political state" to viewing China as a "cultural state." During the war, he reintroduced Confucianism and emphasized using Chinese traditional literature to resist Japanese calls to establish "the central thought" in order to achieve the goal of "Greater East Asia co-prosperity."[5]

We can analyze Zhou's articles from the 1940s to see that his major concerns were Chinese culture and thought. Two years after Zhou wrote this article, he wrote the following in the postscript to a collection of his essays:

> In 1942, I wrote "The Problem of Chinese Thought," which went beyond the scope of literature to touch on the reasons for a nation's rise and fall, as well as the fundamental ways of living ...
>
> I was always worried and apprehensive about the future of China, and became more so recently, not only because I myself am part of it and have the feeling of involvement and drowning, but also because I think that it is China's traditional morality to give one's heart and strength and even one's life to work for the interests of the people, or at least find some ways to achieve that. Every intellectual should take that as a standard, as is indicated in the Confucian classics and commentaries.[6]

After the Japanese occupation of China, the Japanese began controlling Chinese thought and publishing. Therefore, intellectuals in the occupied areas needed to use rhetorical strategies to express their thoughts. China has a long history, and there are large numbers of resources, such as historical allusions and literary quotations, which bring richness to classical Chinese writing. Scholars have observed that intellectuals in occupied Beijing often used strategies such as "the resurrection of concepts, the employment of literary allusions, and the imitation of literature genres."[7] In "The Problem of Chinese Thought," Zhou used three rhetorical strategies to indicate his dissatisfaction with Japan while escaping censorship: the first was to reinterpret political concepts in the direction he wanted, disguising the replacement of their original meaning; the second was to use historical and literary allusions; and the third was to weaken the contemporary setting.

The second of these rhetorical strategies – historical and literary allusion – was the most popular and commonly used by writers in occupied areas. The reason for the popularity of this rhetorical strategy was because, on the one hand, there were abundant resources to use, and on the other hand, writing in literary Chinese or quoting classical Chinese texts was subtler than writing in modern language. Although Zhou was a representative of New Culture or vernacular literature, his articles written during the war utilized a much higher proportion of classical Chinese prose. In the foreword of his book *Yaotang zawen*

(Essays from Yaotang), Zhou explained: "Something changed in the articles I wrote, as if the proportion of classical language increased ... this is not because I wanted to write the article in a classical style ... it is not impossible to use modern things, but in terms of living conditions nowadays, I have to use ancient things."[8]

Reader responses further reveal Zhou's intentions. The strongest response came from Japanese writer Kataoka Teppei (1894–1944). On 27 August 1943, at the second Greater East Asia Writers' Congress, Kataoka made a speech entitled "The Establishment of Chinese Literature" that criticized Zhou as "an old reactionary literary writer who is currently active in the pacified regions."[9] Zhou wrote to the Japanese Literature Patriotic Association to ask Kataoka for a clear explanation. Kataoka wrote in response:

> In my opinion, advocating to tolerate the desires of the Chinese people is in fact a refutation of the current war for the liberation of the Greater East Asia. What is more, if Chinese people are in favour of the liberation of Greater East Asia but do not want to give up their desire to survive, then this implies that Chinese people will not share any pain to assist in the Greater East Asia War. And if such thinking becomes generally accepted, what is the position of China on this war?[10]

Kataoka Teppei directly linked "Chinese thought" with the war and pointed out that Zhou's opinion about the problem of survival was, in fact, a rejection of the Greater East Asia War.

After the war, the article translated below was used as important trial evidence in Zhou's defence. Zhou's friends, the writer and translator Xu Zuzheng (1895–1978) among them, said this article was "Zhou's most significant anti-Japanese text" in their affidavits to the court.[11] The initial verdict of the High Court was that this article "was very insightful in taking loyalty and forbearance as China's original thought."[12] Although reader responses to a certain degree indicated that this article expressed Zhou's dissatisfaction with Japan, there is a great difference between dissatisfaction and resistance. Zhou repeated many times that there was no problem with Chinese thought, but his primary preoccupation was with the concept of turmoil. He replaced the problem of thought with the problem of survival, believing that avoiding turmoil was of the greatest importance. It is difficult to see his intention to resist from reading this article alone.

The final verdict from Zhou Zuoren's trial stated: "Although it is difficult to prove such an article offered strategies for Japan's colonial domination, it was the voice of the puppet government under the oppression of Japan. Therefore, the opposition of Kataoka Teppei, representative of the Japanese Literature Patriotic Association, cannot exempt Zhou from the charge of treason."[13] Zhou Zuoren finally accepted his legal guilt and went to prison in 1946. However, as detailed in the following chapter by Timothy Cronin, Zhou was released amid much controversy in 1949.

TRANSLATION

The Problem of Chinese Thought

ZHOU ZUOREN

The problem of Chinese thought, though important, is not a very serious problem. I am not an easily optimistic person about any other matter, yet I remain optimistic about Chinese thought, and I think that there is hope for its future. Recently Chinese intellectuals have indeed been confused; however, this is merely a superficial and temporary phenomenon. Looking across its distant and deep past, the thought of the Chinese people was once very robust. Based on this robust foundation, if it is properly cultivated, a robust thought will develop from which a robust citizenry will be created.

What is this intrinsic Chinese thought? Some think that China is always lacking a central thought and they labour to find China a new one. This is a difficult task to accomplish and naturally leads to failure. In my opinion, there is no need for such efforts because China's central thought has existed and has not changed for thousands of years. In brief, it is Confucian thought (*Ruxue sixiang*). While it cannot be stated so simply, before it was called Confucianism this thought was already established, and scholars continued to parade the term "Confucianism" even after they focused on the eight-legged essay.[14] If we simply call it Confucianism, there will be confusion and perplexity, so I must restate it clearly and succinctly: The Confucianism of which I speak is represented by Confucius and Mencius, with the sages Yu and Ji as its models. Several examples will make this clearer. The following is from *Mencius,* chapter 4, *Li Lou II:*[15]

> Living in their peaceful times, Yu and Ji used to pass their houses many times without entering the door. For this, Confucius appreciated them. Living in an age of disorder, Yanzi[16] dwelt in a backstreet, living off his simple food and plain water. Though others could not have endured such adversity, he never changed his optimistic attitude. For this Confucius also praised him. "Yu, Ji and Yan acted on the same principle." Mencius commented: "When Yu thought of people across the land getting drowned, he felt as if he had caused them to be drowned. When Ji thought of people across the land going hungry, he felt as if he had caused them to go hungry. That was why they kept engaging themselves in matters of great urgency. If Yu and Ji had been placed in Yan's position, each would have done what the other had done."[17]

Also by Mencius, in chapter 1, *King Hui of Liang I:*[18]

> Let mulberry trees be planted in five *mu*[19] of land around the house, then people in their fifties can be clothed in silk. Let fowls, pigs and dogs be bred at due time, then people in their seventies will have meat for meals. Let no farming schedules be upset, then a fairly large family with a hundred *mu* of land will not suffer from hunger. Let prudent heed be paid to schooling and the sense of fraternal duties be taught to the young, and you won't see a gray-haired on the way carrying a heavy burden on his back. If a state ruler guarantees that his elderly people have silk to wear and meat to eat, if he exempts his people from cold and hunger, it will never occur that he cannot become a unifier of the entire kingdom.[20]

The latter quotation discusses specific matters on what is called benevolent governance. The former shows a benevolent person's diligence. These show that the fundamental thought of Confucianism is benevolence, which can be divided into loyalty and forbearance, and benevolence pervades all of Confucianism. The term "humanitarianism" may be misinterpreted, so perhaps we can say that this is the doctrine of humanity. In *On the Analects and Benevolence,* Ruan Boyuan[21] wrote:

> *The Doctrine of the Mean*[22] states that benevolence is the characteristic element of humanity. Zheng Kangcheng[23] read "humanity" as people in a good relationship. People in a good relationship indicate that there are at least two human beings. Benevolence can be seen only if it is put into practice, and only when there are two people. If someone shuts one's door, closes

> one's eyes, and sits quietly in one's room, although one has virtues and logic in one's mind, one can never be regarded as benevolent in Confucianism. The benevolence of ordinary people is reflected in the circle of one's clans and fellows; the benevolence of emperors, princes, and officials is reflected in their kingdom and their subjects. The meaning of people in a good relationship is that there are two people and then benevolence can be seen.

His explanation of Confucian benevolence is very simple and clear. To be benevolent is to be human, and regarding others likewise as human, meaning do not do to others what you would not have them do to you. Moreover, do to others what you would have them do to you. That is to say, one wishing to establish oneself should also seek to establish others; one wishing to enlarge oneself should also seek to enlarge others, and then do to others what they want done to them and then one will achieve forbearance and even loyalty. In *Subtle Notes from Daohan,* Zhang Taiyan[24] wrote:

> Confucius took an all-pervading unity as his doctrine, and what does unity mean? It is loyalty and forbearance. Many people discuss the principle of regulating one's conduct with a measuring square, and about considering others in one's own place, which can be explained by the word forbearance. Human beings eat food crops, deer eat grasses, centipedes eat snakes, and eagles eat rats; they have different preferences. Although we are human, we like different things, only knowing social regulations and offering others what general people like, while you may happen to offer others what they do not want. How can we know whether we do the right thing and achieve the principle of loyalty? The person who achieved the greatest loyalty and forbearance was Zhuangzi,[25] and his theory of the equality of everything contained loyalty and forbearance. Neo-Confucianists Cheng Yi and Cheng Hao[26] did not understand the doctrine. They stated that Buddhism let people abandon their body, donate their heads, eyes, and brains to others, and this is giving others what they themselves do not want. If so, the emperor of the kingdom of Lu has no need to raise the Aiju bird[27] with beautiful music and rich food. Letting people know the principle is the duty of forbearance, and giving people property and courage is the duty of loyalty.

One who excels in loyalty and forbearance brings benevolence to its extreme. Though the mountain peak is very high and steep, and its roots very deep and vast, people from the sages to the ordinary all share the same thought – to do their part and try their best. Like Ruan Boyuan said, "the benevolence of ordinary people is reflected in the circle of one's clans and fellows; the benevolence of emperors, princes, and officials is reflected in their kingdom and their subjects." This is also like the taste of seawater; no matter a spoon of it or the entire ocean, it tastes the same regardless of the measure. Another significant point is that, when we talk about benevolence, we think it is very illusory, while actually it is very practical or simple, since it is a fundamental human instinct. In *Study Notes on the Book of Changes*, volume 12, Jiao Litang[28] wrote:

> My father told me that life is all about food, drink, and sexual pleasure. One cannot live without food and cannot procreate without sex. I want food and others want it too, I like sexual pleasure and others like it too. Mencius's theory of the fondness of wealth and beauty explains it all. There is no need to abandon one's desire for food and sexual pleasure, but one should not forget that one has survived on food and was born by one's parents. I have studied the *Book of Changes* for thirty years, and thus I can understand what the sages mean. It is not easy to be a sage.

The chapter "Li Yun" in *The Book of Rites*[29] states: "The things that men greatly desire are comprehended in food, drink, and sexual pleasure; those that they greatly dislike are comprehended in death, exile, poverty, and suffering." This is no different from what Jiao Litang said, but Jiao explained it more clearly. Food and drink are necessary for individual survival, while procreation is necessary for the survival of a race. These desires are instinctive for all creatures, and are labelled "the will to live" by evolutionists. Human beings also have such instincts because they too are living creatures. However, regular creatures' will to live is quite simple. They strive to exist through any means necessary, only worrying about their own existence and not hesitating to jeopardize the lives of others. Human beings are not like this. Like animals, they strive to live. However, at first on finding it impossible to achieve this goal all by themselves, they feel the need to connect with others and help each other to live a better life. Later, on finding that others also have their likes and dislikes, they try to live together in harmony. The former is a way to live that some animals can also achieve, while the latter is a kind of survival morality that is unique to humanity. This is similar to what Mencius said: "The difference between human beings and animals is very small." This primitive survival morality is the roots and shoots of benevolence, and is shared by all human beings. However, people's minds vary as much as their faces, and so too does the psychological development of each nation. Some strive to live, seeking immortality yet ending up with destruction, like the theistic tendencies of Jews and Hindus; some chase power on the road to survival, like the establishment of imperialism in the Roman Empire. These are all typical examples. Among all nations, China is the only one sticking to simple secularism by emphasizing actual utility and moderation, thus the pursuit of the Chinese nation is helping each other to go through difficulties, which is the same as the worn-out slogan of coexistence and co-prosperity,[30] and contains no lofty proposals. This, viewed from the surface, is based on creatures' survival instincts; therefore its foundations run deep. Moreover, from a profound perspective, it is completely natural and able to conform to nature's principle and human beings' feelings to put all creatures in their places, which coincides with the sages' diligence and the ordinary people's capabilities. This contributes to the soundness of Chinese thought that I have mentioned above. Being derived from human nature and different from thoughts instilled by external sources, it is certainly better comprehended by well-educated scholars, yet can also be understood by the illiterate who have never read the books of the sages. Thus even the illiterate can get along with others, conforming to rites and laws as the way of the ancient sages. This is why I said I am optimistic for Chinese thought. The foundation of Chinese people's thought is Confucianism, naturally with Confucius as the primary representative. This is not because Confucius established Confucianism and advocated his doctrines with great endeavour, rather, Confucius himself, as a native Chinese, represents and epitomizes the peak of Chinese thought. The thought of a nation is its roots and shoots, and political education is its nutrients, like sunshine and water. No doubt, nutrients are essential, yet the roots and shoots are infinitely more important as innate things that, whether good or bad, are difficult to alter by external forces. Fortunately, the roots and shoots for Chinese thought are good, which is something to be grateful for. In an unpromising age, for me this is the only thing to be optimistic about, and I can positively acclaim that there is absolutely no problem with the roots of Chinese thought.

With these optimistic words said, I do not mean that there is no danger or concern for us to fear now or in the future. As the old saying goes, there is not any advantage without disadvantage; so it is with Chinese thought. This is understandable. People cannot live without water and fire, yet flood and conflagration can also be serious disasters. If mishandled, things that benefit people may turn harmful. We have always found the thought of the Chinese citizenry to be a good thing, helping the people deal with things in past times, and undoubtedly helping us to deal with future matters as well.

As no matter how the world changes, people always need to learn to behave and to survive, thus seeking "coexistence and co-prosperity" with others is the correct path. Yet this is the positive side, and of course there is a negative side that one needs to be concerned with. Chinese people's need for life is quite simple but urgent: they want to survive. With avoiding harming others for their own benefit as their survival morality, they are also unwilling to hurt themselves to benefit others like saints do. People of other religions, dreaming that heaven is near, can walk into boiling water or fire for the sake of eternal life. Chinese people do not have this faith and are not willing to sacrifice their lives for God or religious service. Yet when they feel that there is no hope for life, they too can also walk through water and fire without flinching, risking all in desperation. According to Mencius, a benevolent government focuses on protecting people from hunger and cold. When this is not done, people "do not have enough to support their parents or wives or children, they suffer all the while even in good years, and in bad years they cannot escape death."[31] Such things are signs of turmoil. What Mencius said is very simple, so I quote Confucius to explain it: "There are two ways: benevolence and not benevolence." The manifestation of benevolence is people living and working in harmony and happiness, and its consequence is peace. The manifestation of not benevolence is people living on the edge of starvation, and its consequence is turmoil. As explained above, turmoil is the threat that is our greatest concern. After studying Chinese history and examining Chinese thought, I came to the conclusion that the most terrible thing in China is turmoil, and this turmoil arises in reaction from the people's will to survive. It is not due to any doctrines or theories, but arises because the desires of the people are prevented or left unsatisfied. In more modern times, turmoil arose in the times of Zhang Xianzhong and Li Zicheng in the late Ming dynasty,[32] and Hong Xiuquan and Yang Xiuqing in the Qing dynasty.[33] Though historians have provided a variety of critiques, the different periods of turmoil are fundamentally of the same kind. The process of destruction still shocks people today, and the reason for the periods of turmoil was the desperate living status of people. These are all lessons to be learned. Chinese people generally love peace and sometimes seem to be too tolerant, however, when circumstances are out of control, they may totally change by discarding their original manners and unleashing a wild nature. But who is to blame? It is said that there are neither quarrels with nice words nor fights with weak blows. It is not unfair that not being benevolent brings no benevolence from others. I will reiterate my idea that I see no problem with Chinese thought. The most important thing is to prevent turmoil, and to prevent turmoil our primary task is to stop those who would arouse turmoil. The responsibility for this falls within the realm of politics rather than Confucian training. Again in Mencius's words, even if we are not capable of providing the elderly with good food and clothing and guaranteeing that people do not suffer from hunger and cold, we must do our utmost to ensure that conditions are not so terrible that people "do not have enough to support their parents or wives or children. They suffer all the while even in good years, and in bad years they cannot escape death."[34] Although it is a passive approach, avoiding the creation of conditions and opportunities for turmoil may be much more effective than eliminating and adjusting people's thoughts. Although it may not coincide with Western theories, this method should be more suitable for China's circumstances as it is obtained from thousands of years of Chinese history. History books are indeed national treasures, as they record the whole nation's health and diseases. On reading about the history of roving bandits, we can identify China's problem; on learning how Wang Anshi's[35] political reform injured people, we can realize that the misuse of drugs is also lethal. Ancient people likened history books to mirrors and named them "helpful books to govern the state." This is a very appropriate statement. By reading history books, we take Confucian classics, philosophical writings, essays, and poems as historical records and draw conclusions from them. Their words are often simple but true, and they are indeed better medical records and prescriptions for China than lofty unrealistic ideas. I recall a piece in *Notes from the Old Learning Study,*[36] chapter 1:

> Taoist Shangguan[37] of Mount Qingcheng[38] was a northerner who lived in trees and ate wheat, and he was ninety years old. He only smiled when being visited by people. And when asked questions, he never replied, using illness as an excuse. When I met him in the Taoist temple, all of a sudden he began to talk to himself about how to preserve one's health. According to him, keeping the nation at peace and being alive forever were both impossible tasks for ordinary people. What one should do at the moment is to protect the nation from disorder and wait for a person of extraordinary talent, and to protect people's lives from death and wait for a distinguished person. To keep the nation in order and keep people alive depends not on magic arts but on discretion. I was excited and bowed down to him, but he said no more.

I was impressed and convinced by these words. Although a priest in the Taoist tradition, Taoist Shangguan's theory of keeping people alive and the nation in order accords more closely with Confucianism. It is the minimum requirement of Confucianism's political ideal. However, things are always easier said than done. I used to sigh for the unusual circumstance in which turmoil from the Northern and Southern Song dynasties to the Ming dynasty was almost all caused intentionally, while on second thought, this is not so. Louis XIV had known the flood[39] would come yet chose to do nothing to help his people to survive. Was this not the most inane thing under heaven? I read Du Muzhi's "Ode to E-pang palace" in *Analysis of Ancient Essays,*[40] which ends with the sentence: "People of the Qin dynasty had no opportunity to lament themselves while later generations lamented them. If later generations only lamented the Qin dynasty without learning a lesson from it, their descendants would again lament them." At that time I read it out aloud to appreciate the rhyme. Now, I find the meaning of it even more profound.

What I have stated above is of simple meaning yet too verbose, so I would like to make a summary. I believe that there is no problem with Chinese thought since its main idea exists forever. Its main idea, stemming from people's biological instincts and being bound by human morality, is very solid and sound. In some nations, the supreme ideal is the monarch, while in others it is God. However, ordinary Chinese people serve themselves and their clans, while Confucian scholars serve the people. Actually, these are one and the same. This is not unique to some people or a certain class; rather, it is shared by everyone to different extents, from the narrowest to the widest. It is not created by sages and introduced gradually to the people; on the contrary, it is derived from the ordinary people and gradually improved and expanded on by the sages. Because of this, I see no problem with Chinese thought, and the only thing needed is to cultivate it for a normal development. While Chinese thought is based on people's need for subsistence, with subsistence being jeopardized, the thought will be shaken, leading to the danger of turmoil. As this is not brought about by any theory, it cannot be prevented by language and words. Perhaps some will object to both the optimistic and pessimistic sides of my essay, for their inconformity to foreign theories, but I think my words are very reliable and honest. In the past I studied foreign books with an open mind, yet only to absorb knowledge about the universe and biology. When it comes to Chinese affairs, especially Chinese thought, I think Chinese people know it better or know it more correctly. I will not take the words and deeds of heroes and sages as examples like patriots do, but I think it is in common with observing ordinary people and finding the Chinese outlook of life from their words, and then confirming it with the rise and fall of dynasties in history. The result may not be absurd. So I believe that although what I have stated is simple, my reasoning is correct and can be identified by people with deep insight. These outdated words, although perhaps behind the times, reveal my poor talent but can reflect my sincerity.

(18 November 1942)

Notes

1 Susan Daruvala, *Zhou Zuoren and an Alternative Response to Chinese Modernity* (Cambridge, MA: Harvard University Press, 2000), 2.

2 Zhitang [Zhou Zuoren], "Zhongguo de sixiang wenti" [The problem of Chinese thought], *Zhonghe yuekan* [Zhonghe monthly] 4, 1 (1943): 4–8. Zhitang is one of Zhou Zuoren's pen names. *Zhonghe yuekan* was founded by Qu Duizhi (1894–1973), a Chinese historian and politician, in Beijing on 1 January 1940 and ended publication in 1945.

3 Zhou Zuoren, "Fandong laozuojia" [Reactionary old writer], *Zhitang huixiang lu* [Memoirs of Zhitang] (Taipei: Longwen chubanshe, 1989), 714.

4 Yu, also called Yu the Great, was a legendary person in ancient China famed for his prevention of flood by water control. He also established the Xia dynasty. Ji, also called Hou Ji, was a legendary person famed for his agriculture skills in the Xia dynasty. He taught people how to plant food crops and was claimed as the ancestor of the Zhou dynasty.

5 Zhao Jinghua, "Zhou Zuoren de minzu guojia yishi" [Zhou Zuoren's national consciousness], *Wenxue Pinglun* [Literary review] 1 (2015): 70.

6 Zhou Zuoren, "Lichun yiqian xu" [Postscript of *Before Spring*], in *Zhou Zuoren Wenxuan* [Analects of Zhou Zuoren], ed. Zhong Chuhe (Guangzhou: Guangzhou chubanshe, 1995), 34.

7 For example, see Yuan Yidan, "Yinwei xiuci: Beiping lunxian shiqi wenren xuezhe de biaoda celue" [Subtle rhetoric: The strategies of literati during the occupation of Beiping], *Zhongguo xiandai wenxue yanjiu congkan* [Modern Chinese literature research studies] 1 (2014): 1.

8 Zhou Zuoren, Foreword, *Yaotang zawen* [Essays from Yaotang] (Beijing: Xinmin chubanshe, 1944), 1–2.

9 Nanjing shi danganguan, ed., *Shenxun Wang wei Hanjian bilu* [The trial transcripts of the Wang Jingwei regime traitors] (Nanjing: Fenghuang chubanshe, 2004), 1398.

10 Quoted in Zhi An, *Zhou Zuoren zhuan* [The biography of Zhou Zuoren] (Jinan: Shandong huabao chubanshe, 2009), 240.

11 Nanjing shi danganguan, *Shenxun,* 1390.

12 Ibid., 1434.

13 Ibid., 1439.

14 The eight-legged essay was a special style of essay that was used in imperial examinations during the Ming and Qing dynasties.

15 The book *Mencius,* named after its writer, is one of the Confucian classics. *Mencius* has seven chapters, each named after the first person to appear in the chapter. Li Lou was a legendary person with strong vision.

16 Yanzi (521–481 BCE), also called Yan Hui, was Confucius' best disciple.

17 Wu Guozhen, *Mengzi zuixin yingwen quan yi quan zhu ben* [A new annotated English version of the works of Mencius] (Fuzhou: Fujian jiaoyu chubanshe, 2015), 198.

18 King Hui of Liang (400–319 BCE) was the third king of Wei during the Warring States period.

19 *Mu* is a unit of area equivalent to 667 square metres.
20 Wu Guozhen, *Mengzi,* 31.
21 Ruan Yuan (courtesy name Boyuan, 1764–1849), was a writer and philosopher in the Qing dynasty. In *Lunyu lunren lun* [On the analects and benevolence], he tried to explain the *Analects of Confucius* and the concept of benevolence.
22 *Zhong yong* [The doctrine of the mean] is Chapter 31 of *The Book of Rites* and became one of the Four Books of Confucian philosophy after the Song dynasty. It is a text rich with guidance to gain perfect virtue.
23 Zheng Xuan (courtesy name Kangcheng, 127–200), was a Confucian scholar in the Eastern Han dynasty.
24 Zhang Taiyan (1869–1936), also known as Zhang Binglin, was a revolutionary, philosopher and scholar during the late Qing dynasty and the early Republic. *Daohan weiyan* [Subtle notes from Daohan] is a collection of his philosophical essays discussing Buddhism and Confucianism. Daohan was the name of his study.
25 Zhuangzi (369–286 BCE), also known as Zhuang Zhou, was a Chinese philosopher, littérateur, and one of the foremost representatives of Taoism.
26 Cheng Yi (1033–1107) and his older brother, Cheng Hao (1032–85), were philosophers and educators in the Song dynasty.
27 The Aiju is a seabird in a story from an ancient Chinese history book, *Guoyu* [Discourses of the states].
28 Jiao Xun (1763–1820), courtesy name Litang, was a Chinese philosopher, mathematician and opera theorist in the Qing dynasty. *Yi yu yue lu* [Study notes on the *Book of Changes*] is a collection of his academic notes of his study of the *Book of Changes,* an ancient Chinese divination text.
29 *Li Ji* (*The Book of Rites*) is a collection of texts describing the social forms, administration, and ceremonial rites of the Zhou dynasty. The chapter titled "Li Yun" describes Confucian political thought and historical viewpoints. The "Great Unity" thought in this chapter has had a profound impact on politicians and reformers of China.
30 "Coexistence and co-prosperity" was a popular Japanese propaganda slogan during the war.
31 Wu Guozhen, *Mengzi,* 30.
32 Zhang Xianzhong (1606–47), nicknamed Yellow Tiger, was a leader of a peasant revolt who later became the emperor of the short-lived Da Xi dynasty in Sichuan. Li Zicheng (1606–45), nicknamed Dashing King, was a leader of a peasant revolt that overthrew the Ming dynasty in 1644. Li later became the emperor of the short-lived Da Shun dynasty.
33 Hong Xiuquan (1814–64) was the leader of the Taiping Rebellion during the Qing dynasty and established the Taiping Heavenly Kingdom in Nanjing. Yang Xiuqing (1823–56) was an organizer of the Taiping Rebellion and the east king of the Taiping Heavenly Kingdom.
34 Wu Guozhen, *Mengzi,* 30.
35 Wang Anshi (courtesy name Jiefu, 1021–86), was an ideologist, politician, and littérateur. Wang initiated the socioeconomic reform known as the New Policies in the Song dynasty.
36 *Laoxuean biji* [Notes from the old learning study] was written by Lu You (1125–1209), a Chinese poet in the Song dynasty.
37 Shangguan is a relatively rare Chinese compound surname.
38 Mount Qingcheng, a mountain in Sichuan, is considered one of the birthplaces of Taoism.
39 The flood indicates the French Revolution, which started over seven decades after the rule of Louis XIV.
40 *E-pang gong fu* (Ode to E-pang palace) is an essay written by Du Mu (courtesy name Muzhi, 803–52), a poet and essayist of the late Tang dynasty. E-pang was a palace complex

of the first emperor of the Qin dynasty. Through describing its construction and destruction, Du Mu summarized the historical experience of the Qin dynasty. *Guwen xiyi* (Analysis of ancient essays) is a book written by Lin Yunming (1628–97), a poet and essayist of the late Ming and early Qing dynasties who selected and analyzed Chinese classics by making commentaries and annotations.

23 Zhou Zuoren's Letter to Zhou Enlai

TIMOTHY CRONIN

On 4 July 1949, the day to which this letter to Premier Zhou Enlai (1898–1976) is dated, Zhou Zuoren (1885–1967) was living in the home of his former student You Bingqi[1] in a newly liberated Shanghai. He had resided there since his sudden release from Nanjing's Tiger Bridge Prison in January, scarcely two years into a ten-year sentence for the crime of "collaboration with an enemy nation and conspiracy against his own country."[2] This turn of good fortune accompanied the Kuomintang (KMT) abandonment of the capital, as part of a general amnesty to all state prisoners not serving a life sentence.[3]

Although cut off from his family in Beiping, Zhou was not without moral and financial support, and the months he spent in Shanghai present a picture of relative ease and collegiality atypical even of his life before the 1937 invasion. Among his visitors, for poetry and games of mah-jong, was a veritable who's who of literary luminaries from the Shanghai and Nanjing wartime scene, many of whose reputations were similarly clouded by association with the Wang Jingwei (1883–1944) regime.

After the resumption of regular rail services, Zhou resolved to return north. Although his conviction had been issued by the court of a defunct regime and it was possible that the freshly triumphant Communists might display a measure of magnanimity that the legitimacy-strapped KMT could ill afford in 1946, Zhou's situation remained precarious and many questions hung over his future livelihood and the status of his estate. His impressive library had been requisitioned as "enemy property" and lay piled in a wing of the Palace Museum, while People's Liberation Army soldiers billeted in the front rooms of his old home and his large family rented the rooms around the rear courtyard only at the new government's forbearance.[4]

Zhou Zuoren was anxious to ascertain his status in the regime's eyes, and this letter can be seen as an attempt to accommodate himself to China's new rulers before his return. But Zhou, who believed that he had done much to ameliorate the excesses of the Japanese and their more opportunistic hangers-on, remained quietly aggrieved at his treatment. This was, therefore, equally an opportunity to restate his case before a new authority and partially redeem his sullied reputation.

This letter is the most coherent account we have of Zhou's own views on the circumstances and motivations behind the collaborative act that rendered him *persona non grata* in the world of Chinese letters. The arguments marshalled here, as idiosyncratic as the man himself, confound the common categories of loyalty and disloyalty that Zhou himself rejected as inappropriate standards for action. He was dismissive of any mode of abstract patriotism that privileged political purity over tangible goods delivered to actual people. Indeed, the "scorn of hypocrisy" that Zhou accorded to his intellectual heroes led him to a particular disdain for literary men who fancied themselves warriors, and this attitude coloured his views on resistance itself.

In his mind, years of internecine struggle under warlord and KMT rule alike had sapped China's capacity to defend itself against imperial Japan's military might.[5] But he did not celebrate the Japanese victory he believed inevitable. Before the war, Zhou had written as forcefully as anyone against the tide of fascism that disfigured the Japan of unbound feet, ribald poetry, and reverence for the ordinary that had disclosed itself to him with all the force of revelation as a young exchange student.[6] He regarded Japan's appalling behaviour on the international stage as a tragedy for both victim and victimizer alike.[7]

While ample evidence exists of resistance and insubordination against the Japanese authorities on Zhou's part,[8] these acts were possible only because of the inherent propaganda value his cooperation held for the occupiers and the legitimacy it lent them.[9] Did Zhou's purported ends justify his means? Or does his argument smack too keenly of post facto justification? While these questions remain open to debate, according to Zhou the status of either dedicated resister or opportunistic collaborator appears equally implausible.

This is all in support of Lu Yan's trenchant assertion that "in Zhou Zuoren's case, [Poshek] Fu's three patterns of behaviour – passivity, resistance, and collaboration – seem to coexist in one person, and thus do not fit well. These categories ... are only relevant in an intellectual context dominated by nationalism."[10] For Zhou, the integrity of the nation was not the *summum bonum* of ethical action but was secondary to fundamental questions of individual well-being and maintaining conditions amenable to its flourishing. For Zhou, expecting individuals to sacrifice themselves in the name of the nation was not only a relic of feudal virtue akin to the fetishization of female chastity (valorizing suicide over survival), but was also wasteful and counterproductive.[11] Against these ideas, he invoked the practical virtues of a pristine "proto-Confucianism" and the scientific truths revealed by Western advances in sexual psychology, sociology, and anthropology – dual intellectual streams that buttressed his appeals to the "practicalisation of morality" and "naturalisation of ethics" respectively.[12]

Whatever their ultimate exculpatory power, it is crucial to note that most of Zhou Zuoren's arguments herein predate the outbreak of war. His apparent apprehension of communism's essential correctness through the circuitous path of "the Woman Question" can indeed be traced back to a 1918 essay published in the pages of *Xin qingnian* (New youth).[13] The letter's basic gambit rests in Zhou's attempt to establish his natural sympathy for the Communist cause via his verifiable progressive record, even in the absence of a legitimate socialist pedigree. He hoped to earn a place in the New China as an essentially benign, if not beneficial, member of the body politic.

It remains unclear whether Zhou Enlai ever read the letter, but Zhou Zuoren seems to have copied it out more than once. A copy of the letter made it into the hands of Feng Xuefeng,[14] founding editor-in-chief of the People's Literature Publishing House. Wei Shijing writes that "one day Comrade Xuefeng arrived at the Lu Xun Publishing Society ... and sat across from me. Turning on the desk lamp, he began to read some documents, becoming more and more agitated until exclaiming loudly: 'Look! If Zhou Zuoren had even an ounce of self-awareness, he would know not to write this sort of thing!'"[15] When the letter was first published in May 1987, the editor's note asserted that its provenance was precisely from this copy of Feng's. Indeed, this copying process may explain the conspicuous absence of a named addressee.[16]

This also seems not to have been the only letter Zhou wrote to senior party members. In January 1951, he appears to have written to Mao himself – with a copy sent to Mao's influential cultural czar, Zhou Yang (1908–89). If extant, neither of these letters are publicly available, but some of their content has survived in Hu Qiaomu's correspondence and Zhou Zuoren's diary. Addressing Zhou Yang, Zhou Zuoren wrote:

> I am unwilling, under the People's Government, to be spoken of as either a collaborator with an enemy nation, or a conspirator against his own country. Back in the days of the Kuomintang, concepts of right and wrong were upside-down and so I thought there was no point in arguing with it. But I believe that our present government is imminently possessed of reasonable feelings ... like a drowning man in sight of a rescue vessel, I cannot help but feel a certain sense of hopefulness – this is a thoroughly human weakness, after all. It is with happy heart that I humbly entreat your consideration.[17]

The following week Hu Qiaomu wrote to Mao:

> My opinion is that [Zhou] should completely admit to his wrongdoings and repent in the papers like Li Ji[18] ... He currently translates classical European literature, earning his living from the proceeds of these manuscripts and perhaps he can continue work in this area in the future. Zhou Yang seconds this suggestion. Please indicate your instructions, for or against.[19]

Mao's mark instructs to "proceed as suggested." Zhou Zuoren's diary indicates that he did draft several versions of a confession, but according to Lou Shiyi's[20] later account they were rejected because Zhou "would not admit fault ... and insists that he entered the puppet regime only to preserve our national culture. Our leaders thought that there was no way they could possibly present a confession like this to the People."

These letters did not earn the redress or rehabilitation Zhou had hoped for. Nonetheless, he was treated with relative leniency in these early years, even as his literary endeavours were restricted to reminiscences of Lu Xun and translations from the Classical Greek and Japanese. For the most part, (...) he lived out an anonymous, industrious life – never vindicated, but neglected more than actively persecuted.[21] Tragically, this anonymity failed to protect Zhou at the outbreak of the Cultural Revolution. His old home was stormed by a contingent of Red Guards, and he was subjected to a series of savage beatings before being forced to eke out his final year in a state of malnourishment and appalling privation.[22]

The reigning interpretation of Zhou's collaboration as an ipso facto betrayal of race and nation likely contributed to the brutality of his end, as the young guards – stirred by revolutionary rhetoric – arrogated for themselves the right to execute with violence what they must have believed to be the solemn judgment of history. To the extent to which definitions of patriotism and loyalty remain unreflective and unreconstructed in China and elsewhere, the complicated wartime experience of Zhou Zuoren – one of modern China's most accomplished literary stylists and broad-minded social commentators – will remain relevant and illustrative.

TRANSLATION

A Letter by Zhou Zuoren

Dear Mister XX:

It is with a good deal of hesitation that I write this letter to you, sir, because judged according to old norms, doing so cannot but seem a little inappropriate. If one were to adopt the tone typical of an old-society news reporter, then it might be said of the whole thing that it smacks a bit of unabashed brown-nosery and shameless self-promotion – for the fact remains that there is really no pleasant way of discussing these matters. Yet, after a period of deliberation, I finally made the decision to write. This is because our present time differs markedly from preceding ages, and past concepts of right and wrong are no longer fit guides for present action. It simply behooves us now to speak the truth, and to do so with sincerity. If it happens that one has some matter or other to declare before the People's government – which is to say, my government also – then there is nothing about this that is impermissible. This state of affairs is diametrically opposed to how we were expected, from our position as subjects, to address the authoritarian governments of the past; and it is for this reason that I have resolved to write this letter to you, sir, so as to offer some manner of explanation of my views on New Democracy[23] and give account of some matters of personal significance.

I am not a researcher of the social sciences, and can by no means lay claim to any great understanding of communism's scientific essence, even though

I have had occasion to read a little of its standard texts, and believe, furthermore, that history is (as it has ever been) the history of class struggle, in which prevailing categories of morality and law through the ages have represented nothing so much as the interests of the privileged classes of the day. I also have no specialized knowledge to speak of and, as far as literature is concerned, I am quite conscious of my lack of propensity for it – so I have long since given up that particular game. Yet in saying this, even now I find myself interested in the myths of the Greeks,[24] in the tales of children and their songs, in folklore and popular customs and other things of this sort – and this all happens to be deeply implicated in the so-called Woman Question and Child Question,[25] two issues to which I have devoted a considerable amount of attention in my day. There was a time in which my investigations into this Woman Question also led me to much the same conclusion as the English thinker Edward Carpenter:[26] that that Woman Question had to be solved alongside the "question of the worker." It is from this realization that I came to believe that communism was our only sure way out of this bind, a sentiment from which I have never wavered in all these years since. Coming to the issue obliquely, from the question of women's proper role in society, I came to understand the righteousness of communism's path and believe in its power to solve all of our society's many ills. Those of us who have lived under Kuomintang rule know very little of the formal theories of the Chinese Communist Party, nor much of its current realities – only what information we could glean from the two or three works of Chairman Mao available to us, or from the books of the American journalist Edgar Snow and others like him.[27] But this year, with Tianjin and Beiping liberated one after the other – followed in quick succession by Nanjing and Shanghai – we are finally able to see and hear for ourselves, and it can finally be said of us that we properly understand. But while we know that the theory of communism is correct, we desire most of all to know how its reality will prove. The people have all witnessed for themselves the superb discipline of the People's Liberation Army, but to speak quite plainly, though this is a very positive thing indeed, it is also something that should go without saying. Instead, the more pressing question is how politics will be done, and it is this question that the average person's attention is fixed upon today.

On the topic of north and east China, we are aware of the party's efforts at implementing the principles of New Democracy there. While this is only a very vague characterization of the kind of work underway, the significance of these acts themselves is, in fact, quite monumental. Ever since the founding of the republic, there has been no shortage of "-isms" and theories that have swept across the public stage only to betray themselves as little better than the placards and advertisements they ever were: an interminable series of uncashable cheques. But for there now to be a theory actually put into practice, represents something of an unprecedented miracle for China. And as a person who has long believed in the pressing need for morality to be transformed into a form of practical ethics, naturally I can only express my sincere admiration. It is obviously difficult to encapsulate the full import of this new turning point in Chinese history. Yet speaking generally of what we have witnessed to date, we know that the Chinese Communist Party possesses an established system of self-criticism and a studious spirit and are witness to the rigour and practicality of its dealings, its prudence and industry, and its willingness to "seek truth from facts" (to quote, in the main, the words of Zhang Zhizhong).[28] That these developments represent a new and previously nonexistent direction for China is probably something of which the whole world is well aware. But I think that the most meaningful aspect of this is the fact that theory and practice are unified for the party, and that the traditionalism once so rife in our governing circles is being smashed in favour of a politics characterized by the rustic decency of the peasantry. The value and significance of this is difficult to adequately quantify, of course, but it is a feat at least equal to breaking the military dominance of the feudal aristocracy and one that is in many ways even more challenging for being an act of creation. I mean only to offer here some expression of my admiration for these recent developments, and will refrain from embellishing further, given that these are all things that the party itself is perfectly well aware of – and no doubt more than a few outsiders have expressed similar sentiments, besides.

Because I am not someone with any great understanding of politics or economics, my words cannot help but sound just so crudely superficial as this. But these words are nonetheless true, insofar as they serve to express my meaning. Therefore, I will quit my hemming and hawing and just write my mind as best I can. Perhaps, however, there will be those who will wonder, who does he think he is to say such things? – and because this criticism is a perfectly reasonable one, I think I must also offer a few words of explanation for myself, sir, since I fear that there may be certain aspects of my thought and actions that you may not entirely understand.

Regarding the criticisms that have been levelled at me: before the War of Resistance, they were because I was deemed too leisurely and passive, whereas after the war, it was for my having reputedly betrayed the nation and collaborated with the enemy. As far as my own situation is concerned, severe criticism is entirely warranted and there ought to be a frank admission of fault on my part. However, it is also necessary for me to offer some account of how these circumstances came to pass. And although it is altogether unavoidable for this to smack a little of self-justification, I can claim in all honesty that none of these justifications are of the spurious and sophistic sort and I will categorically admit to whatever errors of mine that emerge from the recounting.

Because of my cursory readings into the Woman Question and its relationship to sexual psychology, my thinking became influenced by the ideas of August Bebel,[29] Edward Carpenter, Havelock Ellis,[30] and others. Through them I was led to conclude that women's sexual and economic liberation could only be found within a communist society, a view from which I have never wavered since. As for Chinese thinkers of the past, there have been three that have significantly influenced my thinking: the first of these is Wang Chong of the Eastern Han dynasty; the second, Li Zhi of the Ming; and the third, Yu Zhengxie of the Qing.[31] All these men were united by their scorn for hypocrisy and falsity, their intimate knowledge of human feelings and the natural order of things[32] and their opposition to the feudalistic ethical codes and Confucian ritualism that prevailed in their days. Li Zhi's example in particular has long been for me a particularly potent source of inspiration, and there was also a period around the May Fourth movement in which everyone was engaged in discussion of him, praising the ideas he espoused in works like *A Book to Burn* (*Fenshu*), *A Book to Keep Hidden* (*Cangshu*) and *Upon Arrival at the Lakeside* (*Chutan ji*) – all books that were roundly condemned during the Ming and Qing dynasties as blasphemous tracts and strictly banned. Li employed new and independent insights to criticize the old historiographical traditions and overturn the moral system of the Three Bonds,[33] while authoring essays that sought to re-evaluate the legacies of such maligned figures as Zhuo Wenjun, female Emperor Wu Zetian, and Feng Dao.[34] Li argued that Confucius's standards of right and wrong were inadequate guides for current norms, despite his own essays being riddled with canonical quotations and classical allusions. Instead he makes it clear, in a letter contained in *A Book to Burn,* that his aim was not to hand down the teachings of the ancients even though he happened to cite their words prodigiously; rather he quoted them simply because of the sheer stock the people placed in such allusions and for the plausible degree of cover that the words of the ancients might be able to provide him and his ideas. I quite categorically do not believe that teachings of Confucius or Mencius can ever be productive of democratic ideals, and I likewise hold a special dislike for the brand of Confucian that emerged from the Han and Song dynasties onward. Even so, in spite of this I frequently cite the words of Confucius and Mencius in the course of my essays and have claimed, furthermore, that there existed "Confucians" predating Confucius and Mencius who possessed certain ideas that remain worthy of our continued consideration today. Their paragons were not Kings Wen or Wu or the Duke of Zhou, but it was rather to Yu the Great and Hou Ji (the Lord of Millet) that they traced their lineage – or perhaps even all the way back to the words of Shennong (the Divine Farmer), who can be sure?[35] Regardless of these questions of lineage, we can say that their common aim lay, first and foremost, in guaranteeing the people's livelihood. And although we can hardly regard their example as "government by the people," it certainly touched on, at the very least, the principle of "government for the people."[36] But it was in this sense, therefore, that I employed much the same tactic as Li Zhi: using the examples of the past for the cause of present reform – well aware that my words were not the truth per se, but finding myself in circumstances that presented few alternatives. "The Problem of Chinese Thought,"[37] "Two Kinds of Chinese Literary Thought," and several other pieces authored in the thirty-second year of the republic (1943) are prime examples of this sort of essay of mine. And indeed, Li Zhi's views and my own were basically of a piece as far as antiquated Confucian ethical codes were concerned. But whereas the tool with which he sought to demolish Confucianism's autocracy was the teaching of Chan Buddhism, those of us in this day and age must naturally arm ourselves with a different tool altogether, that is, with science.

The cannibal nature of the old Confucian orthodoxy is borne out by the bare facts of history, inscribed there – line by line – in the pages of our books.[38] For these past two thousand years, China's governing morality has served the interests of the family head (for whom it was established) and its guiding principle has been the chauvinist ideology of the Three Bonds. For these men, the male as family head represented the absolute centre of the moral universe: wives were his personal possession, and sons and daughters were expected to exert themselves to their utmost in order to ensure his full provision. In times of need they could be sold off as slaves or as prostitutes, or even to act as paid scapegoats for capital crimes. Then, if he fell ill, they would make him medicinal soup prepared from flesh hewn from their own thighs; if enraged, he could simply kill them indiscriminately.[39]

If this "filial bond" between father and child were not bad enough, then the conjugal bond between man and wife was basically intolerable. For if children were his chattel and livestock, then wives and concubines were not only chattel and livestock, but also tools for his personal use. On top of the arbitrary treatment with which we are already familiar, there was added a level of cruelty and abuse born out of the particular sense of jealous entitlement by which this bond is distinguished. For example, on the death of a patriarch it was common practice for his wives and concubines to be buried next to him in the grave alongside his chariots, his horses, his precious garments, buried there so that he might continue to use them in the afterlife. By way of a second example, it was also typical, on encountering the ravages of war, that the first wish of the patriarch (that is, the gentry and scholar-officials familiar to us from later ages) should be for his wives and concubines to promptly hang themselves – or hastily cast themselves into the river – lest they be carried away by the hands of others. This is all to say, since they were his to use and because he could not protect them, it was better they die cleanly than be despoiled. Indeed this act could even be for him a source of honour and glory: on the one hand, when peace was restored he could return and stock his household with new wives and concubines, while on the other hand he could erect an arch in memoriam, nailing up a plaque to extoll the virtue of the most chaste of martyrs[40] and going on to reap, in so doing, even further renown for his house and prestige for his person.

This iniquitous and inhumane brand of morality has dominated our society down to the present day, continuing to flourish especially from the Song dynasty onwards. I have spoken here at some length on the subject of the conjugal bond, not necessarily to make specific reference to the Woman Question itself, but also because it is precisely from this bond that the bond between ruler and subject arises. Therefore, it was necessary to offer some explanation for the former first. Now, there have certainly existed monarchical autocracies in every corner of the world, and in each alike has ruler been exalted and subject demeaned. But where these have differed from China's case is that, in spite of the incredible inequality that has existed between lord and subject in those parts too, the relationship was only ever that of master and slave. While the slave remained at his master's beck and call (and even life and death awaited his master's pleasure), the demands of the relationship nonetheless ended there. In China, however, the relationship between lord and subject was modelled on the bond between man and woman: hence, we find "subjects" and "concubines" referred to as necessary counterpoints and terms such as "virgin-official" and "virgin-maiden" uttered in the very same breath. Indeed, the poetic corpus abounds with lines that analogize the lord-subject relationship to that of a man and a woman – with the clearest and most ubiquitous lines of connection drawn between "faithfulness" and "integrity," clear evidence of the degree to which the statuses of subject and concubine had been reduced to an essential equivalence.

These are ideas that should be regarded as altogether unreasonable in our modern age. Whereas in ancient times this might not have seemed at all outlandish, under a republic it should be a different matter altogether. For while it is good and proper for citizens to hold affection for their country and their people, any standard that would take their measure against the norms once applied to the "virtuous mistress" or the "chaste woman" should simply no longer exist. I believe that a republican morality should represent the interests of the people, nothing more – and I cannot condone any morality founded on such antiquated standards, even if I have no particular desire to go out of my way to destroy them.

One final point on this subject: I find myself utterly dissatisfied with the words of Dong Zhongshu when he wrote: "He makes his relations correct and does not reckon upon profit; he makes clear his way and does not calculate over accomplishments,"[41] because I really cannot escape the feeling that people of old only knew how to speak in platitudes and harp on in tones grandiloquent, while expending little to no effort in actually enacting their high-flown ideals. This is a monumental failing. So, while my advocacy for a "practicalization of morality" has certainly been influenced by Yan Yuan,[42] it can also be said to arise from a place of personal intuition and true feeling.

I have rambled on at such length in hopes of offering some explanation for how this antipathy for traditional Confucian orthodoxy has informed my thinking, since my later actions bear some connection to this fact. Indeed, if one were to pronounce me an iconoclast or a heretic – or to say that I have somehow blasphemed against certain pious orthodoxies, then this is a charge that I can readily accept; but if it were claimed that I had somehow betrayed my people through my actions, then I deny there having been any such intent on my part. I do not offer this by way of justification, but merely as an explanation of fact.

To elaborate on circumstances just a little further, it was in the sixth year of the republic [1917] that I first arrived at Peking University, and by the time of the twenty-sixth year [1937] I had already spent a full two decades there. According to university policy, staff were entitled to a year's sabbatical after having completed five years' employment, but up until that time I had yet to make use of any of my entitled leave. It just so happened that I was finally intending to take leave (the paperwork was just in the process of being formalized) when the Marco Polo Bridge Incident broke out. As Peking University was making its preparations to relocate to Changsha, the professoriate met on two occasions, during which it was agreed that final decisions on whether to remain or to leave should rest with the individual. As such, there were a number of professors, who due either to old age or the heavy burden of family dependants, declined to head south. My mother was still alive at the time, and my younger brother's wife and three children, as well as my daughter and her three children (my son-in-law had gone to the National Northwestern Associated University to teach) were all living under my roof. This amounted, when added to the members of my immediate family, to some fourteen dependants altogether. In light of this I opted to stay put and not to go.[43] The university also designated four elderly professors – Meng Sen, Ma Yuzao, Feng Zuxun, and myself (although I was only fifty-four at the time) – to serve as "Peking University resident professors," entrusted with the job of safeguarding the university's campus and property. Later on, in November, I was sent a telegram with further instructions to this effect from the dean of the university, Mr. Jiang Menglin.

At the end of that year, the custodian of the university's Second College (which is the College of Natural Sciences) located me and informed me that the Kempeitai had recently dispatched people to inspect the college's building, issuing a two-day ultimatum to vacate the premises. At the time, Professor Meng was incapacitated by illness and Ma Yuzao was unwilling to deal with the matter, so it fell upon Feng Zuxun and myself to write to the puppet Provisional Government's minister of education, Tang Erhe,[44] to urge his immediate intervention on the university's behalf. Through his negotiations with the Kempeitai that very evening the building escaped unscathed and was preserved to such an extent that during an inspection tour of Beiping after Japan's defeat, Zhu Jiahua, then the Kuomintang secretary of the Department of Education, gave a speech proclaiming the university's natural science department to be the best preserved in the country.[45] Following this earlier incident, I leveraged my name and position to safeguard the university library and the Department of Literature and History and was able, fortunately, to preserve the original state of the institutions' staff and assets – while I employed similar tactics later on to spare the collection of the National Library.

Following Tang Erhe's death shortly thereafter, it was suggested that I assume his place in the ministry, a proposal I chose to accept in the end following a period of consideration. Since the management of higher education rested entirely with the minister at the time, everyone saw the need for me to fill the position so as to defend against the likes of Wang Yitang[46] and his ilk. In the two years that I spent in the role, the job of actively sustaining the school's activities occupied a place of secondary importance to the pressing demands of passive defence. We strove to offer some manner of resistance, sometimes explicit, sometimes implicit, against the pressures and interference we faced at the hands of the enemy Asia Development Board and the puppet New People's Association.[47] All this was done in hopes of lessening the pains and burdens imposed on students and on the school. Indeed, these can be said to have been the problems that most sorely taxed our minds from day to day. I do not dare to speculate on the efficacy of any of these efforts, of course, but I believed that they were worth doing at the time, if only to bring some small measure of benefit to students and young people alike. I believe that if I had escaped instead to the interior and gone on to teach there for a few years, this would been just so much empty talk for me, quite unequal to having stayed in the midst of occupation and worked – even in the most minute capacity – on the school and students' behalf. For me it was a tangible contribution at any rate.

I do not believe in any of this talk of keeping one's faithfulness or of losing it, I only believe in doing some practical good for the people. Moreover, all these nominal categories of loyalty and disloyalty, right and wrong, are basically malleable: to be entrusted, for example, with the special mission of "suppressing [communist] rebellion" by the Kuomintang government absolutely cannot be deemed an act superior to the job of sustaining a school in the occupied territory. I know that my opinions on these matters cannot avoid some bias, even though I am speaking the truth as I know it. But it is also true that my attention was only ever focused on the concerns of the school and students – the fact that I only considered the needs of the intellectual classes, while neglecting the broader plight of the masses, was certainly a mistake, and one to which I must readily admit.

Collaboration with the enemy is an exceedingly rare thing among the Chinese people, and the act of merely making do and muddling along under trying circumstances certainly cannot genuinely be regarded as collaborative acts. As for those engaged in some form of resistance against the invader – whether implicitly or explicitly – this is naturally even less the case for them. As far as my published thoughts and writings from before and after the occupation are concerned, there are two pieces of evidence I can offer to show that my thinking did not undergo any kind of drastic transformation before and after the outbreak of war.

First, before the War of Resistance I published several articles in the *Guowen Weekly* under the heading of "Limited Views on Japan." The fourth and final instalment of these was published in July 1937, in what would be the magazine's last issue before the outbreak of war. In that essay, I sought to explain how our attempts at understanding the Japanese national character through the prism of culture, with literature and art as our keys, were ultimately futile endeavours. While keys of this sort can certainly be applied to questions of culture, attempting to use them to unpick problems of a military or political nature naturally sends us running into walls that remain, in spite of our best efforts, thoroughly impenetrable. Rather, I argued that it was necessary for us to tackle these questions from the starting point of religion and turn our scrutiny to Shinto as practised in the popular realm – differing so markedly from the foreign imports of Confucianism and Buddhism and characterized, as it so often is, by the mad fervour of one possessed. The spectacle of the divine palanquin[48] on festival day, for example – thrashing about wildly from side to side as it was carried shrine to shrine, often in complete defiance of the established route – is a sight that one would never encounter in the folkways of China. The sheer emotional impulsivity of these displays, above and beyond the bounds of common reason and manifesting in outbursts of sheer irrationality, may hold some explanatory power for the acts of violence perpetrated by Japan both domestically and internationally.

Later, in the winter of the twenty-ninth year of the republic [1940], the Japanese International Cultural Revival Association solicited an essay from me in commemoration of the 2,600th anniversary of the founding of the Japanese nation. Since there was no way that I could possibly refuse, I penned an essay entitled "Re-understanding Japan" for the occasion. This essay duly appeared in print, and readers can verify for themselves that the essay's conclusion is precisely the same as that I have just drawn. In it I made the argument that any attempt at understanding the national character of a people through the lens of culture will always prove fruitless, that for there to be any hope of understanding, such questions must be approached from a religious perspective. This piece can be said to be representative of my published views on Japan.[49]

Second, as far as any writings on the subject of China are concerned, I happened to write quite a few these during the occupation, and of these, "The Problem of Chinese Thought" can be seen as the most representative. This piece was written in the winter of the thirty-first year of the republic [1942], at a time when the Asian Revival Society and the New People's Association were enthusiastically seeking to establish a central ideology on behalf of the Chinese people. That this centre was meant to be found within the bounds of the "New Order of Greater Asia" goes without saying, and it was in direct opposition to these efforts that my essay was written. As per usual practice, I made amply sure to quote the words of Confucius and Mencius and I loudly sang the praises of Yu the Great and Hou Ji's style of governance – all in an effort to argue for China's possession of just such a central system of beliefs from its very earliest days. This set of beliefs, I explained, did not arise merely from the advocacy of the scholar and literatus. Instead, there was no heart that did not possess it innately, whether sage on high or common man and woman below. Therefore, it was possible neither to eliminate it nor to inculcate it either – rather, it was founded on the people's basic will to live. Each individual desired survival, and desired that all others might be able to live as well, and while the saints and sages dignified this desire with the name of "benevolence," even the common folk were able to comprehend its meaning innately, though they may not be able to read it if written down. In ordinary times, the Chinese people are very peaceful and willing to endure considerable hardship if necessary, yet they will refuse to yield if they are brought to a juncture where their survival is threatened. I am well aware that these conclusions are shallow – not to mention vague and full of gross generalities. But the important thing here is less the soundness of these theories than the practical effect they had. In September of the following year, the Japanese army–controlled Patriotic Literature Society organized the Greater East Asia Writers' Congress in Tokyo, during which society member Kataoka Teppei called for the elimination of a certain "old reactionary writer" in China. His speech contained the following assertions:

> I come before you to identify an enemy who must count among those vestigial foes that you honoured gentlemen would recognize all too well. As we speak, this old writer of the reactionary literary establishment continues to sow discord and disruption in the pacified areas; for although he resides within the pacified zone, this enemy of ours insists on setting himself against the literary activities pursued with such vigour and enthusiasm by you honoured gentlemen – using his formidable literary qualifications in order to occupy China's literary arena. This man frequently employs his extremely reactionary thoughts and actions to oppose the Great Asian Thought that you, honoured gentlemen, and I seek to establish. On the road of our struggle, this man is an obstacle and an active saboteur – representing a heretical idol at the heart of East Asia, which must be torn down and smashed

– and so on, and so forth. (The original text of this speech was published in the third issue of *Patriotic Literature* [*Bungaku hōkoku*], the society's official organ, and the full Chinese translation of the speech was published in

Shanghai in the thirty-third year of the republic, in the May issue of *Miscellany [Zazhi].*)

Although Kataoka did not mention any names on that occasion, after direct interrogation, he admitted in a letter that this "vestigial foe" of his did indeed refer to me (the original was delivered as evidence to the high court in Nanjing, where there exists an official copy). The third paragraph of the letter goes on to read:

> If a reader, after reading the "The Problem of Chinese Thought" in full, fails to perceive the reactionary and conservative role played by this text, in light of this present historical moment of ours, it is because the reader in question lacks the necessary perspicacity to perceive the meaning lying beneath the pages' surface. I perceive in its words a position which argues that the supposed "will of the Chinese people" should be left unstifled: which, in fact, constitutes a passive repudiation of the war that struggles even now for the liberation of Greater East Asia. It is for this reason that I delivered the speech I did at the Greater East Asia Writers' Congress in September of last year. The people of China look up to you, sir, as a moral compass; and knowing the powerful influence that essays of yours would necessarily have there, reading them instilled in me no small sense of trepidation. If this essay of yours, sir, is not an outright repudiation of the Greater Asia War, then at the very least it represents the attitudes of a certain subset of the Chinese people whose desire it is to sit on the sidelines of this war and it serves to endow these views with a certain respectability based on traditional morality and to normalize them thereby.[50]

You can see from this something of the tone and quality of the essays I authored under the occupation – such that the enemy itself regarded me as an obstacle on their road of struggle, an active saboteur, and an idol in need of smashing. This sort of evidence should go to show that I was not some willing collaborator. Beyond this one particular essay, there were a few more that I wrote at the time, but none really worth mentioning here and so I will decline to go on any more superfluously.

I had originally hoped to do my very best at writing simply and to the point, and yet now I have already gone and blathered on rather incessantly. It is simply that there were a few areas for which I could not help but try to offer up some manner of explanation, and for this I have to beg your forgiveness. To the delusion of some of my past ideas, and for the errors of my actions, I myself readily confess – and yet I earnestly and sincerely hope that you are able to understand my true nature and intent, sir. It is for this reason that I have written you this letter. I had originally thought to write to Mr. Mao, but knowing how busy he most certainly is, I did not dare to bother him. I hope, therefore, that you might represent to him my case.

(The fourth of July, the thirty-eighth year of the republic [1949])

Notes

1 You Bingqi (1912–84) was an accomplished translator of Japanese and English. Notable translations include Kenneth Grahame's *The Wind in the Willows;* Lu Xun's old friend and publisher, Kanzō Uchiyama's *Ikeru Shina no sugata* (China as it is); and several works of Natsume Sōseki, including his famed novel *Wagahai wa neko de aru* (*I Am a Cat*).

2 Nanjing shi dang'anguan, ed., *Shenxun Wangwei Hanjian bilu* [Records of the trial of Wang puppet regime traitors] (Nanjing: Jiangsu guji chubanshe, 1992), 1486–89.

3 Geng Chuanming, *Zhou Zuoren de zuihou 22 nian* [Zhou Zuoren's final twenty-two years] (Beijing: Zhongguo wenshi chubanshe, 2005), 125.

4 Zhi An, *Zhou Zuoren zhuan* [A biography of Zhou Zuoren] (Jinan: Shandong huabao chubanshe), 267.

5 Kiyama Hideo, *Beijing Kuzhu'an ji: RiZhong zhanzheng shidai de Zhou Zuoren* [Zhou Zuoren in the Time of the Sino-Japanese War], trans. Zhao Jinghua (Beijing: Shenghuo, dushu, sanlian shudian, 2008), 11.

6 Susan Daruvala, *Zhou Zuoren and an Alternative Response to Chinese Modernity* (Cambridge, MA: Harvard University Press, 2000), 59–65; Lu Yan, *Re-understanding Japan* (Honolulu: University of Hawai'i Press), 51–59.

7 For a poignant account of Zhou's outspoken criticisms of Japan, both immediately preceding the war and long before its outbreak, see again Lu Yan, *Re-understanding Japan,* 138–43, 220–29. In a quote that speaks clearly to both Zhou's affection for Japan and sorrow at its actions, Lu cites him angrily exclaiming in 1925: "Those who truly love China naturally should curse China, just as those Chinese who truly love Japan must become absolute Japanophobes" (138).

8 See Nanjing shi dang'anguan, *Shenxun Wangwei Hanjian bilu,* 1424–89, for evidence positively attesting to Zhou's actions during the war, submitted to the court during his 1946 trial.

9 See Qian Liqun, *Zhou Zuoren zhuan* [A biography of Zhou Zuoren] (Beijing: Beijing shiyue wenyi chubanshe, 1990), 450–52. Qian details some of Zhou's more potentially dubious activities during his collaboration. Responding to similar facts, Jianmei Liu, although otherwise sympathetic to Zhou's intellectual accomplishments, takes a dim view of recent attempts to justify Zhou Zuoren's wartime conduct, no doubt speaking for many when she writes:

> Zhou did not have the courage to stand up and fight or the wisdom to avoid disgraceful political involvement – both characteristics he regarded as important components of the Confucian Spirit. Instead, he wore the Japanese military uniform while he inspected a parade of the youth regiment, visited Japan, and lived a luxurious life during the war; all these deeds violated the basic Confucian standard. Without wisdom, courage, loyalty, honesty and benevolence in his behaviour, Zhou Zuoren's talk of "the central theory of Confucian culture" appears very hypocritical and even ironic.

Jianmei Liu, *Zhuangzi and Modern Chinese Literature* (Oxford: Oxford University Press, 2016), 88.

10 Lu Yan, "Beyond Politics in Wartime: Zhou Zhouren, 1931–1945," *Sino-Japanese Studies* 11, 1 (1998): 12, referencing Poshek Fu's influential study on Chinese collaboration with Japan: *Passivity, Resistance, and Collaboration: Intellectual Choices in Occupied Shanghai, 1937–1945* (Stanford, CA: Stanford University Press, 1993). Lu finds the eponymous formulation complicated by the complexities of Zhou Zuoren's case.

11 See especially, his essays "Guanyu yingxiong chongbai" (On the worship of heroes, 1935) and "Yue Fei yu Qin Gui" (Yue Fei and Qin Gui, 1935), both collected in his October 1935 collection of essays *Jottings from Bitter Tea Studio* [Kucha suibi], reissued in 2011 as Zhou Zuoren, *Kucha suibi* [Jottings from Bitter Tea Studio], ed. Zhi An (Beijing: Beijing shiyue huayi chubanshe, 2011). For an English translation of the latter, please see the author's previous translation at: http://www.chinaheritagequarterly.org/features.php?searchterm=028_yuefei.inc&issue=028.

12 Daruvala, *Zhou Zuoren and an Alternative Response,* 110–12; Wang Pu, "Law, Morality, and the Nation-State in the Trial of Zhou Zuoren: Revisiting the Case of Zhou's Collaboration with Japan during the Second Sino-Japanese War," *Frontiers of Literary Studies in China* 7, 4 (2013): 574–83.

13 Li Tonglu, "The Sacred and the Cannibalistic: Zhou Zuoren's Critique of Violence in Modern China," *Chinese Literature: Essays, Articles, Reviews* 36 (December 2014): 40. Zhou had also been a close friend of Li Dazhao, one of the cofounders of the Chinese Communist Party. On Li Dazhao's execution in 1927 at the hands of the forces of Zhang Zuolin, Zhou harboured Li's orphaned son from the authorities until he and the famous calligrapher Shen Yinmo were able to secure him funds and passage, under an assumed name, to the relative safety of Japan. For a detailed account, see Ni Moyan, *Kuyu zhai zhuren* [The Master of Bitter Rain Studio] (Shanghai: Shanghai renmin chubanshe, 2003): 249–50.

14 Feng Xuefeng (1903–76) was an important member of the League of Left-Wing Writers in Shanghai and a close friend and protégé of Lu Xun, instrumental in recruiting Lu to the Communist cause. During the 1950s, Feng occupied prominent positions in China's literary hierarchy, before being branded a "rightist" during the 1957 Anti-Rightist campaign and purged from the party. He was rehabilitated following Mao Zedong's death.

15 Wei Shijing, "Guanyu Zhou Zuoren" [About Zhou Zuoren], *Luxun yanjiu dongtai* [Trends in Luxun Research] 4 (1985): 27, as quoted in Zhi An, *Zhou Zuoren zhuan,* 266.

16 Zhou Zuoren, "Zhou Zuoren de yi feng xin" [A letter by Zhou Zuoren], *Xin wenxue shiliao* [Historical materials on new literature] 2 (1987): 213–16, 221.

17 Zhi An, *Zhou Zuoren zhuan,* 267–86.

18 Li Ji (1892–1967) was an early member of the Communist Party, a distinguished translator of Marxist theoretical literature, and a leader of the Chinese Trotskyists. On 21 December 1950, he and fellow Trotskyist Liu Renjing publicly expressed remorse for their political heterodoxy in the pages of the *People's Daily.* See Wu Jimin, "Purgatory: The Chinese Trotskyists' Ordeal and Struggle," in *Prophets Unarmed: Chinese Trotskyists in Revolution, War, Jail, and the Return from Limbo,* ed. George Benton (Leiden: Brill, 2015), 133.

19 Zhi An, *Zhou Zuoren zhuan,* 268.

20 Lou Shiyi (1905–2001) was a prominent leftist critic and translator. Notably, he was responsible for drafting an open letter to Zhou Zuoren in 1937 urging him to evacuate Beiping and head south, lest he be considered a traitor to the nation. This entreaty was signed by seventeen other prominent writers, including such luminaries as Mao Dun, Ding Ling, Hu Feng, Lao She, and Zhou's close personal friend, the novelist Yu Dafu.

21 Zhi An, *Zhou Zuoren zhuan,* 275–99.

22 Ibid., 300. For a detailed first-hand account of Zhou's final years, including his tragic end, see Wen Jieruo's (1927–) account "Wannian de Zhou Zuoren" [Zhou Zuoren's later years], *Dushu* [Reading] 26 (1990): 127–35.

23 New Democracy refers to a distinctive Chinese revolutionary program promulgated by Mao Zedong and adopted by the Chinese Communist Party. Through a coalition of classes under communist and proletarian leadership it sought to enter directly into socialism via the proactive participation of the people, bypassing the capitalist phase that Marx theorized as the necessary and inevitable sequel to feudalism and colonialism. For information on New Democracy, including a full translation of Mao's essay "On New Democracy" that introduced its tenets, see Timothy Cheek, ed., *Mao Zedong and China's Revolutions: A Brief History in Documents* (New York: Palgrave, 2002), 76–122.

24 Wei Zhang, professor of Greek and Latin classics at Fudan University, regards Zhou as "the foremost translator of ancient Greek literature modern China has yet seen." Particularly pertinent to our discussion here is the cultural connection Zhou drew between ancient Greece and Japan. The formulation was not his own, but rather borrowed from his intellectual idol, British sexologist Havelock Ellis (see note 30 below), who called the Japanese "the Greeks of another age and clime." Nonetheless, the connection was borne out by Zhou's own experiences in Japan, when the twenty-one-year-old was inspired by the sight of the bare and unbound feet of his landlady's daughter, an epiphany on par with his brother Lu Xun's famous (and possibly apocryphal) experience at the medical school in Sendai some months earlier. This revealed to Zhou the "love of the natural and appreciation of the simple" (Lu Yan, "Re-Understanding Japan," 41) inherent to the country and her people, virtues he would soon find echoed in his readings of ancient Greek mythology and literature. His hopes to inculcate the Chinese people with such a spirit by means of his extensive translations from both languages became an integral part of his program for cultural reform. For a detailed discussion of Zhou Zuoren's engagement with and translation of Greek mythology and literature, see Wei Zhang, "Zhou Zuoren and the Uses of Ancient Greek Mythology in Modern China," *International Journal of the Classical Tradition* 22, 1 (2015): 100–15; and Daruvala, *Zhou Zuoren and an Alternative Response*, 59–64.

25 *Funü wenti* is a direct translation from the English "the Woman Question." Although the term is somewhat ungainly to modern ears, it was commonly employed in the nineteenth and early twentieth centuries with reference to the debates that surrounded the changing role of women in society, including such issues as women's suffrage, reproductive rights, property rights, and other legal privileges, and extending into questions of women's sexuality and criticism of the institution of marriage. These issues were a major fixture of intellectual debate during the May Fourth and New Culture Movements.

26 Edward Carpenter (1844–1929) was a British poet, philosopher, socialist propagandist, and early proponent of many and various social causes, including homosexual rights, women's rights, and vegetarianism. See Sheila Rowbotham, *Edward Carpenter: A Life of Liberty and Love* (London: Verso Books, 2009).

27 See Edgar Snow, *Red Star over China* (London: Victor Gollancz, 1937).

28 Zhang Zhizhong (1895–1969) was an important KMT general and close confidant of Chiang Kai-shek. As governor of Hunan during the War of Resistance, he was infamous for accidentally causing the devastating Great Fire of Changsha after ordering key positions and building razed in anticipation of a Japanese attack that never materialized. Later, he represented the Kuomintang in peace talks with the Communists, before defecting in the final round. Presumably, Zhou is referring to public affirmations of support that Zhang would have made in favour of the Communists following his defection. S.C.M. Paine, *The Wars for Asia: 1911–1949* (Cambridge: Cambridge University Press, 2012), 148–49, 291.

29 August Bebel (1840–1913) was a German socialist statesman and cofounder of the Social Democratic Party. He was author of the influential treatise *Woman under Socialism* (1883) and an outspoken proponent of women's social, economic, and sexual liberation.

30 Victorian-era social reformer and "sage of sex" Havelock Ellis (1859–1939) was, according to Zhou Zuoren, "the thinker I most admire," and Susan Daruvala views Ellis as the most important of all the Western thinkers Zhou was exposed to. Ellis's holistic world view sought to reconcile science, through biology, with an aesthetic sense of "the world as a vision of beauty," according the organic desires of men and women an appropriate place in the affective and moral life of human beings. Chief among these desires was sex, seen as innate, good, and ultimately blameless. Ellis's philosophical campaign against prevailing ethical norms of Victorian Britain caused considerable controversy, a fact that would have appealed strongly to Zhou who, along with Lu Xun and other progressive compatriots, was likewise engaged in the struggled against the "feudal" norms still pervasive in Chinese society, particularly around sexuality. Indeed, Daruvala writes, "Ellis' rejection of norms of false modesty as destructive to women, physically and morally, struck a deep chord in Zhou and was part of the May Fourth ethos." Naturally this greatly influenced his later ideas around the "naturalisation of ethics." Daruvala, *Zhou Zuoren and an Alternative Response,* 87, 207–10.

31 Wang Chong (courtesy name Zhongren, 27–c. 100) was a Han dynasty thinker best known for his collection *Lunheng* (Discourses weighed in the balance), which was distinguished by its broad investigations into history and the natural sciences and notable for its skeptical and materialist approach toward the received wisdoms of the day. See Rafe de Crespigny, *A Biographical Dictionary of Later Han to the Three Kingdoms (23–220 AD)* (Leiden: Brill, 2007). Li Zhi (courtesy name Zhuowu, 1527–1602) was a philosopher and historian from the Ming dynasty, whose iconoclastic writings ultimately saw him arrested by the authorities on charges of heresy; he eventually killed himself in prison. See Rivi Handler-Spitz, Pauline C. Lee, and Haun Saussy, eds., *A Book to Burn and a Book to Keep (Hidden)* (New York: Columbia University Press, 2016), for selected translations of his most prominent and controversial works (mentioned below in the text). Yu Zhengxie (courtesy name Lichu, 1775–1840) was a noted mid-Qing scholar famous for his remarkable memory. Today Yu is often cited as a kind of Confucian proto-feminist, having been uncharacteristically outspoken for his time regarding the hypocrisies inherent in traditional notions of gender. Among other things he wrote against widow chastity, footbinding, and the notion of "women's jealousy." Two of his most famous works are *Guisi leigao* (Categorized manuscripts from the Guisi year [1833]) and *Guisi cungao* (Further writings from the Guisi year), collections of notes made on an array of topics such as history, the classics, folklore, anthropology, medicine, economics, and geography.

32 Here I have borrowed Susan Daruvala's translation of the term *renqing wuli* in her discussion of this important concept and its place in Zhou Zuoren's thought. See Daruvala, *Zhou Zuoren and an Alternative Response,* 87, 211.

33 The Three Bonds (or Three Cardinal Guides, *san gang*) refers to the three asymmetrical relationships – ruler-subject, father-son, and husband-wife – that served as the foundations of the Confucian social order from the early imperial period onwards. They were characterized by a system of mutual, albeit unequal, social obligations that served to reify an ideal social hierarchy. See Xinzhong Yao, ed., *The Encyclopedia of Confucianism* (Abingdon, UK: Routledge, 2003), 522.

34 The mainstream historiographical tradition took a dim view of these figures, and they were often portrayed as cautionary examples of moral deficiency; therefore, for Li Zhi to seek to re-examine or even rehabilitate their legacies was a considerable and controversial departure from common historical wisdom. Zhuo Wenjun (c. 179–after 117 BCE) was a renowned writer of *fu* rhapsodies in the Han dynasty, whose elopement with fellow poet Sima Xiangru, following the death of her husband, was the cause of considerable controversy. For a detailed biographical treatment, see Lily Xiao Hong Lee and A.D. Stefanowska, eds., *Biographical Dictionary of Chinese Women: Antiquity through Sui, 1600 B.C.E.–618 C.E.* (Abingdon, UK: Routledge, 2015), 257–59. Emperor Wu Zetian

(624–705) was the founder of the short-lived Zhou dynasty and China's only female monarch to reign in her own name. The facts of her rule are often difficult to untangle from the scandalous deeds attributed to her by later scholars and historians. For a study on her life and times, see C.P. Fitzgerald, *The Empress Wu* (Vancouver: UBC Press, 1968). Feng Dao (882–954) was officially credited with overseeing the first systematic printing of the Confucian classics during the tumultuous Five Dynasty era. In later ages his reputation proved contentious for his willingness to serve at the courts of no less than ten different emperors. For a comprehensive treatment of these issues, see Wang Gungwu, "Feng Tao: An Essay on Confucian Loyalty," in *Confucian Personalities,* ed. Arthur F. Wright and Denis Twitchett (Stanford, CA: Stanford University Press, 1962), 123–45.

35 For a detailed discussion of Zhou Zuoren's political and rhetorical uses of these ancient culture heroes, who traditionally bequeathed the Chinese people the tools of flood-taming, agriculture, and medicine, see Edward M. Gunn, *Unwelcome Muse: Chinese Literature in Shanghai and Peking, 1937–1945* (New York: Columbia University Press, 1980); and Daruvala, *Zhou Zuoren and an Alternative Response,* 111–12.

36 See Lyon Sharman, *Sun Yat-sen: His Life and Its Meaning* (Stanford, CA: Stanford University Press, 1968), 94, 271, for a discussion on the direct influence of Lincoln's Gettysburg Address on Sun Yat-sen's formulation of the Three Principles of the People, whose tenets of nationalism, democracy, and livelihood echo Lincoln's language: "Of the people, by the people, for the people."

37 Please see Xue Bingjie's complete translation of this essay in Chapter 22 of this volume.

38 For a thorough and enlightening discussion of Zhou's scholarly and literary meditations on violence, including his extensive use of cannibalistic symbolism in his discussions of Confucianism and ideology, see Li Tonglu, "Sacred and the Cannibalistic," 25–60.

39 For a recent and comprehensive study of many of these practices and social phenomena, including "filial slicing" and "chastity suicides," see Jimmu Yu, *Sanctity and Self-Inflicted Violence in Chinese Religions, 1500–1700* (Oxford: Oxford University Press, 2012).

40 For a detailed discussion of the cult of chastity and the role of women in late-imperial China, see Jane Theiss, *Disgraceful Matters: The Politics of Chastity in Eighteenth-Century China* (Berkeley: University of California Press, 2004).

41 Dong Zhongshu (179–104 BCE) was an influential Han dynasty Confucian scholar who played a decisive role in establishing Confucianism as the state cult of the imperial Chinese realm, as well as being the first thinker to formally classify the aforementioned Three Bonds.

42 Yan Yuan (courtesy name Xizhai, 1635–1704) founded a practical and empirical school of Confucianism in fervent opposition to the dominant Zhu-Cheng neo-Confucianism of his day. A considerable proportion of his works deal with pragmatic issues of governance, agriculture, and the livelihood of the people. For a detailed study of his life and works, see Jui-sung Yang, *Body, Ritual and Identity: A New Interpretation of Yan Yuan* (Leiden: Brill, 2016).

43 Zhou Zuoren is referring here to his brother Zhou Jianren's first wife, who was the younger sister of Zhou Zuoren's Japanese wife. Curiously he does not mention Lu Xun's estranged wife, Zhu An, who had lived with Zhou Zuoren since Lu Xun's departure from Beiping in 1926.

44 For more on Tang Erhe (1878–1940), see Chapter 21 in this volume.

45 For corroboration of Zhu Jiahua's (1893–1963) speech, as well as Hu Shi's testimony on behalf of Zhou Zuoren, see Nanjing shi dang'anguan, *Shenxun Wangwei Hanjian bilu,* 1458, 1477.

46 Wang Yitang (1877–1948) was a former member of the Anhui warlord clique and close ally of Duan Qirui who sought refuge with the Japanese on the collapse of Duan's government in 1928. He later served in the Hebei-Chahar Political Council and then in the

Provisional Government of the Republic of China. For a discussion of Wang and his postwar fate, see Dongyoun Hwang, "Wartime Collaboration in Question: An Examination of the Post-war Trials of the Chinese Collaborators," *Inter-Asia Cultural Studies* 6, 1 (2005): 75–97.

47 For a discussion of the New People's Association as north China's principal "mass mobilisation" organization, including its important role in the dissemination of the "New People's Principles" (concocted to supplant Sun Yat-sen's Three Principles of the People) and their relation to the "Kingly Way" of Manchuria, see Kitamura Minoru and Lin Si-Yun, *The Reluctant Combatant: Japan and the Second Sino-Japanese War* (Lanham, MD: University of America Press, 2014), 73–75. Notably, Zhou Zuoren's primary competition for the minister of education position vacated by Tang Erhe was the head of the New People's Association, Miao Bin (1899–1946), whose role as an enthusiastic propagandist for the Japanese spurred concerned parties to encourage Zhou to nominate himself. See Wang Dingnan, "Wo dui Zhou Zuoren de ren weizhi yishi de shengming" [My statement regarding the matter of Zhou Zuoren's assumption of a false office], *Xin wenxue shiliao* [New literature historical documents] 2 (1987): 220–21. For more on Miao, see Frederic Wakeman Jr., "Hanjian (Traitor)! Collaboration and Retribution in Wartime Shanghai," in *Becoming Chinese: Passages to Modernity and Beyond,* ed. Wen-hsin Yeh (Berkeley: University of California Press, 2000), 323–24.

48 *Mikoshi;* see Brian Bocking, *A Popular Dictionary of Shinto* (Abingdon, UK: Routledge, 2005), 92.

49 For a deeper discussion of these two essays, including Zhou's ruminations on the particular religious character of the Japanese people, see Lu Yan, *Re-understanding Japan,* 239–43, which takes its title from the latter essay. An excellent translation of this piece by Richard Rigby – which he translates as "Japan Re-encountered" – can be found in *Renditions* 26 (1986): 97–106.

50 For a detailed discussion of this incident in English, see Gunn, *Unwelcome Muse,* 165–71.

24 Lin Yutang

Non-Aligned Intellectual on the Japanese Occupation

SON YOO DI

In the mid-twentieth century, Lin Yutang (1895–1976) was a rare example of a Chinese writer and intellectual who enjoyed fame both at home and abroad. Part of his legacy was built on his English-language publications, but he was even more prolific in Chinese. Between 1917 and 1920, Lin studied at Harvard University, publishing copiously before returning to China. Lin's literary work featured in the popular journals *Lunyu* (The analects) and *Ren jian shi* (This human world), coedited with Shao Xunmei (1906–68) and Zhang Kebiao (n.d.), through which he advocated *xingling* (personality), *youmo* (humour), and *xianshi* (light leisure). He became increasingly political in the 1920s and 1930s, when he established the Chinese League for the Protection of Civil Rights (*Zhongguo minquan baozheng tongmeng*) with Song Qingling (1893–1981), Cai Yuanpei (1868–1940), and Yang Xingfo (n.d.). Lin's biographer Suoqiao Qian has praised the critic as China's foremost advocate of democracy and human rights in the early twentieth century, deserving recognition as one of the "three pillars of modern Chinese intellectuality" alongside Lu Xun (1881–1936) and Hu Shi (1891–1962).[1] The translations below confirm these aspects of Lin's liberal critique in fierce and poetic denunciations of Japanese occupation that while removed from any affiliation to political parties remain unquestionably political.

Chinese leaders faced difficult challenges in the mid-nineteenth century as they struggled to imagine the fate of the Qing dynasty (1644–1912), and such problems carried over into the fate of China in the twentieth century. May Fourth Chinese authors, such as Lu Xun and Zhou Zuoren (1885–1967), hoped to strengthen the country on the global stage and attempted to raise national awareness through numerous new publications, such as *Xin qingnian* (New youth), which predominated in literary circles in the 1920s. In 1924, Lin and Sun Fuyuan (n.d.) contributed to this movement when they founded the pro-revolution periodical *Yu si* (Threads of conversation), to which Lin regularly contributed essays. It was during this time that Lin established himself as a liberal critic and a fierce proponent of democracy, yet his writings remained critical of both China's major political parties.

Literature cannot be separated from society; thus, an author's literary direction is often determined by political disposition. Lin did not lean toward either the Kuomintang (KMT) or the Communist Party (CCP). He criticized the KMT's passive anti-Japanese resistance and, although he did view communism as in many ways superior to feudalism, he nevertheless deemed it too impersonal, institutional, and incompatible with human nature.[2]

Heavily influenced by Enlightenment ideas, Lin was opposed to intellectuals' support of political parties.[3] He was disappointed by writers who produced exceedingly politicized works and their efforts to inject ideology into literature under the slogans of enlightenment and the reconstruction of the national character. Hence, Lin gradually dissociated himself from both the KMT and the CCP to write at his own leisure.

Lin moved to Shanghai during a very tumultuous time; his 1927 move coincided with Chiang Kai-shek's anticommunist massacre. Initially, Lin associated with Lu Xun and energized the Chinese literary scene, but he shifted to the political centre in the 1930s. The city was attacked by Japan in 1932. Despite this horrendous violence, Lin re-established *Lunyu* in 1932, and soon earned himself the title "The Ambassador for Humour." In fact, Lin coined the term *youmo* as a Chinese transliteration of the English word "humour."[4] His writings were so well-loved by readers that they dubbed 1933 "The Year of Humour." Coincidentally, George Bernard Shaw (1856–1950), one of the greatest English-language playwrights, visited Shanghai in 1933 while travelling around the world. Lin, then the editor-in-chief of *Lunyu,* hosted Shaw, who greatly influenced Lin's own literary philosophy.

Lin produced more than a hundred essays while he lived in China. He left China for the second time in 1936 and spent most of the rest of his life in America. He was later banned in China for his anticommunist stance, and his writings were all but forgotten for decades. His works began to be translated into Chinese and attracted more scholarly attention only in the 1980s. In 1966, he settled in Taiwan, after having become more positive toward the KMT. Lin's Taiwan-era literature is unique and liberal, yet did not lead to nationwide Chinese interest and garnered attention only from a handful of scholars in his hometown, Xiamen. In the process of transitioning from his short essay writing style in Chinese to an English, novel-writing style, he wrote two lengthy essays called "My Country and My People" (*Woguo womin*) (1935) and "The Importance of Living" (*Shenghuo de yishu*) (1937).

In 1931, after Japan invaded Manchuria, Lin turned to writing about war. Below, I translate two of Lin's essays from this period: "Wuzi de piping" (Criticism without words) published in *Ren jian shi* on 20 August 1934; and "Guanyu Beiping xuesheng 'yier-jiu' yundong" (On the "December 9" students' movement in Beiping), published in *Yuzhou feng* (Cosmic wind) on 1 January 1936. These are representative of a non-aligned liberal critic's rejection of Japanese occupation. Lin was very optimistic for the KMT and CCP to work together during the United Front to oppose Japanese aggression and forge a new China.[5] These two essays show this spirit and foreshadow the brief political unity that was to come. The essays focus on two cities struggling under Japanese control, Shenyang and Beiping respectively, showcasing Lin's understanding of Chinese national issues and politics and reflecting a noted Chinese intellectual's understanding of China under Japanese occupation.

"Criticism without Words" displays Lin's frustration with efforts by Japan and the US-based Council on Foreign Relations to obscure truth in order to justify invasion and occupation under international law. Lin himself was involved in the council's debates on the occupation and struggled to make sense of the injustice and his own impotence to influence events.

While "Criticism" is a philosophical essay, "On the 'December 9' Students' Movement in Beiping" offered angry and direct support for the mass student movement. In 1939, Mao Zedong (1893–1976) mentioned the December Ninth Movement as a major student movement alongside the 1911 Revolution, the May Fourth Movement, and the May Thirtieth Movement.[6] However, almost no research has been published on this movement since the 1960s.[7] In this article, Lin also compares the December 9 Movement to the May Fourth and May Thirtieth Movements, fiercely arguing for the importance of such mass movements as "the people's lament and the people's cry" and refuting Japanese attempts to stifle and silence students in occupied Beiping.

These translations allow readers to visualize Lin's perspective on Japan's invasion of Manchuria, particularly illuminating China's student and youth movement during this pivotal time as understood by a prominent Chinese author with first-hand experience of the May Fourth Movement and China's revolutionary history.

— TRANSLATIONS —

Criticism without Words[8]

LIN YUTANG

Mendelssohn titled his composition "Songs without Words," and Hans Christian Andersen called his book "A Picture-Book without Pictures." Similarly, "A Speech without an Audience" or "A Letter without a Recipient" could have been excellent book titles, but, sadly, nobody has attempted these. Beyond these, Zhuangzi's similar expression, "Disputation without Argument,"[9] contains significant meaning, and the expression is not very different from "criticism without words."

Zhuangzi indicated that the truth of the world is vague and every single individual has their own truth and falsehood; the more one argues, the more fragmented those become. Therefore, the more that people argue with each other, the more arguments can be found in writings, consequently obscuring the meaning of truth. The Way which can be spoken of is not the eternal Way.[10] The title "Disputation without Argument" implies that people should learn from self-experience. "Self-experience" refers to an internal concept of truth and falsehood that readers usually have within their selves. To see the essence of the Way, ordinary people require neither profound theory nor trained logic. They can implicitly understand right and wrong. Thus, the word "self-experience" is far from the mystical enlightenment discussed in the Buddhist text *Understanding of Zen* (*Wu Chan*) or Lu Jiuyuan's *Understanding of the Way* (*Wu Dao*).

Logically speaking, there is deep academic meaning to the phrase, "The Way which can be spoken of is not the eternal Way." The Way is by nature chaotic and unenlightened, but when it undergoes scholars' analysis and disputation, it loses its unity and becomes fragmented. After such disputation, the Way, divided and broken, is stripped of its original meaning and completely shattered. Because of this brokenness, the cunning person can argue and cover themselves with rhetoric; thus the more they argue, the more the Way suffers. For example, an outstanding argument can be written in defence of Japan's invasion of the three eastern provinces if one wished to defend it. By listing historical, economic, and realistic reasons, one can explain why Japan had to invade Shenyang and Jinzhou. The renowned Council on Foreign Relations in New York once held a meeting regarding this issue, during which an international law expert came to the conclusion that "Japan's occupation of Shenyang was never in violation of international law." Here, we can see how empty argument and theoretical analysis are unreliable. I happened to be at the meeting, and I made two statements without making a counterargument: "Japan's occupation of Shenyang is lawful according to international law. This is proven by experts, so it may very well be true. However, I absolutely do not believe in what lawyers have said." We do not need experts' theories unless we are going to use an ordinary way of speaking. Japan's occupation of Shenyang is torturing people and is clearly an invasion and forced occupation. Therefore, the Way is chaotic and unenlightened, and theories of analysis are unreliable. And this is Zhuangzi's profound meaning in "Disputation without Argument."

This is the reason why the Chinese are said to be an illogical people who rely on intuition for all things. Intuition is general and non-analytical, and hence prone to logical disputes. This is the true essence of the Way. Women tend to rely on intuition without reasoning; when a situation strikes, I depend on women's ability to improvise the decision and not on men, because intuition is realistic and allows one to understand the overall situation. Men's arguments seem logical and methodological, but when they speak of point A, they forget point B; when they talk of point B, they forget point C. Their various points all contradict one another. Furthermore, men have often already formed their own opinions, and only assert all these points to comfort themselves. The saying that a revolution led by a scholar cannot succeed even after three years comes from this context as well. Past dynasties' founding emperors, Zhu Yuanzhang and Liu Bang in particular, were all mere street hoodlums who achieved success not because of their studies, but because their intuition made them more capable than scholars in responding to events. These emperors took no heed of studies and theories, but still they founded great dynasties that lasted for a long time. The Chinese know that theories cannot be trusted, so they base their relationships on affection (*qing*). A characteristic principle of Chinese ideology holds that through both an affirmation of affection and an affirmation of reasoning anything can be achieved.

While Zhuangzi spoke of "disputation without argument," people in the modern era prefer argumentation. Magazines and newspapers lure readers with rumours about people. Also, criticism, which Western scholars find difficult, has become an easy task for people of today in spite of the fact that criticizing others' weaknesses does not accentuate one's own strengths. The critics should be criticized by readers as well. When readers criticize the critic, then the critic becomes the criticized; however, the counterpart may not respond. Most readers do not criticize by writing – rather, their impression of a certain critic is enough to make them stop arguing and keep silent. This silence is "criticism without words." For instance, if someone on the street were to shout: "Shit!" then passersby would pour their "criticism without words" onto the person who shouted, implying: "Why is this person shouting out dirty words?"

In another example, someone stands on a stage criticizing today's teachers for inadequate language skills. If the language used by the critic is the same language as that used by the teachers, people will have no choice but to keep silent. And such silence is "criticism without words." It is unfortunate that no one has discovered a method through which to criticize others' language skills while speaking a foreign language. Such an approach would be masterfully proficient. Silent argumentation is superior to vocalized argumentation. Disputation without words is superior to disputation with words.

Some critics have also cursed others for not participating in revolutions – they are timid and reside in foreign concessions. Readers may then wonder why the critics themselves are not fighting in battles in Jiangxi, and this is also considered silent and odourless criticism without words.

Critical essays are all confined within the realm of writing. Such writings remain bound by points of view, opinions, theories, perspectives, styles, and motives. A point of view can be lofty or deficient, just as an opinion can be deep or shallow. Theories can be well structured or disordered. Perspectives can be wide or narrow. Styles can be eloquent or coarse. Motives can be true or false. If a piece of writing has a deficient point of view, shallow opinion, disorderly theory, narrow perspective, coarse style, and false motive, it will give such an impression and then receive people's "criticism without words."

Regrettably, people's wisdom is often not unlike that of a sow, but one thinks of oneself as an exception. A person who writes short essays and states "I hate short essays" is a common phenomenon. Zhuangzi said that every single individual has their own truth and falsehood. If someone falls into a right or wrong dispute, the more one fights one reveals one's narrow-minded, servile-hearted, cowardly, shallow, evil, and silly character. Whether writings fill up papers with righteousness, ideology, or manners is meaningless, because the writings have already received criticism without words by their readers.

People fear that critics might argue that clay is jade or that deer are horses, and that if nobody criticizes the critics, there will always be traces left behind. Then, the next generation determines someone's criticism with only two or three sentences of argument that clay is jade or that fish eyes are pearls. A recent example is how people falsely believe that Wu Yuseng opposed written vernacular Chinese in the twenty-second year of the Republic of China [1933] and that Dai Jitao converted to Buddhism in the twenty-third year [1934].[11] These examples of disputation without argument can be terrifying.

On the "December 9" Students' Movement in Beiping[12]

LIN YUTANG

Newspapers report that Suma visited Tang Youren to protest against the Beiping student movement.[13] Was it necessary for Suma to visit Tang Youren? Suma could have simply called, but the fact that he personally visited him illustrates how much importance he placed on the movement. Moreover, since Suma did not protest when He Yingqin moved north, but did protest politely against the student movement, one can conclude that Suma feared the student movement more than the Chinese military.[14] How brilliant Suma is! Who said there are no men of talent in Japan? What Japan wants is a quiet and stable China without mass movements and protests. How can one explain this? The reason is that both the Tanggu Agreement, which resulted in the loss of national sovereignty, and the impending Tanggu Truce were formed through the indirect actions of people behind the scenes. The Treaty of Versailles, which received global attention, was destroyed by the clamouring, nonviolent May Fourth Movement of the Chinese masses, demonstrating how the power of the masses is like a blazing fire – much more fearsome than the Chinese military. Rethinking the May Thirtieth Movement,[15] we see that it forced the British to surrender; the Kuomintang youth movement brought down the northern government, while the combined forces of the Revolutionary Army and the masses achieved the glorious historical achievement of the party-state Northern Expedition, based on movements by the masses and students. Dr. Sun Yat-sen and Japanese politicians all knew this, which is why Dr. Sun Yat-Sen wrote in his last will and testament the phrase, "Awaken the people!" (*huanxing minzhong*) to bring prosperity to the nation.

Politicians in neighbouring countries also know this, so they have paid extra attention to student movements. I say to Suma that the current movement against the independence of north China follows the protocol of the May Fourth Movement, with great strength and vigour, so the result will be unimaginable. If the Beiping student protests aim to protect the government and preserve Chinese territory, then can the Beiping military police stop them by force? They will never be able to do so. Then what will the police do? The police will surround the universities and confine the students to prevent them from participating in protests. Then, if Peking University students are willing to be confined at the Third Garden, just as in the May Fourth Movement, student strikes might spread to other universities in Beiping, just as in the May Fourth Movement. Students and chambers of commerce across the country might participate, just as in the May Fourth Movement. Would this not complicate the situation? Would it not revive the dying national spirit? At this time, if the Chinese government wishes to pursue friendly diplomatic policies toward neighbouring countries, it must carefully observe public sentiment. Against my protests, the response of the Chinese government was that it was unable to put a stop to it – not that it did not try. The government is incapable because of public sentiment and also because territorial integrity and independence of administration are demanded by academic and economic circles. At this time, I cannot blame the Chinese government. The movement in north China is a domestic issue of China and is thus difficult for Japanese to interfere with but, if things play out as such, this change in circumstances will allow the Ju Ren Tang (Ju Ren Hall) and its Third Floor Officials to easily take advantage of the north China region![16] This is the perspective of foreigners and, from a Chinese perspective, Japan's request to eliminate mass movements in China is the same as erasing the phrase, "Awaken the people!" from the last will and testament of the Kuomintang's president and founding father. Beiping's student movement is the people's lament (*minxu*) and the people's cry (*minhu*) proposed by propagandists such as Ye Chucang and Yu Youren.[17] How much territory did China lose twenty to thirty years ago? How much territory did we lose today? People lamented then – why can we not lament today? As we lose our territory, people can lament and cry. If the people do not stand up when north China is being occupied, people cannot lament and cry, because China has lost all of its vitality. Never mind the destruction of north China, the end of the entirety of China is not far away. Even dogs kick their legs twice when they die, should not the people do the same? Were I to cut off a dog's leg today, and that dog did not breathe or struggle, this would mean that the dog was already dead. The dog would have died regardless of me cutting off its leg, so why try to beautify this by covering it up with the word "calm" (*zhenjing*)? Much in the same way, the fall of China has not been caused by Japan. Even if it were not for Japan, another country would have destroyed China. If I were Japan, I would take wretched and discarded China; I would rather kill a living rooster than a dead dog. Mass movements are like a patient's pulse. Doctors say that a patient's pulse determines the course of a disease. If the pulse is healthy, there is nothing to worry about even when symptoms are severe. However, light symptoms can prove lethal for a patient with a weak pulse. I think that the pulse of education leaders and students in Beiping is healthy. Does China have hope?

(12 December [1935])

Notes

1 Suoqiao Qian, *Lin Yutang and China's Search for Modern Rebirth* (Singapore: Springer, 2017), 15, 26.

2 Wang Zhaosheng, *Lin Yutang di wenhua qinghuai* [Lin Yutang's cultural sentiments] (Beijing: Zhongguo shehui kexue chubanshe, 1998).

3 Lin Taiyi, *Lin Yutang zhuan* [A biography of Lin Yutang] (Taipei: Lian jing chubanshe ye gongsi, 1989).

4 Qian, *Lin Yutang and China's Search,* 21–22.

5 Qian, *Lin Yutang and China's Search,* 18.

6 Mao also indicated the importance of the December Ninth Movement in ending the Civil War in 1937. See Mao Zedong, *Selected Works of Mao Tse-tung,* vol. 2 (Beijing: Foreign Languages Press, 1965), 23, 322.

7 This included John Israel's article as well as comments by Israel, Edgar Snow, and Hao-Jan Chu in the 1966 and 1967 editions of the *China Quarterly.* John Israel, "The December 9th Movement: A Case Study in Chinese Communist Historiography," *China Quarterly* 23 (1965): 140–69.

8 Lin Yutang, "Wuzi de piping" [Criticism without words], *Ren Jian Shi* [This human world] 10, 20 (August 1934): 6–8.

9 Zhuangzi, *Qi wu lun* [On levelling all things], ch. 2.

10 This is the first line of the Taoist classic, the *Tao Te Ching.* Lin Yutang, *The Wisdom of Laotse* (New York: Greenwood, 1948).

11 Wu Mi (Wu Yuseng, 1894–1978) was a famous scholar of Western literature. He was born and died in Shenyang. Dai Jitao (Dai Chuanxian, 1891–1949) was an important politician and intellectual associated with the Kuomintang.

12 Lin Yutang, "Guanyu Beiping xuesheng 'yier-jiu' yundong" [On the "December 9" students' movement in Beiping], *Yuzhou Feng* [Cosmic wind] 8 (1936): 355–56.

13 Suma Yakichiro (1892–1970), consul general of Japan in Nanjing; Tang Youren (1893–1935), undersecretary of national government diplomacy. Unknown assassins killed Tang for having pro-Japanese sentiments in December 1935, after student-led large-scale protests against Japanese efforts to encourage North China independence.

14 He Yingqin (1890–1987), senior general of the Republic of China Army.

15 The May Thirtieth Movement (*Wusi yundong*) was a 1925 labour and anti-imperialist movement.
16 Ju Ren Tang – the "Hall where Benevolence Resides," originally called Hai Yan Tang in Zhongnanhai – was the building where Yuan Shikai lived and worked; Third Floor Officials were the core leadership who usually gathered on the third floor.
17 Ye Chucang (1887–1946), general secretary of the Central Executive Committee; Yu Youren (1879–1964), premier of the Executive Yuan.

25 Struggles between Local Powers and Collaboration

Yan Xishan, the CCP, and the Western Shanxi Incident

TIMOTHY CHEEK

This news report from the Chinese Communist Party's (CCP) main newspaper of the day, *Jiefang ribao* (Liberation daily) in Yan'an, provides an emblematic example of how the CCP cast collaboration with the Japanese by 1944. The text is doubly useful because it is both a piece of central propaganda of the CCP, therefore likely to reflect central party policy, and was personally revised by Mao. The case has to do with the independent local general, Yan Xishan (1883–1960), and efforts of the CCP between 1936 and early 1940 to cooperate with his armies in resisting the inroads of the Japanese Imperial Army. These were the early days of the Second United Front between the Communists and the Nationalists under Chiang Kai-shek (1887–1975). Yan Xishan was nominally aligned with the Nationalists but was, in fact, quite independent of Chiang's forces. Thus, the Communists, who had invaded the western counties of Yan's Shanxi province in early 1936 only to be knocked back, shifted later that year to the nonconfrontational, "let's all work together" spirit of the United Front to woo Yan Xishan. However, Yan was no more interested in working under the Communists than he was in submitting to the Nationalists, and ultimately Yan and the Communists fell out.

The specific case – which is detailed in this report – has to do with fighting in 1939 between the CCP forces, in which Han Jun served as political commissar, and Yan's forces.[1] Han Jun had been a leader in the "Dare-to-Die Corps" and other units tied to the Communists. In a complicated series of manoeuvres, the Communist forces were overwhelmed and forced to leave the area by early 1940. The interpretation of what happened was still contested in 1944; this news article is a response to a press conference Yan had given a few days earlier.[2] The issue at hand was, of course, who was at fault for the split between these two Chinese forces. Historians might write the conflict off as local competition, but the actors at the time sought to make their justifications in terms that had national significance. Yan cast the Communist forces as "rebels" and "bandits" who helped the Japanese; the Communists denounced Yan for "working with the Japanese."[3] Regardless of the merits of each side's case, this shows the status of Japanese collaborators among the Communists and independent local forces under Yan Xishan: nothing less than traitors.

This text was reportedly edited by Mao Zedong (1893–1976) himself and is included in a collection of his works on journalism. This report was extended in the days that followed through further articles by senior CCP leaders such as Bo Yibo elaborating the claim that Yan Xishan "colluded with the enemy to sell out the nation."[4] The fact that Mao, as the newly anointed supreme leader "Chairman Mao," took a personal interest in this historical case reflects the propaganda significance of being cast as a "traitor working with the Japanese." Mao could not let Yan Xishan's claim that Communist forces were collaborating with the Japanese stand without a vigorous rebuttal. In all, the Communist propaganda on the case stressed that Yan Xishan had made a secret peace deal with the Japanese.[5]

Two further contexts are worth considering when reading this document. First, in 1944, the CCP had not yet unequivocally made its case as the revolutionary party of China. The Kuomintang (KMT), or Nationalists, continued to present themselves as China's revolutionary party. Indeed, one of the reasons that the CCP pursued a renewed United Front with the KMT in the mid-1930s was because of the success of news and propaganda in the Nationalist press that presented the CCP as a puppet of the Soviet Union rather than as a force for change in China.[6] Second, Mao's vision here was a minority voice in China at the time, only one in a segmented public sphere in which media and information was divided among spheres controlled by the Nationalist government and its forces, Japanese forces and their subordinates, and areas controlled by Communist forces. Of the three, the Communist voice reached the smallest audience at the time, but its message of social revolution was one that increasingly appealed to young Chinese as the Japanese occupation faltered and the Nationalist government seemed unable to restore order and prosperity. Mao's version came to dominate in the new People's Republic after 1949. Only in recent decades has newer scholarship (even abroad) challenged the Communist narrative of resistance and revolution.[7]

This text is also interesting for showing that the CCP had firmly embraced a hard line of zero tolerance for any collaboration or accommodation with Japanese forces during the resistance war. The language and arguments of the text are thus useful for illustrating how the CCP made its case and its claim for public support.

TRANSLATION

Han Jun Tells the Inside Story of the Western Shanxi Incident[8]

HAN JUN
(WITH TEXT IN ITALICS ADDED BY MAO ZEDONG)

(New China News Agency, *Yan'an, 13 August [1944]*) In Yan Xishan's talk with the delegation of Chinese and foreign reporters carried in the *Western Capital Daily* in Xi'an, he discussed the betrayal of the Second Column of the New Army led by Han Jun in 1939 when Yan Xishan was preparing for the winter offensive. In order to let the Chinese people know the inside story of this incident, which saddens friends but pleases the enemy, our reporter conducted a special interview with Comrade Han Jun, who endured all the hardships and dangers himself. First, Comrade Han Jun told the reporter that in the past he had concealed the facts and remained silent on the cruel and vicious inside story of the Western Shanxi Incident and had never made it public in the press, in the hopes that Mr. Yan would come to his senses. This time, because Yan Xishan reversed fact and fiction, and openly confused the truth before the Chinese people and people abroad, Comrade Han could no longer remain silent. Therefore, Comrade Han Jun gave us a detailed description of the process of the incident.

Yan Xishan Is Hostile to the People

After the fall of Taiyuan [in November 1937], Yan Xishan became shaky and was preparing to surrender and compromise. After Wang Jingwei's surrender, Yan Xishan called a meeting of senior cadres to feel out the possibilities for peace. He said: "Resistance and peace are political issues; we cannot say that those who are for resistance are correct and those who are for peace are wrong." At that moment Comrade Bo Yibo said: "The enemy invaded our country and occupied our territory; we want national independence. We can only resist to the very end. Peace and appeasement are surrender; this is to be a traitor to China." Yan remained silent. It was not the first time that he talked in this way, but this was always exposed and opposed by the Sacrifice League and the New Army.[9] However, Yan's preparation for surrender never stopped. The Sacrifice League and the New Army believed that to win victory in the War of Resistance, we had to implement democracy and mobilize the masses. Yan is against democracy. He dismissed the popularly elected county heads, district heads, village heads, and other popularly elected institutions. He said: "Political power is a dagger; if it is in our hands, we will be able to rule; but if it is in the hands of the people, we will be in danger, hence we cannot have democracy." He was also against the establishment of the Peasants' Anti-Japanese National Salvation Association, of the self-defence army, and so on (but these are the foundations of the Chinese resistance forces). He said:

> The peasants are tigers; once they are mobilized it will be dangerous (he is afraid the peasants will fight to the end of the War of Resistance and refuse to obey him), but it is an opportunity if they are not mobilized (he is afraid that the Communists will come and mobilize the peasants). Now it is not a question of whether to mobilize; instead, it is a matter of controlling the electric whip (an electric whip is used to control tigers).

The reason he was against democracy and mobilizing the masses can be attributed entirely to his desire to surrender and compromise. He also said: "Survival is everything, and resistance is only the means." During the 7 July Incident,[10] in order to survive he had to resist a few days; later, when he found out that the War of Resistance will be long and difficult, he wanted to surrender. This was also for survival. There are no such words as justice, self-evident truth, or sense of state and nation in his dictionary. While making these preparations, he pretended to be resisting, but in fact he was already collaborating with the enemy and was secretly against the Communists. He held meetings with the enemy in Liucun and Anping. Many of his diplomatic envoys collaborated with the enemy on the road between Xingji and Taiyuan. The commander of the Dare-to-Die Corps repeatedly expressed: "The purpose of our cooperation with you is to fight the War of Resistance to its very end, not to surrender and compromise. We are against anybody who wants to surrender and compromise." Consequently, Yan Xishan regarded the New Army as the biggest obstacle in his way to surrender and compromise. He could not make the Dare-to-Die Corps give in, through persuasion or other means, so naturally he began to carry out his "wise counsel." "Unconsciously" he "transformed" the New Army into a "rebel army" and began to "send armed forces to suppress it." This is the true inside story of the Western Shanxi Incident.

The Converging Attack on the Dare-to-Die Corps by the Yan and Japanese Armies

In terms of the Western Shanxi Incident itself, it was Yan Xishan who first broke faith and started the Civil War. Yan Xishan attempted to get rid of the New Army, and he had planned for it for a long time. By October 1939, he ordered Wang Jingguo and Chen Changjie[11] to prepare to attack the New Army. He met with the anticommunist generals and lobbied *them one by one*, telling them that the strength of the Communists and the Eighth Route Army was expanding every day. With the addition of cooperation from the Sacrifice League and the Dare-to-Die Corps, there would be no place for our Shanxi-Suiyuan army to survive. Now was the time to get rid of the New Army and the Sacrifice League, using mutual assistance between China and Japan as proposed by the Japanese, in order to achieve our goal of survival. One reactionary officer (Liu Wuming) asked how to get rid of them. Wang and Chen answered that we should first reshuffle the Fourth Column of the Dare-to-Die Corps and transform it into the "Chinese Anti-Japanese Vanguard Army of Loyal Braves." Then we will muster six armies in western Shanxi, in cooperation with the Japanese army, to get rid of the Second Column of the Dare-to-Die Corps. Finally, we will get rid of the First and Third columns in coordination with the Japanese army. Not unexpectedly, Yan Xishan soon appointed Chen Changjie as the commander-in-chief of the "rebel suppression" army. On 29 November *1939* (nine days before the Western Shanxi Incident), Chen sent out a secret order to attack the New Army from three directions. The southern column consisted of the Sixty-First Army, Eighty-Third Army, and the Seventy-Third Division of the Garrison Army. Chen held concurrent command. It attacked Yiquan and Huangtu (the location of the headquarters of the second column of the Dare-to-Die Corps) in Xi county. The commander-in-chief of the northern column was Liang Peihuang. He commanded the Nineteenth Army and part of the Thirty-Third Army attacking the Shuitou-Shikou-Damaijiao area (at that time this was the location of the western Shanxi detachment of the Eighth Route Army) in Xi and Xiaoyi counties. The right column consisted of the New First Brigade and others, commanded by Cui Daoxiu; it attacked the

Quanziping area in Xi county. Meanwhile, the enemy also gathered the more than five thousand garrison troops between Linfen and Pingyao and stationed them along the Hanxinling area. So on 1 December *1939,* Yan Xishan ordered that the second column of the Dare-to-Die Corps prepare to attack and destroy the Tongpu rail line[12] on the fifth to implement the "winter offensive." When we were just mobilizing the troops to carry out the order of attack and destruction, *Yan's* army and the Japanese army began to attack us simultaneously. Our second column was encircled and suffered the converging attack of the Japanese and of *Yan's* army. The situation was extremely dangerous, and we were facing the danger of being completely exterminated. If we did not engage in self-defence, we would be dead. We *had to* fight against the enemy with bayonets, on the one hand, and defend ourselves against the Old Army,[13] on the other. We fought for twenty days before breaking through the encirclement of the Japanese invaders and the Old Army, and then moved to northwest of Shanxi. This is the "rebellion of the Dare-to-Die Corps." Ever since then, the Dare-to-Die Corps began to be called the "rebel army."

Who in the End Is the Rebel Army?

Who in the end is the rebel army? Who works hand in glove with the enemy against the people, sabotages the War of Resistance, and betrays the nation? Is it the New Army, or Yan Xishan? The New Army did not work against the people, regarding them as fierce tigers, nor did it attend the Linfen meeting or the Anping meeting to *collaborate with the enemy and betray the nation,* nor did it send Zhao Chengshou, Liang Yanwu, Wang Qianyuan, or anyone else to Taiyuan, Beiping, or Nanjing to call on the enemy and the traitor Wang Jingwei, nor did it conclude the "present territorial agreement" with the enemy. On the contrary, it was Yan Xishan himself who did these things. It is quite clear that Yan himself knows that the Dare-to-Die Corps is not the rebel army. Before 1939 he praised the Dare-to-Die Corps in every possible way, saying that they were revolutionary youth and all their methods were revolutionary, and he felt ashamed that his Old Army was all muddle-headed, backward, unprogressive, and unable to keep up with the Dare-to-Die Corps. Let us put aside all this for the time being. Even after the Western Shanxi Incident, he once said in his small circle of a few "faithful comrades": "The Dare-to-Die Corps was revolutionary and was the most resolute in the War of Resistance"; "Bo Yibo is not a serviceman, but the troops trained by him and his men are capable of fighting the enemy. This is because his methods are revolutionary and progressive." Then why does he insist that the Dare-to-Die Corps is the rebel army? "The Old Tippler's delight is not in the wine (he has ulterior motives)."[14] His aim is to use this to conceal his ugly collaboration with the enemy against the people and the Communists, and his real image as a traitor or quasi traitor. It was not the "Han Jun betrayal" or the "conflict between the New Army and the Old Army"; on the contrary, it was a struggle between surrender and antisurrender, between disintegration and unity, and between progress and retreat. Action speaks louder than words. Even if Yan Xishan had one hundred mouths, it would be hard for him to talk his way out of it.

In this affair not only can Bo Yibo, Han Jun, and other Communists and non-Communists who worked in the Dare-to-Die Corps and the Sacrifice League confirm this from their personal experience but also Mr. Xu Fanting (1893–1947), a senior figure in the KMT (who was appointed the commander of the Provisional First Division by Mr. Yan and later became the general commander of the New Army) can also confirm it from his personal experience. More important, all the ordinary people in Shanxi province can tell of Yan's crimes against the public as if enumerating their family treasures.

Notes

1 Han Jun (1912–49) joined the CCP in 1932 but was soon imprisoned along with fellow Communist Bo Yibo (1908–2007). They were released in September 1936 to join the United Front. Bo brought Han Jun to work in Shanxi and both took leading positions in the Sacrifice League.

2 Yan Xishan gave interviews to *Xijing ribao* (Western capital daily) that were published on 21 and 22 July 1944.

3 According to Odoric Y.K. Wou, the clash with the Communists did force Yan "to make friends with the Japanese," something not at all out of line with the other cases documented in this volume. See Edwin Pak-wah Leung, ed., *Historical Dictionary of Revolutionary China, 1839–1976* (New York: Greenwood Press, 1992), 484.

4 "Bo Yibo tongzhi jielu Yan Xishan tongdi panguo neimu" [Comrade Bo Yibo exposes the secret plot of Yan Xishan to collude with the enemy to sell out the nation], *Jiefang ribao* [Liberation daily], 14 August 1944.

5 The official CCP version is given in "Xu Fanting Shanxi fanzhan ji" [Xu Fanting's Resistance War diary], in the "Archives of Chinese Leading Cadres" section of *Zhongguo gongchandang xinwen wang* [CCP news net], 21 July 2015. This is the same figure Mao mentions as proof at the end of the 1944 report, http://dangshi.people.com.cn/n/2015/0721/c85037-27335933-4.html.

6 Joseph Esherick, "The CCP in the 1930s: The View from Defectors' Declarations," *PRC History Review* 2, 2 (April 2017), http://prchistory.org/review-april-2017.

7 Diana Lary, *China's Republic* (Cambridge: Cambridge University Press, 2007); and Hans van de Ven, *China at War: Triumph and Tragedy in the Emergence of the New China* (Cambridge, MA: Harvard University Press, 2018).

8 [Mao Zedong], "Han Jun tan jin xi shibian zhenxiang" [Han Jun tells the inside story of the Western Shanxi Incident], *Mao Zedong xinwen gongzuo wenxuan* [Selected Writings by *Mao Zedong* on journalistic work] (Beijing: Xinhua, 1983), 309–13, giving the date 13 August 1944, being a news report from *Jiefang ribao* of 14 August 1944 plus material from the CCP Central Archives. The original text was an unsigned article in *Jiefang ribao*.

9 The Sacrifice League for National Salvation was a Communist front organization that Yan Xishan was persuaded to endorse. Founded on 18 September 1936, the fifth anniversary of the Mukden Incident of 1931 (in which the Japanese took over Manchuria), this patriotic association allowed Communists, such as Bo Yibo, to organize troops legally in Shanxi to resist the looming Japanese presence in north China. The "New Army" (also known as the Dare-to-Die Corps) was the military wing of the Sacrifice League. See Feng Chongyi, "The Making of the Jin Sui Base Area," in *North China at War: The Social Ecology of Revolution, 1937–1945* (Boulder, CO: Rowman and Littlefield, 2000), ed. Chongyi Feng and David S.G. Goodman, 157–62.

10 That is, the start of the war with Japan with the Marco Polo Bridge Incident on 7 July 1937.

11 Wang Jingguo (1893–1952) was one of Yan Xishan's leading generals; Chen Changjie (1897–1968) was the Nationalist general in western Shanxi.

12 The Tongpu rail line was the major railroad in Shanxi, running from Datong in the north, through the capital in Taiyuan and to Puzhou, near Xi'an in the southwestern corner of the province.

13 The "Old Army" refers to Yan Xishan's forces that had turned on the CCP-backed forces.

14 This literary phrase, *Zui weng zhi yi buzai jiu* (the Old Tippler's delight is not in the wine), draws from a poem by the Song period literatus, Ouyang Xiu (1007–72). The full line reads in translation: "The Old Tippler's delight is not in the wine but in the mountains and waters."

26 Tapping into the Premodern Work-Contracting System

ZHANG YUANFANG

This selected excerpt is from Nakamura Takatoshi's (n.d.) study on the local work-contracting system (*batou zhidu*) that Japan's wartime companies utilized in the area of the North China–Manchukuo border during the Second Sino-Japanese War (1937–45). The *batou* system was the coolie-recruitment mechanism employed in foreign-owned industries in China. This mechanism reduced the cost of managing workers by contracting the task to local labour organizers. Unlike modern capitalist enterprises, which employ workers through contracts, the *batou* system relied on Chinese contractors to recruit and control unskilled coolies. These contractors recruited poor peasants in groups that usually came from the same village. Two types of contractors are mentioned in this text: the group leader (*zuzhang*) and his underling, the team leader (*duizhang*). The group leader was responsible for delegating the daily workload to the team leader and passing wages to his underlings. The team leader managed the coolie workers, including supervising their work, and determining and paying their wages. These organizers used their own reputation and influence to deal with recruitment, the managing of coolies' lives, and the supervision of coolies working on the shop floor.

The unskilled Chinese coolies were an important part of the *batou* system. Nakamura notes that unlike modern disciplined industrial workers, Chinese coolies coming from the countryside worked for industries only during winter fallows. The seasonal migration of labour from rural agriculture to mining endowed Chinese coolies with a specific characteristic coded by Nakamura as "semi-industrial and semi-agrarian." Interestingly, Nakamura treats the so-called backwardness of Chinese agrarian workers not as an impediment to but as a condition for the development of wartime industry in occupied China. The hiring and management of Chinese coolie labourers during the war constituted the condition for Japanese wartime industries to intervene in, negotiate, and restructure indigenous social mechanisms as one solution to the labour deficiency magnified by the wartime controlled economy.

Nakamura's research took place in the context of the wartime national mobilization of labourers[1] and the expansion of production in Manchukuo (1932–45), a puppet state of Japan in Northeast China and Inner Mongolia. In 1942, heavy industrial production was about to reach its pinnacle.[2] His research was sponsored by the Labour Science Institute, an organization conducting research on workers across the territory of the Japanese empire. In Japan, labour science research organizations were responsible for designing policies that nurtured labourers in order to promote their technical level.[3] In Japanese-occupied Manchukuo, labour research institutes were also charged with collecting, differentiating, and disseminating biopolitical information on colonial labourers to make sure that they fit labour market niches in response to the expansion of wartime production in the empire's periphery regions.

For example, the word "coolie" denoted a politics of categorization. It was not simply a pejorative term but referred to peasants from China proper who migrated to become cheap labourers for Manchukuo's heavy industries. These people lacked skills and were exclusively Han Chinese. The word itself embodied some finer distinctions between Chinese coolie workers and Japanese labourers in Manchukuo's industry along the fault line of race.[4] The document translated below reflects how mining workers in Manchukuo were differentiated in terms of ethnicity, and how Chinese workers were coded as unskilled coolies who were placed at the bottom rank of labour differentiation.

In fact, the utilization of unskilled coolies against the background of heavy industrialization contained a structural ambiguity concerning the role of precapitalist social forms not only in Manchukuo but also in Japan's political economy. As a late-developed country, Japan started its state-driven industrialization in the Meiji Restoration in the late nineteenth century. In its transition to capitalism, the Meiji government instituted reforms that laid the foundation of Japan's modern rise as a new power in the region of East Asia. The Japanese state played a pivotal role in promoting reforms effectively. It redistributed the wealth and income accumulated since the Tokugawa period for the political and economic expansion of Meiji oligarchies. It also established foundations for building urban industries through its introduction of modern technologies from the West. Aside from that, the Meiji oligarchs launched land-tax reforms in the 1870s, unleashing small peasants from their bondage to feudal tenancy that centred on the complicated relation between landowning and land-leasing; at the same time, land ownership was legalized as a commodified title that was free to be traded on the market. Unlike its Western counterparts, in Japan there was no institutionalized land enclosure that forced landless peasants to become workers necessary for the development of capitalist social relations. As a result, small peasantry survived in the countryside. Thus, the social change accompanied by land reform cannot be characterized as a typical capitalist revolution. Rather, the Meiji Restoration successfully established a dual economy constitutive of a modern industrial sector and residual precapitalist social forms that remained partially separated from the new modern economy.

The dual structure of the national economy paved the way for Japan's rise as a modern power in several respects. First, the countryside became a main source of cheap labour for urban industries. Because the process of peasant expropriation advanced more rapidly than the development of capitalism, the dispossessed peasantry were converted into tenants or part-time tenants who depended largely on domestic industries, such as spinning, weaving, and sericulture.[5] The presence of "backward," low-skilled peasants brought down the wage levels of industrial workers in cities, which was conducive to capitalists' profit-reaping activities. Second, during the time of crisis, the countryside became a buffering space that offset the negative effects of capitalism. Jobless workers who had agrarian connections with the countryside were channelled back to their villages, which helped urban industries to dispense with social care for rural workers.

The co-presence of different social forms was also fundamental to the development of the colonial economy in association with Japan's imperial expansion between the 1860s and the 1940s. For example, in Okinawa, along with its national incorporation into Japan as a prefecture, the development of capitalism did not dissolve its traditional rural social relations. Rather, the government enacted a preservation policy to keep the existing social structure and agrarian productive forces intact. This policy benefited the home market of Japan because the inland merchants could import sugar, the most important commodity exported from Okinawa, at a lower price than the market.[6] In Korea, the formal colonization of the country in 1910 and the inflow of Korean workers to Japan enabled Japanese colonialism to racially classify and identify Korean workers, who were then institutionally channelled into the day-labour market. In the meantime, the state gave preferential treatment to Japanese workers by securing their niche in factories and other long-term positions.[7]

The doubling effect of feudal elements could also be found in occupied China during the Sino-Japanese War (1937–45). As can be seen from the translated excerpt below, Nakamura held an ambivalent attitude toward the local work-contracting system. On one hand, he argues that this system should undergo reform in the future, which corresponds to the discourse on the establishment of a modern productive mechanism. On the other hand, he concedes that the wartime expansion of production could take advantage of the existing local system to manage coolie workers in order to reduce costs.

This text should not be read simply as a work that documents the contrast between modern and coolie workers. Neither can the observation be interpreted simply as an imperialist and condescending view of the colonized. Rather, it is evidence attesting to the specific way in which the occupied economy was organized and developed.

TRANSLATION

A Study of the *Batou* System[8]

NAKAMURA TAKATOSHI

The General Definition of the *Batou* System

After the Marco Polo Bridge Incident [hereafter the Incident],[9] the economic development and the expansion of productions under Japan's supervision were highly reliant on coolies' manual labour, and furthermore, labour reinforcement. This fact does not have to be understood as an exigent strategy due to the shortage of resources. It will be clear, if facts are contrasted against their background, that mining industries operated by foreign capitalists failed to employ the mechanized means that had been used in other countries. Even though there is an enormous amount of potentially stagnant surplus population, modern companies are still distressed by the shortage of modern workers. It is for this reason that these industries have customized production to the hiring of semi-agrarian coolies characterized by their lack of discipline and skills, rather than to the use of machines characterized by programmatic planning and high-quality yields. Rather than developing the central-organized production system, industries take advantage of the local *batou* system, or the work-contracting system – an indigenous institution inherited from the past – to organize workers in production.

The *batou* system is not rooted in *petit* commodity production.[10] Its formation is rooted in the development of capitalism, especially the separation of owner and manager in the capitalist production (though maintaining the traditional traits of capitalism) and the extensive recruitment of unskilled coolies (who cannot be regarded as modern labourers). Moreover, this system is not a developed form of "guild." It is not an inherent system that foreign-run industries utilize, and there are unexpectedly many opinions that confuse this system with labour management by Chinese agents in a foreign-run industry. In Chinese industries, since the development of capitalist relations is shrouded by bureaucracies and warlords, capitalism managed to prove its presence in capitalists' direct control of mechanisms in the sphere of circulation and their indirect control of production. Doubtless, this tendency forms the hotbed for the development of the work-contracting system. The application of the contracting system can be found not only in mines, but also in textile industries. The use of the *batou* system, whose tenacious presence could be found in project-contracting (*sakugyō ukeoi*) and work-contracting (*rōdō ukeoi*) arrangements, must be distinguished from the daily hiring system (*hamba*)[11] that was applied in Japan's coal mines in the past.

The other element persistently supporting the *batou* system is the semi-agrarian and semi-industrial nature of Chinese coolies. In this case, it must be made explicit that this nature cannot be understood in generic terms. Rather, the *batou* system demonstrates the qualities of coolie workers. Afflicted by hunger and poverty, coolies must become migrant workers to supplement their family budget. This type of worker must also be distinguished from Japanese semi-agrarian labourers who work in different fields. The semi-agrarian and backward type of worker constitutes the foundation for the presence of the *batou* system.

Although the *batou* system is deeply rooted in Chinese society, this does not mean that it has never changed. Its evolution throughout history invites a realistic understanding of its cause, which is influenced by two factors. The first is the priority for the expansion of production, which will absolutely help overcome shortcomings of the feudal production system, namely, the absence of overall planning and the presence of limits constraining technical progress. With the disintegration of China's rural society, the semi-agrarian nature of coolies – the second factor – has been gradually changed with respect to its structure; and this change has also weakened the dependent relations of coolies with others, which shakes the foundation of the *batou* system. The establishment of the planned economic system itself is a question of adopting a specific operational mechanism. In this report I will address these two conditions as the leverage for the development of the *batou* system.

The Particularity of the *Batou* System in the Ryūen Iron Mine

According to Andersson's survey,[12] the Ryūen iron mine company was inaugurated as a joint state-private business in 1918 during the First World War with an initial capital of 2 million *yuan*. In 1919, with another 5 million *yuan* invested into the company, the company was renamed Mount Yantong coal mine and proceeded to manage mining activities. However, due to the poor development after the war, it was shut down, and mines were sealed. The Nanjing national government took over the mine after the Northern Expedition. After the Incident, it was again taken over by the Kōchū company.[13] In this way, twenty years after its abandonment by China's government, it was reopened by Japan without intervention of foreign capital. It was run in this disadvantaged condition in face of the deficiency of resources and the lack of historical experience. At the same time, due to the commodified nature of ores, there was no room to shift the burden caused by higher prices for the means of subsistence in the area near the mining locations. In addition, regarding the production mechanism, unlike coal mines, drilling for iron ores cannot be carried out simply through manual labour; rather, the industry must rely to a large extent on the use of machines. Finally, with respect to the source of workers coming to the mining area, the industry must depend on poor coolies from Henan and Shandong provinces. These conditions, which constitute the basis for the running of the company, are very different from other mines in north China. At the same time, the *batou* system shows its particularity in many ways. Nevertheless, the organization of the semi-agrarian and semi-industrial coolies in the feudal production system has always been consistent in different areas. Hence, it is imperative for us to master and understand the diversified aspects of Chinese coolies in north China as well as the *batou* system.

Before Japan took over Ryūen, the production was contracted to five superior *batou*. These five superior *batou* had two to five underlings respectively, and each underling had almost a hundred workers. In total, there were fifteen *batou* and fifteen hundred workers. Most of the *batou* came from Tangshan. After the ore mine was sealed, most *batou* returned to Tangshan, and some of them ended up in Mongolia as *batou* in construction industries. The takeover of industry by the Kōchū company marked the restoration of the *batou* system under the direct control of the company itself, rather than the superior *batou*. The working camp consisted of fewer coolies.

Although the company made efforts to recruit more *batou* supervised by the superior *batou* in 1939, it failed due to the lack of suitable candidates. As a trial, some competent candidates were invited from Manchuria to take the position of superior *batou*, but they had difficulty adapting to the environment because of their identity as outsiders. The local *batou* clique persisted in denigrating them to the technicians. Those outsiders were forced to leave because of circulating rumours. The Ryūen mine decided to accept small-scale *batou* units that consisted of *batou* born in Hebei.

The Ryūen mine is different from other mines in north China because its operation represented Japan's national interest. Production plans are accordingly installed in response to commands from the imperial Japanese state. The core section of production is controlled by the company. In other words, basic equipment, such as dowsing tools and explosives, are either well integrated into other means of mining dynamics or are strictly controlled by the company. In this regard, the *batou* system is to a large extent limited in terms of its functioning as a project-contracting mechanism; on the contrary, its functioning as a work-contracting mechanism is strongly reinforced. It is for this reason that only a small portion of capital has been invested into the maintaining of the *batou* system.

Because they could no longer benefit from working as an agent of labour supply, *batou* have to make every effort to recruit coolies and manage their dormitories. For this reason, although their engagement have to make every effort to recruit coolies and manage their dormitories requires the investment of an amount of capital, the financial burden has been largely relieved, since distribution of the means of subsistence has been taken up by the company. In this way, the company can dispense with the need for a large amount of capital. In addition, since the section of fixed capital constitutes only a small portion, and since this amount of capital is mainly invested into the recruiting and managing of migrant coolies, the foundation for the *batou* system becomes unstable due to the migratory nature of coolies. Forming a small clique allows these *batou* to present themselves as a community, while it still does not help improve *batou*'s reputation. I think this aspect has laid the foundation for the dramatic fluctuation of *batou,* accompanying social changes.

The instability and vulnerability of the *batou* system cannot help but impact the lives of coolies. This could be reflected in the frequent migration of coolies, the difficulty of nurturing a professional mining worker, and decreases in productivity. In April 1941, thanks to the rising price of the means of subsistence because of the drought in Mongolia, coolies' lives were on the verge of collapse. This event laid foundations for the urgent reform of the *batou* system in the next year. However, since this reform rushed to an end, the state was not ready to install a new mechanism in place of the *batou* system. In addition, this reform also caused some components of the *batou* system to fail to take effect. At the same time, *batou* who took advantage of this reform experienced a change: in the past, they played a dominant role in directly docking a portion from coolies' wages as their extra income; now, they had to distribute an amount to coolies to pay for the means of subsistence. This reform was not thoroughly carried out and it was flawed in two aspects: the preservation of the remnants of the old system, and the failure to establish a new mechanism. Now the pressing question is how to understand comprehensively the *batou* system in order that a real reform could be launched.

The Semi-agrarian and Semi-industrial Nature of Coolies

I have already outlined the nature of the impoverished coolies who must migrate to other places to make a living as mine workers. This semi-agrarian and semi-industrial nature lays the foundation for the *batou* system. The "semi-agrarian" coolies will not stay in the industry throughout their lives; hence the management in modern companies becomes uneasy and unbearable. In addition, their backwardness obstructs the full realization of mechanization, as it is difficult for them to adapt themselves to the application of machines. The insufficiency of mechanization furthermore entails the maintaining of the *batou* system as a remnant of the old society. There are two conditions pivotal to the existence of the *batou* system, namely, coolies bearing the semi-agrarian and semi-industrial character, and the company lacking a planned production system. These two conditions do not have equal weight in each industry; rather, each element is present to a certain degree. The degree of presence for each element is also in constant flux.

A gross generalization of the semi-agrarian and semi-industrial nature of coolies is far from enough. Its combination with premodern heterogeneous social elements, and the structural change of this combination, must be taken into consideration for further analysis. In the case of the Ryūen mine, coolies are divided into different groups. First, professional mining workers only constitute a small part of the whole coolie group. Second, most workers are long-term migrant workers; sojourners who are mainly engaged in mining but return to agrarian production during the farming seasons; migrant peasants who come to mine industries during the winter fallow; and part-time workers who only commute to the mine. These five types of workers are differentiated according to the degree of their "semi-agrarian" nature. The category that a coolie belongs to is determined largely by their social stratum in the rural society. Most peasants who can afford the means of subsistence and can raise their families by engaging in agrarian work become migrant workers during the winter fallow. Regarding seasonal workers who make a living mainly by mining during the fallow time, most of them come from the class in which they can barely make their ends meet through agrarian production. In the case of long-term migrant workers, many of them are landless peasants or coolies who are even less engaged in agrarian work. As for the professional mining workers, due to their low real wage and their inability to support their families, most of them are homeless and lead a precarious life before they settle down in the mining industries.

At mines, migrant workers who engaged in sporadic agrarian activities in their rural origins build relationships with others coming from the same village. The origin of *batou* must be traced back to the reproduction of relations shaped by the spatial linkages in the working sites of an enterprise. At the very beginning, *batou* are mainly from the stratum of farmers who own land in their hometown. The notion of hometown mediates the relationship between the shared rural locality and personal networking at industrial working sites. As the communal life at the company proceeds, a new interpersonal relationship is developed centring on the worksite, leading to dilution of the meaning of *batou,* whose importance emanates from the relationship of shared locale. However, the interdependent relationship between *batou* and their underling coolies from the same village continued in the company's worksites.

The above-mentioned reform is also negatively influenced by mining workers' poverty. Rising prices caused by inflation have a great impact on peasants in the rural society, including coolies at worksites. The increasing price of the necessities of life, namely, the price for the means of subsistence, plunges workers' lives into bankruptcy, forces them to migrate in search of a better life, and loosens their ties to the company. *Batou* receive more and more pressures coming from the contracted production, and finally those pressures are shifted toward their role in supervising workers' everyday lives. Coolies' consciousness of criticism of the *batou* will be nurtured against the essence of the *batou* system (insofar as the transformation of the role of the *batou* system unfolds in this way).

Restraints of the Indigenous Feudal Production System

In order to achieve the prior goal of the expansion of production during the war, the company must take control of production plans and apply partially mechanical means in the mining industry. I have already argued that the effect of work contracting is partly restricted due to the direct control of the means of production by the company. However, this effect should not be underrated.

It is only because the company has not fully established the planned production system that it has to rely to a greater or lesser degree on the indigenous feudal production system. There are two conditions for establishing the modern production system, namely, the complete development of modern labourers and reform of the production mechanism, based on the introduction of machinery. In reality, however, before the introduction of machinery, it is imperative for the company to take control of the production mechanism in order to install central plans for production. In view of this fact, it is very important to assess the function of the *batou* system.

The fundamental question is that, when the *batou* system is paradoxically incorporated into the production mechanism, it will be inevitably restructured as the coolie-organizing system bearing dualistic ambiguities. As the leader in charge of his working team, *batou* must secure interests at each working team, as the stake he has in the process of work contracting, rather than his working experience at mining industries, constitutes the condition for the presence of this system. To squeeze profits from the process of production, a group leader will require the team leader under his command to supervise production. On the company's side, from the points of view of the production planning and profitability, the company convenes its technicians and gives its orders through these technicians to the team leader, who takes charge of the supervision of production on the shop floor. Hence, the team leader epitomizes the double-faced character of the *batou*. This has brought about many difficulties.

In order to carry out production plans, it is necessary to establish a consistent system for supervising coolies working on the shop floor via a team leader. This system encompasses different positions that range from technicians to workers. In the first place, for this reason, it becomes very important to nurture the team leader as a skilled leader. Second, team leaders must be fully trained as pre-eminent leaders in terms of technical ability and physical endurance. Chinese technicians are especially needed for this purpose. Third, it is imperative to train the backbone workers who play a pioneering role among the workers by following guidance from the team leader. Finally, it is necessary to give Chinese technicians, team leaders, and backbone workers, all of whom are involved in the production mechanism, a wage generous enough for them to devote everything they can to mining production. These are the conditions for pushing for the establishment of planned production in place of the *batou* system.

Reform of the production mechanism through the installation of a planned production system is now unfolding faster than the partial mechanization carried out in early years. Moreover, it is not accurate to say that reform cannot be realized without the full achievement of mechanization. In fact, in the case of most developed mines, reform is based upon the reconstitution of the *batou* system. In Kailuan coal mine, a British-run mine in Hebei, foremen coming from training schools are organized into the supervision system. Placed under the direction of specialists and made to follow production plans in the coal mine, these foremen play a key role in changing the nature of the *batou* system. In Fushun mine, a Japanese-run mine in Fengtian province in Manchukuo, Japanese technicians are appointed as leaders of working teams at production sites. This measure creates the basic condition for putting one part of the *batou* system under the direct control of the mining company. As I have discussed, the lack of Japanese technicians and the low quality of available technicians have made resuscitation of the *batou* system inevitable after the Incident. Hence, in contrast to general understandings, the reason for the reliance on the *batou* system does not include difficulty in recruitment. At Fushun coal mine, the partial progression of mechanization adds difficulty to simply reviving the old *batou* system. The nurturing of technicians coming from Manchuria has already been accepted as an option for providing a positive solution to this problem. Regarding reforms that took place in the two areas, while it is interesting to note the continuing difference between Japanese-run and British-run mines, it is necessary to fully assess reform of the production mechanism as the basic condition for the resuscitation of the *batou* system, despite the specific running conditions shown in each case and the unfolding of mechanization as one way to reform the production mechanism. (The pace of the reform does not have to be directly proportional to the rate of mechanization, though.)

Alongside the unfolding of reform, on the other hand, the *batou* system must be situated into the frame of the work-contracting system, and furthermore, *batou* must be temporarily converted into the employees of the company. While reform of the production mechanism creates the basic condition for facilitating reform of the *batou* system toward the mechanism of work contracting, at the same time, reform of the *batou* system will also in turn enable the reform of production mechanism.

The Role of the Team Leader in the Determination and Payment of Wages for Coolies

The determination and payment of wages for a coolie not only becomes the material basis for sustaining the management of a working team, but also determines the basic life of miners. Moreover, how is the wage determined and paid? What relation does the team leader have to the determination and payment of wages? Although the team leader has a stake in the formation of such relations, I have not seen a satisfactory published survey on these people. For the time being, I will put together data concerning one survey taken from team leaders on the wage of a certain group. First, let me talk about the determination of wages. Wages distributed from the company are passed to the team leader, who determines the paid amount as the subcontracting fee for the whole working team, rather than determining the individual wage for each coolie. In this regard, what standards does the team leader follow to assess the output and skill of each coolie before distributing wages? In most cases it is the team leader who determines the wage. There is also an instance in which, besides the team leader, the senior coolie is also involved in making decisions. In some cases, the team leader makes a decision based on the discussion he has with the senior coolie. It is impossible to learn details just from a survey on team leaders. From the data that has already been disclosed to me, in Group One, the team leader, surnamed Ma, decides all wages for twelve out of twenty-eight workers. These workers also get paid directly by the leader. For the rest of the coolies, Ma's relative, surnamed Li, takes charge of them, rents a house for them in the village, and is responsible for the preparation of food for their communal life. Li determines the amount of wages for these coolies and distributes wages once he has received the total amount from Ma. Similar to the instance in which the dormitory is not distinguished from the dining place, just like the one managed by Li, in other circumstances in which coolies from the same group are divided according to their working locations, there are very few instances in which the senior coolie still does not have a decisive say in the determination of wages. The dependence on senior coolies is not limited to the formation of relationships at worksites as they also provide crucial introductions to new coolies during the recruitment process. In two or three instances, the team leader distributes wages to these coolies, including the senior coolie. However, the range of personal relationships that this determination fits is still unclear. Does it imply that the percentage of wage distribution by the team leader via the senior coolies is high?

Another question is what standard the determination of wage follows. In a working team, coolies are divided into first-class workers and second-class workers. However, how do leaders distinguish between the first class and the second class? Among the factors enumerated by different team leaders, physical strength is the factor that most leaders mentioned. Here is a chart [see Table]:

Criteria for the determination of experienced/inexperienced workers

Criteria		Cases
Stamina and spiritual power	Physical strength	21
	Passion	7
	Attendance	5
Technical ability		20

We can divide all the criteria that leaders have listed into three categories: the inherent physical strength and spiritual endurance of the body, technical capability, and a certain degree of leadership. As is shown in the chart, physical strength is the most required condition. The degree of physical strength is not determined by scientific standards but merely depends on the team leader's judgment. Technical capability centres on coolies' proficiency in craft skills, such as the use of rock-drilling machines, the designation of spots for drilling, and the speed of drilling. The first and second classes are determined in this way.

Once the division is made, does it remain unchanged, or keep changing all the time? It is hard to come to a universal conclusion that applies in every work team. In most cases, the division is made two weeks or one month after the first payment, and it becomes fixed upon the implementation; but there are quite a few cases in which the first-class workers have been relegated to the lower class due to their slacking in work. This supports the fact that enthusiasm will also be considered as an important factor in addition to physical strength for assessing unskilled coolies. Regarding the standard for deciding wages for workers, the role of the leader is an important factor, and the determination should always be dependent on his judgment.

The categorization of workers varies from group to group, and its significance for each group also differs. We can catch a glimpse of this variation from the numbers of each type of worker in every group. Take the data for one work group as an example. In the first work team, the team leader Pan has two first-class workers and seventeen second-class workers; while in the second work team, the leader Ma has two first-class workers and twelve second-class workers. The categorization of workers in these two teams corresponds to the criteria that I have discussed. In the third work team, under the leadership of Wang, however, there are forty first-class workers and six second-class workers. The ratio between the two types is inverted. The working obligation of this team is drilling, and unlike other drilling teams that assess coolies by their skill of choosing preferred spots and by the direction they take during the drilling process, in this team, it is the cooperation of two or three coolies in the process of operation that determines the condition for ranking the workers. As a result, most coolies can participate in the working process. Therefore, only child and old coolies are considered to be second-class workers. Even within one group, the distinction between the two classes and the significance deriving from this distinction cannot be normalized. With respect to the allocation of real wages corresponding to working days, there is a difference of 10 to 30 *qian* per day per group. This difference even varies between teams in one group. Regarding this point, we now understand that the determination of wages is dependent on the team leader's own preference rather than his respect for fixed rules or standards. With respect to the wage difference between the two classes of workers, we still do not have enough details on whether the difference is kept as constant as 20 *qian* or if it varies among different groups. With respect to the absolute value of the wage, if the wage of the second-class workers in one team is higher than the wage of the first-class workers in another team, in case of other values kept unchanged, as a cumulative effect, workers will move to advantageous positions. The criteria for categorizing workers vary from one team to another. At the same time, because the complexity of workload differs, the internal mobility of workers driven by differences in the absolute value of nominal wage does not take place easily. In most cases in which the team leader decides the amount of wage, even if the leader an arbitrary decision, he always figures it out based on some basic facts, and he makes decisions in such a context that his calculations will not be isolated from other factors.

One thing that must be noted is that the wage is not represented as a fixed amount paid to each worker; rather, it is represented as the daily wage at an average level calculated as the ratio of the everyday output of each team to the attendance of every worker. Each worker's attendance record is usually approved by the team leader as well, and in some instances by the first-class worker. The team leader reports his record to the accountant, based on which the accountant makes his own record. There is a slight difference between the two records.

With respect to payment, as I have mentioned, the group leader receives the total amount from the company, deducts food costs, and passes the remaining amount to each team leader, who is responsible for the payment of wages to coolie workers. Sometimes the team leader relies on the senior coolie, as the person in direct charge of work, for the distribution of wages. There is another instance in which the team leader deducts food costs for his workers himself. In this case, the fees docked for paying means of subsistence become an important source for the team leader's income.

How do those agents, such as group leaders, team leaders, and senior coolies, charge the fees from coolies? Due to its subtlety, this matter is an issue on which we cannot get details. Very few team leaders respond by answering that their boss, the group leader, has never docked an amount from them. In one group, according to the leader of the working team responsible for transporting ore from the mine, the group leader charges 1 *qian* per mining car. In one team at another group, the team leader docks 10 *qian* per coolie per day. One tendency shown is that the amount skimmed off varies from team to team, even within the same group. Coolies under the organization of the team leader will be charged more by the group leader than coolies under the direct organization of the group leader.

Conclusion

The *batou* system is a work-contracting mechanism in China under the condition in which the modern industrial system has not yet established a planned production mechanism, though it has already controlled the means of production.

The two conditions for maintaining the *batou* system are the not-yet-established condition of planned production based on the absence of mechanization, and the presence of backward half-agrarian coolies. The nature of the *batou* system has also been altered as the two conditions changed.

The effect of the *batou* system is represented as project contracting (*sakugyō ukeoi*) based on the supremacy of planned production. However, as the system is gradually limited by social conditions, it undergoes a transition to the effect of work contracting (*rōdō ukeoi*).

In this regard, it is highly possible that the *batou* system would undertake the guidance of everyday life for coolies. For this reason, the education of *batou*, the preparation for life guidance, and the establishment of recruiting mechanisms based on coolies' regional connections must be assured as prerequisite conditions.

The establishment of the modern planned production system is premised on the adoption of mechanization. However, before this takes place, production must rely on an operation command system that is founded on a structure consisting of technicians, team leaders, and coolies.

For this purpose, it is necessary to coordinate team leaders as the underlings of Chinese contractors to recruit coolies. In addition, these leaders must be trained to acquire technical skills and leadership qualities.

It is also necessary to select and train coolies who have the potential to be disciplined, modern workers. In order to achieve this goal, conditions must be created to facilitate discipline through bringing into full play everyday training and creativity. There is a long way to go in reforming the *batou* system.

(Tōkyō: Rōdō Kagaku Kenkyūjo, 1944)

Notes

1 From the founding of Manchukuo, the government imposed labour control to restrict coolie immigration from north China to Manchukuo. This ban was removed in 1938 after the passing of the National Mobilization Law, which allowed enterprises to mobilize workers in a more extensive way. See David Tucker, "Labour Policy and the Construction Industry in Manchukuo: Systems of Recruitment, Management and Control," in *Asian Labour in the Wartime Japanese Empire: Unknown Histories,* ed. Paul Kratoska (London: Routledge, 2002), 25–60.

2 The fact that the wartime expansion of production in heavy industries in imperial Japan reached its zenith around 1942 and 1943 can be inferred from existing data and historiography. After attacking Pearl Harbor in 1941, Japan declared war on the United States, which spurred Japan to gear up production in wartime industries. Take the production of steel as an example. According to the Outline of Resource Mobilization in the Japanese Empire between 1941 and 1945, the amount of steel required peaked in 1943. The high consumption of steel appeared in the period between 1941 and 1942. The supply of steel

relied heavily on colonies within the Sphere of Co-Prosperity; the import of steel from Manchuria reached its apex in 1942.

3 See Sugiyama Mitsunobu, "Civil Society Theory and Wartime Mobilization: On the Intellectual Development of Uchida Yoshihiko," in *Total War and Modernization,* ed. Yasushi Yamanouchi, Victor Koschmann, and Ryuichi Narita (Ithaca, NY: East Asia Program, Cornell University, 1998), 117–36.

4 Descriptions and connotations of "coolies" come from my summary of many studies of their social background in documents and published articles in Manchukuo journals from between 1932 and 1945, such as *Mantetsu Chōsa Getsuhō* (Monthly reports of the South Manchuria Railway Company) and *Manshū Hyōron* (Manchuria forum).

5 E.H. Norman, *Japan's Emergence as a Modern State: Political and Economic Problems of the Meiji Period,* 60th anniversary ed. (1940; Vancouver: UBC Press, 2000), 157.

6 See Wendy Matsumura, *The Limits of Okinawa: Japanese Capitalism, Living Labor, and Theorizations of Community* (Durham, NC: Duke University Press, 2015), ch. 4.

7 See Ken Kawashima, *The Proletarian Gamble: Korean Workers in Interwar Japan* (Durham, NC: Duke University Press, 2009).

8 Nakamura Takatoshi, *Hatō seido no kenkyū* [A study of the *batou* system] (Tōkyō: Bunkyūdō Shoten, 1944).

9 The Marco Polo Bridge Incident on 7 July 1937 marked the beginning of the Anti-Japanese War of Resistance (1937–45).

10 *Petit* commodity production is based on the private ownership of means of production. Political economists contrast it with capitalist commodity production in order to emphasize a teleological and lineal development of social economy in human history.

11 According to Ken Kawashima's research, *hamba* was a basic unit of labour organization in the mining and construction industries. Built like a camp to provide transitory respite, protection, and subsistence, a *hamba* was the site where day workers worked and lived. They paid a fee for using the *hamba* from their wages, which constituted the main source of income for the labour bosses who managed the *hamba*. See Kawashima, *Proletarian Gamble,* 75–76.

12 Johan Gunnar Andersson, a Swedish archaeologist and geologist, served as mining adviser to China's government in the late 1910s.

13 Established in 1935 in Japanese-occupied north China as one of the important conglomerates under the direct control of Japanese government, the Kōchū company developed heavy industries and carried out economic goals for sustaining the control economy under the supervision of Japan.

27 An Anarchist Popular Resistance

The *Awakening* and China's Resistance War at Home and Abroad

MORGAN ROCKS

Founded in 1937, the Chengdu-based journal *Jingzhe* (The Awakening) sought to link China's Anti-Japanese War of Resistance to global anarchist antifascist struggle. Founded by long-time anarchists Lu Jianbo (1904–91), his wife, Deng Tianyu (n.d.), and their colleague, Zhang Lüqian (n.d.), the journal represents a final attempt to push anarchism, which had been overshadowed by the rise of the Kuomintang (KMT) and the Chinese Communist Party (CCP) in the 1920s, as a tool by which to save China.[1] Attempting to address wartime and anarchist agendas, Lu's group filled its pages with articles that joined anarchist revolution to anti-Japanese resistance, offered an anarchist perspective as to why and how the Japanese should be resisted, and linked China's struggles to antifascist resistance in Spain and the rest of the world. The *Awakening* stopped publishing in 1940, but, for a brief moment, it provided an anarchist voice in the war.

The article translated here, "Wuzhengfuzhuyi yu Zhongguo kangzhan" (Anarchism and China's War of Resistance), by Li Min, was published in the *Awakening* in January 1939.[2] In it, Li outlines anarchism's use in China's Anti-Japanese War of Resistance as a means for social revolution, mass participation, and international solidarity. To Li and the *Awakening* group, the war against Japan was not just a conflict between states; it was a chance at a revolution to end state power altogether. In order to do so, anarchists needed to aid and educate the masses so they could resist Japanese imperialists, and afterwards, whoever of the KMT or CCP tried to take charge of the country.[3]

In making this case, Li called for an anarchist-inspired "war of popular resistance" against Japan. Li's arguments for mass participation in a war of popular resistance were not unique. Discussions on "war of popular resistance" and "war of total resistance" had been ongoing in CCP-affiliated journals and newspapers, and the party itself had issued its Ten Guiding Principles (*Shi da gangling*) on the war in August 1937.[4] The *Awakening* group acknowledged this, however, they remained skeptical of the ability of the CCP's Ten Guiding Principles, or even the KMT's Three Principles of the People, to fully mobilize and organize the masses.[5] For Li and the *Awakening* group, the masses ultimately had to lead themselves. They may have shared in the vocabularies of communist and other leftist discourses, but his vision for a war of popular resistance remained true to their anarchist principles.

Furthermore, the extraordinary violence of the Japanese invasion would only be replaced by the everyday violence of the state, so the people needed to arm themselves to ensure their rights in postwar society. While Li recognized that, philosophically, anarchist thought opposed war, given the alternative of Japanese conquest, exceptions had to be made.[6] Li and the *Awakening* group drew their support for an anarchist war of popular resistance from the thought of Errico Malatesta (1853–1932), an influential Italian anarchist who recognized the place of violence in achieving revolution.[7] Li's use of Malatesta's argument, of course, went beyond Malatesta's original intent. Malatesta had famously denounced anarchist participation in the First World War and had characterized war as nothing more than a tool of capitalism and the state.[8] However, for Li and the others at the *Awakening*, Japan's invasion of China was not just an affair between states. It pitted the forces of capitalism against the labouring peoples of China and Japan, threatening any hope for social revolution in China. In this sense, Li's use of Malatesta, though made to fit China's current wartime situation, kept its meaning. For the *Awakening* group, an anarchist war of popular resistance was as much a tool of wartime mobilization as it was a tool to prevent any future Chinese "demon king from ascending the throne and demanding supplication and tribute from the masses."[9]

Resistance in China lay at the forefront of the *Awakening's* agenda, but anarchist internationalism also influenced its message. From the first appearance of Chinese anarchist groups, engaging in international solidarity and revolution claimed equal importance with fomenting revolution within China. This solidarity went beyond translating the writings of European and American anarchists. It included forming personal and working relationships with international anarchists and, in some cases, even participating in international movements or inviting international anarchists to China.[10] By the time of the *Awakening*'s founding, a new international cause came to occupy Chinese anarchist attention: the Spanish Civil War. The prominence and early victories of anarchists in the Spanish Civil War encouraged the remaining anarchists in China. They saw their own country's plight in the Spanish anarchists' struggle against Franco's fascist Falangist party. International antifascist solidarity became a rallying point for Chinese anarchists, and the *Awakening* was an important outpost for this.

For Li Min and the *Awakening* group, Spain provided both aspirational and operative examples for China's own resistance. "Anarchism and China's War of Resistance" explicitly links Chinese anarchist efforts to Spain as well as to the Abyssinian wars against fascist Italy.[11] Lu Jianbo, in an April 1938 article entitled "Kang faxisizhuyi zhi dong xi zhan" (Antifascist wars of resistance, East and West), outlines the similarities in Spanish anarchists' fight against Franco and China's war against Japan. Demanding his comrades' solidarity with the Spanish anarchists, he declares: "We and our Spanish comrades are thoroughly antifascist. As we fight against fascism, we will follow in their successes and learn from their failures."[12] These calls were not just rhetorical. Lu Jianbo and his colleagues attempted to establish a Chengdu-based branch of the Solidaridad Internacional Antifascista. The SIA was an anarchist organization founded in May 1937 in Valencia, Spain, which sought to garner support for the Spanish anarchist cause and to provide aid to global antifascist movements. Soon after, it opened branches across the world, including China. The April 1938 issue of the *Awakening* contained the bylaws and statutes of the organization, contact information, and solicited members and inquiries for the Chinese branch.[13] The importance the *Awakening* placed on the internationalism of China's antifascist struggle served both as a marker of just how connected China's political and social plight was to other parts of the world and as a reminder of the acute conditions China faced against Japan.

The *Awakening* folded in 1940, after four volumes and twenty-two issues. Its readership and effect on any practical anarchist organizing remains unknown and understudied. But, in the group's writings, other sides of the anti-Japanese struggle may be seen. As a whole, the journal sought to revitalize Chinese anarchist practice for a collaborative war effort that included China's various factions and for social revolution. In so doing, it synthesized existing threads of anarchist thought and contemporary discourse and vocabulary used by Chinese leftist intellectuals

27.1 Morgan — "Qian jin, xiongdi!," Ba Jin, "Xibanya de shuguang." *Source:* Sina Collection, http://collection.sina.com.cn.

so as to create a Chinese anarchist plan for a war of popular resistance. At the same time, it continued to connect China's problems to the world's, letting its audience know that China's Anti-Japanese War was both a domestic and international affair.

TRANSLATION

Excerpts from "Anarchism and China's War of Resistance"[14]

LI MIN[15]

Introduction

Wishing to see the advent of an emancipatory communist society, anarchists cannot separate themselves from the struggles of the workers and peasants oppressed, exploited, and enslaved by capitalist society, and they cannot shirk the real battles against authoritarian control in society.

China's present War of Resistance is against the power of Japan's imperialists and capitalists. This war is to destroy the threats to the world and to human peace and freedom that Japanese imperialist and capitalist powers represent. In other words, the Chinese masses, in continuing and safeguarding the strength and successes of Abyssinian and Spanish antifascist efforts, are shedding their former slave status and becoming liberated individuals who oppose Japanese fascist conquest – who oppose Japanese fascist violence!

[The author here cites antifascist struggles in Abyssinia and Spain as bellwethers for Chinese anarchist efforts, with Spain being a prominent example throughout the journal.]

Section 2: Eliminating War through War

In the aftermath of the First World War, there were some 9,879,000 deaths, 6,259,512 heavy casualties, and 14,002,039 minor casualties. Total military costs of the war were $190 billion. Property losses totalled roughly $310 billion. Production losses totalled $47 billion. Relief costs came to around $1.1 billion, with other miscellaneous costs totalling some $160 billion.[16]

These numbers were reached through the flesh and blood of humans. They reminded humanity of the high cost of war, yet in paying such a terrible price, what was achieved? Pay heed to this,[17] as an even more brutal, violent, and bitter Second World War is set to begin.

From the First World War, we can observe the utter failure of disarmament conferences as military spending and expansion has reached epic proportions across the globe. All those contracts for peace have been ripped asunder by fascist nations, and the weak and small peoples[18] are being trampled underfoot by fascists' iron boots.

In such an age pervaded by the scent of sulphur and gunpowder, where the hands of imperialists are stained crimson through their sacrifice of weak and small peoples, and war is a constant possibility, the prospect of peace has reached a nadir.

In such an age, hope for peace can only be guaranteed through war.

As such, every individual should recognize that in this age of fascist and imperialist fanaticism, war is unavoidable. To shout "peace," "justice," and "humanity" at these fascist butchers is simply to demand *laohu kouzhong tao sui gu chi* (broken bones to eat inside a tiger's mouth).[19]

Hence, we must realize that we cannot oppose fascist imperialism through "pacifistic propaganda or movements," and that we must answer war with war. Simply put, as enemies bomb us from the skies, killing us, we must defend ourselves from such bombings, sending a warning to our enemies.

From such a stance it is only natural that we reach this conclusion: we must end war through war.

Errico Malatesta, in *Anarchism's Guiding Principles,* wrote: "It is quite clear that the masses' only hope of liberation lies in resisting violence with violence."[20]

In *Toward Anarchism,* Malatesta has also written:

> There is in every country a government which, with brutal force, imposes its laws on all; it compels all to be subjected to exploitation and to maintain, whether they like it or not, the existing institutions. It forbids the minority groups to actuate their ideas, and prevents the social organizations in general from modifying themselves according to, and with, the modifications of public opinion. The normal peaceful course of evolution is arrested by violence, and thus with violence it is necessary to reopen that course. It is for this reason that we want a violent revolution today; and we shall want it always – so long as man is subject to the imposition of things contrary to his natural desires. Take away the governmental violence and ours would have no reason to exist.[21]

Japanese fascist imperialists have not stopped at using violence to both hinder the advance of peace in Japanese society and oppress the masses of workers and peasants. They have spread their violence to China so as to oppress its society. For us to liberate the Chinese people and aid the Japanese workers and peasants in emancipating themselves, we must engage a twofold path in resisting the Japanese fascist imperialists' war. We must both actively and aggressively engage in war and revolution and utilize war as a tool of self-defence.

To clarify, we have not forgotten the savagery of war and its potential to extinguish human civilization. We have not overlooked war's tragic, inhumane, blood-besotted history of brutality and crime in some sort of reverence. In reality, for the safety, happiness, peace, and freedom of people across the world, it is necessary for us to be armed in self-defence and to "wash blood away with blood."[22]

Everyone knows that animals, in order to protect their own lives, naturally adopt strategies of defence and attack.

Among reptiles, tortoises are known as strict vegetarians. They do not invade or torment other animals, yet they have numerous enemies. In order to protect themselves from the dangers these enemies – buzzards, wild dogs, and others – present, they will hide their entire bodies, from their heads to their tails, inside their shells.

Now, swans are the most inspiring of birds. They are like poems, paintings, or musical notes in harmony, and they are absolute vegetarians. Yet, in order to deal with their shared enemies, they will, with a courage fiercer than that of an eagle snatching away a hatchling, set out to kill a wild dog or break the ribs of a human.

In another example, J.A. Thompson has described how in Florida, an Englishwoman[23] kept a grey parrot. One day, a guest gave the bird some matches. It pecked at the match heads, setting them alight. The parrot never forgot this incident, and never forgave that guest. After a few months, that same guest returned, and the bird ruthlessly bit him.

Learning from the punitive actions taken by tortoises, swans, and parrots in preserving their freedom of existence, we respond to the Japanese fascist imperialists' invasion with war. We attack the attackers and punish the invaders. Moreover, we must enter into a war of resistance if we are to defend ourselves and have revolution.

In truth, we know that should we discuss peace and humanity with the Japanese fascist imperialists, we will only be answered with bombs. A very clear example of this is how a peaceful assembly against the bombing of defenceless cities, held in Paris on 20 July 1938, did not prevent the Japanese from viciously bombing defenceless Chinese cities.[24]

Therefore, we anarchists, in following the principle of returning violence upon the violent, must engage in armed self-defence and a war for peace in answering the Japanese fascist imperialist invasion. We agree that we will end war through war!

Section 3: Strengthening the Organization of Workers and Peasants

Even though the banner of the Republic of China has been hanging for twenty-seven years, none of the individuals involved in its government came to their post through merit. Instead, they are the leftover dregs of feudalism. Not one of these individuals can be called a true representative of the Chinese citizenry.

The constitution outlines civilized regulations on gender equality, people's right to publicly assemble and form associations, and freedom of speech. However, in reality, women are still kept in the kitchen tied to men, with no freedom to have public lives, and all business, scholarly, and artistic organizations discriminate against women, refusing their participation. In terms of freedoms of assembly, association, and speech, they are not only restricted under security laws, they are also thoroughly squeezed in Communist-controlled and special administrative regions. Such permissive freedom is as worthless as KMT-issued money![25]

This situation leads some to remark that the Chinese republic is, in fact, really the Chinese Republic of Officials. After China's ordinary citizens overthrew the Manchu Qing [dynasty] in revolution, their social status has not risen.[26] In turn, they have become a throng of "Adou"-type characters.[27]

What people in China have felt, body and soul, over the past twenty-seven years is not [just][28] famine, death, and homelessness brought about by civil war, but is the loss of home and livelihood, and the proliferation of banditry and thievery, and begging caused by foreign pressure.

China's struggling and helpless masses, in this way, daily grow in number, while any sense of independence and autonomy slip away. Of its four hundred million people, only 5 percent can afford to live in luxury apartments, wear fine clothes, and eat fancy foods. The other 95 percent wear tattered rags, starve, and take shelter in shacks, struggling through the elements. Living through such extremes of suffering, nothing remains of their will to live.

Chinese society is either mired in mirth or buried in tragedy. It truly is either heaven or hell.

As the present social situation is so horrible, it only further immiserates, numbs, and weakens the people, transforming them into perfect, tame little lambs.

However, during the May Fourth and May Thirtieth Movements, the Chinese masses began to wake up to life's oppressions, long for freedom, understand society's gradations, and to know life is struggle, and that to give in is death.[29] They have gone from being meek little lambs to violently fierce tigers, determinedly seeking to beat away those enemies who enslaved, oppressed, and exploited them.

Further, within China, they oppose feudal warlords and the false flags of international capitalists. They are forming numerous and different revolutionary groups and holding demonstrations and strikes.

Yet, as the conditions the people have endured are so terrible, and the suppression they've felt under the guns of the military, police, and laws of the feudal warlords, their organizing is incomplete, and their arming for self-defence is not enough. Under the guns and cannons of cooperating imperialists and feudal warlords, swords and knives invariably give way.

The May Fourth and May Thirtieth Movements' opposition to imperialists and feudal warlords has failed. But failure is the mother of success!

The Chinese masses, especially the proletarian workers and peasants, have twice experienced the bloody lessons of failed revolution. This and their previous hardships have only made the need for revolution more urgent. They recognize that feudal warlords and imperialists are of the same ilk, and they fervently desire the quick outbreak of social revolution in China.

Living under China's present man-eating political and economic conditions, though, has limited their political and economic freedoms. Working to feed themselves, they work days, nights, months, and years with no time to train themselves, organize themselves, or form revolutionary groups. The strong among them, those who cannot stand life's oppressions, rush into danger and head to Mount Liang to begin a life of looting.[30] As for the weak, they float around begging and end their lives dying in ditches and along the roads. As such, China's masses can only wait for the times to change and the chance for China's social transformation to present itself.

The chance inherent in 9/18, 1/28, 7/7, and 8/13 has arrived.[31] China's masses have all gathered under the banner of opposition to Japanese fascist imperialist invasion. They demand a war of resistance! Unanimously, they prepare their weapons to exact long-held blood debts from their enemies, and are truly prepared to fight on the front lines of the war of resistance.

At the same time, we must not be afraid to recognize that the abilities of the Chinese masses to engage in a resistance war are not yet fully formed or solidified. Any talk of their abilities right now is optimistic. There has been no real or solid organization or arming of the masses for a war of resistance.

We anarchists believe that any revolutionary work that departs from the masses, especially the proletarian worker and peasant masses, will not be successful. Conversely, should workers, peasants, and the rest of the masses not be adequately organized for revolution – here we mean being armed for self-defence and determined to carry out their revolutionary tasks – revolution will not be successful.

Hence, we anarchists down to the last individual must throw our physical efforts into going to the worker and peasant masses, and with our comrades there, help strengthen their revolutionary groups and solidify their organizations. This is our primary task.

We know that relying only on propaganda to establish an anarcho-communist society is not enough. We must rely both on anarcho-communists from all kinds of movements and on the struggles of the broader worker and peasant masses if we want to transform society.

Malatesta, in *Anarchism's Guiding Principles,* states:

> As we oppose all forms of government, and demand integral liberty, we should aid any struggle for partial liberation. I believe that it is through struggle that we learn of struggle [...]. We must stand with the masses, and we must be able to guide them to demand their complete freedom. Then, from the sidelines, we will help them in planning to achieve their goals. We must demonstrate our most sincere strength to earn their trust. Whatever their goal may be, should they truly desire it, they must obtain it through their own means. Once they believe, then they will have power, and having power, they will stand up to their detested and despised enemies.[32]

In the short piece "Our Principles," Malatesta again stated:

> For this, we must spread our propaganda among the masses and make sure that they hear our voice. In every worker's struggle, in every movement held by the masses, we should propagate our actions. No matter the time or place, we must help all those who have suffered become conscious of their sacrifices, inequities, and ignorance, and from there appeal to their interests so that they may place faith in their own strength and rise up with their fellow sufferers and comrades to take action themselves.[33]

In *Towards Anarchism,* Malatesta adds this: "From this we can see that, to arrive at Anarchism, material force is not the only thing to make a revolution; it is essential that the workers, grouped according to the various branches of production, place themselves in a position that will ensure the proper functioning of their social life – without the aid or need of capitalists or governments."[34]

China's current War of Resistance has already entered its fourth phase. During this time, our greatest lesson has been "mobilizing the masses," which until now has been more slogan than actuality. China's past failures in this war have come from the lack of solid organizing by the masses behind the battle lines. Yet news from occupied areas tells us that the masses currently under the iron boot of the Japanese fascist imperialists have already organized themselves to oppose the Japanese fascist imperialist war of conquest. Moreover, in those areas not yet occupied, people across all levels of society are taking up arms and organizing themselves so as to militarily resist the Japanese fascist imperialists' thievery and cruelty!

We anarcho-communists, in order to help the masses rationalize their actions so as to reach a true free and liberated existence, must join them in the War of Resistance. We must never separate ourselves from the masses. Our task in this war is to not merely resist the Japanese fascist imperialists' invasion, but also to guarantee that the political and economic liberties gained through the masses' sacrifices do not accrue to some "privileged class" or are stolen away by bandits. So, from the masses' own struggles, we shall solidify and strengthen their organization so that they may resist all power and brutality!

To strengthen the organization of the people's power so that they may undertake the arduous work of revolution, this is the great task we anarcho-communists set for ourselves in this war of resistance!

Notes

1 Jiang Jun, "Lu Jianbo xiansheng zaonian de wuzhengfuzhuyi xuanchuan huodong jishi" [An account of Mr. Lu Jianbo's early anarchist propaganda activities], in *Wuzhengfuzhuyi sixiang ziliao xuan* [A selection of materials on anarchist thought], ed. Ge Mouchun, Jiang Jun, and Li Xingyi (Beijing: Beijing daxue chubanshe, 1984), 1019–20.

2 Li Min, "Wuzhengfuzhuyi yu Zhongguo kangzhan" [Anarchism and China's War of Resistance], in ibid., 889–96. This article originally appeared in *Jingzhe* [The awakening] 3, 5 (1939). Li Min could possibly be one of Lu Jianbo's pen names. In the journal, he used at least three: Wu Yun, Tian Shenyu, and Da Ji (see n15 for further discussion). Until this question is resolved, I will treat Lu Jianbo and Li Min as separate individuals. *Jingzhe* was also the name of a Guangzhou-based journal in the 1930s. The earlier journal was printed in Chengdu and operated by Lu Jianbo and Zhang Lüqian; see Ge Mouchun, Jiang Jun, and Li Xingyi, *Wuzhengfuzhuyi*, 1020–21, for further details.

3 Ibid., 896.

4 The Ten Guiding Principles came from the 22–25 August 1937 Luochuan Conference, and would serve as a blueprint for how the CCP believed total war of resistance against the Japanese should be fought. The document advocated the total mobilization of China's military resources and its populace for the war effort. In addition, it called for political reform, directing economic production to produce materiel for the war, eliminating traitors, implementing anti-Japanese propaganda in school curricula, and improving the daily lives of the people.

5 Wu Yun, "Kangzhan zhu fangmian" [Aspects of the Resistance War], in Ge Mouchun, Jiang Jun, and Li Xingyi, *Wuzhengfuzhuyi*, 880. This article originally appeared in *Jingzhe* 2, 4 (1938), 2–7.

6 Li Min, "Wuzhengfuzhuyi yu Zhongguo kangzhan," 891.

7 Ibid.

8 Errico Malatesta, "Anarchists Have Forgotten Their Principles," *Anarchist Library*, https://theanarchistlibrary.org/library/errico-malatesta-anarchists-the-war-and-their-principles. Originally published 1914.

9 Yin Lizhi, "Yi zhanzhang qu fandui zhanzheng" [Opposing war through war], in Ge Mouchun, Jiang Jun, and Li Xingyi, *Wuzhengfuzhuyi*, 878. This article originally appeared in *Jingzhe* 2, 1 (1937), 1–2.

10 Lu Jianbo, for example, wrote to Emma Goldman in France and collaborated with Ray Jones, an immigrant Chinese anarchist living in San Francisco. After the KMT White Terror in 1927, Jacques Reclus, a French anarchist who taught at Labour University, helped Lu to safety after it became apparent KMT forces were targeting him. In late 1926, anarchists in China even floated the idea of forming an East Asian Anarchist League. The proposed organization would join together anarchists from China, Korea, Japan, and other Asian countries with the aim of fighting colonialism and nationalism. See Liu Xu, "Zhuzhang zuzhi dongYa wuzhengfuzhuyizhe dalianmeng" [On organizing an East Asian Anarchist League], in Ge Mouchun, Jiang Jun, and Li Xingyi, *Wuzhengfuzhuyi,* 716–19.

11 Li Min, "Wuzhengfuzhuyi yu Zhongguo kangzhan," 889.

12 Wu Yun, "Kang faxisizhuyi zhi dong xi zhan" [Antifascist wars of resistance, East and West], *Jingzhe* 2, 5 (1938): 8.

13 Tian Shen, "Guoji kang faxisi huzhu hui" [International antifascist solidarity], *Jingzhe* 2, 5 (1938): 20–23. Tian Shen seems to be an abbreviation of one of Lu Jianbo's pen names, Tian Shenyu.

14 *Jingzhe* 3, 5 (January 1939). The text used in this translation comes from the transcribed version collected in Ge Mouchun, Jiang Jun, and Li Xingyi, *Wuzhengfuzhuyi.*

15 Li Min could be a pseudonym, possibly of Lu Jianbo or others involved in the magazine. In the third and fourth volumes of *Jingzhe,* four articles under this name appeared. Three of these articles, including the one translated here, argue for an anarchist line on the war against Japan. The other is on the duplicity of the Soviet Union's 1939 Non-Aggression Pact with Germany. In terms of tone, rhetoric, and the prominent place of Malatesta's thought, these articles share similarities with those written under Lu Jianbo's more established pen names. However, there is, as of yet, no clear evidence linking the two. Further, the byline Li Min appeared frequently in the journal *Shi yu chao* (Time and tide) on translations of Japanese articles on the war. Around twenty-one articles under the name Li Min appeared in *Shi yu chao* in 1938–39, but after 1940, articles under this name are scarce.

16 The author does not provide a source for these statistics, but the total deaths and casualties are in line with current estimates.

17 Here the phrase *zhuyi* (ideology) is used, instead of its homonym "to pay heed."

18 *Ruoxiao minzu,* here translated as "weak and small peoples," was a common term during this period. It was used to denote nationalities and peoples labelled "backwards" and oppressed by Western and Japanese-led imperialism.

19 This phrase seems to be a play on a riddle, most likely the phrase *laoshu zuili taosui gu moxiang,* which is used to describe an impossible situation.

20 Errico Malatesta was an Italian anarchist. He spent much of life outside Italy, travelling in Europe and the United States, where he interacted with immigrant anarchist movements. He edited a number of radical journals and had quite a following whenever he gave public speeches. As an anarchist, Malatesta supported the use of violence only in response to state oppression, or to end state repression. He was adamant about the need for the lower classes to organize and lead themselves to revolution, and he believed that revolution was a gradual process, with numerous revolutions coming before anything resembling anarchist society came to pass. The quotation here is taken from a series of speeches he made in July 1920 during a conference in Bologna that established the Italian Anarchist Union. The *Awakening* group obtained a transcript of the speeches, which were translated and published in English in *Man!* 2, 8 (1934). *Man!* was a San Francisco–based anarchist journal edited by Marcus Graham (1893–1985) that had close ties to the Bay Area Italian anarchist community. This quotation appears on p. 25 of the Chinese

translation, "Wuzhengfu gongchan zhuyi gangling" [Principles of anarcho-communism], *Jingzhe* 2, 4 (1938): 21–34.

21 This quotation can be found on pp. 17–18 of the translation by Chun Fei, "Zouxiang an'naqi" [Towards anarchism], *Jingzhe* 2, 5 (1938): 16–20. This Chinese translation, along with a companion piece on Fascism and a translator's introduction, were taken from French versions published in *Le Reveil* 978 (24 July 1937). *Le Reveil* and its Italian sister paper, *Il Risveglio,* were edited by Luigi Bertoni (1872–1947) and disseminated from Geneva, Switzerland. The English translation used here follows Malatesta, *Towards Anarchism,* https://theanarchistlibrary.org/library/errico-malatesta-towards-anarchism, which is taken from a translation that first appeared in *Man!*

22 This phrase comes from the *Jiu Tangshu* (Old book of Tang), *Yuan Xiu zhuan* [Yuan Xiu chapter], vol. 127, Biographies 77. The original text is *ru guo yi sha tu dong deng, wu you sha ru, you yi xue xi xue, wu sheng shen er.* (Your state has already killed Tu Dong and others. Were I to kill you, it would be to wash blood away with blood. It would merely pollute matters a great deal further.)

23 It is not entirely clear to whom the author is referring.

24 Existing records of this rally appear to be sparse. Since the author does not mention how he learned of it, it is to be assumed that the rally was reported either in the overseas Chinese language press or through foreign wire services.

25 The then-current legal tender issued by the KMT. The KMT government took China off the silver standard in 1934 and thereafter printed money by fiat. During the Anti-Japanese Resistance War and 1946–49 Civil War, the KMT printed extraordinary amounts of paper money to cover wartime costs, leading to severe hyperinflation.

26 Such critiques of developments since the 1911 Revolution were common across the political spectrum.

27 "Adou" refers to the Three Kingdoms ruler Liu Shan. Used as a term of disparagement, "Adou" means an incompetent, incapable individual.

28 There seem to be some missing characters in the transcription.

29 The metaphor of China awakening from slumber was widespread in intellectual discourse at the time. An authoritative account of this metaphor can be found in John Fitzgerald, *Awakening China: Politics, Culture, and Class in the Nationalist Revolution* (Stanford, CA: Stanford University Press, 1996).

30 Mount Liang is the protagonists' stronghold in the well-known classical novel *The Water Margin.*

31 These dates refer to important events in the Sino-Japanese War: 9/18, of course, refers to the Mukden Incident of 1931; 1/28 refers to the Japanese attack on Shanghai in 1932; 7/7 refers to the 7 July 1937 Marco Polo Bridge Incident, largely seen as the point when full-scale war erupted; 8/13 is the Japanese invasion of Shanghai in 1937.

32 Malatesta, "Wuzhengfu gongchan zhuyi gangling," 32. The order of the text differs between the *Jingzhe* translation and the quotation here.

33 The Chinese title used here is "Women de gangling" (Our principles), and this piece seems to be a separate text from the previously cited two. It should also be noted that the July 1938 edition of *Jingzhe* included advertisements for the group's translations of Malatesta's writings. The article cited here could be in the advertised collection, or it could have come from other existing Chinese translations of Malatesta's work.

34 Malatesta, "Zouxiang an'naqi," 19. See n21.

28 Resolutions on Preventing *Hanjian* Activities and Espionage

YUN XIA

The Chinese Nationalist government issued the "Resolutions on Preventing *Hanjian* Activities and Espionage" (hereafter, the Resolutions) in 1939, during the stalemate stage of China's War of Resistance against Japan (1937–45). The Resolutions reveal important features of law-making in wartime China that in an overly broad fashion penalized transgressions against political morality upheld by the resistance state and patriotic groups. This document shows how the criminal categories of *Hanjian* – traitors to the Han (Chinese) – and "spy" could be easily applied to various groups of social misfits, who were then left to the judgment of local communities. The Resolutions also demonstrate a populist dimension of the War of Resistance, as the Nationalist state utilized existing local networks and turned civilians into proxies for law enforcement and counterespionage agents.

Understanding the term *Hanjian* is vital for gauging the political and legal significance of this document. Often translated as "collaborator" or "traitor," *Hanjian* is a powerful epithet with connotations that neither translation fully conveys. The character *Han* in *Hanjian* refers to people of Han ethnicity, the earliest members and the majority of the Chinese population. The term thus connotes a Han ethnocentrism in the Chinese national identity, which gained much of its vitality in the struggles against the Manchu rulers and foreign imperialism. *Jian* in the traditional Chinese lexicon means "illicit sex" as a criminal category, "treacherous" or "cunning" as an adjective, and "to trespass" as a verb.[1] The modern character inherits all these pejorative connotations, and refers to a range of illicit sexual conduct and criminal activities including espionage.[2] Implied in *Hanjian,* therefore, is a deep contempt toward Han

Chinese who betray the collective well-being of the national/ethnic community through working with an external enemy for personal gain.

The term *Hanjian* gained its full dynamism during China's War of Resistance, as a catchword in popular patriotic discourse and in law. Japan had been encroaching on Chinese territory for decades before 1931, and by 1937 had established several local collaborationist regimes. Condemnation of, and pre-emptive attacks on, "*Hanjian* behaviours" thus became one of the most vocal parts of the national salvation movement.[3] In August 1937, one month after the war broke out in full scale, the Nationalist government stipulated "Regulations on Punishing *Hanjian*." These regulations, together with their multiple revisions and amendments made during wartime, including the Resolutions, defined the crime of *Hanjian* through an extensive list of activities and provided guidelines for their punishment. Considering the exigency of the wartime situation and its lack of full judicial capacity, the Nationalist government allowed extralegal arrests and execution of *Hanjian* by its military and intelligence, and by grassroots patriotic groups.[4]

The anti-*Hanjian* laws were so widely circulated and celebrated by the media that they functioned as law and propaganda in one. Jurists annotated such laws and regulations for clarification and for their easy dissemination.[5] Complementing these legal texts was a genre of literature that championed the eradication of *Hanjian: chujian wenxue* (literally, "weeding-out traitors literature"). Some publications of this category instructed the common people step by step on how to identify *Hanjian* among themselves and what actions to take against them. Others cheered on the arrests and execution of *Hanjian* in various war zones.[6] In general, such literature condemned *Hanjian* both as individuals and figuratively as rotten parts of Chinese culture and society that needed to be exorcized.

The Resolutions, in particular, addressed both the necessity and methods of catching *Hanjian* during the stalemate stage. By 1939, the Nationalist government had lost its capital and key cities along with the most developed areas in China to the Japanese Imperial Army. Chiang Kai-shek (1887–1975), head of the Nationalist government and party, was commanding China's resistance efforts from the remote inland city of Chongqing. Meanwhile, for the Japanese, a quick conquest of China as originally planned seemed impossible, so they resorted to a strategy of "using the Chinese to rule Chinese." At the national and local levels, the Japanese enticed or coerced numerous members of the Chinese elite into collaborationist regimes, which were all labelled *Hanjian* by the Nationalist state. Espionage was a type of *Hanjian* behaviour that was deemed most detrimental to national security. Indeed, the Japanese Imperial Army recruited Chinese from all social strata to spy on or sabotage the resistance forces. Those executed as *Hanjian* spies ranged from top officials in the Nationalist government to the unemployed who ran small errands for the Japanese on a temporary basis for survival.[7]

Mindful of Japan's wartime strategy and the plight of ordinary people in occupied regions, the Nationalist government took pre-emptive measures against those who were likely to become *Hanjian*. The Resolutions targeted social groups that the state had always treated with suspicion because of their particular employment profiles, appearances, behaviours, familial structure, or social interactions. The vague description of some of these groups, such as "those who are generally ill-behaved," "those who are unemployed yet often appear busy," "those who frequently interact with foreigners," and "all other individuals who do not appear normal," rendered a significant portion of the population "potential *Hanjian*" in the eyes of the state.[8]

The Resolutions reflected long-held stereotypes and prejudices in Chinese society. Among the places deemed at risk of penetration by *Hanjian* and spies were main transportation routes, docks, temples, stations, theatres, hotels, and "suspicious news agencies." Many such places were gathering places and temporary homes for unsettled members of the population: travellers, itinerant monks, boatmen, performers, and so forth, who had always been outside the effective reach of "mutual surveillance units" (*baojia*). This floating population kept increasing due to natural and manmade disasters that had plagued China since the late nineteenth century, including war-induced poverty and dislocation. Consequently, to sift out the traitorous elements among the socially marginalized groups became a daunting task.

Chiang Kai-shek, the national leader, considered the people and local militia key to catching enemies from within and defending the nation.[9] The Resolutions elaborated on Chiang's call with specific instructions. Local police, volunteer groups, village heads, and common villagers were required to identify individuals and activities that appeared suspicious and to patrol "high-risk locations." Once spotted, such individuals would be followed, questioned, and possibly reported to the local authorities.

To gauge the implementation of the Resolutions at the national level is impossible, but wartime journalism and case studies do show an expansive web for catching *Hanjian*. Resistance news agencies reported on numerous incidents of *Hanjian* spies caught by local militia and patriotic citizens.[10] In many localities, the *baojia* system that the Nationalist government had constructed for eliminating "Communist bandits" was fortified for catching *Hanjian* and spies. In August 1939, for instance, the Jiangxi provincial government mobilized local people into squads with various functions, among which was a "self-defence squad" (*ziweidui*) with the mission of destroying *Hanjian* and spy networks.[11] Wanzai county, in particular, followed the Resolutions diligently. The county government updated household registration and maps of its towns to reinforce the *baojia* system and boost local defence. Heads of the *baojia* system were to take charge of the *Hanjian*-elimination work at the village level. The county government also paid special attention to those who lived on boats, in temples, and in other "high-risk locations."[12]

The Resolutions issued by the Nationalist government had national significance despite the government's curtailed jurisdiction. As Chiang Kai-shek's wartime ally against the Japanese, the Chinese Communist Party (CCP) carried out campaigns against *Hanjian* in areas under its control following the Nationalist guidelines. The Shanxi-Hebei-Shandong-Henan base area, for instance, reprinted the Nationalist army's *Fangdie jiaoling* (Instructions on preventing spy activities) to prevent the infiltration of *Hanjian*.[13]

The Resolutions reflect what the Nationalist government and its allies sought to achieve through the War of Resistance and what they considered key to their victory. The Resolutions were issued by the Nationalist Ministry of Internal Affairs, rather than by a legislative or judicial branch. Similarly, the CCP's Central Office of Social Affairs (*Gongchandang zhongyang shehuibu*) was in charge of campaigns against *Hanjian* and spies.[14] For both parties, campaigns against *Hanjian* also served to purify their own organizations and the nation's people. An inherent paradox of the Resolutions, however, was that the suspicion of *Hanjian* being ubiquitous contradicted the myth that the Chinese majority was on the resistance side.

— TRANSLATION —

The Resolutions on Preventing *Hanjian* Activities and Espionage (1939)[15]

Article I With the purpose of preventing *Hanjian* activities and espionage, these resolutions are drafted and implemented for safeguarding our nation.

Article II Local law enforcement is responsible for preventing *Hanjian* and spies from sabotaging resistance efforts. In counties and villages without a standing police force, heads of villages and mutual surveillance units (*baojia*) will take charge.

Article III All people of the Chinese nation, regardless of age and gender, are responsible for investigating and exposing *Hanjian* and spies.

Article IV Localities are allowed to organize voluntary groups and police to supervise, command, and facilitate the surveillance against *Hanjian* and spies. The structure of such groups, as well as the training and management of their members, shall be approved by local governments at different levels and reported to the Ministry of Internal Affairs.

Article V All those who are engaged in the prevention of *Hanjian* and spy activities shall, under all circumstances, obey the offices in charge and follow orders strictly.

Article VI To prevent *Hanjian* activity and espionage, special attention will be paid to the following groups and activities:

A. Suspicious groups and individuals:

1 Those who are generally ill-behaved
2 Those who have no regular job and frequently take part in social gatherings
3 Those who are unemployed yet are often quite occupied
4 Those who are without jobs or property yet are living comfortable lives
5 Those who are employed yet are more engaged in activities that few know about

6 Those who have been poor yet suddenly make a fortune
7 Those whose household profiles are unclear
8 Those who have suspicious visitors
9 Those who interact with individuals with complicated backgrounds
10 Those who have an inconsistent style of dressing or carry particular marks
11 Those who overdress for their activities and overspend for their social status
12 Those who seem anxious or disturbed in their expressions and speech
13 Travellers or visitors with suspicious backgrounds
14 Travellers with abnormal luggage
15 Those who come out in dark night or early morning to meet with others in public places
16 Pedestrians with faces covered by hats or sunglasses
17 Pedestrians who often look back to see if they are followed
18 Pedestrians who appear to be in a panic
19 Monks, beggars, rickshaw pullers, and peddlers who do not fit into their respective groups
20 Those who suddenly have an increasing quantity of telegraphs or correspondence
21 Those whose words are unpatriotic or sympathetic to the enemy
22 Those who suddenly bequeath gifts or money to people who are not their close acquaintances
23 Those who are dressed in the Chinese way but do not seem Chinese in their speech, habits, or behaviours
24 Those who frequently interact with foreigners
25 Nationals of the enemy state
26 All other individuals who do not appear normal.

B. Suspicious activities:

1 Holding gatherings without approval by the government or without state surveillance

2 Hosting weddings, funerals, or birthday banquets that are of an unusual format
3 Intentionally leaking confidential information of political or military importance
4 Spying on national defence mechanisms or plans for the enemy
5 Colluding with the enemy
6 Being used by the enemy
7 Disturbing the social order and provoking panic
8 Sabotaging the financial order
9 Stirring up student protests
10 Stirring up strikes
11 Damaging important transportation lines or infrastructure of other types
12 Taking photos or making drawings of government or military headquarters, strategic regions, roads, bridges, and other strategic points without permission
13 Other suspicious activities.

C. High-risk locations:

1 Train stations, bus stations, and airports
2 Docks, ports, and places along the coasts or riverbanks where people can easily get on or get off
3 Entrances and exits of cities and artery roads
4 Parks and libraries
5 Theatres and other public entertainment centres
6 Hotels, clubs, dormitories, youth associations, hospitals, and factories
7 Places where poor people and refugees gather
8 Suspicious residences, stores, and houses
9 Suspicious news agencies, post offices, and other social organizations
10 Offices and schools with members of mixed backgrounds
11 Temples and monasteries
12 Places where nationals of the enemy nation cohabit or associate
13 Other places with suspicious visitors or layouts.

Article VII	Constant attention and caution should be exercised toward individuals, activities, and places listed in Article VI.
Article VIII	Suspicious individuals shall be followed and questioned. Those who seem particularly dangerous must be arrested and taken to offices in charge of local security.
Article IX	Local residents who are informed of *Hanjian* activities and espionage should immediately report to the offices in charge.
Article X	Responsible authorities should immediately and secretly carry out investigations and interrogations when a *Hanjian* or spy case is brought in. Those who are innocent should be set free. Those who are guilty should be taken to the local garrison headquarters.
Article XI	Local governments should keep clear household records at a time of emergency. Changes to household numbers should be reported to the local police in a timely manner. Withholding such information is not allowed.
Article XII	Local stores, schools, office buildings, hotels, clubs, public residences, youth clubs, hospitals, factories, social organizations, theatres, teahouses, restaurants, brothels, temples, stations, docks, and other places are not allowed to accommodate suspicious-looking strangers. Those who break this rule will be punished severely. If those sheltered turn out to be *Hanjian* or spies after investigation, the hosts will be charged with the same offence.
Article XIII	Local law enforcement should pay close attention to suspicious households and be ready to investigate at any time.
Article XIV	Local law enforcement should work with village heads to identify unemployed wanderers, keep a registry, and help them get settled and get employed, so that they will not be used by the enemy. Wanderers who do not comply or do not behave should be monitored or detained for penal labour, depending on how potentially dangerous they are.
Article XV	Offices in charge should reward those who help discover or investigate *Hanjian* or spy cases.
Article XVI	Hoaxing and extortion in the name of preventing *Hanjian* and spy activities are strictly forbidden. Those who frame others will be punished according to the laws.
Article XVII	Anyone who clandestinely colludes with the enemy, *Hanjian,* spies, or bandits will be severely punished.

Article XVIII	Local governments and offices in charge shall draft specific policies regarding the prevention of *Hanjian* and spy activities, and rewarding informants. Such policies shall be kept on file by the Ministry of Internal Affairs.
Article XIX	*Hanjian* and spy cases processed by the local governments and garrison headquarters shall be reported to their superiors in a timely manner, so that these cases will reach the Military Council and the Ministry of Internal Affairs for approval.

Notes

Acknowledgment | The translation of "Resolutions on Preventing *Hanjian* Activities and Espionage" in this chapter originally appeared in Yun Xia, *Down with Traitors: Justice and Nationalism in Wartime China* (Seattle: University of Washington Press, 2017). Reprinted with permission from the University of Washington Press.

1 See Zhang Yushu, *Kangxi zidian* [Kangxi dictionary] (reprint; Beijing: Zhonghua shuju, 1958), 255, 260.

2 For discussion of the evolution of the term *Hanjian*, see Yun Xia, *Down with Traitors: Justice and Nationalism in Wartime China* (Seattle: University of Washington Press, 2017), 14–22.

3 Trading Japanese products, for instance, was considered "*Hanjian* behaviour." Following the Shanghai Incident in 1932, the Shanghai Coal Association received a letter from patriotic citizens that warned against continuing to deal in Japanese coal. Ibid., 57–58.

4 Ibid., ch. 2.

5 See, for instance, Qian Qinglian, *Chengzhi Hanjian fa* [Laws and regulations targeting *Hanjian*] (Nanjing: Zhengzhong shuju, 1941).

6 See, for instance, Yi Zhenhua, *Zenyang qingchu Hanjian* [How to eradicate *Hanjian*] (Shanghai: Shenghuo shudian, n.d.); Bing Ying, *Hanjian xianxingji* [Exposure and elimination of *Hanjian*] (Xi'an: Zhanshi chubanshe, n.d.).

7 See, for instance, the case of Huang Jun, secretary of the Confidential Affairs Office in the Nationalist government. Xia, *Down with Traitors*, 25–26.

8 The Resolutions, Article VI.

9 Yang Ji'an, *Minguo shiqi Wanzai xian jiceng zhengquan jianshe* [A study of local state-building in Wanzai, Jiangxi, during the republic] (Beijing: Zhongguo shehui kexue chubanshe, 2014), 83.

10 See Bing Ying, *Hanjian xianxingji*.

11 See, for instance, Yang Ji'an, "Minguo shiqi xianggan bianjie baojia zhidu de shishi jiqi xiaoneng: Yi Jiangxi Wanzai xian wei ge'an" [A case study of the *baojia* system in Wanzai, Jiangxian during the Republican era], *Jinggangshan daxue xuebao* [Jinggangshan University journal] 9 (2012): 11–15.

12 Ibid.

13 Ouyang Hua, *Kangzhan shiqi Shaan-Gan-Ning bianqu chujian fante fazhi yanjiu* [A study of the laws against *Hanjian* spies in the Shaan-Gan-Ning base area] (Beijing: Zhonghua zhengfa daxue chubanshe, 2013), 214.

14 Ibid.

15 Qian, *Chengzhi Hanjian fa*, 74–79.

29 Kishida Kunio and the Problems of Culture

TIMOTHY ILES

It is a superficial truism that the Meiji era brought sweeping changes to all aspects of Japanese life, but it nonetheless remains true. One of the most significant of these changes was war: for the first time in over 250 years, Japan was embroiled in violent conflict not only internally but internationally as well, as it embarked on a program of imperial expansion. This expansion stretched over four decades and came to an abrupt end in 1945 with Japan's surrender following the atomic bombings of Hiroshima and Nagasaki, but the effects of that period of imperialism still exist in Japan today. Indeed, Japanese imperialism has not ended but rather shifted away from the "hard power" imperialism of invasion and colonialism to the "soft power" imperialism of cultural exportation. This shift points to an enduring question from the first half of the twentieth century that continues to resonate around the problem of culture and its exportation. In the relationship between citizenry and nation, which is to serve the other? This question was addressed by Kishida Kunio (1890–1954) in a series of articles and lectures during the Shōwa period. His primary answer is that the citizenry exists to uphold and fulfill the aims of the nation, through focused and coordinated cultural activity.

Kishida Kunio was a product of Japan's modernization. Born in 1890 to a military family, he entered the Tokyo Imperial University at the age of twenty-six to study French literature. Soon attracted to the theatre, he became a playwright and theatre critic and was influential in the Shingeki (New Theatre) movement that brought Western-styled drama to Japan. Shingeki focused on issues of daily life and the tensions therein between the demands of social responsibility on the one hand, and individual choice and liberty on the other. This central issue of responsibility also runs through the social commentaries that Kishida wrote in the late 1930s and 1940s, while he was associated with the Taisei Yokusankai (Imperial Rule Assistance Association, 1940–45). This organization had as its mandate the mobilization of the citizenry to support the colonial aspirations of the Japanese government. Part of its operations, under the supervision of the Cultural Division, included the coordination of citizens' movements, about which Kishida often wrote.

Although Kishida was writing primarily for a Japanese audience, expressing an official view towards policy on the home islands to encourage and support the imperial project abroad, by 1942 the conception of what constituted "Japan" had grown to include significant territory overseas. Indeed, the Greater East Asia Co-Prosperity Sphere may be considered nothing more than a euphemism for "Japan-beyond-Japan," that is, for a Japan whose territory stretched from the home islands to Southeast Asia, and whose culture, despite the existence of diverse ethnicities, languages, histories, and cultural practices among the peoples living in those territories, was essentially "Japanese."

The Japanese state of Manchukuo serves as a good model for this way of thinking about "Japan beyond Japan," with a citizenry that was to be "Japanese," even while ethnically diverse. International observers during the 1930s and early 1940s noted the extensive investments in infrastructure (especially in rail lines to facilitate the transportation of goods) made by Japanese concerns, while simultaneously acknowledging the extensive control the Japanese government exercised over Manchukuo. Indeed, a contemporary assessment is blunt: "Manchukuo's vaunted independence exists only in the imagination of Japanese propagandists. As at present constituted, the Manchukuo 'government' amounts to little more than a polite fiction invented to obscure the fact that Japan has gone in for imperialism in a big way."[1]

This imperialism involved not only the acquisition of territory and natural resources but also the spread of Japanese colonists of a variety of types. "Between 1932 and 1935 only a few thousand colonists came, but from 1935 on their numbers grew every year so that by 1945 at least 270,000 Japanese colonists were living in Manchuria," as Ronald Suleski notes.[2] The Japanese colonial project brought Japanese farmers, industrialists, and army members from Japan, but also young people – boys often below the age of eighteen – as part of the Youth Corps:

> All of the publicity surrounding the Youth Corps emphasised the positive role it was to play in regard to the Chinese who lived in

> Manchukuo. Based on the slogan, "Harmony between the Japanese and Chinese Peoples" (*minzoku kyōwa*), the boys were supposed to cooperate with the Chinese peasants to increase agricultural output, implement better methods of sanitation, and generally improve the living standards of the region. At the end of their three years of service in the Youth Corps it was expected that they would settle down in Manchukuo, raise families, work the land, and become a sort of cadre for the other colonists who would come from Japan.[3]

This expectation of emigration to Manchukuo highlights the function of cultural transformation or "development" within the imperial project. Japan's goal was to *change* the ways of living of the peoples in the territories it acquired, to create greater similarity between their lifestyles and those of the Japanese (colonists and "home islanders" alike). Norman Smith points out the example of cultural policies around gender:

> The reconstitution of gender ideals was an essential element of the Japanese cultural agenda in Manchukuo. In officially sanctioned media, conservative constructs of womanhood were promoted. Without exception, "model" women were portrayed as submissive, meek, and, most of all, obedient. Any perceived deviation was denounced. New women were criticised for lewd, selfish, and self-centred behaviour.[4]

Chinese women were to "embrace the 'beautiful customs' of Japanese women."[5]

Although the population goals of the colonial project – bringing Japanese people into Manchukuo – would prove problematic, the cultural goals at least held out the promise of success. Japanese news media in the early 1940s were optimistic about the maintenance of Japan's overseas territories and the "harmony" possible between Japanese and non-Japanese there: "The basic purpose of the colonisation of the continent should be to assist Manchukuo in her endeavour to build up a land where the ideal of concord among all races is realized."[6]

All aspects of culture had a role to play in the transformation of the peoples of the various colonies. The Japanese language itself had a fundamental power to help change people's behaviour and ideals. As Andrew Hall writes, policy makers in Manchukuo believed in the late 1930s that

> Japanese language instruction was the most effective tool for cultivating loyalty among a subjected people, and could overcome even the lack of blood ties. Many expressed their belief that the Japanese language was infused with a living spirit that could be experienced by anyone who became immersed in the language. They were convinced that if the colonised peoples could be made to speak Japanese and learn Japanese customs, their characters would naturally become more refined, and they would appreciate and become allies in Japan's mission to lead a unified East Asia.[7]

Kishida's involvement in the Imperial Rule Assistance Association made direct contributions to this project of harmonious coexistence under the umbrella of a "Japanese culture" covering the home islands and colonial territories. Significantly, Kishida himself writes directly that his own project is to help change *Japanese* people as well, to create a proud, culturally aware population able to transmit the benefits of Japanese culture both from generation to generation, and from ethnic group (the Japanese) to ethnic group (the non-Japanese peoples living in greater Japanese "territory"). This goal of transformation was vital to guarantee the ongoing legitimacy of Japan's position as a vanguard Asian nation; for Japan to rule, it must "deserve" to do so by virtue of its cultural leadership.

In Kishida's view, it was important to inculcate in the youth of Japan a "correct" view of and appreciation for the particular aspects of Japanese culture that would permit them to assume a position of leadership in future development, both at home and abroad as an internationally leading nation. For Kishida, culture served as the foundation on which politics and economics stood, not as separate or superior enterprises, but as manifestations of a cultural identity that had to be, first and foremost, "wholesome" rather than "high." Culture was that which existed within every activity of every Japanese person but was also the "responsibility" that the Japanese people had for supporting and advancing their nation. Cultural movements and citizens' activities were part of the nation's war preparations, alongside expansion of production capacity and the rationing of consumption.

One of Kishida's longest works, *Chikara toshite no bunka* (Culture as strength) consists of a series of lectures that together argue for a particular reawakening of the value of traditional Japanese values, hand in hand with an adaptation of modern political ideals. Kishida writes that the "subject's path" (*shindou*) has to be practical in order to achieve results. He criticizes the government for having lost sight of the value of culture as a foundation for national mobilization and cooperative effort, and urges the youth of Japan to demonstrate to their elders their pure ambitions for creating a new world of accomplishments.

Throughout his work, Kishida remained a firm advocate for the unique abilities and potential of Japan, stemming from its culture, traditions, and history. This made him both a product and an exemplar of his times. He used his position as an intellectual and artist to promote a particular view of Japanese culture and Japan's role in the world, and while that view may be especially germane to the imperial period, it is not without value even today. The problem of culture – of what is particular in an increasingly globalized world – remains significant. While Japan has lost its militarism, it remains a model for the amalgamation of history and modernity, as well as a soft-power force. For Kishida, culture is what made this possible.

TRANSLATION

Foreword to *Culture as Strength: Five Lectures during a Time of War*[8]

KISHIDA KUNIO

For the past two years, I have undertaken work for the Culture Division of the Imperial Rule Assistance Association; I have conducted considerable research on cultural mechanisms, which we should establish as national organizations and, further, on the various types of cultural matters that we should adopt as national movements. After inviting opinions from every field, I have come to realize that this matter is limitlessly broad, and that each particular issue stands on extremely deep roots. I have often been at a loss as to which point we should take in hand first.

In accordance with current needs, and first of all keeping separate those concrete problems that we must dispose of quickly, I believe that the most important matter, in order to establish the foundation for the nation's next one-hundred-year plan, is, after all discussion, the resurrection of the traditions of what we know to be Japanese culture in the hearts and minds of every single citizen of the nation.

In particular, for the benefit of our youth, who carry responsibility for future generations and who burn with ambition, we absolutely must clearly explain the significance of culture and create a correct perception concerning the culture of our own country. It is extremely important for us to depend on the abilities of our educators in this.

The word "culture" already appears in the upper-primary textbooks of our National Schools, and I, at least, keenly hope that educators will pay special attention to this matter and will themselves wish to fulfill their roles as cultural leaders in an age such as today's, in which the word is abused in every field.

However, on the one hand, educators may be hesitant to limit the meaning of this *raw unprocessed* word in Japanese in their own ways. They should probably fully study the explanations of specialists or philosophers. I believe, however, that even my own attempts at stating a profoundly realized, unified "view of culture" that runs through the whole range of citizens' movements, growing from the practical work that I have encountered in my responsibilities in the Culture Division of the Imperial Rule Assistance Association, may serve, to some extent, and if I may restate my own hopes, certainly and directly as a reference for educators and for our youth.

The custom of considering whether a country has a high or a low culture has existed till today. However, whether that culture is wholesome or not has not been especially problematic. Here, we find the shape of change and development in culture till today.

If we ask where the crisis in culture in countries that have boasted of so-called high cultures lies, it is not in a separate strength that jeopardizes that culture, but rather it has now become clear that something exists within the culture itself that can infiltrate those high aspects. That is, within the standard of value of those high aspects, the fact has been revealed that the condition of "health" has been completely lacking.

In that regard, it seems that some people have come to believe the paradox that high culture is consequent upon unhealthiness. In fact, that isn't really the case, but that opinion alone seems to circulate with substantial force among the public. Indeed, we meet scholars and thinkers in particular who have concluded, from the general state of contemporary Western culture, that even there, too, the advance of culture comes together with pursuing the paths of decadence; this is based on the trends and propensities of contemporary Western thought that have not yet realized the complete relationship between culture and the people or the nation.

Moreover, the special qualities of Japanese culture, despite the superficial confusion of modern times, even now preserve a lively vitality, based on the shining history of its people and the rich traditions of its realms. Responding to the times, this vitality has become the "do or die!" spirit of the people, displaying their efforts to pulverize formidable enemies. However, in regard to one aspect, we cannot say that there are no weak points among the Japanese people. Further, we cannot give assurances that our enemies are not in fact plotting a counter-offensive against this very aspect. As to what that weak point may be, it is, in a word, nothing other than the delays we face in those areas that have cultural ability. I believe that so long as we do not take corrective measures in these areas, we will not be able to boast of perfect preparations for a long-term war of attrition.

These measures, together with considerations for the construction of a new culture, growing from the singular perspective of "culture as strength," must be precisely the central aims of practical movements worthy of the great efforts to raise up the country.

I cover this in the main text, but what we mean by "culture" is not everything that exists under the crowning name of "culture," and is not only the features and customs of Japan, ranging over every aspect of national life, or permeating every action, both public and private, connected with everyone; it is also the amount of responsibility that everyone must bear in this regard.

A single young person, in a sense, in every respective position demonstrates Japanese culture through himself, but this is not only a matter of past and present. In fact, his is a young existence that is entrusted with the state of tomorrow's Japan, together with its great dreams.

In September of Shōwa 16 [1941], I published the following. I hereby reprint it, expressing my tremendous hopes and expectations for our youth:

> Japan now stands at a crossroads that will determine its vicissitudes. We must before all else have this reality clearly in mind. Do not conclude that the pride of our people will be built through such philosophical questions as "What shall we do?"
>
> The people, similarly, imagine in their hearts where tomorrow's Japan must go. However, the contemporary government is still full of contradictions and confusion, and its leaders cannot in the least predict the appearance of our shining future.
>
> Of course when we speak of new systems and the establishment of the national polity and national defence, vast ideals are undoubtedly included

in these words, but our job, from now on, will surely be to call up images that will stir the breasts of every single citizen.

It is my personal consideration that the voices of our youth, who carry many dreams and responsibilities for future generations, will be the driving force of this new government. Because they are young, these voices are loud, but because they are pure, no one can obstruct them.

What the young seek is neither power nor greed. They seek nothing more than truth, goodness, and beauty – in other words, the highest expression of human life.

For a long time, the Japanese government has lost sight of these aims. The instincts of the people are finally about to realize this. The commencement of the new Japan is the hope itself of the youth.

However, the character of government is not something that can change overnight. Youth must wait patiently. Waiting is not standing with folded arms, doing nothing. Those who seek must seek greatly; they must prepare for the day that must come; and what we are able to accomplish, we must accomplish together.

The slogan of the Imperial [Rule] Assistance Movement is "The subject's path leads to results." One may say that the paths of our youth, as citizens of the nation, are for those who have work to be zealous in their respective jobs, or for those who are at school to be dedicated to their schoolwork; but if that was all they were to be, there would be no need to restate this now. Under the current conditions, what I particularly hope for our youth is that, for the sake of our Japan, they will not insist on the "ways of living" which they crave in their hearts. We can find therein a particular spirit that suggests that, as Japanese, we must live in that way; but it is precisely that disposition, which longs to live thusly, that will move the youths' elders, and will for the first time put the new government of Japan on the right track.

If one were to say that it is still too early to discuss the issue of government, my friends, you need not hesitate in the least. It is best to speak frankly and boldly about "life." You, more than anyone else, must keenly feel that for Japan to be strong, for Japan to be right, the present-day Japanese cannot carry on this way. If you look around you, you will see what is preventing us from displaying our inherent, practical abilities. What thing worthy of the name of wholesome culture has been started at the hands of modern Japan? We have cluttered up daily life under the pretense of cheering you all up.

Now that the matter has come this far, I must say a few brief remarks about the form of the new youth that contemporary Japan is seeking.

In fact, this problem is an extremely significant one, and even though I myself hope to refrain from dealing with this issue according to my own predilections, as someone has said, this topic has already become a subject of public conversation. Further, it is a fact that in every region young men and women whom we must regard as this "new type" have already started to appear.

Certainly, the era creates types of people, and so these are the types who will be met by the new era and who will offer the spectacle of fashion to their times. Accordingly, people who are opposed to these types have also appeared.

But what value is there in the type of person who merely reflects the atmosphere of the times? What we are looking for is the archetype of Japanese people who will truly *live* their times, who will *guide* their times. For me, nothing is more pleasant than imagining the appearance of the singular, youthful spirit of the young men and women who forecast the growth towards this archetype, though incomplete, still vital and vigorous and possessing rich connections with our ancestors, and who fully exhibit the potentialities stretching to the still-unknown future world.

Nonetheless, the "appearance of this spirit" is not something easily depicted in literary expressions or if one has limited powers of imagination. Perhaps we can allow one particular, concrete type to come to the common imagination, some sort of "ideal this or that," some type who has accomplished some particular growth within a set of limited conditions – for example, the "ideal teacher" or the "ideal farming village youth." In these cases, though, I often see the word "ideal" being pulled down by a categorical, vulgar tone. Even if we grant that, at a glance, this indicates an impeccable, exemplary kind of youth in each of their respective standpoints, therein is always an emphasis on something utilitarian and results-oriented, and it's rare to problematize the quality or "intentions" of Japanese youth. In particular, from time to time under the rubric of the "exemplary youth" we find extreme cases of types stinking of a discrimination or flattery that is unbecoming to the young; these can even reach intolerable degrees.

In short, anyone can be fooled by people who do nothing more than superficially put on the airs of their times as merely a temporary guise. However, that type will at once reveal its frivolous aspects as soon as anyone looks, and we cannot say that there will not be the phenomena of cynicism and self-deprecation, which exist as reactions against the pretentions that are rampant as the outrageous manners of the age.

Today, even though we intend to call up the country, burning with the conviction of certain victory, and with every citizen living day by day in readiness to serve on the battlefields, even so, if we tend towards the impression that the enemy is still distant, or the front is still remote, a momentary slackness will be born in our hearts. People already underestimate the situation, saying, "Victory is assured," or else, "So long as we win the battle, all will be well." Even though that may well be, I have the feeling that a simplistic mood has raised its head somewhere in our minds, and we no longer pay heed to what may lie ahead after this moment.

As a result of the issue of Japanese culture – which should be at the foundation of every rallying cry of every significant movement, such as those to enhance national morale, expand production capacity, increase the population, or encourage savings – *not* always coming to the forefront, I believe we do not give enough consideration, even in those functions that aim at the training of the people, to comprehensively elevating the nature of the Japanese people and their abilities, in which they should feel pride in their authority as the vanguard nation.

My deliberate intention of dedicating this book to "Young People," even while myself feeling ashamed of its inadequacies, did not at all come from the arrogance of believing today's youth to be unsatisfactory. Rather, I have tried to state, as frankly as possible and mainly through self-reflection, the one idea that the numerous projects that our generation has not been able to achieve must all be accomplished by the next; I have tried to express the spirit that must become the basis upon which we will aim for the formation of tomorrow's Japanese people, after first creating a new type of youth.

From the outset, such an attempt must be undertaken by many people. If my own inexperienced and hurried considerations were at least to hasten even a little such an opportunity, then it would not only be fortunate, but if it could become the foundation for training and self-reflection of young men and women themselves, I would have achieved one of my longed-for life goals; there would be nothing to surpass such joy for this author.

(11 February, Shōwa 18 [1943])

Notes

1 H.J. Timperley, "Japan in Manchukuo," *Foreign Affairs* 12, 2 (January 1934): 295.

2 Ronald Suleski, "Northeast China under Japanese Control: The Role of the Manchurian Youth Corps, 1934–1945," *Modern China* 7, 3 (July 1981): 352.

3 Ibid., 354.

4 Norman Smith, "Disrupting Narratives: Chinese Women Writers and the Japanese Cultural Agenda in Manchuria, 1936–1945," *Modern China* 30, 3 (July 2004): 301–2.

5 Ibid., 302.

6 *Tokyo Gazette* 4, 10 (April 1941): 396–401, quoted in "Japanese Population Policy," *Population Index* 7, 4 (October 1941): 266.
7 Andrew Hall, "The Word Is Mightier Than the Throne: Bucking Colonial Education Trends in Manchukuo," *Journal of Asian Studies* 68, 3 (August 2009): 897.
8 Kishida Kunio, *Chikara toshite no bunka* [Culture as strength] (Tōkyō: Kawade shobō), 1943.

Contributors

Timothy Cheek is a professor and the Louis Cha Chair in Chinese Research at the Institute of Asian Research and Department of History at the University of British Columbia. His most recent books include *The Intellectual in Modern Chinese History* and *Voices from the Chinese Century.*

Timothy Cronin is the program manager of the China Economy Program and a research officer at the East Asian Bureau of Economic Research at the Crawford School of Public Policy, Australian National University. A graduate of ANU College of Asia and the Pacific majoring in Chinese language and history, he was awarded first-class honours for his unpublished thesis, "Zhou Zuoren and the Consolations of Bitterness."

Annika A. Culver is an associate professor of East Asian History at Florida State University and a scholar in the US-Japan Network for the Future. She is also the author of *Glorify the Empire: Japanese Avant-Garde Propaganda in Manchukuo* and the coeditor of *Manchukuo Perspectives: Transnational Approaches to Literary Production.* Her current work examines how consumer capitalism developed in modern Japan, while another project on Japanese science delves deeply into questions of empire and the continuity of transwar elites.

Matthew Galway is a lecturer at the Australian National University. He has published peer-reviewed articles in scholarly journals *Cross-Currents: East Asian History and Culture Review, China Information, Review of Religion and Chinese Society,* and *Asian Ethnicity.* His current manuscript, entitled "Global Maoism: China's Red Evangelism and the Cambodian Communist Movement, 1949–1979," is under review with Cornell University Press.

Weiting Guo is a postdoctoral scholar in history at Aix-Marseille Université. He was previously an assistant professor of history and director of Taiwan

Studies Group at Simon Fraser University (2015–19). He has published peer-reviewed articles in *Cross-Currents: East Asian History and Culture Review, Journal of the Canadian Historical Association,* and several edited volumes. He is currently revising his first monograph, "Justice for the Empire: Summary Execution and Legal Culture in Qing China."

Jonathan Henshaw is a research associate at the Institute of Asian Research at the University of British Columbia. He recently completed a doctorate in modern Chinese history at UBC with funding from the Chiang Ching-kuo Foundation and the Social Sciences and Humanities Research Council of Canada. He has previously written on the internment of Allied civilians in China and Chinese commemorations of the Second World War, and is now writing a biography of Kiang Kang-hu.

Hua Rui is a PhD candidate of History and East Asian Languages at Harvard University, and an incoming postdoctoral associate with the Program in Agrarian Studies at Yale University. His dissertation, entitled "The Legal Topography of Empires: Transnational Civil Justice in Manchuria, 1900–1950," examines how vernacular legal cultures shaped the game of great powers in the Northeast Asian borderland.

Timothy Iles is an associate professor of Japanese Studies at the University of Victoria. He is the author of *Crisis of Identity in Contemporary Japanese Film: Personal, Cultural, National* and *Abe Kōbō: An Exploration of His Prose, Drama, and Theatre.*

Naoko Kato is an instructor at St. Mark's College and a senior intern at the North American Coordinating Council on Japanese Library Resources. While at the University of British Columbia as the Japanese language librarian, she co-curated and edited the Meiji at 150 Digital Teaching Resource, which was published as *Digital Meijis: Revisualizing Modern Japanese History at 150.* Her doctoral dissertation was titled "Through the Kaleidoscope: Uchiyama Bookstore and Sino-Japanese Visionaries in War and Peace." A book on Uchiyama Bookstore is forthcoming with Earnshaw Books.

Jennifer Junwa Lau is a sessional lecturer at the University of Toronto and the associate editor of Chinese Canadian cultural platform, Fête Chinoise. Her doctoral dissertation explored discursive connections between Canada and China from 1868 to 1938 with the support of the Social Sciences and

Humanities Research Council of Canada and the W. Garfield Weston Foundation Doctoral Fellowship Program. Her interests include issues of translation, revisionist histories, and Chinese diasporic studies.

Jonghyun Lee is an associate professor at Bridgewater State University who has published on Korean history and social work, including the book chapter "Unfaithful Angels: Social Work in Colonial Korea," and articles in journals including *Community Mental Health Journal, Fudan Journal of the Humanities and Social Sciences, Social Work in Mental Health,* and *Affilia.*

David Luesink is a historian of modern China with particular interests in the history of medicine and science. He completed his PhD at the University of British Columbia in 2012. He is currently completing a book manuscript on the history of anatomy in China. Publications related to this research have appeared in the *Journal of Asian Studies* and elsewhere. He coedited *China and the Globalization of Biomedicine* and is developing a new research project on early laboratory science in China.

Brian G. Martin is a visiting fellow at the Australian Centre on China in the World, Australian National University. He has published widely on wartime collaboration and Chinese organized crime, including *The Shanghai Green Gang: Politics and Organized Crime, 1919–1937.*

Janice Matsumura is an associate professor in the Department of History at Simon Fraser University. Her more recent research focuses on the relationship between state ideology and medical knowledge, and she has published in journals such as *Modern Asian Studies, Gender & History, War in History,* and the *Bulletin of the History of Medicine.*

Norio Ota is an associate professor in the Department of Languages, Literatures and Linguistics at York University. He is the co-translator of Reginald Bibby's *Mosaic Madness: The Poverty and Potential of Life in Canada,* published in Japanese as *Mozaiku no Kyōki.*

Christopher Rea is a professor of Asian Studies and former director of the Centre for Chinese Research at the University of British Columbia. His book *The Age of Irreverence: A New History of Laughter in China* won the 2017 Association for Asian Studies Joseph Levenson Book Prize (post-1900 China).

His recent books include *The Book of Swindles: Selections from a Late Ming Collection, Imperfect Understanding: Intimate Portraits of Modern Chinese Celebrities,* and *China's Chaplin: Comic Stories and Farces by Xu Zhuodai.*

Morgan Rocks is a PhD candidate in Chinese history at the University of British Columbia. He is currently researching Chinese participation in transnational anarchist networks from the 1920s to the 1950s and is involved in projects to translate key writings by contemporary Chinese public intellectuals.

Bill Sewell is a professor of history at Saint Mary's University. He is the author of *Constructing Empire: The Japanese in Changchun, 1905–45.* Other publications include "Missions to Manchuria," *Canadian Journal of History,* and his coedited volume with John Lee, *Seven Crucial Centuries: Changes in Premodern Chinese Society and Economy, 499 BCE–1800 CE.*

Craig A. Smith is a lecturer at the University of Melbourne. His articles have appeared in *Modern Chinese Literature and Culture, Twentieth-Century China,* and *Modern Asian Studies.* His monograph *Chinese Asianism* is forthcoming from the Harvard University Asia Center.

Norman Smith is the author of two monographs, *Resisting Manchukuo* (awarded the 2008 Canadian Women's Studies Association Book Prize) and *Intoxicating Manchuria* (awarded the 2013 Gourmand Wine Books Award – Best Drink History Book, Canada [English]). He has edited one collection of essays, *Empire and Environment in the Making of Manchuria,* and coedited seven books (six in Chinese). His work has been generously funded by the Social Sciences and Humanities Research Council of Canada.

Son Yoo Di holds a PhD in Asian Diaspora Studies and Literature from Korea University, where she is now a lecturer at the Institute for General Education. Her dissertation and previous publications concerned Lin Yutang and his writings.

Ronald Suleski is a professor of history and also director of the Rosenberg Institute for East Asian Studies at Suffolk University Boston. Prior to joining Suffolk he was assistant director of the Fairbank Center for Chinese Studies at Harvard University. He worked in Japan for twenty years in the field of international publishing. His most recent book is *Daily Life for the Common People of China, 1850 to 1950: Understanding* Chaoben *Culture.*

Wang Yu received his PhD in history from the University of Toronto. He is currently a post-doctoral fellow at the University of Macau. He has a wide range of research interests, ranging from the circulation of knowledge in the late Qing to the technologies of sound and propaganda in twentieth-century China. Currently he is working on a book manuscript, tentatively entitled "Rethinking Propaganda: Radio and Technopolitics of Sound in Mao's China."

Torsten Weber is a historian of modern East Asia and Principal Researcher at the German Institute for Japanese Studies (DIJ Tokyo). He holds an MA in Chinese Studies from the School of Oriental and African Studies (SOAS, University of London) and a PhD in Japanese Studies from Heidelberg University. His research focuses on the history of Japanese-Chinese relations and interactions from the modern to the contemporary era, including the politics of history and memory. His current project "Testifying and Contesting War Experiences–John Rabe's Nanjing Diaries" (rabediaries.hypotheses.org) studies wartime diaries and other witness accounts of the Japanese invasion of China. He is the author of *Embracing 'Asia' in China and Japan. Asianism Discourse and the Contest for Hegemony, 1912–1933.*

Yun Xia is a professor of history at Shanghai University, China. Previously, she taught at Seattle University and obtained tenure at Valparaiso University, IN. She is the author of *Down with Traitors: Justice and Nationalism in Wartime China* and is currently working on an edited volume and a monograph on the history of law and crime in Taiwan.

Xie Miya Qiong is an assistant professor of Chinese literature and culture in the Asian Societies, Cultures, and Languages Program at Dartmouth College. She is currently working on her first book manuscript, "Borderland Matters: Manchuria and the Making and Unmaking of National Literatures in East Asia (1920–1950)," and her second book project on ethnic Korean literature in China.

Xue Bingjie graduated from the Chinese Academy of Social Sciences in 2018. Her PhD dissertation focused on the composition of classical poetry under the occupation, with a particular focus on works written in Beijing, from 1937 to 1945. She is currently working for China's National Ethnic Affairs Commission.

Zhang Yuanfang is a PhD candidate in the Department of East Asian Studies at the University of Toronto. His dissertation examines the discursive production of the agrarian question in Manchukuo between 1932 and 1941.

Index

Note: "(f)" following a page number indicates a figure